THE FACTS ON FILE DICTIONARY OF

Allusions

THE FACTS ON FILE DICTIONARY OF

Allusions

MARTIN H. MANSER

David H. Pickering, Associate Editor

The Facts On File Dictionary of Allusions

Checkmark Books
An imprint of Infobase Publishing
132 West 31st Street
New York NY 10001

Library of Congress Cataloging-in-Publication Data

Manser, Martin H.
Dictionary of allusions / Martin H. Manser; David H. Pickering, associate editor.
p. cm.
Includes bibliographical references and index.
ISBN 978-0-8160-7105-0 (hc : alk. paper) 1. Allusions—Dictionaries. I. Pickering, David, 1958– II. Title
ISBN-10 : 0-8160-7105-5 (hc : alk. paper)
ISBN-13 : 978-0-8160-7907-0 (pbk)
ISBN-10 : 0-8160-7907-2 (pbk)

PN43.M25 2008
422'.03—dc22 2007051375

Checkmark Books are available at special discounts when purchased in bulk quantities for businesses, associations, institutions, or sales promotions. Please call our Special Sales Department in New York at (212) 967-8800 or (800) 322-8755.

You can find Checkmark Books on the World Wide Web at http://www.factsonfile.com.
Visit the author's Web site at www.martinmanser.com

Text design by Kerry Casey
Cover design by Salvatore Luongo

Printed in the United States of America

MP BVC 10 9 8 7 6 5 4 3 2 1

This book is printed on acid-free paper and contains 30 percent postconsumer recycled content.

Contents

Acknowledgments

The Editors wish to thank Rosalind Fergusson for her meticulous editing, Rosalind Desmond and Lynda Drury for their very careful checking and typing of the manuscript, and Martin Selman, Stephen Curtis, John Barton, and Angela Gluck Wood for their helpful comments on earlier drafts of the text.

Reference resources included the British National Corpus, the use of which we gratefully acknowledge.

—Martin H. Manser
David H. Pickering

Introduction

An allusion is a reference that evokes a certain set of aspects or features of a person or thing. For example, a kind and selfless person may be referred to as a *Good Samaritan;* a musical genius may be hailed as a *Mozart;* a political, administrative, or financial scandal may be referred to by name with the suffix*–gate*, after *Watergate;* a large-scale nuclear accident may be referred to as another *Chernobyl;* a fatal weakness may be referred to as a person's *Achilles' heel;* something that rises anew in the face of defeat may be compared to *a phoenix rising from the ashes;* and *9/11* has become synonymous with terrorist atrocity.

The *Facts On File Dictionary of Allusions* builds on the earlier volume of the *Facts On File Dictionary of Classical and Biblical Allusions*, doubling the content to provide a comprehensive reference to allusions in the English language. Entries have been selected not simply because they are well-known events, places, people, phenomena, etc., but also because they have generally acquired some wider linguistic significance, conveying a particular message beyond a mere reference. This method of selection distinguishes this volume from other references on the same subject, including other dictionaries of allusions as well as more expansive (but less focused) works such as *Brewer's Dictionary of Phrase and Fable.*

Allusions in this volume are drawn from a wide range of sources, including Shakespeare and the Bible; Greek, Roman, Norse, and other types of mythology; literary texts from all ages; historical events; and popular culture, including film and television.

Arrangement of entries

Allusions are listed in their original form and under the source of the original reference. Entries are listed in strict letter-by-letter alphabetical order:

go and do thou likewise

gobbledygook

Godfather, the

God save the king/queen

God's in his heaven, all's right with the world

Godwin's oath

Godzilla

Goebels

go from strength to strength

Pronunciation

Pronunciation is given in parentheses for a word or words that include a proper name, are of non-English origin, or are not a common English expression:

expede Herculem (eks peday herkyoolem)

valley of Jehoshaphat (jăhōshăfat)

Stress is shown by an underscore in the pronunciation. Pronunciation is as in American English and uses the following key:

a (cab)
ă (about)
ah (car, lawn, flaunt)
air (flair)
ay (day, state)
b (but)
ch (chip)
d (danger)
e (sell)
ee (feet)
eer (clear)
er (robber, thirst)
f (fine)
g (get)
h (hand)
i (ill)
ī (wine)
j (jolly)
k (kitten, can)
ks (mix)
kw (quell, quake)
l (lie)
m (mole)
n (nine)
ng (longer)
n(g) (restaurant)
o (fog)
ō (telephone)
oi (ploy)
oo (loose, glue)
or (sore)
ow (cow)
p (pink)
r (red)
s (silent)
sh (shut)
t (tip)
th (theater)
TH (this)
u (luck)
uu (bulletin)
v (very)

w (wet) yoor (European)
y (young) z (fizz)
yoo (unisex) zh (fusion)

Definitions

Each entry begins with an explanation of the use of the word or phrase in contemporary English.

Indiana Jones . . . A dashing, even roguish adventurer, especially one with a seemingly unexciting academic background. . . .

painting the Sistine Chapel . . . Undertaking a demanding and seemingly endless task, especially one of a creative nature. . . .

The origin and background of the allusion is then explained:

cut the Gordian knot . . . To take a direct route in solving a complex problem. The allusion is to the story of the intricate knot with which Gordius, a peasant who became king of Phrygia, attached his wagon to the yoke. It was said that any person who could untie the knot would become ruler of all Asia. When Alexander the Great was presented with the challenge of unloosing the knot he simply cut through it with his sword.

Examples

Examples of allusions are given for nearly every entry. They may come from English literature or contemporary citations (in case they are in quotation marks), or they may be sentences constructed by the editors to show typical usage (in which case they are italicized).

fall by the wayside To give up or fail at something; to become useless. . . . "While other internet bosses have fallen by the wayside, he remains in charge after overseeing his company's flotation and sale" (*The Guardian,* April 23, 2001).

Mozart (mōtzahrt) The embodiment of musical genius. . . . *It is probably too early to be sure, but some are saying we have another Mozart in our midst.*

Additional Information and Derived Forms

Additional information, variants, and phrases derived from the main allusion are included in many entries.

fast lane The most direct route to success, fame, wealth, etc. The allusion is to the lane on a highway or expressway that is reserved for vehicles overtaking slower traffic. The phrase is often encountered in the expression ***life in the fast lane***.

phoenix (feeniks) Something that rises anew in the face of defeat or adversity. This legendary bird appears in the mythology of ancient Egypt, ancient Greece, and early Christianity and was widely considered a symbol of immortality and life after death. According to most traditions the phoenix resembled an eagle, with gold and scarlet feathers, and lived for about 500 years. When the time came for it to die, it lay down on a pyre and allowed itself to be burned in the flames. It then emerged renewed from the ashes, hence the expression a ***phoenix rising from the ashes.***

See References

See references direct the reader to the full entry where the allusion is considered.

Bluto *See* POPEYE.

eye of a needle *See* CAMEL: GO THROUGH AN EYE OF A NEEDLE.

rest on one's laurels *See* LAURELS.

Biblical quotations are from the King James Version of the Bible.

A

Aaron *See* AARON'S BEARD; AARON'S ROD; AARON'S SERPENT.

Aaron's beard (airănz) Popular name of one of a variety of wild plants, including meadowsweet, Saint-John's-wort *(Hypericum calycinum)*—which is also known as rose of Sharon—and ivy-leaved toadflax. The name comes from Psalm 133:2: "It is like the precious ointment upon the head, that ran down upon the beard, even Aaron's beard: that went down to the skirts of his garments." According to Exodus 4:14, Aaron was the brother of Moses and became the first high priest of the Israelites. His name may come from *haaron* (meaning "ark"). *Among the plants she identified as having magical powers was Aaron's beard.*

Aaron's rod (airănz) Popular name of a widespread plant *(Verbascum thapsus)* with woolly leaves and tall spikes of yellow flowers. The allusion is to the rod used by Aaron to perform various miracles in Egypt prior to the Exodus. According to Numbers 17:1–13, when Aaron's rod was placed among 12 rods representing the tribes of Israel in the tabernacle, it blossomed overnight and produced almonds. It was by this sign that Aaron was recognized as having the strongest claim to the priesthood. Henceforth his rod was, according to the apostle Paul, kept in the ARK OF THE COVENANT itself. Aaron's rod is today a symbol of authority and, in the East, also of travel. *Aaron's rod makes an attractive addition to any garden border. See also* AARON'S SERPENT.

Aaron's serpent (airănz) Something that is so powerful it easily consumes lesser beings or entities. The allusion is to Exodus 7:8–12 and to AARON'S ROD, which turned into a serpent and devoured the rods of his Egyptian enemies after they too had turned into serpents. *Like Aaron's serpent, the new conglomerate has swallowed up virtually all the smaller companies that were once its rivals.*

Abaddon (ăbadon) Alternative name for the devil, the ruler of hell. He is described at Revelation 9:11 as "the angel of the bottomless pit" who rules over an army of locusts with stings like scorpions. His name means "destruction" in Hebrew, although he is sometimes referred to by his Greek name ***Apollyon.*** "And my father preached a whole set of sermons on the occasion; one set in the morning, all about David and Goliath, to spirit up the people to fighting with spades or bricks, if need were; and the other set in the afternoons, proving that Napoleon (that was another name for Bony, as we used to call him) was all the same as an Apollyon and Abaddon" (Elizabeth Gaskell, *Cranford,* 1851–53).

Abbott and Costello (abăt, kostelō) A comical or incompetent duo or outfit. The allusion is to the celebrated comedy team of Bud Abbott (1895–1974) and Lou Costello (1906–59), whose routines were hugely popular with radio, television, and cinema audiences in the 1930s and 1940s. *Observing the dads putting up the tent was like watching Abbott and Costello. See also* LAUREL AND HARDY.

Abednego *See* FIERY FURNACE.

Abel *See* CAIN AND ABEL.

Abelard and Héloïse (abălahrd, elōeez) Archetype of a pair of tragic lovers. Peter Abelard (1079–1142) was a gifted scholar who incurred the wrath of the church authorities after he fell in love with the beautiful Héloïse (1101–64), niece of Canon Fulbert of Notre Dame, while acting as her tutor. After marrying in secret and having a son together, the pair were persecuted by the girl's father (who had Abelard castrated) and forcibly parted: Abelard became a monk and Héloïse a nun. Their remains were laid to rest together after death. *Her bitter complaints about their treatment suggested that Abelard and Héloïse had got off lightly by comparison.*

abigail (abigayl) A lady's maid; female domestic servant. The reference is to Abigail, the wife of Nabal according to 1 Samuel 25. When Nabal, the wealthy owner of goats and sheep in Carmel, refuses to provide food for David's followers, Abigail apologizes for her husband's ungenerosity and offers sustenance to David, thus forestalling an attack upon their own people. Abigail calls herself "thine handmaid" no less than six times in the space of 17 verses and, after Nabal dies 10 days later, becomes David's wife. Sir Francis Beaumont and John Fletcher subsequently gave the name to a lady's maid in their play *The Scornful Lady* (1610) and thus popularized it as an informal name for any woman engaged in such a post. Its identification with such subservient roles was further cemented by the notoriety of Abigail Hill Masham, a lady-in-waiting to Queen Anne of Great Britain who used her influence over the monarch to advance her own interests. *Her grandmother served as an abigail in one of the great Scottish castles.*

abomination of desolation Something loathsome or disgusting. The expression comes from the Old Testament book of Daniel (9:27; 11:31; 12:11; see also Matthew 24:15–21) and is thought to allude to a pagan altar to Zeus that was erected in the Temple on the orders of Antiochus Epiphanes. In Daniel, the sacrilege was seen as an abomination, a horror that made the Temple emptied, or desolate, of God. "In truth all that night had been the abomination of desolation to me" (Joseph Conrad, *The Arrow of Gold,* 1919).

Abraham (aybrăham) Archetypal patriarch. One of the most important figures of the Old Testament, Abraham is usually considered the father of the Hebrew people and the ancestor of all Jews and is referred to as "the father of many nations" in Genesis 17:5. His name is often invoked as an image of patriarchal values or wisdom or as a symbol of fertility. "In the latter quarter of each year cattle were at once the mainstay and the terror of families about Casterbridge and its neighbourhood, where breeding was carried on with Abrahamic success" (Thomas Hardy, *The Mayor of Casterbridge,* 1886). *See also* ABRAHAM'S BOSOM; ABRAHAM'S SUPREME TEST.

Abraham Lincoln (aybrăham linkăn) Archetype of a resolute, honest politician. Abraham Lincoln (1809–65) was president of the United States during the traumatic years of the Civil War. He was a stalwart opponent of slavery but strongly believed in sustaining the Union, even at the cost of thousands of dead on both sides in the war. Adored and hated in almost equal measure, he had a reputation for great nobility of spirit, and was popularly dubbed "Honest Abe." He died just after the end of the war when he was assassinated at Ford's Theater on April 14, 1865, by the deranged actor John Wilkes Booth. *The late ambassador had the patient steadfastness of an Abraham Lincoln. See also* GETTYSBURG ADDRESS.

Abraham's bosom (aybrăhamz) The Christian paradise; heaven as the restful abode of the blessed dead. The phrase comes from Luke 16:19–31, in which Jesus relates the parable of Lazarus and the rich man: "The beggar Lazarus died, and was carried by the angels into Abraham's bosom." It has been suggested that the image of leaning on the bosom of a friend may relate to the classical custom of reclining on a friend's chest when dining (hence the expression a "bosom friend"). "The sons of Edward sleep in Abraham's bosom" (William Shakespeare, *Richard III,* c. 1592).

Abraham's supreme test (aybrăhamz) An ultimate challenge or sacrifice. The reference is to God's command to Abraham to sacrifice his only son, Isaac, as a burned offering on Mount Moriah. Abraham readily agreed to comply and was about to kill Isaac with his knife when God, satisfied that Abraham's faith was genuine, intervened by providing a ram caught in a thicket to take Isaac's place (Genesis 22:1–19; see also Romans 4; Hebrews 11:8–19; James 2:20–26). *The president faces his own version of Abraham's supreme test, being forced to choose between instinctive loyalty to his vice president or to his own political principles.*

Absalom (absălom) Archetype of a rebellious son, especially one who meets a tragic end. Absalom is identified in 2 Samuel 13–18 as the third son of King DAVID, remarkable for his great beauty and adored by both his father and his people. Unfortunately, he sided with Ahithophel in rebellion against David and was consequently slain by Joab after getting his long hair entangled in the branches of a tree while trying to escape. David's grief over his slain son was overwhelming and gave rise to his famous lament "O my son Absalom, my son, my son Absalom! Would God I had died for thee!" (2 Samuel 18:33). "Sometimes, the worthy gentleman would reprove my mother for being over-indulgent to her sons, with a reference to old Eli, or David and Absalom, which was particularly galling to her feelings" (Anne Brontë, *The Tenant of Wildfell Hall,* 1848).

absurd, theater of the *See* THEATER OF THE ABSURD.

academia (akădeemeeă) The academic world. The word comes from the Greek *Akademeia,* the name of the public garden (with a grove) in Athens where the philosopher Plato instructed his pupils toward the end of the fourth century B.C. The grove in turn was named after the legendary hero Academus. In modern usage students may still be said to toil in the GROVES OF ACADEME. Other words from the same root include ***academy, academe***, and ***academic***. *The announcement has sent a ripple of concern through academia.*

according to Hoyle (hoil) Acting fairly or honestly. Edward Hoyle (1672–1769) is remembered for his codification of the rules for various card games, and as the supreme authority on such games as whist. Thus, a person who acts "according to

Hoyle" is observing both the letter and the spirit of the rules, whether at card-playing or in life more generally. *His conduct toward the women present was not exactly "according to Hoyle."*

Aceldama (ăseldămă) A battlefield or any other place where much blood has been spilled. The name means "field of blood" in Hebrew and refers to the field that was reputedly bought by Judas with the THIRTY PIECES OF SILVER he had received in payment for betraying Christ. According to Peter in Acts 1:18–19, once Judas had purchased the field he fell headlong onto it and "burst asunder in the midst, and all his bowels gushed out," hence the field's name. "Is there any haunting of the Bank Parlour, by the remorseful souls of old directors, in the nights of these later days, I wonder, or is it as quiet as this degenerate Aceldama of an Old Bailey?" (Charles Dickens, *The Uncommercial Traveller,* 1860). *See also* POTTER'S FIELD.

Achates (ăkayteez) Archetype of a loyal friend. Achates appears as the devoted friend of the hero Aeneas in Virgil's *Aeneid* (30–19 B.C.), sometimes referred to as *"fidus Achates"* (meaning "faithful Achates"). *He proved a true fidus Achates, sticking by his friend through thick and thin.*

Acheron (akăron) The underworld, the abode of the dead. According to Greek mythology, Acheron was one of the four rivers surrounding Hades, although Homer's *Iliad* (c. 700 B.C.) identifies it as the only river flowing through the underworld. The name itself means "river of woe." "Mrs. Grantly, as she got into the carriage, smiled slightly, thinking of the battle, and as she sat down she gently pressed her daughter's hand. But Mrs. Proudie's face was still dark as Acheron when her enemy withdrew, and with angry tone she sent her daughter to her work" (Anthony Trollope, *Framley Parsonage,* 1861).

Achilles and Patroclus (ăkileez, patrăklăs) Archetypes of devoted friendship. The fondness and loyalty of the Greek heroes Achilles and Patroclus during the Trojan War was legendary, and when Patroclus was killed after Achilles absented himself from the battlefield (*see* SULK IN ONE'S TENT), the latter was inconsolable. He eventually returned to the fray to avenge his friend by killing Patroclus's slayer, Hector. "Or perchance he was some Achilles, who had nourished his wrath apart, and had now come to avenge or rescue his Patroclus" (Henry David Thoreau, *Walden,* 1854).

Achilles' heel (ăkileez) A fatal weakness; a place where an otherwise strong person or thing is vulnerable. The allusion is to the legends surrounding the great Greek hero Achilles, who became virtually invulnerable after being dipped by his mother, Thetis, in the waters of the River Styx as a child. But in order to dip him, Thetis had to hold him by his heel, so this one area was not touched by the water and remained the one part of his body in which he could be wounded. Ultimately, Achilles met his death when he was shot in the heel by a poisoned arrow fired by Paris during the Trojan War. On the basis of the same legend, the fibrous cord that connects the heel to the muscles of the calf is known as the ***Achilles tendon***. *Her sense of vanity is her Achilles' heel, and all her enemies know it.*

Acres, Bob *See* BOB ACRES.

acropolis (ăkropălis) A citadel within an ancient Greek city, usually housing the headquarters of the city's administrative and legislative institutions. The original Acropolis was a group of temples that surmounted the fortified hill around which the city of ancient Athens was built. Chief among these buildings was the Parthenon, dedicated to the goddess Athena. *The townsfolk retreated to the acropolis, leaving the lower part of the city to be sacked by the invaders.*

Actaeon (akteeăn) Archetype of a hunter. According to Greek mythology Actaeon was a hunter who accidentally caught sight of the goddess Artemis bathing and as punishment was transformed by her into a stag. He was then torn apart by his own hounds. A variant of the legend explains that Actaeon was put to death as punishment for boasting that he was more skilled at hunting than Artemis. Because Actaeon was turned into a stag and cuckolds according to ancient tradition had horns, the name Actaeon may also be applied to a man whose wife is unfaithful. "In a minute, a gentleman-farmer, panting with Actaeonic excitement, rode up to the two pedestrians, and Grace being a few steps in advance he asked her if she had seen the fox" (Thomas Hardy, *The Woodlanders,* 1887).

Action Man *See* G.I. JOE.

Actium (akteeăm) A decisive defeat. The promontory of Actium in western Greece overlooks the waters in which the Roman fleet of Octavian destroyed that of Mark Antony and Cleopatra VII in 31 B.C. *The scale of the defeat was such that, as for Mark Antony after Actium, there was no prospect of a recovery.*

Adam (adăm) The archetypal man, especially one who is completely alone or in a state of innocence. The allusion is to the biblical Adam, who became the first man on earth. The human race as a whole has often been referred to as ***sons of Adam***. Christ is sometimes called the ***new Adam, second Adam,*** or ***last Adam*** (1 Corinthians 15:45). "But here . . . shut in by the stable hills, among which mere walking had the novelty of pageantry, any man could imagine himself to be Adam without the least difficulty" (Thomas Hardy, *The Return of the Native,* 1880). *See also* ADAM AND EVE; ADAM'S ALE; ADAM'S APPLE; ADAM'S CURSE; ADAM'S PROFESSION; ADAM'S RIB; EVE; GARDEN OF EDEN; KNOW SOMEONE FROM ADAM, NOT TO; WHIP THE OFFENDING ADAM.

Adam and Eve (adăm, eev) The archetypal man and woman. According to Genesis 2, Adam and Eve were the man and woman created by God to inhabit the GARDEN OF EDEN. Their names may be invoked in a variety of contexts, variously with reference to their state of happy innocence before the FALL, to their nakedness, to their fallibility, to their disobedience, or to their joint guilt for committing the first sin. "'O pooh! He is the fallen Adam with a soured temper. We are Adam and Eve unfallen—in paradise'" (George Eliot, *The Mill on the Floss,* 1860). *See also* ADAM; EVE.

Adam's ale (adămz) Water. This humorous epithet refers ironically to the fact that the biblical ADAM had only water to drink. Sometimes called ***Adam's wine***. *He said he owed his longevity to his refusal to drink anything stronger than Adam's ale.*

Adam's apple (adămz) The visible projection of the thyroid cartilage of the larynx in the throat. According to legend, when ADAM bit from the fruit of the forbidden tree a piece of the fruit lodged in his throat, and ever since men have had this visible projection from their throat in remembrance of this first sin. This incident is not, however, mentioned in the book of Genesis, and nowhere is the forbidden fruit identified as an apple. *She could remember little about her assailant beyond the fact that he had bulging eyes and a prominent Adam's apple.*

Adam's curse (a̲dămz) Ironic colloquialism for work. After ADAM committed the sin of eating of the fruit of the tree of knowledge, against God's command, he and EVE were expelled from the GARDEN OF EDEN. Ever since, as part of their punishment, they and their descendants have known the toil and onerousness of work: "In the sweat of thy face shalt thou eat bread" (Genesis 3:19). Related terms include the ***penalty of Adam***, which refers to the labors implicit in living a life governed by nature and the turn of the seasons in comparison with the easier life enjoyed by people in urban surroundings. *Too many people's lives today are ruled by Adam's curse than by their life outside work.*

Adam's profession (a̲dămz) Gardening or agriculture. The allusion is to the one occupation that, according to the book of Genesis, was available to ADAM in the GARDEN OF EDEN prior to the FALL (Genesis 2:15). "There is no ancient gentlemen but gardeners, ditchers, and grave-makers; they hold up Adam's profession" (William Shakespeare, *Hamlet,* c. 1600).

Adam's rib (a̲dămz) A woman. The phrase alludes to the biblical origin of EVE, who, according to Genesis 2:21–23, was fashioned by God from a rib plucked out of ADAM's body while he slept so that he might have a companion in Eden: "And the LORD God caused a deep sleep to fall upon Adam and he slept: and he took one of his ribs, and closed up the flesh instead thereof; And the rib which the LORD God had taken from the man, made he a woman, and brought her unto the man. And Adam said, This is now bone of my bones, and flesh of my flesh: she shall be called Woman, because she was taken out of Man." As a consequence of the biblical tradition, for many years it was popularly believed that men had one rib less than women. *The minister muttered something beneath his breath about how life would be a lot easier without the problematic legacy of Adam's rib and left shortly after.*

Adam's wine *See* ADAM'S ALE.

add a colophon *See* COLOPHON.

add a cubit to his stature To exceed one's natural limitations. The phrase is biblical in origin, appearing in Matthew 6:27: "Which of you by taking thought can add one cubit unto his stature?" The cubit was a measure of length equivalent to the distance from a person's elbow to his or her fingertips. "For his temperament (not uncommon in a misty climate) had been born seven feet high; and as a man cannot add a cubit to his stature, so neither can he take one off" (John Galsworthy, *The Forsyte Saga,* 1922).

Addams Family (a̲dămz) A group of people who are grotesque or horrific in appearance or character. The comical misadventures of the Addams family, a bizarrely spooky group of individuals, became hugely popular in the 1960s both as a newspaper comic strip and in television and (later) film stories. Prominent among them were Gomez and Morticia Addams, their children Pugsley and Wednesday, Uncle Fester, Cousin Itt, and the butler LURCH, all of whom bore a disturbing resemblance to well-established characters of the horror genre. *By the time he had fought his way through the* *swamp he looked like something out of the Addams Family. See also* MUNSTERS, THE.

Adler, Polly *See* POLLY ADLER.

Admah and Zeboiim (admah, zebōeem) Places of wickedness and sin. The citizens of Admah and Zeboiim are identified in Deuteronomy 29:23 as having abandoned themselves to lives of sin and debauchery, and in consequence their cities suffer much the same fate as the better-known SODOM AND GOMORRAH, both being destroyed as punishment for offending God. *The two villages were shunned by people living in the surrounding hills, who considered them modern versions of Admah and Zeboiim.*

Admetus *See* ALCESTIS.

Admirable Crichton (krītăn) An archetype of the perfect butler. The name appeared as the title of a 1902 play by J. M. Barrie, in which a butler called Crichton emerges as the most capable person when shipwrecked on a desert island with the aristocratic family he serves. Barrie himself borrowed the name from that of a celebrated multitalented Scottish scholar called James Crichton (1560–82), whose many gifts earned him the nickname "the Admirable Crichton." *What we need here is a really reliable pair of hands—someone like the Admirable Crichton, if we can find one. See also* JEEVES.

Adolf Hitler *See* HITLER.

adonis (ădōnis) An exceptionally handsome young man. According to Greek mythology, Adonis was a beautiful youth who attracted the amorous attentions of Aphrodite, the goddess of love. When he was killed while hunting a boar (possibly the jealous god of war, Ares, in disguise), he was brought back to life by Persephone. The flower called the anemone sprang up where his blood had spilled. Spending part of the year in the underworld with Persephone and part on earth with Aphrodite, Adonis was worshiped as a nature god, and his absence in the underworld accounted, in myth, for the dormancy of nature in winter. His name came from the Phoenician *adoni* (meaning "my lord"), a title borne by the god Tammuz. "'I really can't see any resemblance between you, with your rugged strong face and your coal-black hair, and this young Adonis, who looks as if he was made out of ivory and rose-leaves'" (Oscar Wilde, *The Picture of Dorian Gray,* 1891).

adullamite (adulămīt) A refugee or fugitive. Adullam is identified at 1 Samuel 22:1–2 as the name of the cave in which DAVID sought shelter when fleeing from the wrath of King Saul, being joined there by a host of other individuals seeking similar refuge: "And every one that was in distress, and every one that was in debt, and every one that was discontented, gathered themselves unto him." The term is generally reserved today for dissident members of political groups who leave to form their own cliques. It was first employed with reference to members of the British Liberal Party who withdrew to form their own group in 1866. *These latter-day adullamites gathered in the lobby of the House of Commons and joined in noisy discussion of their outrage at the behavior of their cabinet colleagues.*

Aegean (ijeeăn) The sea, part of the Mediterranean, between Greece and Turkey. It was named after Aegeus, king of Athens and father of the hero THESEUS. According to Greek mythology, before Theseus sailed to Crete to bring about an end to the payments Athens had to pay to King Minos, he promised his father that if he was successful, he would hoist white sails on his return to indicate that he was safe. If he perished, then his ship would hoist black sails, and Aegeus would know his son was dead. Unfortunately, on his return Theseus forgot his promise and his ship sailed in with black sails. Seeing this and presuming his son dead, Aegeus threw himself into the sea, which has borne his name ever since. "After an extended cruise in the Aegean and the Black Sea on their steam-yacht *Ibis,* Mr. and Mrs. Mortimer Hicks and their daughter are established at the Nouveau Luxe in Rome" (Edith Wharton, *Glimpses of the Moon,* 1922).

aegis (eejis) Auspices; protection. The word is Greek in origin (deriving from a word meaning "goat skin") and has its roots in mythology. It was the name of the shield of Zeus, which was forged for him by Hephaestus, and covered with the skin of the goat Amalthea. By shaking this shield Zeus created storms and thunder. Those who enjoyed his protection were thus ***under his aegis,*** the context in which the word usually appears today. (Athena was also depicted carrying an aegis with the head of the gorgon Medusa in its center.) "So saying, she turned her fine shoulders twice, once this way and once that, and went out. She had never told even Stanley her ambition that at Becket, under her aegis, should be laid the foundation-stone of the real scheme, whatever it might be, that should regenerate 'the Land'" (John Galsworthy, *The Forsyte Saga,* 1921).

Aeneas (ăneeăs) Archetypical classical hero and man of destiny: the legendary forefather of the Romans. As described in Virgil's epic poem the *Aeneid* (30–19 B.C.), Aeneas was a Trojan prince, the son of Anchises and Aphrodite, who escaped the fall of Troy and embarked on a long and arduous voyage in search of a new home. In the course of his many adventures he effectively prepared the way for his descendants Romulus and Remus to found the city of Rome. "Thus he proceeded, like Aeneas with his father" (Thomas Hardy, *The Return of the Native,* 1880, referring to Virgil's account of how Aeneas carried his old, frail father on his back out of the burning city of Troy). *See also* DIDO AND AENEAS.

aeolian (ayōleeăn) Of or relating to the wind. Aeolus was identified in Greek mythology as a god of the winds. In modern usage the word Aeolian is usually employed in relation to sounds produced naturally by the wind as it passes over a stretched string, as in the case of an ***aeolian harp.*** In musical theory, an ***Aeolian mode*** is a natural diatonic scale from A to A that forms the basis of the modern minor key. Stones that have been deposited or worn by the wind may sometimes be referred to as ***aeolian rocks.*** "I do love a good tree. . . . How grand its voice is, too, when it talks with the wind: a thousand aeolian harps cannot equal the beauty of the sighing of a great tree in leaf" (H. Rider Haggard, *Allan Quatermain,* 1887).

Aeschylean (eeskăleeăn) Tragic on a grand or epic scale. The allusion is to the tragedies of the celebrated Greek playwright Aeschylus (525–456 B.C.), whose dramas typically dealt with tragedies resulting from pride or defiance of the gods. Of his 90 or so plays, just seven survive, including the trilogy known as the *Oresteia* (458 B.C.). Aeschylus is said to have been killed when an eagle, mistaking his bald head for a stone, dropped a tortoise on it in order to break its shell. "A few minutes after the hour had struck something moved slowly up the staff, and extended itself upon the breeze. It was a black flag. 'Justice' was done, and the President of the Immortals, in Aeschylean phrase, had ended his sport with Tess" (Thomas Hardy, *Tess of the D'Urbervilles,* 1891).

Aesculapius *See* STAFF OF AESCULAPIUS.

Aesop (eesop) A teller of simple tales with a moral. The allusion is to the deformed Phrygian slave Aesop (c. 620–560 B.C.), who is traditionally identified as the author of a collection of animal fables illustrating a variety of morals. In reality, many of these tales seem to predate his era by hundreds of years. Nonetheless, several later writers have been dubbed Aesops of their age, including the English writer John Gay (1685–1732), called the Aesop of England, and the French fabulist Jean de la Fontaine (1621–95), known as the Aesop of France. "But how moral you've become all of a sudden, at twelve o'clock at night! Instead of being Mrs. Radcliffe, I shall think you're Mr. Aesop'" (Anthony Trollope, *Doctor Thorne,* 1858).

Agamemnon *See* BRAVE MEN BEFORE AGAMEMNON, THERE WERE; WRATH OF AGAMEMNON.

Aganippe *See* HELICON.

Agatha, Aunt (agăthă) A formidable aunt or, alternatively, any older woman of fearsome disposition. The original Aunt Agatha featured in the Bertie Wooster stories of P. G. Wodehouse (*see* JEEVES), her chief role apparently being to make unwarranted demands upon her hapless nephew's time and talents. *His mother swept into the room and glared at the intruders for all the world like Bertie Wooster's Aunt Agatha.*

Agatha Christie (agăthă kristee) Mysterious, unfathomable, sinister, or otherwise reminiscent of the detective thrillers of Agatha Christie (1890–1976). Featuring such memorable sleuths as MISS MARPLE and HERCULE POIROT, her novels were notable for their inventive plots, which readers struggled to unravel before the final unmasking of the culprit. *"It's all very Agatha Christie," she said with furrowed brow as she gave up the search for clues as to the whereabouts of her diary.*

age of Aquarius *See* AQUARIUS, AGE OF.

Aglaia *See* THREE GRACES.

Ahab (ayhab) Archetype of an arrogant, wicked tyrant. Ahab is identified in 1 Kings 16:29–22:40 as a king of ancient Israel and the husband of the evil JEZEBEL: "But there was none like unto Ahab, which did sell himself to work wickedness in the sight of the LORD, whom Jezebel his wife stirred up" (1 Kings 21:25). He colluded in the introduction of pagan worship and, when Naboth refused to hand over his vineyard (see NABOTH'S VINEYARD), had him stoned to death. Subsequently he was warned by ELIJAH that he faced divine vengeance and the fall of his dynasty, which duly occurred, Ahab himself being killed in battle and his blood being licked up by dogs. *Like the biblical Ahab, he ignored all warnings that he would have to answer for his wicked ways, possibly with his life.*

Ahab, Captain *See* CAPTAIN AHAB.

Ahasuerus *See* ESTHER; WANDERING JEW.

Ajax (ayjaks) Archetype of a brave, strong warrior. The Greek hero Ajax is depicted in Homer's *Iliad* (c. 700 B.C.), which tells the story of the

Trojan War, as second only to Achilles in courage and strength but also as arrogant and foolish. Ajax was deeply offended when Achilles' armor was won by Odysseus and in his rage slaughtered a flock of sheep. When he recovered he was overcome with shame and killed himself. "She sat as helpless and despairing among her black locks as Ajax among the slaughtered sheep" (George Eliot, *The Mill on the Floss,* 1860).

Aladdin's cave (ăladănz) A confined space full of wonderful, typically valuable things, especially if stolen or otherwise illicit. The allusion is to a story in ARABIAN NIGHTS, in which the penniless Aladdin becomes rich after stealing a magic lamp from a magician's cave. *The police discovered a veritable Aladdin's cave of stolen curios and antiques.*

Aladdin's lamp (ăladănz) Something that enables a person to attain great treasure or otherwise fulfil his or her desires. In the story of Aladdin and his lamp in ARABIAN NIGHTS, Aladdin finds himself trapped inside a wicked magician's cave, but manages to escape with the aid of a magic lamp and the GENIE it contains. *As we have no Aladdin's lamp to solve the mystery, we shall have to resort to old-fashioned policing methods.*

Alamo *See* REMEMBER THE ALAMO.

alarums and excursions (ălahrămz) Chaos and disorder. The origin of the phrase lies in Elizabethan theater scripts, which might include such a stage direction to indicate noise offstage to simulate the sound of battle or other frenetic activity. The archaic word "alarum" was a variant of "alarm," while "excursion" signified a military assault on an enemy. "It was only a bit of acting, however, for Duke was an old dog, had suffered much, and desired no unnecessary sorrow, wherefore he confined his demonstrations to alarums and excursions, and presently sat down at a distance and expressed himself by intermittent threatenings in a quavering falsetto" (Booth Tarkington, *Penrod*, 1914).

alas, poor Yorick! (yorik) An expression of lamentation over someone dead or otherwise fallen. The phrase comes from William Shakespeare's tragedy *Hamlet* (c. 1600), specifically from act 5, scene 1, in which Hamlet muses upon the skull of a long-deceased court jester called Yorick. In modern usage, this overfamiliar expression is only ever employed facetiously. *The dreams I once had of becoming head of this department and making life hell for everyone else I have reluctantly had to let go—alas, poor Yorick!"*

Alastor (ălastor) A vengeful god or spirit. The name was one of several titles borne by Zeus, ruler of the gods in Greek mythology. "Their impulse was well-nigh to prostrate themselves in lamentation before untimely rains and tempests, which came as the Alastor of those households whose crime it was to be poor" (Thomas Hardy, *The Mayor of Casterbridge,* 1886).

albatross around one's neck A burden that constitutes a real hindrance to progress. The allusion is to the poem "The Rime of the Ancient Mariner" (1798) by Samuel Taylor Coleridge, in which a luckless sailor finds himself cursed after he has killed an albatross, which he is forced by the rest of the crew to wear around his neck in penance (the albatross being a lucky bird that sailors believed should be left unharmed). "Michael Banks was suddenly a very expensive albatross around Paul Lexington's neck" (Simon Brett, *Murder Unprompted*,

1984). The allusion is widely known and is sometimes abbreviated to ***albatross***: *That building is a real albatross, costing more in upkeep than it earns in rent. See also* ANCIENT MARINER.

Alberich's cloak (albăriks) A cloak of invisibility, or anything else that allows a person to operate undetected. In Scandinavian mythology, Alberich appears as a king of the dwarfs, although in Richard Wagner's operatic *Ring* cycle (1869–76) he is transformed into an ugly gnome who steals the treasure of the Nibelungs but is later forced by the gods to give up his ill-gotten gains. His magical cloak is stolen by Siegfried. *The program acts like an Alberich's cloak, allowing a hacker to get behind firewalls and other cyber defenses without being detected.*

Albion (albeeăn) A poetic name for England. The name may be derived from the Latin *albus* (meaning "white"), or else from the Celtic *alp* (meaning "rock" or "crag"). In either case, the allusion is thought to be to the white cliffs of Dover, which have for centuries symbolized the English nation. "You are going out, Micawber, to this distant clime, to strengthen, not to weaken, the connexion between yourself and Albion" (Charles Dickens, *David Copperfield*, 1849–1850). *See also* PERFIDIOUS ALBION.

Al Capone (kăpōn) A gangster, specifically someone who acts as (or as though) head of a criminal organization, in a habitually illicit manner. Al Capone (1899–1947) was a notorious leader of organized crime in Chicago during the Prohibition years of the 1920s and 1930s, who long evaded arrest until eventually tried on charges of tax fraud and imprisoned in ALCATRAZ. "He ruled the streets in his territory like a budding Al Capone" (Jack Caplan, *Memories of the Gorbals*, 1991).

Alcatraz (alkătraz) A place of imprisonment, especially one in which prisoners are held in harsh conditions and from which it is virtually impossible to escape. The original Alcatraz was a prison situated on the island of this name in San Francisco Bay, opened in 1868. Dangerous tides surrounding the island made any attempt to escape from the prison a highly perilous prospect. The prison (which closed in 1963 and is now a tourist attraction) housed, among other notorious felons, the gangster AL CAPONE. *He had turned the house into an Alcatraz, from which none of the family were permitted to depart.*

Alcestis (alsestis) Archetype of a woman who sacrifices herself for others. The allusion is to the Greek legend of Alcestis, the wife of King Admetus of Thessaly, who volunteered to die in her husband's place when Apollo agreed to spare his life if he could find someone to take his place. Persephone (or Hercules) subsequently rescued her from Hades and restored her to her husband, as described in the tragedy Alcestis (438 B.C.) by Euripides. The headmistress appeared ready to play Alcestis for the sake of her secretary, but such a monumental sacrifice on her part was not necessary in the end.

Alcibiades (alsibīădeez) Archetype of a debauchee. Alcibiades (c. 450–404 B.C.) was an Athenian statesman and general who won notable victories at Abydos (411 B.C.) and Cyzicus (410 B.C.). His many lovers may have included Socrates, who, according to Plato's *Symposium,* demonstrated his tremendous self-control by spending the night with the beautiful Alcibiades without attempting to make love to him. *The field marshal was the Alcibiades of his day, combining undoubted military prowess* *with scandalous exploits in the casinos and brothels of Paris.*

Alecto *See* FURIES.

Aldershot (oldăshot) The British military establishment. The town of Aldershot in Hampshire has been home to one of the largest British army camps since 1854. *I'm not sure what Aldershot will make of the decision to make substantial cuts in the lower ranks. See also* SANDHURST.

Alexander the Great (alekszander) Archetype of a great military commander. Alexander the Great (356–323 B.C.) was the son of Philip II of Macedon and studied as a youth in Athens under Aristotle. He became king of Macedon at 20 and soon established a reputation as a brilliant military leader, conquering Greece (336 B.C.), Egypt (331 B.C.), and the Persian Empire (328 B.C.) before his premature death from fever at the age of 32. He was well known for treating any women who became his prisoners with respect, and the ***continence of Alexander*** acquired proverbial status. *The president appears to think himself Alexander the Great, but his critics prefer to liken him to Donald Duck.*

Alf Garnett *See* ARCHIE BUNKER.

Ali, Muhammad *See* MUHAMMAD ALI.

Ali Baba *See* OPEN SESAME.

Alice in Wonderland Fanciful or fantastic in nature. The allusion is to the classic children's book *Alice's Adventures in Wonderland* (1865) and its sequel *THROUGH THE LOOKING-GLASS* (1872) by Lewis Carroll, which depict the extraordinary adventures of a young girl in illogical fantasy worlds that she unwittingly enters. In modern usage, if something is described as "Alice in Wonderland," it is usually with negative overtones. *The committee's decision is completely unrealistic, totally Alice in Wonderland.*

all animals are equal, but some animals are more equal than others All human beings are entitled to the same rights and privileges, but some will always claim they have a special right to preferential treatment. The allusion is to George Orwell's satire *ANIMAL FARM* (1945), in which this is one of the slogans that the pigs use to defend their superior lifestyle before less privileged animals. Sometimes shortened to ***some are more equal than others***, the slogan is often used to comment on a situation in which certain people are perceived to enjoy more privileges than others. *As far as tax relief goes, it seems that all animals are equal, but some animals are more equal than others.*

Allan Quatermain (kwortămayn) A rugged hero, especially one with long experience of Africa. The allusion is to the hero of that name in the adventure novels of H. Rider Haggard (1856–1925), including the best-seller *King Solomon's Mines* (1886). His extensive experience of the dangers of the African interior made him a capable guide for the various Europeans drawn to unknown regions of the African continent and in many ways established the model that decades later produced INDIANA JONES. *Her father had spent his life in the Australian outback and had all the qualities of a grizzled antipodean Allan Quatermain.*

all flesh is grass *See* FLESH IS GRASS.

all for one and one for all Each individual will aid his or her fellows, just as he or she in turn can rely upon their aid. This was the slogan of the heroes of

Alexandre Dumas's *The Three Musketeers* (1844), who often fought side by side in the course of their joint adventures. *"All for one and one for all!" he yelled as he leapt into the fray with a grin. See also* THREE MUSKETEERS.

all Greek to me, it's *See* IT'S ALL GREEK TO ME.

all is for the best in this best of all possible worlds *See* BEST OF ALL POSSIBLE WORLDS, THE; PANGLOSSIAN.

all is vanity *See* VANITY OF VANITIES.

all quiet on the western front Nothing is happening, or at least nothing is being admitted to happening. The formula dates from World War I, during which it frequently appeared in German newspapers when nothing beyond the usual sniping or minor exchanges of fire were reported as taking place in the trenches of the western front. The phrase was later poignantly employed as the title of a classic war novel (1929) by the German writer Erich Remarque, who used it to emphasize the fact that even when no major attacks were taking place, men were still dying in large numbers. In modern usage, the phrase may be applied in various contexts when what is really happening is being (deliberately or negligently) ignored publicly. *Public relations officers were rushing about the building, but officially it was still "all quiet on the western front."*

all roads lead to Rome All the alternatives will lead to the same result. The allusion is to the road system that was built to connect all parts of the far-flung Roman Empire with Rome. "All roads lead to Rome, and there were times when it might have struck us that almost every branch of study or subject of conversation skirted forbidden ground" (Henry James, *The Turn of the Screw,* 1898).

all the days of one's life *See* DAYS OF ONE'S LIFE, ALL THE.

all the president's men The political establishment, especially when employed in covering up dubious actions by a president or other prominent leader. The allusion is to a 1974 book and a 1976 film of the same title, which depicted the attempts of various U.S. political agents to cover up the WATERGATE scandal that eventually resulted in the resignation of President Richard Nixon. "We are the President's men and we must behave accordingly" (Henry Kissinger, quoted in M. and B. Kalb, *Kissinger*, 1974). *See also* DEEP THROAT.

all the world's a stage Life has no more permanence or reality than a play enacted in a theater. This comparison between life and a theatrical performance comes from Shakespeare, specifically from his play *As You Like It* (c. 1599): "All the world's a stage, / And all the men and women merely players; / They have their exits and their entrances; / And one man in his time plays many parts. . . ." *All the world's a stage, and there sometimes seems to be little difference between politics and acting.*

all things are possible with God Anything can happen, especially if willed by God. The proverb in its current form is biblical in origin, appearing in Matthew 19:26: "With men this is impossible; but with God all things are possible." A similar sentiment had been voiced in earlier times, as in Homer's *Odyssey* (c. 700 B.C.): "With the gods all things can be done." *No one thought he would make it, but all things are possible with God.*

all things in common The shared ownership of property, goods, and possessions. The phrase comes from Acts 2:44–45, which describes how the first Christians gathered in communal groups, sharing their wealth and possessions equally and owning nothing individually. *All those who enter the monastery surrender their right to ownership of property, as the rules demand holding all things in common.*

all things to all men Compromising and flexible adaptation of opinions, actions, etc., regardless of principle, in order to appease a variety of conflicting interests. The expression comes from 1 Corinthians 9:22, in which Paul, explaining how he seeks converts among both Jews and Gentiles, writes, "I am made all things to all men, that I might by all means save some." *The church leader was criticized for not making his own views clear and for attempting to be all things to all men.*

alpha and omega (alfă, ōmaygă) The entirety or most important part of something; the first and last of something. The phrase appears in Revelation 1:8, 21:6, and 22:13 and, according to the *NIV Study Bible,* means, "God is the beginning and the end. . . . He rules sovereignly over all human history. In 22:13 Jesus applies the same title to himself." Alpha and omega are respectively the first and last letters of the Greek alphabet, which was adopted around 1000 B.C. *Engine performance is the alpha and omega of all research done at this facility.*

Alpheus and Arethusa (alfeeăs, arăthooză) Archetypes of lovers who are so close they appear indivisible. According to Greek mythology, Alpheus was a river god who fell in love with the nymph Arethusa. The virginal Arethusa fled from Alpheus and, at her own request, was transformed by the goddess Artemis into a sacred spring on the island of Ortygia, near Sicily. Alpheus, however, transformed himself into a river and flowed under the Peloponnesus to mingle with her. The legend may have been inspired by the fact that the Alpheus River does indeed flow underground in certain places. *They're like Alpheus and Arethusa, more or less joined at the hip!*

Althaea's brand (altheeăz) An event that has fatal consequences. The allusion is to Greek mythology and the legend of Althaea and her son Meleager, who was fated to live as long as a certain log of wood remained unburned. After Meleager murdered her brothers, Althaea threw the log into the fire and brought about her son's death, as related in Ovid's *Metamorphoses* (A.D. 1–8). "As did the fatal brand Althaea burned" (William Shakespeare, *Henry VI,* 1592).

Amalekite (ămalăkīt) Archetype of a wicked, untrustworthy enemy. The Amalekites are described in the Bible as a nomadic warlike tribe descended from Amalek (Esau's grandson) and the perpetual enemies of the Israelites: "The LORD will have war with Amalek from generation to generation" (Exodus 17:16). *The troops regard their opponents as modern-day Amalekites, quick to resort to violence and on no account to be trusted.*

Amalthea *See* CORNUCOPIA.

Amaryllis (amărilis) A shepherdess or country girl. It is the name of a shepherdess featured in the pastorals of Theocritus and (c. 310–250 B.C.) and Virgil (70–19 B.C.). In modern usage it is best known as an alternative title for the belladonna lily or of several other related plants. "Were it not better done as others use, / To sport with Amaryllis in the shade / Or with the tangles of Neaera's hair?" (John Milton, *Lycidas,* 1637).

amazon (amăzon) A large, robust, or aggressive woman. The Amazons were, according to Greek mythology, a race of warrior women who inhabited Scythia, on the shores of the Black Sea. They were called Amazons (meaning "without breast") because of their practice of removing the right breasts in order to facilitate the drawing of a bow. They only consorted with men for the purpose of procreation. Led by their queen, Hippolyta, they were renowned for their fierceness in battle. The Amazon River in South America is said to have been so called by the Spanish explorer Francisco de Orellana, who reported seeing female warriors in the region in 1541. In 1997 the discovery in southern Russia of ancient graves of what appeared to be female warriors suggested a possible source of the legend of the Amazons. In modern usage, anyone with a clean-shaven face may be said to have an ***Amazonian chin.*** *I didn't offer to break down the door, since if the door needed breaking down this amazon looked quite capable of doing the job herself.*

ambrosia (ambrōzhă) A delicious or sweet-smelling food. The allusion is to Greek mythology and the belief that the gods on Olympus fed on such food, which gave them immortality. "We feasted that evening as on nectar and ambrosia" (Charlotte Brontë, *Jane Eyre,* 1847). *See also* NECTAR.

Amelia Earhart (ămeeleeă erhahrt) The archetype of an adventurous female aviator. Amelia Earhart (1897–1937) was a U.S. pilot who, in 1932, became the first woman to fly solo across the Atlantic. She is presumed to have died with her navigator after her aircraft went missing over the Pacific during a round-the-world flight in 1937. *Her grandmother was an intrepid pilot who earned a modest reputation as a second Amelia Earhart without ever flying outside her home continent.*

American Dream The notion that the United States is a land of freedom and opportunity for all people, of whatever color, gender, religion, or class. More cynical observers, however, tend to associate the phrase with the disappointment of naive optimism about what the United States really has to offer. The phrase appears to have been in use since at least the early years of the 20th century, when hundreds of thousands of immigrants flocked to the United States from all over the world in search of better lives. *His first impression of downtown Detroit sat uneasily with the image in his head of the American Dream.*

American Gothic That aspect of the American provincial character that is stiff, conservative, and narrow-minded. The allusion is to a famous painting of the same title painted by Grant Wood (1891–1942) in 1930, which depicts a stern-faced pitchfork-wielding farmer and his wife before their immaculate, white-painted home. Today, the painting is celebrated as a satirical comment on American provincial life, although Wood himself protested that he was simply portraying the values of the rural communities of Iowa in which he grew up. *The family represented to him all that was stifling and hateful in American Gothic.*

America's Sweetheart An overly sweet girl. The title was originally bestowed on silent-movie star Mary Pickford (1892–1979), who was famed throughout the world for her winning performances in the role of the pure, vulnerable young heroine, complete with blonde locks and pretty smile. In modern usage, the term tends to be applied sarcastically to girls whose cloying, saccharine sweetness some may find off-putting. *Tell America's Sweetheart over there that we don't want to contribute to whatever it is she's collecting for.*

amid the alien corn In a foreign land or among strangers. This is a quotation from the poem "Ode to a Nightingale" by the British poet John Keats (1795–1821), in which he refers to the exile of the biblical RUTH: "Perhaps the selfsame song that found a path / Through the sad heart of Ruth, when, sick for home, / She stood in tears amid the alien corn." *He spent his last years in sad seclusion amid the alien corn.*

amillennialism *See* MILLENNIUM.

Am I my brother's keeper? *See* MY BROTHER'S KEEPER.

ammonia (ămōnyă) A colorless soluble gas widely used in making fertilizers and other compounds. The word comes from the name of the Egyptian god Ammon (meaning "the hidden one"), as the salt or gum resin that is the source of ammonia was supposedly first obtained from plants growing near a temple dedicated to him in Libya. *This machine measures the amount of ammonia produced in the process.*

Amos 'n' Andy (aymăs) Stereotypes of the rural black population of the United States. *Amos 'n' Andy* was massively popular both as a long-running radio comedy, first broadcast in 1929, and later as a television series, with Freeman S. Gosden as the hardworking Amos and Charles Correll as his slower-thinking friend Andy. Because both characters were played by white actors in "blackface" makeup, the series eventually fell foul of civil rights activists and the show was canceled in 1958, despite having become a national institution with a huge following. Nowadays, the names are sometimes applied to black people who appear to fit the characters depicted in the program, usually by virtue of their dim-wittedness or naive incompetence. *That pair are about as reliable as Amos 'n' Andy.*

Amphitrite (amfitrītee) A woman who loves the sea. Amphitrite was identified in Greek mythology as a goddess of the sea, the wife of Poseidon and mother of Triton. The name itself comes from the Greek for "wearing away on all sides." *She stood in the vessel's prow, staring at the distant horizon, Amphitrite in her element at last.*

Amyclaean silence (amikleeăn) A self-imposed silence. According to ancient Greek legend, the inhabitants of Amyclae were so scared by repeated rumors that the Spartans were attacking that they forbade any mention of the subject. Thus, when the Spartans really did attack, no one spread the news, and the town was captured. *The senior members of the government seem to have agreed to answer the questions of the press with an Amyclaean silence.*

Anacreontic (ănakreeontik) In praise of love or wine; convivial. Anacreon was a celebrated Greek lyric poet who lived in the sixth century B.C. He was well known for his verses on the glories of love and wine, and his name has subsequently been applied to many poets and artists whose work deals with similar themes. *The following week the magazine published a collection of Anacreontic lyrics by anonymous readers.*

Ananias club (anănīăs) A band of liars or deceivers. The allusion is biblical, referring to a rich man called Ananias who, in expectation of Christ's Second Coming, attempted to join the devout community led by the apostle Peter. Ananias and his wife, Sophia, had sold a piece of property. With his wife's full knowledge, Ananias had retained some of the money from the sale for himself and brought the rest and put it at the apostle's feet. Ananias claimed to have given all his money, but Peter knew that the offer was insincere. He accused Ananias of dishonesty, and the latter was immediately struck dead. According to the account in Acts 5:1–12, the same fate also befell Ananias's wife, when she, unaware of her husband's demise, also came to Peter and maintained that they had laid before him all their worldly wealth. Ever since, the name has often been applied to liars, but it was U.S. president Theodore Roosevelt (1858–1919) who coined "Ananias club," directing it specifically at his political enemies and at journalists who betrayed his confidence. *The Ananias club of news reporters and paparazzi was barred from entering the building so that the various leaders could discuss matters without the fear that their words would be publicly distorted.*

anathema (ănathămă) Something or someone deemed detestable or otherwise accursed or intolerable. Originally a Greek word implying "something hung up in a temple and dedicated to a god," it took on a more negative connotation through the Hebrew practice of "dedicating" their defeated enemies to God by sacrificing them. In the New Testament the word thus came to denote anything abhorrent to the Lord and by extension anything evil or accursed. The Book of 1 Corinthians ends with the apostle Paul writing, "If any man love not the Lord Jesus Christ let him be Anathema Maranatha" (16:22). (*Maranatha* means "the Lord cometh" and is intended merely as a closing benediction to the letter but sometimes is mistakenly treated as an intensification of *anathema*). It also came to be applied to formal denunciations or the curse of excommunication (or curses in general). *The idea of taking a vacation in a country where women were treated as second-class citizens was anathema to her.*

Anchises (ankīseez) Archetype of an aged but respected parent. According to Greek mythology, the goddess of love, Aphrodite, fell in love with Anchises when he was a handsome young Trojan prince and in due course bore him the hero AENEAS. When Aeneas was allowed to go free after the sack of Troy by the Greeks, who greatly respected his prowess, and permitted to take the one thing he most valued with him Aeneas chose the now aged and infirm Anchises, carrying him on his shoulders through the flames. Anchises subsequently accompanied Aeneas on his voyages and died in Sicily aged 80. "Ay, as Aeneas our great ancestor / Did from the flames of Troy upon his shoulder / The old Anchises bear, so from the waves of Tiber / Did I the tired Caesar" (William Shakespeare, *Julius Caesar,* 1599).

ancien régime (on(g)seeon(g) rayzheem) The old order or system. The allusion is to the Bourbon regime that was overthrown by the French Revolution of 1789. The implication is usually that things were much worse under the old order. *With this latest round of elections within the university the last of the ancien régime has been swept away.*

ancient mariner A person, typically an old man, who insists upon telling his story, which is usually lengthy and melodramatic in nature. The allusion is to the epic poem *The Rime of the Ancient Mariner* (1798) by Samuel Taylor Coleridge, in which the Ancient Mariner himself unfolds his extraordinary and extended life history to a hapless passer-by on his way to a wedding party. *There was absolutely no escaping this ancient mariner and his tedious stories.* *See also* ALBATROSS AROUND ONE'S NECK; FLYING DUTCHMAN.

Andersen, Hans Christian *See* HANS CHRISTIAN ANDERSEN.

and now for something completely different Now for a complete change of subject. The expression is usually associated with the BBC television comedy series *Monty Python's Flying Circus* (*see* MONTY PYTHON), in which it was used to link unrelated sketches, usually by John Cleese in the guise of a BBC announcer. Before that it was already familiar to viewers as a formula used in the children's program *Blue Peter* to introduce new items. *"And now for something completely different," said the minister as he closed the book.*

Androcles and the lion (andrăkleez) Legendary incident illustrating the moral that those who behave kindly to others may reap the benefit of their generosity later. Androcles (or Androclus) was a Roman slave who was sentenced to be killed by wild beasts in the circus. When he was placed in the arena with a fierce lion, however, the lion did not kill him but greeted him with every sign of friendship. It transpired that some time earlier Androcles, having escaped from his master, had befriended the lion in the wilderness by removing a thorn from the animal's paw, thus relieving its agony. Duly impressed, the authorities released Androcles and presented him with the lion. The legend is perhaps best known today through its dramatization as *Androcles and the Lion* (1912) by British writer George Bernard Shaw. *It was like Androcles and the lion: The magistrate descended from his bench and warmly embraced the felon who had been brought in for admonishment.*

Andromeda (andromădă) A constellation in the Northern Hemisphere, located between Cassiopeia and Pegasus. It was named after the legendary Andromeda, daughter of King Cepheus of Ethiopia and Cassiopeia, who was greatly admired for her beauty. When Cassiopeia boasted that her daughter was more beautiful than the sea nymphs known as the Nereids, they persuaded the sea god Poseidon to send a monster to ravage Cepheus's land. In order to appease the monster, Andromeda was chained to a rock and offered as a sacrifice. She was rescued by Perseus, who killed the monster by showing it the severed head of Medusa, who turned all who looked at her into stone. Perseus and Andromeda subsequently married. After her death she was placed among the stars. "With these were to be seen at intervals some of maturer years, full-blown flowers among the opening buds, with that conscious look upon their faces which so many women wear during the period when they never meet a single man without having his monosyllable ready for him,—tied as they are, poor things! on the rock of expectation, each of them an Andromeda waiting for her Perseus" (Oliver Wendell Holmes, *Elsie Venner,* 1861).

and so to bed *See* PEPYS.

and that's the way it is That is how things are. This was the stock phrase with which U.S. news presenter Walter Cronkite (born 1916) signed off at the end of the news bulletins he hosted on CBS Evening News for 19 years (1962–81). *"And that's* *the way it is," he said, putting an end to any further questioning.*

Andy Hardy Archetype of an all-American boy or the idealized American way of life. Wholesome teenager Andy Hardy, played by Mickey Rooney in a series of 15 films made between 1937 and 1947, was a member of the equally wholesome and cheery Hardy family, who with their clean-living and optimistic outlook on life epitomized mid-20th century middle-class American values. *She came from a town in the Midwest that was all very respectable and Andy Hardy.*

angel of death Personification of death. The angel of death is usually assumed to be of biblical origin, being variously identified as Apollyon (*see* ABADDON), Azrael, or Michael. "Some day soon the Angel of Death will sound his trumpet for me" (Bram Stoker, *Dracula,* 1897).

anger of Juno *See* JUNOESQUE.

angry young man A disenchanted young man, especially one who rails against conventional society and the current establishment. The tag was applied to a group of British playwrights and novelists of the 1950s, whose ranks included John Osborne, author of the play *Look Back in Anger* (1956), which featured the seething ***Jimmy Porter*** and from which the term originally came. *He was an angry young man in those days, not the comfortable old codger we know today. See also* KITCHEN-SINK; REBEL WITHOUT A CAUSE.

Animal Farm A totalitarian regime in which the ordinary order of things has been turned upside down. The allusion is to the satirical novel (1945) of the same title by George Orwell. Orwell's vision of a farm taken over by the livestock was intended as a satire of Stalinist Russia, in which the possibilities presented by the 1917 revolution had been squandered. *The danger is that we will see Animal Farm relived in several tottering African states. See also* ALL ANIMALS ARE EQUAL, BUT SOME ANIMALS ARE MORE EQUAL THAN OTHERS.

Anna Karenina (kărenină) Archetype of a tragic, doomed heroine. Anna Karenina is the central character in a novel bearing her name written by the Russian novelist Leo Tolstoy (1828–1910). Married to a dull bureaucrat, the beautiful but lonely Anna falls in love with the handsome ***Count Vronsky***, but is rejected by society for her indiscretion and is eventually driven by despair to throw herself under the wheels of a train. *Like Anna Karenina, she could see no way out of her misery except to kill herself.*

Annie Oakley (ōklee) An expert female sharpshooter. Annie Oakley (Phoebe Ann Mozee Butler; 1860–1926) became famous for her rifle-shooting skills as a member of Buffalo Bill's Wild West Show in the late 19th century. Her trademark feat involved shooting the pips out of playing cards (as a consequence of this, punched railroad tickets and passes to baseball games, and by extension free tickets or benefits of any kind, are nicknamed "Annie Oakleys"). *My daughter's been shooting since she was five—a regular Annie Oakley, she is.*

anointed of the Lord The clergy, or others deemed to have been chosen by God. The phrase comes from 1 Samuel 24:10, in which David protests accusations that he plotted the death of King Saul: "I will not put forth mine hand against my lord; for he is the LORD's anointed." *It was his mother's dearest wish that he would elect to join the* *church and enjoy the respect deserving the anointed of the Lord.*

another fine mess *See* LAUREL AND HARDY.

Anschluss (anshlăs) The enforced annexation of another country, company, organization, etc. The original Anschluss (meaning "junction" or "union" in German) was the annexation of Austria by Nazi Germany in March 1938. *Many observers were worried that Serbia was planning an "Anschluss" against its neighbor.*

Antaeus (anteeăs) A powerful person who has to renew his or her strength periodically. The allusion is to the giant Antaeus, who, according to Greek mythology, was in the habit of killing any opponent who could not defeat him at wrestling. The son of Poseidon and the earth goddess Gaea, he depended for his strength on being in contact with the earth, so when Hercules held him off the ground, he was powerless to prevent himself being strangled to death. *The big man was uneasy in the abstract realms of thought, needing, like Antaeus, to keep his feet firmly on the ground.*

anthropophagi (anthrăpofăgī) Cannibals. According to Greek mythology, the Laestrygones were a race of cannibalistic anthropophagi (meaning "eaters of human beings") encountered by the Greek hero Odysseus, who only narrowly escaped them. "And of the Cannibals that each other eat, / The Anthropophagi, and men whose heads / Do grow beneath their shoulders" (William Shakespeare, *Othello,* 1603–04).

Antichrist A person who opposes Christ or is the implacable enemy of all that is good. The Antichrist is described in the Bible as the enemy of Christ (1 John 2:18–21), who will inflict great wickedness upon the world prior to being overcome in a final battle by Christ at the Second Coming. The Antichrist denies the fundamental truths about Jesus Christ; instead, Christ coming is seen as a sign of the "last days." Similar biblical figures include the "man of lawlessness" (2 Thessalonians 2:3–12) and the beast (Revelation 11:7). The title "Antichrist" has been bestowed upon many notorious figures and institutions over the centuries, among them the Roman emperors Caligula and Nero, the Roman Empire in general, Muhammad, the papacy, Napoléon Bonaparte, and Adolf Hitler. *His excesses over the years had turned him into an Antichrist-type figure as far as the rest of his family was concerned.*

Antigone (antigănee) Archetype of a woman who sacrifices herself for her family. The allusion is to the Greek myth about Antigone, daughter of Oedipus and his mother, Jocasta. Antigone was condemned to death by being buried alive for having given burial rites to the body of her brother Polyneices against the order of her uncle, King Creon of Thebes. Antigone committed suicide. "As Antigone said, 'I am neither a dweller among men nor ghosts' " (Thomas Hardy, *Jude the Obscure,* 1895).

Antiphates' wife (antifayteez) Epitome of ugliness. According to Greek mythology, the wife of Antiphates, leader of the cannibalistic Laestrygones, was appallingly ugly. *Not since Odysseus laid eyes upon Antiphates' wife had any man been so revolted by the physical form of a woman.*

Antisthenes *See* CYNIC.

Antony and Cleopatra (antănee, kleeōpatră) Archetypes of doomed lovers. The Roman general

Mark Antony (82–30 B.C.) became a member of the Second Triumvirate, alongside Octavian and Lepidus, in 43 B.C. and had responsibility for Rome's eastern provinces. He repudiated his wife to join Cleopatra VII (69–30 B.C.), queen of Egypt, but their joint forces were defeated by Octavian at ACTIUM in 31 B.C., after which Antony committed suicide having been told (inaccurately) that Cleopatra was dead. Cleopatra killed herself shortly afterward, letting a poisonous asp bite her. "Passion is destructive. It destroyed Antony and Cleopatra, Tristan and Isolde" (William Somerset Maugham, *The Razor's Edge,* 1944).

Anubis (ănoobis) Personification of death. The jackal-headed Anubis was identified in ancient Egyptian mythology as the son of Osiris and as the god of the dead who escorted the deceased to judgment. The Greek equivalent was Hermes. *The gloom that concealed this melancholy spot might have been the shadow of Anubis himself.*

apartheid (ăpahrtīd, ăpahrtīt) Separation of one section of society from another, especially if officially sanctioned. Derived from an Afrikaans word meaning "separateness," apartheid became notorious as a policy adopted in 1948 by the Republic of South Africa against its black population, who were barred from sharing the privileges of the country's white residents. After much internal unrest and condemnation from outside South Africa, the system was finally abandoned in 1991. *Young people in this country are subject to a kind of cultural apartheid, which denies them any significant voice.*

Aphrodite (afrōdītee) A beautiful or sexually desirable woman. The goddess of love in Greek mythology, Aphrodite was variously described as having been born from the foam *(aphros)* of the sea or, according to Homer, as the daughter of Zeus and Dione. She was forced to marry the ugly Hephaestus and was notoriously unfaithful to him, allegedly possessing a magic girdle (also called the ***cestus*** or, by the Romans, the ***girdle of Venus***) supposed to have the power to make her sexually irresistible to any person she might wish to attract. Her name inspired the word ***aphrodisiac,*** which describes any substance or other influence that is deemed to excite sexual desire. "No, her mood now was that of Aphrodite triumphing. Life—radiant, ecstatic, wonderful—seemed to flow from her and around her" (H. Rider Haggard, *She,* 1887).

Apicius (apishăs) A gourmand. The name belonged to three celebrated Roman epicures, the most famous of whom was Marcus Gavius Apicius, who lived in the first century A.D. and was the author of a book of recipes known as *Of Culinary Matters.* When he was faced through financial difficulty with having to restrict himself to a plain diet, he killed himself rather than suffer such privation. *This Apicius dedicated his life to seeking out new taste sensations in the restaurants and hotels of Manhattan.*

apocalypse (ăpokalips) A catastrophic or climactic event involving total destruction. The book of Revelation, in which John reveals how the world will end, is sometimes referred to as the Apocalypse. The word itself comes from the Greek *apokalyptein* (meaning "to disclose"). The derivative adjective is ***apocalyptic.*** "The events of September 11 were so apocalyptic that it seemed in the immediate aftermath that the landscape of travel would be altered forever" (*The Guardian,* September 7, 2002). *See also* FOUR HORSEMEN OF THE APOCALYPSE.

apocryphal (ăpokrăfăl) Of dubious authenticity or authorship; sham. The word refers to the Apocrypha, the books appended to the Old Testament but not forming part of the Hebrew canon and not included in the Protestant Bible. It comes from the Greek *apokryptein* (meaning "to hide away"). *The story that it was here that the conquistadores held their first mass is probably apocryphal.* The apocryphal books are also know as the deuterocanonical (secondarily canonical) books. For many centuries, they were read as part of the Latin (Vulgate) Bible, having been included in the Septuagint, or Greek translation of the Old Testament, but not the Hebrew Bible; despite their inclusion, their value was regarded as somewhat ambiguous. At the Reformation, however, the Roman Catholic Church fixed their number at twelve and included them in their editions of the Bible, whereas the Protestant denominations formally excluded them. They include some additions to the books of Esther, Daniel (including the history of Susanna and the Song of the Three Holy Children), and Jeremiah, as well as a number of historical works (1 and 2 Maccabees and 1 Esdras), an apocalyptic book (2 Esdras), three short stories (Tobit, Judith, and Bel and the Dragon), two wisdom books (Ecclesiasticus, or Sirach, and the Wisdom of Solomon) and three other works of various kinds (the Prayer of Manesses, the Letter of Jeremiah, and Baruch). They have been preserved in Greek but many were probably written originally in Hebrew or Aramaic (Selman and Manser, *The Hearthside Bible Dictionary*).

Apollonian (apălōneeăn) Serene, harmonious, ordered. The word alludes to the Greek sun god Apollo, the son of Zeus and Leto, who represented such positive attributes as light, music, poetry, healing, and prophecy. He was conventionally depicted as a handsome youth, and even today a beautiful young man may be termed an ***apollo.*** *Nietzsche contrasts the Apollonian need for light, order, and harmony with the Dionysian urge for darkness, wild passion, and destruction.*

Apollyon *See* ABADDON.

apostle (ăposăl) A devoted follower of a particular belief, faith, movement, etc. From the Greek *apostolos* (meaning "a messenger"), the word acquired new significance through the work of Christ's apostles—originally the 12 disciples (Matthew 10:2)—who were chosen by Christ to preach the gospel. It is also used to refer to Paul, commissioned to be an apostle by the risen Christ. The apostles' basic qualification was that they had been with Jesus during his earthly ministry and had witnessed his resurrection. The apostles were recognized as the founders of the church. The word *apostle* is also used more generally to refer to a representative or messenger of a particular church. Subsequently the term came to be applied to any individual who sought to spread Christianity around the world and more generally to anyone publicly espousing a particular cause or movement. *Over the last two years he has emerged as a leading apostle of the political Left.*

appeal from Philip drunk to Philip sober To seek a decision or complete some other task at a more favorable time. The allusion is to a legendary incident in which a Macedonian noblewoman sought a legal ruling from Philip II of Macedon (382–336 B.C.), but found her petition refused by the king, who was in a drunken, unsympathetic mood. The woman announced her intention to appeal against the decision. When the outraged king demanded to whom she intended to make her appeal, she replied, undaunted, "To Philip sober." Legend has it that she subsequently won her case. *When her husband returned home late that night, somewhat the worse for wear, he refused to countenance her suggestion and she resolved to wait until the following morning, when she might appeal from Philip drunk to Philip sober.*

appease his manes (mayneez) To observe the wishes of a dead person. According to Roman belief, the spirit, or *manes,* of the deceased would rise up in anger if survivors failed to show due respect to his or her wishes. *In order to appease his manes, they scattered the old man's ashes on the cliff top, as he had instructed.*

Appleby, Sir Humphrey *See* HUMPHREY, SIR.

apple of discord A cause of argument. The allusion is to Greek mythology and the golden apple that was offered by Eris, the goddess of discord, to the most beautiful of the guests at the wedding of Peleus and Thetis, to which she had not been invited. The resulting contest between the goddesses Hera, Athena, and Aphrodite was settled by Paris (*see* JUDGMENT OF PARIS) but resulted in much resentment and bloodshed and ultimately the outbreak of the Trojan War. In modern usage, to ***throw the apple of discord*** means to provoke conflict. "I suppose he specified sincere because it was no longer sincere: he hurled the offer into Musgrove Cottage by way of an apple of discord—at least so I infer from the memorandum, with which he retired at present from the cash hunt" (Charles Reade, *Hard Cash,* 1863).

apple of knowledge *See* FORBIDDEN FRUIT.

apple of one's eye Someone or something that is very precious to a particular person. The phrase is biblical in origin, appearing in Deuteronomy 32:10, which describes God's love for Israel—"He kept him as the apple of his eye"—and again in Psalm 17:8 and Proverbs 7:2. The apple is understood to be a metaphor for the pupil of the eye, which is not dissimilar in shape. " 'He's the only minister I ever had much use for. He's God's own if ever a man was. And he loves you—yes, sir, he loves you like the apple of his eye' " (Lucy Maud Montgomery, *The Chronicles of Avonlea,* 1912).

apple pie A symbol of the household values that lie at the heart of the American national character. The image of apple pie as a thoroughly American dish dates back to its association with the Pilgrim Fathers, who were the continent's first permanent European settlers. It is often linked with "motherhood" in the phrase ***motherhood and apple pie.*** *Little league baseball is as American as apple pie.*

Appleseed, Johnny *See* JOHNNY APPLESEED.

apples of Sodom *See* DEAD SEA FRUIT.

apples of the Hesperides *See* LABORS OF HERCULES.

après moi le déluge (apray mwah lă dayloozh) Everything will collapse after I am (or we are) gone. The sentiment (which translates from French literally as "after me the flood") is usually attributed to Louis XV of France (1710–74), who thus prophesied the chaos that would follow the overthrow of the French monarchy. Other sources credit it to Louis's mistress Madame de Pompadour (1721–64), reacting to the defeat of the French and Austrian armies by Frederick the Great at Rossbach in 1757. *The general appeared to be* *resigned to pulling out of the country, warning darkly "après moi le déluge."*

April is the cruelest month Early spring can be a time of great struggle and contrasting fortunes, a time when survival may be hardest and when new life exists alongside death. The allusion is to the opening of T. S. Eliot's poem *The Waste Land* (1922): "April is the cruelest month, breeding / Lilacs out of the dead land, mixing / memory and desire, stirring / Dull roots with spring rain." *The spring tides have wreaked havoc all along the coast—April has proved once again the cruelest month.*

Aquarius, age of (ăkwaireeăs) An astrological era in which humanity enters into a new period of peace, freedom, and understanding. For many people the phrase is linked inextricably with the HIPPIE culture of the 1960s, specifically the opening song of the 1967 musical *Hair*, and has thus become a synonym for childish naivety and optimism. "This is not the age of Aquarius, as the 1960s song so misleadingly supposed: it is the age of imminent judgment" (Andrew Walker, *Enemy Territory*, 1988).

Arabian Nights (ăraybeeăn) A set of fantastical tales of Eastern origin, widely perceived as representing the exotic and fascinating character of the Arabian region and culture. *The Arabian Nights Entertainments* (or *The Thousand and One Nights*) comprise an immense series of folk tales purportedly told by an Arabian princess called ***Sheherezade*** to her captor in an attempt to dissuade him from having her executed (he eventually agrees and marries her instead). They are thought to have been compiled around A.D. 1500. "It's like living in the Arabian Nights" (John Fowles, *The Collector*, 1989). *See also* ALADDIN'S CAVE; ALADDIN'S LAMP; BARMECIDE FEAST; OLD MAN OF THE SEA; OPEN SESAME; SINBAD.

Arabs, fold their tents like the *See* FOLD THEIR TENTS LIKE THE ARABS.

arachnid (ăraknid) An anthropod of the class Arachnida, characterized by eight legs and simple eyes. The arachnids, which include spiders, owe their name to Greek mythology, specifically to a girl from Lydia named Arachne who offended the goddess Athena after challenging her to a weaving contest. When Arachne won the contest Athena destroyed Arachne's tapestry, prompting the latter to attempt to hang herself. Instead, Athena turned the rope into a cobweb and Arachne into a spider. The study of arachnids is known as ***arachnology***. *Ever since she was a child she had nursed a terror of all arachnids, especially spiders.*

Aramis *See* THREE MUSKETEERS.

Arbeit macht frei (ahbīt makt frī) Work sets free. This German slogan was mounted over the entrance to the Nazi concentration camps at AUSCHWITZ and Dachau and has consequently acquired a hugely controversial reputation. Nonetheless, it is occasionally heard today in jocular fashion, typically in reaction to the imposing of some unwelcome task. "Arbeit Macht Frei says the sign on the gate, with typically gruff and undesigning eloquence" (Martin Amis, *Time's Arrow*, 1991).

Arcadian (ahrkaydeeăn) Rustic, pastoral, harmonious, idealized. According to Greek mythology, Arcadia was a mountainous area of the Greek Peloponnese whose inhabitants were said to pursue peaceful, harmonious lives in bucolic surroundings.

The notion of Arcadia representing an idealized rural setting was taken up with some enthusiasm by English poets of the late 16th century. "I had not forgotten Sebastian. He was with me daily in Julia; or rather it was Julia I had known in him, in those distant Arcadian days" (Evelyn Waugh, *Brideshead Revisited,* 1945).

Arcati, Madame *See* MADAME ARCATI.

Archie Bunker (ahrchee bunker) A garrulous bigot. Archie Bunker was the central character in the U.S. television series *All in the Family*, broadcast between 1971 and 1991. Archie Bunker represented the narrow, bigoted views of the working classes and regularly voiced his prejudices to the consternation and amusement of his family, his neighbors, and anyone else unlucky enough to cross his path. The show was based on the British television series *Till Death Us Do Part*, in which the Archie Bunker character ranted and railed under the name ***Alf Garnett***. *It seems likely that we will always have our Archie Bunkers decrying the way that society is.*

Archilochian bitterness (arkilōkeeăn) Mocking, personalized satire. The allusion is to the writings of the seventh-century B.C. Greek satirical poet Archilochus, who expressed personal resentments and bitterness in his verse. *It was just as well that the author of such Archilochian bitterness had elected to remain anonymous as he or she would doubtless have been sued for libel.*

Archimago (ahkeemaygō) An arch-hypocrite. Archimago appears in Edmund Spenser's *The Faerie Queene* (1590, 1596), in which he is depicted as an evil sorcerer who uses his powers to deceive. *The Republicans now have their own Archimago, voicing opinions that no one in the White House actually shares.*

Archimedean (ahrkămeedeeăn) Of or relating to the mathematical or physical theories of Archimedes. A Greek mathematician and scientist, Archimedes (c. 287–c. 212 B.C) made many notable and profoundly influential discoveries in such fields as geometry, mechanics, and hydrostatics, such as the ***Archimedes principle*** and the ***Archimedes screw.*** "It was at this juncture that Mr. Monck Mason (whose voyage from Dover to Weilburg in the balloon Nassau occasioned so much excitement in 1837) conceived the idea of employing the principle of the Archimedean screw for the purpose of propulsion through the air" (Edgar Allan Poe, "The Balloon-Hoax," 1850). *See also* EUREKA!

Arden *See* FOREST OF ARDEN.

Ares (aireez) Personification of war. Ares was identified in Greek mythology as the son of Zeus and Hera and the god of war. In Roman mythology he was called Mars. *The spirit of Ares loomed over the conference table and made any substantial agreement well nigh impossible.*

Arethusa *See* ALPHEUS AND ARETHUSA.

argonaut (ahrgănot) A seafarer, especially one who embarks in a spirit of adventure. In Greek mythology the Argonauts were the heroes who accompanied Jason in his pursuit of the GOLDEN FLEECE. Including such famous names as HERCULES and ORPHEUS among their number, they took their name from their vessel, the *Argo* (meaning "swift"). "This was our second parting, and our capacities were now reversed. It was mine to play the Argonaut, to speed affairs, to plan and to accomplish—if need were, at the price of life; it was his to sit at home, to study the calendar, and to wait" (Robert Louis Stevenson, *The Wrecker,* 1892).

Argus (ahrgăs) An eagle-eyed watchkeeper or guardian. Argus Panoptes appears in Greek mythology as a monster with 100 eyes who was appointed by Hera to guard over the heifer into which Io had been transformed by Zeus. He was, however, lulled to sleep by the music Hermes played on his lyre. Hermes then killed him, and his 100 eyes were placed by Hera in the tail of the peacock, her favorite bird. In his memory, anyone who proves himself or herself vigilant may be described as being ***Argus-eyed.*** "Now Argus, the poets say, had an hundred eyes, and was set to watch with them all, as she does, with her goggling ones" (Samuel Richardson, *Pamela,* 1741).

Ariadne *See* LABYRINTH.

Ariel (aireeăl) An ethereal fairy spirit, especially one who seems otherworldly and remote from human concerns. Ariel appears as a supernatural character in Shakespeare's *The Tempest* (1611), using his powers of invisibility to serve his master PROSPERO, who ultimately rewards him by granting him his freedom. In modern usage, his name is sometimes invoked to describe a person of either sex who is sylphlike in his or her delicate form and lightness of touch. "But for him Ayala would run about as though she were a tricksy Ariel" (Anthony Trollope, *Ayala's Angel*, 1881).

Arion (ărīon) A musician. According to Greek mythology, Arion was a celebrated poet and player of the kithara who lived in the seventh century B.C. When threatened by the crew of the vessel in which he sailed home victorious from a musical contest, he played his kithara and then hurled himself into the sea, from which he was rescued by music-loving dolphins and carried home. "But then there were some sceptical Greeks and Romans, who, standing out from the orthodox pagans of their times, equally doubted the story of Hercules and the whale, and Arion and the dolphin; and yet their doubting those traditions did not make those traditions one whit the less facts, for all that" (Herman Melville, *Moby-Dick,* 1851).

Aristotelian (aristăteeleeăn) Of or relating to the philosophical ideas of Aristotle. The Greek philosopher Aristotle (384–322 B.C.) studied under Plato and later became tutor to Alexander the Great. Founder of the Peripatetic School in Athens, he wrote influential works on logic, ethics, politics, poetics, rhetoric, biology, zoology, and metaphysics. In modern usage, this adjective is usually used in reference to his work on logic or to philosophical positions that incorporate some of his ideas, notably his recommendation that a philosopher should adopt an objective viewpoint independent of social or moral contexts. "In morals he was a profest Platonist, and in religion he inclined to be an Aristotelian" (Henry Fielding, *Tom Jones,* 1749).

Aristotle Onassis (aristotăl ōnasis) Archetype of a billionaire tycoon. Aristotle Onassis (1906–75) was a Turkish-born Greek shipowner who built up one of the largest independent shipping lines in the world, making a vast fortune in the process. After a lengthy relationship with opera singer Maria Callas, he married Jackie Kennedy, widow of assassinated U.S. president John F. Kennedy, in 1968. *You'd need the wealth of an Aristotle Onassis to buy a house around here.*

ark A large boat or other vessel that serves as a means to rescue people, animals, or something else under threat of annihilation. The allusion is to the floating Ark that, according to the book of Genesis (6:14), Noah built on God's orders and in which he preserved his family and two of every species of animal on earth when the world was inundated by the Flood. Related phrases include ***out of the ark,*** signifying something that is so old or out of date that it may well date back to the Ark itself. "In ancient times some Mr. Bell was sailing this way in his ark with seeds of rocket, saltwort, sandwort, beach-grass, samphire, bayberry, poverty-grass, &c., all nicely labelled with directions, intending to establish a nursery somewhere; and did not a nursery get established, though he thought that he had failed" (Henry David Thoreau, *Cape Cod,* 1865).

Ark of the Covenant Something considered sacrosanct or greatly revered, especially a ruling or opinion widely regarded as irrefutable. According to Exodus 25:10–12, the original Ark of the Covenant was the gold-covered wooden chest in which were kept the two tablets inscribed with the Ten Commandments. The ark was the most sacred symbol of the covenant formed between God and the Israelites and was carried by them into battle against the Philistines, who captured it. It was subsequently returned to Israel and enshrined in the HOLY OF HOLIES in the Temple at Jerusalem on the orders of Solomon but vanished, presumably destroyed, when the city fell to Nebuchadnezzar in 586 B.C. Some claim that it is now located in the church of St. Mary of Zion in Axum (Aksum), northern Ethiopia. Related phrases include to ***lay hands on the ark,*** meaning to abuse a sacred object, opinion, etc. *The attendant handled the casket with such care it might have been the Ark of the Covenant itself.*

Armada *See* SPANISH ARMADA.

Armageddon (ahrmăgedăn) A decisive, cataclysmic confrontation; the end of the world. From the Hebrew *Har Magedon* (meaning "hill of Megiddo"), the term refers to the Palestinian city of Megiddo, which was located between Mount Carmel and the coast. Because of its favorable location, the city was frequently fought over in ancient times and thus became synonymous with bloodshed and war. Armageddon is identified in the book of Revelation 16:14–16 as where the climactic battle between the forces of good and evil will be fought. In modern usage, the term is widely employed in referring to any catastrophic conflict that threatens universal disaster, often specifically to nuclear war. "'Armageddon Now,' declared *Kommersant,* the Russian business daily" (*Daily Telegraph,* September 13, 2001). *See also* JUDGMENT DAY.

Arnold, Benedict *See* BENEDICT ARNOLD.

Arnold Schwarzenegger (shwortsănieger) A muscle-bound strong man. Born in Austria in 1947, Arnold Schwarzenegger was a successful bodybuilder and winner of seven Mr. Universe titles before turning to movie acting and becoming a leading star of big budget Hollywood action movies, notably in such roles as CONAN THE BARBARIAN and the TERMINATOR. He then quit the acting world to enter politics, becoming governor of California in 2003. "He was stripped to the waist, and she could see the lunar map of dead skin and fresh scars that was stretched tautly over his

Schwarzenegger musculature" (Kim Newman, *Bad Dreams*, 1990).

Artemis (ahrtămis) Personification of youthful female vigor and athleticism. Artemis, or Diana in Roman mythology, was the ancient Greek goddess of the hunt and the moon, a virgin armed with bow and arrow, twin sister of Apollo. She appeared in numerous legends, including the stories of ACTAEON and THESEUS. "Ah! here is the duchess, looking like Artemis in a tailor-made gown" (Oscar Wilde, *The Picture of Dorian Gray,* 1891). *See also* DIANA OF THE EPHESIANS; EIGHTH WONDER OF THE WORLD.

Artful Dodger A youth who is adept at thieving and other criminal activities. The character (properly, Jack Dawkins) appeared originally in the Charles Dickens novel *OLIVER TWIST* (1837–38), in which he was the most talented of FAGIN's gang of child pickpockets. Though an accomplished petty thief, he is redeemed to some extent by his natural charm and quick wits. "Meg made many moral rules, and tried to keep them, but what mother was ever proof against the winning wiles, the ingenious evasions, or the tranquil audacity of the miniature men and women who so early show themselves accomplished Artful Dodgers?" (Louisa May Alcott, *Little Women*, 1868–69).

Arthur, King *See* KING ARTHUR.

as a tree falls, so shall it lie A person's end corresponds to the life that he or she has led, and any last-minute changes of opinion or belief will not change this. This proverb is of biblical origin, appearing in Ecclesiastes 11:3: "In the place where the tree falleth, there it shall be." It was first recorded in its present form in 1678. "She sent a message . . . to the old father to come and see her before she died . . . His answer was, 'As a tree falls so shall it lie'" (W. H. Hudson, *Traveller in Little Things,* 1921).

Ascalaphus (askălayfăs) According to Greek mythology, when Persephone was rescued from the underworld, it was Ascalaphus who revealed the fact that she had eaten some pomegranate seeds while in Hades, thus breaking the condition that she must not eat anything during her abduction. As a result, Persephone was condemned to spend six months in the underworld and six months on earth for the rest of her life. In revenge for this betrayal, Persephone transformed Ascalaphus into an owl. *The pair resolved to have their revenge upon their former colleague who, like Ascalaphus betraying Persephone, had brought about their utter ruin when they were within sight of victory.*

as game as Ned Kelly *See* NED KELLY.

Asgard *See* VALHALLA.

as happy as Larry Deliriously happy. An Australian phrase, it alludes to a famous boxer called Larry Foley (1847–1917), though it may also have been influenced by the slang term "larrikin," which described a well-dressed young hooligan and was itself an elaboration of the first name Larry. "Ten years later Burton would have been as happy as Larry" (Melvyn Bragg, *Rich: The Life of Richard Burton*, 1989).

Ashcan School An artistic style that deals with unattractive, realistic subjects from the seamier side of life. The term was applied initially to a group of artists specializing in painting such subjects in the early years of the 20th century, their leader being Robert Henri (1865–1929). Later recruits to the movement included Edward Hopper (1882–1967). *The subjects of his writing lent him a spurious ashcan school credibility. See also* KITCHEN-SINK.

ashes *See* SACKCLOTH AND ASHES.

ashes to ashes *See* UNTO DUST SHALT THOU RETURN.

Ashtoreth (ashtăreth) Symbol of fertility or sexuality. Ashtoreth (Ashtorath) is identified in the Bible as the Phoenician fertility goddess Astarte, equivalent to the Greek Aphrodite, whom the Israelites briefly adopted as an idol, to the great offense of God: "And the children of Israel did evil again in the sight of the LORD, and served Baalim, and Ashtaroth" (Judges 10:6). "The bailiff was pointed out to Gabriel, who, checking the palpitation within his breast at discovering that this Ashtoreth of strange report was only a modification of Venus the well-known and admired, retired with him to talk over the necessary preliminaries of hiring" (Thomas Hardy, *Far from the Madding Crowd,* 1874).

ask and it shall be given you If you want something, you must take positive action to get it, rather than do nothing at all. The proverb is of biblical origin, appearing in Matthew 7:7, and is sometimes encountered in its fuller form: "Ask, and it shall be given you; seek, and ye shall find; knock, and it shall be opened unto you." Variants include ***ask and thou shall receive*** and the more colloquial ***them as asks, gits; them as don't ask, don't git.*** *The old woman handed over the envelope of money with a smile and whispered, "Ask and it shall be given you."*

ask not what your country can do for you Think what you can do for others, not what others can do for you. This worthy sentiment was voiced by President John F. Kennedy (1917–63) in the course of his inauguration speech on January 20, 1961: "Ask not what your country can do for you; ask what you can do for your country." It remains one of Kennedy's most oft-quoted lines, though not always given in full and often with the word "country" replaced with something else. *Ask not what your computer can do for you . . .*

Aslan *See* NARNIA.

as mad as a hatter *See* MAD AS A HATTER.

as old as Methuselah (methoozălă) Very old, ancient. Methuselah is the oldest man mentioned in the Bible who, according to Genesis 5:27, died at the advanced age of 969. "Now, you are my witness, Miss Summerson, I say I don't care—but if he was to come to our house with his great, shining, lumpy forehead night after night till he was as old as Methuselah, I wouldn't have anything to say to him'" (Charles Dickens, *Bleak House,* 1852–53). A ***methuselah*** is also an oversized wine bottle with a capacity of eight standard wine bottles.

Aspasia (aspayzhă) A prostitute. Aspasia was a celebrated Athenian courtesan of the fifth century B.C. whose devoted admirers included Pericles, who made her his mistress. "The man who acts, decides, and achieves; the woman who encourages, applauds, and—from a distance—inspires: the combination is common enough; but Miss Nightingale was neither an Aspasia nor an Egeria" (Lytton Strachey, *Eminent Victorians,* 1918).

as rich as Croesus (kreesăs) Immensely wealthy. Croesus (d. 546 B.C.) was the last king of Lydia and, through his conquests, the possessor of seemingly unlimited wealth. He was overthrown by Cyrus of Persia. "'And as for Lizzie—she's your cousin, and all that. And she's ever so pretty, and all that. And she's as rich as Croesus, and all that'" (Anthony Trollope, *The Eustace Diamonds,* 1873).

assume the mantle of Elijah *See* MANTLE OF ELIJAH.

Astaire, Fred *See* FRED ASTAIRE.

as you sow, so shall you reap *See* REAP WHAT YOU SOW.

Atalanta's race (atălantăz) A contest that is won through trickery. The allusion is to Greek mythology and the race that was run between the fleet-footed huntress Atalanta and her suitor Hippomenes (sometimes identified as Melanion). If Hippomenes won the race, according to the agreement, Atalanta would become his wife, but if he lost he would be put to death, like all her previous suitors. Before the race, Aphrodite gave Hippomenes the three golden apples of the Hesperides, which Hippomenes dropped along the route so that Atalanta would pause to pick them up. By this ruse Hippomenes won the race, and they were married. "Laurie reached the goal first and was quite satisfied with the success of his treatment, for his Atalanta came panting up with flying hair, bright eyes, ruddy cheeks, and no signs of dissatisfaction in her face" (Louisa May Alcott, *Little Women,* 1868–69).

Ate (aytee) Personification of mischief. According to Greek mythology, Zeus was so incensed at the goddess Ate's mischief making that he hurled her from Olympus. Ever since she has busied herself making trouble among inhabitants of the mortal world. "Caesar's spirit, ranging for revenge, / With Ate by his side, come hot from hell, / Shall, in these confines with a monarch's voice, / Cry 'havoc' and let slip the dogs of war" (William Shakespeare, *Julius Caesar,* 1599).

at ease in Zion (zīon) Living a life of comfort and luxury. The phrase comes from Amos 6:1, in which the prophet Amos criticizes the complacency of those who live indolent, comfortable existences: "woe to them that are at ease in Zion." *It was a long time since the regiment had seen action. The general accused them of having grown soft, living at ease in Zion. See also* ZION.

Athena (ătheenă) Personification of female wisdom and civilization. Known as Minerva by the Romans, Athena was depicted in Greek mythology as a virgin goddess who embodied practical skills and prudence in warfare. She was identified as the patron goddess of Athens (the city being named after her) and sided with the Greeks in the Trojan War. Legend had it that she was not born but sprang fully armed from the head of Zeus. *She held court at her mansion like some Athena presiding over the doings of lesser mortals. See also* PALLADIUM.

Athos *See* THREE MUSKETEERS.

Atkins, Tommy *See* TOMMY.

Atlantis (atlantis) A fabled lost city or land. The name was first applied to a lost continent described by Plato (c. 427–c. 347 B.C.) in *Timaeus* and *Critias* that was home to a great civilization existing some

9,000 years before the emergence of ancient Greece. According to legend, Atlantis sank beneath the waters of the east Atlantic, destroyed by earthquakes and floods as punishment for the wickedness of its citizens. It has been suggested that this lost land of fable may have been inspired by the Canary Islands or the Azores. "As for Owen Ford, the 'Margaret' of his book, although she had the soft brown hair and elfin face of the real girl who had vanished so long ago, 'pillowed where lost Atlantis sleeps,' had the personality of Leslie Moore, as it was revealed to him in those halcyon days at Four Winds Harbor" (Lucy Maud Montgomery, *Anne's House of Dreams,* 1917).

atlas (atlăs) A book of maps. The word refers to Greek mythology, specifically to Atlas, one of the Titans who attempted to overthrow Zeus. When the rebellion was defeated, Atlas was condemned to support the heavens upon his shoulders as punishment. One legend had it that he was transformed into the Atlas Mountains in northern Africa after Perseus, offended at Atlas's refusal to offer him hospitality, showed him the head of Medusa and turned him to stone. Any person who has to bear a heavy burden may be dubbed an Atlas or said to have ***Atlantean shoulders.*** The association with cartography dates from 1595, when maps compiled by Rumold Mercator included a depiction of Atlas supporting the earth on the title page. "Maple White Land it became, and so it is named in that chart which has become my special task. So it will, I trust, appear in the atlas of the future" (Sir Arthur Conan Doyle, *The Lost World,* 1912). *See also* CHARLES ATLAS.

Atlas, Charles *See* CHARLES ATLAS.

Atreus *See* HOUSE OF ATREUS.

Atropos *See* FATES.

at the eleventh hour At the last moment; in the nick of time. The expression is biblical in origin, appearing in Matthew 20:1–16, which relates the parable of the laborers in the vineyard and describes how workers who started work at the 11th hour received the same payment as those who had begun much earlier. "I am not easily shocked; and I can be implicitly trusted.' I hesitated even now, at the eleventh hour, sitting alone with him in his own room" (Wilkie Collins, *Armadale,* 1866).

at the Greek calends (kalendz) Never. The CALENDS marked the first day of the month in the Roman calendar. (They were unknown to the Greeks.) *He promised to repay the loan "at the Greek calends" and disappeared before anyone could ask when that might be.*

attic The space beneath the roof of a building. The word has its origins in the Attic style of architecture developed in ancient Athens (Attica) in the classical era. It acquired its modern meaning in the 18th century when Attic-style pilasters were widely used to decorate the outer walls of upper stories of classical facades. ***Attic salt*** describes a refined, biting wit, alluding to the reputation for sophisticated wit possessed by the inhabitants of ancient Attica. ***Attic faith*** is synonymous with trustworthiness or dependability, a reflection of how ancient Athenians believed themselves honorable and civilized. "'I see well enough you're going to get that old dress suit out of the cedar chest in the attic, and try to make me put it on me'" (Booth Tarkington, *Alice Adams,* 1921).

Attila the Hun (ătilă) Nickname for someone who behaves in a barbaric, cruel, and destructive manner. The historical Attila the Hun (A.D. c. 406–453) was the leader of the Huns, a nomadic people from central Asia who ravaged swaths of the Roman Empire in the fifth century, causing great destruction and loss of life. He was eventually defeated by the Romans and Visigoths at Châlons-sur-Marne. His men were widely feared for their barbaric behavior, hence the modern appropriation of their leader's name for anyone who behaves in a similar manner. *The heart of the city became a wasteland, as if the contract for redeveloping it had been given by mistake to Attila the Hun. See also* GENGHIS KHAN.

Augean stables *See* LABORS OF HERCULES.

August The eighth month of the year. The name comes from the Roman emperor Octavian (63 B.C.–A.D. 14), who was granted the title Augustus (meaning "venerable") by the Senate in recognition of his life's work. He named August after himself in imitation of his predecessor Julius Caesar, who had renamed July in his own honor. In order that Augustus's month should have no fewer days than Caesar's, he transferred one day from February to August so that both July and August would have 31 days. *By noon the day was as sultry as August, but she still felt a chill in her heart.*

Augustan Age (ogăstăn) A time of great prosperity and cultural achievement. The allusion is to the reign of the first Roman emperor, Augustus Caesar (63 B.C.–A.D. 14), which witnessed a great flowering of the arts and commerce in the peace following lengthy civil war. Notable products of this golden era included the building of many roads and aqueducts, the rebuilding of Rome, and the creation of many fine sculptures and literary masterpieces, among them the works of Horace, Ovid, and Virgil. In modern usage, the term is often employed in reference to literature (for instance, that of early 18th-century England). "You will perceive that I demand something which no Augustan nor Elizabethan age, which no culture, in short, can give" (Henry David Thoreau, *Walking,* 1851).

Aunt Agatha *See* AGATHA, AUNT.

Auntie The British Broadcasting Corporation (BBC). The nickname was originally intended as a condemnation of what was seen as the comfortable, uncontroversial outlook of the organization as a whole, but has since been adopted as a fond epithet by staff, listeners, and viewers alike. *Auntie is planning a few surprises for its younger viewers over the coming months.*

aurora (ororă) Atmospheric phenomenon in which bands or curtains of light move across the sky in polar regions (called the ***aurora australis*** over the South Pole and the ***aurora borealis*** over the North Pole). The phenomenon was named after Aurora, the Roman goddess of the dawn, equivalent to Eos in Greek mythology. The term is also used as a poetic description of the dawn. "It was morning; and the beautiful Aurora, of whom so much hath been written, said, and sung, did, with her rosy fingers, nip and tweak Miss Pecksniff's nose" (Charles Dickens, *Martin Chuzzlewit,* 1843).

Auschwitz (owshvits) A place or situation in which prisoners are treated with inhuman barbarity and are likely to be tortured and put to death in large numbers. Auschwitz (or Oświęcim) in southwest Poland was the site of a notorious Nazi death camp, in which some 2 million Jews from all over occupied Europe were executed in gas chambers. Even today, allusions to Auschwitz tend to be reserved for only the worst similar contexts, such is the horror associated with its name. *Recent rumors that the regime has discussed building a prison that could become another Auschwitz are troubling.* See also FINAL SOLUTION; HOLOCAUST.

Austerlitz (owsterlits, osterlits) An individual's greatest success. The Battle of Austerlitz was fought in 1805 between the armies of Napoleonic France and those of Austria and Russia in what is now the Czech Republic. Napoleon's crushing victory represented his greatest military success; although he did win further victories, it was never surpassed in scale and completeness by his armies. "The sun came up without a cloud, and shone brightly on his face. He sprang to his feet and said to Burleson, as he saluted him: 'The sun of Austerlitz has risen again.'" (Amelia Barr, *Remember the Alamo*, 1888).

auto-da-fé (otōdăfay) A trial, especially one in which the final outcome is predetermined and results in a death sentence. Meaning "act of faith" in Portuguese, the phrase originally described a ceremony during which officials of the Spanish Inquisition delivered their verdict and sentence on accused heretics, often ordering their execution at the stake at the hands of the church authorities. The term is usually applied today to judicial proceedings that are perceived to be both harsh and unfair. *The hearings were nothing more than an auto-da-fé in which the victims were not allowed an opportunity to be heard.*

Autolycus (otolikăs) Archetype of a cunning thief. Autolycus was identified in Greek mythology as the son of Hermes and grandfather of Odysseus and had a reputation as a crafty robber, being able to change the appearance of the property he stole. He attempted to refute charges that he had stolen the cattle of Sisyphus by changing their color but was undone by the fact that Sisyphus had marked his cattle under their feet. A pickpocket named Autolycus is a character in William Shakespeare's *The Winter's Tale* (1609). *This Autolycus was well known by the local police, who had arrested him on countless occasions in the past for petty larceny of one form or another.*

automatic pilot An approach to doing something while not thinking consciously about it or giving it much attention. The allusion is to a device that allows aircraft and other mechanical systems to be operated for a time without direct human intervention. When applied to ways of doing things, it tends to suggest they are being done in a lazy or negligent manner. *She appeared to be on automatic pilot, barely registering the content of the papers she was signing.*

Avalon (avălon) Paradise. It was to Avalon that, according to Celtic legend, KING ARTHUR was carried by his sister ***Morgan le Fay*** when mortally wounded at the Battle of Camlan. The word itself means "land of apples." *For years many of the party faithful continued to hope their leader would emerge from her self-imposed retirement in Avalon to lead them once more to victory.*

avatar (avătar) The embodiment of an idea or phrase. The avatars of Hindu mythology were the earthly forms in which various deities visited the human realm. Vishnu himself had ten such avatars, which included a lion (Narasimha), a boar (Varaha), and a fish (Matsya). *Through its policy of investment and expansion, the company has made itself an avatar of excellence within the industry.*

avenging angel Person bent on exacting retribution. According to Judeo-Christian tradition, the avenging angels, whose task it was to punish those who broke the laws of God, were among the first angels created by God. Twelve in number, they included Gabriel, Michael, Nathanael, Raphael, Satanel, and Uriel. "Harry smiled blandly till they were well on the pavement, saying some nothing, and keeping the victim's face averted from the avenging angel; and then, when the raised hand was sufficiently nigh, he withdrew two steps towards the nearest lamp-post" (Anthony Trollope, *Doctor Thorne,* 1858).

Avernus (ăvernăs) Hell; the underworld. In Roman mythology, a cave beside the volcanic lake of Avernus in Campania, central Italy, was identified as the entrance to the underworld and thus the name of the lake became synonymous with hell itself. The name itself means "without birds," a reference to the ancient belief that the sulphurous exhalations of the lake killed any birds flying in the area. Avernus is often referred to in the context of a line from Virgil's *Aeneid* (30–19 B.C.), *"Facilis descensus Averno"* (easy is the descent to Avernus). "Little boys at school are taught in their earliest Latin book that the path of Avernus is very easy of descent" (William Makepeace Thackeray, *Vanity Fair,* 1847–48).

axis (aksis) An alliance of two or more states, organizations, or other entities, often with what is perceived as being a nefarious end in mind. The original Axis was the international political alliance that was forged between Nazi Germany, Fascist Italy, and Japan in 1936, linking their militaristic ambitions. It was later extended to include Hungary, Bulgaria, Romania, Slovakia, and Croatia. The term itself was introduced in 1939, when it was coined by Italy's Fascist dictator Benito Mussolini, hailing the Pact of Steel agreed between Italy and Germany that year. In 2002, President George W. Bush brought the term back into currency with his warnings about an ***axis of evil*** being created to attack U.S. interests around the world. *The press took up the notion of an axis of evil comprising Iran, Iraq, and North Korea.*

axis of evil *See* AXIS.

ax to grind *See* HAVE AN AX TO GRIND.

ayatollah (īătolă) A repressive, authoritarian figure. The term is used among Shia Muslims to refer to their religious leaders, who deliver pronouncements upon Islamic law. The word acquired negative associations throughout the Western world with the rise of the ayatollahs in Iran in 1979 and their calling for the institution of strict Islamic states around the world. The title itself means "manifestation of God" in Arabic. *This suggestion is unlikely to go down well with the ayatollahs at head office. See also* FATWA.

ay, there's the rub *See* THERE'S THE RUB

B

Baal (bahl) A false god; an idol. The name, from the Hebrew *ba'al* (meaning "lord"), was originally applied to various ancient Semitic fertility gods and also appeared in Phoenician mythology as the name of the supreme sun god and god of fertility. Baal is identified in the Bible as the false pagan idol to which the Israelites briefly devoted themselves at the prompting of JEZEBEL (1 Kings 16–21). "What had he now brought down upon himself by sojourning thus in the tents of the heathen? He had consorted with idolaters round the altars of Baal, and therefore a sore punishment had come upon him" (Anthony Trollope, *Barchester Towers,* 1857).

Babbitt (babit) A person who lacks any interest in culture, a philistine. The allusion is to the novel *Babbitt* (1922), by the U.S. writer Sinclair Lewis, the central character of which is a simpleminded businessman whose life is filled with the mundane preoccupations of his work, to the exclusion of any cultural activity. *The streets were full of Babbitts chasing the elusive buck.*

Babel *See* TOWER OF BABEL.

babes and sucklings, out of the mouths of *See* OUT OF THE MOUTHS OF BABES AND SUCKLINGS.

babes in the wood A group of people whose innocence of the world is seen as making them vulnerable. The allusion is ultimately to an English broadside ballad entitled "The Children in the Wood; or, the Norfolk Gentleman's Last Will and Testament," which first appeared in Percy's *Reliques* in 1595 and at around the same time as an early melodrama. It has since, in much changed form, been adapted as the basis of popular Christmas pantomimes. The original tale concerns two young children who are left in the care of a wicked uncle after their father, the master of Wayland Hall in Norfolk, dies. Seeking to steal the children's inheritance, their uncle pays two thugs to murder the infants. One of the men is overcome with pity for the victims' plight and kills his confederate before abandoning the children deep in the woods. The children die and their tiny bodies are covered with leaves by a robin redbreast. In punishment for his crime, the wicked uncle suffers a series of terrible misfortunes, culminating in his own death in prison. In modern versions of the tale the tragic ending is usually revised so that the children are restored to their inheritance, often through the intervention of the folk hero ROBIN HOOD. "This is marriage, Trot; and Heaven bless you both, in it, for a pair of babes in the wood as you are!" (Charles Dickens, *David Copperfield*, 1849–50).

Babylon (babilon) A city, place, society, etc., notorious for corruption or depravity. The reference is to the biblical city of Babylon, the wealthy capital of ancient Babylonia on the Euphrates River. In the New Testament, Babylon is a symbol for a prosperous human society that has no time for God. Its fall is described in Revelation 18. Many cities have since been identified as modern Babylons. "There is iron-dust on everything; and the smoke is seen through the windows rolling heavily out of the tall chimneys to mingle with the smoke from a vaporous Babylon of other chimneys" (Charles Dickens, *Bleak House,* 1852–53). *See also* BABYLONIAN CAPTIVITY; BABYLONIAN NUMBERS; WHORE OF BABYLON.

Babylonian captivity (babilōneeăn) A lengthy period of exile or subjugation. The original Babylonian captivity was the time the Jews spent in exile in Babylon in the years 587–538 B.C. (2 Kings 25). The term was subsequently revived to describe the period of exile of the popes to Avignon in the years 1309–77, during which time they were dominated by the French monarchy and presided over a corrupt, materialist court. *He spent the next five years in a kind of willing Babylonian captivity, submitting himself to her every whim.*

Babylonian numbers (babilōneeăn) The involved and unreliable forecasts of astrologers and fortune-tellers. The phrase comes from a quotation from Horace's *Odes* (24–13 B.C.), which in translation reads, "Do not make trial of Babylonian calculations." In classical times Babylonian astrologers were considered among the most sophisticated of their kind. *Her interest in what are sometimes termed Babylonian numbers quickly exasperated her entourage.*

Baca, Valley of *See* VALE OF TEARS.

Bacchae *See* BACCHANTE.

bacchanalia (bakănaylyă) A drunken orgy; any outburst of dissolute, riotous behavior. The word alludes to the orgiastic celebrations that took place in ancient Rome in honor of BACCHUS, the god of wine (himself the equivalent of the Greek god Dionysus). Celebrants abandoned themselves to all manner of licentious excess, including singing, dancing, drinking, and unrestrained sexual indulgence. The festival, which was imported to Rome around 200 B.C., was banned by the Senate in 186 B.C. "The learned profession of the law was certainly not behind any other learned profession in its Bacchanalian propensities" (Charles Dickens, *A Tale of Two Cities,* 1859). *See also* BACCHANTE.

bacchante (băkantee) A drunken female reveler. In ancient Rome the bacchantes, also known as ***bacchae*** or ***maenads,*** were women who followed BACCHUS, the god of wine, and were notorious for their indulgence, sexual immorality, and drunkenness—central features of the celebrations known as the BACCHANALIA. (The male form of the word is ***bacchant,*** but the female form is far more common.) "The praise of folly, as he went on, soared into a philosophy, and Philosophy herself became young, and catching the mad music of Pleasure, wearing, one might fancy, her wine-stained robe and wreath of ivy, danced like a Bacchante over the hills of life, and mocked the slow Silenus for being sober" (Oscar Wilde, *The Picture of Dorian Gray,* 1891).

Bacchus (bakăs) The god of wine and thus, by extension, of any alcoholic drink. Bacchus was the son of Zeus and Semele and the Roman equivalent of Dionysus, the Greek god of wine. He was variously depicted as a bearded, merry man or as a beautiful youth crowned with vines and ivy. Those who imbibe too enthusiastically may be termed ***sons of Bacchus*** or ***priests of Bacchus.*** "Raphael's face was found boldly executed on the underside of the moulding board, and Bacchus on the head of a beer barrel" (Louisa May Alcott, *Little Women,* 1868–69). *See also* BACCHANALIA; BACCHANTE.

backroom boys People who work behind the scenes, out of the public view, especially scientists and technicians. The phrase dates to World War II, when hundreds of such experts worked tirelessly on radar and other innovations that might help the Allied war effort. The ultimate origin of the term lies in the song "See what the boys in the back room will have," made famous by MARLENE DIETRICH in the film *Destry Rides Again* (1939). "I think you'd better be a financial adviser—one of the bank's backroom boys" (J. R. L. Anderson, *Death in the City*, 1980).

back to square one Back at the very beginning of a project, task, etc. The origins of this phrase are much debated, but the most popular theory is that it alludes to early radio broadcasts of soccer matches, in which listeners were provided with a grid of the pitch, divided into numbered squares, so that they could visualize where the action described was taking place as the commentators gave the number of the relevant square; after a goal, play restarted in the middle, on square one. "I took him back because I love him and can't do without him, so now I'm back to square one" (Sue Sharpe, *Falling for Love*, 1987).

bad day at Black Rock A disappointing, even disastrous state of affairs. The allusion is to a classic 1955 film of the same title, starring Spencer Tracy as a stranger who incurs the wrath of the unwelcoming residents of a remote township called Black Rock when he starts to uncover the truth behind a local murder. *It was a bad day at Black Rock when the band sacked their lead singer.*

Baedeker (bīdekă) A guide book. Karl Baedeker (1801–59) was the German publisher of a series of celebrated guidebooks that came to be widely trusted by travelers around the world. During World War II, commanders of the German air force were rumored to be using the Baedeker guidebook to the United Kingdom to decide which historic British cities they should bomb in what became known as "Baedeker raids." In modern usage, guidebooks and of any kind may be referred to as "Baedekers." *"Don't forget your Baedeker," said Terry, tossing Roger his guide to places of interest in southern Canada.*

Balaam's ass (baylamz) Someone or something that serves to remind a person of the correct way to act. The allusion is to the biblical story of Balaam, a Mesopotamian prophet who was commanded by Balak, king of Moab, to curse the Israelites. Balaam set out to do the king's bidding, but on the prompting of his talking donkey prophesied instead future glory for them (as related at Numbers 22–23). People who follow a religion for reasons of profit or gain are sometimes dubbed ***Balaamites.*** "'By my hilt!' cried the archer, 'I though I be not Balaam, yet I hold converse with the very creature that spake to him'" (Sir Arthur Conan Doyle, *The White Company,* 1891).

balkanization (bolkănīzayshăn) The fragmentation of a country, organization, etc., into smaller, separate, and often warring parts. The term refers to the countries of the Balkan region of southeast

Europe, which have been the scene of internal conflict motivated by ethnic and historical differences for generations, most recently in the 1990s following the disintegration of the former Yugoslavia. In modern usage, the term often refers to the deliberate splintering of a larger country or other entity in order to limit the power it might exert as a coherent unit. *The balkanization of what was formerly a public corporation has effectively ended its dominance of the market.*

ballpark figure A rough estimate. The allusion, which dates to the 1950s, is to the stadiums in which games of baseball are played, the size of which makes calculating the extent of the playing area and the number of spectators a matter of conjecture. A figure that is thought to be approximately correct may be said to be ***in the right ballpark.*** *I know you can't tell me precisely what you might be prepared to pay, but at least give me a ballpark figure.*

balm in Gilead (gileead) A remedy or consolation in times of trouble. The allusion is to Jeremiah 8:22, in which God laments that his people are not yet healed of their sins: "Is there no balm in Gilead; is there no physician there?" There is another reference to Gilead in Genesis 37:25 that runs, "Behold, a company of Ishmeelites came from Gilead with their camels bearing spicery and balm and myrrh, going to carry it down to Egypt." Gilead is the name of a desolate region east of the Jordan, which was well known for the production of aromatic herbs and balm, a resin extracted from the mastic tree *Pistacia lentiscus* and noted for its medicinal properties. " 'My garden was all smashed flat,' he continued mournfully, 'but so was Dora's,' he added in a tone which indicated that there was yet balm in Gilead" (Lucy Maud Montgomery, *Anne of Avonlea,* 1908).

balthazar (balthăzahr) A large wine bottle equivalent to 16 standard bottles. The allusion is to King BELSHAZZAR, who provided huge quantities of wine for guests at a great banquet (*see* BELSHAZZAR'S FEAST). *It is many years since balthazars of fine wine were supplied to the restaurant on a regular basis in advance of royal visits. See also* MAGI.

Bambi (bambee) A youthful person or animal, especially one that is depicted as innocent and vulnerable. The allusion is the Walt Disney cartoon film *Bambi* (1942), about the adventures of a young deer fawn, which was based on a 1923 novel of the same title written for children by Felix Salzman (or Salten). The name Bambi was derived from the Italian *bambino*, meaning "baby." *He looked like Bambi caught in the glare of the world's press.*

band of merry men *See* ROBIN HOOD.

Banquo's ghost (bankwōz) An unwished-for reminder of a past crime or misdeed. The allusion is to William Shakespeare's tragedy *Macbeth* (1606), in which the ghost of the murdered Banquo materializes during a banquet to torture the guilty conscience of Macbeth, who ordered his killing: "Thou canst not say I did it; never shake thy gory locks at me." *The memory of their former boss kept springing to mind, like Banquo's ghost.*

baptism of fire An arduous initiation or introduction to something. The phrase was coined by early Christians in referring to the spiritual purification given by the presence of the Holy Spirit at the time of Pentecost (Acts 2:1–4). "New Environment Secretary, Mr. Tom King, faces a baptism of fire over his decision to withdraw and re-draft the latest rules on council spending" (*Guardian,* January 14, 1983).

Barabbas (Bărabăas) A criminal who evades punishment for his crimes. According to Matthew 27:16 and John 18:40, Barabbas was a thief condemned to be crucified at Passover time. At the public crucifixion, the mob was, by long-established custom, offered the choice of one of the men to be pardoned; the group chose Barabbas. He is variously described in the books of Luke and Mark as a seditionist or murderer. Jocularly he is sometimes thought of as a publisher, an identification attributed to the English poet Lord Byron. The story goes that Byron was presented with a beautiful edition of the Bible by his publisher John Murray, but the poet returned the gift after having changed the word *robber* ("Now Barabbas was a robber," John 18:40) to *publisher. Like some latter-day Barabbas, he had successfully hoodwinked the courts and spent much of his adult life enjoying moneyed freedom in the Seychelles.*

Barathron (bărathrăn) A place where garbage is dumped. The original Barathron, or ***Barathrum,*** was a deep ditch behind the Acropolis in Athens into which criminals were thrown to their death. *The alley was a veritable Barathron, full of all description of trash.*

Barbara Cartland (bahrbără kahrtlănd) The embodiment of romantic fiction. The British novelist Barbara Cartland (1901–2000) became the world's best-selling author in the world by virtue of the hundreds of light romantic stories that she produced over a long writing career. Derided by critics, she strongly defended her role as a champion of old-fashioned romance. *With the softest of furnishings and everything in pastel shades it was all very Barbara Cartland.*

barbarian A brutish, uncivilized person. The term was coined by the ancient Greeks, who called anyone who could not speak Greek *barbaros* (because the unintelligible Germanic dialects of many such people sounded like "bar-bar-bar" to the Greek ear). In due course the term came to be applied to the cultures of such foreign peoples in general. ". . . a silly, painful, and disgusting ceremony, which can only be considered as a relic of barbarian darkness, which tears the knees and shins to pieces, let alone the pantaloons" (William Makepeace Thackeray, *Adventures of Major Gahagan,* 1839).

Barbie An attractive but superficial female, typically one with blonde hair and an overly sweet manner. The original Barbie (whose full name was Barbara Millicent Roberts) was a child's doll first marketed under the Barbie tradename by the Mattel Toy Company in 1959. Dressed like a trendy teenaged girl of the late 1950s, Barbie (and her wardrobe) kept pace with the times, becoming a widely recognized cultural and fashion icon, though also a target of outraged feminists. She even acquired a boyfriend called ***Ken***. Her name was borrowed from Barbara (or 'Barbie') Handler, who as a young girl on holiday with her parents Ruth and Elliot Handler, the cofounders of Mattel, took a liking to a doll (named Lilli) that she spotted in a Lucerne shop window. She bought the doll, which became the prototype for Barbie. Ken, when he appeared, was named after Barbara's brother. *Some people call Britney Spears a real Barbie, but I think she's cool.*

Bardolph (bahrdolf) A coarse, swaggering drunkard, especially one with a drinker's red nose. The allusion is to a character of the name in William Shakespeare's *Henry IV, Parts I and II* (1597) and *Henry V* (1598). One of Falstaff's drinking companions, Bardolph is called "the knight of the burning lamp" because of his bulbous red nose. Such a nose is sometimes described as ***Bardolphian***. "His cheeks were plump and sanguine, his eyes bright and cheerful, and the tip of his nose glowed with a Bardolphian fire,—a flame, indeed, which Hugh was so far a vestal as to supply with its necessary fuel, at all seasons of the year" (Nathaniel Hawthorne, *Fanshawe*, 1828). *See also* FALSTAFFIAN.

Bardot, Brigitte *See* BRIGITTE BARDOT.

bare ruined choirs A ruined building or other entity that has been reduced to a mere relic of its former self. The phrase comes from William Shakespeare's Sonnet 73, in which it is employed as an image of the ravages of time: "That time of year thou mayst in me behold / When yellow leaves, or none, or few, do hang / Upon those boughs which shake against the cold, / Bare ruined choirs where late the sweet birds sang." *Gavin felt moved to tears as he surveyed the bare ruined choirs of the aircraft carrier in the breaker's yard.*

Barkis is willin' (bahrkis) An expression of willingness. The phrase came originally from the Charles Dickens novel *David Copperfield* (1849–50), in which Barkis is a carrier who sends the message "Barkis is willin'" to his sweetheart Clara Peggotty to indicate that he is ready to marry her. *You can tell my boss that now we've sorted out the pay Barkis is willin'.*

Barmecide feast (bahrmăsīd) An illusory advantage or valueless promise. The allusion is to the ARABIAN NIGHTS, which includes the tale of a rich nobleman called Barmecide who mocks a starving beggar called Schacabac by offering him a banquet of nonexistent food and wine. The beggar pretends to eat, but after drinking the imaginary wine he feigns drunkenness and strikes his host. Barmecide is so pleased that his guest has played along with him that he offers Schacabac real food and wine. "Your lighter boxes of family papers went up-stairs into a Barmecide room, that always had a great dining-table in it and never had a dinner . . ." (Charles Dickens, *A Tale of Two Cities*, 1859).

Barnum, P.T. *See* P. T. BARNUM.

baroque (bărok; bărōk) Exceedingly ornate, convoluted, or overembellished. The allusion is to a decorative style in art and architecture that enjoyed a huge vogue between the 16th and 18th centuries. The style of the baroque incorporated florid swirls and lavish details such as cherubs and other figures picked out in gilt and gold. The word itself comes from the Portuguese *barroco*, meaning "a pearl of irregular shape." *The baroque complexity of Einstein's calculations exceeded the grasp of most of his contemporaries. See also* ROCOCO.

Barsetshire Archetypal of English rural life and the values of its inhabitants. The imaginary county of Barsetshire was created by British novelist Anthony Trollope as the setting for a series of celebrated novels, beginning with *The Warden* (1855) and ending with *The Last Chronicle of Barset* (1867). Barchester, the county town, was modeled on the real English cities of Salisbury and Winchester. *The surroundings were all very Barsetshire, with the shadow of the cathedral slowly lengthening as the sun set over the distant hills and woods.*

Bashan, bull of *See* BULL OF BASHAN.

Basil Fawlty *See* FAWLTY TOWERS.

basilisk stare (basălisk; bazălisk) A cold stare; a glance that exerts a profound, even deadly influence over the person at whom it is directed. The basilisk (virtually synonymous with the COCKATRICE) was a serpent of mythological origin, hatched by a reptile from the egg of a cock and reputed to be able to kill its victim with a mere glance or with the exhalation of its breath. In modern usage, the word *basilisk* may refer to any example of the genus *Basiliscus* of tropical America, which includes a variety of small arboreal semiaquatic lizards (the males of which often have an inflatable head crest used in display). "Without softening very much the basiliks nature of his stare, he said, impassively: 'We are coming to that part of my investigation, sir'" (Joseph Conrad, *The Secret Agent,* 1907).

Bastille (basteel) A formidable or impregnable prison. The Bastille prison in Paris, built originally as a fortress in the 14th century, was the most notorious prison in France prior to the French Revolution of July 14, 1789, when the mob stormed its gates and freed all the prisoners inside. The prison was subsequently sacked; ever since then July 14 has been celebrated as Bastille Day. The word itself comes from the Old French *bastir*, meaning "to build." In modern usage, the name Bastille may be used figuratively of any bastion of oppression. "Yet the other half was as determined as ever and in a better position for defence, since it consisted of enormous convents and monasteries with walls like the Bastille, which could not be so easily brushed out of our way" (Arthur Conan Doyle, *The Adventures of Gerard*, 1896).

Bates Motel (bayts) An unappealing and sinister hotel, boardinghouse, or other building. The allusion is to the terrifying 1960 movie *PSYCHO,* directed by Alfred Hitchcock, the action of which takes place largely in the lonely Bates Motel and in the neighboring house occupied by its owner, the psychotic, mother-obsessed ***Norman Bates***. "Most travellers with their wits about them and an eye for aesthetics would have preferred to rest at the Bates Motel" (Paul Bryers, *The Adultery Department*, 1993).

Bathsheba *See* DAVID AND BATHSHEBA.

Batman and Robin Archetypal comic-book superheroes, who seek to right wrongs and defend the innocent in a crime-ridden world. Dressed in a distinctive bat-like cape and mask, Batman (otherwise known as the ***Caped Crusader***) was the alias of rich Gotham City socialite ***Bruce Wayne***. The creation of Bob Kane (1915–98), he made his first appearance in *Detective Comics* in 1939 and subsequently became a star of television and film. Robin, the ***Boy Wonder***, was introduced as Batman's equally heroic assistant, while Batgirl was added in 1967. The somewhat camp flavor of the 1960s U.S. television series based on the original characters means that modern references to Batman and Robin are usually jocular and intended to point out deficiencies in the people to whom the tag is applied. *You look like Batman and Robin in those anoraks. See also* GOTHAM.

batrachomyomachia (bătrakōmīōmakeeă) A great deal of fuss about something trivial; much ado about nothing. The word, which means "the battle of the frogs and mice," originated as the title of a mock heroic epic formerly attributed to Homer (eighth century B.C.) but more probably is the work of Pigres of Caria (c. fourth century B.C.). *Billed as an epic struggle, the contest turned out to be more of a batrachomyomachia.*

Battle of Hastings *See* HASTINGS, BATTLE OF.

Battle of the Bulge *See* BULGE, BATTLE OF THE.

Baucis *See* PHILEMON AND BAUCIS.

Bauhaus (bowhows) In a modernistic style reminiscent of that championed by German architect Walter Gropius (1883–1969). The Bauhaus itself was the name of the art and design school established by Gropius in Weimar, Germany, in 1919 to further the principle of combining art and craft in building design, with the emphasis on form following function. The name Bauhaus was arrived at by inverting the German word *Hausbau* (building of a house). The school was closed by the Nazis in 1933 but the movement it represented continued to exert a profound influence throughout the 20th century. "Its full-length windows give the appearance, appropriately enough, of a power house, and the quantity of glass gives it a modern, almost Bauhaus feel" (Jeffrey Richards and John M. MacKenzie, *The Railway Station: A Social History*, 1988).

Bay of Pigs A military fiasco, a foiled invasion. The allusion is the disastrous U.S.-backed invasion of Cuba launched on April 25, 1961, which ended catastrophically as a result of poor organization and lack of air cover. *It was the nation's greatest humiliation since the Bay of Pigs.*

beam in one's own eye, the *See* MOTE AND BEAM.

beam me up, Scotty I wish I could escape this awkward or embarrassing situation. The line is a quotation from the popular long-running U.S. science-fiction television and film series *STAR TREK*, first broadcast on television in 1966. Members of the crew were transported from the starship *Enterprise* to other locations by means of a matter-transference beam, often in order to escape extreme danger. Lieutenant Commander 'Scotty' Scott, played by James Doohan (1920–2005), was the ship's chief engineer, who oversaw such transfers. Though the line has become a catchphrase, it is claimed that the line is never actually delivered in precisely this form anywhere in the televised adventures. *"Beam me up, Scotty," he breathed as his wife walked into the room, her brow dark with fury.*

Bean, Mr. *See* MR. BEAN.

bear/carry/take one's cross To suffer a trial affliction patiently. The expression alludes to Christ's words to his disciples: "If any man will come after me, let him deny himself, and take up his cross, and follow me" (Matthew 16:24). "You must try and be strong and bear it bravely. We all have our cross to bear" (Aldous Huxley, *Limbo,* 1920). "'Still, this isn't the time really, is it?' And she smiled, and was carrying her cross ever so bravely really" (G. W. Target, *The Teachers,* 1960).

bear the burden and heat of the day To assume the most laborious or exacting part of a task, particularly in comparison to the lesser efforts of others. The phrase is a quotation from the parable of the vineyard in which Christ compares the differing contributions of the workers, some of whom have worked all day long, while others have arrived much later when the bulk of the work has been done (Matthew 20:1–16). "We do not wish to tax your energies too much. We will bear some of the burden and heat of the day ourselves" (Mark Twain, *The Innocents Abroad,* 1869).

beast with ten horns *See* WHORE OF BABYLON.

beast with two backs The act of lovemaking. The phrase is usually credited to William Shakespeare, who employed it in his tragedy *Othello* (c. 1603), in which IAGO uses it to provoke DESDEMONA's father concerning the elopement of his daughter and her lover OTHELLO: "I am one, sir, that comes to tell you your daughter and the Moor are now making the beast with two backs." In reality, the phrase is older and of French origin, appearing in the works of Rabelais (c. 1494–c. 1553). *He had long since given up trying to persuade her to make the beast with two backs with him.*

Beat Generation (beet) The young of the 1950s and early 1960s, especially young U.S. writers and artists of the period known for their unconventional, Bohemian lifestyle and espousal of antiestablishment values. Notable figures of the Beat Generation, who were largely motivated by despair at the state of the world around them, included the writers Jack Kerouac (1922–69), Allen Ginsberg (1926–97), and William Burroughs (1914–97). The name Beat Generation was based on the slang usage of the word "beat" meaning "exhausted," although Kerouac also linked it to "beatitude." *She was one of the last of the Beat Generation to settle in Greenwich Village.*

beatitude (beeatitood) A blessing, especially one of a formulaic nature. The original Beatitudes were the eight sayings spoken by Christ in the Sermon on the Mount, as recorded at Matthew 5:1–12. In these, Christ promises that the poor in spirit, those who mourn, the meek, those who thirst for righteousness, the merciful, the pure in heart, the peacemakers, and those who are persecuted for righteousness's sake will receive the blessing of heaven. "Indeed, throughout all the great soft-coal country, people who consider themselves comparatively poor may find this consolation: cleanliness has been added to the virtues and beatitudes that money can not buy" (Booth Tarkington, *Alice Adams,* 1921). *See also* MEEK SHALL INHERIT THE EARTH, THE.

Beatrice *See* BENEDICK; DANTE AND BEATRICE.

beat swords into plowshares To make peace; to adapt the weapons of war for peaceful purposes. The phrase is biblical in origin, appearing in Isaiah 2:4 (and also Micah 4:3), as follows: "And he shall judge among the nations, and shall rebuke many people: and they shall beat their swords into plowshares, and their spears into pruninghooks: nation shall not lift up sword against nation, neither shall they learn war any more." The same imagery recurs at Joel 3:10, but with the reverse meaning: "Beat your plowshares into swords." *On the surface, this latest nuclear disarmament treaty amounts to the most determined attempt in recent years to beat the swords of the two superpowers into plowshares.*

Beau Brummell (bō brămăl) A fop, a person obsessed with fashion. George Bryan Brummell (1778–1840) was a celebrated trendsetter during the regency of the future George IV and moved in the highest social circles, championing a restrained elegance of dress in fashionable society. His nickname Beau, meaning "dandy," reflected his love of fine clothes. He gambled away most of his money and fell out with the future king in 1812, however, eventually dying in poverty in a hospital for the insane in France. *He was the Beau Brummell of the* *group, always wearing a jacket and tie and a pair of highly polished shoes.*

Beau Geste (bō zhest) A romantic hero, or a dashing adventure story. The allusion is to the novel *Beau Geste* (1924) by P. C. Wren, which relates the adventures of the disgraced hero Michael "Beau" Geste in the French Foreign Legion. The title of the novel may also be invoked to describe places that are apparently deserted, an allusion to a famous scene in the novel in which an abandoned fort is made to appear defended through the arranging of dead bodies to look like guards manning the walls. *He stood on the wall waving the flag like something out of Beau Geste.*

beauty and the beast Two people or other entities of contrasting qualities, especially as regards physical appearance. The allusion is to a famous fairy tale of the same title in which a beautiful girl is forced to live with an ugly monster in order to save the life of her father. She gradually falls in love with the "beast" as she learns to appreciate the inner beauty that lies behind the unappealing exterior. The story is many centuries old, early versions including Strapola's *Le Piacevoli Notti* (1550). "However, when the Parkers passed by, some were cruel enough to refer to the minister and his attractive wife as 'The Beauty and the Beast'" (James Munson, *The Nonconformists*, 1991).

beauty contest A competition that is decided by superficial factors, such as physical appearance. The term referred originally to contests, popular around the middle of the 20th century, in which beautiful women were judged chiefly or wholly according to their looks. In modern usage the term is also applied in U.S. politics to the selection of delegates to nominating conventions in primary elections. *The politicians are treating the issue as if it's a beauty contest, not something that affects people's lives.*

because it's there The only reason for doing something is that it is there to be done. This sentiment is usually attributed to British mountaineer George Mallory (1886–1924) as his reply (while on tour in the United States in 1923) when asked why he wanted to climb MOUNT EVEREST. He died in an attempt on the mountain a year later; his body was found below the summit in 1999. Another theory attributes the phrase to a reporter named Benson, who wrote up Mallory's U.S. tour in the *New York Times*. *The only reason he could give for wanting to embark on such a difficult and dangerous enterprise was because it was there.*

Becky Sharp (bekee) An unscrupulous, ambitious, opportunistic young woman. Becky Sharp is the memorably self-serving heroine of the novel *VANITY FAIR* (1847–48) by the British novelist William Makepeace Thackeray (1811–63). An orphan, Becky Sharp determines to make the best of her opportunities and uses all the means at her disposal, including marriage, to make her way in society. By the end of the book she is a rich woman, though many others have suffered through knowing her. "She was the Becky Sharp of the cat world" (Jean Bow, *Jane's Journey*, 1991).

bedlam (bedlăm) A state of chaos, confusion, and uproar. The allusion is to the priory of St. Mary of Bethlehem at Bishopsgate, London, which took in mentally ill patients from the 14th century. In due course the name of this asylum was abbreviated to Bedlam, hence the modern word. Fashionable people of the 17th and 18th centuries enjoyed touring Bedlam to see the chaos and disorder in which the inmates lived. *There was bedlam when the stars appeared at the stage door.*

bed of Procrustes *See* PROCRUSTEAN.

Beelzebub (beeelzebăb) A devil, demon, or very wicked person. Beelzebub is identified in 2 Kings 1:2 as a god of the Philistines and is listed in the Bible as one of the devil's closest allies—sometimes his name is even used as a synonym for SATAN. The word comes from the Hebrew *ba'al zebub* (originally meaning "lord of the heavenly habitation" but later reinterpreted as meaning "lord of the flies"). "Had this history been writ in the days of superstition, I should have had too much compassion for the reader to have left him so long in suspense, whether Beelzebub or Satan was about actually to appear in person, with all his hellish retinue; but as these doctrines are at present very unfortunate, and have but few, if any believers, I have not been much aware of conveying any such terrors" (Henry Fielding, *Tom Jones,* 1749).

beer and skittles A comfortable situation, an easy way of life. The allusion is to a proverbial expression, "Life is not all beer and skittles." The skittles in question are those used in the British game of ninepins. *Life here is pretty good at the moment, but it hasn't all been beer and skittles since we arrived.*

before the Flood *See* FLOOD.

be fruitful and multiply To prosper, usually as measured by the production of offspring. The phrase is a quotation from Genesis 1:28, in which God commands Adam to "be fruitful, and multiply, and replenish the earth." It appears once again in Genesis 9:1, in which God repeats the instruction to Noah. The phrase is sometimes cited in defense of arguments against contraception or clerical celibacy. The expression is also found as ***go forth and multiply,*** in allusion to God's words to Noah: 'Go forth of the ark, thou, and thy wife, and thy sons, and thy sons' wives with thee. Bring forth with thee every living thing that *is* with thee, of all flesh both of fowl, and of cattle, and of every creeping thing that creepeth upon the earth; that they may breed abundantly in the earth, and be fruitful, and multiply upon the earth" (Genesis 8:16–17). *The settlers took their duty to be fruitful and multiply very seriously and within five years their small community had doubled in number.*

beginning was the Word, in the *See* IN THE BEGINNING WAS THE WORD.

behemoth (biheemăth) A huge beast or thing. The name appears in Job 40:15–24, where it probably refers to a hippopotamus (although when John Milton described the behemoth in *Paradise Lost* he clearly had an elephant in mind). The word itself comes from the plural form of the Hebrew *behemah* (meaning "beast"). "Adolph tripped gracefully forward, and Tom, with lumbering tread, went after. 'He's a perfect behemoth!' said Marie" (Harriet Beecher Stowe, *Uncle Tom's Cabin,* 1852). *See also* LEVIATHAN.

behind the eight ball In an awkward, even dangerous position. The allusion is to pool, in which the black eight ball (distinguished by a white number eight) should not be pocketed until the end of the game. A player is disadvantaged, therefore, if the eight ball lies in front of the ball he or she wishes to pocket and is thus in danger of being pocketed out of order. *When the project* *landed on his desk he found himself behind the eight ball, unwilling to approve it but not wanting to be taken off the job.*

behold the man *See* ECCE HOMO.

Belial (beeleeăl) Archetypal demon; a personification of wickedness or lawlessness. The word is mentioned several times in the Old Testament, where it is synonymous with "worthlessness" (1 Samuel 1:16 and 2 Samuel 25:17), and is also used in the New Testament as another name for SATAN (2 Corinthians 6:15). John Milton identified Belial in *Paradise Lost* as one of the fallen angels: "Belial came last, than whom a spirit more lewd / Fell not from heaven." The word itself comes from the Hebrew *beliy* (meaning "without") and *ya'al* (meaning "worth"). Rebellious, lawbreaking people are sometimes referred to as ***sons of Belial.*** "The Presbyterian sternly raised his eyes. 'After the world, and according to the flesh, she is my daughter; but when she became a child of Belial, and a company-keeper, and a trader in guilt and iniquity, she ceased to be a bairn of mine'" (Sir Walter, Scott, *The Heart of Midlothian,* 1818).

bell, book, and candle The ceremony of excommunication from the Roman Catholic Church. The phrase alludes to features of the ceremony, namely, the symbolic shutting of the Bible, the quenching of a candle, and the tolling of a bell, all of which represent the ending of a person's life within the church. *She removed all trace of him from her life, as though by bell, book, and candle.*

belle dame sans merci, la *See* LA BELLE DAME SANS MERCI.

belle époque, la *See* LA BELLE ÉPOQUE.

Bellerophon *See* LETTER OF BELLEROPHON.

bell the cat To undertake a dangerous mission. The allusion is to the fable attributed to the Greek writer AESOP (c. 620–564 B.C.) that relates how some mice agreed that it would be a good idea to hang a bell around a cat's neck so that they would know when it was approaching but were then faced with the daunting question of who should attempt to attach the bell in the first place. ". . . as he was made of sterner stuff than they, so would it be more difficult to reconcile him to the alterations which were now proposed in the family arrangements. Who was to bell the cat?" (Anthony Trollope, *Ayala's Angel,* 1881).

below the belt *See* HIT BELOW THE BELT.

below the salt Of humble, lower-class origins. The allusion is to a custom observed in baronial halls during the medieval period. This involved the salt being placed at the center of the long tables at which diners sat to eat. The better-connected people sat at the end nearest the lord and his family (above the salt) and the rest at the far end (below the salt). "Cyrus Vance, the U.S. secretary of state, the Iranian foreign minister, and other senior officials were well below the salt" (William Shawcross, *The Shah's Last Ride*, 1989).

Belphegor (belfegor) Archetype of a misanthropic lecher. He is identified in Numbers 25:3 as the Assyrian version of BAAL, the pagan god whose veneration took the form of licentious orgies. In later medieval legend Belphegor was identified as a demon who was sent to earth to investigate the realities of marital bliss. Having probed the truths behind married life, Belphegor fled earth to escape the horrors of female companionship. *After his* *divorce, he assumed the mantle of Belphegor, muttering darkly about the vagaries of woman and avoiding all contact with the fairer sex.*

Belshazzar (belshazăr) A corrupt or decadent ruler, especially one who is threatened by imminent disaster. The reference is to the biblical Belshazzar, who was the last Chaldean king of Babylon (Daniel 5). His name literally means "Bel protect the king." "To have been Belshazzar, King of Babylon; and to have been Belshazzar, not haughtily but courteously, therein certainly must have been some touch of mundane grandeur" (Herman Melville, *Moby-Dick,* 1851). *See also* BALTHAZAR; BELSHAZZAR'S FEAST; BELSHAZZAR'S PALSY; WRITING ON THE WALL.

Belshazzar's feast (belshazărz) An example of decadent indulgence. The allusion is to the banquet hosted by Belshazzar, who was the last Chaldean king of Babylon, as described in Daniel 5. The feast, attended by a thousand nobles, was remarkable for the magnificence of the gold and silver utensils, which had been seized from the Temple in Jerusalem. "'I always like this room,' said Spandrell as they entered. 'It's like a scene for Belshazzar's feast'" (Aldous Huxley, *Point Counter Point,* 1928). *See also* BELSHAZZAR'S PALSY; WRITING ON THE WALL.

Belshazzar's palsy (belshazărz) A fever, especially one caused by fear. The allusion is to the episode of BELSHAZZAR'S FEAST, a magnificent banquet hosted by BELSHAZZAR, king of Babylon, at which the WRITING ON THE WALL appeared. The shock caused Belshazzar to be seized by a shaking fever, as described at Daniel 5:6: ". . . his thoughts troubled him, so that the joints of his loins were loosed, and his knees smote one against another." *The effect of this news upon the general was startling. His face went deathly pale and his hands shook uncontrollably. Though no doctor, the priest was inclined to diagnose a severe case of Belshazzar's palsy.*

Benedick (benădik) A confirmed bachelor who finds himself snared into marriage. The allusion is to a fictional character of the name (sometimes given as ***Benedict***) in William Shakespeare's romantic comedy *Much Ado About Nothing* (1598). Despite his avowed intention, Benedick falls in love with ***Beatrice*** and agrees to marry her by the end of the play. *No Benedick could have been more determined to avoid the altar.*

Benedict Arnold (benădikt ahrnăld) A traitor, especially a man who betrays his country on a massive scale. The original Benedict Arnold (1741–1801) was an American general who distinguished himself in the Continental army during the American Revolution. Having got heavily into debt, and feeling embittered toward Congress, he then changed allegiances and plotted to hand over the fort of West Point, New York, to the British. The plot was uncovered and Arnold fled to safety with the British, subsequently fighting alongside them against his fellow Americans. He eventually retired to England and remained there for the rest of his life in disgrace. *After he reported the company to the authorities his former colleagues regarded him as a Benedict Arnold and would have nothing to do with him.*

Ben Gunn Archetype of a mad old man, especially one of wild appearance or one who has spent many years in isolation. Ben Gunn is a character from Robert Louis Stevenson's adventure novel *Treasure Island* (1883), in which he appears as a former member of the pirate crew of Captain Flint who has become deranged after being marooned for many years on the island of the title. More than anything else he has missed over the long years, as he explains, he has dreamed of toasted cheese. *He looked like Ben Gunn, with his long straggly white beard and tattered clothes.*

Benjamin (benjămin) The youngest, favorite son in a family. The allusion is to the biblical Benjamin, who is identified in Genesis as the youngest and most loved son of Jacob and Rachel and the brother of Joseph. When Joseph provides a feast for Jacob's sons, Benjamin is offered five times as much as his other brothers; hence, the largest share of something may be called ***Benjamin's mess.*** 'He got up, put the cage on the table, and paused for a moment to count the mice in it. 'One, two, three, four—Ha!' he cried, with a look of horror, 'where, in the name of Heaven, is the fifth—the youngest, the whitest, the most amiable of all—my Benjamin of mice!'" (Wilkie Collins, *The Woman in White,* 1860).

Bennet, Elizabeth *See* MR. DARCY.

Beowulf (bayăwălf) Archetypal warrior hero. Beowulf is the central character in an Old English epic poem of unknown authorship dating from the early eighth century. Set in Denmark or Sweden, the Germanic tale relates how the warrior Beowulf volunteers to kill the dreadful monster Grendel, who has been making nightly raids upon the court of King Hrothgar. After a ferocious struggle Grendel is killed, but the following night Beowulf has to do battle with Grendel's equally formidable mother, who seeks revenge for her son's death. Beowulf triumphs and in due course becomes king. Ultimately, many years later, he dies in combat with a dragon. *To his followers he seemed like a warrior from a long past age, a Jason or a Beowulf perhaps.*

Berkeley, Busby *See* BUSBY BERKELEY.

Berlin Wall A substantial wall or other barrier. The allusion is to the formidable concrete wall (initially just a barbed-wire fence) that was constructed by the authorities in communist East Germany in 1961 to control contact between people living in the two parts of the divided country. It quickly became a symbol of the divide between the communist East and the capitalist West. The wall was broken down following the political upheavals of 1989. *There was no getting past the Berlin Wall that the family had created. See also* CHECKPOINT CHARLIE; IRON CURTAIN.

Bermuda Triangle (bermyoodă) An area or situation in which things go inexplicably missing. The original Bermuda Triangle is a triangular area of ocean between Bermuda, Florida, and Puerto Rico that acquired a reputation as a region where many ships and aircraft went missing in the second half of the 20th century. The mysterious disappearance of five U.S. Navy torpedo bombers while on a training flight in the area in December 1944, described by Charles Berlitz in his best-selling book *The Bermuda Triangle* (1974), is thought to have been the inspiration for speculation about the menacing properties of the region. The Bermuda Triangle has entered the annals of modern folklore, despite the fact that observers have claimed that statistically the area is no more dangerous than any other. *This desk is a Bermuda Triangle for pens and pencils.*

berserk (băzerk) Frenzied; uncontrollably violent or destructive. The term was first applied to certain ferocious Norse warriors, who customarily worked themselves up into a wild frenzy before going into battle, often without armor. They were sometimes identified as the descendants of Berserk. The word itself comes from the Icelandic *björn* (bear) and *serkr* (shirt), a reference to the fact that the berserks were often clad in bearskins. "The Professor, with his face flushed, his nostrils dilated, and his beard bristling, was now in a proper berserk mood" (Sir Arthur Conan Doyle, *The Lost World,* 1912).

Bertie Wooster *See* JEEVES.

best-laid plans gang aft agley, the (ăglay) Things rarely go according to plan, however well they may have been planned. The expression is a mangled quotation from the 1775 poem "To a mouse, on turning her up in her nest with the plough" by the Scottish poet Robert Burns (1759–96): "The best-laid schemes o' mice an' men / Gang aft agley, / An' lea'e us nought but grief an' pain, / For promis'd joy!" The phrase ***the best-laid plans of mice and men*** has also entered the common vocabulary as a description of schemes and projects that are fated to go wrong. *We intended to get to the airport well before boarding time, but the best-laid plans gang aft agley.*

best of all possible worlds, the An optimistic view of our world. The expression was first used by the German philosopher and mathematician Baron Gottfried Wilhelm von Leibnitz (1646–1716) and subsequently ridiculed by Voltaire in *CANDIDE* (1759), in which it was the credo of the disaster-prone Dr. Pangloss (*see* PANGLOSSIAN). "All is for the best in this best of all possible worlds, he mused, blowing a great cloud of smoke into the air above him" (M. Lewes Kilby, *Man at the Sharp End*, 1991).

best of times, it was the worst of times, it was the *See* IT WAS THE BEST OF TIMES, IT WAS THE WORST OF TIMES.

bethel (bethăl) A Nonconformist chapel. The word comes from the Hebrew *beth El,* meaning "house of God," and appears in Genesis 28:19 as the name of the town on the west bank of the Jordan River where Jacob had his dream about God and heaven. "His family was a little Bethel, for the Worship of God constantly and exactly maintained in it" (Cotton Mather, "The Life of John Eliot," 1702).

Bethesda, pool of *See* RISE, TAKE UP THY BED, AND WALK.

better a dinner of herbs than a stalled ox where hate is It is better to be poor or to eat modest fare among friends than to be rich or to eat well in hostile surroundings. The saying comes from the Bible, appearing in Proverbs 15:17: "Better is a dinner of herbs where love is, than a stalled ox and hatred therewith." "Well has Solomon said—'Better is a dinner of herbs where love is, than a stalled ox and hatred therewith.' I would not now have exchanged Lowood with all its privations for Gateshead and its daily luxuries" (Charlotte Brontë, *Jane Eyre,* 1847).

better to give than to receive *See* IT IS BETTER TO GIVE THAN TO RECEIVE.

better to marry than to burn It is preferable to enjoy the satisfactions of marriage than to be tortured by inappropriate passions as an unmarried person. This proverbial advice is of biblical origin, a quotation of Paul (himself a bachelor), as recorded in 1 Corinthians 7:8–9: "I say therefore to the unmarried and widows, It is good for them if they abide even as I. But if they cannot contain, let them marry: for it is better to marry than to burn." "'It is better to marry than to burn,' says St. Paul, where we may see what it is that chiefly drives men into the enjoyments of a conjugal life" (John Locke, *Essay Concerning Human Understanding*, 1690).

Betty Grable (graybăl) A person who resembles in some way the U.S. film actress Betty Grable (1916–73). Comparisons to Betty Grable are usually in relation to her famous legs, which featured prominently in pin-ups of the star printed during World War II and which were supposedly insured for one million dollars. They might also, however, relate to her distinctive piled-up hairdo. *Her mother sported a Betty Grable hairdo of the sort that was considered extremely stylish in her youth.*

between Scylla and Charybdis (silă, kăribdis) Having to confront one or the other of two equally dangerous hazards. The allusion is to Greek mythology and the Strait of Messina. Scylla aroused the jealousy of the goddess Amphitrite by attracting the amorous attentions of Amphitrite's husband, Poseidon. Transformed by Amphitrite into a monster with six dogs' heads, each with three rows of teeth, Scylla made her home in a cave in the Strait of Messina directly opposite the abode of the equally horrific Charybdis, who was the daughter of Poseidon and Gaea and had been turned into a monster by Zeus. Any vessel that passed between the two was likely to be attacked and the sailors devoured; the more they tried to evade one threat, the more likely they were to fall prey to the other. In more prosaic terms, Scylla was identified as a vast promontory of rock, while Charybdis was described as a whirlpool. *Louis considered which woman to choose, feeling himself caught like a hapless seaman between Scylla and Charybdis.*

Beulah See LAND OF BEULAH.

Beulah, peel me a grape (byoolă) Ironic expression of satisfaction at being pampered. This is a quotation from the movie *I'm No Angel* (1933), in which it is delivered by MAE WEST to her black maid, thus blithely dismissing speculation that she might be upset after her lover has stormed out on her. *"Beulah, peel me a grape!" he whooped as he threw himself onto the couch.*

beware of Greeks bearing gifts Do not trust gifts or favors if they come from an enemy. This advice has its roots in the story of the TROJAN HORSE, the treacherous subterfuge by which the Greeks finally overcame their Trojan adversaries at the end of the Trojan War. It is occasionally encountered in its Latin form ***timeo Danaos et dona ferentes*** (meaning "I fear the Greeks, even when they offer gifts"). *This offer of the Democrats looks suspicious to their opponents, a case of "beware of Greeks bearing gifts."*

beyond the pale Beyond the bounds of reasonable behavior or acceptability. The Pale was the name given to that part of Ireland over which the English exercised control during the medieval period. Thus, anything that lay outside that area was considered beyond the limits of contemporary civilization. The word "pale" itself means "stake," and refers to the palisades made of such stakes used to fence off particular areas. *The way he* *carried on at the wedding, in front of all the guests, was totally beyond the pale.*

Bhopal (bōpahl) A serious industrial accident, especially one on a big scale. The allusion is to the disastrous leaking of methyl isocyanate gas from the Union Carbide insecticide plant that occurred at Bhopal, India, on December 3, 1984. Some 2,000 people died and many more suffered severe side effects. There were also serious environmental effects. *Steps have been taken to prevent another Bhopal taking place.*

bible An authoritative book or other source of information. The word is most familiar as the name for the collected sacred writings of Christianity, consisting of the Old and New Testaments and in certain versions the Apocrypha. The word itself comes from the Greek *biblion* (meaning "book"), which in turn derives from *biblos* (meanings "papyrus"), named after Bublos, the Phoenician port where the Greeks obtained Egyptian papyrus. *This pamphlet is a bible for everyone in the motivational seminar industry.*

Bibulus (bibyoolăs) An idler; an office holder who does no actual work. The allusion is to Bibulus, an ally of Julius Caesar who held high office but acted merely as a cipher for his friend. *The deputy president of the company is widely regarded as a yes-man for the board, a real Bibulus.*

Bickle, Travis *See* TRAVIS BICKLE.

Big Apple The city of New York, or any other major city. According to one theory, the nickname was coined by black jazz musicians who saw the cities, particularly New York, as the places where they would have the best chance of getting a "bite of the apple." Another theory claims that the nickname was first applied to New York City in the 1920s by the journalist John J. FitzGerald, who had heard it in use among black stable hands in New Orleans when referring to the city's racetracks. *They left the Midwest to set up a chain of restaurants in the Big Apple.*

big bad wolf A villain or other threat. The allusion is to the traditional story of *The Three Little Pigs*, who are menaced one after another in their respective homes of straw, twigs, and bricks by the Big Bad Wolf, who seeks to blow the houses down and eat their owners. The tag is often applied to men who have the reputation of being sexual predators. "I do get a bit tired of being the permanent Big Bad Wolf" (Diane Pearson, *Voices of Summer*, 1993).

big bang A major event that triggers a significant change or the beginning of something. The term is particularly associated with the immense explosion that is believed to have given birth to the universe, but it has also been applied to the modernization of the British Stock Exchange in 1986, among a range of other events. *We are preparing for the big bang that will transform the country's civil administration in six months' time.*

Big Bertha (berthă) A large machine, especially a large weapon. The allusion is to a massive cannon used by the Germans to shell the Allied positions at Liège and Namur during World War I. It was nicknamed Big Bertha after Bertha Krupp, a member of the Krupp family of armaments manufacturers, though in fact the gun had been made at the Skoda works. The nickname was also applied to another big gun used to shell Paris in 1918, and is sometimes given insultingly to oversized women. *The Iraqi supergun was a modern Big Bertha,* *proof that the military mind sometimes moves very slowly.*

Big Brother An oppressive government, organization, person, etc., that maintains a vigilant watch over the lives of individuals. The concept was a creation of British writer George Orwell (1903–50) in his novel *Nineteen Eighty-Four* (1949), in which Big Brother is the all-seeing dictator whose regime exercises stifling control over the lives of citizens. The name has acquired new meaning in recent years with the advent of the popular *Big Brother* television programs screened in many countries around the world, in which disparate groups of individuals spend several weeks living in confinement together under the watchful eye of the camera. "Fear of big brother is abroad in the land" (Stewart Lamont, *In Good Faith*, 1989). *See also* ROOM 101; THOUGHT POLICE.

Biggles (bigălz) A pilot, especially one with a daring, adventurous character. The allusion is to James Bigglesworth, the hero of the Biggles adventure novels of Captain W. E. Johns (1893–1968), beginning with *The Camels are Coming* (1932). Johns based his hero upon a real man, Air Commodore Cecil George Wigglesworth (1893–1961), with whom Johns flew in the Royal Flying Corps during World War I. *Tell Biggles up there in the cockpit that if he doesn't get us into the air soon he'll have a riot on his hands.*

big lie A lie, especially one told by a politician. The phrase is particularly associated with the Nazi Party and the often outrageous propaganda disseminated to the German people under the direction of Josef Goebbels. Adolf Hitler himself admitted in *Mein Kampf* (1925), "The broad mass of a nation . . . will more easily fall victim to a big lie than to a small one." *The government has refused to be drawn on the issue, presumably afraid it will be caught out in its big lie.*

Big Rock Candy Mountain An idealized place where everything a person could possibly want is in ready supply. The allusion is to a U.S. folk song recorded in the 1920s by Mac McClintock and later by Burl Ives. The song identifies Big Rock Candy Mountain as a kind of heaven were cigarettes grow on trees and whiskey forms in lakes. *She thought of her husband's family home as a Big Rock Candy Mountain, supplying every luxury she had dreamed of as a girl.*

big sleep, the Death. The phrase is indelibly associated with U.S. crime writer Raymond Chandler (1888–1959), whose first novel was *The Big Sleep* (1939): "What did it matter where you lay once you were dead? . . . You were dead, you were sleeping the big sleep." *We never saw him again, so I guess after all these years he's sleeping the big sleep.*

big stick The use of force, or the threat of force, to persuade others to act in a certain way. The concept of "big stick" diplomacy was introduced by President Theodore Roosevelt in 1901, in discussions of U.S. policy toward Latin America. He was drawing on a West African proverb, which advises "Speak softly and carry a big stick." "After the big stick came the carrot: he offered to pay my first month's rent at a hostel he knew" (Michael Falk, *Part of the Furniture*, 1991).

bikini (băkeenee) A revealing two-piece woman's bathing suit. The allusion is to the Pacific atoll called Bikini (in the Marshall Islands), which was the site of U.S. nuclear weapons tests in 1946. The name of the island was first applied to this then-controversial new item of beachwear in 1947 in the magazine *Le Monde Illustré*, the expectation being that it would have a similarly explosive effect to a nuclear device. The lower part of the garment worn alone, or any highly revealing one-piece swimsuit, came to be dubbed a monokini, while attempts were also made to introduce to the market a three-piece garment called a trikini. "Riborg showed her a photograph album, with herself by a fjord in a minuscule bikini" (Jean Bow, *Jane's Journey*, 1991).

Bill Gates (gaytz) A very rich man, especially one connected with the computer industry. The original Bill Gates (b. 1955) founded the software company Microsoft in 1975 and ended the century as the richest man in the world. His name is now commonly applied to any highly successful business operator although, less flatteringly, it may also be applied to people who might otherwise be labeled "computer nerds." *Over the last few years he has become well known in business circles as the Bill Gates of toy manufacture.*

Bill Sikes *See* NANCY.

Billy Liar A daydreamer, someone who readily confuses fantasy and reality. The novel *Billy Liar* (1959) by Keith Waterhouse (b. 1929), subsequently adapted for stage and screen, introduced the world to undertaker's clerk William Fisher, who escapes mundane reality by imagining himself in a range of more glamorous roles. In the film version (1963) the character was played by Tom Courtenay. *He told me he was a war reporter but now I know he's a Billy Liar. See also* WALTER MITTY.

Billy the Kid Archetype of a reckless young outlaw of the Wild West. U.S. bank robber and bandit William H. Bonney Jr. (1859–81) was dubbed Billy the Kid as a result of the many acts of violence in which he was implicated during his relatively brief but murderous criminal career. He may have gunned down as many as 27 men before being shot dead himself by Sheriff Pat Garrett at Fort Sumner in New Mexico in 1881 and becoming enshrined as one of the central legends of the Wild West. In modern usage his name may be applied to anyone who is seen as being relatively young in a particular context. *The newspaper is being run by a crew of Billy the Kids who think they know everything about the business but have no real idea of what their readers expect.*

Bing Crosby (krozbee) Archetypal crooner. Harry Lillis "Bing" Crosby (1903–77) was the most popular singer of his day and also enjoyed a long and successful Hollywood career. His lasting popularity was in no small part due to his easy, affable manner, which endeared him to audiences until the end of his life. *Her father fancied himself as a Bing Crosby and seized the microphone whenever it was free.*

bionic man (bīonik) A man who appears to have superhuman strength or other capabilities. The allusion is to the popular U.S. television series *The Six Million Dollar Man* (1973–78), in which Lee Majors played former test pilot Steve Austin, an accident victim whose injured parts were replaced by electronic "bionic" limbs that endowed him with a range of superhuman powers. The series itself was based on a 1972 novel, *Cyborg*, by Martin Caidin. In modern usage, the label may be applied more loosely to any man who is deemed capable of apparently superhuman feats. By the same token, a woman who exhibits similar capabilities may be called a ***bionic woman***. A further spin-off television series about the adventures of a so-called bionic woman featured Steve Austin's girlfriend, remade with cybernetic limbs following a skydiving accident. *If they think I can shift this lot all by myself they must think I'm the Bionic Man.*

Bircher, John *See* JOHN BIRCHER.

Birnam Wood (bernăm) An ominous sign, something that is interpreted as a portent of imminent disaster. The allusion is to William Shakespeare's Scottish tragedy *Macbeth* (1606), specifically to a passage in which the title character is reassured that his throne will remain secure until he sees distant Birnam Wood come to his castle at Dunsinane, an event that appears to be practically impossible. When Macbeth's enemies subsequently invade Scotland, however, they disguise their numbers as they approach Dunsinane by cutting boughs from the trees of Birnam Wood and carrying them, thus giving the impression that the wood itself is moving. When he sees this, Macbeth knows he is doomed. Though no one knows if Shakespeare himself ever visited Scotland, both Dunsinane Castle and Birnam Wood are real places, around a dozen miles apart. *They watched as the huge crowd held up their placards to form a vast logo, which shimmered and shifted like Shakespeare's Birnam Wood.*

birthright, sell one's *See* SELL ONE'S BIRTHRIGHT FOR A MESS OF POTTAGE.

bite the bullet To become resigned to enduring a necessary or unavoidable burden of some kind or to making a difficult decision. The allusion is to the former custom of providing a patient about to be subjected to a painful surgical procedure with a soft lead bullet or something similar to bite on in response to the agony. This helped patients to stifle their screams and also lessened the chance of them biting their tongue off. The custom thankfully ended with the introduction of modern anesthetics. "When fate marks you down for immortality you'd just better bite the bullet and lace your boots up tight" (Robert Rankin, *The Suburban Book of the Dead*, 1993).

Blackbeard (blakbeerd) A piratical rogue, especially one with a formidable appearance or black beard. The allusion is to the notorious pirate captain Blackbeard (Edward Teach; d. 1718), who terrorized shipping off the east coast of America for 18 months leading up to his eventual death in battle when surprised by a pair of Royal Navy sloops. This most infamous of pirates was renowned for his unpredictable temper and wild appearance, especially his long black beard, which he wore tied in braids. *Her father was a mild-mannered type, but when he'd had a drink or two he turned into a real Blackbeard.*

Black Beauty A horse or something else of a rich black hue. The allusion is to the children's book *Black Beauty* (1877) by Anna Sewell, which tells the life story of a black horse from the point of view of the horse itself. The horse is known by several other names by its various owners, among them Black Auster, Darkie, and Jack. The book, which Anna Sewell felt moved to write in response to the cruel treatment suffered by many horses, has been filmed several times. *As a girl she had dreamed of owning her very own Black Beauty.*

blackboard jungle The violent and chaotic world of inner-city schools. The term is a reference to the 1955 movie *The Blackboard Jungle*, which was set in a run-down New York City school. The movie was based on an earlier novel of the same title by Evan Hunter (Salvatore Albert Lombino; 1926–2005). Appropriately enough, Hunter is said to have got the name Evan Hunter from the names of two schools he attended, Evander Childs High School and Hunter College. His other pseudonyms included Ed McBain, under which he published popular crime fiction. *His hair had turned white after ten years in the blackboard jungle.*

Black Death A disease of uncontrollable, epidemic proportions. The allusion is to the disease that originated in Asia and swept Europe between 1348 and 1351, killing about one third of the entire population. There were further epidemics in 1361–62 and 1379. The disease has since been identified as pneumonic and bubonic plague. *Scientists are worried that modern civilization could be devastated by a second Black Death.*

black hole A void into which vast amounts of money or other resources disappear. The allusion is to the black holes of astronomy, hypothetical entities of negative energy that result from the gravitational collapse of stars. Anything that falls into a black hole is trapped within it forever, hence the modern interpretation of a black hole as any place into which things disappear irrevocably. "The worst thing about cocaine is that once it has exhausted all the dopamine from the brain, then what's left is a black hole of depression so big and so awful that not all the misery in the world can fill it" (Bernard Cornwell, *Crackdown*, 1990).

Black Hole of Calcutta (kalkătă) A place of cramped, overcrowded confinement. The allusion is to the tiny dungeon in Fort William, Calcutta, into which 146 captured British soldiers of the British East India Company were locked overnight by Siraj-ud-daula, Nawab of Bengal, on June 20, 1756. By dawn all but 23 of the prisoners (including the one female prisoner) had died from heat exhaustion and suffocation. The incident led to an outcry in Britain. "The former they ran to earth at last at the smithy, a tiny Black Hole of Calcutta where Matthew Grimble, the blacksmith, lived with his portly wife and ten portly children" (Mary Gervaise, *The Distance Enchanted*, 1983).

Black Lagoon, Creature from the *See* CREATURE FROM THE BLACK LAGOON.

Black Monday A day when stock prices fall dramatically. The allusion is to Monday October 19, 1987, when the Dow Jones average on WALL STREET fell by 500 points, triggering fears that the economies of the Western world would slide into a depression of a severity not seen since the GREAT DEPRESSION of 1929. *The market lives in fear of a new Black Monday.*

Black Rock, bad day at *See* BAD DAY AT BLACK ROCK.

Black Sox scandal *See* SAY IT AIN'T SO, JOE.

Blanche DuBois (blahnch doobwah) Archetype of a faded Southern belle. Blanche DuBois is a central character in the 1947 play *A Streetcar Named Desire* by Tennessee Williams (1911–83). Brutalized by her brother-in-law Stanley Kowalski, Blanche's already tenuous hold on reality quickly disintegrates and she descends into madness. The play ends with her touchingly pathetic and deluded observation that she has always relied upon ***the kindness of strangers***. The character was memorably brought to life by Vivien Leigh in the 1951 film version of the play. *She wants to spend the summer in the Deep South, lounging on a verandah like some superannuated Blanche DuBois.*

blarney *See* KISS THE BLARNEY STONE.

blessed are the meek *See* MEEK SHALL INHERIT THE EARTH, THE.

Bligh, Captain *See* CAPTAIN BLIGH.

Blimp, Colonel *See* COLONEL BLIMP.

blind leading the blind A situation in which those who show the way are as misguided or ignorant as those they lead. The phrase appears in Matthew 15:14, in which Christ responds to the suggestion that he has offended the Pharisees: "Let them alone: they be blind leaders of the blind. And if the blind lead the blind, both shall fall into the ditch." It is also used in Luke 6:39. "The staff of the Archaeological Department are insufficiently trained by precept and experience—indeed as regards the students and junior members it is a case of the blind leading the blind, and the quality of the department is likely to deteriorate progressively" (Mortimer Wheeler, *Still Digging,* 1955). "Neil Hannon's 20s coincided with the 1990s when the bland led the bland" (*Guardian,* October 22, 2001).

blitz (blits) A sudden, overpowering assault or effort. The word comes from the German *Blitzkrieg*, meaning "lightning war," and became current during the early years of World War II, when the German armed forces conducted such attacks by land and air against Poland, the Low Countries, and France, relying upon fast movement of armored columns deep into enemy territory. When German bombers carried out mass raids on London and other British cities the campaign rapidly became known among the British as "the Blitz." Since the war, the term has been used much more widely of efforts in other fields. *What this house needs is a proper blitz to get it ready for our guests tomorrow evening.*

blockbuster Something of enormous size or power. The allusion is to the heaviest caliber of bombs dropped by the RAF during World War II, which were capable of destroying whole blocks of buildings at a time. The term has since been applied in a wide range of contexts, especially to epic Hollywood movies. *Several releases are competing for the title of top summer blockbuster this year.*

blood crieth from the ground The guilt of those who have committed murder or other acts of violence cannot be concealed. The expression is a quotation from Genesis 4:10, in which God confronts Cain after the latter has put his brother Able to death: "What hast thou done? the voice of thy brother's blood crieth unto me from the ground." "In the book that our teachers worship I have heard it read, that the voice of blood crieth from the ground! This is the voice—Hermanric, this is the voice that I have heard! I have dreamed that I walked on a shore of corpses, by a sea of blood!" (Wilkie Collins, *Antonina,* 1850). *See also* BLOOD WILL HAVE BLOOD.

blood for blood *See* BLOOD WILL HAVE BLOOD.

blood of the lamb *See* WASHED IN THE BLOOD OF THE LAMB.

blood, sweat, and tears Extreme effort and sacrifice, both mental and physical. The phrase is a loose quotation from a speech delivered by British prime minister Winston Churchill (1874–1965) in the House of Commons on May 10, 1940, at a point when Britain faced imminent invasion by

Nazi Germany: "I have nothing to offer but blood, toil, tears and sweat." It has been suggested that he may have been drawing on similar constructions previously used by the poets Lord Byron and John Donne. "We've put blood, sweat and tears into this campaign and now you're dismissing it out of hand!" (Angela Wells, *Viking Magic*, 1993).

blood will have blood Violence breeds violence. In this form the proverb dates from the 16th century, but it is of biblical origin, appearing in Genesis 9:6: "Whoso sheddeth man's blood, by man shall his blood be shed." A variant form is ***blood for blood.*** "It will have blood; they say blood will have blood" (William Shakespeare, *Macbeth,* 1606).

bloody shirt *See* WAVING THE BLOODY SHIRT.

Bluebeard (bloobeerd) A man who murders his wives, or otherwise treats them badly. In the fairy tale (1697) by the French writer Charles Perrault (1628–1703), Bluebeard is a rich but very ugly noble with a blue beard who murders each of his six wives in turn when he tires of them, keeping their corpses in a locked room. His seventh wife, Fatima, is driven by curiosity to disobey her husband's instructions and looks inside the locked room, upon which Bluebeard threatens to kill her too; she is saved from this fate by the timely arrival of her two brothers, who rescue her and kill her husband. A morality tale warning women against giving in to their curiosity, the story may have been inspired by the similarly bloodthirsty reputation of the historical Gilles de Rais (1404–40), a bearded Breton nobleman who was said to have murdered over 140 children, or else by the fates of the various wives of HENRY VIII, who sported a ginger beard. "Your tone would seem to imply that I am some sort of Bluebeard who keeps her incarcerated" (Lindsay Clarke, *The Chymical Wedding*, 1989).

blue bird of happiness The elusive source of happiness. The phrase comes from the play *The Blue Bird* (1908) by Maurice Maeterlinck, in which Tyltyl and Mytyl, the children of a poor woodcutter, go in search of the blue bird of happiness. *She sought in vain for the right man all her life, but the blue bird of happiness evaded her.*

Bluto *See* POPEYE.

Blyton, Enid *See* ENID BLYTON.

Boadicea *See* BOUDICCA.

Boanerges (bōănerjeez) A fiery preacher or orator; any man with a tempestuous nature. The allusion is to the apostles James and John, the sons of Zebedee, who in Mark 3:17 were dubbed Boanerges—meaning "sons of thunder"—by Christ in acknowledgment of either their impassioned calls for retribution against the Samaritans after they rejected Christ or their generally turbulent temperaments. "At first she resisted, and told him she was not used to be taken to task by her confessors. But he overpowered her, and so threatened her with the Church's curse here and hereafter, and so tore the scales off her eyes, and thundered at her, and crushed her, that she sank down and grovelled with remorse and terror at the feet of the gigantic Boanerges" (Charles Reade, *The Cloister and the Hearth,* 1861).

Bob Acres (aykerz) A natural coward, especially a man who boasts of his own bravado until put to the test. The allusion is to Richard Brinsley Sheridan's comedy *The Rivals* (1775), in which mild-mannered Bob Acres agrees to fight a duel for the hand of Lydia Languish, only to find his courage "oozing out at the palms of his hands" when he finally has to face his rival suitor. "'If you are busy, another time will do as well,' continued the bishop, whose courage like Bob Acres' had oozed out, now that he found himself on the ground of battle'" (Anthony Trollope, *Barchester Towers*, 1857).

Bob Cratchit (krachit) A loving but impoverished father. Bob Cratchit is the hapless clerk of Ebenezer SCROOGE in *A Christmas Carol* (1843) by Charles Dickens (1812–70). He receives only a meager wage from his employer to support his wife and five children, but does not allow his straitened circumstances to prevent him being a loving and devoted husband and father, especially to his sickly son ***Tiny Tim***. *The office was crowded with a group of miserable Bob Cratchits clearly struggling to make ends meet.*

Body-Snatchers, Invasion of the *See* INVASION OF THE BODY-SNATCHERS.

Boeotian (beeōshăn) Dimwitted, stupid, uneducated. The allusion is to Boeotia, a rural region of ancient Greece whose inhabitants were reputed to be very slow witted (supposedly caused by the cloyingly damp climate of their homeland). By the same token any person suspected of lacking any sensitivity toward music was accused of having ***Boeotian ears.*** Contrary to their reputation, however, the Boeotians included among their number such intellectual luminaries as Hesiod, Pindar, and Plutarch. "At the same time, who can avoid smiling at the earnestness and Boeotian simplicity (if indeed there be not an underhand satire in it), with which that 'Incident' is here brought forward . . .'" (Thomas Carlyle, *Sartor Resartus*, 1833–34).

boldly go where no man has gone before, to *See* *STAR TREK*.

Bolshevik (bolshăvik) Revolutionary or radical in nature. The original Bolsheviks were members of Lenin's Russian Revolutionary Party, who came to power in 1917 in the wake of the overthrow of the Russian monarchy. The name Bolshevik came originally from the Russian *bol'she*, meaning "more." It was inspired by the fact that at the party conferences of 1902–03 there were more Leninists present than supporters of other factions. During the era of the Soviet Union, the term was commonly applied to communists anywhere; in modern usage, any obstreperous person, particularly one with Leftist leanings, may be labeled a Bolshevik, or ***bolshie***. *This announcement did not go down well with the Bolsheviks in the gallery, who began throwing paper cups onto the heads of the delegates below.*

Bonaparte *See* NAPOLEON.

Bond, James *See* JAMES BOND.

bone of my bones *See* FLESH OF MY FLESH.

bones, dry *See* VALLEY OF DRY BONES.

bonfire of the vanities A symbol of the destruction of the follies and delusions of mankind. The phrase refers ultimately to the reformist preaching of the radical Dominican leader Girolamo Savonarola (1452–98), who urged the people of Florence to purge themselves of material vanities by throwing paintings, mirrors, musical instruments, cards, rich clothing, etc., onto huge heaps and setting fire to them. Savonarola's extreme views brought him into conflict with the pope and resulted in riots throughout the city. Savonarola was eventually arrested, tortured, and hanged. Tom Wolfe's novel *The Bonfire of the Vanities* (1987), filmed in 1990, makes fleeting references to the events surrounding Savonarola's tempestuous career. *Some members of the Christian right call regularly for a modern bonfire of the vanities.*

Bonnie and Clyde (bonee, klīd) Archetype of a pair of outlaws, one male and one female. The original Bonnie and Clyde were Bonnie Parker (1911–34) and Clyde Barrow (1909–34), who embarked on a four-year career of murder and bank robbery in the southwestern United States in the early 1930s. They were eventually ambushed and shot dead by Texas Rangers in Louisiana in May 1934. Their bloodthirsty reign of terror was subsequently romanticized in the 1967 film *Bonnie and Clyde*, in which they were played by Faye Dunaway and Warren Beatty. The notion that the pair were lovers, as portrayed in the 1967 film, is probably erroneous, as Clyde was homosexual. *The pair ruled the playground like an underage Bonnie and Clyde, threatening to pinch and slap anyone who did not hand over their pocket money.*

book of life Life itself, the experience of living, or a record of how a life has been spent. The original Book of Life, in which the names and deeds of those who will be saved on JUDGMENT DAY are listed, is described in Revelation 3:5, 20:12–15, and 21:27. It is also sometimes called the ***book of fate.*** "Now, Mr. Copperfield, I hope that you will not render it necessary for me to open, even for a quarter of an hour, that closed page in the book of life, and unsettle, even for a quarter of an hour, grave affairs long since composed" (Charles Dickens, *David Copperfield,* 1849–50).

books, of making many *See* OF MAKING MANY BOOKS.

Boone, Daniel *See* DANIEL BOONE.

Borden, Lizzie *See* LIZZIE BORDEN.

boreal (boreeăl) Pertaining to the north; cold, bleak. The word has its origins in Boreas, who was identified in Greek mythology as the god of the north wind. He was the son of Astraeus (one of the Titans) and Eos (the goddess of the dawn) and the brother of Zephyrus (the west wind), Notus (the south wind), and Eurus (the east wind). He was said to live in a cave on Mount Haemus in Thrace. "He knew, and she knew, that, though the fascination which each had exercised over the other—on her part independently of accomplishments—would probably in the first days of their separation be even more potent than ever, time must attenuate that effect; the practical arguments against accepting her as a housemate might pronounce themselves more strongly in the boreal light of a remoter view" (Thomas Hardy, *Tess of the D'Urbervilles,* 1891).

Borgias, the (borzhăz) A family with a reputation for ruthlessness and unscrupulous behavior. The allusion is to the historical Borgia family, who wielded immense power in RENAISSANCE Italy. Chief among them were Pope Alexander VI (1431–1503) and his children Cesare Borgia (1476–1507) and ***Lucrezia Borgia*** (1480–1519). The fondness of the Borgias for disposing of enemies by making them take pledges in poisoned wine prompted the metaphorical ***glass of wine***

with the Borgias, signifying a "fatal honor" of some kind. Other evils associated with the family included various acts of treachery, murder, and incest, although they were also noted patrons of the arts and many of the accusations leveled against them were probably the inventions of their rivals. "I watched her recoiling from that poulet en casserole, as if it had been something dished up by the Borgias" (P. G. Wodehouse, *Cocktail Time*, 1958).

Boris Karloff (kahrlof) A person with a menacing, ugly appearance. The allusion is to the Hollywood movie actor Boris Karloff (William Henry Pratt; 1887–1969), who starred in *Frankenstein* (1931) and *The Mummy* (1931) among numerous other black-and-white horror movies, often heavily made up. *He was so badly beaten up that after the fight he looked like Boris Karloff.*

born-again Of or relating to conversion to a particular cause, often specifically referring to a renewed zeal for the Christian faith. The term has biblical origins, appearing in John 3:3 in Christ's explanation to Nicodemus that only by being reborn spiritually could he reach heaven: "Verily, verily, I say unto thee, Except a man be born again, he cannot see the kingdom of God." "They take the risk of financial insecurity in order to be born again workers" (*Guardian,* December 7, 1984).

Bosch, Hieronymus *See* HIERONYMUS BOSCH.

Boston Strangler (bostăn) Archetype of a vicious serial murderer. The Boston Strangler was Albert DeSalvo (1933–73), who strangled 13 women in Boston, Massachusetts, between June 1962 and January 1964, causing widespread panic. He was eventually caught and sentenced to life in prison, but was ultimately stabbed to death by a fellow inmate. *After what she had been told about her daughter's new boyfriend she had expected a cross between Quasimodo and the Boston Strangler.*

Boston Tea Party An act signalling the start of a rebellion. The Tea Act of 1773 allowed the East India Company to ship tea to America at advantageous tax rates, to the detriment of American merchants, who were deprived of any say in the levying of such taxes. In 1773 outraged patriots disguised themselves as Native Americans and boarded British ships in Boston, tipping their cargoes of tea into the harbor. This act presaged the outbreak of the American Revolution, which began two years later. *This open act of defiance reminded some observers of the Boston Tea Party.*

Boswell (bozwel) A person who records the events of another's life, especially one who knows his subject intimately. James Boswell (1740–95) was the Scottish writer who compiled a detailed and illuminating *Life* of the celebrated lexicographer Samuel Johnson (1709–84), recording his conversations and describing his travels around the British Isles. Published in 1791, Boswell's *Life of Samuel Johnson* set the standard for all subsequent biographies. *He played Boswell to the rock star's Johnson, recording every quip that fell from his lips.*

bottomless pit A person, project, or other entity that consumes an apparently endless supply of money or other resources; a pit or hole that seems to have no end. In its original biblical context the phrase refers to the pit of hell (Revelation 9:1–2, 11), variously identified elsewhere by such epithets as the Abyss or the pit of the dragon. "Now, what is Costaguana? It is the bottomless pit of 10 per cent loans and other fool investments. European capital has been flung into it with both hands for years" (Joseph Conrad, *Nostromo,* 1904).

Boudicca (boodikă) Archetype of a formidable woman. Boudicca (sometimes less accurately called ***Boadicea***) was a queen of the Iceni tribe of eastern England, who rose up in revolt against the Roman occupation. She sacked Colchester. London, and St. Albans before being defeated by the Roman legions under Suetonius Paulinus. She committed suicide by taking poison in A.D. 62. *She stormed into the party like some Boudicca on a chariot.*

Bountiful, Lady *See* LADY BOUNTIFUL.

Bounty, the *See* CAPTAIN BLIGH.

Bovary, Madame *See* MADAME BOVARY.

bowdlerize (bōdlărīz, bowdlărīz) To expurgate a piece of writing by removing any obscene or other controversial content. The reference is to the retired British physician Dr. Thomas Bowdler (1754–1825) who in 1818 published a 10-volume edition of the works of William Shakespeare, with any vulgarity that might cause offense to contemporary readers removed or rewritten. The most notorious of his changes included substantial cuts to celebrated speeches made by Juliet and King Lear. His version of Shakespeare's plays became a best-seller, as did his "improved" versions of other classics designed to be suitable for a family audience, but he is remembered today as the quintessence of censorious prudishness. *He gave the detective a bowdlerized account of what had taken place in the bedroom prior to the shooting.*

bowels of compassion The source of a person's sympathy or pity. In biblical times the bowels were commonly believed to be the seat of a person's emotions, as illustrated by 1 John 3:17: "Whose hath this world's good, and seeth his brother have need, and shutteth up his bowels of compassion from him, how dwelleth the love of God in him?" Other examples include 2 Corinthians 6:12; Colossians 3:12. Jeremiah in his sorrows laments, "My bowels! My bowels!" (4:19), and Job in his mental suffering similarly complains, "My bowels boiled" (30:27). Thus, to ***shut up the bowels of compassion*** is to behave without compassion or mercy. "It is the proper language—working upon her father's bowels of compassion. Fathers always have bowels of compassion at last" (Anthony Trollope, *Ayala's Angel,* 1881).

boycott (boikot) To shun someone or something. The allusion is to Captain Charles Boycott (1832–97), a land agent of County Mayo who treated his Irish tenants very harshly, becoming highly unpopular. In 1880 his disgruntled tenants, their families, and most of the rest of the local population adopted a policy of refusing to talk to him or deal with him in any way until he agreed to reduce their rents, a tactic that became known as "boycotting." *We have decided to boycott the store until they take these publications off their shelves.*

Boy Wonder *See* BATMAN AND ROBIN.

Bracknell, Lady *See* LADY BRACKNELL.

Brady Bunch (braydee) A group of wholesome all-American children. The allusion is to the U.S. television series *The Brady Bunch* (1969–74), which revolved around the suburban Brady family, comprising a couple and their six children (three each from previous marriages). All the children were lively, good-natured, and cheerful, embodying the way in which a certain stratum of middle-class America of the period liked to see itself. *Good-looking, clean-living, and always smiling for the cameras, they were marketed as pop's equivalent of the Brady Bunch.*

Braggadocio (bragădōsheeō) Boastfulness, or a person who boasts a lot. The allusion is to Edmund Spenser's *The Faerie Queene* (1590, 1596), the characters of which include the boastful Braggadocchio (a name arrived at through the combination of "braggart" and the suffix *-occhio*, meaning "big"). The word "brag" referred originally to the discordant braying of a trumpet. Spenser is thought to have based the character on a real person, the French nobleman the duc d'Alençon. "It might amuse him to rub salt into her wound, to display that notches-on-the-bedhead braggadocio shared by so many of his fellows" (Stella Shepherd, *Black Justice*, 1988).

brand of Cain *See* MARK OF CAIN.

brave men before Agamemnon, there were (agămemnon) No person, place, or era has a monopoly on achievement or glory. The saying is a quotation from the *Odes* of the Roman poet Horace (65–8 B.C.), whose original Latin version ran "*Vixere fortes ante Agamemnona.*" In Greek mythology, Agamemnon was the king of Mycenae who led the Greeks during the Trojan War. *The current national squad are being hailed as the best ever to represent the country, but there were brave men before Agamemnon.*

brave new world A greatly changed new situation or prospect. The phrase is a quotation from William Shakespeare's play *The Tempest* (1611), in which MIRANDA exclaims, on laying eyes on other human beings for the first time: "O, wonder! / How many goodly creatures are there here! / How beauteous mankind is! O brave new world, / That has such people in't!" The negative overtones connected with the phrase date from the publication in 1932 of the Aldous Huxley novel *Brave New World*, in which the author depicts a nightmarish future. "Our lives in this brave new world will be tough, my friends" (Gareth Roberts, *The Highest Science*, 1993).

Bray, Vicar of *See* VICAR OF BRAY.

bread alone, by *See* MAN CANNOT LIVE BY BREAD ALONE.

bread and circuses Food and entertainment as means to keep the masses content. The cynical notion that a populace provided with plenty of free food and entertainment *(panem et circenses)* would never rise up in revolt was familiar to the ancient Romans, as evidenced by the writing of the satirist Juvenal (A.D. c. 55/60–127): "People long eagerly for two things . . . bread and circuses." Successive emperors sponsored spectacles in the circuses of Rome in the belief that these superficial palliatives would preserve them from the anger of the mob over more serious issues. *TV dinners and Monday night football, it has been cynically suggested by observers, are the bread and circuses with which the masses are kept in their place in modern society.*

bread cast upon the waters *See* CAST THY BREAD UPON THE WATERS.

bread of affliction Suffering or trouble. This metaphor is biblical in origin, appearing in 1 Kings 22:27 and in 2 Chronicles 18:26: "Feed him with bread of affliction and with water of affliction." "When I reflect, Brother Toby, upon Man; and take a view of that dark side of him which represents his life as open to so many causes of trouble—when I consider, brother Toby, how oft we eat the bread of affliction, and that we are born to it, as to the portion of our inheritance—I was born to nothing, quoth my uncle Toby, interrupting my father—but my commission" (Laurence Sterne, *Tristram Shandy,* 1759–67).

break a leg! Good luck! The allusion is to the world of the theater, in which the phrase is a traditional expression of good luck to someone about to go on stage. Various origins for the expression have been suggested. These include the general notion that wishing a person well simply invites the fates to interfere, therefore wishing a person ill should make it less likely that anything bad will happen. The expression may, on the other hand, have its origins in the Elizabethan theater, specifically in the kneeling of actors to pick up coins tossed onto the stage by an appreciative audience or in the bending of the leg when taking repeated bows in response to enthusiastic applause. A less plausible theory links the saying to the assassination of ABRAHAM LINCOLN in his box at Ford's Theater in Washington, D.C., in 1865 and the fact that as he leapt to the stage his assassin, actor John Wilkes Booth, broke his leg (*see also* ONE'S NAME IS MUD). Equally colorful is the link suggested with the story of English actor Samuel Foote (1720–77) who was granted a valuable royal patent to perform spoken drama at the Haymarket Theatre in London as compensation for breaking a leg (which then had to be amputated) in the course of boisterous horseplay with the duke of York: the patent enabled Foote to make his fortune, giving him cause to be grateful for what might otherwise have been a disastrous setback. "Charles wanted to say something to help, but all he could think of was 'Break a leg' " (Simon Brett, *Murder Unprompted*, 1984).

break Priscian's head (prishănz) To break the rules of grammar. The allusion is to Priscianus Caesariensis, a Roman grammarian of the sixth century A.D. "Some free from rhyme or reason, rule or check, / Break Priscian's head and Pegasus's neck" (Alexander Pope, *The Dunciad,* 1728).

breath of life Life or something considered as essential as life itself. According to the book of Genesis, God brought Adam to life literally by breathing life into him: "And the LORD God formed man of the dust of the ground, and breathed into his nostrils the breath of life; and man became a living soul" (Genesis 2:7). "Ah, but she won't abandon you. Poetry and art are the breath of life to her. It is poetry you write, Mr. Winsett?" (Edith Wharton, *The Age of Innocence,* 1920).

Brechtian (brekteeăn) Of or relating to the plays of German playwright Bertolt Brecht (1898–1956). Through such plays as *Mother Courage and Her Children* (1939) and *The Caucasian Chalk Circle* (1944), Brecht became well known for his didactic approach to the theater and for his Marxist ideas, as well as for his espousal of techniques designed to restrict the emotional response of an audience at the expense of the underlying message. "Modernist cinema is cast in a Brechtian mould of distantiation and bears formalist characteristics" (Scott Lash, *Sociology of Postmodernism*, 1990).

bricks without straw Work that is expected to be done under difficult conditions or without the necessary tools or materials. The phrase refers to the biblical incident in which Pharaoh refused to provide the Hebrews with the straw they needed to make bricks, insisting that they find it themselves: "And Pharaoh commanded the same day the taskmasters of the people . . . saying, Ye shall no more give the people straw to make brick, as heretofore: let them go and gather straw for themselves" (Exodus 5:6–7). Bricks made with mud from the Nile had to include straw to prevent them from cracking as they dried. *The union complained that as a result of the cutbacks, their members were effectively being asked to make bricks without straw.*

Brideshead (brīdzhed) A magnificent stately home, a symbol of the high English aristocracy. Brideshead is the name of the palatial home of the lordly Flyte family in Evelyn Waugh's novel *Brideshead Revisited* (1945). When the novel was televised in 1981, the role of Brideshead was taken by Castle Howard in Yorkshire. *The view was all very Brideshead, couples in evening dress sauntering between the follies above the shining lake, on which the swans floated.*

bridge too far, a A step that when taken proves to be one too many. The allusion is to Cornelius Ryan's book *A Bridge Too Far* (1974), filmed in 1977, which relates the events surrounding the disastrous Allied advance into the Netherlands in 1944. The phrase itself was supposedly first spoken by General Frederick Browning in response to Field Marshal Montgomery's plans for the capture of 11 bridges, including that at Arnhem: "But, sir, we may be going a bridge too far." *This latest acquisition may ultimately prove a bridge too far for the company.*

brief encounter A short-lived love affair or other relationship. The allusion is to the 1945 romantic film *Brief Encounter*, written by Noël Coward and directed by David Lean, which told the story of the ill-starred and ultimately unfulfilled romance of a couple (played by Trevor Howard and Celia Johnson) whose relationship blossoms during meetings at a suburban railroad station. The real station used for the film, in the English town of Carnforth in Lancashire, is a place of pilgrimage for the many fans of the movie. *We had a brief encounter a few years ago, but haven't seen much of each other since then.*

Brigadoon (brigădoon) Idealized vision of a rural village, especially one that seems cut off from the realities of everyday life. The fictional Scottish village of Brigadoon is the setting for the 1947 musical of the same title, by Frederick Loewe and Alan Jay Lerner. Possibly inspired by Brig o' Doon in Ayrshire, the village in *Brigadoon* is curiously divorced from life in the real world, being subject to a magic spell that means it comes alive for just one day every hundred years. "It's a bit like coming back to Britain and finding you've committed yourself to living in Brigadoon" (Ann Granger, *A Season for Murder*, 1991).

Brigitte Bardot (brijit bahrdō) A beautiful, sexually alluring blonde, especially one who enjoys the status of a sex symbol. Brigitte Bardot (b. 1934) became an international star after appearing in such films as *And God Created Woman* (1956) and was one of the most widely recognized faces of the late 1950s and early 1960s, appearing in movies, pin-ups, and glossy magazines. *His second wife was a Brigitte Bardot with long blonde locks and a sultry, pouting face.*

brimstone and fire *See* FIRE AND BRIMSTONE.

broad is the way *See* STRAIT AND NARROW.

Broadway (brahdway) The U.S. popular theater. The Broadway district of New York City is famous for its theaters, which over the years have hosted countless musicals and other large-scale productions. In modern usage, the name is often applied more generally to the theatrical world as a whole. Broadway itself, otherwise known as the GREAT WHITE WAY, is a street that runs through the West Side of Manhattan. *She dreamed of making a name for herself in Broadway musicals.*

Brobdingnagian (brobdingnageeăn) On a vast, gigantic scale. The land of Brobdingnag, in which all the inhabitants are 60 feet tall, is one of the places visited by Lemuel GULLIVER in Jonathan Swift's *Gulliver's Travels* (1726). It has been suggested that the name came about as an anagram of "grand big nob(le)." "Death or injury lies in wait for the imprudent in Brobdingnagian chasms below" (Eric G. Holland, *Coniston Copper*, 1986). *See also* LAPUTA; LILLIPUTIAN; YAHOO.

Brodie, Miss Jean *See* MISS JEAN BRODIE.

broken reed A weak or damaged person or thing. The phrase is biblical in origin. In Isaiah 36:6 King Hezekiah is advised not to trust the Egyptians: "Lo, thou trustest in the staff of this broken reed, on Egypt; whereon if a man lean, it will go into his hand, and pierce it." In Matthew 12:20 Christ echoes this passage in his words "A bruised reed shall he not break." "'God help thee, my son! He can help when worldly trust is a broken reed.'—Such was the welcome of the matron to her unfortunate grandson" (Sir Walter Scott, *The Black Dwarf,* 1816).

Bronx cheer (bronks) A "raspberry," a derisive noise made with the tongue and lips. The Bronx district of New York is one of the rougher areas of the city, long notorious for the vulgar behavior of its inhabitants. *The only response to my request was a Bronx cheer from one of the teenagers.*

Brothers Grimm *See* GRIMM'S FAIRY TALES.

brother's keeper *See* MY BROTHER'S KEEPER.

Brown, John *See* JOHN BROWN.

Bruce, Robert *See* ROBERT THE BRUCE.

Bruce Wayne *See* BATMAN AND ROBIN.

bruised reed *See* BROKEN REED.

Brummell, Beau *See* BEAU BRUMMELL.

Brute *See* ET TU, BRUTE?

Bucephalus (byoosefălăs) Archetype of a noble, courageous horse. Bucephalus was the name of the horse that Alexander the Great rode in the course of his celebrated military campaigns. Legend has it that only Alexander proved capable of breaking the horse, whose name—from *bous,* meaning "ox," and *kephale,* meaning "head"—referred to its resemblance to a bull. "Close-reefing top-sails in a gale, there he was, astride the weather yard-arm-end, foot in the Flemish horse as 'stirrup,' both hands tugging at the 'earring' as at a bridle, in very much the attitude of young Alexander curbing the fiery Bucephalus" (Herman Melville, *Billy Budd,* 1924).

Buckingham Palace (băkingăm) A large and magnificent home. Buckingham Palace in London is the official residence of the British monarchy. It was named after the first duke of Buckingham, who built the original palace in 1703, and became a royal residence when bought by George III in 1762. In modern usage, homes may be compared with Buckingham Palace ironically to highlight their relatively humble character. *It's very cozy, but it's hardly Buckingham Palace.*

Buck Rogers (băk rojerz) A person who makes use of futuristic technology, or the technology itself. The archetypal space hero Buck Rogers, created by Philip Francis Nowlan, made his first appearance in a space adventure story in the magazine *Amazing Stories* in 1928. A year later, drawn by Dick Calkins, he became the star of his own long-running comic strip *Buck Rogers in the 25th Century*, which continued until the late 1960s, by which time he had become a universally recognized symbol of science fiction. The futuristic adventures of Buck Rogers were also brought to life on the radio and in the cinema, with Rogers himself played by former swimmer Buster Crabbe. *They selected for the young couple a shiny silver Buck Rogers toaster.*

buck stops here, the There is no one else to whom responsibility can be passed. The expression supposedly has its roots in the game of poker, in which players formerly placed a buckhorn knife on the table to remind players whose turn it was to deal next. The phrase "to pass the buck," meaning "to pass responsibility to someone else," dates back to the 19th century. In the 1940s, President Harry S. Truman kept a sign on his desk reading "the buck stops here" to remind himself that he bore ultimate responsibility for decisions to be made. *Running your own company can be very satisfying and rewarding, but you have to remember that if anything goes wrong, the buck stops here.*

Buffalo Bill (bufălō) Archetype of a dashing cowboy figure. William Frederick Cody (1846–1917) became internationally famous for his Wild West Show, which toured the world with a cast of sharpshooters, cowboys, and Native Americans. Cody's stagename recalled his past as a buffalo hunter, in which role he was said to have killed nearly 5,000 buffalo over an 18-month period to supply railroad workers with meat in the 1870s. *His prowess as a rider and marksman brought him Buffalo Bill status locally.*

build a better mousetrap To come up with something that is sure to prove a success. The philosopher and essayist Ralph Waldo Emerson (1803–82) is credited with formulating this phrase to express the truth that if an idea is good enough it is bound to enjoy success. He used it in one of his lectures: "If a man can write a better book, preach a better sermon, or make a better mousetrap than his neighbor, though he builds his house in the woods the world will make a beaten path to his door." *It's just as true today as it ever was—if you want to make your fortune all you have to do is build a better mousetrap.*

Bulge, Battle of the (bulj) The struggle to stay slim. The allusion is to the so-called Battle of the Bulge that took place in the Ardennes region of Belgium and Luxembourg in December 1944 when the German armed forces launched an unexpected counterattack against the Allies in the closing stages of World War II. The Allies were pushed back by the determined armored assault until a "bulge" in the front line some 60 miles deep had opened up. It was not until the end of January 1945 that the German advance was reversed and the bulge was flattened out. The phrase has since been taken up in the world of dieting to describe the unending battle of many people to keep flabbiness at bay. *This new product could prove a useful weapon in the Battle of the Bulge for many people.*

Bull, John *See* JOHN BULL.

bull of Bashan (bashăn) A very strong or ferocious man; a cruel tyrant. Og was a brutish giant who ruled Bashan, an area east of the Sea of Galilee and famous for its cattle (Deuteronomy 32:14; Psalm 22:12; and Ezekiel 39:18). Og and all his followers were killed in battle against Moses and the Israelites (Deuteronomy 3:1–11). Among the trophies taken by the Israelites after the battle was Og's huge iron bedstead, which measured nine by four cubits (around 13 by 16 feet). To ***roar like a bull of Bashan*** means to make an excessive noise. ". . . man and steed rushing on each other like wild bulls of Bashan!" (Sir Walter Scott, *Ivanhoe,* 1819).

Bunbury (bunbăree) A fictitious friend, especially one invented for convenience. Bunbury is the name given to the fictitious, ailing friend invented by Algernon Moncrieff in Oscar Wilde's comedy *The Importance of Being Earnest* (1895) as an excuse to make himself absent from town when he has appointments he would like to avoid, particularly with his aunt LADY BRACKNELL. *I think I may need to invent a Bunbury in order to avoid to get out of this meeting.*

Bunker, Archie *See* ARCHIE BUNKER.

Bunker Hill (bunker) An opening skirmish, especially one that proves a source of inspiration to a cause. The allusion is to the Battle of Bunker Hill, one of the first battles of the American Revolution, which took place during the siege of Boston on June 17, 1775. The American forces put up a spirited defense before being driven from Bunker Hill by the British, having run out of ammunition. Though defeated, the Americans took great heart from the encounter. *This turned out to be the women's movement's Bunker Hill.*

bunker mentality (bunker) A defensive state of mind. The expression dates from World War II, when millions of people were forced to seek shelter from bombing and artillery shelling in fortified underground dugouts called bunkers. With the Russians on the outskirts of Berlin, Adolf HITLER himself was driven into his bunker, where he was seemingly driven to paranoid madness and eventually suicide by the imminence of the threats surrounding him. *After such an extended run of defeats, the team management have surrendered to bunker mentality and are now obsessed with damage limitation.*

bunkum (bunkăm) Nonsense, empty talk. The word "bunkum" originated in the first half of the 19th century, prompted by a speech to Congress made by one Felix Walker, who represented the district of Buncombe in North Carolina. Such was the inanity and dullness of Walker's speech, addressed to the people of Buncombe, that ever afterward any insincere, meaningless speech became known as "buncombe" or "bunkum." "De mortuis nil nisi bonum, and all that bunkum" (Stella Shepherd, *Black Justice*, 1988).

bunnyboiler *See* FATAL ATTRACTION.

Bunyan, Paul *See* PAUL BUNYAN.

burden of Isaiah (īzayă) A prophecy of disaster; a complaint against hardships imposed by others. The reference is to ISAIAH's prophecy against Babylon, as described, for example, in 13:1. *He seemed weighed down, as if with the burden of Isaiah, by this realization of the inevitable catastrophe to come.*

burden of Sisyphus *See* SISYPHEAN.

Buridan's ass (băridănz) A person who finds it impossible to choose between two alternatives. The allusion is to the French philosopher Jean Buridan (c. 1300–c. 1358), who conceived the notion of an ass that finds itself unable to choose between equally attractive heaps of hay and therefore starves to death. *He was like Buridan's ass, torn between the two women and thus fated to lose both of them.*

Burke and Hare (berk, hair) Bodysnatchers. William Burke (1792–1829) and his accomplice William Hare (d. 1860) became notorious as suppliers of cadavers for dissection by the Edinburgh surgeon Dr. Robert Knox. Their activities eventually attracted the attention of the authorities, who uncovered the fact that in their search for fresh bodies the pair had been guilty of 15 murders. Hare was spared the death penalty after turning King's Evidence, dying many years later, but Burke was hanged. *The modern demand for genetic material raises the ugly prospect of a generation of latter-day Burke and Hares.*

burning bush A source of revelation, especially one of a miraculous nature. The allusion is to the biblical episode concerning the burning bush from which God addressed Moses, as related in Exodus 3:2: "And the angel of the LORD appeared unto him in a flame of fire out of the midst of a bush; and he looked, and behold, the bush burned with fire, and the bush was not consumed." The passage goes on to detail God's instructions to Moses to lead the Israelites out of Egypt and guide them to the Promised Land. The bush has been tentatively identified as a bramble or blackberry bush. The name is now applied to several shrubs or trees with bright red fruits or seeds, as well as to a number of plants with bright red foliage. In medieval times a burning bush was commonly adopted as a symbol of the Virgin Mary. "I think, sir, when God makes His presence felt through us, we are like the burning bush: Moses never took any heed what sort of bush it was—he only saw the brightness of the Lord" (George Eliot, *Adam Bede,* 1859).

burnt offering A jocular reference to an overcooked meal. The allusion is to the various offerings of animals killed and ritually burned, as described in the Old Testament. These included the offering made to God by Noah in Genesis 8:20: "And Noah builded an altar unto the LORD; and took every clean beast, and of every clean fowl, and offered burnt offerings on the altar." "The sleep-walker had wakened to bitter knowledge of love and life, finding himself a failure in both. He had made a burnt offering of his dreams, and the sacrifice had been an unforgivable hurt to Mary" (Booth Tarkington, *The Turmoil,* 1915).

bury the dead *See* LET THE DEAD BURY THE DEAD.

Busby Berkeley (buzbee bahrklee) A spectacular choreographed sequence in a movie or stage show. The U.S. movie director and choreographer Busby Berkeley (William Berkeley Enos; 1895–1976) is usually remembered for the carefully synchronized kaleidoscopic dance sequences in such movies as *42nd Street* (1933) and *Gold Diggers of 1933* (1933). "'A Busby Berkeley line-up in front of his bed couldn't wake Sam in the middle of the night' Clare said" (Shirley Conran, *Crimson,* 1992).

bushel, hide one's light under a *See* HIDE ONE'S LIGHT UNDER A BUSHEL.

buskin Symbol of tragic drama. The buskin, or ***cothurnus,*** was originally a style of boot with a thick sole that was conventionally worn by performers of tragic roles in the Greek and Roman theater to give actors a few inches of extra height and thus contribute to the grandeur of their performance. "But in that bitter tirade upon Chantilly, which appeared in yesterday's 'Musee,' the satirist, making some disgraceful allusions to the cobbler's change of name upon assuming the buskin, quoted a Latin line about which we have often conversed" (Edgar Allan Poe, "The Murders in the Rue Morgue," 1841). *See also* SOCK.

Buster Keaton (buster keetăn) Archetype of an inventive physical comedian. Buster Keaton (1896–1966) is remembered as one of the most gifted clowns of the early silent-movie industry, famous for his deadpan expression and for performing his own death-defying stunts. "He gained a reputation as the Buster Keaton of the cricket world, a man who rarely seemed to have any expression on his face and who was not one for the excited cavortings that greet the fall of a wicket; yet behind the mask a good deal of thought was given to his bowling, and he was liked and respected by his fellow players" (Gerry Cotter, *England versus West Indies*, 1991).

Butch Cassidy and the Sundance Kid (buuch kasidee, sundans) Archetypal outlaws of the Wild West. Robert LeRoy Parker, otherwise known as Butch Cassidy, and Harry Longbaugh (or Longabaugh), otherwise known as the Sundance Kid (having robbed a bank in Sundance, Nevada) entered folklore by virtue of the crimes they committed in the late 19th century and their inventive attempts to evade the posse that pursued them. Forced south by their pursuers, they are believed to have died in a shoot-out with soldiers in Bolivia in 1909. A romanticized version of their story was presented in the classic Western movie *Butch Cassidy and the Sundance Kid* (1969), in which the outlaws were winningly played by Paul Newman and Robert Redford. *With those hats on they look like Butch Cassidy and the Sundance Kid. See also* WILD BUNCH.

Butler, Rhett *See* GONE WITH THE WIND.

by bread alone *See* MAN CANNOT LIVE BY BREAD ALONE.

by Jove (jōv) Exclamation of surprise or admiration. The allusion is to the chief Roman god Jupiter, whose Latin name was Jovis. Jupiter was traditionally regarded as a source of good humor, hence the related term ***jovial,*** meaning "jolly" or "good-humored." "'Oh, by Jove!' said Captain Donnithorne, laughing. 'Why, she looks as quiet as a mouse. There's something rather striking about her, though'" (George Eliot, *Adam Bede,* 1859).

Byronic (bīronik) In a grand, dark, romantic, passionate manner. The British poet George Gordon, Lord Byron (1788–1824) became one of the most celebrated men of his age through such epic works as *Childe Harold's Pilgrimage* (1812–18). Both in his writing and in his personal life, Byron was renowned for his tempestuous, passionate character. He had several scandalous love affairs and caused a sensation wherever he went before ultimately dying in Greece after committing himself to the fight for Greek independence. "But civil strife and political violence, the quick and easy expedients of the gun and the bomb, already had for him a romantic and almost Byronic aura"

(F. Selwyn, *Hitler's Englishman*, 1987). *See also* MAD, BAD, AND DANGEROUS TO KNOW.

by their fruits ye shall know them *See* FALSE PROPHET.

by the rivers of Babylon (babilon) In exile from a cherished but far-distant place or time. The phrase comes from Psalm 137:1, in which the Israelites in exile in Babylon lamented their lost homeland of ZION: "By the rivers of Babylon, there we sat down, yea, we wept, when we remembered Zion." *The refugees, like the Israelites who wept by the rivers of Babylon, were inconsolable in their lamentations for their lost homeland.*

by the skin of one's teeth *See* SKIN OF ONE'S TEETH, BY THE.

Byzantine (bizănteen; bizăntīn) Labyrinthine, intricate, convoluted, complicated. The allusion is to the intrigue and deviousness that characterized political and bureaucratic dealings in the Byzantine Empire between the time of its foundation in the fourth century A.D. and its dissolution upon invasion by the Turks in 1453. *It took the detectives some considerable time to unravel the Byzantine convolutions of the case, but in due course they conceded reluctantly that they had been pursuing the wrong man.*

C

cabal (kă<u>bal</u>) A group of close advisers or conspirators, a junta. It is popularly believed that the word dates from the 17th century, and that it referred originally to a group of ministers who controlled Britain under Charles II, being formed from the initials of their names (Clifford, Ashley, Buckingham, Arlington, and Lauderdale). In 1672 this group of men acted entirely without the consent of Parliament when they entered a Treaty of Alliance with France, thus leading to war with Holland. In fact, the word made its first appearance in English some 50 years earlier, when it was incorporated into the language from the French *cabale*. The ultimate origins of the word lie in the Hebrew *cabala*, which refers to a collection of writings conveying the mystical secrets of the Torah. "This was not a powerful cabal, and they had little expectation of early success" (James Hinton, *Protests and Visions*, 1989).

cabbages and kings A wide and contrasting range of subjects. The phrase, which implies that the subjects named are so disparate that any connection between them would be nonsensical, comes originally from the poem "The Walrus and the Carpenter" in Lewis Carroll's *Through the Looking-Glass* (1872): "'The time has come,' the Walrus said, / 'To talk of many things: / Of shoes—and ships—and sealing wax— / Of cabbages—and kings.'" The phrase was later adopted by O. Henry (William Sydney Porter; 1862–1910) as the title of a volume of otherwise unconnected short stories (1904). *For many years he wrote a cabbages and kings article in the paper in which he discussed anything that took his fancy.*

Cadillac (<u>kad</u>ilak) An expensive, luxurious automobile, or anything that is considered the best of its kind. The original Cadillac car was assembled by General Motors at its factory in Cadillac, Michigan. Since then the term (also rendered as ***Caddy***) has been applied more widely to luxury cars in general and is also used in nonautomotive contexts. *This is the Cadillac of rock bands.*

Cadmean letters (<u>kad</u>meeăn) The 16 letters of the Greek alphabet. They were named after the legendary Cadmus, king of Phoenicia and Telephassa in Greek mythology, who founded the city of Thebes and was credited with introducing the alphabet to Greece from Phoenicia. *By the end of the term all these young scholars are expected to be familiar with the Cadmean letters and other basics of rhetoric.*

Cadmean victory *See* PYRRHIC VICTORY.

caduceus (kădooseeăs) Emblem of the medical profession: a staff entwined with two serpents. In classical mythology the caduceus was carried by Hermes (or Mercury) as a symbol of his role as messenger of the gods. Such staffs were also traditionally carried by Greek heralds and ambassadors on peace missions. According to legend, the mere touch of this staff could put a person to sleep or revive a corpse. Its adoption as a symbol of medicine relates to its similarity to the STAFF OF AESCULAPIUS. "I had not hopped far before I perceived a tall young gentleman in a silk waistcoat, with a wing on his left heel, a garland on his head, and a caduceus in his right hand" (Henry Fielding, *A Journey from this World to the Next,* 1743).

Caesar (seezer) An emperor, dictator, or other powerful ruler or military commander. The allusion is to the Roman general and statesman Gaius Julius Caesar (100–44 B.C.), who conquered Gaul and Britain before returning to Rome and becoming the effective sole ruler of the Roman state from 49 until his death. He made many important reforms before being assassinated by a group of senators who feared he had become too powerful. After his death, his adopted son and heir Gaius Octavius (later called Augustus) took the name Caesar to help legitimize his reign, and subsequently all Roman emperors up to Hadrian adopted Caesar as a title. The title was revived by rulers of the Holy Roman Empire in the 10th century and became transformed into *kaiser* by the German monarchy. It was also adopted by the Russian royal family, in the form *czar,* and by the Arabs, as *qaysar. The fanfare played, the crowd cheered, and Caesar stepped up to the microphone to address the victorious faithful. See also* CAESAR IS NOT ABOVE THE GRAMMARIANS; CAESAR'S WIFE MUST BE ABOVE SUSPICION; CESAREAN SECTION; I CAME, I SAW, I CONQUERED.

caesarean section *See* CESAREAN SECTION.

Caesar is not above the grammarians (seezer) No one, however exalted his or her rank, can be excused for bad grammar. The reference harks back to the legend of the Roman emperor Tiberius, who was once corrected in his grammar. A courtier purportedly stated that as the emperor had said the mistake, the slip would henceforth be considered good Latin. A grammarian present, however, immediately objected, reminding the emperor, "*Tu enim Caesar civitatem dare potes hominibus, verbis non potes*" ("Caesar, you can grant citizenship to men, but not to words"). *The chief editor sighed and with a rueful smile crossed out what he had written. Even Caesar is not above the grammarians.*

Caesar's wife must be above suspicion (seezerz) People who occupy prominent social positions need to maintain unsullied reputations. The expression alludes to the story of Julius Caesar's second wife, Pompeia, who around 62 B.C. became embroiled in rumors that she was involved in an adulterous affair with the notorious philanderer Publius Clodius. Disguised as a woman, Publius Clodius had apparently infiltrated the all-female rites held at Caesar's house in honor of the goddess Bona Dea and there attempted to seduce the emperor's wife before being discovered. Although the accusations remained unsubstantiated and there was no reason to believe Pompeia had responded to the advances of Publius Clodius, Caesar still insisted on divorcing her on the grounds that even the suggestion that she might be guilty was damaging to him. Thus, any person in such an elevated position may be reminded that they must be ***like Caesar's wife***—free of all taint of misdeed. "I am as free as the air. I feel myself as far above suspicion as Caesar's wife" (Charles Dickens, *Bleak House,* 1852–53).

Caiaphas (kayăfas) Archetype of a ruthless, hypocritical politician. Caiaphas appears in the Bible as a Jewish high priest who tries Jesus (John 18:14–28) on the grounds that it is "expedient for us, that one man should die for the people, and that the whole nation perish not" (John 11:50). "Leaving Kennetbridge for this place is like coming from Caiaphas to Pilate!" (Thomas Hardy, *Jude the Obscure,* 1895).

Cain and Abel (kayn, aybăl) Archetype of two brothers whose relationship ends in violent disagreement. The allusion is to the story of Cain and Abel, related in Genesis 4:1–16, which details how Cain, the first son of Adam and Eve and described as a "tiller of the ground," came to murder his brother Abel, a shepherd, through envy: "And Cain talked with Abel his brother: and it came to pass, when they were in the field, that Cain rose up against Abel his brother, and slew him" (Genesis 4:8). "Cain's envy was the more vile and malignant towards his brother, Abel, because when his sacrifice was better accepted there was nobody to look on" (Francis Bacon, "On Envy," 1601). *See also* CAIN'S CITY; MARK OF CAIN; MY BROTHER'S KEEPER; RAISE CAIN.

Cain's city (kayns) A city with a reputation for corruption and evil. The allusion is to the city supposedly founded by Cain after he was banished by God for the murder of his brother Abel. According to Genesis 4:17, Cain "builded a city, and called the name of the city, after the name of his son, Enoch." *The settlement was founded with the best of motives but like Cain's city soon became a notorious den of iniquity.*

cake, let them eat *See* LET THEM EAT CAKE.

cakes and ale The material pleasures of life. The phrase occurs in William Shakespeare's play *Twelfth Night* (1601): "Dost thou think, because thou art virtuous, there shall be no more cakes and ale?" It was used as the title of a 1930 novel by W. Somerset Maugham and is also sometimes encountered in the expression "Life is not all cakes and ale," meaning that no person's life is without its moments of hardship. "So supposing you never marry, and if you go on being so fussy you probably never will—are there to be no cakes and ale?" (Lynne Reid Banks, *The L-Shaped Room*, 1960).

Calamity Jane (kălamitee) A reckless, adventurous female, or one who predicts or seems prone to accidents and other misfortunes. The allusion is to the frontierswoman Martha Jane Burke (c. 1852–1903), who became famous for her riding and shooting skills while working (often dressed as a man) as a teamster supplying mining camps during the gold rush that swept the Black Hills of Dakota in the 1860s and 1870s. Her nickname Calamity Jane arose from the fact that she is supposed to have threatened "calamity" to any man who approached her with a view to romance. *His daughter came home with minor scrapes and scratches so often the rest of the family knew her as Calamity Jane.*

Calchas (kalkas) Archetype of a wise prophet. In Greek mythology, Calchas was a soothsayer who advised the Greeks during the Trojan War. It was Calchas who recommended the sacrifice of

Iphigenia to appease Artemis before the Greek fleet set sail, persuaded Agamemnon to surrender his prize Chryseis to her father in order to halt a plague sent by Apollo, and advised the Greeks to build the TROJAN HORSE. He died of a broken heart after Mopsus proved himself superior in his skills as a prophet of future events. *The president will miss his closest aide, who has acted as Calchas to the party for over a decade.*

Caleb (kayleb) A faithful servant. According to Numbers 13:6 and 32:12, Caleb was one of those chosen by Moses to spy out the land of Canaan. Of the 12 men sent, only Caleb and Joshua returned with a favorable report. For his loyal service Caleb was eventually granted Hebron as his inheritance. "It is for you to say, with the faith of a Caleb, 'Give me this mountain'" (F. B. Meyer, *Joshua,* 1893).

calends (kalendz) The first day of the month. The calends, or ***kalends,*** (meaning "proclamation day") had particular significance for the ancient Romans and was so called because it was originally marked by high priests calling the people together to hail the new month and announcing the festivals and sacred days to be observed in the coming weeks. *She celebrates the calends each month by clearing everything off her desk and concentrating on new projects. See also* AT THE GREEK CALENDS.

calf, fatted *See* KILL THE FATTED CALF.

calf, golden *See* GOLDEN CALF.

Caliban (kaliban) A brutish, uncivilized man. Caliban is the stupid, resentful, unkempt, and monstrous son of the witch Sycorax in William Shakespeare's play *The Tempest* (1611). He rails against his master PROSPERO and lusts after Prospero's daughter MIRANDA, but is helpless against Prospero's magical powers. His name may have been suggested by the Romany *kaliban*, meaning "blackener," or may have come about through juggling the letters of "cannibal." *The streets were full of drunken Calibans.*

Caligari, Doctor *See* DOCTOR CALIGARI.

Caligula (kăligyoolă) Archetype of a cruel and eccentric ruler. Gaius Caesar (A.D. 12–41), nicknamed Caligula, ruled as emperor of Rome for a relatively short time (37–41) and quickly became notorious for his unpredictable and vicious nature. Among his excesses, he declared himself a god, made his horse Incitatus a consul, and ordered his army to collect seashells. His reign ended prematurely when he was murdered. *This fledgling Caligula of the new Asia is full of surprises, even renaming the days of the week according to personal whim.*

Calliope *See* MUSES.

Calpurnia (kalperneeă) Archetype of a devoted wife, who is concerned for her husband's welfare. The wife of the Roman emperor Julius Caesar, Calpurnia was greatly troubled by various portents of death that appeared to threaten her husband. Caesar, however, ignored her warnings and was duly murdered by members of the senate in 44 B.C. *Like Caesar's Calpurnia, she seemed to realize the danger her husband was in but could find no way to make him change his plans.*

calvary (kalvăree) A place or experience that causes intense suffering, especially mental anguish. In the Bible, Calvary is identified as the hill in Jerusalem upon which Christ was crucified (Luke 23:32). The name comes from the Latin *calvaria,* itself a translation of the Greek *kranion* (meaning "skull"). Its other names include ***Golgotha*** (from the Aramaic *gulguta*, or "skull") and ***place of skulls*** (Matthew 27:33; Mark 15:22; John 19:17). The actual site of Calvary is disputed, with some identifying it with a vaguely skull-shaped hill near the Garden of Gethsemane and others indicating the site of the Church of the Holy Sepulchre. Legend has it that the skull of Adam was kept at the church. "The horse, a dangerous animal . . . whose martyrdom, and man's shame therein, he has told most powerfully in his Calvary, a tale with an edge that will cut the soft cruel hearts and strike fire from the hard kind ones" (George Bernard Shaw, *Captain Brassbound's Conversion,* 1900).

Calvinist (kalvinist) Of a joyless, puritan nature, according to a strict moral code. The allusion is to the teachings of the French-born Protestant theologian Jean Calvin (1509–64), who stressed the authority of the Bible and the importance of personal discipline in daily life and recommended the pursuit of thrift, industry, and sobriety. "My Afrikaner grandfather was fond of repeating that a man needs six hours, a woman seven, and a bloody fool eight hours' sleep—a sentiment which nicely incorporated both his simple male chauvinism and a Calvinist abomination of indulgence" (Jacob Empson, *Sleep and Dreaming*, 1989).

Calydonian boar hunt (kalădōneeăn) An epic pursuit of a ferocious prey. The original Calydonian boar hunt was a chase in which Meleager, the ruler of ancient Calydon, and various other heroes, including Jason and Theseus, set off in pursuit of a massive boar that had been sent by Artemis to ravage the land. Meleager himself finally succeeded in killing the beast and presented its head to Atalanta, who had inflicted the first wound. *The three operatives privately agreed never to let up on their pursuit of the gangsters, viewing the investigation as a type of modern Calydonian boar hunt.*

calypso (kălipsō) Popular style of West Indian ballad, characterized by syncopated percussion and topical lyrics. It is thought to have been named after Calypso, a sea nymph of Greek mythology who fell in love with Odysseus and detained him for seven years on the island of Ogygia. There, Odysseus spent his nights as Calypso's lover but passed his days in longing for his wife, Penelope. Ultimately, Odysseus refused Calypso's offer of immortality if he would remain with her on the island forever, and on the command of Zeus, Calypso allowed him to continue his journey home to his wife. The island Ogygia is sometimes tentatively identified as Gozo, near Malta. *Tonight the strains of the calypso seemed to lack their usual cheerfulness, reminiscent even of the original Calypso pining for the absent Odysseus.*

camel: go through an eye of a needle A feat that is considered very difficult, if not impossible to achieve. The reference is to the words of Christ related in Matthew 19:23–24, Mark 10:23–25, and Luke 18:24–25, describing the challenge faced by the rich man who wished to enter heaven: "Then said Jesus unto his disciples, Verily I say unto you, That a rich man shall hardly enter into the kingdom of heaven. And again I say unto you, It is easier for a camel to go through the eye of a needle, than for a rich man to enter into the kingdom of God" (Matthew 19:23–24). One theory suggests the imagery used by Christ was intended as a reference to a gate called the "needle's eye" that was so narrow a camel—the largest animal in ancient Palestine—could not pass through it. "It is as hard to come as for a camel / To thread the postern of a small needle's eye" (William Shakespeare, *King Richard II,* 1595). "It is easier for a cannibal to enter the Kingdom of Heaven through the eye of a rich man's needle than it is for any other foreigner to read the terrible German script" (Mark Twain, *Notebook,* 1898).

Camelot (kamălot) A place of government or an inner circle of advisers or colleagues. The allusion is to Camelot, the legendary court of KING ARTHUR in English folklore. The home of the knights of the ROUND TABLE, it was envisioned as a palace in which the ideals of medieval chivalry were celebrated and defended. Its site is variously identified with Cadbury Castle in Somerset or Camelford in Cornwall, among other possible locations. The name later came to be strongly associated with the short-lived administration (1961–63) of President John F. Kennedy, which ended with the assassination of this dashing, modern-day King Arthur in Dallas. Significantly, Kennedy's period in office coincided with the success on BROADWAY of the Lerner and Loewe stage musical *Camelot*, which was reportedly a great favorite of the president and his wife. The name Camelot itself comes from the Celtic word *cant*, meaning "circle" or "edge." *You need to have the right connections to be admitted to this particular Camelot.*

Camilla (kămilă) Personification of a fast runner. Camilla was identified in classical mythology as a Voscian princess and a servant of Diana. She was described as being so fleet of foot that she could run over a field of corn without bending the stalks and could cross the sea without getting her feet wet. "Margaret ran, swift as Camilla, down to the window" (Elizabeth Gaskell, *North and South,* 1854–55).

Camille (kămeel) A prostitute with a heart of gold. The title character of the 1848 novel *La Dame aux camélias* by Alexandre Dumas *fils*, which is known as *Camille* in some English adaptations, she is a Parisian courtesan who renounces her former life to be with her lover Armand, but is then persuaded to abandon him in order to protect his reputation. Tragically, she dies of tuberculosis shortly after a tearful reconciliation with Armand, who has just learned of her sacrifice. *She felt like the fictional Camille, sacrificing herself for love.*

Camp David (dayvid) A country retreat, particularly one associated with political negotiations. The allusion is to the U.S. presidential retreat at Catoctin Mountain Park, Maryland, to which various presidents over the years have invited prominent foreign statesmen and stateswomen for private top-level discussions (notably the Camp David agreements between Israel and Egypt in 1978). It was first used for such purposes by Franklin D. Roosevelt, who called it SHANGRI-LA; it acquired the name Camp David in 1953 when Dwight D. Eisenhower renamed it after his grandson David. *What this country needs is a Camp David where international issues could be discussed and resolved.*

Cana, marriage in *See* WATER INTO WINE.

Canaan, land of *See* PROMISED LAND.

Can any good thing come out of Nazareth? *See* GOOD THING COME OUT OF NAZARETH.

canary in a coal mine A sign of imminent danger. The allusion is to a former practice whereby miners took canaries into mines to warn them of the presence of poisonous gases, the birds being more susceptible to the effects of such gases than the humans, giving them time to escape if a bird died. *This decline in consumer sales could be a canary in a coal mine warning of a loss of public confidence in government policy.*

Canary Wharf (kănairee worf) The financial establishment in the United Kingdom. Canary Wharf is the name of the area surrounding the skyscraper called Canary Wharf Tower in London's Docklands, which since redevelopment in the 1990s has become home to the head offices of various major financial and business companies. *It's anyone's guess what they will make of this announcement in Canary Wharf.*

Candid Camera A situation in which unsuspecting people are caught unawares and exposed to humiliation or embarrassment. The allusion is to a popular long-running television program first screened in the 1950s in which ordinary people were secretly filmed in unexpected situations. *Everything was so bizarre that for a minute I thought I was on Candid Camera.*

Candide (kandeed) Stereotype of a naive optimist. The allusion is to *Candide, ou l'Optimisme* (1759), a satirical novel by Voltaire in which the author lampoons the gullible innocence of the central character Candide, a young man who (until experience teaches him otherwise) bears all misfortunes philosophically, encouraged by his tutor Dr. Pangloss into believing that "all is for the best in this best of all possible worlds." *Like Voltaire's Candide, he strove to find something positive in every disaster that befell him.* *See also* PANGLOSSIAN.

candle under a bushel *See* HIDE ONE'S LIGHT UNDER A BUSHEL.

Cannae (kanee) A disastrous defeat that brings to an end a run of previous successes. The allusion is to the battle of Cannae that took place in 216 B.C. during the Second Punic War between Rome and Carthage. The Roman army had won the First Punic War, but after the Carthaginian general Hannibal invaded Italy, Rome was soundly defeated and suffered heavy losses at the village of Cannae in southeastern Italy. The Roman generals Lucius Aemilius Paulus and Gaius Terentius Varro, who had made the reckless decision to attack the center of the Carthaginian force (thus allowing their enemy to encircle them), spent the rest of their lives in disgrace, and the name of the battle became forever associated with catastrophic defeat. *After so many years in undisputed power, this electoral disappointment is already being described as the party's Cannae.*

Canossa, go to *See* GO TO CANOSSA.

Canute, King *See* KING CANUTE.

Caped Crusader *See* BATMAN AND ROBIN.

Capone, Al *See* AL CAPONE.

Captain Ahab (ayhab) A person who is obsessed to the point of madness in pursuing a particular goal. The original Captain Ahab was the captain of the whaling ship *Pequod* in Herman Melville's 1851 novel *Moby-Dick*, who is determined to have his revenge upon the white whale that cost him his leg many years before. *He stood on the bow of the vessel, like Captain Ahab, and announced that he would not eat or sleep until he had received an apology. See also* MOBY DICK.

Captain Bligh (blī) Archetype of a pitiless master or employer. Captain William Bligh (1754–c. 1817) was the commander of the *Bounty*, which was taken over by its crew (objecting to the harsh discipline Bligh imposed) on its way to the South Sea Islands in 1787. In what was to become the most notorious of all mutinies at sea, the tyrannical Captain Bligh and several other members of the crew were overpowered by the mutineers (led by Fletcher Christian) and set adrift in a small boat. The rest of the crew eventually sought safety on remote Pitcairn Island, and Captain Bligh managed to get back to England, where he brought charges against the mutineers. *He regarded his workforce with the same lack of compassion as Captain Bligh.*

Captain Hook A piratical villain, or a roguish person who lacks a hand. Captain Hook is the wicked pirate captain in J. M. Barrie's *Peter Pan* (1904), whose one aim in life is to defeat his enemy PETER PAN, whom he blames for the loss of his hand (bitten off by a crocodile and replaced with a metal hook). *With that evil smirk and artificial hand he looked more like Captain Hook than a captain of industry.*

Captain Kirk *See STAR TREK.*

Captain Marvel (mahrvăl) A person who can seemingly achieve superhuman feats. Captain Marvel was one of the most popular of the superheroes to feature in Marvel Comics, making his debut in 1940. Having acquired his superhuman powers after meeting a wizard, he changes into a superhero whenever he utters the word ***shazam*** (an acronym composed of the first initials of the classical heroes Solomon, Hercules, Atlas, Zeus, Achilles, and Mercury). *We never thought we would get to see the president, but our guide turned out to be a Captain Marvel.*

Captain Oates (ōts) A person who heroically sacrifices himself or herself to save others. The allusion is to Captain Lawrence Oates (1880–1912), who was a member of Captain Scott's doomed expedition to the South Pole in 1912. Suffering badly from frostbite, and concerned that his incapacity would prevent his companions from reaching safety when caught in a blizzard, Oates walked out of the tent to die in the snow with the memorable last words: "I am just going outside and may be some time." His gesture failed to save the rest of the expedition, but has been celebrated ever since as the quintessence of heroic self-sacrifice. *When he realized that his girlfriend was in love with his best friend he resolved to behave with the gallantry of a Captain Oates. See also* SCOTT OF THE ANTARCTIC.

Captain Queeg (kweeg) A tyrannical but cowardly leader or boss. Captain Queeg is the vicious but cowardly commander of the minesweeper *Caine* in the 1954 movie *The Caine Mutiny*, based on a 1951 novel by Herman Wouk. Played in the movie by Humphrey Bogart, Queeg is revealed as a petty-minded bully whose bravado quickly disintegrates when he is faced with a real challenge to his authority. *It was no fun working for a Captain Queeg who insisted upon knowing where every item of stationery had gone to and who threatened his underlings with dismissal for the smallest infringement of his rules.*

Capua corrupted Hannibal (kapyooă, hanibăl) Decadence will ruin anyone. The reference is to the winter the Carthaginian leader Hannibal spent in the Italian city of Capua, which was renowned as a center of idleness and luxury, during his campaign on the Italian mainland. Until then he had been victorious everywhere; afterward he failed to reach anew the same degree of success. *As heavyweight champion it seemed for a time that he would never be defeated, but just as Capua corrupted Hannibal, soft living fatally undermined his stamina in the ring.*

Capulet *See* PLAGUE ON BOTH YOUR HOUSES, A.

cardigan (kahdigăn) A knitted sweater, buttoned at the front. The garment was named after the seventh earl of Cardigan (1797–1868), who was commander of the Light Brigade on the day it was committed to a disastrous charge against Russian guns at the Battle of Balaclava in 1854, during the Crimean War. Many of the British troops wore such garments to keep out the bitter cold during the Crimean campaign. "Ahead of him a morose-looking man in a cardigan was sorting through slabs of meat in plastic containers" (Nigel Williams, *The Wimbledon Poisoner*, 1990).

Carey Street (kairee) Bankruptcy. Carey Street in the City of London was the location of the city's Bankruptcy Court, hence "to be in Carey Street" meant "to be bankrupt." The connection is sometimes made with the expression ***in Queer Street***, which also means "bankrupt" or "short of funds," but this would appear to have different origins, in the word "crooked" or "cross." *The sixth earl squandered the family's fortunes and ended up in Carey Street.*

Carmen (kahrmăn) A passionate, reckless femme fatale. Carmen is the gypsy girl who is the focus of the action of the 1846 novel *Carmen* by the French writer Prosper Mérimée (1803–70), brought to life in 1875 as an opera by Georges Bizet. Carmen's tempestuous career in love famously ends with her being stabbed to death by her jilted lover Don José. *Carmen herself could not have made a more dramatic entrance.*

Carnaby Street (kahrnăbee) The British fashion world, particularly that of the 1960s. Carnaby Street in central London was the location of several influential boutiques whose customers included rock stars and many other well-known public faces. It had declined in importance by the mid-1970s. "The trendies of Carnaby Street flounced around in military uniforms, sporting flowers of peace where medals once had hung" (Simon Brett, *Murder Unprompted*, 1984).

carpe diem (kahrpay deeăm) Make the most of one's opportunities, as they may not come again; seize the moment. The slogan comes from the *Odes* of the Roman poet Horace (65–8 B.C.), in which he wrote: *"carpe diem, quam minimum credula postero"* ("enjoy today, trusting little in tomorrow"). It is also rendered as ***seize the day*** and ***take time by the forelock.*** "When a man had nothing left in life except his dinner, his bottle, his cigar, and the dreams they gave him—these doctors forsooth must want to cut them off! No, no! Carpe diem! while you lived, get something out of it" (John Galsworthy, *The Forsyte Saga,* 1922).

carpetbagger An unprincipled opportunist. The word made its first appearance in the years following the U.S. Civil War, when the ravaged southern states provided rich pickings for politicians and traders who arrived from the north with no more than a carpet traveling bag of personal belongings. They quickly acquired an unenviable reputation for corruption, selfishness, and greed. The term has since been applied to political candidates who have no real connection with the area they seek to represent. *Shares in the company have been pounced on by carpetbaggers hoping to make an easy profit.*

carry coals to Newcastle *See* COALS TO NEWCASTLE.

Carry Nation (karee) A supporter of the temperance movement. Carry Nation (1846–1911) became a dedicated crusader against the drinking of alcohol after her first marriage was wrecked by her husband's alcoholism. As leader of the Women's Christian Temperance Union, she campaigned to have the illegal saloons of Kansas closed, even wielding a hatchet herself to destroy bars until arrested and imprisoned for destruction of property. *She stormed into the bar like Carry Nation herself, overturning tables and scattering startled partygoers.*

carry one's cross *See* BEAR/CARRY/TAKE ONE'S CROSS.

Carson, Kit *See* KIT CARSON.

Carter, Nick *See* NICK CARTER.

Cartesian (kahrteezeeăn) Of or relating to the theories of French philosopher and mathematician René Descartes (1596–1650). Descartes argued that it was possible to apply mathematical logic to any field of human knowledge, using it to satisfy himself of the existence of the material world and even of the existence of God. He is best remembered for his formulation of the statement ***cogito ergo sum***, which is translated as "I think, therefore I am." "This Cartesian illusion is directly linked with the universal belief that 'we' (people like us) can be distinguished from 'they' (people who are like us in external form but not like us in their inner essence)" (Edmund Leach, *Social Anthropology*, 1986).

Carthaginian peace (kahrthăjineeăn) A peace treaty or other agreement that is extremely harsh and punitive for the loser. The allusion is to the state of affairs that existed following the Punic wars fought between Carthage and Rome. Having suffered defeat in the First and Second Punic Wars, Carthage lost various colonial territories, but the North African state was still substantially intact. The third war, however, ended with the Romans invading the African mainland and setting siege to Carthage itself. The city fell after two years and was utterly devastated, never to regain its past glory. *The Carthaginian peace imposed on Germany after World War I sowed the seed for the growth of nationalism in that country. See also* PUNIC FAITH.

Cartland, Barbara *See* BARBARA CARTLAND.

Carton, Sydney *See* IT IS A FAR, FAR BETTER THING THAT I DO.

caryatid (kareeatid) An architectural column in the shape of a female figure. Such columns were a feature of many ancient Greek temples. They were named after the women of Caryae in Laconia, which had unwisely sided with the Persians against the Greeks at the battle of Thermopylae. The victorious Greeks subsequently ravaged Caryae and carried off the women as slaves. To emphasize their subservience to Greece, the sculptor Praxiteles used these women as models for pillars in the place of conventional columns. "As they stepped out into the darkness, a sheet of rain was driven in upon their faces, and the hall lamp, which dangled from the arm of a marble caryatid, went out with a fluff" (Sir Arthur Conan Doyle, *Round the Red Lamp,* 1894).

Cary Grant (karee grant) A debonair, handsome man in the mold of U.S. film actor Cary Grant (1906–86). Cary Grant was actually born in Bristol, England, under the name Archibald Leach. He became the quintessence of the suave romantic hero in such films as *Bringing up Baby* (1938), *To Catch a Thief* (1954), and *North by Northwest* (1959). *She had dreamed of marrying a Cary Grant type, but ended up an embittered spinster surrounded by cats.*

Casanova (kasănōvă) A prolific seducer of women. Giovanni Jacopo Casanova de Seingalt (1725–98) was a Venetian adventurer and conman who acquired a notorious reputation as a libertine whose many sexual conquests were recorded (with varying degrees of reliability) in his scandalous *Mémoires* (1826–38). Casanova traveled extensively throughout Europe, and his colorful reputation did not prevent him from being appointed to the respectable posts of director of the state lottery in Paris and librarian to Count Waldstein in Bohemia. "I don't pretend to be a monk, exactly, but I'm no Casanova, either" (Eleanor Rees, *Hunter's Harem,* 1992). *See also* DON JUAN; LOTHARIO.

Casey at the bat (kaysee) A hero who against all expectation fails to deliver at the crucial moment. The allusion is to a popular poem by Ernest Lawrence Thayer, first published under this title in the *San Francisco Examiner* in 1888, which tells the tale of Mighty Casey, star of the Mudville baseball team, whose overconfidence leads him to strike out on the crucial last pitch in a vital game: "Oh somewhere in this favored land the sun is shining bright. / The band is playing somewhere, and somewhere hearts are light; / And somewhere men are laughing, and somewhere children shout, / But there is no joy in Mudville; Mighty Casey has struck out." *There is no joy in Mudville—the new president is turning out to be another Casey at the bat.*

Casey Jones (kaysee) A locomotive driver, especially one of stalwart, heroic character. The original Casey Jones was U.S. locomotive engineer John Luther Jones (1864–1900) whose courage saved the passengers of the Cannonball Express when it crashed between New Orleans and Chicago, at the cost of his own life. The incident was the inspiration for a number of folk ballads and even a television series of the 1960s. *The new owner of the miniature railway explained that he had always fancied himself as a Casey Jones.*

Caspar *See* MAGI.

Caspar Milquetoast (kasper milktōst) A timid person. Caspar Milquetoast was the creation of U.S. cartoonist H. T. Webster, who introduced him in the cartoon *The Timid Soul* in the *New York World* in May 1924. A hesitant, easily put-upon middle-aged man with a droopy white mustache and pince-nez, he is one of the world's most long-suffering victims. "Milktoast" is toast soaked in milk, a bland foodstuff recommended for small children and invalids. *There was no way a proud woman like her would ever fall for a Caspar Milquetoast like him.*

Cassandra (kăsandră) A prophet of doom, specifically one whose prophecies are ignored but who is later proved correct. The allusion is to Cassandra, the daughter of King Priam of Troy, who was granted prophetic powers by Apollo but later fated never to be believed as punishment for her having refused his advances. Consequently, when she foretold the fall of Troy no one heeded her warnings. After the fall of Troy, Cassandra was taken by Agamemnon to Greece, where she prophesied Agamemnon's death but was again ignored. Ultimately, she and Agamemnon were murdered by Clytemnestra. "But Cassandra was not believed, and even the wisdom of *The Jupiter* sometimes falls on deaf ears" (Anthony Trollope, *Barchester Towers,* 1857).

Cassidy, Butch *See* BUTCH CASSIDY AND THE SUNDANCE KID.

Cassidy, Hopalong *See* HOPALONG CASSIDY.

Castalian spring (kastayleeăn) A source of inspiration. The allusion is to a sacred spring on Mount Parnassus that was believed by the ancient Greeks to bestow the gift of poetry upon anyone who drank from its waters. "The Aeneid, you know, begins just as he says an epic ought not to begin; and the Aeneid is the greatest Latin epic. In the next place the use of Modesty is to keep a man from writing an epic poem at all but, if he will have that impudence, why then he had better have the courage to plunge into the Castalian stream, like Virgil and Lucan, not crawl in funking and holding on by the Muse's apron-string" (Charles Reade, *Hard Cash,* 1863). *See also* PARNASSIAN.

casting couch The exchange of sexual favors for employment opportunities or other benefits. The phrase is of theatrical or cinematic origin, referring to the (largely mythical) couch upon which aspiring young actresses were supposedly encouraged to demonstrate their talents to directors casting plays or films. "She described the Hollywood of the late 1940s as 'an overcrowded brothel' but was no stranger to the casting couch herself" (Robin Smith, *The Encyclopaedia of Sexual Trivia,* 1990).

cast in one's teeth To insult; to revile; to throw a reproof at someone. The idiom comes from Matthew 27:44: "The thieves also, which were crucified with him, cast the same in his teeth." "All his faults observed, / Set in a notebook, learn'd and conn'd by rote, / To cast in my teeth" (William Shakespeare, *Julius Caesar,* 1599).

cast into Dante's Inferno *See* DANTE'S INFERNO.

cast into outer darkness *See* OUTER DARKNESS.

cast money changers out of the temple To criticize or take action against inappropriate commercialism. The allusion is to the biblical episode in which Christ ejected the money changers from the Temple, which had become a place of business, as related at Matthew 21:12–13: "And Jesus went into the temple of God, and cast out all them that sold and bought in the temple, and overthrew the tables of the moneychangers, and the seats of them that sold doves, and said unto them, It is written, My house shall be called the house of prayer; but ye have made it a den of thieves." The money changers had originally been allowed into the Temple to facilitate the selling of doves for ritual sacrifices and the payment of Temple taxes by exchanging Roman currency for Hebrew coinage. *The accountants rule Hollywood, and there is little likelihood that* *anyone will succeed in casting these money changers out of the temple. See also* DEN OF THIEVES.

cast of thousands A large number of people involved in a particular project. The phrase comes from publicity releases for movies of the 1920s, specifically one for the first screen version of *Ben Hur* (1925), which boasted "a cast of 125,000." "A cast of thousands may have to be cut to seven" (Stafford Whiteaker, *A Career in Advertising and Public Relations*, 1986).

Castor and Pollux (kastor, polăks) Archetypes of devoted brothers. Castor and Pollux were identified in Greek mythology as twin brothers, sometimes called the ***Dioscuri.*** As the son of the god Zeus and the mortal Leda, Pollux enjoyed the gift of immortality, but Castor, being the son of Leda and the mortal Tyndareus, was mortal. When Castor died, Pollux asked to be allowed to die with him so that they might not be parted. Zeus granted his wish and placed the two brothers in the sky as stars (in the constellation of Gemini). *Like Castor and Pollux, the brothers were inseparable as teenagers and maintained this closeness well into adulthood.*

cast pearls before swine *See* PEARLS BEFORE SWINE.

cast the first stone *See* LET HIM WHO IS WITHOUT SIN CAST THE FIRST STONE.

cast thy bread upon the waters To give generously, as acts of generosity or kindness will be rewarded eventually. The sentiment comes from Ecclesiastes 11:1: "Cast thy bread upon the waters: for thou shalt find it after many days." *He little expected that he would ever benefit from this casting of bread upon the waters, but many years later he was pleasantly surprised to find his generosity was paying dividends.*

catbird seat An advantageous position. The phrase was popularized by radio sportscaster Red Barber (1908–92), who claimed to have borrowed it from a fellow poker player. The catbird *(Dumetella carolinensis)* is related to the mockingbirds and has a distinctive catlike cry. *The team are well and truly in the catbird seat now.*

Catch-22 (twenteetoo) A situation in which one outcome depends on another, which itself depends upon the first outcome, and thus cannot be resolved. The allusion is to the novel of the same title by Joseph Heller (1923–99), published in 1961. At the heart of the novel are the attempts of Captain ***Yossarian***, an officer in the U.S. Air Force stationed in Italy during World War II, to avoid taking part in further suicidal missions by pretending he is mad. His campaign falters when his superiors argue that by trying to escape such danger he is merely demonstrating his sanity (as made clear in regulation 22 laid down by the military bureaucracy): "There was only one catch and that was Catch-22 which specified that concern for one's own safety in the face of dangers that were real and immediate was the process of a rational mind." "Asserting herself as a conceptual artist, considering all her work as creative, whether working with other people or developing ideas for further projects, Jane nevertheless sees spending time on other people's creativity as a Catch-22 situation" (S. Townsend, *Women's Art*, 1992).

catcher in the rye *See* HOLDEN CAULFIELD.

Catherine wheel (kathrin) A small circular firework that spins rapidly on a pin, shooting out bright sparks. The firework refers to the death of Saint Catherine of Alexandria, who was executed in Alexandria around A.D. 310. Born into a wealthy Egyptian family, she converted to Christianity and was put on trial for her faith. Her eloquence at her trial resulted in the conversion of 50 pagan philosophers, all of whom were subsequently put to death on the orders of the emperor Maxentius. Catherine refused to renounce her faith and was sentenced to be tortured to death on a spiked wheel (hence the name of the modern firework). When this wheel broke she was beheaded. *The Catherine wheel spun several times then flew off the fence at high speed, making the guests scatter in all directions.*

Cathy *See* HEATHCLIFF.

Cato (kaytō) Archetype of an austere moralist and critic. Marcus Porcius Cato (234–149 B.C.) was a Roman statesman and writer who was well known for his contempt for decadence and his implacable hatred of Carthage, which he believed should be destroyed because of the threat it posed to Rome's future prosperity (*see* DELENDA EST CARTHAGO). His grandson, Marcus Porcius Cato (95–46 B.C.), was also a statesman, who in his turn became well known for his opposition to Catiline and Caesar. In modern usage, any person who becomes known for strictness of habits or bluntness of speech may be dubbed a Cato. *For years the paper has acted Cato, calling for an end to the contemporary obsession with celebrity culture.*

cattle of the sun Something forbidden that if enjoyed will bring disaster upon the guilty party. The allusion is to Greek mythology and the cattle on the Island of the Sun, upon which Odysseus and his crew landed in the course of their long voyage home. Odysseus was told that on no account should the cattle be harmed, but when Odysseus temporarily left his hungry men in order to pray to the gods, they killed and ate some of the cows. The sun god vented his rage by killing them all but Odysseus and destroying their ship. *Like the ancient Greeks who were all slaughtered for eating the cattle of the sun, those who were tempted to help themselves during the power failure have paid heavily for their crimes.*

Caulfield, Holden *See* HOLDEN CAULFIELD.

cave of Trophonius (trăfōneeăs) A cause of depression or fear. According to Greek mythology, Trophonius was an architect who was deified after his death and worshiped at a cave near Lebadeia in Boeotia. Those who entered the cave to consult his oracle were said to be so overawed by the place that they never smiled again. Thus, any person who seems unusually gloomy or scared may be said to have ***visited the cave of Trophonius.*** "The gardens were arranged to emulate those of Versailles. . . . There is the Trophonius' cave in which, by some artifice, the leaden Tritons are made not only to spout water, but to play the most dreadful groans out of their lead conches" (William Makepeace Thackeray, *Vanity Fair,* 1847–48).

Cecil B. DeMille (dămil) Archetype of a movie mogul. Cecil B. DeMille (1881–1959) was one of the first generation of great movie directors, responsible for such epics as *The Ten Commandments* (1923) and *The Greatest Show on Earth* (1952). The ambitious scope of his movies made his name synonymous with cinematic spectacle on a vast scale. His name is often invoked in a quotation from the 1950 film *Sunset Boulevard*, in which Norma

Desmond delivers the celebrated line "Mr. DeMille, I'm ready for my close-up now." "He was a fabulous showman, the Cecil B. DeMille of the dinner party trail, equally happy embracing Henry Kissinger or Liza Minnelli or Andy Warhol or Elizabeth Taylor, who was one of the more celebrated of his many lovers" (William Shawcross, *The Shah's Last Ride*, 1989).

Celestial City Heaven. The allusion is to John Bunyan's religious allegory *PILGRIM'S PROGRESS* (1678, 1684), in which the Celestial City is identified as Christian's ultimate destination. According to Bunyan, the Celestial City is made of pearls and precious gems, and the streets are paved with gold. "And it was as if she had glimpsed the celestial city knowing that she could never enter in" (Winifred Beechey, *The Reluctant Samaritan*, 1991).

centaur (sentor) One of a race of mythical creatures having the head, arms, and torso of a man and the lower body and legs of a horse. Centaurs belonged to Greek mythology and were deemed to represent the bestial aspects of human nature, although later tradition generally depicts them as benevolent, gentle creatures. They may have been inspired by the appearance of the ancient Thessalians who were the first to tame horses and learn how to ride. According to legend, the centaurs were defeated in battle by the human Lapiths, an epic encounter depicted in the celebrated friezes that decorated the Parthenon. "He was dressed in a Newmarket coat and tight-fitting trousers; wore a shawl round his neck; smelt of lamp-oil, straw, orange-peel, horses' provender, and sawdust; and looked a most remarkable sort of Centaur, compounded of the stable and the play-house" (Charles Dickens, *Hard Times,* 1854). *See also* CHIRON.

center cannot hold, the *See* THINGS FALL APART, THE CENTER CANNOT HOLD.

central casting A source of personnel who conform exactly to what is expected. The allusion is to Central Casting, an organization set up in 1926 to supply extras for Hollywood movies. "All black suede shoes and double-breasted pinstripe, he seemed central casting's idea of the ideal Establishment man" (Jeremy Paxman, *Friends in High Places*, 1990).

Cephalus *See* UNERRING AS THE DART OF PROCRIS.

Cerberus (serbărăs) A guardian; a watchkeeper. The allusion is to the fierce three-headed dog that, according to Greek mythology, guarded the entrance to the underworld. It has been suggested that the legend of Cerberus may have been inspired by the ancient Egyptian practice of guarding graves with dogs. "When a woman knows that she is guarded by a watch-dog, she is bound to deceive her Cerberus, if it be possible, and is usually not ill-disposed to deceive also the owner of Cerberus. Lady Glencora felt that Mrs. Marsham was her Cerberus" (Anthony Trollope, *Can You Forgive Her?* 1864). *See also* LABORS OF HERCULES; SOP TO CERBERUS.

cesarean section (săzaireeăn) A surgical incision through the abdominal and uterine walls to allow for the delivery of a baby. This procedure (also spelled ***caesarean section*** and often referred to simply as a ***cesarean***) traces its name back to the Roman emperor Julius Caesar (100–44 B.C.), who was reputed to have been born in this way. Medical experts however, have questioned whether Caesar's mother could possibly have survived such an operation given the limited knowledge of medical practitioners of the day, and the word, instead, may come simply from *caesus,* past participle of the Latin *caedere* (meaning "to cut"). *The cesarean section left a long vivid scar that did not fade with time.*

c'est la guerre (say la gair) Such things must be expected in these particular circumstances. The allusion is to World War I, when the phrase (meaning "it is the war" or "that's war") was widely quoted among members of the French military and civilian establishments, who were increasingly inclined to blame any misfortune upon the war. It was similarly used by British soldiers fighting in France during World War I, and later during World War II, and has since been employed throughout the English-speaking world as an excuse for (or as a general expression of resignation in the face of) any setback or disappointment caused by prevailing circumstances. *"C'est la guerre," he said with a shrug of the shoulders. "You must expect prices to rise when supplies are so scarce."*

c'est magnifique, mais ce n'est pas la guerre (say manifeek may să nay pa la gair) It is a grand but futile or misdirected gesture. The phrase (meaning "it is magnificent, but it is not war") was first uttered by the French general Pierre Bosquet in reference to the dashing but disastrous CHARGE OF THE LIGHT BRIGADE at the Battle of Balaclava on October 25, 1854. "Another leading pacifist, Cyril Joad, put the same point more succinctly: 'Ce n'est pas magnifique, mais ce n'est pas la guerre'" (James Hinton, *Protests and Visions*, 1989).

cestus See APHRODITE.

chain reaction A series of changes set in motion by a single event. The term was first used to describe chemical or nuclear reactions around the 1930s, but since the 1970s has come to be applied in a much wider range of contexts. *This move led to a chain reaction that resulted in hundreds of employees changing their job descriptions.*

Chamber of Horrors A place full of horror or unpleasantness, or what is found there. The allusion is to the Chamber of Horrors, the most popular part of the Madame Tussaud's waxworks exhibition in London, where wax figures of notorious murderers, torturers, etc., are displayed. "About a week after he had taken the stable, a Land Rover swept round the drive at high speed and disgorged its chamber of horrors—his family" (Jean Bow, *Jane's Journey*, 1991).

Chan, Charlie See CHARLIE CHAN.

Chandleresque (chandlăresk) In a manner reminiscent of the detective thriller novels of Raymond Chandler (1888–1959). Chandler's stories, many of which were subsequently made into successful Hollywood movies, have a dark, brooding atmosphere and even the heroes are cynical about the corrupt and violent world they inhabit. Stylistically, the term suggests a bleak, realistic tone interspersed with unexpectedly lyrical and even poetic images and turns of phrase, often inspired by the argot of the street. *He hailed from a Chandleresque background of slum tenements and sinister back alleys. See also* PHILIP MARLOWE.

Chaney, Lon See LON CHANEY.

Chang and Eng See SIAMESE TWINS.

chaos (kayos) A state of disorder or confusion. The word is Greek; in Greek mythology it described the state of the universe prior to the birth of the gods. Chaos itself was personified as the parent of Night and of Erebus (representing darkness). ". . . order began to emerge from chaos and the vision of a home made happy and comfortable by her skill and care came to repay and sustain her" (Louisa May Alcott, *An Old Fashioned Girl,* 1870).

Chaplinesque (chaplinesk) In a manner reminiscent of silent-movie star Charlie Chaplin (Sir Charles Spencer Chaplin; 1889–1977). Comparisons to Chaplin usually involve reference to the celebrated tramp character in which he appeared in many of his earlier movies. Such comparisons may be inspired by echoes of his physical appearance in the role, complete with baggy trousers and battered derby hat, or by a perceived connection with the hapless but likable persona of his most famous creation. *He cut a Chaplinesque figure with his ill-fitting suit and shy demeanor.*

Chappaquiddick (chapăkwidik) A scandalous event in the past that continues to blight a person's present reputation. The allusion is to Senator Ted Kennedy (b. 1932), who on July 19, 1969, drove his car off a bridge on the island of Chappaquiddick in Massachusetts. Kennedy was found guilty of leaving the scene of the accident, which resulted in the death by drowning of his 28-year-old passenger Mary Jo Kopechne. The shadow cast by the incident is thought to have ended Kennedy's chances of standing for the presidency of the United States and has remained a permanent blot on his public record. *This unfortunate episode looks set to become a Chappaquiddick that will haunt the party for years to come.*

Charge of the Light Brigade A heroic but doomed, even tragic, gesture against impossible odds. The allusion is to the cavalry charge made by the British Light Brigade against Russian batteries at the Battle of Balaclava on October 25, 1854, during the Crimean War. The charge, which was the result of a catastrophic misunderstanding of orders, caused the deaths of 247 of the 637 soldiers who took part in it and was vividly commemorated in a poem written that same year by Alfred, Lord Tennyson, entitled simply "The Charge of the Light Brigade." "Although you have not been in the manager's seat very long, you have done nothing to alter my original opinion that your appointment makes about as much sense as the Charge of the Light Brigade" (M. Gist, *Life at the Tip*, 1993). See *also* C'EST MAGNIFIQUE, MAIS CE N'EST PAS LA GUERRE; OURS NOT TO REASON WHY.

chariot of fire An apparently miraculous mean of overcoming a natural obstacle or other difficulty. The allusion is to the "fiery chariot" that transported ELIJAH to heaven, as recorded in 2 Kings 2:11: "Behold, there appeared a chariot of fire, and horses of fire, and parted them both asunder; and Elijah went up by a whirlwind into heaven." *With a last wave to the admiring crowd she leapt onto the bike, gunned the engine, and moments later was roaring off toward the horizon on this veritable chariot of fire.*

charity covers a multitude of sins Those who are of a kind and loving disposition will forgive the wrongdoing of others; sometimes used to state that such charity may also be a cloak for bad behavior or a sign of a guilty conscience. The proverb comes from 1 Peter 4:8: "And above all things have fervent charity among yourselves: for charity shall cover the multitude of sins." Sometimes the phrase is encountered with other words replacing *charity,* such as ***beauty covers a multitude of sins.*** "'John is so sensible, I'm afraid he will think I'm stupid if I ask questions about politics and things.' 'I don't believe he would. Love covers a multitude of sins, and of whom could you ask more freely than of him?'" (Louisa May Alcott, *Little Women,* 1868–69).

Charlemagne (shahrlămayn) Archetype of a wise, chivalrous ruler. Charlemagne (742–814), otherwise called Charles the Great, became the first Holy Roman Emperor in 800, and he and the adventures shared by the paladins who joined his court inspired many legends (*see* ROLAND). Charlemagne himself was said to be at least eight feet tall and immensely strong, being able to bend three horseshoes at once with his bare hands. ". . . at all events Steelkilt was a tall and noble animal with a head like a Roman, and a flowing golden beard like the tasseled housings of your last viceroy's snorting charger; and a brain, and a heart, and a soul in him, gentlemen, which had made Steelkilt Charlemagne, had he been born son to Charlemagne's father" (Herman Melville, *Moby-Dick,* 1851).

Charles Atlas (atlăs) A man with a well-developed physique, a bodybuilder. The original Charles Atlas (Angelo Siciliano; 1892–1972) was a U.S. bodybuilder who transformed himself from an underweight weakling into "the world's strongest man." Subsequently he became widely known through advertisements for a bodybuilding course that he promoted under the slogan "You too can have a body like mine." His name deliberately evoked comparison with the Greek Titan ATLAS, especially as depicted in books of maps, supporting the sky or the world itself on his muscle-bound shoulders. *As an old man he lost his Charles Atlas physique and resembled once more the puny youth of his early years.*

Charles Manson (mansăn) Archetype of a deranged serial killer, especially one who is addicted to drugs. Charles Manson (b. 1934) was the charismatic leader of an informal "cult" family which, in August 1969, went on a drug-fuelled killing spree in Beverly Hills. The so-called "Manson gang" entered the home of film director Roman Polanski and there viciously murdered his pregnant wife, actress Sharon Tate, and four others. Another spate of murders followed two nights later before the gang were captured and sentenced to death; their sentences were later commuted to life imprisonment. *The police are anxious to find and arrest the man before he turns into another Charles Manson.*

Charlie Chan A person of Chinese descent, especially one who proves both resourceful and well-mannered. The original Charlie Chan (properly, Inspector Charles Chan) was a Chinese detective created in 1925 by U.S. novelist Earl Derr Biggers. He featured in six novels and was the star of numerous movies of the 1930s and 1940s. A native of Honolulu, Chan was distinguished by his witty aphorisms and unfailing courtesy. He was rumored to have been based upon a real Hawaiian police detective, one Chang Apana. *The bureau badly needed a Charlie Chan who knew his way around the immigrant Chinese community and understood the cultural issues involved in the case.*

Charon (karăn) Personification of death; a ferryman. According to Greek mythology, Charon was the name of the ferryman who rowed the dead across the rivers Styx or Acheron to Hades, the abode of the dead. He was conventionally depicted as a hideous old man dressed in rags. In ancient times a coin, known as ***Charon's toll,*** was often placed in the mouth of a corpse prior to burial as payment to Charon, to ensure the deceased was seen safely into the underworld. "There stands a gig in the gray morning, in the mist, the impatient traveller pacing the wet shore with whip in hand, and shouting through the fog after the regardless Charon and his retreating ark, as if he might throw that passenger overboard and return forthwith for himself; he will compensate him" (Henry David Thoreau, *A Week on the Concord and Merrimack Rivers,* 1849).

Charybdis *See* BETWEEN SCYLLA AND CHARYBDIS.

Chatterley, Lady *See* LADY CHATTERLEY.

Chaucerian (chahrseereeăn) Of or relating to the literary works or world of English poet Geoffrey Chaucer (c. 1343–1400). The term is applied especially to works that are distinctly ribald in nature, reflecting the outrageous events depicted in "The Miller's Tale" and other stories that form Chaucer's celebrated *Canterbury Tales* (c. 1387). *His sense of humor verged on the Chaucerian and included frequent references to parts of the anatomy that are usually left out of the conversation in more refined circles.*

chauvinism (shōvinizăm) Blind patriotism, or the taking of a superior attitude toward others. The allusion is to Nicolas Chauvin of Rochefort, a French soldier who fought under Napoleon Bonaparte, to whom he was deeply devoted, in the early 19th century. He is reputed to have been wounded 17 times in the service of his emperor, but never to have faltered in his fanatical loyalty, continuing to sing his commander's praises even after the emperor's downfall (perseverance that led to Chauvin himself being lampooned in various popular plays and becoming a laughingstock on both sides of the Atlantic). The term was originally applied to exaggerated patriotic feeling for one's country, but has since been extended to blind belief in various other things, notably (in the phrase ***male chauvinism***) the assumption of male superiority over females. "His chauvinism and arrogance sent a shiver up my spine" (Peter Lewis, *The Fifties: Portrait of a Period*, 1989).

Checkpoint Charlie A military or police checkpoint. The original Checkpoint Charlie was one of the few crossing-points between East and West Berlin during the COLD WAR. Located at the junction of Friedrichstrasse and Kochstrasse, it was the only crossing-point in the BERLIN WALL that was open 24 hours a day and became notorious as the scene of various spy exchanges and other cloak-and-dagger activities in popular thrillers of the period. The original buildings that constituted the actual checkpoint (on the U.S. side little more than a wooden shed) were removed after reunification of Germany in 1990, but a copy of the simple shed was later reinstated on the site as a tourist attraction. *The school decided to set up a Checkpoint Charlie where students could be checked for knives and other weapons.*

Chekhovian (chekōveeăn) Reminiscent of the themes or writing style of the Russian playwright Anton Chekhov (1860–1904). In his plays, which include *The Three Sisters* (1901) and *The Cherry Orchard* (1904), he dealt with such themes as unfulfilled yearning, frustration, and the decline of the Russian aristocracy. *The building was infused with a Chekhovian melancholy that spoke evocatively of a lost empire.*

Chernobyl (cher<u>nō</u>băl) A nuclear accident, especially one on a large scale. The reference is to the nuclear power station at Chernobyl in the former Soviet Union, which exploded on April 26, 1986, resulting in around 250 (indirectly, possibly many more) deaths, the evacuation of a substantial area of what is now Ukraine, and radioactive contamination of large parts of Europe. The reactor itself was subsequently encased in concrete to prevent further radioactive leaks. The incident, which remains the worst nuclear accident ever to take place, is often referred to in discussions of the dangers of nuclear power, but is also invoked in wider contexts. *Some claim that the influence of television has led to western civilization facing a cultural Chernobyl. See also* CHINA SYNDROME; MELTDOWN; THREE MILE ISLAND.

cherub (<u>cherăb</u>) A sweet, angelic child. The word was used in the Bible to refer to a class of angels attending upon the throne of God in heaven (for example, Ezekiel 10:2–7). They are generally represented in art as plump, winged babies. "To think o' that dear cherub! And we found her wi' her little shoes stuck i' the mud an' crying fit to break her heart by the far horse-pit" (George Eliot, *Adam Bede,* 1859).

che sarà, sarà (kay să<u>rah</u> să<u>rah</u>) Whatever will be, will be. This familiar acceptance of the inevitable, in Italian, was the motto of the dukes of Bedford, although it became more widely familiar in the form ***que sera, sera*** in the 1950s as the title of a popular song by Jay Livingston and Ray Evans and recorded by Doris Day. *It wasn't what I wanted, but che sarà, sarà.*

Cheshire Cat (<u>chesh</u>er) Resembling in some way the Cheshire Cat in Lewis Carroll's *Alice's Adventures in Wonderland* (1865). The Cheshire Cat is remarkable both for its wide smile and (in Carroll's work) for its ability to vanish repeatedly until all that is left is its grin. A person who smiles broadly, especially at some private joke or satisfaction, is likely to be said to ***grin*** (or ***smile***) ***like a Cheshire Cat***. Though made famous by Carroll, the Cheshire Cat was not his invention, being referred to in literature of the late 18th century, and possibly earlier. It has been suggested that the concept of the Cheshire Cat may derive from the custom of stamping Cheshire cheeses with the image of a grinning cat. *She came into the kitchen, smiling like a Cheshire Cat and brandishing the letter that said she'd won a scholarship.*

chiaroscuro (keeară<u>skoor</u>ō) Light and shade, especially in paintings. From the Italian for "light-dark," the term became current during the RENAISSANCE with reference to contemporary painting but has since been applied more widely. "But I was getting a trifle chilled—just a trifle, you know, and on this beautiful day—he waved a gloved hand at the brilliant sky and the buildings, dazzling in a chiaroscuro of stone and snow, the snow making the grey stone look black, the stone making the snow blindingly pure" (Peter Carter, *Bury the Dead*, 1986).

chicken in every pot, a The prospect of prosperity for all. The first expression of this assurance to a whole nation appears to date from the late 16th century, when Henry IV of France told the French people: "I wish that there would not be a peasant so poor in all my realm who would not have a chicken in his pot every Sunday." Centuries later, in 1928, the phrase became linked with U.S. presidential candidate Herbert Hoover—although in fact he never actually said it in quite this form.

During the depression, when hard times came to millions, many recalled how he had promised a chicken in every pot and a car in every garage.

Chicken Little An alarmist, especially one who spreads fear and despondency on very little evidence. The allusion is to a nursery tale character, a chicken otherwise called Chicken-Licken, who after being hit on the head by an acorn tells everyone that the sky is falling down. The creatures who hear this are thoroughly alarmed and fall easy prey to a cunning fox, who lures them all into the dubious shelter of his den. *The president cursed him for being a Chicken Little and banned him from the Oval Office.*

Childe Roland to the dark tower came (chīld rōlănd) An acknowledgment of peril on approaching a hazard of some kind. The line is a quotation, which appears as the title of a poem written by Robert Browning in 1855 and, before that, in a passage from William Shakespeare's tragedy *King Lear* (1605): "Child Rowland to the dark tower came; / His word was still 'Fie, foh, and fum, / I smell the blood of a British man.'" Shakespeare in turn was referring to an ancient Scottish ballad in which the Childe (apprentice knight) Roland (variously identified as a son of KING ARTHUR or a nephew of CHARLEMAGNE) is helped by MERLIN to rescue his sister from a castle in which she has been imprisoned by fairies. *"Childe Roland to the dark tower came," he muttered as he lifted the latch with trembling fingers. See also* ROLAND.

children of a lesser god People with disabilities. The phrase became well known as the title of a 1979 play by Marc Medoff (b. 1940) about the relationship between a deaf girl and a speech therapist. The ultimate origin of the expression lies in *Idylls of the King* (1859–85) by Alfred, Lord Tennyson, which contains the lines: "For why is all around us here / As if some lesser god had made the world, / But had not force to shape it as he would." The phrase has since come to be applied more widely to any group considered disadvantaged or inferior in some way. "Brian was so thoroughly weak that marriage to Evelyn, dire as it was, was better than no framework to his life, since his working-class parents were children of a lesser god" (Jean Bow, *Jane's Journey*, 1991).

children of light Those who are enlightened or otherwise alive to virtue, culture, faith, etc. The phrase is biblical in origin, appearing in Luke 16:8 and John 12:35–36 when Christ addresses those attending the feast of the Passover: "Yet a little while is the light with you. Walk while ye have the light, lest darkness come upon you . . . While ye have light, believe in the light, that ye may be the children of light" (John 12:35–36). "But the heart of man is the same everywhere, and there are the children of this world and the children of light there as well as elsewhere. But we've many more Methodists there than in this country" (George Eliot, *Adam Bede,* 1859).

children's hour A period during which the interests or influence of children, or people acting in a childish manner, are perceived to be predominant. The allusion is to a popular BBC children's radio program with this title, broadcast between 1922 and 1964. It featured such long-term favorites as presenter Uncle Mac (Derek McCulloch; 1897–1967) and the fictional occupants of Toytown, notably Larry the Lamb. The title was actually a quotation from the poem *Birds of Passage* (1860) by H. W. Longfellow: "Between the dark and the daylight / When the night is beginning to lower, / Comes a pause in the day's occupations, / That is known as the Children's Hour." *It was children's hour in the conference chamber, with delegates spouting much hot air and very little sense.*

children's teeth set on edge How a person behaves reflects on the rest of his or her family or associates. The image appears in Jeremiah 31:29–30, in which this piece of proverbial wisdom is refuted in favor of each person being responsible for his or her own behavior: "In those days they shall say no more, The fathers have eaten a sour grape, and the children's teeth are set on edge. But everyone shall die for his own iniquity." It is also included in Ezekiel 18:2–3. *When, as a young man, he was faced with having to answer for his progenitor's controversial policy, it was a case of the father having eaten a sour grape and the children's teeth being set on edge.*

chimera (kīmiră) An idle fancy; a fantastic, wild, or implausible product of the imagination. The allusion is to a fire-breathing monster of Greek mythology, described as having the head of a lion, the body of a goat, and the tail of a serpent. She was killed by the arrows of Bellerophon, mounted on the winged horse Pegasus. The creature's name may have been borrowed from that of a volcano similarly named in Lycia; flames shot forth from its summit, while lions prowled its upper slopes and goats and snakes lurked lower down. The name subsequently came to be used to describe any fabulous creature comprising the body parts of several different animals. By extension, anything unlikely or fantastical may be described as ***chimerical***. ". . . her spontaneous appeal to that sacred name dissolved his chimera; and let him see with his eyes, and hear with his ears" (Charles Reade, *The Cloister and the Hearth,* 1861).

China syndrome A theoretical scenario in which a nuclear MELTDOWN in the United States would result in the radioactive material burning its way through the earth's core and reemerging in China, on the other side of the world. This alarming possibility was raised in a film starring Jane Fonda and Jack Lemmon, *The China Syndrome*, which was released in 1979, the same year as the nuclear accident at THREE MILE ISLAND; it appeared to be even closer to becoming a reality following the CHERNOBYL disaster in 1986. The phrase is sometimes applied in nonnuclear contexts. *This error by the department could trigger a China syndrome that burrows its way through the whole government structure.*

Chinese wall *See* GREAT WALL OF CHINA.

Chingachgook *See* LAST OF THE MOHICANS.

chinless wonder An ineffectual, typically dim-witted, upper-class male. The expression, which appears to date only from the 1960s, was probably inspired by the "Boneless Wonder," the name under which circus contortionists were traditionally billed. A receding chin has long been interpreted as a sign of pusillanimous character, just as a jutting jawline has been seen as a sign of physical and mental strength. "She'd been waylaid within ten feet of the front door, which didn't surprise me, by a chinless wonder in a baggy suit and powder blue trainers (nobody wears trainers with a suit any more)" (Mike Ripley, *Just Another Angel*, 1989).

chips with everything Summary of the traditionally insular, culturally unambitious attitude of the British working class. Best known as the title of a 1962 play by Arnold Wesker (b. 1932), the phrase refers to the popularity of chips (French fries) among the working class in the postwar period, when they were served as an accompaniment to almost any kind of dish. In his play, Wesker lamented this lack of a sense of adventure in ordinary British working-class life: "You breed babies and you eat chips with everything." *This survey shows that the popular "chips with everything" image of the British working class has changed little over the years.*

Chiron (kīron) Archetype of a wise teacher. According to Greek mythology Chiron was unique among the CENTAURS in being wise and kind in nature. He was skilled at hunting and in various arts and in his turn served as tutor to many heroes, including Achilles and Jason. When accidentally hit by a poisoned arrow fired by his friend Hercules while in battle with the other centaurs, Chiron chose to die and passed his immortality on to Prometheus. His name is preserved today as that of a minor planet between Saturn and Uranus discovered in 1977. "Something less unpleasingly oracular he tried to extract; but the old sea Chiron, thinking perhaps that for the nonce he had sufficiently instructed his young Achilles, pursed his lips, gathered all his wrinkles together, and would commit himself to nothing further" (Herman Melville, *Billy Budd,* 1924).

Chloe (klōee) A rustic maiden; a shepherdess. A character of the same name appears in the Greek pastoral romance *Daphnis and Chloe* by the Greek writer Longus, who lived in the third century A.D. *Asleep on the haystack, her flock idly grazing all around, she seemed a true Chloe, as though she had lived in the country all her life. See also* DAPHNIS AND CHLOE.

chosen few A select group of people who enjoy particular favor. The expression comes from Matthew 22:14: "For many are called, but few are chosen." "He considered the years to come when Kim would have been entered and made to the Great Game that never ceases day and night, throughout India. He foresaw honour and credit in the mouths of a chosen few, coming to him from his pupil" (Rudyard Kipling, *Kim,* 1901). *See also* CHOSEN PEOPLE.

chosen instrument A person entrusted with a particular responsibility. The phrase appears in Acts 9:15, in which God tells Ananias that he has selected Paul to represent him among men: "Go thy way: for he is a chosen vessel unto me, to bear my name before the Gentiles, and kings, and the children of Israel." "I was wondering, in my own mind, whether the day of his downfall had come at last, and whether you were the chosen instrument for working it" (Wilkie Collins, *The Woman in White,* 1860).

chosen people A group of people considered select or particularly marked out. In the Bible the phrase is associated with Israel, and in the New Testament the church: "But ye are a chosen generation, a royal priesthood, an holy nation, a peculiar people" (1 Peter 2:9). "The folk here are civil, and, like the barbarians unto the holy apostle, hae shown me much kindness; and there are a sort of chosen people in the land, for they hae some kirks without organs that are like ours, and are called meeting-houses, where the minister preaches without a gown" (Sir Walter Scott, *The Heart of Midlothian,* 1818). *See also* CHOSEN FEW.

Christian *See* PILGRIM'S PROGRESS.

Christie, Agatha *See* AGATHA CHRISTIE.

Christmas, Father *See* SANTA CLAUS.

Churchillian (cherchileeăn) In a manner reminiscent of the British wartime leader Sir Winston Churchill (1874–1965). The word is variously employed with reference either to his policies or, more often, to his phlegmatic, determined character or distinctive speaking manner, preserved in recordings of his many celebrated speeches and broadcasts during and after World War II. "'We shall nevah surrendah!' came a Churchillian voice from the lads" (Bette Howell, *Dandelion Days*, 1991). *See also* WE SHALL FIGHT THEM ON THE BEACHES.

Ciceronian (sisărōneeăn) Eloquent; erudite. The word alludes to Marcus Tullius Cicero (106–43 B.C.), the Roman consul, orator, and writer who was widely admired for his eloquence and the purity of his Latin prose style. According to Plutarch, he was given the name Cicero—from *cicer* (meaning "wart")—because of the lump on the end of his nose. By extension, a person who guides sightseers around museums or similar places may be called a ***cicerone.*** *Epitaphs for the great man in the national newspapers emphasized his power as a speaker and included extracts from some of his more Ciceronian pronouncements.*

Cimmerian (simireeăn) Very dark or gloomy. According to Greek mythology, as recorded by Homer (eighth century B.C.) the Cimmerians were a tribe who inhabited a land of perpetual gloom situated at the remotest edge of the world and neighboring Hades itself. "A kind of landscape and weather which leads travellers from the South to describe our island as Homer's Cimmerian land, was not, on the face of it, friendly to women" (Thomas Hardy, *The Return of the Native,* 1880).

Cincinnatus (sinsinatăs) Archetype of a great man in retirement. Lucius Quinctius Cincinnatus (c. 519–438 B.C.) was a Roman general and statesman who was widely admired for his frugality and integrity. Assuming dictatorial powers, he saved Rome when it was threatened by invading armies on two occasions (in 458 and 439 B.C.) but each time surrendered his powers as soon as the danger had passed and returned to live quietly on his farm. Many celebrated public figures, including George Washington and Napoléon Bonaparte, have been dubbed a Cincinnatus for their time after giving up their powers and going into retirement. The city of Cincinnati in Ohio was named after the Society of the Cincinnati, made up of retired officers who had served in the Continental army in the American Revolution, that offered help to the dependents of fallen comrades. The name was transferred to the two-year-old city of Losantiville in 1790 by General Arthur St. Clair, president of the Cincinnati society and first governor of the Northwest Territory. "How rude you look, pushing and frowning, as if you wanted to conquer with your elbows! Cincinnatus, I am sure, would have been sorry to see his daughter behave so" (George Eliot, *Middlemarch,* 1871–72).

Cinderella (sindărelă) A neglected or underfunded person or thing. The allusion is to the traditional fairy tale about Cinderella, a young girl who is mistreated by her stepsisters (*see* UGLY SISTERS) until enabled by her FAIRY GODMOTHER to go to the royal ball and there win the heart of PRINCE CHARMING. The story most familiar today is of French origin, appearing in Charles Perrault's *Contes du temps passé* (1697), but versions of the tale are common to many other cultures. A ***Cinderella story*** is one in which a person who has previously failed to make much of an impact is suddenly transformed into a great success. "This was another powerful signal that primary education had ceased to be the Cinderella of the education service in Leeds" (R. Alexander, *Policy and Practice in Primary Education*, 1992).

Circe (sersee) A dangerous temptress. According to Homer's *Odyssey* (c. 700 B.C.), Circe was a beautiful enchantress of the island of Aeaea who was in the habit of transforming men who approached her palace into swine. Several of Odysseus's companions suffered such a fate but Odysseus remained immune to Circe's power with the help of Hermes, who advised him to protect himself by eating some of a mysterious herb called "moly," and obliged her to restore his men to their original form. Odysseus subsequently remained with the enchantress for a year, during which time he visited the underworld with her assistance, before continuing on his voyage. "Wolf Larsen it was, always Wolf Larsen, enslaver and tormentor of men, a male Circe and these his swine, suffering brutes that grovelled before him and revolted only in drunkenness and in secrecy" (Jack London, *The Sea-Wolf,* 1904).

circle the wagons To form a defensive posture against a threat of some kind. The phrase dates back to the pioneering journeys undertaken by migrants to the American West in the 19th century, when wagon trains were customarily drawn up into circles for defense each night to guard against attack by hostile Native American tribes. The image of pioneers resisting attack from within their circles of wagons became a standard image of Western movies in the 20th century. *The White House has decided to circle the wagons against this sustained media attack.*

Cisco Kid (siskō) Archetypal cowboy hero. The Cisco Kid first appeared in the guise of a Mexican bandit in a short story by O. Henry called "The Caballero's Way" in 1907. Depicted as a Wild West version of ROBIN HOOD, he went on to appear in a host of early silent movies, radio shows, and television series. *In that big hat and that shirt he looks just like the Cisco Kid.*

cities of the plain *See* SODOM AND GOMORRAH.

Citizen Kane (kayn) Archetype of a hugely wealthy but personally troubled tycoon. The 1941 movie *Citizen Kane*, starring Orson Welles as newspaper proprietor Charles Foster Kane, was controversially based upon the life of publishing magnate William Randolph Hearst (1863–1951) and regularly tops polls as the greatest movie ever made. *The press have decided to depict him as a second Citizen Kane, but the truth is more complicated than that. See also* ROSEBUD.

city of refuge A place of safety from one's enemies. The allusion is to Exodus 21:13 and Joshua 20:3, which describe how Moses and Joshua named six cities of refuge "that the slayer that killeth any person unawares and unwittingly may flee thither: and they shall be your refuge from the avenger of blood" (Joshua 20:3). People who had committed accidental homicide were admitted to one of these walled cities (Ramoth, Kedesh, Bezer, Shechem, Hebron, and Golam) in order to evade those who might seek vengeance. "He has been deprived of his city of refuge, and, in my humble opinion, has suffered infinite wrong!" (Nathaniel Hawthorne, *The House of the Seven Gables,* 1851).

city on a hill Utopia; a utopian community or shining example of some kind. The phrase comes from Christ's Sermon on the Mount: "Ye are the light of the world. A city that is set on an hill cannot be hid. Neither do men light a candle, and put it under a bushel, but on a candlestick; and it giveth light unto all that are in the house. Let your light so shine before men, that they may see your good works, and glorify your Father which is in heaven" (Matthew 5:14–16). *Most of her followers eagerly accepted her vision of a city on a hill where all might live in harmony together.*

Clark Gable (gaybăl) A suave, good-looking man. The U.S. movie star Clark Gable (1901–60) was Hollywood's most celebrated leading man during the 1930s and 1940s, appearing in such epics as *Mutiny on the Bounty* (1935) and *GONE WITH THE WIND* (1939). He was renowned for his romantic good looks, though critics lampooned him for his big ears and bad breath. *Her husband's not unattractive, but he's no Clark Gable. See also* FRANKLY, MY DEAR, I DON'T GIVE A DAMN.

Clark Kent *See* SUPERMAN.

clay in the potter's hand Easily led; malleable; pliable. The phrase is biblical in origin, appearing at Jeremiah 18:6, in which God's influence on earth is likened to a potter shaping clay: "As the clay is in the potter's hand, so are ye in mine hand." *The soldier easily roused the mob to fury, working them like clay in the potter's hand.*

clean the Augean stables *See* LABORS OF HERCULES.

Cleopatra *See* ANTONY AND CLEOPATRA; CLEOPATRA'S NOSE.

Cleopatra's nose (kleeōpatrăz) An apparently insignificant thing that is actually of extreme importance and has major consequences. The phrase was popularized by the French philosopher Blaise Pascal (1623–62), who speculated how history would have been different if Cleopatra VII (69–30 B.C.) had not been so beautiful, reflecting in his *Pensées:* "If the nose of Cleopatra had been shorter, the whole face of the earth would have been changed." It was the beauty and charm of the queen of Egypt that beguiled both Julius Caesar and Mark Antony and thus exerted a profound influence on the history of the ancient world. As it was, both Caesar and Mark Antony offered Cleopatra military assistance and thus preserved her throne from the rival claim of her brother. Some historians have, however, questioned the accuracy of modern assumptions about Cleopatra's beauty, pointing out that the few surviving contemporary portraits of her suggest she was somewhat plain, with prominent cheekbones. *It seems strange, looking back, how that one detail, like Cleopatra's nose, decided everything that was to follow later.*

cliff-hanger A point in a story or series of events where the outcome teeters on a knife-edge and is as yet unknown. The allusion is to early silent movie serials in which the hero was often left in a perilous situation, such as clinging to a cliff top, to be resolved in the next episode. The device later became a favorite ploy of radio drama serials and television soap operas. "It is a good 'cliffhanger' scene at the end of Book V, as Pippin falls in the black blood of the troll, to have his fate decided by events of which we have no knowledge" (T. A. Shippey, *The Road to Middle-Earth*, 1982).

climb Parnassus *See* PARNASSIAN.

Clio *See* MUSES.

clockwork orange A person who has been brainwashed to fit into society. The allusion is to the 1962 Anthony Burgess novel (and 1971 movie) *A Clockwork Orange*, which depicts the violent mayhem caused by a rebellious gang of teenagers who are eventually subjected to forcible conditioning designed to adjust their antisocial characters. Burgess himself adapted his title from a cockney expression, ***queer as a clockwork orange***, meaning "homosexual." *She felt as if the family was turning her into a clockwork orange who no longer had ideas of her own.*

close encounter Intimate contact of some kind, especially with alien beings. The allusion is to the 1977 movie *Close Encounters of the Third Kind*, directed by Steven Spielberg, in which human beings and aliens come into direct contact for the first time. A close encounter of the first kind involves a sighting of a UFO, a close encounter of the second kind involves an alien landing, a close encounter of the third kind involves actual contact, and a close encounter of the fourth kind involves abduction by aliens. The phrase is now commonly used to describe any kind of meeting, whether with aliens, people, animals, or sensations. "The pain is severe and no predator would risk a second close encounter with these snakes" (Desmond Morris, *Animal Watching—A Field Guide to Animal Behaviour*, 1991).

clothed and in one's right mind Fully aware and ready to perform any undertaking. The phrase alludes to an exorcism carried out by Christ on a man possessed by demons, as related at Luke 8:35: "Then they went out to see what was done; and came to Jesus, and found the man, out of whom the devils were departed, sitting at the feet of Jesus, clothed, and in his right mind: and they were afraid." *The rest of the family was surprised to find this matriarch, despite her years, clothed and very much in her right mind.*

Clotho *See* FATES.

cloud by day, pillar of fire by night Unfailing guidance or advice. The phrase comes from Exodus 13:21–22, which relates how the Israelites were guided on their journey from Egypt to Canaan by a pillar of cloud by day and a pillar of fire by night. "When I was a boy, I always thought a pillar of cloud by day and a pillar of fire by night was a pit, with its steam, and its lights, and the burning bank,—and I thought the Lord was always at the pit-top" (D. H. Lawrence, *Sons and Lovers,* 1913). *See also* PILLAR OF FIRE.

cloud cuckoo land A realm of fantasy or foolishness; something that exists only in the imagination. The phrase has its origins in the comedy *The Birds,* by the Greek playwright Aristophanes (445–c. 388 B.C.): It is the name of an imaginary city built by the birds where two Athenians hope they will be able escape the attentions of the legal authorities who are pursuing them. *If they think I'm going all that way just to be bored to death then they're living in cloud cuckoo land.*

cloud nine *See* ON CLOUD NINE.

cloud no bigger than a man's hand A relatively insignificant portent of something much greater about to happen. The phrase alludes to 1 Kings 18:44–45, which describes how, having defeated the prophets of Baal, Elijah eagerly awaits the coming of rain in response to his prayers. The rain duly arrives after Elijah has dispatched his servant to keep watch from Mount Carmel a seventh time: "And it came to pass at the seventh time, that he said, Behold, there ariseth a little cloud out of the sea, like a man's hand . . . And it came to pass . . . that the heaven was black with clouds and wind, and there was a great rain." "The prospect was bright, and the air sunny. In the midst of all which there rose in the horizon a cloud, like that seen by Elijah's servant, a cloud no bigger than a man's hand" (Charles Reade, *Put Yourself in His Place,* 1870).

Clouseau, Inspector *See* INSPECTOR CLOUSEAU.

cloven hoof An evil nature; some physical indicator of such a nature. According to the law as laid down by Moses, only animals with cloven hoofs were suitable as food or as sacrificial offerings (Deuteronomy 14:3–8). The devil was conventionally depicted by medieval artists as having cloven hoofs, a detail probably borrowed from pagan gods, hence the modern significance of the term. According to popular belief, the devil, no matter his disguise is unable to hide his cloven hoofs and can always be detected in this way. To ***show the cloven foot*** means to reveal a base motive or innate wickedness. *Several people who witnessed the great man's actions that evening privately agreed that they might have caught a first glimpse of his cloven hoof.*

clowns, send in the *See* SEND IN THE CLOWNS.

Clytemnestra (klītemnestră) Archetype of a vengeful mother or faithless wife. In Greek mythology Clytemnestra was the daughter of Leda and King Tyndareus of Sparta and became the wife of Agamemnon, leader of the Greeks during the Trojan War. With the help of her lover Aegisthus, she murdered Agamemnon in his bath upon his return from the war in revenge for the sacrifice of her daughter Iphigenia, who had been put to death to appease the goddess Artemis after the Greek fleet was becalmed at Aulis. She, in her turn, was murdered by her son Orestes. *The duchess turned out to be a Clytemnestra in disguise, plotting a bloody revenge upon her husband.*

coals of fire *See* HEAP COALS OF FIRE.

coals to Newcastle Something taken to a place where it is already in plentiful supply. Newcastle upon Tyne, in the northeast of England, lies at the center of what was the thriving British coal industry, and thus to carry coal there would have been pointless. The expression dates from the 17th century. *Providing the Inuit with ice-making machines is rather like carrying coals to Newcastle.*

coat of many colors A multicolored garment. The original coat of many colors was the coat presented by Jacob to his favorite son, Joseph, as a sign of his special love for him, as related in Genesis 37:3: "Now Israel loved Joseph more than all his children, because he was the son of his old age: and he made him a coat of many colours." The gift made Joseph's brothers so jealous that they stole the coat, stained it with blood, and told their father that Joseph had been killed by wild animals, while selling Joseph into slavery. In some translations the coat is perhaps more accurately described as being a long robe with sleeves or a richly ornamented robe. *His mother's latest acquisition was a truly hideous coat of many colors, guaranteed to cause alarm wherever she dared to wear it.*

Cockaigne *See* LAND OF COCKAIGNE.

cock and bull story An unbelievable story. Various suggestions have been made as to the origins of this phrase. It may allude to the various medieval fables in which cocks and bulls commonly feature, or it may be a reference to the fact that many English pubs, where tall stories abounded, were called the Cock or the Bull. Perhaps significantly, in Stony Stratford, Buckinghamshire, travelers by coach formerly swapped stories with each other as they exchanged coaches between the Cock and Bull inns. "Nobody believes this cock and bull story about the sacking incident" (M. Kilby, *Man at the Sharp End*, 1991).

cockatrice (kokătris) A monster who can kill with a single glance; by extension, a dangerous, treacherous person. The cockatrice was a legendary serpent hatched by a serpent from a cock's egg. It could kill any enemy with a single glance or with its breath. The creature appears in Isaiah 11:8, 14:29, and 59:5 and also in Jeremiah 8:17. "This will so fright them both that they will kill one another by the look, like cockatrices" (William Shakespeare, *Twelfth Night,* 1601). *See also* BASILISK STARE.

Cockpit of Europe Belgium and the surrounding region of northwest Europe. This nickname alludes to the area's long history as the scene of armed conflict between the major nations of western Europe, from medieval times to World War II. Important battles fought in the region have included WATERLOO (1815) and the SOMME (1916). *The shape of the modern world was decided in the Cockpit of Europe. See also* FLANDERS.

cogito ergo sum *See* CARTESIAN.

Cold Comfort Farm An untidy, comfortless place, especially one in a rural setting. The allusion is to a comic novel of the same title by the British novelist Stella Gibbons, published in 1932. The plot, which parodied the genre of rustic novels then fashionable, revolves around the arrival of a lively young woman in the bleak surroundings of Cold Comfort Farm, home to the eccentric Starkadder clan. "The decor expresses an uneasy marriage between *Cold Comfort Farm*, the house behind the garage in *The Big Sleep*, and the Hole-in-the-Wall gang's hideaway on the morning after the shoot-out" (Ellen Galford, *The Dyke and the Dybbuk*, 1993). *See also* SOMETHING NASTY IN THE WOODSHED.

Colditz (kōldits) A forbidding, prison-like building. Colditz Castle, not far from the German city of Leipzig, became notorious as a high-security prison for captured Allied officers during World War II. The many ingenious escape attempts (some successful) devised by the inmates inspired books and the popular television series *Colditz* (1972–74). "This Colditz estate is to be pulled down" (Beatrix Campbell, *Wigan Pier Revisited*, 1985).

cold war A state of mutual hostility between two parties, short of actual confrontation. The original cold war broke out between the Soviet Union (together with its communist satellite states) and the United States (together with the rest of the free, capitalist West) at the end of World War II and lasted until the collapse of the Soviet regime in the late 1980s. Contact between the two blocs was restricted, and both sides sought to undermine their opponents through propaganda, spying, and economic pressure. The term is thought to have been coined in 1947, suggested by former newspaper editor Herbert Bayard Swope for a speech delivered by U.S. politician and economist Bernard

Baruch (1870–1965): "Let us not be deceived—we are today in the midst of a cold war." "At least the easing of the cold war lessened Anglo-American tensions over trade with communist countries" (C. J. Bartlett, *The Special Relationship*, 1992). *See also* BERLIN WALL; CHECKPOINT CHARLIE; COME IN FROM THE COLD.

coliseum (kolăseeăm) A large theater or other building used for entertainment, sports, and other events. The original Colosseum was the vast amphitheater in Rome that was begun by the emperor Vespasian and completed by Titus in A.D. 80. The venue for a wide variety of entertainments, ranging from gladiatorial combats and naval battles to executions, the Colosseum was so named in reference to a huge statue (colossus) of Nero that once stood nearby. *In this utopia every town was well furnished with facilities for public entertainment, including at least one major coliseum for the performance of spectacles on a large scale.*

Colonel Blimp A hidebound old soldier, or anyone who is pompously at odds with new methods or thinking. Colonel Blimp was a creation of British cartoonist David Low in the *London Evening Standard* in the years following World War I and was later the subject of a popular but controversial film, *The Life and Death of Colonel Blimp* (1943), which incurred the wrath of prime minister Winston Churchill, who feared that by criticizing senior military figures it would damage wartime morale. "The grand council of the movement was dominated by retired military officers of the Colonel Blimp type, die-hard conservatives, landed gentry and emancipated middle-class women" (R. Thurlow, *Fascism in Britain: 1918–1985*, 1987).

colophon (kolăfon) A publisher's emblem, traditionally placed at the end of a book. The allusion is to the ancient Ionian city of Colophon, whose horsemen were renowned for turning the tide of battle with last-minute charges. By the same token, to ***add a colophon*** means to add the finishing stroke. "Master Gridley took out a great volume from the lower shelf,—a folio in massive oaken covers with clasps like prison hinges, bearing the stately colophon, white on a ground of vermilion, of Nicholas Jenson and his associates" (Oliver Wendell Holmes, *The Guardian Angel*, 1887).

colossus (kălosăs) Something that is very large in size. The reference is ultimately to a huge statue of ancient Egypt, described by the Greek historian Herodotus (c. 484–c. 430/420 B.C.) but is more usually associated with the Colossus of Rhodes, a massive bronze statue of Apollo that formerly stood at the entrance to the harbor of Rhodes. Erected around 292–280 B.C., it was destroyed by an earthquake in 225 B.C. The modern conception that the statue actually bestrode the harbor entrance is thought to be erroneous. In due course the word came to be applied to any large statue and may now be used to refer to any person or thing of impressive size, reputation, power, etc. "I found the wall—it was only a foot or two beyond my reach. With a heave I had my foot on the spike, and turning, I had both hands on the opposite wall. There I stood, straddling like a Colossus over a waste of white waters, with the cave floor far below me in the gloom" (John Buchan, *Prester John*, 1910). *See also* EIGHTH WONDER OF THE WORLD.

Columbus (kălămbăs) Archetype of a great explorer, especially one who discovers what many considered a new world. The Italian explorer

Christopher Columbus (1451–1506), a native of Genoa, is generally identified as the discoverer of the American continent (although the Vikings may have got there centuries earlier), setting foot on the Bahamas in 1492 in the course of a voyage paid for by Ferdinand and Isabella of Spain. *NASA has assumed the mantle of the modern world's Columbus.*

come, let us reason together An appeal to someone to come to terms, especially someone who might otherwise be considered beyond salvation. The phrase is a quotation from Isaiah 1:18: "Come now, and let us reason together, saith the LORD: though your sins be as scarlet, they shall be as white as snow; though they be red like crimson, they shall be as wool." *Management has made friendly overtures to the union, clearly believing that a "come, let us reason together" approach will do them more good in the long run than being belligerent.*

comédie humaine (komaydee yoomen) The human condition. Employed in its original French form (meaning "human comedy"), the expression was applied by the French novelist Honoré de Balzac (1799–1850) to his epic series of 90 novels, which encompassed the whole breadth of human society as he perceived it in the first half of the 19th century. *Scenes like this are shocking and unexpected, but such is the extraordinary and unpredictable nature of the comédie humaine.*

come in from the cold To return from a state of exile, isolation, or peril far from safety. The expression has been especially associated with the world of espionage since the publication of the COLD WAR spy thriller *The Spy Who Came in from the Cold* by John Le Carré in 1963, which related the events surrounding the return of a British agent from East Germany. "Said his friend-cum-mentor, Irving Layton, in looking back over the period, 'I had a very sharp feeling in the early fifties that poetry in Canada had come in from the cold and was starting to gain momentum'" (Loranne S. Dorman and Clive L. Rawlins, *Leonard Cohen: Prophet of the Heart*, 1990).

comforter, Job's *See* JOB'S COMFORTER.

comin' in on a wing and a prayer Narrowly succeeding in making it back to safety. The allusion is to a song written by Harold Adamson and Jimmy McHugh in 1943, during World War II, about a pilot struggling to land a badly damaged plane: "Tho' there's one motor gone, we can still carry on / Comin' in on a wing and a pray'r." *With their best player injured, the team is comin' in on a wing and a prayer.*

Comstockery (komstokăree) Censorship of literature and the arts. The word was inspired by the campaigning efforts of Anthony Comstock (1844–1915) to oppose obscenity in the arts and in the wider community in his role as secretary of the New York Society for the Suppression of Vice, a position he occupied for 42 years. Among his targets in the literary world were the works of George Bernard Shaw, who responded in 1905 by coining the word "Comstockery." *This proposed new law against the distribution of mildly pornographic advertising smacks of Comstockery.*

Conan the Barbarian (kōnăn) Archetype of a muscle-bound, unsophisticated warrior-hero of limited intelligence. He made his first appearance in the 1930s in short stories written by Robert E. Howard for *Weird Tales* magazine and later became a popular comic-strip hero. He was brought to the big screen in the movies *Conan the Barbarian* (1982) and *Conan the Destroyer* (1984), both of which starred former bodybuilder ARNOLD SCHWARZENEGGER in the title role. *Visiting the former heavyweight champion was like having tea with Conan the Barbarian.*

Concordia (konkordeeă) Personification of peace. Concordia was identified in Roman mythology as the goddess of peace and harmony. *The warring parties quickly reached a compromise and for a time Concordia reigned over the entire scene.*

Connecticut Yankee (kănetikăt) Someone or something that is out of place and time, an anachronism. The allusion is to the novel *A Connecticut Yankee in King Arthur's Court* (1889) by U.S. writer Mark Twain (1835–1910), which relates the experiences of a Connecticut factory worker after he is struck on the head with a crowbar and wakes to find himself transported back in time to the court of KING ARTHUR. *He enjoyed playing a Connecticut Yankee to the people of the remote tribes he encountered in the Amazon rainforests.*

consider the lilies *See* LILIES OF THE FIELD.

Contemptibles, Old *See* OLD CONTEMPTIBLES.

continence of Alexander *See* ALEXANDER THE GREAT.

continence of a Scipio (sipeeō) Self-restraint or moral integrity; the ability to refuse temptation. According to Roman legend, the Roman general Publius Cornelius Scipio Africanus (237–183 B.C.), who led the Roman army against the Carthaginians during the Second Punic War, was once offered the chance to meet a beautiful princess whom his men had taken prisoner but declined the opportunity on the grounds that he might be tempted to forget his principles. *To work in such company and not be tempted to try one's luck with one of the ladies would require the continence of a Scipio.*

cook someone's goose To spoil someone's chances or plans. The allusion is allegedly to an episode in the reign of Eric IV of Sweden, who surprised his enemies by marching his small army out to attack their town. His enemies expressed their scorn at this temerity by hanging a live goose from their battlements to provide Eric's men with a target. Eric responded by telling his opponents he would cook their goose, and then set about laying waste to the surrounding region. His enemies soon gave in, and Eric cooked and ate their goose. *The management planned to develop a new range of products, but their rivals cooked their goose for them.*

Cook's tour An excursion or roundabout journey, especially one that allows for only a cursory look at local places of interest. British missionary Thomas Cook (1808–92) was a pioneer of the travel industry, arranging his first excursion in 1841 in order to get customers from Leicester to Loughborough for a temperance meeting. He went on to arrange numerous similar trips, dubbed Cook's tours, both within the United Kingdom and to the continent of Europe. *They made a quick Cook's tour of the theater.*

copperhead A secret enemy or traitor, especially one who operates covertly and undetected. The term copperhead, which first appeared in this sense in the *New York Tribune* on July 20, 1861, was applied to Northerners who secretly favored the Southern cause during the U.S. Civil War of the 1860s, although it had previously been variously employed to describe the original Native American inhabitants of the United States and the country's early Dutch colonists. The term ultimately alludes to the venomous copperhead snake which, unlike the rattlesnake, lacks a rattle that might warn of its presence. *There are too many copperheads in the party to keep big secrets from leaking to the press.*

Cordelia (kordeeleeă) Archetype of an ideal, loving daughter. Cordelia is the youngest of the king's three daughters in William Shakespeare's tragedy *KING LEAR* (1605) she is the only one to tell her father the truth and the only one to offer the king comfort after he goes mad. She is also admired for her soft and gentle voice. *In the end she proved a Cordelia to her father's deranged and dispossessed Lear.*

cordon bleu (kordon(g) blă) Of the highest standard, especially as regards cooking. A French term meaning "blue ribbon," it referred originally to the blue ribbon from which French knights of the Order of the Holy Ghost suspended the order itself. The knights were famous for their superb dinners, hence the link with high cuisine. In modern usage, however, the phrase is often applied to matters unrelated to cookery. *The race established itself as a cordon bleu event attracting the cream of society.*

cordon sanitaire (kordon(g) sanitair) A barrier created around a particular area that is considered infectious in some way. A French phrase meaning "sanitary line," it was originally applied to areas that had to be put in quarantine to prevent the spread of disease. In modern usage, the expression is applied more widely, especially in international politics. *A cordon sanitaire has been placed around several countries considered ripe for revolution.*

Corinth, it is not for every man to go to (korinth) Some things, such as great wealth, are fated to be enjoyed by only a few. This is a quotation from the *Epistles* of Horace (65–8 B.C.). Corinth, which was famed for its great wealth, was deemed difficult to get to either because of the expense required to travel there or because it was awkwardly situated between two seas. *As a young man he had dreamed of making his million, but it is not for every man to go to Corinth. See also* CORINTHIAN.

Corinthian (kărintheeăn) Licentious, dissolute. The lax morals of the inhabitants of Corinth were widely known throughout the ancient world. The word *Corinthian* also denotes the most richly decorated of the five orders of Greek architecture. "He never passed the line which divides the spruce vices from the ugly; and hence, though his morals had hardly been applauded, disapproval of them had frequently been tempered with a smile. This treatment had led to his becoming a sort of regrater of other men's gallantries, to his own aggrandizement as a Corinthian, rather than to the moral profit of his hearers" (Thomas Hardy, *Far from the Madding Crowd,* 1874). *See also* DORIC; IONIC; TUSCAN.

Coriolanus (koreeōlaynăs) Archetype of an arrogant politician. According to Roman legend, Gaius Marcus Coriolanus was a Roman general who threatened to lead his army against Rome in the fifth century B.C. until dissuaded from so doing by his mother and wife. His contempt for the public in general was memorably depicted in William Shakespeare's play *Coriolanus* (1608), in which he was portrayed lamenting the fact that he was obliged to recruit popular support for his cause. *The press was unforgiving in its accounts of the minister's arrogance, calling him a Coriolanus for his time.*

corners of the earth The remotest, most distant parts of the globe. The notion that the earth has corners comes from Isaiah 11:12, which describes how God will "assemble the outcasts of Israel, and gather together the dispersed of Judah from the four corners of the earth." "'I can run out of the house,' cried her ladyship, wildly. 'I can fly to the uttermost corners of the earth; but I can not hear that person's name mentioned!'" (Wilkie Collins, *Man and Wife,* 1870).

cornucopia (kornăkōpeeă) A great abundance of something; a plentiful supply, especially of food and drink. The reference is to Greek mythology and one of the horns of Amalthea, the goat that suckled Zeus. Zeus presented the horn to the daughters of Melisseus, king of Crete, and it overflowed immediately with whatever food or drink its owners desired. Also known as the ***horn of plenty,*** the cornucopia subsequently became a symbol of plenty widely used in art and literature. "The last time they had had a big basket with them and all their Christmas marketing to do—a roast of pork and a cabbage and some rye bread, and a pair of mittens for Ona, and a rubber doll that squeaked, and a little green cornucopia full of candy to be hung from the gas jet and gazed at by half a dozen pairs of longing eyes" (Upton Sinclair, *The Jungle,* 1906).

corruptible and incorruptible That which is flawed may yet prove perfect. The expression comes from 1 Corinthians 15:42–44, 52–54, in which Paul discusses the resurrection, through which the weak and perishable body is made strong and imperishable: "It is sown in corruption, it is raised in incorruption: it is sown in dishonour, it is raised in glory" (1 Corinthians 15:42–43). "Now that the incorruption of this most fragrant ambergris should be found in the heart of such decay; is this nothing? Bethink thee of that saying of St. Paul in Corinthians, about corruption and incorruption; how we are sown in dishonour, but raised in glory" (Herman Melville, *Moby-Dick,* 1851).

Corybantian (koreebanteeăn) Wild, ecstatic, noisy, or unrestrained in manner. The allusion is to the Corybantes of Greek mythology, who were attendants of the goddess Cybele and were well known for their frenzied rituals, which featured the repeated crashing of cymbals and wild dancing. Legend had it that the infant Zeus escaped death at the hands of his father when his crying was drowned out by the noise made by the Corybantes. "Again, at Eleusis, home of Ceres, I see the modern Greeks dancing, I hear them clapping their hands as they bend their bodies, I hear the metrical shuffling of their feet. I see again the wild old Corybantian dance, the performers wounding each other" (Walt Whitman, *Leaves of Grass,* 1855).

Corydon (koridăn) A rustic or shepherd. A lovesick shepherd of this name appears in Virgil's *Eclogues* (42–37 B.C.). "'Gad, what a debauched Corydon!' said my lord—what a mouth for a pipe!'" (William Makepeace Thackeray, *Vanity Fair,* 1847–48).

Coryphaeus (korifeeăs) A leader, especially the most active member of a board, expedition, etc. The term was originally reserved in ancient Greek theater for the leader of the chorus. By extension, the leading dancer of a ballet troupe may sometimes be termed a ***Coryphée.*** *This Coryphaeus dominated the meeting, and by the end of the evening few of the directors had any doubts about which way they should vote.*

Cosa Nostra *See* MAFIA.

Costello, Lou *See* ABBOTT AND COSTELLO.

cothurnus *See* BUSKIN.

Cotton Mather (maTHer) Archetype of a strict, intolerant Puritan. The writer and clergyman Cotton Mather (1663–1728) was a committed Puritan, although he probably does not deserve the reputation for rigid intolerance that is now associated with his name. *Her father was a Cotton Mather who did not smoke, drink, or think anyone in his family should have a good time.*

counsel of perfection A commendation of something beyond a minimum; an unattainable ideal. The phrase alludes to the biblical episode in which Christ told a rich young man what he needed to do in order to reach heaven: "Jesus said unto him, If thou wilt be perfect, go *and* sell that thou hast, and give to the poor . . . But when the young man heard that saying, he went away sorrowful, for he had great possessions" (Matthew 19:21–22). *Advocating better manners among sports fans smacks of a counsel of perfection.*

Count of Monte Cristo, the (montay kristō) A person who seeks revenge for wrongs done to him or her in the past. The 1844 novel *The Count of Monte Cristo* by the French writer Alexandre Dumas *père* (1802–70) recounts the adventures of Edmond Dantès, who is framed for crimes he did not commit and then seeks to have his revenge after spending 20 years in prison. *He fancied himself as a cheap version of the Count of Monte Cristo, wanting to rid the world of the lowlife who had put him away.*

count the cost To consider the advantages, disadvantages, or risks before deciding to do something; consider the possible effects or results of something. The expression comes from Jesus' words as recorded in Luke 14:28: "For which of you, intending to build a tower, sitteth not down first, and counteth the cost, whether he have sufficient to finish it?" *You must count the cost before you make up your mind to take off a year from school to travel around Europe.*

court of the Gentiles Those people who are not Jews, not one of God's chosen. The court of the Gentiles was a feature of Herod's Temple and is described in Josephus and the Mishnah; it is alluded to in Revelation 11:2, and since it was where the money changers carried on their business, it is also referred to indirectly in Matthew 21:12. In biblical times Jews were tried by their own court in the Jewish Temple, while others appeared before court of the Gentiles. *Such a superior attitude was unlikely to be welcome in the court of the Gentiles. See also* CHOSEN PEOPLE.

Cousin Itt *See* ADDAMS FAMILY.

cover a multitude of sins *See* CHARITY COVERS A MULTITUDE OF SINS.

Cowardly Lion *See* FRIEND OF DOROTHY.

Crane, Ichabod *See* ICHABOD CRANE.

Cratchit, Bob *See* BOB CRATCHIT.

Creature from the Black Lagoon A person of monstrous appearance. The reference is to the classic 1954 horror movie *The Creature from the Black Lagoon*, which features a monster that is half man and half fish. "God alone knew what she must look like—a creature from the black lagoon probably—and suddenly, unexpectedly, she began to chuckle" (Emma Richmond, *A Stranger's Trust*, 1991).

Cressida *See* TROILUS AND CRESSIDA.

Cretan bull *See* LABORS OF HERCULES.

Crichton, Admirable *See* ADMIRABLE CRICHTON.

Crippen, Doctor *See* DOCTOR CRIPPEN.

critical mass The point at which a buildup of elements triggers a particular event. The allusion is to nuclear physics, in which the term refers to the amount of material needed to set in motion a sustained nuclear CHAIN REACTION. *He hoped to build up a critical mass of support that would make his claim to the candidacy impossible to resist.*

Crockett, Davy *See* DAVY CROCKETT.

crocodile tears Insincere, hypocritical tears. The allusion is to the traditional story that the crocodile makes pitiful sobbing sounds to deceive its prey into coming close enough to be snatched up in its jaws, a practice mentioned in William Shakespeare's play *Henry VI, Part II* (1590): "As the mournful crocodile / With sorrow snares relenting passengers." The crocodile is also said to continue weeping as it consumes its prey, a belief possibly inspired by the fact that a gland in the top of the crocodile's mouth releases tears while the creature is eating. "In a few days Riddle's body might be found and the two women would almost certainly arrange an elaborate funeral which they would attend and shed a few crocodile tears" (W. J. Burley, *Wycliffe and the Scapegoat*, 1987).

Croesus *See* AS RICH AS CROESUS.

Cronos (krōnus) Personification of time. Cronos (also rendered as ***Cronus*** or ***Kronos***) was identified in Greek mythology as the youngest of the Titans, a son of Uranus and Gaea and the equivalent of the Roman Saturn. Entrusted with the government of earth, he presided over a GOLDEN AGE. He devoured his own children by Rhea because of a prophecy that one of them would overthrow him but failed to kill his son Zeus, who tricked him into disgorging his siblings. He was defeated in battle by his offspring and imprisoned in Tartarus. *They hoped to get to the ancient ruins in time to see the dawn, but it seemed that Cronos had decreed against them as the sky was already growing pink to the east.*

crooked shall be made straight Things will be made right in the end. The phrase appears in Isaiah 40:4, which foretells how all will be made well at the coming of the Messiah: "The crooked shall be made straight, and the rough places plain." It is also quoted in the New Testament in Luke 3:5. *It is hoped that through the introduction of these new standards the crooked shall be made straight and performance will be improved across the board.*

Crosby, Bing *See* BING CROSBY.

crossing of the Red Sea A miraculous escape, especially one made with divine assistance. The allusion is to the crossing of the Red Sea by the Israelites from Egypt to Sinai, under the guidance of Moses. According to the biblical narrative, the waters of the Red Sea parted at Moses' command but closed behind them, blocking the Egyptians who followed in pursuit (Exodus 14:21–30). *A path through the rain suddenly opened up for them and* *they dashed for it, like the Hebrews at the crossing of the Red Sea.*

cross over Jordan To die and enter heaven. The reference is to the biblical episode in Joshua 3 describing how the Israelites invaded Canaan under the leadership of Joshua. When they came to the Jordan River the water parted as promised by God (verse 7) to allow the Israelites to cross into Canaan, the PROMISED LAND. *The old lady crossed over the Jordan last night, and the family is therefore in mourning.*

cross the Rubicon (roobăkon) To take an irrevocable step, especially a decision from which there is no going back. Under the laws of ancient Rome it was illegal for a military commander to lead troops over the Rubicon River, which divided Cisalpine Gaul from Italy. (Such a measure was intended to prevent any wayward general seizing power by force.) In 49 B.C. Julius Caesar defied the prohibition by leading his army over the Rubicon, went on to defeat Pompey in the ensuing civil war, and became the effective head of state. If he had failed, he would have faced the death penalty. *With this act the state legislature has crossed the Rubicon. There is no going back now. See also* DIE IS CAST, THE.

Crow, Jim *See* JIM CROW.

crown of thorns A symbol of great suffering and humiliation. According to the biblical account of Christ's crucifixion, Jesus was forced to wear a crown of thorns in mockery of his claim to be king of the Jews, as related in Matthew 27:29: "And when they had platted a crown of thorns, they put it upon his head . . . and they bowed the knee before him, and mocked him, saying, Hail, King of the Jews!" (See also Mark 15:17 and John 19:2–5.) *He wore his injured pride like a crown of thorns, appealing for sympathy from anyone who would hear his story.*

Cruella De Vil (kroo<u>e</u>lă dă <u>vil</u>) A ruthless, cold-hearted woman, especially one who behaves cruelly toward animals. Cruella De Vil is the evil villain in Dodie Smith's novel *The Hundred and One Dalmatians* (1956), which was later made into two highly successful Walt Disney movies (1961 and 1996). Dressed entirely in black and white, she covets the black-and-white dalmatian fur she needs to make herself a spotted fur coat. *Once confirmed as head of the organization she stopped behaving like Mary Poppins and turned into Cruella De Vil.*

crumbs that fall from the rich man's table The meager benefits that are left to the poor after the rich have taken their fill of something. The expression is biblical in origin, appearing in the Gospels. It features, for example, in the story of the Gentile woman who professes her faith in Christ with the words, "Truth, Lord: yet the dogs eat of the crumbs which fall from their masters' table" (Matthew 15:27). (See also Mark 7:24–30.) In Luke 16:20–21, it appears in the story of the beggar Lazarus: "And there was a certain beggar named Lazarus, which was laid at his gate, full of sores. And desiring to be fed with the crumbs which fell from the rich man's table: moreover the dogs came and licked his sores." 'I mean that I am content to give what I have given and must always give, and take in payment those crumbs that fall from my mistress's table, the memory of a few kind words, the hope one day in the far undreamed future of a sweet smile or two of recognition, a little gentle friendship" (H. Rider Haggard, *She,* 1887).

Crusoe, Robinson *See* ROBINSON CRUSOE.

crying in the wilderness *See* VOICE CRYING IN THE WILDERNESS.

cry of blood *See* BLOOD CRIETH FROM THE GROUND.

Cui bono? (kwee bōnō) For what purpose? For whose benefit? This legal phrase is of Roman origin, being attributed ultimately to the Roman judge Lucius Cassius Longinus Ravilla (fl. second century B.C.), who was in the habit of posing this question in cases brought before him. "'And may I not paint one like it for you?' 'Cui bono? No'" (Charlotte Brontë, *Jane Eyre,* 1847).

cult of personality The redefinition in totalitarian states of a national leader as a semireligious figure. The expression was first uttered, in reference to Joseph Stalin, by Soviet president Nikita Khrushchev in a speech made to the 20th Party Congress on February 25, 1956. Other substantial cults of personality sprang up around Mao Zedong in China and Kim Il Sung and his son Kim Jong Il in North Korea. "So developed did the cult of personality in Northern Nigeria become that even in dealing with rude and warlike pagans it was bad form to stoop to securing their acquiescence in the will of the government by resort to force" (Kathryn Tidrick, *Empire and the English Character*, 1992).

Cumaean sibyl *See* SIBYL.

cunctator (kănktaytor) Delayer; someone who employs delay as a tactic. The title is most closely associated with Quintus Fabius Maximus (d. 203 B.C.), the Roman general who cunningly adopted delaying tactics against the invading Carthaginian armies of Hannibal, avoiding any direct confrontation. Initially held in contempt for his apparent cowardice, Fabius eventually won hero status after the wisdom of his policy was realized. *The managing director's colleagues privately dubbed him cunctator because of his reputation for putting things off time and time again. See also* FABIAN.

Cupid (kyoopid) Personification of love. The son of Aphrodite, Cupid was the god of love in Roman mythology and the equivalent of the Greek god Eros. He was usually depicted as a winged naked boy, sometimes blindfolded, carrying a bow from which he fired arrows of desire. To ***play Cupid*** means to act as matchmaker, while ***Cupid's bow*** describes the shape of the upper lip in humans. "And off I started, cursorily glancing sideways as I passed the toilet-table, surmounted by a looking-glass: a thin irregular face I saw, with sunk, dark eyes under a large, square forehead, complexion destitute of bloom or attraction; something young, but not youthful, no object to win a lady's love, no butt for the shafts of Cupid" (Charlotte Brontë, *The Professor,* 1857).

cup is full *See* MY CUP RUNNETH OVER.

cup runneth over, my *See* MY CUP RUNNETH OVER.

cup that cheers, the A cup of tea, in contrast to a drink of alcohol. The allusion is to the poem *The Task* (1783) by William Cowper (1731–1800): "And, while the bubbling and loud-hissing urn / Throws up a steamy column, and the cups, / That cheer but not inebriate, wait on each." "'Well, are yer comin' or ain't yer?' he asked after a long and noisy sip at the cup that cheers" (M. Kilby, *Man at the Sharp End*, 1991).

curate's egg Something that is good in some parts but bad in others. The allusion is to a cartoon published in *Punch* magazine in November 1895, in which a nervous young curate sharing breakfast with his bishop is asked about his egg: "'I'm afraid you've got a bad egg, Mr. Jones.' 'Oh no, my Lord, I assure you! Parts of it are excellent!'" *The official report into the civil administration was a curate's egg, some departments coming out well, but others being revealed to have major deficiencies.*

curse God and die *See* JOB'S WIFE.

curse of Cain *See* MARK OF CAIN.

curse the day I was born An expression of despair at the situation one finds oneself in. The expression comes from Job 3:1–11, in which Job laments the pain he suffers from the boils with which he is afflicted: "After this opened Job his mouth, and cursed his day . . . Let the day perish wherein I was born, and the night *in which* it was said, There is a man child conceived . . . Why died I not from the womb? *Why* did I *not* give up the ghost when I came out of the belly?" *At this latest blow the general loudly cursed the day he was born and retired to his room, where he remained for the next three days, sulking.*

Custer's Last Stand (kustăz) A heroic but futile last stand made against overwhelming odds. The allusion is to the Battle of ***Little Bighorn*** in Montana on June 25, 1876, during which the celebrated General George Armstrong Custer (1839–76) and his 200 men of the Seventh Cavalry were annihilated by a strong force of Cheyenne and Sioux Indians under the leadership of Crazy Horse and Sitting Bull. Subsequent analysis of the encounter has suggested that the defeat resulted largely from confusion and recklessness among the army's officers; despite this the clash is cherished in the national imagination as a generally heroic affair. *He was tempted to stage a Custer's Last Stand against the demands of the rest of the family, but eventually wisely decided to back down.*

customer is always right, the It is good policy to agree with the customer, or do what he or she wants, if only in order to retain his or her future custom. This familiar commercial slogan was devised originally in 1909 by U.S.-born H. Gordon Selfridge (1858–1947) for his famous London department store Selfridge's, the staff of which were sternly forbidden to argue with customers, whoever was really in the right. It has since been adopted as a principle if not a slogan by many other commercial ventures. "In education no single customer is always right, people aren't all looking for the same things" (Mike Sullivan, *Marketing your Primary School*, 1991).

cuts, death by a thousand *See* DEATH BY A THOUSAND CUTS.

cut the Gordian knot (gordeeăn) To take a direct route in solving a complex problem. The allusion is to the story of the intricate knot with which Gordius, a peasant who became king of Phrygia, attached his wagon to the yoke. It was said that any person who could untie the knot would become ruler of all Asia. When Alexander the Great was presented with the challenge of unloosing the knot he simply cut through it with his sword. "When he became prime minister last April, Koizumi was supposed to be the clean-up kid who would cut through Japan's Gordian knot of bureaucratic inertia and political torpor to bring about reform" (*Guardian Weekly,* February 14, 2002). "'Is not such the doom of all speculative men of talent?' said she. 'Do they not all sit wrapt as you now are, cutting imaginary silken cords with their fine edges, while those not so highly tempered sever the everyday Gordian knots of the world's struggle and win wealth and renown?'" (Anthony Trollope, *Barchester Towers,* 1857).

cutting-room floor The trash can or other destination where rejected ideas, things, etc., are dumped. The allusion is to the movie industry and the process of editing footage down into a finished movie in the days before computerization, when the pieces of film not needed were cut out and literally ended up on the cutting-room floor. The term is now widely used in noncinematic contexts. *She was very annoyed when she found that all her suggestions for future expansion had been left on the cutting-room floor.*

cut off at the pass To intercept someone or something at a point further on. The allusion is to Western movies and the often-filmed horse chases through wild country in which such a line might be delivered. It enjoyed renewed coverage in 1973 when it was heard being used by President Richard Nixon in the WATERGATE tapes. The phrase is also encountered in the form ***head off at the pass***. *He was cut off at the pass by his superiors as soon as they were told what he had in mind.*

cut off one's nose to spite one's face To do something against one's own interests. This expression is French in origin and is sometimes associated with the French nobleman Henry of Navarre. In 1589, the Protestant Henry ascended the throne of France, in which role he was faced with strong Catholic opposition in Paris. When Henry contemplated destroying Paris, his advisers dissuaded him with the argument that he would simply be damaging his own interests if he thus "cut off his nose to spite his face." Henry conceded and decided to revert to Catholicism in order to reclaim the city. *When her agent announced that he would no longer be handling her money-spinning tours it was felt that he had cut off his nose to spite his face.*

Cyanean rocks *See* SYMPLEGADES.

Cybele (sibilee) Personification of the Earth or of nature. Cybele was identified as the Phrygian goddess of nature, equivalent to the Greek Rhea or Demeter. Her worshipers were noted for their orgiastic rites, which included much spilling of blood. "He had scarce finished his story, when a most violent noise shook the whole house . . . The priests of Cybele do not so rattle their sounding brass" (Henry Fielding, *Tom Jones,* 1749).

cyclopean (sīklōpeeăn) Anything one-eyed or limited in vision; a building style characterized by the use of large undressed blocks of stone. The allusion is to the Cyclops of Greek mythology, one of a breed of giants (Cyclopes) with only one eye, located in the middle of the forehead. The poet Hesiod (c. 800 B.C.) said there were just three Cyclopes, who were cannibals and lived in Sicily and the western coast of Italy. Others claimed they lived on volcanoes, forging thunderbolts for Zeus, and that Mount Etna was their chief abode. To them were attributed various massive edifices erected by otherwise unknown hands in prehistoric times. The word itself comes from the Greek *kuklos* (meaning "circle") and *ops* (meaning "eye"). "He had forgotten that the dead seldom plan their own houses, and with a pang he discovered the name he sought on the cyclopean base of a granite shaft rearing its aggressive height at the angle of two avenues" (Edith Wharton, *The Touchstone,* 1900). *See also* POLYPHEMUS.

cynic (sinik) A person who is inclined automatically to think the worst of people or things. The word was originally applied, for obscure reasons, to the followers of the Greek philosopher Antisthenes (c. 445–c. 360 B.C.), whose number included Diogenes (411–322 B.C.). One suggestion is that the group acquired the name from *kunikos* (meaning "doglike"), a reference to their coarse manners, while another has it that they used to meet in a school called the Kunosarges (meaning "white dog"). The Cynics rejected the conventions and standards of society and instead emphasized self-discipline of the individual. "There is very little intelligent design in the majority of marriages; but they are none the worse for that. Intelligence leads people astray as far as passion sometimes. I know you are not a cynic" (Joseph Conrad, *Chance,* 1914).

Cynthia (sintheeă) Personification of the Moon. As a surname of Artemis and Diana in classical mythology, Cynthia was so called after Mount Cynthius in Delos, where she was reputed to have been born. In Elizabethan times the name became one of the epithets by which several leading poets addressed Elizabeth I (1533–1603). *The pale orb of Cynthia dominated the scene, casting a wan glow over the lawns leading down to the river.*

Cyrano (sirănō) A tragicomic figure, especially one with a large nose. The reference is to the eponymous hero of Edmond Rostand's verse drama *Cyrano de Bergerac* (1897), a multitalented cavalier with a big nose. The play centers on Cyrano's heroic self-sacrifice when he discovers that Roxanne, the woman he loves, is in love with someone else. The character of Cyrano was based on a real person, the French writer and soldier Savinien Cyrano de Bergerac (1619–55), whose adventurous life included fighting more than 1,000 duels and success as a playwright. *With his romantic persona and misshapen nose he was constantly likened to Cyrano de Bergerac.*

D

Dada (dahdah, dada) In the arts, characterized by outrageous eccentricity and rejection of convention. The Dada movement developed as a challenge to the complacency of art critics and middle-class society in general in the wake of World War I, led by such innovative surrealist artists as Salvador Dali (1904–89) and Man Ray (1890–1976). The name of the movement was chosen by the Alsatian artist Hans (or Jean) Arp (1887–1966), who decided upon it by stabbing a French dictionary with a knife and thus picking out the French word for "hobby-horse." The term ***Dadaist*** (or ***Daliesque***) may be applied today to any instance of apparently outlandish or nonsensical thinking or behavior. *He awoke unrefreshed after eight hours of disturbing Dadaist nightmares.*

Dad's Army A group of men, or people generally, who are considered too old to act in a competent manner. The allusion is to the Home Guard that was assembled by the British government to defend the country from German invasion during World War II. Though evidently as willing and courageous as troops in the other armed forces, many Home Guard recruits were too old to fight in the regular army, hence their reputation for bumbling feebleness. The nickname Dad's Army was later taken up as the title of a popular BBC television series of the 1970s that lovingly and comically dramatized the misadventures of a Home Guard platoon. *The railway is manned by a Dad's Army of volunteer rail enthusiasts, most over the age of 60.*

Daedalian (didayleeăn) Skillful, ingenious, or labyrinthine. The adjective, also encountered in the variant forms ***Daedalean*** or ***Daedalic,*** refers to the legendary Athenian craftsman Daedalus, who was renowned for his skill as an inventor and engineer. Having fled his native Athens after murdering his pupil Talos in a fit of professional jealousy, he was employed by King Minos of Crete and built the wooden cow with which Queen Pasiphae coupled and consequently gave birth to the monstrous Minotaur. Daedalus also designed the labyrinth at Knossos in which the Minotaur was imprisoned until its eventual destruction at the hands of Theseus. The outraged King Minos, realizing that Theseus could never have escaped from the labyrinth without the help of its creator, had Daedalus and his son Icarus confined there, knowing that not even they could find the way out without aid. Daedalus, however, overcame the problem by designing two pairs of wings with which he and his son were able to soar into the air and escape from Crete. Unfortunately, Icarus ignored his father's warning not to fly too high as the heat of the sun's rays would melt the wax holding the wings together, and the lad plummeted into the Aegean Sea and was drowned. Daedalus completed his flight safely and found refuge at the court of the king of Sicily. As further proof of his ingenuity, Daedalus was also credited with the invention of the saw, the ax, and the gimlet, among other devices. *The engineers were confronted by a problem of such Daedalian complexity that for a time it seemed a solution would be beyond any of them.*

Dagon (daygon) A sea monster or whale. In the Bible, Dagon is a Philistine god, possibly with a human upper half and fishlike lower half (Judges 16:23–24 and 1 Samuel 5:1–5). Other authorities do not consider him to be a fish god but rather a storm or grain god, since *Dagon* is related to a Hebrew word for "grain." Samson destroyed the temple to Dagon at Gaza, and Dagon himself died when the ark of God was brought to his house, his body being found next morning with severed head and hands. John Milton, meanwhile, in *Paradise Lost* (1667) identifies Dagon as one of the fallen angels. "In fact, placed before the strict and piercing truth, this whole story will fare like that fish, flesh, and fowl idol of the Philistines, Dagon by name; who being planted before the ark of Israel, his horse's head and both the palms of his hands fell off from him, and only the stump or fishy part of him remained" (Herman Melville, *Moby-Dick,* 1851).

daily bread The income or sustenance necessary in order to live. The phrase has its origins in the Lord's Prayer, where it appears in the form of the petition "Give us this day our daily bread" (Matthew 6:11). ". . . these true gentlefolk showed Polly their respect and regard, put many pleasures in her way, and when they paid her for her work, gave her also the hearty thanks that takes away all sense of degradation even from the humblest service, for money so earned and paid sweetens the daily bread it buys, and makes the mutual obligation a mutual benefit and pleasure" (Louisa May Alcott, *An Old Fashioned Girl,* 1870).

Daliesque *See* DADA.

Dallas (dalăs) The glossy, cutthroat, superficial world of multimillionaire wheeler-dealing. The allusion is to the highly popular U.S. television series *Dallas*, which ran from 1978 to 1991 on the strength of barely credible melodramatic plots and the glitzy, bitchy romantic relationships of ***J. R.*** and Sue Ellen Ewing and the other central characters. *It was like a scene out of Dallas, with rival lovers slugging it out in the swimming pool as their respective wives shrieked their anger at being ignored.*

Damascus, road to *See* ROAD TO DAMASCUS.

Damien (daymeeăn) Archetype of a badly behaved or evil young boy. Damien Thorn was the name of the central character (actually the Antichrist) in the 1976 horror film *The Omen* and its sequels. *Everyone thought her son was a sweet child, but he turned out to be a real Damien who took advantage of anyone who showed him kindness.*

Damocles, sword of *See* SWORD OF DAMOCLES.

Damon and Pythias (daymăn, pitheeas) The archetype of perfect friendship. Damon and Pythias (or ***Phintias***) were two close friends who lived in Sicily under the tyrannical rule of Dionysius of Syracuse in the fifth century B.C. Pythias was a philosopher and follower of Pythagoras who found himself under a death sentence on charges of treason. Dionysius agreed to the condemned man's request to be allowed to go home to settle his affairs on condition that he find someone willing to take his place if he did not return by the due date. Damon immediately volunteered to take his friend's place, and Pythias set off for home. When Pythias was delayed on his return, it seemed Damon would have to be executed in his stead, but at the last moment Pythias rushed back to save his friend's life. Dionysius was deeply moved by the pair's willingness to sacrifice themselves for each other and, having pardoned Pythias, asked to be allowed to participate in their friendship. "Papa, I am really longing to see the Pythias to your Damon. You know, I never saw him but once, and then we were so puzzled to know what to say to each other that we did not get on particularly well" (Elizabeth Gaskell, *North and South,* 1854–55). *See also* DAVID AND JONATHAN.

damsel in distress A female in apparent need of assistance. The allusion is to the archetypal story of a fairy-tale heroine being rescued from danger by her hero-lover, typically in the form of a KNIGHT IN SHINING ARMOR. The word damsel itself comes from the Old French *damoisele*, which described the feminine equivalent of a *damoisel* (squire). "I've never met Sir Brian or Sir Oliver and have only met Sir Bernard a few times, but I instinctively feel that all six would lay down their lives without hesitation for a damsel in distress" (Marti Caine, *A Coward's Chronicles*, 1990).

dance of death *See* DANSE MACABRE.

Dan Dare Archetype of a dashing male hero, especially one connected with space flight. The original Dan Dare was the hero of a long-running boys' comic book series created by Frank Hampson, which began in 1950 and finally ended in 1967. As a colonel in the Interplanetary Space Fleet, Dan Dare battled the ***Mekon*** and other formidable foes on Venus and elsewhere. In modern usage, the name tends to be applied facetiously. *He was a bit of a Dan Dare in his youth, but you wouldn't think it to look at him now.*

danegeld (dayngeld) Payment made to ward off a threat of some kind. The word was coined in the 10th century to describe the payments made by the English on the orders of their king, Ethelred II (978–1016), to appease the Danes, who otherwise threatened to extend their settlements in England. In the event, the policy failed to work, and Ethelred was forced to flee the country in 1013. Danegeld continued to be collected under Canute and subsequent kings even though the threat from the Danes no longer existed. *The shopkeepers carried on paying danegeld to the mafia for decades before plucking up the courage to put up some resistance.*

dangerous age, a A time in life when a person is deemed particularly susceptible to various temptations or otherwise likely to behave unpredictably. The phrase is associated chiefly with the age of 40, although it may be equally validly applied to any other period in a person's life, as illustrated by the title of the 1967 Dudley Moore film *Thirty is a Dangerous Age, Cynthia*, which did much to popularize a saying that was already fairly well known. The ultimate source may be a book entitled *Den farlige alder* ("The Dangerous Age") by the Danish writer Karin Michaelis, published in 1910. "Thirteen is a dangerous age: nothing is more subtle. The boy, inspired to play the man, is beset by his own relapses into childhood, and Hedrick was near a relapse" (Booth Tarkington, *The Flirt*, 1912). *See also* LIFE BEGINS AT FORTY; SEVEN-YEAR ITCH.

Daniel Boone (boon) Archetype of a pioneer frontiersman. Daniel Boone (1734–1820) responded to the lure of the wilderness at an early age and spent his life helping to open up the unexplored regions of Kentucky and Missouri. He also served in the U.S. militia and defended the many settlements he had helped to found against attack by Native American tribes. *Her father emerged from the store wearing a Daniel Boone hat and leather jacket.*

Daniel come to judgment, a (danyăl) A person who reaches a wise conclusion about something that has left others bewildered, especially one who displays wisdom beyond his or her years. The allusion is to the biblical Daniel, as described in Daniel 5 (where he explained the meaning of the WRITING ON THE WALL). The phrase in its modern form comes from William Shakespeare's *The Merchant of Venice* (c. 1596), in which Shylock hails Portia with the following words: "A Daniel come to judgment! yea a Daniel! / O wise young judge, how I do honour thee!" In a story related in the apocryphal book of Susanna the youthful Daniel successfully defends Susanna against the accusation of being found committing adultery in the shade of a tree by asking her two accusers what kind of tree it was. The two men give different answers and Susanna's innocence is proved. By much the same token any judge who earns respect for his great wisdom might be referred to simply as a ***Daniel.*** *It was in this moment of crisis that this young prodigy really proved himself a Daniel come to judgment.*

Daniel in the lions' den (danyăl) A person who is in a position of great danger. The phrase alludes to the biblical story of Daniel in which the Hebrew prophet is accused of defying the rulers of Babylon and is thrown into a cage full of hungry lions: "Then the king commanded, and they brought Daniel, and cast him into the den of lions" (Daniel 6:16). Daniel's courage and faith is rewarded when God saves his life by sealing the lions' mouths so they cannot eat him. By the same token, a ***den of lions*** signifies any situation in which a person finds himself or herself surrounded by others who mean the person harm. *Finding himself suddenly surrounded by rogues and bandits of all description, the journalist quickly appreciated that he was like Daniel in the lions' den.*

danse macabre (dahns măkahbră) A series of events seemingly moving inexorably toward destruction and death. The danse macabre (or dance of death) was a well-known motif of medieval art, typically depicting a skeletal figure of Death leading a string of mortals away to the grave. The motif became widespread throughout Europe with the eruption of the Black Death in the middle of the 14th century. *The countries of the Middle East seem to be engaged in a danse macabre that can only end in bloodshed.*

Dante and Beatrice (dantay, dontay; beeătris) An idealized, unfulfilled, platonic romance. The allusion is to the Italian writer Dante Alighieri (1265–1321) and Beatrice Portinari (1266–90), the beautiful young girl with whom the writer fell hopelessly in love on first seeing her in 1274, when both were still children. Dante's love for Beatrice remained pure and unblemished, although he had little chance to express it and she went on to marry an Italian nobleman and died in her twenties. She remained for Dante an unattainable ideal and the subject of some of his greatest poetry. "But Will wanted to talk with Dorothea alone, and was impatient of slow circumstance. However slight the terrestrial intercourse between Dante and Beatrice or Petrarch and Laura, time changes the proportion of things, and in later days it is preferable to have fewer sonnets and more conversation" (George Eliot, *Middlemarch*, 1871–72).

Dante's Inferno (dantayz, dontayz) A place of terrifying heat, violence, or demonic confusion. The Italian writer Dante Alighieri (1265–1321) has been celebrated for generations for his vivid depiction of hell in *Inferno*, the first part of his epic poem *La Divina Commedia* (*The Divine Comedy*; 1307–21). His descriptions of the infernal regions to which condemned souls are doomed had a profound effect upon the medieval imagination and remain influential today, as much for their poetical qualities as for their theological content. To be ***cast into Dante's Inferno*** is to be thrown, actually or metaphorically, into a seething cauldron of fire or confusion and horror. Anything that is reminiscent of Dante's vivid imaginings may be similarly dubbed ***Dantean*** or ***Dantesque***. *As he opened the door to the blast furnace it was like stepping into Dante's Inferno.*

Dan to Beersheba, from (dan, beersheebă) Everywhere; from one end of a kingdom to the other. The biblical town of Dan was located in the north of Canaan and marked the northern limit of ancient Israel, while Beersheba was situated on the southern limit of the kingdom. The phrase appears in Judges 20:1, in which the Israelites are described as being "gathered together as one man, from Dan even to Beer-sheba." *News of his downfall spread quickly, and soon everyone from Dan to Beersheba knew that his star had been eclipsed.*

Danvers, Mrs. *See* MRS. DANVERS.

Daphne (dafnee) The archetype of a woman who seeks to defend her chastity. Daphne was a NYMPH who attracted the amorous attentions of the god Apollo. He pursued her until she called on the other gods to help her and was transformed by them into a laurel, or bay, tree. Apollo swore that from thenceforth he would wear bay leaves in tribute to her. "A spasm passed through Grace. A Daphnean instinct, exceptionally strong in her as a girl, had been revived by her widowed seclusion" (Thomas Hardy, *The Woodlanders,* 1887).

Daphnis and Chloe (dafnis, klōee) An archetypal pair of young lovers. A celebrated ancient Greek pastoral romance relates how Daphnis and Chloe fell in love and eventually married. Their story was subsequently retold in Allan Ramsay's *Gentle Shepherd* (1725) and Jacques-Henri Bernardin de Saint-Pierre's *Paul et Virginie* (1787), as well as the ballet *Daphnis et Chloe* (1912), with music by Maurice Ravel and choreography by Michel Fokine. *A couple sauntered among the trees and flowers, for all the world like a latter-day Daphnis and Chloe. See also* CHLOE.

Darby and Joan Archetype of a comfortable, devoted, elderly married couple. They first appeared as characters in a ballad by Henry Woodfall, published in the *Gentleman's Magazine* in 1735: "Old Darby, with Joan by his side, / You've often regarded with wonder: / He's dropsical, she is sore-eyed, / Yet they're never happy asunder." The characters may have been based on real people, John Darby being the man under whom Henry Woodfall served an apprenticeship, although another tradition identifies them as a Yorkshire couple. "He found her at home, and with her was her husband. 'Here is a Darby and Joan meeting, is it not?' she said, getting up to welcome him" (Anthony Trollope, *Phineas Finn*, 1869).

Darcy, Mr. *See* MR. DARCY.

Dare, Dan *See* DAN DARE.

Dark Ages A period in which intellectual progress has given way to ignorance and barbarism. The term was originally applied to the period of history that extended from the end of the Roman Empire in the fifth century A.D. to the medieval period beginning around A.D. 1000, an obscure era of which relatively few historical records survive. The term is generally avoided by modern historians, who point out that the period in question witnessed significant cultural advances and developments in social organization. In modern usage, the term is often applied to people or practices that seem to belong to another outdated, unsophisticated, or prejudiced time. *The way he goes on about the evils of computers and the Internet, you'd think he was still living in the Dark Ages.*

Darkest Africa The remotest, least-known parts of the African continent, where all is mystery and, probably, horror. The phrase dates back to the early exploration of Africa by white adventurers, who called the region the ***Dark Continent*** because so little was known about it. The British explorer and journalist ***Henry Morton Stanley*** (1841–1904) wrote books with the titles *Through the Dark Continent* (1878) and *Through Darkest Africa* (1890). "Thus even in darkest Africa was the light of German civilization commencing to reflect itself upon the undeserving natives just as at the same period, the fall of 1914, it was shedding its glorious effulgence upon benighted Belgium" (Edgar Rice Burroughs, *Tarzan the Untamed*, 1920).

Dark Lady A woman of mysterious nature or identity, especially one who is unfaithful. The allusion is to the otherwise unidentified "Dark Lady of the Sonnets" to whom William Shakespeare addressed some of his best-loved poetry of the 1590s, notably Sonnets 127–152: "Two loves I have of comfort and despair, / Which like two spirits so suggest me still; / The better angel is a man right fair, / The worser spirit a woman colour'd ill" (Sonnet 144). She has been tentatively identified by modern scholars as one of a number of real historical characters, including ladies by the name of Mary Fitton, Penelope Rich, Mrs. Davenant, and Lucy Parker. The historian A. L. Rowse made out a strong case for her being Emilia Lanier, the daughter of a Venetian court musician, who may have had an affair with Shakespeare around the end of 1592. Because of the strong suggestion of infidelity in the sonnets, the term "Dark Lady" is often applied to women who are suspected of being unfaithful to their husbands or lovers. It may also, however, be applied more broadly to any brunette, or any woman with a dark complexion. *Everyone likes her, but my wife thinks she may be a "Dark Lady" who wouldn't think twice about running off with someone else's husband.*

darkness *See* EGYPTIAN DARKNESS.

darkness, outer *See* OUTER DARKNESS.

darkness at noon The extinguishing of hope, freedom, optimism, etc., especially through the agency of an oppressive regime. The allusion is to a 1940 novel of the same title by Arthur Koestler (1905–83), in which he depicted life under the repressive Soviet regime in Stalinist Russia. He, in turn, may have borrowed the phrase from John Milton's *Samson Agonistes* (1671), which includes the line "O dark, dark, dark, amid the blaze of noon," or from William Cowper's "The Progress of

Error" (1782), which has "Judgment drunk, and brib'd to lose his way / Winks hard, and talks of darkness at noon-day." "She could not trust God, and in the bitterness of doubt her spirit was like darkness at noon" (Os Guinness, *Doubt*, 1976).

dark night of the soul A period of intense mental or spiritual anguish. The phrase, in its Spanish form *La noche oscura del alma*, was used by the Christian mystic St. John of the Cross (1542–91) as the title of a religious treatise published around 1578. The phrase originally denoted a time of spiritual isolation through which a mystic might achieve union with God. Now, however, it refers to any period of deep depression or hopelessness, as in F. Scott Fitzgerald's famous line: "In a real dark night of the soul it is always three o'clock in the morning." "And during his dark night of the soul while he was at Cuddesdon, part of the darkness was the behavior of the House of Commons" (Owen Chadwick, *Michael Ramsey: A Life*, 1991).

dark satanic mills An industrial setting, or industry in general, especially with regard to what may be seen as its dirty, inhuman nature. The phrase was coined by the English poet William Blake (1757–1827) in what is now the much-loved hymn 'Jerusalem,' which first appeared as part of the longer *Milton* (1804): "And was Jerusalem builded here / Among these dark Satanic mills." Blake himself intended his lines to be a criticism not of England's factories, but of England's churches. *He had never felt at home among the dark satanic mills of the city and longed to escape to the rural shires from which he had come.*

Darling, Grace *See* GRACE DARLING.

D'Artagnan *See* THREE MUSKETEERS.

Darth Vader (dahrth vaydă) A thoroughly evil, menacing person, sometimes with a slightly comical aspect. Helmeted and dressed entirely in black, Darth Vader was the archvillain in the original trilogy of *Star Wars* films made by George Lucas, beginning with *Star Wars* itself in 1977. The original idea was that his name was a version of "dark father" (it is ultimately revealed that he is the father of the young hero Luke Skywalker, lured to the dark side). The name is sometimes applied to people who have a similar rasping voice. *Kitted out in his black bike gear he looked like a paunchy Darth Vader, lacking only the long black cloak. See also* EVIL EMPIRE.

Dartmoor (dahrtmor) A forbidding high-security prison. Dartmoor Prison in Devon is one of the most notorious of British prisons, being located at Princetown in the middle of a windswept moorland wilderness, which makes escape doubly difficult. It was built to house French prisoners-of-war during the Napoleonic Wars and has since housed many hard-bitten convicts. *If the police find out about this it'll be Dartmoor for the lot of us.*

Darwinian (dahrwineeăn) Of or relating to the evolutionary theories of the British naturalist Charles Darwin (1809–82). As proposed in his celebrated book *On the Origin of Species by Means of Natural Selection* (1859), Darwin emphasized the role of the SURVIVAL OF THE FITTEST in the course of evolutionary progress. In fact, similar theories were already in circulation before Darwin, but it was his book that brought them to public notice. "So how did it come to evolve by slow, steady, infinitesimally small Darwinian improvements?" (Richard Dawkins, *The Blind Watchmaker*, 1986).

Dastardly, Dick *See* DICK DASTARDLY.

Daughter of Zion *See* ZION.

daughters of Eve *See* EVE.

daughters of men Women. The phrase is biblical in origin, appearing in Genesis 6:1–4 in the course of a passage describing how men or possibly angels began to couple with any woman they chose: "When men began to multiply on the face of the earth . . . the sons of God saw the daughters of men that they were fair; and they took them wives of all which they chose . . . and they bare children to them, the same became mighty men which were of old, men of renown." "She might have been—except for that something radiant in her that marked her apart from all the other daughters of men" (Joseph Conrad, *The Arrow of Gold,* 1919).

David (dayvid) A person noted for his wisdom, courage, chastity, or skill as a musician. In the Bible David was a hero, born the son of Jesse, who slew the giant Goliath and eventually became king of Judah and Israel. According to the Gospel of Luke, he was also an ancestor of Christ. His skill as a harpist brought him the favor of Saul, who found solace in his musicianship, as related in 1 Samuel 16:23: ". . . when the evil spirit from God was upon Saul, that David took an harp and played with his hand: so Saul was refreshed, and was well, and the evil spirit departed from him." The link between David and chastity alludes to the story of the aged David sharing his bed with a young woman named Abishag so that she might chastely warm his body with hers: "The damsel was very fair and cherished the king, and ministered to him: but the king knew her not" (1 Kings 1:4). "You make me feel as I have not felt these twelve months. If Saul could have had you for his David, the evil spirit would have been exorcised without the aid of the harp" (Charlotte Brontë, *Jane Eyre,* 1847). *See also* DAVID AND BATHSHEBA; DAVID AND GOLIATH; DAVID AND JONATHAN; EWE LAMB.

David and Bathsheba (dayvid, bathsheebă) A guilty or treacherous love affair. The allusion is to the biblical episode of 2 Samuel 11, 12, in which King David falls in love with the beautiful Bathsheba and arranges to have her husband, Uriah, sent into the heat of battle to be killed, leaving David free to claim Bathsheba as his wife. The couple later have a child who dies. Psalm 51 records David's repentance. *They looked as guilty as David and Bathsheba, and it was not difficult to guess what had been going on.*

David and Goliath (dayvid, golīăth) A contest in which the two sides are unequally matched. The allusion is to the biblical story of David, a humble but devout shepherd boy, who alone faces and defeats the Philistine giant GOLIATH by killing him with a slingshot: "[David] smote the Philistine in his forehead, that the stone sunk into his forehead; and he fell upon his face to the earth" (1 Samuel 17:49). "It is David and Goliath; the man in overalls against the suits in Brussels; UK sovereignty versus burgeoning European power" (*Guardian,* April 10, 2001).

David and Jonathan (dayvid, jonăthăn) The epitome of close friendship between two members of the same sex. The biblical hero David, Saul's heir, and Jonathan, the son of Saul, are described as inseparable companions: "It came to pass . . . that the soul of Jonathan was knit with the soul of David, and Jonathan loved him as his own soul" (1 Samuel 18:1). When Saul subsequently became jealous of David, Jonathan attempted to mend relations between his father and his friend, and when Jonathan was ultimately killed in battle, David uttered a sincere lamentation for him. *The pair were inseparable, like David and Jonathan.*

David and Nathan *See* EWE LAMB.

da Vinci, Leonardo *See* LEONARDO DA VINCI.

Davy Crockett (krokăt) The epitome of a rugged, experienced backwoodsman. Davy Crockett (1786–1836) had many unlikely adventures during the years he spent living in the wild frontier lands of the American West, as recounted in his fictionalized autobiography, published in 1834. One of the most celebrated pioneer frontiersmen of U.S. folklore, he was sent to the House of Representatives in 1827 and ultimately died at the Alamo in 1836. "That do-or-die Davy Blooming Crockett spirit" (Jack Yeovil, *Krokodil Tears*, 1990). *See also* REMEMBER THE ALAMO.

Day, Doris *See* DORIS DAY.

day of infamy A day marked by an act of exceptional evil or deceit. The allusion is to Sunday, December 7, 1941, when the U.S. naval base at PEARL HARBOR on Hawaii was unexpectedly attacked by Japanese aircraft. The attack was condemned the following day, when President Franklin D. Roosevelt (1882–1945) addressed a shocked Congress: "Yesterday, December 7, 1941—a date which will live in infamy—the United States of America was suddenly and deliberately attacked by the naval and air forces of the Empire of Japan." Congress responded by consenting to a declaration of war. The phrase has since been used sparingly of other extreme events, most notably the terrorist attacks of September 11, 2001 (*see* 9/11). *That was a day of infamy that no one around this table is ever likely to forget.*

day of judgment *See* JUDGMENT DAY.

day of small things Apparently insignificant details may in time prove to be the beginning of much greater things. The expression appears in the Bible in Zechariah 4:10, in which God reassures Zechariah after some of his people scoff at the relatively unimpressive beginnings of his rebuilding of the Temple: "For who hath despised the day of small things? for they shall rejoice." "I am but the incumbent of a poor country parish: my aid must be of the humblest sort. And if you are inclined to despise the day of small things, seek some more efficient succour than such as I can offer" (Charlotte Brontë, *Jane Eyre,* 1847).

days of one's life, all the For as long as a person lives. The expression comes from Psalm 23:6, in which it appears in the form: "Surely goodness and mercy shall follow me all the days of my life: and I will dwell in the house of the LORD for ever." *That is something to remember all the days of one's life.*

days of our years A person's lifetime, emphasizing the relatively brief time that mortals have on earth. The phrase comes from Psalm 90:10, where it appears in the passage: "The days of our years are threescore years and ten." *Modern science threatens to prolong the days of our years beyond anything our forebears would have believed possible.*

D-day The day set for a particular event to take place. The original D-day was June 6, 1944, when the Allies launched the invasion of Europe by landing troops on the Normandy beaches. The culmination of months of preparation, D-day is remembered as one of the most decisive dates in world history. In fact, D-day was initially set for June 5, but had to be postponed for 24 hours due to adverse weather conditions. The D in D-day was an abbreviation of "Day." *Next Monday is D-Day for Wall Street. See also* LONGEST DAY.

dead . . . and never called me mother! An expression of mock dismay, as typified by melodramatic 19th-century drama and fiction. Though associated particularly with the hugely popular sentimental novel *EAST LYNNE* (1861) by Mrs. Henry Wood, the line does not actually appear in the original book, but was added in a successful 1874 stage adaptation of the novel. The line occurs in a scene during which a mother grieves over her young son, who has died unaware of his mother's true identity. *It was one of those "dead . . . and never called me mother!" performances that would never convince any modern audience.*

dead bury their dead, let the *See* LET THE DEAD BURY THE DEAD.

dead-end kids Youths who seem doomed to a disappointing future by virtue of their unpromising, impoverished backgrounds. The allusion is to a group of U.S. child actors called the Dead End Kids, who appeared in the role of street hooligans in a series of films during the 1930s, among them *Angels with Dirty Faces* (1938). *He was a dead-end kid in his youth but grew up to become one of the most influential men in the city.*

dead lion *See* LIVING DOG IS BETTER THAN A DEAD LION, A.

dead man's hand A stroke of bad luck, or an unlucky omen. The allusion is to the hand of cards that Sheriff ***Wild Bill Hickok*** was holding when he was shot in the back in a Deadwood saloon on August 2, 1876 (supposedly black aces and black eights or, according to another tradition, two jacks and two eights). Ever since then a similar combination of cards has been called a "dead man's hand." *He froze when he saw that he had been dealt the fabled dead man's hand.*

dead man walking A person who is considered as good as dead. The phrase, which became more widely known through the 1995 film *Dead Man Walking*, was traditionally called out by prison guards escorting condemned prisoners from death row to the execution chamber in U.S. prisons. In modern usage, the phrase is sometimes applied to officials who are considered to be clinging to office long after their resignation or dismissal has become inevitable. *Since that defeat the leader of the party has been a dead man walking.*

dead parrot Something that is totally defunct. The allusion is to the celebrated "dead parrot sketch" first performed on British television in the 1970s by the MONTY PYTHON comedy team, in which a disgruntled customer attempts to return a dead parrot to a pet store only to be met with the store owner's blank refusal to admit that the bird is actually dead. *This policy is a dead parrot as far as the rest of the government is concerned. See also* SICK AS A PARROT.

Dead Sea fruit A bitter disappointment or disillusion. The allusion is biblical in origin, referring to the fruit trees grown on the shores of the Dead Sea by the morally degenerate Sodomites. The fruit of these trees was said to be beautiful to look at but bitter to the taste and "within full of ashes," in the words of the French traveler Jean de

Thevenot (1633–67). It is also known by the name ***apples of Sodom***. "Like to the apples on the Dead Sea shore, / It is all ashes to the taste" (Lord Byron, *Childe Harold,* 1817).

Dean, James *See* JAMES DEAN.

Dear John letter A letter from a lover ending a relationship. The phrase dates from World War II, when many men serving in the armed forces overseas received such letters from their sweethearts at home after the latter tired of their long separation. In modern usage, the term may also be applied to similar letters of rejection from other parties, such as employers. *He had just received a Dear John letter from head office, informing him that his services were no longer required.*

death by a thousand cuts A painful and prolonged process of destruction or humiliation. The allusion is to a traditional method of execution developed originally in ancient China, which involved the victim being slowly cut to pieces by "a thousand knives." *This gradual reduction of public services is simply death by a thousand cuts.*

death is nothing at all Death is an insignificant event, which is not to be feared. The phrase is a quotation from a piece of writing by Henry Scott Holland (1847–1918), which is often recited at funerals: "Death is nothing at all. I have only slipped away into the next room. I am I and you are you. Whatever we were to each other, that we are still. Call me by my old familiar name, speak to me in the easy way which you always used . . ." Scott Holland was a canon of St. Paul's Cathedral in London and the author of various sermons and other writings. It has been suggested that he first wrote these lines to be recited after his own death. *They keep telling me that death is nothing at all, but people still look both ways when they cross the road.*

Death, where is thy sting? Death is nothing to fear. The expression comes from 1 Corinthians 15:55, which questions the significance of mortal death when compared with everlasting life in heaven: "O death, where is thy sting? O grave, where is thy victory?" In modern usage, the phrase is best known for its inclusion in funeral services. *He died with a smile on his face, as if to say, "Death, where is thy sting?"*

death's door, at At the point of death; very ill. The phrase derives from Miles Coverdale's translation of Psalm 107:18, as found in the *Book of Common Prayer*: "Their soul abhorred all manner of meat: and they were even hard at death's door." "He had had more than one attack of delirium tremens after his father's death, and had almost been at death's door" (Anthony Trollope, *Doctor Thorne,* 1858).

Deborah (debră) A courageous woman, especially one noted for her virtue or devotion to God. The original Deborah was a biblical prophet and judge who urged Barak to lead an army against the invading Canaanites, spurring him on to victory at the Kishon River, a triumph she celebrated in a memorable victory ode dubbed the "Song of Deborah" (Judges 5:1–31). "Stay, stay thy hands! Thou art an Amazon / And fightest with the sword of Deborah" (William Shakespeare, *Henry VI, Part 1,* 1589).

deep calleth unto deep A metaphor evoking a profound spiritual or philosophical understanding between two individuals, parties, etc. The phrase comes from Psalm 42:7, which interprets waterfalls or cataracts as representing the soul's restless yearning for God: "Deep calleth unto deep at the noise of thy waterspouts: all thy waves and thy billows are gone over me." *There existed an immediate bond of mutual understanding between the two great men, a vivid illustration of deep calleth unto deep.*

Deep Throat A covert source of information, usually otherwise unidentified. The original Deep Throat was the person who leaked information about the WATERGATE scandal to *Washington Post* journalists Carl Bernstein and Bob Woodward in 1972–74. In 2005 he was revealed as being Mark Felt, deputy director of the FBI. The code name itself was an allusion to the 1972 sex film *Deep Throat* starring Linda Lovelace. *What we need is a Deep Throat on the inside of the organization to spill the beans. See also* ALL THE PRESIDENT'S MEN.

Defarge, Madame *See* MADAME DEFARGE.

defenestration (deefenăstrayshăn) The act of throwing someone or something out of a window. The word came to prominence through its association with an incident involving a breakdown in relations between Roman Catholic and Protestant members of the Bohemian National Council sitting in the castle at Prague in 1618 prior to the start of the Thirty Years' War. Two of the Catholics present were thrown out of the window by their Protestant opponents, fortunately escaping serious injury by landing in the moat. The incident has since become known as the Defenestration of Prague. In modern usage the term has been used figuratively of the dismissal of a person from high office. *The senior management has been much reduced as a result of recent defenestrations.*

Deimos (daymăs) A personification of fear. In Greek mythology, Deimos was identified as the god of fear, son of Ares and Aphrodite. *The spirit of Deimos had possessed them and they charged as one for the exit.*

Deirdre (deerdră, deerdree) The archetype of a woman whose beauty causes only tragedy. According to Irish legend, Deirdre was the daughter of a storyteller whose beauty, it was predicted, would bring about the ruin of Ulster. King Conchobar's plans to marry her were disrupted when she eloped with Naoise, one of the three sons of Usnech, and fled with him to Scotland. Conchobar lured them back with promises of forgiveness, but when they returned, he had the three brothers killed. Deirdre is variously said to have committed suicide or to have died of grief a year later. Her story was dramatized by both William Butler Yeats (*Deirdre*, 1907) and John Millington Synge (*Deirdre of the Sorrows,* 1910). *What with all her moaning and grieving she's a regular Deirdre and no mistake.*

Delectable Mountains A place or situation that offers a view of wonderful things almost within reach. The allusion is to John Bunyan's great religious allegory *PILGRIM'S PROGRESS* (1678, 1684), in which Christian finally gets a view of the CELESTIAL CITY (heaven) from the peaks of the Delectable Mountains. "We call this hill the Delectable Mountain, for we can look far away and see the country where we hope to live some time" (Louisa May Alcott, *Little Women*, 1868–69).

delenda est Carthago (delendă est kahrthahgō) Any obstacle that stands in the way must be removed at all costs. This proverbial phrase is a quotation from Cato the Elder (234–149 B.C.), who took to ending every speech he made in the Roman senate with these words after visiting Carthage in 157 B.C. and realizing that it was becoming a serious rival to Rome. *The president will not be moved on this issue. It's a case of delenda est Carthago.*

Delilah (dă<u>lī</u>lă) A seductive, treacherous woman; a temptress. The biblical Delilah, whose name means "dainty one," was a Philistine whore who at the command of the Philistine leaders used her seductives wiles to trick SAMSON into revealing the secret of his great strength (his long hair) and then used this knowledge to bring about his ruin, having his hair cut short as he slept in her lap, as related at Judges 16:4–20. "What is the good of the love of woman when her name must needs be Delilah?" (H. G. Wells, *The Invisible Man,* 1897).

deliver us from evil A prayer for protection against harm. The expression comes from the Lord's Prayer: "And lead us not into temptation, but deliver us from evil" (Matthew 6:13). In modern usage it is sometimes quoted ironically in the form of a plea for relief from some minor irritation. "'Lead us not into temptation but deliver us from evil. But what is temptation? What is evil?'" (Anthony Trollope, *Barchester Towers,* 1857).

Delphic (<u>del</u>fik) Obscure in meaning; enigmatic; ambiguous. The Delphic oracle was a shrine situated at Delphi on the slopes of Mount Parnassus, thought by ancient Greeks to be the center of the world. Here a priestess known as the Pythia, seated upon a tripod, communicated messages from the god Apollo on a wide range of topics, from domestic matters to international affairs, often at the request of rulers or other powerful political figures. Many of these pieces of advice were obscure in meaning and open to a variety of interpretations, hence the use of the term *Delphic* to describe anything that sounds important but is in fact unclear in meaning. At one point in the fifth century B.C. the pronouncements of the oracle at Delphi became noticeably more specific, recommending that the Greeks give up their hopeless resistance against the Persians. When the Persians were subsequently defeated, the oracle was heavily criticized, and future pronouncements were wisely delivered with more of their former ambiguity. The temple at Delphi was finally closed down in A.D. 390 on the command of the emperor Theodosius. ". . . it was his wont to relapse into grim silence when interrogated in sceptical sort as to any of his sententious oracles, not always very clear ones, rather partaking of that obscurity which invests most Delphic deliverances from any quarter" (Herman Melville, *Billy Budd,* 1924).

Demeter (dă<u>mee</u>ter) A personification of fertility. In Greek mythology, Demeter was a corn goddess equivalent to the Roman Ceres. She was the goddess of fruit, crops, and vegetation and the mother of Persephone. When Persephone was carried off to the underworld by HADES, Demeter threatened that the earth would remain barren until Persephone was returned to her. It was eventually agreed that Persephone would spend nine months of the year with her mother, when crops would grow and plants would bear fruit, and three months with Hades, when the earth would remain barren. *There was real warmth in the spring sunshine, suggesting that Demeter had at long last been released from the underworld and returned to the light.*

DeMille, Cecil B. *See* CECIL B. DEMILLE.

Demon Barber of Fleet Street *See* SWEENEY TODD.

Demosthenic (demos<u>then</u>ik) Eloquent; persuasive; possessing or showing great powers of oratory or eloquence. The Athenian statesman Demosthenes (384–322 B.C.) was greatly admired as an orator, although as a youth he struggled with a weak voice and stammer. He improved his speaking technique by such devices as learning to talk clearly with his mouth stuffed with pebbles and competing in volume with the sound of the waves crashing on the shore. Ultimately, his skill as an orator proved his undoing after his criticisms of Philip of Macedonia incurred the latter's wrath and he was obliged to kill himself by taking poison when the Macedonians invaded. "Those are distinctions which we hardly understand on this thick-headed side of the water. But demagogues, democrats, demonstrations, and Demosthenic oratory are all equally odious to John Eustace" (Anthony Trollope, *The Eustace Diamonds,* 1873). *See also* PHILIPPIC.

denarius (denahreeăs) Ready money; cash. The denarius was the basic silver coin in ancient Rome. *I bet that car cost a pretty denarius.*

Denmark, something is rotten in the state of *See* SOMETHING IS ROTTEN IN THE STATE OF DENMARK.

Dennis the Menace An unruly young boy. Dennis the Menace made his first appearance in the British children's comic book *The Beano* in 1951 and soon became a firm favorite. That same year he also made his debut in U.S. comic strips, although depicted as blond and much younger than the British prototype, who was distinguished by his mop of thick black hair. *Her boy is a real Dennis the Menace, and destroys just about everything he lays his hands on.*

den of lions *See* DANIEL IN THE LIONS' DEN.

den of thieves A place where thieves or other dishonest characters are likely to be found. According to Matthew 21:13 Christ entered the Temple only to find that it had been taken over as a place of business by money changers, causing him to lament, "It is written, My house shall be called the house of prayer; but ye have made it a den of thieves." Christ then overturned their tables and threw the money changers out of the Temple. In modern usage the phrase is often applied to any financial institution or business suspected of using unscrupulous methods. "The ordinary of Newgate preached to women who were to swing at Tyburn for a petty theft as if they were worse than other people,—just as though he would not have been a pickpocket or shoplifter, himself, if he had been born in a den of thieves and bred up to steal or starve!" (Oliver Wendell Holmes, *Elsie Venner,* 1861). *See also* CAST MONEY CHANGERS OUT OF THE TEMPLE.

Denver boot A wheel clamp. Comprising a metal clamp that fits around the tire of a car, the device is commonly employed to immobilize vehicles that have been illegally parked until their owners have paid an appropriate fine. The name alludes to the introduction of the first such clamps in Denver, Colorado, in 1949. *His new car, which attracted attention with its whitewall tires and red paint job, fell victim to the Denver boot far more frequently than any of his previous cars.*

depart in peace *See* NUNC DIMITTIS.

Desdemona (dezdămōnă) Archetype of an innocent female victim of intrigue and deceit. Desdemona is the hapless wife of OTHELLO in William Shakespeare's tragedy *Othello* (c. 1603). Thanks to the evil machinations of the treacherous IAGO,

Othello wrongly comes to believe that Desdemona has been unfaithful to him and murders her. Her name is based on the Greek *dusdaimōn*, meaning "ill-fated." *She played Desdemona in this unhappy sequence of events that resulted in all involved being exposed to public humiliation in the press.*

Desert Rats A military force that specializes in operations in desert areas. The allusion is ultimately to the British Seventh Armoured Division, which distinguished itself in action against the German Afrika Korps in Libya during World War II. Members of the division wore a badge depicting a desert rat (jerboa). The nickname was subsequently applied to the Seventh Armoured Brigade, which went on to see action in Bosnia and Iraq. *A new generation of Desert Rats are adding fresh honors to the regimental records.*

desert shall blossom, the The land will be returned to its rightful owners one day. The phrase comes from Isaiah 35:1–2, which consists of the prophecy that the Israelites shall one day reclaim their homeland in Zion: "The desert shall rejoice, and blossom as the rose. It shall blossom abundantly, and rejoice even with joy and singing." This was originally a promise that the Babylonian exiles would return to their homeland in Palestine, but in modern times the prophecy has been quoted many times by those defending the controversial extension of Israeli settlements into areas formerly populated by Palestinians. *The Israeli government has promised that the desert shall bloom, but without detailing the cost they are prepared to pay in lives.*

deus ex machina (dayăs eks makină) An unexpected or contrived solution to an apparently insoluble difficulty. Literally translated from Latin as "a god from a machine," the expression referred originally to the practice of Euripides (c. 484–406 B.C.) and other classical Greek dramatists of bringing their plots to an artificial resolution in the final act through the sudden appearance on stage of a god, who used his powers to make everything right. It is thought that such characters were lowered from above the stage using some kind of mechanical device, hence "from a machine." "Dr Gwynne was the Deus ex machina who was to come down upon the Barchester stage and bring about deliverance from these terrible evils" (Anthony Trollope, *Barchester Towers,* 1857).

devil *See* SATAN.

De Vil, Cruella *See* CRUELLA DE VIL.

devil chained A potentially harmful individual, creature, organization, etc., that has been placed under restraint. The expression alludes to the image given to John of Satan being put in chains: "And he laid hold on the dragon, that old serpent which is the Devil, and Satan, and bound him a thousand years" (Revelation 20:2). *The vicious old man thrashed and strained in the arms that held him back, like a devil chained.*

devil's advocate A person who takes an opposing view in order to test the strength of an argument. The phrase, which was originally rendered in Latin as *advocatus diaboli*, was used as a title in the Roman Catholic Church for an official who was appointed to seek out weaknesses in the cases of individuals proposed for beatification or canonization. In modern usage, the term is often applied to any person who adopts an unpopular or mischievous stance on something, usually motivated by the urge to express a contrasting opinion to that generally held. *Her father liked playing devil's advocate,* *suggesting all manner of outrageous reasons why something that was perfectly obvious to everyone else could not possibly be right.*

devils believe and tremble Even the most wicked people have a conscience or lingering belief in good that may trouble them. The sentiment appears in the Bible: "Thou believest that there is one God; thou doest well: the devils also believe, and tremble" (James 2:19). *Fear convulsed the murderer's face when he was shown photographs of his victim, proving that even devils believe and tremble, as the saying goes.*

Devil's Island A forbidding place of confinement or isolation, from which a person may well not return. The original Devil's Island was an island off the coast of French Guiana, which was formerly the site of a notorious penal colony. Due to the harsh conditions on the island, many prisoners died there. The prison was closed in 1953 and the island was remarketed as a tourist resort. *He felt as if he was being sent to some remote Devil's Island, and that soon no one back home would even remember his name.*

Diana of the Ephesians (dīană, efeezhănz) Someone or thing that serves to distract attention from the truth. According to Acts 19:24–28, Diana of the Ephesians was a fertility goddess with many breasts. Paul urged Diana's worshipers to give her up but met with objections from the local silversmiths, who were earning a great deal of money selling trinkets at the temple of Diana. The followers of Diana shouted "Great is Diana of the Ephesians," and ever since then the phrase has been quoted in circumstances when a person stands accused of being blinded by his or her own self-interest. "Then he wad rather claver wi' a daft quean they ca' Diana Vernon (weel I wet they might ca' her Diana of the Ephesians, for she's little better than a heathen—better? she's waur—a Roman, a mere Roman)" (Sir Walter Scott, *Rob Roy,* 1817). *See also* ARTEMIS.

diaspora (dīaspără) The dispersion of people through migration or forced removal. The word was originally applied to the scattering of the Jews after the Babylonian exile. In modern usage the word has been applied much more generally, though it is still often understood to refer specifically to Jewish communities scattered throughout the world. *The extent of the Scottish diaspora means that a Scotsman abroad can be confident of finding sympathetic hosts in any major city in the developed world.*

Dick Dastardly (dastărdlee) A villainous rogue, especially an incompetent one. Dick Dastardly was one of the central characters in the Hanna-Barbera television cartoon series *WACKY RACES*. Sporting the long mustache of villains in 19th-century melodrama, and assisted by his sniggering but resentful dog-companion ***Muttley***, Dick Dastardly sought to win each race by a range of devious ruses, all of which came disastrously undone. His escapades continued in the spin-off series *The Perils of Penelope Pitstop* and *Dastardly and Muttley in their Flying Machines*. *He drove with total disregard for other road users, snarling at other drivers to get out of the way like Dick Dastardly.*

Dickensian (dikenzeeăn) Reminiscent of the atmosphere, settings, themes, or style of British novelist Charles Dickens (1812–70). One of the most celebrated novelists of the Victorian era, Dickens created a lively, vivid world that encompassed many aspects of life in 19th-century

England. Settings depicted in his many works ranged from the squalid slums and factories of major cities to scenes of pastoral charm. Characters varied from jolly squires and cheerful servants to starving orphans and villainous clerks and thieves. In modern usage, the term "Dickensian" tends to be employed broadly to imply a panoramic, detailed and colorful, even grotesque, satirical depiction of the real world, especially one that harks back to the 19th century. "There is a Dickensian quality about Cairo: the dense narrow lanes, the rubbish and stench of the streets, the jostling crowds, the animals, the dramatic disparity between rich and poor, the spectacle of young children hard at work, the host of people scraping a living from the most menial of tasks: porters, scavengers, match-sellers, bootblacks, water-carriers" (Stanley Stewart, *Old Serpent Nile: A Journey to the Source*, 1991).

Dick Tracy (traysee) Archetype of a tough police detective. Dick Tracy made his debut in a U.S. comic strip in 1931, drawn by Chester Gould. He was a tireless, square-jawed opponent of injustice and wrongdoing, driven by the urge to avenge himself upon the criminals for the kidnapping of his girlfriend and the murder of her father. *He worked long into the night, doggedly poring over the details of the case like Dick Tracy.*

Dido and Aeneas (dīdō, ăneeas) An archetype of tragic love. The love affair between the Trojan adventurer Aeneas and Dido, queen of Carthage, was told in Virgil's *Aeneid* (29–19 B.C.). Dido fell in love with Aeneas after the latter was shipwrecked off Carthage but was ultimately unable to dissuade him from sailing on to Italy on the command of Jupiter. After he left she committed suicide by throwing herself onto a pyre. *One had the feeling that their love was doomed from the start, like Dido and Aeneas. See also* AENEAS.

die is cast, the An irrevocable step has been taken; there is no going back now. This common expression, in its Latin form *alea jacta est,* originated in a saying by Julius Caesar as he ordered his army across the Rubicon River toward Rome in 49 B.C., a step tantamount to an act of war. The reference is to gambling with dice (from the obvious truth that once a die is thrown, the cast cannot be taken back). "'But I have no purpose of debating these points with you, my lord,' waving his hand, as if to avoid farther discussion; 'the die is cast with you; allow me only to express my sorrow for the disastrous fate to which Angus M'Aulay's natural rashness, and your lordship's influence, are dragging my gallant friend Allan here, with his father's clan, and many a brave man besides'" (Sir Walter Scott, *A Legend of Montrose,* 1819). *See also* CROSS THE RUBICON.

die like Roland *See* ROLAND.

Dien Bien Phu (dyen byen foo) A disastrous military defeat, especially one that is self-inflicted. Dien Bien Phu, in northern Indochina, was the site of a French fortification that fell to communist Vietminh guerrillas in May 1954 after a siege of 55 days. The defeat was blamed on overconfidence among the French commanders, who had failed to realize the threat posed by the guerrilla army and had allowed their enemies to occupy the strongest positions. *Spokesmen for the army are denying that this reverse represents a Dien Bien Phu for U.S. forces.*

dies irae (deeayz eeray) A day of reckoning. Latin for "day of wrath," the phrase appears at Zephaniah 1:15, in which Zephaniah foresees a "day of wrath, a day of trouble and distress," generally interpreted as a reference to the Day of Judgment. Subsequently it became widely familiar as the opening words of a medieval Latin hymn used in funeral and requiem masses. "One thing is certain,—that there is a mustering among the masses, the world over; and there is a dies irae coming on, sooner or later" (Harriet Beecher Stowe, *Uncle Tom's Cabin,* 1852). *See also* JUDGMENT DAY.

Dietrich, Marlene *See* MARLENE DIETRICH.

different drummer *See* MARCH TO THE BEAT OF A DIFFERENT DRUMMER.

dii penates *See* LARES AND PENATES.

dilemma, horns of a *See* HORNS OF A DILEMMA.

Dillinger, John *See* PUBLIC ENEMY NUMBER ONE.

dinner of herbs *See* BETTER A DINNER OF HERBS THAN A STALLED OX WHERE HATE IS.

Diogenes (dīojăneez) A seeker of truth and honesty, especially one who is cynical about his or her chances of finding it. The original Diogenes (c. 412–320 B.C.) was a Greek philosopher who founded the Cynics, a school of philosophers whose ideals included the pursuit of asceticism and independence. According to tradition, he lived in an earthenware tub and carried a lantern in broad daylight to further his search for an honest man. His name may also be encountered in that of the ***Diogenes crab,*** which is a West Indian hermit crab that inhabits the abandoned shells of other creatures (reminiscent of the philosopher in his tub), and also in that of the ***Diogenes cup,*** the hollow formed in the palm of the hand when the fingers are unstraightened (a reference to the simple lifestyle associated with the Cynics). "The magistrate took the light out of the servant-maid's hand, and advanced to his scrutiny, like Diogenes in the street of Athens, lantern-in-hand, and probably with as little expectation as that of the cynic, that he was likely to encounter any especial treasure in the course of his researches" (Sir Walter Scott, *Rob Roy,* 1817).

Diomedean exchange (dīomeedeeăn) A bargain in which one side gets all the benefit. The phrase alludes to an episode in Homer's *Iliad* (c. 700 B.C.) in which Glaucus and Diomedes exchange suits of armor. Glaucus hands over a fine suit of armor "of gold divinely wrought," whereas all Diomedes has to offer is an almost worthless suit of brass armor "of mean device." Also known as a ***Glaucus swap.*** *With the benefit of hindsight it seems clear that this was a Diomedean exchange, with the government getting nothing out of it.*

Diomedes *See* LABORS OF HERCULES.

Dionysian (dīoneezheeăn, dīoneeshăn) Wild, frenzied, uninhibited, abandoned, orgiastic. In Greek mythology Dionysus was the son of Zeus and Semele and the god of wine, fruitfulness, and vegetation, equivalent to the Roman Bacchus. It was Dionysus who, according to myth, invented wine and developed the cultivation of grapes. The five festivals held in Athens each year in his honor were notorious for the frenzied and licentious behavior of the celebrants, who indulged freely in drink and sex. These festivals gave birth to the Greek theater. *As a student he had pursued a Dionysian lifestyle, holding riotous parties and rarely spending an evening at home.*

Dioscorea (dioskoreeă) A genus of plants belonging to the yam family. It was named in honor of the Greek physician Dioscorides Pedanius (C. A.D. 40–c. 90), who studied a wide variety of plants in order to gather information about their medicinal properties while serving as a surgeon in the Roman army. He was later recognized as one of the fathers of modern botany. *There are probably many more secrets to learn about* Dioscorea.

Dioscuri *See* CASTOR AND POLLUX.

Dirty Harry A maverick policeman, or someone else who employs heavy-handed or ethically dubious tactics to achieve his or her aims. The 1971 film *Dirty Harry* introduced the eponymous Harry Callaghan, a self-willed San Francisco police inspector (played by Clint Eastwood) who thought nothing of breaking the rules in order to outwit criminals who might otherwise escape legal retribution. He continued to break the rules in a series of sequels. *We don't approve of Dirty Harry tactics in this company. See also* GO AHEAD, MAKE MY DAY.

disciple A follower or pupil of a religious teacher or other leader. The word is most familiar from its application in the Bible to the 12 apostles and to followers of Christ more generally. ". . . the doctrine it contain'd was by degrees universally adopted by the philosophers of Europe, in preference to that of the abbé; so that he lived to see himself the last of his sect, except Monsieur B—, of Paris, his élève and immediate disciple" (Benjamin Franklin, *Autobiography,* 1793).

discord, apple of *See* APPLE OF DISCORD.

dismal science Economics. It was Thomas Carlyle (1795–1881) who gave economics this label, which has haunted it ever since, in his 1849 essay "On the Nigger Question": "The social science—not a 'gay science,' but a rueful—which finds the secret of this Universe in 'supply and demand' . . . what we might call, by way of eminence, the dismal science." In coining the label, he may have been influenced by contemporary economists who held the gloomy view that population growth would outstrip food production. *If we are to believe the purveyors of the dismal science, we are heading for another period of recession.*

Disneyfication (diznifikayshăn) The trivialization of historical fact or real places, people, etc., in order to maximize their commercial appeal. U.S. filmmaker Walt Disney (1901–66) made his reputation with brilliant but often sentimentalized cartoons and live-action films in which the less pleasant or controversial aspects of nature or human existence were either ignored or made more palatable and unchallenging. The same approach typified the various Disney resorts that his corporation later built. Many critics have found fault with the tendency of many commercial organizations to indulge in similar "Disneyfication" of historical truth and the realities of life. *As a scholar, I deplore the Disneyfication of the slave issue in early American history.*

Disneyland (dizneeland) An unreal, fantasy world. The original Disneyland was a hugely popular amusement park opened by U.S. filmmaker Walt Disney (1901–66) in Anaheim, California, in 1955. Featuring many of the fictional characters made famous in the Disney films, Disneyland presented a view of the world far removed from daily reality. Its success over the decades has spawned many other similar parks all over the world. A person "living in Disneyland" is someone who fails to appreciate the true situation. *If he thinks the problem is going to go away by itself he's living in Disneyland.*

Dives (d<u>ī</u>veez) A very rich man, especially one who is obsessed with material concerns and ignores the interests of others. In the Bible, Christ tells the story of a rich man named Dives who ignores the plight of the beggar Lazarus at his gate and is consequently condemned to an eternity in hell while Lazarus goes to heaven (Luke 16:19–31). The rich man is not actually named in the original text but acquired the name in the Latin version of the New Testament, apparently from the Latin *dives,* meaning "rich." "Remember, we are bid to work while it is day—warned that 'the night cometh when no man shall work.' Remember the fate of Dives, who had his good things in this life" (Charlotte Brontë, *Jane Eyre,* 1847).

divided against itself *See* HOUSE DIVIDED AGAINST ITSELF, A.

divide the sheep from the goats *See* SEPARATE THE SHEEP FROM THE GOATS.

Doctor Caligari (kali<u>gah</u>ree) A mysterious villain. Doctor Caligari is an evil magician and hypnotist in the celebrated 1919 silent German horror movie *The Cabinet of Dr. Caligari*, in which he was played by Werner Krauss. In the original film, Caligari uses his powers of hypnotism to make a sleepwalker carry out murders on his orders, but he is later revealed to be a character in the dreams of a patient in the asylum for the insane of which Caligari is director. *He felt as if his fate was in the hands of a powerful Doctor Caligari, and that he was powerless to resist any instructions he was given.*

Doctor Crippen (<u>krip</u>ăn) A wife-murderer or other evil, criminally-minded person. American-born London doctor Hawley Harvey Crippen (1862–1910) hit the headlines in the United Kingdom in 1910 when he was discovered to have murdered his wife Belle, a former music-hall performer. After killing his wife with the poison hyoscine hydrobromide, dismembering her body, and hiding the remains under the basement of their home, Crippen attempted to flee the country with his mistress Ethel le Neve on board the cargo ship *Montrose*. He was arrested when the ship docked in Canada (thus becoming the first person to be arrested as the result of messages sent by wireless telegraphy), brought back to London, and hanged. *Who would have thought from that quiet, charming demeanor that we were dealing with a second Doctor Crippen?*

Doctor Dolittle (<u>doo</u>lităl) A person who is very good with animals and seems to understand the way they think and behave. The allusion is to the books of British writer Hugh Lofting (1886–1947) depicting the adventures of the animal-loving Dr. John Dolittle, who possesses the power to talk with the various creatures that come to him for treatment. The books, published over three decades from 1920 to 1952, have since inspired several films. *The way she communicates with those horses, you would think she was Doctor Dolittle.*

Doctor Fell, I do not like thee, *See* I DO NOT LIKE THEE, DOCTOR FELL.

Doctor Jekyll and Mr. Hyde *See* JEKYLL AND HYDE.

Doctor Kildare (kil<u>dair</u>) Archetype of a handsome, caring young doctor. In the U.S. television medical series *Dr. Kildare* (1961–66), he was played with suitable suavity by Richard Chamberlain. *Say what you like, but old Doc Stevens with his bald head and half-moon spectacles is no Doctor Kildare.*

Doctor Livingstone, I presume? (livingstăn) An ironic greeting on meeting someone. The allusion is to the supposed words of greeting uttered by the British explorer and journalist ***Henry Morton Stanley*** (1841–1904) on finally locating Dr. David Livingstone (1813–73) at Ujiji in central Africa in 1871, after the latter had been out of contact with the rest of the world for some considerable time. Stanley's words have since been lauded, or lampooned, as a perfect example of British understatement and good etiquette, even in the most unlikely of circumstances. *"Doctor Livingstone, I presume?" Charles giggled as he lifted the blanket covering Edward's head.*

Doctor Spock A child care expert. Dr. Benjamin Spock (1903–98) challenged many established conventions concerning child care with his *Common Sense Book of Baby and Child Care* (1946), which became a best-seller and profoundly influenced parents for years to come. His liberal views on discipline were especially controversial and were blamed by many for a decline in behavior among the young. *As children they were brought up on the Doctor Spock model, but this did not mean they were allowed to do what they liked.*

Doctor Strangelove (straynjlăv) Archetype of a mad scientist who is so obsessed with his work that he does not appreciate the possible consequences of it. In the classic 1964 film comedy *Dr. Strangelove: Or, How I Learned to Stop Worrying and Love the Bomb*, directed by Stanley Kubrick, the eponymous scientist was brilliantly played by Peter Sellers, who portrayed him as an ex-Nazi boffin with an uncontrollable urge to bring about a catastrophic nuclear confrontation. *Supposing a Doctor Strangelove got in here and started pressing buttons? See also* DOOMSDAY MACHINE.

Doctor Watson A devoted companion or assistant. The allusion is to the character of the name who is the right-hand man of the gifted detective SHERLOCK HOLMES in the mystery stories of Arthur Conan Doyle. He has seen service as a medical officer with the British army in India before becoming Holmes's amanuensis and chronicler of his many adventures. *Every great detective must have his Dr. Watson. See also* ELEMENTARY, MY DEAR WATSON.

Dodge City A lawless, dangerous, urban environment. The frontier town of Dodge City, Kansas, had a notorious reputation as a haven for gunfighters and other rough elements of the old Wild West until finally cleaned up by Wyatt Earp in 1876. *Take care—it's like Dodge City out there.*

Dogberry A petty bureaucrat, an officious person. The allusion is to the overbearing constable Dogberry in William Shakespeare's *Much Ado About Nothing* (1598) and his pompous but ignorant nature. Like Mrs. Malaprop in a much later generation of fictional characters, he is given to using long words that he does not really understand (*see* MALAPROPISM). *The Dogberrys at City Hall proved to be of no use at all in offering any useful advice.*

dog days The hottest days of summer. The concept is of ancient Roman origin, having its roots in early astronomy and the fact that the star SIRIUS, the brightest star in the night sky and commonly called the dog star, rose with the Sun at this time of year. Romans believed that the dog star, so-named because it was placed at the head of the constellation Canis Major (meaning "greater dog"), added its heat to that of the Sun and exerted a baleful influence upon human affairs, making mortals drowsy and listless and bringing forth droughts and disease. Changes in the movements of the stars over the centuries mean that Sirius today rises some time later in the year in the Northern Hemisphere. *The long-standing difference of opinion ignited once more during the dog days of summer, when the heat made everybody irritable and argumentative.*

dog has his day, every *See* EVERY DOG HAS HIS DAY.

dog in the manger, a A person who selfishly prevents others from enjoying what he or she cannot enjoy himself or herself. The expression comes from a fable by the Greek writer Aesop (620–560 B.C.) in which a surly dog sits on a pile of hay in a manger, preventing some cows from eating it, even though he cannot eat it himself. "'I suppose it is wrong and selfish,' he said. 'I suppose I am a dog in a manger. But I do own that there is a consolation to me in the assurance that she will never be the wife of that scoundrel'" (Anthony Trollope, *The Last Chronicle of Barset,* 1867).

dog in the nighttime, the A seemingly innocuous event that, by not happening, provides a vital clue in the solution of a crime or other mystery. The allusion is to the short story "Silver Blaze" (1892) by Sir Arthur Conan Doyle, in which the detective SHERLOCK HOLMES solves the crime by reasoning that a dog did not bark when a racehorse was stolen from some stables because it knew the person stealing the horse: "'Is there any point to which you would wish to draw my attention?' 'To the curious incident of the dog in the night-time.' 'The dog did nothing in the night-time.' 'That was the curious incident,' remarked Sherlock Holmes." The phrase subsequently provided the title of a 2003 novel by Mark Haddon, *The Curious Incident of the Dog in the Night-Time. The nonappearance of the professor may prove to be the dog in the nighttime that solves this case.*

dog must be bad indeed that is not worth a bone, the *See* LABORER IS WORTHY OF HIS HIRE, THE.

dog returneth to his vomit, a Fools and criminals tend to be drawn irresistibly back to their follies or crimes. This proverb is biblical in origin, appearing in Proverbs 26:11, "As a dog returneth to his vomit, so a fool returneth to his folly," and in 2 Peter 2:22. In modern usage the proverb is usually quoted with reference to criminals who cannot resist returning to the scene of their crimes. *The gang came back to the scene of the murder that very evening, drawn like dogs to their vomit.*

dogs of war Mercenary soldiers. The phrase appears in William Shakespeare's *Julius Caesar* (1599): "Cry havoc, and let slip the dogs of war" and became doubly familiar to a more modern audience through the title of Frederick Forsyth's 1974 thriller *The Dogs of War*, which recounted the involvement of a group of mercenaries in a coup in central Africa. The term is occasionally employed more widely, as in its original Shakespearean context, to describe the horrors of war generally. *After leaving the army he contemplated taking up a career as one of the dogs of war who drift from continent to continent in search of money and adventure.*

dolce vita, la *See* LA DOLCE VITA.

Dolittle, Doctor *See* DOCTOR DOLITTLE.

Don Giovanni *See* DON JUAN.

Don Juan (jooăn, wahn) A serial seducer of women. A figure of Spanish legend who features in numerous operas, plays, stories, and poems, Don Juan Tenorio (or ***Don Giovanni***) is a young nobleman of Seville, who in one version of the story is said to have seduced no less than 2,594 women in five countries. His undoing comes when he seduces the young daughter of the commandant of Ulloa. The girl's father objects, so Don Juan kills him and then, in a fit of foolish bravado, invites a statue of the dead man to dine with him: The statue duly answers the invitation and carries Don Juan off to hell. *Her brother is a regular Don Juan and no pretty girl is safe with him. See also* CASANOVA; LOTHARIO.

do not let your left hand know what your right hand is doing *See* LEFT HAND KNOW WHAT YOUR RIGHT HAND IS DOING, DO NOT LET YOUR.

Don Quixote (kihōtee, kwiksăt) A dreamy, romantic idealist, especially one with little grasp of practical realities. Don Quixote is the central character in the epic novel *Don Quixote* (1605, 1615) by the Spanish writer Miguel de Cervantes Saavedra (1547–1616). Depicted as gaunt, dignified, and simple-minded, he embarks on an absurd heroic knightly quest to right wrong, mounted on the broken-down old horse ***Rosinante*** and accompanied by his squire ***Sancho Panza***. A person who evinces a similar taste for the romantically unrealistic may be summed up as ***quixotic***. "De Gaulle was often depicted as a Don Quixote tilting at windmills or King Canute trying to turn back the waves, while the reality was that France was a middle-sized power with no prospect of returning to its Napoleonic glories" (Andrew Shennan, *De Gaulle*, 1993). *See also* DULCINEA; TILT AT WINDMILLS.

don't fire until you see the whites of their eyes Wait until the last moment before firing or otherwise committing yourself. The allusion is ultimately to a clash that occurred during the American Revolution near Charlestown Neck on June 17, 1775. Though outnumbered by the British forces, the Americans calmly held their fire on the orders of their commander, Colonel William Prescott (1726–95), who told his men "Don't fire until you see the whites of their eyes." The Americans successfully threw back two assaults before being forced into retreat, having run out of ammunition. *In photography as in warfare, don't fire until you see the whites of their eyes.*

don't give up the ship Don't give up the fight. This famous exhortation to keep fighting dates back to June 1, 1813, when the U.S. frigate *Chesapeake* found itself locked in a duel to the death with the British ship HMS *Shannon* off the U.S. coast during the War of 1812. The U.S. captain, Commander James Lawrence (1781–1813), was mortally wounded during the engagement and on being carried below deck urged his officers to resist the British boarding party that even then was swarming aboard: "Don't give up the ship! Sink her! Blow her up!" Unfortunately, the British took control of the ship before it could be destroyed by its crew—but Lawrence's rallying cry entered U.S. history and his words are often quoted in extremis. *I know we're eight points behind and the game is half over, but don't give up the ship!*

don't go to bed angry *See* SUN GO DOWN ON ONE'S ANGER, DON'T LET THE.

Doolittle, Eliza *See* ELIZA DOOLITTLE.

doomsday (doomzday) A final, terrible day of reckoning, especially one marking the end of the world. In Anglo-Saxon England the word *doom* signified a "legal ruling," but in modern usage the word evokes images of the destruction accompanying the end of the world as described in the Book of Revelation. "'I was all riled up, Anne, and I said she might stay till doomsday if she waited for that; and I stuck to it'" (Lucy Maud Montgomery, *Anne of Avonlea,* 1909). *See also* JUDGMENT DAY.

doomsday machine (doomzday) A machine that threatens to bring about the destruction of the world. The concept was first voiced by U.S. mathematician Herman Kahn in his book *On Thermonuclear War* (1960) and is particularly associated with nuclear weapons and the threat of mutual destruction that they represent. Such a machine plays a central role in Stanley Kubrick's film *DOCTOR STRANGELOVE* (1964). *In the wrong hands such a device could become a doomsday machine that will kill us all.*

Dorcas Society (dorkăs) A women's group that makes clothing for charity. These Anglican church groups take their name from the biblical Dorcas (also called Tabitha), a Christian woman of Joppa who, according to Acts 9:39, was noted for her good works, which included making "coats and garments" for needy widows. When she died and was laid out for burial, Peter brought her back to life through his prayers. "'Do any of you wish to take articles home, to do at odd times?' said Fan, who was president of this energetic Dorcas Society" (Louisa May Alcott, *An Old-Fashioned Girl,* 1870).

Dorian Gray (doreeăn) A person who looks unaccountably younger than his or her years. The allusion is to Oscar Wilde's novel *The Picture of Dorian Gray* (1891), in which the eponymous Dorian Gray retains his youth while a portrait of him in the attic steadily degenerates, reflecting his dissolute life of vice and corruption. *The manufacturers of antiaging creams have turned their attention to the male market, targeting older men with advertisements that suggest anyone can be a Dorian Gray.*

Doric (dorik) Simple, rustic, or uncouth. The inhabitants of the mountainous region of Doris in ancient Greece and their way of life (especially the dialect of Greek that they spoke) were considered simple and unrefined in comparison with other Greek peoples and their more sophisticated lifestyles (*see* ATTIC). The term *Doric* is still used today to imply a rustic, pastoral character, especially in relation to rural dialects and the arts: Pastoral poetry is occasionally called the ***Doric reed,*** for example. The ***Doric order*** in ancient Greek architecture was similarly denoted by its strong and relatively plain, unsophisticated character. "When, early in a summer afternoon, we have been shaking the dust of the village from the skirts of our garments, making haste past those houses with purely Doric or Gothic fronts, which have such an air of repose about them, my companion whispers that probably about these times their occupants are all gone to bed" (Henry David Thoreau, "Walking," 1851). *See also* CORINTHIAN; IONIC; TUSCAN.

Doris Day Archetype of the indomitably cheerful girl-next-door. The U.S. actress and singer Doris Day (Doris Kappelhoff; b. 1924) starred in a series of uplifting film musicals and comedies of the 1940s and 1950s, becoming a symbol of healthy, exuberant American youth. *Her mother was the Doris Day type, a plump woman with rosy cheeks and an ever-present smile.*

Dormouse A sleepy, quiet individual. The allusion is to the Dormouse in Lewis Carroll's *Alice's Adventures in Wonderland* (1865), one of the characters present at the Mad Hatter's tea party. He repeatedly falls asleep, despite the efforts of the others to keep him awake by pinching him: "'Wake up, Dormouse!' And they pinched it on both sides at once. The Dormouse slowly opened his eyes. 'I wasn't asleep,' he said in a hoarse, feeble voice: 'I heard every word you fellows were saying.'" *Her son was like the Dormouse, nodding off in a corner where he wouldn't be disturbed.*

Dorothy, friend of *See* FRIEND OF DOROTHY.

Dotheboys Hall (dooTHăboiz) A school where the pupils are subject to the harshest of discipline and conditions. Dotheboys Hall is the name of the fearsome private boarding school run by the brutish ***Wackford Squeers*** and his wife in the novel *Nicholas Nickleby* (1839) by Charles Dickens. The outrage provoked by Dickens's novel led to the closure of many such schools in real life. *He remembered his school as a real-life Dotheboys Hall where the boys suffered regular thrashings and other humiliations.*

do thou likewise *See* GO AND DO THOU LIKEWISE.

doublespeak The use of language to conceal the truth. The origins of the word lie ultimately in George Orwell's vision of a nightmarish future in his novel *Nineteen Eighty-Four* (1949), in which he introduced the concepts of DOUBLETHINK and NEWSPEAK to describe the dishonest use of language by a totalitarian government in order to subdue the population. The word "doublespeak" does not appear in Orwell's book, but was coined by others in the early 1970s, who were inspired to combine the author's doublethink and newspeak to form a new word encompassing the meaning of both. "In this typical example of scientific doublespeak, the burden of proof is, as usual, thrown on to conservationists to show that a fishing technique has an unacceptable effect, rather than on the fishing nations to show that the method is ecologically sound" (Michael Donoghue and Annie Wheeler, *Dolphins: Their Life and Survival*, 1990).

doublethink The hypocritical holding of contradictory ideas or beliefs at the same time, as achieved through propaganda and political indoctrination. The phrase was introduced by George Orwell in his futuristic novel *Nineteen Eighty-Four* (1949). "Doublethink had entered so completely into Ceausescu's soul by the 1980s that he could genuinely bask in what he took to be sincere affection at the same time as he knew how stage-managed the whole event was" (Mark Almond, *The Rise and Fall of Nicolae and Elena Ceausescu*, 1992). *See also* DOUBLESPEAK; NEWSPEAK; THOUGHT POLICE.

double whammy (wamee) A twofold blow, or one with double the impact. Widely heard in the 1990s, the term double whammy (or even ***triple whammy***) provoked much debate as to its actual meaning and origins. Perhaps its earliest appearance was in the Al Capp comic strip *L'il Abner* in July 1951, in which the character Evil-Eye Fleegle explains what it means: "*Evil-Eye Fleegle* is th' name, an' th' '*whammy*' is my game. Mudder Nature endowed me wit' eyes which can putrefy citizens t' th' spot! . . . There is th' '*single whammy*'! *That*, friend, is th' full, *pure power* o' *one* o' my evil eyes! It's *dynamite*, friend, an' I do not t'row it around lightly! . . . And, lastly—th' '*double whammy*'—namely, th' *full power o' both eyes*—which I hopes I never *hafta* use." *This announcement of job losses is a double whammy for the unions, who were already reeling from a loss of support among members.*

doubting Thomas (tomăs) A person who remains unconvinced about something until firm proof is proffered. The allusion is to the biblical Thomas, the apostle who declined to believe in Christ's resurrection until allowed to see and touch Christ's wounds for himself: "But he said unto them, Except I shall see in his hands the print of the nails, and put my finger into the print of the nails, and thrust my hand into his side, I will not believe" (John 20:25). Christ eventually showed himself so that Thomas might satisfy his doubts but rebuked him for his lack of faith. *His uncle remained stubbornly unconvinced and it seemed nothing would persuade this doubting Thomas.*

do unto others *See* GOLDEN RULE.

dove of peace A symbol of peace and reconciliation. The association between doves and peace is biblical in origin, arising from the story of the dove that was sent out by Noah to see if the Flood was receding (Genesis 8:8–12). When the dove returned with an olive branch in its beak, Noah interpreted this as a sign that God was reconciled with humankind once more and that the waters were retreating. Because the Holy Spirit descended to Christ in the form of a dove at his baptism, the bird may also be treated as a symbol of the Holy Spirit, purity, or divine inspiration. *The dove of peace has settled on this land today and the sound of gunfire is heard no more. See also* OLIVE BRANCH.

down for the count Out of contention, finally overwhelmed. The allusion is to boxing and the flooring of a fighter in the ring as the seconds are counted out: he is declared the loser if he cannot rise before ten seconds have passed. The phrase is also commonly employed, sometimes in the variant form ***out for the count***, to describe someone who has fallen asleep and is deemed unlikely to wake up any time soon. *They got back late last night and are still down for the count.*

down the rabbit hole Into a weird or surreal situation. The allusion is to Lewis Carroll's *Alice's Adventures in Wonderland* (1865), in which Alice finds herself in a strange fantasy world after following the White Rabbit into its rabbit hole. *He felt like he had fallen down the rabbit hole when he realized just what was expected of him in his new role. See also* ALICE IN WONDERLAND.

draconian (drăkōneeăn, draykōneeăn) Excessively harsh or severe. The word alludes to Draco, the lawyer who in 621 B.C. drew up the first written code of justice for his fellow Athenians. The laws imposed in Draco's name, supposedly written in blood rather than ink, were notorious for their severity, with the death sentence being imposed for even relatively petty offenses, hence the modern use of the term *draconian*. In reality, Draco's code did not last very long, and in 590 B.C. a less exacting code of laws was devised by the Athenian statesman Solon. Although popular in his own time for putting the law in some kind of order, albeit harsh, Draco himself came to a premature end when he was smothered under the heaps of garments and flowers that admiring

Athenians showered on him during a visit to the theater. "Such an attitude should hearten China's draconian womb police, who have spent two decades trying to control the nation's burgeoning population through any means possible" (*Time,* July 30, 2001).

Dracula (drakyoolă) An evil-minded person who drains others dry of money, ideas, etc. The evil Count Dracula was created by Bram Stoker in his novel *Dracula* (1879), in which he is depicted as a hypnotic bloodsucking vampire of Transylvania who can only be killed by having a stake driven through his heart or by exposure to sunlight. The story inspired numerous films and Dracula has long since entered modern world folklore as one of the most terrifying yet strangely seductive of supernatural monsters. Stoker is said to have drawn on various inspirations for his famous creation, among them stories surrounding the historical Transylvanian ruler ***Vlad the Impaler*** (1470–76) and a visit to Slains Castle near Aberdeen, which provided a model for Dracula's castle. In modern usage, anyone with a similar cadaverous complexion, black hair, and dark clothing may be likened to Dracula, regardless of his or her actual character. "Under a massive front-page headline, HUNT FOR DRACULA FIEND (*Star*), the report indicated that a 13-year-old was able to tell detectives that her attacker 'had short dark hair streaked with grey and deep-set eyes that made him "look a bit like Dracula"'" (S. Walby and K. Soothill, *Sex Crime in the News*, 1991).

dragon's teeth *See* SOW DRAGON'S TEETH.

dreadnought A powerful battleship. The launching of HMS *Dreadnought* in 1906 heralded the introduction of a whole new class of battleships in the Royal Navy, collectively known as dreadnoughts. Faster and better armed than any other ships then sailing the seas, the dreadnoughts outclassed all opponents and triggered a naval arms race as other nations sought to match this new threat. Since that era large naval vessels of various kinds have often been referred to as dreadnoughts. *The U.S. Navy will send in its dreadnoughts to dissuade powers in the region from starting anything.*

Dresden (drezdăn) Archetype of a city destroyed by war. The bombing of the historic city of Dresden in eastern Germany by Allied aircraft on February 13, 1945 remains one of the most controversial episodes of World War II, especially since the city had little military significance. Most of the city was destroyed in the firestorm that resulted from the bombing and many thousands of its citizens were killed. *No one wanted Sarajevo to be turned into a second Dresden.*

Dreyfus, Alfred *See* J'ACCUSE.

drink hemlock To voluntarily sacrifice oneself by resigning, committing suicide, etc. The phrase alludes to the death of the Athenian philosopher Socrates (469–399 B.C.), who was obliged to kill himself by drinking hemlock after speaking out against the ruling elite in Athens and being sentenced to death at the subsequent trial. *The head of the party took the honorable way out, drinking hemlock by giving up his post and throwing himself on the mercy of the press.*

droit du seigneur (drwah dă saynyer) A person's right to take the first share in something or have the first say. The allusion is to the (largely apocryphal) belief that in certain medieval European countries a feudal lord had the right to have sex with the bride of any of his vassals on her wedding night. Nowadays, the term is applied to any person who exercises a privilege at the expense of others, particularly when this is seen as being overbearing or unjust. *The director exercised his droit du seigneur and took first choice of the company cars.*

drop in the ocean A tiny or insignificant amount; something that makes little real difference. The phrase is biblical in origin, having its roots in Isaiah 40:15, which compares the relatively minor importance of nations with the immense grandeur of God: "Behold, the nations are as a drop of a bucket, and are counted as the small dust of the balance: behold, he taketh up the isles as a very little thing." "And what is our life? One line in the great story of the Church, whose son and daughter we are; one handful in the sand of time, one drop in the ocean of 'For ever'" (Charles Reade, *The Cloister and the Hearth,* 1861).

dryad *See* NYMPH.

dry bones, valley of *See* VALLEY OF DRY BONES.

DuBois, Blanche *See* BLANCHE DUBOIS.

dulce et decorum est pro patria mori (doolkay et dekorăm est prō patreeă moree) It is sweet and becoming to die for one's country. This patriotic sentiment is a quotation from the *Odes* of Horace (65–8 B.C.). In modern times, however, the phrase is frequently encountered as an ironic invocation of the virtue of patriotic valor, sometimes in the abbreviated form ***dulce et decorum est***. It is often associated with the slaughter of World War I, having been taken up as the title of one of the most celebrated poems of Wilfred Owen (1893–1918), a description of a gas attack written shortly before his death in the final week of the war: "My friend, you would not tell with such high zest / To children ardent for some desperate glory, / The old Lie: *Dulce et decorum est / Pro patria mori.*" "My breast heaved—my form dilated—my eye flashed as I spoke these words. 'Tyrants!' said I, 'dulce et decorum est pro patria mori.' Having thus clinched the argument, I was silent" (William Makepeace Thackeray, *The Adventures of Major Gahagan,* 1839).

Dulcinea (dălsinayă) A sweetheart, especially one of humble origins. Dulcinea is the name bestowed upon a pretty young village girl otherwise called Aldonza Lorenzo by the romantic idealist DON QUIXOTE, who conceives an unrealistic passion for her in the comic novel *Don Quixote* (1605, 1615) by Miguel de Cervantes Saavedra. The name itself is based on the Spanish *dulce*, meaning "sweet." "Well, sir, 'come what come might,' I stole under cover of the darkness to the dwelling of my Dulcinea. All was quiet. At the concerted signal her window was gently opened" (Washington Irving, *Tales of a Traveller*, 1824).

Dunkirk (dănkerk) A miraculous escape from disaster, especially one involving the successful retreat of a substantial armed force. The allusion is to the rescue of the surrounded British army from Dunkirk, on the northeast coast of France, in early June 1940 during World War II. Around 340,000 men were brought back to Britain, many of them in small boats sent over from the ports of southern England. The success of the operation meant that a German invasion of Britain would be much more difficult. A substantial victory of sorts was thus snatched from the jaws of defeat, and ever since then, people in times of crisis have been urged to show some ***Dunkirk spirit***. *Not* *since Dunkirk has such a large force been rescued from so extreme a crisis.*

dust, unto *See* UNTO DUST SHALT THOU RETURN.

dust bowl The Great Plains area of the central United States. The nickname was heard with increasing frequency from the 1930s, when the agriculture of this prairie region was devastated by prolonged drought, causing severe hardship to the local population. The term has since been applied to various parts of the world that have suffered similar droughts. *The Chinese government is concerned that environmental changes may bring about dust bowl conditions.*

dust to dust *See* UNTO DUST SHALT THOU RETURN.

dybbuk (dibăk) A demonic spirit or machine that has the power to take over a person. The dybbuk appeared early in the annals of Jewish folklore, being described originally as a type of malevolent wandering soul that could possess a living person until formally exorcised. The term became more widely familiar through the classic Yiddish play *The Dybbuk* (1920) by Solomon Ansky. *His grandmother decided that his behavior was so untypical the only explanation was that he had been taken over by a dybbuk.*

E

Earhart, Amelia *See* AMELIA EARHART.

ears to hear The ability to hear or understand. The phrase is biblical in origin, coming from Matthew 13:43, and on certain other occasions at the conclusion of Jesus' parables: "Who hath ears to hear, let him hear." A misprint in an 1810 version of the Bible that read "Who hath ears to ear, let him hear" led to that version being known as the "Ears to Ear Bible." "One of those wretches whose hearts the Lord had hardened, who, having ears, heard not, having eyes, saw not, and who should find no place for repentance though they sought it even with their tears" (Samuel Butler, *The Way of All Flesh,* 1903). *The headmaster said, "If any student has ears to hear, then will he please note the school rule that smoking is strictly forbidden on all school premises at all times."*

earthshaking Momentous; of fundamental importance. The notion that some events and ideas are so important they make the earth shake has its roots in Greek mythology. The sea god Poseidon was often referred to as "Earthshaker" because he could raise storms and tidal waves. Homer also identified Poseidon as the god of earthquakes. *This discovery could have earthshaking consequences for everyone involved in deep space research.*

ease in Zion *See* AT EASE IN ZION.

east is east and west is west Sometimes there is no alternative but to accept the essential difference between two parties. The phrase is usually (though not always) used in reference to the contrasting cultures of Western and Eastern civilizations. It first appeared in Rudyard Kipling's "The Ballad of East and West" (1892): "Oh, East is East, and West is West, and never the twain shall meet." *You'd think this kind of thing would be frowned upon anywhere in the world, but east is east and west is west, as they say.*

East Lynne (lin) An overtly sentimental, melodramatic tale or situation. The novel *East Lynne* (1861) by Mrs. Henry Wood told the tearjerking story of a mother who deserts her family for a new lover, but then returns in disguise to care for her children. It was hugely popular with 19th-century audiences both as a novel and a play, and though little read today is remembered as the archetype of lachrymose melodrama. "Sa-a-ay, girl, this ain't goin' t' be no scene from East Lynne. Be a good kid. The rest of the bunch can go" (Edna Ferber, *Dawn O'Hara*, 1911). *See also* DEAD . . . AND NEVER CALLED ME MOTHER!

east of Eden (eedăn) A featureless, desolate place or situation; a place of wandering or exile. According to Genesis 4:16, it was to an area "on the east of Eden" that Cain was exiled after he murdered his brother Abel. The phrase is best known today as the title of a 1952 novel by John Steinbeck that relates the events that unfold after Adam Trask moves to California with his warring sons Caleb and Aaron. *He lives somewhere east of Eden, out beyond the bounds of civilized society. See also* LAND OF NOD.

eat crow To have to apologize or do something humiliating. The allusion is to a probably apocryphal event that is said to have occurred during the War of 1812, in which a New Englander accidentally crossed the British lines while hunting and shot a crow. A British officer took the American's gun from him and then forced him to take a bite out of the crow as punishment for his trespassing. When the American was given his gun back, he immediately pointed it at his tormentor and forced him to eat what was left of the bird. The phrase has not been traced back further than the 1870s and is unlikely to be as old as it is sometimes claimed to be. Another version of the story sets it in the time of the Civil War during the 1860s, with the two people concerned being a Federal soldier and a Southern plantation owner. *It looks like the manager will be forced to eat crow if he is to keep his position.*

eat, drink, and be merry Enjoy yourself while you have the chance. The expression comes from the parable of the rich fool related at Luke 12:16–21, in which Christ describes a rich farmer who stores up his wealth for future indulgence and dies before ever enjoying the benefits of it. The parable serves as a warning to those who see the enjoyment of material wealth rather than devotion to God as the ultimate ambition of their lives. The phrase also appears at Ecclesiastes 8:15 in the form "a man hath no better thing under the sun, than to eat, and to drink, and to be merry." In modern usage the phrase is equally likely to be quoted as a criticism of those who indulge in worldly pleasures without thought for the future and, paradoxically, as a justification by those making the most of an immediate opportunity to indulge themselves in the knowledge that the chance may not be there for long. The sentiment is often extended to ***eat, drink, and be merry, for tomorrow we die***, as found in Isaiah 22:13 and 1 Corinthians 15:32. "Such a man, nevertheless, was the Reverend Samuel Pentecost, and such a woman was the Reverend Samuel's mother; and in the dearth of any other producible guests, there they were, engaged to eat, drink, and be merry for the day at Mr. Armadale's pleasure party to the Norfolk Broads" (Wilkie Collins, *Armadale,* 1866).

eater, out of the *See* OUT OF THE STRONG CAME FORTH SWEETNESS.

eat from the tree of knowledge *See* TREE OF KNOWLEDGE.

Ebenezer chapel (ebăneezer) A Nonconformist chapel. This informal title alludes to the biblical episode related in 1 Samuel 7:12 in the course of which Samuel sets up a memorial stone in thanks to God for his victory over the Philistines, giving it the name Ebenezer (meaning "stone of help") and explaining, "Thus far has the LORD helped us." *The family attended the local Ebenezer chapel and took their religion very seriously.*

ecce homo (ekay hōmō) A depiction of Christ wearing a crown of thorns. A Latin phrase usually translated as "behold the man," it appears in John 19:5 as the words spoken by Pontius Pilate when he presented Christ to the people. In modern usage, the phrase is sometimes applied in both its Latin and English forms more widely to any person who is presently a subject of attention. *"Ecce homo!" exclaimed the bishop as the inspector entered the room.*

echo A repetition of a sound or other radiation when reflected by some solid medium; any repetition or imitation of an idea, event, etc. In Greek mythology, Echo was a mountain nymph who fell in love with the beautiful youth Narcissus but wasted away when he ignored her until all that was left of her was her voice. *The echo of breaking glass reverberated through the empty house.*

Eden, Garden of *See* GARDEN OF EDEN.

Edison (edisăn) A brilliant inventor. Thomas Alva Edison (1847–1931) is famous for his many epoch-making inventions, which included the electric light, the telephone transmitter, and the phonograph. On most occasions, however, his name is employed sarcastically to ridicule the underachievements of those whose inventions fall well short of the original Edison's record. *The classroom was full of budding Edisons, none of whom had the faintest idea of how to put their scintillating ideas into practice.*

Edsel (edsăl) A disappointing failure, an anticlimax. Edsel B. Ford (1893–1943) was the son of the pioneer U.S. car manufacturer Henry Ford. In 1957 much publicity attended the launch of a new Ford model, called the Edsel in honor of the founder's late son. Unfortunately, the new car failed catastrophically to win favor and its name became a synonym for a disastrous flop, especially one that is announced with great fanfare. *This latest model looks like being damned as the Edsel of home breadmakers.*

Eeyore (eeor) A person with a melancholic, pessimistic nature. The original Eeyore was a gloomy gray donkey in the *Winnie-the-Pooh* stories written by A. A. Milne in the 1920s. Seemingly resigned to eternal disappointment in life, he was allegedly inspired by Sir Owen Seaman (1861–1936), the editor of *Punch* under whom Milne worked for eight years. *Her grandfather had always been a bit of an Eeyore, pooh-poohing any expression of hope for the future.*

Egeria (ăjeereeă) A woman counselor or adviser. According to Roman mythology, the original Egeria was a nymph who gave valuable advice to Numa Pompilius (753–673 B.C.), the second king of Rome; thus, her name is sometimes cited in describing any female source of inspiration. "Thus, false to his nation, yet true to the new Egeria of his thoughts and actions—traitor to the requirements of vengeance and war, yet faithful to the interests of tranquillity and love—did he seek, night after night, Antonina's presence" (Wilkie Collins, *Antonina,* 1850).

Egyptian darkness (ăjipshăn) Impenetrable darkness. The phrase alludes to the all-enveloping darkness that fell upon Egypt at God's command, constituting the ninth of the 10 plagues with which the Egyptians were afflicted, according to Exodus 7–12. The phrase may sometimes also describe deep melancholy or some other mental state making a person's thoughts inaccessible to others. "And one, more grave, lost in a man's hat and feather, walked in Egyptian darkness, handed by a girl; another had the great saucepan on his back, and a tremendous three-footed clay-pot sat on his head and shoulders, swallowing him so as he too went darkling led by his sweetheart three foot high" (Charles Reade, *The Cloister and the Hearth,* 1861). *See also* NINTH PLAGUE OF EGYPT; PLAGUES OF EGYPT.

Egyptian gold (ăjipshăn) Something of value whose theft or borrowing from its former owners is felt to be justified on the grounds that it may now be put to better use. The phrase alludes to the theft of jewels and vessels of gold and silver from the Egyptians on the flight of the Israelites from the country, as described in Exodus 12:35. Some Christian theologians interpreted the episode as justification for borrowing from pagan tradition anything that could be put to a better Christian purpose. *This Egyptian gold was now put to much better use, funding the establishment of various small enterprises throughout the region that otherwise might never have found backing.*

Egypt's firstborn *See* PLAGUES OF EGYPT.

eighth wonder of the world An outstanding edifice or achievement of some kind; alternatively and ironically, a remarkable failure. The ancient world boasted just seven wonders, as recorded by the Greek historian Herodotus in the fifth century B.C. Although his was not the only list and there was some debate about what should be included prior to medieval times, the list is now generally accepted as including the Pyramids at Giza, the Hanging Gardens of Babylon, the Statue of Zeus at Olympia, the Temple of Artemis at Ephesus, the Mausoleum of Halicarnassus, the Colossus of Rhodes, and the Pharos of Alexandria. Many lists of remarkable buildings or other feats have since been compiled following much the same pattern. "A handsome man was an eighth wonder of the world, at Miss Wigger's school" (Wilkie Collins, *Evil Genius,* 1886).

Einstein (īnstīn) A person with a brilliant mind, especially one who excels in science. The German-born U.S. physicist Albert Einstein (1879–1955) was the archetypal eccentric scientific genius, making important breakthroughs relating to relativity, space and time, and energy. In modern usage, his name is usually invoked sarcastically to challenge someone's intellectual pretensions: *All right, Einstein, show us how it's done if you're so clever.*

Elba A place of exile, especially one of a temporary nature. The island of Elba is located in the Mediterranean west of Tuscany in Italy and is famous chiefly as the place to which the deposed French emperor NAPOLEON was exiled in 1814. He remained there for just 10 months before escaping and rallying his troops for his final campaign (*see* HUNDRED DAYS), which ended at the Battle of WATERLOO in 1815 and was followed by another (this time permanent) exile on the island of SAINT HELENA. *Her disgraced husband was exiled for the rest of the summer to his personal Elba, a resort in the Florida Keys.*

Eldorado (eldărahdō) A source of immense wealth. Spanish conquistadors of the 16th century were captivated by tales of a fabulous city or country of gold supposedly located somewhere in Peru, although repeated expeditions deep into the South American jungle by both Spanish and English adventurers failed to reveal any such place. The name Eldorado (meaning "the gilded one") has since been applied to any source of fabulous riches and, more loosely, to any illusory paradise said to offer a life of ease and luxury. "Would it not be well to call Jack, and hear his account of the matter once more, now we appear to be so near the Eldorado of our wishes?" (James Fenimore Cooper, *Jack Tier*, 1848).

Electra complex (ălektră) The subconscious sexual attraction of a daughter to her father or a father figure, often to the exclusion of the mother. This Freudian concept takes its name from the Greek myth about Electra, which was brought to life in great dramas by Aeschylus, Euripides, and Sophocles. Electra was the daughter of Agamemnon, king of Mycenae, and Clytemnestra. Electra helped her brother Orestes kill their mother and her lover after Clytemnestra had murdered their father. *She gave up on her psychoanalyst and stormed off in a high temper after he had the temerity to suggest she might be suffering from some kind of an Electra complex. See also* OEDIPUS COMPLEX.

elementary, my dear Watson The conclusion reached is obvious. This somewhat overused expression alludes to the detective stories of Sir Arthur Conan Doyle, in which it is supposedly said by his observant sleuth SHERLOCK HOLMES to his slower-witted companion DOCTOR WATSON, typically decrying the latter's astonishment at the detective's brilliant deductive powers. In reality, the phrase does not appear in its popular form anywhere in the *Sherlock Holmes* tales (although on one occasion Holmes does remark "Elementary!" to Watson, in the 1894 story "The Crooked Man"). In its usual form the expression appears to date back to the 1929 film *The Return of Sherlock Holmes*, which ends with the line "Elementary, my dear Watson, elementary." In modern usage, the phrase is often employed with sarcastic intent after someone has made a completely obvious connection. *Of course you have to turn the computer back on before the new program is installed—elementary, my dear Watson!*

Elephant Man A grotesquely ugly individual. The original Elephant Man was Joseph Merrick (1862–90), whose facial deformities (probably the result of the rare Proteus syndrome) made him a fairground attraction and the subject of considerable interest to the medical establishment of 19th-century Britain. Awareness of the tragic life story of Joseph Merrick grew with the release of the 1980 film *The Elephant Man*, and unwittingly promoted use of the epithet as a jocular insult directed at anyone with less than perfectly attractive looks. *He asked her to go out with him, but she said she wouldn't be seen dead with the Elephant Man.*

Eleusinian mystery (elyoosineeăn) Any obscure ritual or process. The original Eleusinian mysteries were the rituals observed in strict secrecy in honor of the corn goddess Demeter and her daughter Persephone at Eleusis, near Athens. Only the participants knew what took place at the rituals. The purpose of the rites was to ensure divine protection of crops in the year ahead. The rituals, which also had significance for devotees of Dionysus, were eventually abolished by the emperor Theodosius toward the end of the fourth century A.D. "They were, and felt themselves to be, the only true depositaries left of certain Eleusinian mysteries, of certain deep and wondrous services of worship by which alone the gods could be rightly approached" (Anthony Trollope, *Barchester Towers,* 1857).

eleventh hour, at the *See* AT THE ELEVENTH HOUR.

Elijah (ălījă) A prophet, especially one who foresees coming disaster. The biblical prophet Elijah warned King Ahab of a forthcoming drought (1 Kings 17:1) and mocked the king's false prophets (1 Kings 18:27) and their god Baal before fleeing the country. *This Elijah on the loose stormed* *through the Capitol, haranguing any member of Congress who ventured out of his or her office to see what the commotion was. See also* CHARIOT OF FIRE; MANTLE OF ELIJAH.

Elijah's fiery chariot *See* CHARIOT OF FIRE.

Elijah's mantle *See* MANTLE OF ELIJAH.

Eliot Ness *See* UNTOUCHABLE.

Elisha (ălīshă) A devoted follower; a disciple. According to 2 Kings 2:13, Elisha was the son of a prosperous farmer who was made the heir of Elijah when the latter rose to heaven in a fiery chariot. His name may also be invoked when a person is taunted of the grounds of baldness, Elisha being himself bald headed. *He was surprised to find that in the intervening years his cousin had lost all his hair and was now as bald as Elisha.*

Elizabeth Bennet *See* MR. DARCY.

Eliza Doolittle (ălīză doolităl) A woman who seeks to transform herself socially. The allusion is to the fictional character of the name created by George Bernard Shaw in his play *Pygmalion* (1913), and later reintroduced in the musical based on Shaw's play, *My Fair Lady* (*see* PYGMALION). Shaw's Eliza Doolittle is a humble flower vendor who becomes the subject of an experiment to pass her off in polite society by working on her use of language. *She rose like Eliza Doolittle from the gutter to the heights of society.*

Ellis Island *See* STATUE OF LIBERTY.

Elmer Gantry Archetype of an evangelizing preacher. The name is a reference to the 1927 novel *Elmer Gantry* by Sinclair Lewis about the impact of a charismatic evangelist upon his legion of female admirers. *His family had come under the disastrous influence of an Elmer Gantry who seemed bent on parting them from their life savings.*

Elm Street *See* NIGHTMARE ON ELM STREET.

Elvis the Pelvis *See* KING, THE.

elysian fields (ălīzhăn) Heaven, paradise, or some other idyllic place. ***Elysium*** (meaning "happy, delightful") was the name of paradise in Greek and Roman mythology, a pastoral place situated "at the world's end" and ruled by Rhadamanthus, judge of the dead. At Elysium heroes could take their ease after death. It is described as a place of perpetual springtime and sunlight, where there are no storms, rain, or snow. The name has since been featured in a number of addresses in the real world, among them the Champs-Elysées in Paris and the Elysian Fields district of New Orleans. "To the eyes of the frequenters of these Elysian fields, where so many men and shadows daily steal recreation, to the eyes of all drinking in those green gardens their honeyed draught of peace, this husband and wife appeared merely a distinguished-looking couple, animated by a leisured harmony" (John Galsworthy, *The Forsyte Saga,* 1922).

éminence grise (ayminahns greez) A guiding hand behind the scenes, someone who exercises real power from the shadows. Historically, the phrase éminence grise (or "gray eminence") came to be associated particularly with François Joseph Leclerc du Tremblay (1577–1638), a gray-habited priest who served as right-hand man to Cardinal Richelieu in the first half of the 17th century and was widely believed to wield considerable influence over the policies espoused by the cardinal in his role as head of the French government. Since that time, the term (in both its English and its French forms) has been routinely applied to people who are suspected of exerting a controlling influence out of the general public view. *The press sought a response from the president's secretary, considered by many to be an éminence grise behind the throne.*

Emma Bovary *See* MADAME BOVARY.

emperor's new clothes Something that is accepted as real, though actually lacking any reality at all. The allusion is to a fairy tale of the same title written by the Danish writer HANS CHRISTIAN ANDERSEN in 1836. The story relates how two cunning weavers fool their emperor into buying robes made of a fabric so fine it is impossible to see, when actually the fabric is entirely nonexistent. When the emperor parades in what he thinks are his fine new clothes, most of the crowd (warned that only stupid people unfit for office cannot see the material) convince themselves that indeed he looks very smart, wilfully ignoring the fact that he is naked. *I have read the opposing party's policies and as far as I am concerned it appears to be a case of the emperor's new clothes.*

empiric A person who pretends to be something he or she is not; a quack. The word was applied originally to the school of medicine founded by Serapion of Alexandria (c. 200–150 B.C.), who placed particular emphasis on observation and experiment in treatment rather than on the opinions of conventional medical authorities. This led to the practitioners of this school acquiring reputations as quacks. "He once more endeavored to pass the supposed empiric, scorning even the parade of threatening to use the knife, or tomahawk, that was pendent from his belt" (James Fenimore Cooper, *The Last of the Mohicans,* 1826).

empty the vials of one's wrath *See* VIALS OF WRATH.

empyrean (emp<u>ī</u>reeăn) Alternative name for heaven or the heavens. The Greek astronomer, mathematician, and geographer Ptolemy (second century A.D.) developed the theory that there are five heavens, the fifth of which (the Empyrean) is the abode of God himself. This ultimate heaven is supposedly composed of elemental fire, hence its name, derived from the Greek *empuros* (meaning "fiery"). In modern usage the word is often employed in references to the sky. "She would be able to arrange her life as she pleased, to soar into that empyrean of security where creditors cannot penetrate" (Edith Wharton, *The House of Mirth,* 1905).

encomium (en<u>kō</u>meeăm) A hymn of praise; a eulogy. The word is Greek in origin, being derived from *komos* (meaning "revel"). In ancient Greece encomiums were usually delivered in praise of victors of the Olympic Games as they were carried home in triumph. "He said the alliance was such as he sincerely wished; then launched forth into a very just encomium on the young lady's merit" (Henry Fielding, *Tom Jones,* 1749).

end is not yet, the There is more yet to happen before something is finished. The expression is biblical in origin, appearing in Matthew 24:6: "And ye shall hear of wars and rumours of wars: see that ye be not troubled: for all these things must come to pass, but the end is not yet." "'I joke very seldom,' Blunt protested earnestly. 'That's why I haven't mentioned His Majesty—whom

God preserve. That would have been an exaggeration. . . . However, the end is not yet. We were talking about the beginning' " (Joseph Conrad, *The Arrow of Gold,* 1919).

end of the beginning An event that signals the start of slow progress toward the eventual completion of something, though that may still be a very long way off. The allusion is to a speech delivered by Winston Churchill on November 10, 1942, greeting news of the Allied victory against Nazi Germany at El Alamein: "This is not the end. It is not even the beginning of the end. But it is, perhaps, the end of the beginning." Churchill may have had in mind a speech delivered nearly 150 years earlier by the French statesman Talleyrand, in which he greeted the news that Napoleon had been defeated in battle with the words "It is the beginning of the end." *Well, we might have a long way to go, but I think we can call this the end of the beginning.*

end of the rainbow A distant, almost unreachable paradise where all the problems of life are finally solved. The allusion is to the traditional belief that a pot of gold lies buried at the point where a rainbow touches the earth, if only the viewer can get to it before the rainbow moves on. The notion was substantially expanded in the 1939 film *The Wizard of Oz*, which located the magical land of Oz "somewhere over the rainbow." *She dreams that some day she will reach the end of the rainbow and she will be able to leave behind her troubled past.* *See also* WIZARD OF OZ.

Endor, Witch of *See* WITCH OF ENDOR.

Endymion (endimeeăn) The archetype of a beautiful young man. In Greek mythology, Endymion was a handsome young shepherd who attracted the attention of the moon goddess Selene while sleeping on Mount Latmus. Having fallen passionately in love with Endymion, Selene begged Zeus to grant the youth a wish. Wishing to remain perpetually youthful, Endymion asked for the gift of eternal sleep. Selene was thus able to embrace him each night without him knowing. Today his name is most familiar from the celebrated poem *Endymion* (1818) by John Keats. *Washed and restored, he looked like some young Endymion, so it was doubly unfortunate when he turned out to have the table manners of a satyr.*

enemy of the people A person whose anarchic or reformist views place him or her outside popular society and thus vulnerable to official persecution. The allusion is to Henrik Ibsen's 1882 play *An Enemy of the People*, which concerns the efforts of a local doctor to close a profit-making municipal bath because of the risk it poses to public health. The threat of financial collapse unites popular opinion against the doctor, who finds himself rejected by the rest of society. "There was no one to understand; no one he could take into the confidence of Decoud's fate, of his own, into the secret of the silver. That doctor was an enemy of the people—a tempter . . ." (Joseph Conrad, *Nostromo*, 1904).

enforcer *See* MURDER, INC.

England expects It is a matter of honor to perform the duty that presents itself. The allusion is to the signal that Admiral NELSON had hoisted from his flagship HMS *Victory* at the start of the Battle of Trafalgar on October 21, 1805: "England expects that every man will do his duty." In fact, Nelson's original message had contained the word "confides," but this was changed to "expects" as the latter was much easier to convey using signal flags. *England Expects that Every Man will Do His Duty and Join the Army Today* (World War I recruiting poster).

Enid Blyton (eenid blītăn) Childish or sickly sweet in character. The allusion is to the best-selling children's novels of the British writer Enid Blyton (1897–1968), creator of such characters as Noddy and the FAMOUS FIVE. Though decried by critics and other adults for their simplistic, sentimental style and unchallenging, unrealistic plots, her stories were hugely popular with children around the world and are still widely read today. *That film was a bit too Enid Blyton for me.*

Enlightenment A liberal, tolerant mode of thinking. The Enlightenment was an intellectual and literary movement of the 17th and 18th centuries that championed reason and freedom of thought in preference to more restrictive traditional approaches toward politics, religion, etc. Modern Western civilization depends largely upon the ideals of the Enlightenment, and the term is now widely used in its allusive sense. *This forward-looking policy is a product of modern Enlightenment thinking.*

Ennius (eneeăs) Epithet sometimes applied to a poet or writer considered to be the founder of, or first outstanding figure in, a nation's literature. The original Ennius (239–169 B.C.) was a Roman writer who was dubbed the Father of Roman Poetry by his admirers. Later writers considered to share such a founding role included England's Layamon (fl. 1200) and Geoffrey Chaucer (c.1340–1400), France's Guillaume de Lorris (fl. 1230) and Jean de Meun (c. 1240–c. 1305), and Spain's Juan de Mena (1411–56). *Who is the German Ennius? Wagner presumably thought it was Hans Sachs.*

Enoch (eenok) An upright, virtuous man. According to Genesis 5:21–24, Enoch was the father of Methuselah; he is described as one who "walked with God." Enoch and Elijah were both taken away into the presence of God without experiencing death (2 Kings 2:11; Hebrews 11:5). ". . . I, in whose daily life you discern the sanctity of Enoch—I, whose footsteps, as you suppose, leave a gleam along my earthly track, whereby the Pilgrims that shall come after me may be guided to the regions of the blest" (Nathaniel Hawthorne, *The Scarlet Letter,* 1850).

enter into one's closet To retire to a private place, especially for prayer or contemplation. The phrase comes from Christ's Sermon on the Mount, as related in Matthew 6:6, in which Christ urges the faithful to pray in private rather than in public, where they may be tempted to do so only to impress others: ". . . when thou prayest, enter into thy closet, and when thou hast shut thy door, pray to thy Father which is in secret; and thy Father which seeth in secret shall reward thee openly." *At the bishop's invitation the two men entered into his closet so that their conversation might not be overheard.*

Eos *See* AURORA.

epicurean (epikyooreeăn) Having a refined taste in food and wine. The word alludes to the Greek philosopher Epicurus (341–270 B.C.), who encouraged his followers to indulge in simple pleasures with moderation and self-control, although his suggestion that the pursuit of pleasure is the primary goal of life means that *epicurean* today is often interpreted as signifying unrestricted hedonistic indulgence in physical pleasure. By the same token, any person who is believed to have discrimination in food matters may be described as an ***epicure.*** "Rose knew very well that the Epicurean philosophy was not the true one to begin life upon, but it was difficult to reason with Charlie because he always dodged sober subjects and was so full of cheery spirits, one hated to lessen the sort of sunshine which certainly is a public benefactor" (Louisa May Alcott, *Rose in Bloom,* 1876).

epiphany (epifānee) A revelatory appearance, manifestation, or realization. In the Bible the word is applied to the presentation of the infant Christ to the Three Wise Men (Matthew 2:11), as commemorated by the Feast of Epiphany (commonly called Twelfth Night) on January 6. The word itself comes from the Greek *epiphaneia* (meaning "manifestation"). *This epiphany was followed by the most extraordinary and unexpected series of events.*

epithalamium (epithălaymeeăm) A wedding song. In ancient Greece such songs were sung by young boys and girls outside the bridal chamber. The genre was developed by such classical poets as Pindar and Sappho circa the sixth century B.C. and was adopted many centuries later by such notable writers as Edmund Spenser, whose wedding poem *Epithalamion* (1595) is counted among his finest works. "And then, with one of those extraordinary transitions of which I have already spoken, she again threw off her veil, and broke out, after the ancient and poetic fashion of the dwellers in Arabia, into a paean of triumph, or epithalamium, which, wild and beautiful as it was, is exceedingly difficult to render into English, and ought by rights to be sung to the music of a cantata, rather than written and read" (H. Rider Haggard, *She,* 1887).

e pluribus unum (ee plooribăs oonăm) Out of many (made) one. This line from "Moretum," a Latin poem attributed to the Roman poet Virgil (70–19 B.C.), is best known today as the motto on the seal of the United States of America. "The more you examine the structure of the organs and the laws of life, the more you will find how resolutely each of the cell-republics which make up the E pluribus unum of the body maintains its independence" (Oliver Wendell Holmes, *Medical Essays,* 1883).

Erato *See* MUSES.

Erebus (erebăs) Darkness. In Greek mythololgy Erebus was the personification of dark, the brother of Nyx (night) and son of Chaos. His name was later applied to the gloomy caverns through which the souls of the dead had to pass on their way to HADES and eventually became more or less synonymous with hell. "Walking to the taffrail, I was in time to make out, on the very edge of a darkness thrown by a towering black mass like the very gateway of Erebus" (Joseph Conrad, *The Secret Sharer,* 1912).

Erinyes *See* FURIES.

Eris *See* APPLE OF DISCORD.

erotic Provoking sexual desire. The word comes from the name of the Greek god Eros, who personified sexual love and whose name now represents the sexual instinct, or libido. Conventionally depicted as a blindfolded youth with wings and carrying a bow and arrows, Eros was the son of Ares, the god of war, and Aphrodite, goddess of love, and combined elements of both their characters. Equivalent to the Roman CUPID, he fired arrows at both gods and men, thus causing them to fall in love. The term *erotic* appears to have entered the English language around the middle of the 17th century. Related words include ***erotica,*** sexually provocative topics and material. *The erotic content of the book caused a sensation at the time but seems fairly mild by today's standards.*

Errol Flynn (erăl flin) A dashing, romantic adventurer. Errol Flynn (1909–59) was a Tasmanian-born U.S. film actor who became Hollywood's greatest player of romantic heroes in the 1930s and 1940s, appearing in a variety of swashbuckling roles such as pirate captains and Robin Hood. *His attempts to play the company's very own Errol Flynn backfired at the office Christmas party when he was chased out of the building by the financial director's drunken mother-in-law.*

Erymanthean boar *See* LABORS OF HERCULES.

Esau (eesah) A person who allows himself to be parted with something of value without receiving much in return. According to Genesis 25:24–34, Esau foolishly sold his birthright to his treacherous twin brother, Jacob, in exchange for a dish of soup or stew (*see* SELL ONE'S BIRTHRIGHT FOR A MESS OF POTTAGE). His name may also be applied to people who are unusually hairy or red haired, Esau himself being described in the Bible as "an hairy man" with red hair, while Jacob was smooth shaven. "'He's of a rash, warm-hearted nature, like Esau, for whom I have always felt great pity,' said Dinah" (George Eliot, *Adam Bede,* 1859).

escape by the skin of one's teeth To make a narrow escape from something. The expression is biblical in origin, appearing in Job 19:20 in the following form: "I am escaped with the skin of my teeth." *The stuntman only escaped serious injury by the skin of his teeth, rolling aside as the tower came crashing down on top of the place where he had been sitting.*

Esther (ester) The archetype of a beautiful, virtuous heroine. The biblical Esther was chosen to become the queen of King Ahasuerus (Xerxes) of Persia on account of her beauty (Esther 2:17). As queen she protected the captive Israelites from persecution by her husband, thereby becoming a heroine to the Jews. The name itself means "star" and was probably originally derived from that of Ishtar, the Babylonian goddess of love. "Mrs. van der Luyden beamed on her with the smile of Esther interceding with Ahasuerus; but her husband raised a protesting hand" (Edith Wharton, *The Age of Innocence,* 1920). *See also* FOR SUCH A TIME AS THIS.

Estragon *See* WAITING FOR GODOT.

état c'est moi, l' *See* L'ÉTAT C'EST MOI.

Eternal City The city of Rome. This commonly heard nickname for Rome is of ancient origin, having been used by Ovid (43 B.C.–A.D. 17) and Tibullus (c. 55–c. 19 B.C.), among other writers. "Then ensued an eager description, by the two women, of what had been done, and what should be done, to penetrate the thick wall of fees, commissions, and chicanery, which stood between the patrons of art and an unknown artist in the Eternal City" (Charles Reade, *The Cloister and the Hearth,* 1861).

Ethiopian change his skin *See* LEOPARD CANNOT CHANGE ITS SPOTS, A.

E.T. phone home A reaction, impressed or otherwise, to some scientifically outlandish suggestion, often relating to the possibility of communication with and between alien life forms. The original E.T. (short for "extra-terrestrial") was the bizarre but lovable space alien depicted in the 1982 Steven Spielberg film *E.T.: The Extra-Terrestrial*. Stranded on earth, E.T. befriends some human children, who look after him until the opportunity comes for him to "phone home" (a phrase he manages to utter in strangled English) and be rescued by his alien family. *The professor argued that some signals from deep space appeared to follow predetermined patterns—very E.T. phone home!*

Et tu, Brute? (et too brootay) Expression of reproachful surprise at a betrayal (usually a relatively minor act of disloyalty) by a friend or colleague. The words, meaning "You too, Brutus?" were allegedly spoken by Julius Caesar when he discovered his close friend Marcus Junius Brutus (85–42 B.C.) among his murderers on the Ides of March in 44 B.C. According to Suetonius (A.D. c. 69–c. 122), Caesar actually spoke the line in Greek, but the Latin form is more familiar today from its use in William Shakespeare's tragedy *Julius Caesar* (1599–1600). "Some months afterwards, when the much-belaboured head of affairs was in very truth made to retire, when unkind shells were thrown against him in great numbers, when he exclaimed, 'Et tu, Brute!' till the words were stereotyped upon his lips, all men in all places talked much about the great Gatherum Castle confederation" (Anthony Trollope, *Framley Parsonage,* 1861).

Eucharist *See* LAST SUPPER.

Euclidean (yooklideeăn) Of or relating to a system of geometry based on the discoveries of the Greek mathematician Euclid, who lived in Alexandria in the third century B.C. Euclid's teachings dominated geometry for some 2,000 years. Such was his dominance that for many years geometry itself was informally known as ***Euclid.*** The term *Euclidean* may also be interpreted more generally as meaning "clearly presented" or "well ordered." "Quoin is not a Euclidean term. It belongs to the pure nautical mathematics. I know not that it has been defined before" (Herman Melville, *Moby-Dick,* 1851).

euhemerism (yooheemărizăm) The belief that the gods of mythology were derived from real historical characters. The word comes from the name of the Sicilian Greek philosopher Euhemerus, who lived in the fourth century B.C. and first suggested the theory in his book *Sacred History.* According to Euhemerus, the idea came to him after he read an inscription supporting the theory on a gold pillar on an island in the Indian Ocean. *The discovery of the temple did little to discourage those scholars who were passionately attached to the theory of euhemerism, the idea that the heroes of myth were based on real characters.*

Eumaeus (yoomayăs) A swineherd. Going back to Greek legend, the original Eumaeus was a slave and swineherd under Ulysses. *The pigs are kept in a state-of-the-art piggery and tended by scientists, a far cry from the Eumaeus of legend.*

Eumenides *See* FURIES.

Euphorbia (yooforbeeă) A genus of plants of the spurge family. This popular ornamental plant takes its name from Euphorbus, a Greek physician who flourished in the first century A.D. Tradition claims that the plant was named in honor of Euphorbus by one of his patients, King Juba II of Mauritania. *She planted some* Euphorbia *around the front gate.*

Euphrosyne *See* THREE GRACES.

Eureka! (yooreekă) Expression of delightful triumph at making a discovery of some kind or in reaching a solution to a problem. According to tradition, the Sicilian mathematician Archimedes (287–212 B.C.) uttered "Eureka!" (meaning "I have found it!") after solving the problem of how to assess the amount of gold in a supposedly solid-gold crown. The crown, made on the orders of Heiron II of Syracuse, was suspected of having been adulterated with cheaper alloys, the presence of which could not be detected by visual examination or by weight. The king called on the mathematician to find a way to verify its content without damaging the crown. As he lay in his bath, Archimedes noticed how his body displaced some of the water and realized that the answer lay in comparing the volume of water displaced by the crown and that displaced by the equivalent amount of pure gold when both were immersed, as the density of gold was known to be different to that of any other metal. If there was a difference between the two, the king had been cheated—as proved the case. "Eureka!" is also the motto of California, recalling the gold rush that took place there. "In one place I suddenly found myself near the model of a tin-mine, and then by the merest accident I discovered, in an air-tight case, two dynamite cartridges! I shouted 'Eureka!' and smashed the case with joy" (H. G. Wells, *The Time Machine,* 1895).

Euryalus *See* NISUS AND EURYALUS.

Eurydice *See* ORPHEUS.

Euterpe *See* MUSES.

Eve (eev) The archetypal woman. According to the Book of Genesis, Eve was the first woman, created by God as a companion for ADAM and named by Adam himself: "And Adam called his wife's name Eve; because she was the mother of all living" (Genesis 3:20). The name Eve itself comes from the Hebrew *hawwah* (meaning "life"). It was Eve who succumbed to the persuasion of the serpent to eat the forbidden fruit of the tree of knowledge and thus brought about the expulsion of Adam and Eve from the GARDEN OF EDEN. The Virgin Mary is sometimes referred to as "the new Eve." Woman in general are sometimes referred to as ***daughters of Eve.*** "Joanna the faithless, the betrayer: Joanna who mocked him, whispered about him behind his back, trapped and tortured him. Joanna Eve" (Fay Weldon, *The Cloning of Joanna May,* 1989). *See also* ADAM AND EVE; ADAM'S RIB.

even Homer nods *See* HOMER SOMETIMES NODS.

Everest *See* MOUNT EVEREST.

every dog has his day Even the most lowly and humble will eventually get their opportunity for glory or success. This proverb has its roots in a Roman saying and was popularly attributed to a legend concerning the death (in 406 B.C.) of the Greek playwright Euripides, who was reputedly torn to pieces by dogs set upon him by his rivals Arrhidaeus and Crateuas. "Let Hercules himself do what he may, the cat will mew, and dog will have his day" (William Shakespeare, *Hamlet,* c. 1600).

Everyman The common man, the ordinary man in the street. Everyman appeared as a character in English literature as early as the 15th century, probably for the first time in a morality play of around 1500 in which he is challenged by Death to account for his life. "The immigrant is the Everyman of the twentieth century" (Hanif Kureishi, *The Buddha of Suburbia*, 1990).

evil empire A hostile state that seems opposed to all the virtues of peaceful, democratic coexistence. The phrase featured strongly in the *STAR WARS* films of George Lucas, beginning in 1977, in which it was applied to the alien empire controlled by DARTH VADER and other villains. During the 1980s the description was applied by U.S. president Ronald Reagan to the Soviet Union and its satellite states (although he retracted the comparison after the political reforms that took place in that part of the world later in the decade). Since then it has been revived periodically to condemn one undesirable regime or another, especially those with territorial ambitions. *North Korea has many of the attributes of the old evil empire that was the Soviet Union.*

ewe lamb A greatly prized possession. The phrase alludes to 2 Samuel 12:1–14, in which Nathan tells King David a parable about a rich man who seizes a poor man's "little ewe lamb" that he has nurtured as though it was his own daughter. When David expresses his rage at this injustice, Nathan accuses David of similar wickedness in having Bathsheba's husband killed so that he can marry her. Later, the child born to Bathsheba and David dies. "'Jane, I never meant to wound you thus. If the man who had but one little ewe lamb that was dear to him as a daughter, that ate of his bread and drank of his cup, and lay in his bosom, had by some mistake slaughtered it at the shambles, he would not have rued his bloody blunder more than I now rue mine'" (Charlotte Brontë, *Jane Eyre,* 1847).

Excalibur (ekskaliber) A mighty weapon wielded by a righteous warrior. In English legend, Excalibur was the name of the magical sword given to KING ARTHUR by the ***Lady in the Lake***. Other versions of Arthurian myth identify Excalibur as the sword that Arthur pulled from the stone, thus proving his right to the English throne. In modern usage the term has been applied to a wide variety of weapons and other tools, from space lasers to the humble telephone. "She held the pole two handed, as if administering the death thrust with Excalibur, plunging it up and down in the soggy mass with a ferocity that had little to do with getting the clothes clean" (A. B. Lancaster, *The Americas*, 1984).

exile *See* BABYLONIAN CAPTIVITY.

exodus A mass migration or departure. The word comes from the Greek *exodos* (meaning "marching out") and in the Old Testament describes the departure of the Israelites from Egypt (Exodus 12:31) under Moses and their subsequent 40-year wanderings in the wilderness before coming to the PROMISED LAND. "Away streamed the Members, but still the noble lord went on speaking, struggling hard to keep up his fire as though no such exodus were in process" (Anthony Trollope, *Can You Forgive Her?,* 1864).

ex pede Herculem (eks peday herkyoolem) By examining a small sample of something, much may be learned about the whole. The phrase literally means "from the foot of Hercules" and alludes to a calculation supposedly made by the Greek mathematician Pythagoras (c. 580–c. 500 B.C.). In order to work out the height of the great hero Hercules, Pythagoras began by comparing the length of the average Greek stadium (600 feet) with that of the stadium of Hercules at Olympia and from this calculated the size of Hercules' foot, with which he would have paced out the distance. Having gleaned this information, it was relatively simple to calculate his height as there is a certain ratio between foot size and height. An alternative phrase with much the same meaning is ***ex ungue leonem*** (meaning "from the claw of the lion"). ". . . and as for Testacio, one of the highest hills in modern Rome, it is but an ancient dust heap; the women of old Rome flung their broken pots and pans there, and lo—a mountain. 'Ex pede Herculem; ex ungue leonem'" (Charles Reade, *The Cloister and the Hearth,* 1861).

extra mile *See* GO THE EXTRA/SECOND MILE.

Exxon Valdez (ekson valdeez) An environmental disaster, especially one involving a spillage of oil. The *Exxon Valdez* was a massive oil tanker that went aground in Alaska's Prince William Sound in 1989, causing catastrophic damage to thousands of miles of shoreline. It has since become a benchmark for all such environmental calamities. *What the world really doesn't need is another Exxon Valdez.*

eye for an eye, an Retribution by extracting like for like. The phrase comes from Exodus 21:24: "Eye for eye, tooth for tooth, hand for hand, foot for foot." *He was an old-fashioned judge who believed in an eye for an eye when it came to crimes against the person.*

eye hath not seen Something invisible to ordinary sight or not readily perceived by the senses. Paul uses the phrase in 1 Corinthians 2:9 in describing the wondrous rewards that God has prepared in heaven for those who are faithful to him: "But as it is written, Eye hath not seen, nor ear heard, neither have entered into the heart of man, the things which God hath prepared for them that love him." "Vast chain of being, which from God began, / Natures aethereal, human, angel, man, / Beast, bird, fish, insect! what no eye can see, / No glass can reach!" (Alexander Pope, *Essay on Man,* 1733–34).

eyeless in Gaza (gahză) Reduced to a state of wretched helplessness in hostile surroundings. The phrase alludes to the ill treatment suffered by SAMSON at the hands of the Philistines, who, according to Judges 16:1–3 and 21, captured him and put out his eyes before imprisoning him "with fetters of brass" at Gaza. The image of the mighty Samson thus pitifully reduced has since been variously adopted by writers over the centuries, from John Milton, who depicted Samson as "eyeless in Gaza at the mill with slaves" in *Samson Agonistes* (1671), to Aldous Huxley, who wrote an autobiographical novel entitled *Eyeless in Gaza* (1936). "Ask for this great deliverer now, and find him Eyeless in Gaza, at the mill with slaves. It is the same story. Great power reduced to impotence, great glory to misery, by the hand of Fate . . ." (Anthony Trollope, *The Last Chronicle of Barset,* 1867).

eye of a needle *See* CAMEL: GO THROUGH AN EYE OF A NEEDLE.

Eyre, Jane *See* JANE EYRE.

F

Fabian (faybeeăn) Cautious; avoiding direct confrontation. The word alludes to the Roman general Quintus Fabius Maximus (d. 203 B.C.), nicknamed CUNCTATOR (delayer), who adopted the tactic of harassment instead of making a direct challenge against the invading Carthaginian armies of Hannibal during the Second Punic War. This policy of avoiding pitched battles provoked accusations of cowardice in Rome but ultimately proved successful. During the American War of Independence, George Washington adopted a similar approach against the British and was consequently known as the American Fabius. In 1884 a group of British Socialists who preferred to achieve their aims through democratic methods rather than through violent revolution opted to call themselves the Fabian Society to emphasize their nonconfrontational ***Fabian tactics.*** *The government would appear to have adopted Fabian tactics in dealing with the threat posed by the unions.*

Fabricius (făbrishăs) Archetype of incorruptibility and honesty. Gaius Fabricius Luscinus (d. c. 270 B.C.) was a Roman consul who became famous for his refusal to accept bribes or in any other way compromise his principles. He lived a frugal life and left nothing to his daughters when he died, but the Senate decided to provide for their future. *He is widely regarded as the Fabricius of the White House, the one person who can be relied on to give an honest appraisal of the situation.*

face that launched a thousand ships *See* HELEN OF TROY.

faction A minority group within a large body, especially one that holds dissenting views. The original factions were the chariot-racing teams, or *factiones,* of ancient Rome. Identified by a particular color, the *factiones* were well-organized sporting enterprises, and each had a committed following, who in time came to wield considerable political influence. The most famous were the Blues, who enjoyed the support of the aristocracy, and the Greens, who were the most popular team among the general populace. On occasion, clashes between the *factiones* could lead to wider unrest, culminating in a full-scale riot in A.D. 509. "All these things tended to make us excessively obnoxious to the great sacerdotal clan, the most powerful because the most united faction in the kingdom" (H. Rider Haggard, *Allan Quatermain,* 1887).

Fagin (faygin) A villainous rogue, especially one who corrupts the young. In the Charles Dickens novel *OLIVER TWIST* (1837–38), Fagin is a cunning and evil old Jew who persuades the runaway

Oliver into joining his wily gang of young pickpockets, but is eventually brought to justice and executed. It is thought that Dickens based his memorable character on a real person, Isaac "Ikey" Solomons (c. 1785–1850). *His father's an old Fagin who won't rest until he's got his hands on everything you've got. See also* ARTFUL DODGER.

Fair Deal A policy that offers the prospect of everyone being fairly treated. A favorite slogan of modern politicians introducing new political solutions, it recalls the original Fair Deal introduced by President Harry S. Truman (1884–1972) in January 1949. Truman's measures aimed to improve the lot of the poorly paid and the poorly housed as well as advancing the cause of civil rights and better social security. *The governor unveiled his Fair Deal apparently convinced that the press would approve wholeheartedly.*

fairy godmother A person or organization that proves to be a generous source of much-needed financial or other help. The fairy godmother is a stock character of fairy tales and pantomimes, the most famous example being the fairy godmother who provides CINDERELLA with the clothes and magic coach she needs to attend the royal ball. "Mrs. Adams's conception of a glue factory as a fairy godmother of this family was an absurd old story which Alice had never taken seriously" (Booth Tarkington, *Alice Adams*, 1921).

faith, hope, and charity The three theological virtues (in contrast to the cardinal virtues of prudence, temperance, fortitude, and justice). Paul identifies the virtues in 1 Corinthians 13:13, using "charity" as a synonym for "love" and singling out charity as the most important of the three: "And now abideth faith, hope, charity, these three; but the greatest of these is charity." "Still—if I have read religious history aright—faith, hope, and charity have not always been found in a direct ratio with a sensibility to the three concords, and it is possible—thank Heaven!—to have very erroneous theories" (George Eliot, *Adam Bede*, 1859).

faith will move mountains With faith anything is possible. This saying comes from Matthew 17:20: "If ye have faith as a grain of mustard seed, ye shall say unto this mountain, Remove hence to yonder place; and it shall remove; and nothing shall be impossible unto you." A variant form is ***faith can move mountains.*** *She firmly believes that she can make him change his ways, and faith will move mountains, so she may yet succeed.*

faith without works A person's good intentions are meaningless unless supported by good actions. The phrase comes from the Book of James 2:14–26: "Yea, a man may say, Thou hast faith, and I have works: show me thy faith without thy works, and I will show thee my faith by my works. . . . But wilt thou know, O vain man, that faith without works is dead? Was not Abraham our father justified by works, when he had offered Isaac his son upon the altar?" (James 2:14–21). *The government has expressed good intentions but failed to do much about them, and critics have observed that it is a case of faith without works.*

Falernian (fălerneeăn) Of or having to do with a wine of a superior quality. The term refers to a particularly fine wine that was made in the Falernian region of Campania in Roman times. Its qualities were praised by Horace and Virgil among others. "Sand-banks, marshes, forests, savages,—precious little to eat fit for a civilized man, nothing but Thames water to drink. No Falernian wine here, no going ashore" (Joseph Conrad, *Heart of Darkness,* 1902).

Fall, the A lapse from a previously happier state. The allusion is to the Fall of the human race as described in the Book of Genesis, when ADAM and EVE disobeyed God's command not to eat the fruit of the tree of knowledge of good and evil (Genesis 3:6), so committing the first sin. As a punishment for their disobedience they were expelled from the Garden of Eden. "What Eve, what serpent hath suggested thee / To make a second fall of cursed man?" (William Shakespeare, *Richard II,* 1595). *See also* ORIGINAL SIN.

fall among thieves To find oneself among bad company or at the mercy of wicked people. The phrase comes from the parable of the GOOD SAMARITAN, in which a man on his way from Jerusalem to Jericho "fell among thieves, which stripped him of his raiment, and wounded him, and departed, leaving him half dead" (Luke 10:30). *Her son was a harmless enough kid, but he fell among thieves and by the time he was out of his teenage years was well known to the local police.*

fall by the wayside To give up or fail at something; to become useless. The phrase is biblical in origin, appearing in the parable of the sower and the seed related in Matthew 13:4, which describes how some seeds inevitably fall by the wayside and fail to germinate. "While other internet bosses have fallen by the wayside, he remains in charge after overseeing his company's flotation and sale" (*Guardian,* April 23, 2001). *See also* PARABLE OF THE SOWER.

fallen angel A person who has suffered a lapse in fortune or reputation. The original fallen angels were Lucifer and other rebels, who according to Christian tradition tried unsuccessfully to overthrow God and were consequently consigned to hell, as related in Isaiah 14:12 and Revelation 12:7–9. The term entered common currency after the publication of Milton's *Paradise Lost* (1667), which retold the story. "'Mr. Finn knows,' said Lady Laura, 'that since he first came into Parliament I have always believed in his success, and I have been very proud to see it.' 'We shall weep over him, as over a fallen angel, if he leaves us,' said Lady Cantrip" (Anthony Trollope, *Phineas Finn,* 1869).

fall from grace To fall in status; to lose a privileged position or favor. The expression comes from Galatians 5:4, in which the Galatians are reprimanded for relying on their own efforts to observe the law rather than depending on God's help: "Christ is become of no effect unto you, whosoever of you are justified by the law; ye are fallen from grace." *Few remember now how he dominated the world of business prior to his sensational fall from grace.*

fall of a sparrow Even the most insignificant events are not outside the care and knowledge of God (or others in authority), who governs everything. The phrase comes from Matthew 10:29–31: "Are not two sparrows sold for a farthing? and one of them shall not fall on the ground without your Father. . . . Fear ye not therefore, ye are of more value than many sparrows." *He ran the estate with a gimlet eye, to the extent that not even the fall of a sparrow took place without his knowledge.*

fall of Jericho *See* WALLS OF JERICHO.

Fall of the House of Usher *See* HOUSE OF USHER.

fall on stony ground To receive an unfavorable reception; to be ignored or fail to prosper. The phrase appears in Mark 4:5–6, which relates the PARABLE OF THE SOWER and the seed: "And some fell on stony ground, where it had not much earth; and immediately it sprang up, because it had no depth of earth: But when the sun was up, it was scorched; and because it had no root, it withered away." *The young woman made several suggestions at her first board meeting, but most of her ideas fell on stony ground.*

fallout The secondary consequences of something. The allusion is to the radioactive fallout that results from the explosion of an atomic or nuclear device, as a consequence of which particles of radioactive material are typically deposited over a wide area. The term is normally employed in the context of events that are seen as disastrous or in some way unexpected or shocking. *The fallout from this shuffle of senior positions in the government will go on for months.*

false prophet A person who purports to speak the truth, but whose words are not in fact to be trusted. The phrase appears several times in the Bible, for example, in Matthew 7:15–17: "Beware of false prophets, which come to you in sheep's clothing, but inwardly they are ravening wolves. Ye shall know them by their fruits. Do men gather grapes of thorns, or figs of thistles? Even so every good tree bringeth forth good fruit; but a corrupt tree bringeth forth evil fruit." "The clergyman had not, it would seem, forgot the observation which ranked him with the false prophets of Dunbar, for he addressed Mr. Maxwell upon the first opportunity" (Sir Walter Scott, *Waverley,* 1814). *See also* WOLF IN SHEEP'S CLOTHING.

Falstaffian (folstafeeăn) Of a jolly, roguish, larger-than-life character. The allusion is to William Shakespeare's Sir John Falstaff, a life-loving comical old knight who appears in *The Merry Wives of Windsor* (c. 1597) and *Henry IV, Parts 1 and 2* (1597). His death is also mentioned in *Henry V* (c. 1598). The term is often applied to people who share not only Falstaff's cheerful, self-indulgent character and his love of wine and women but also his impressive girth. *With his vast paunch and ruddy cheeks, he cut a Falstaffian figure as he leaned on the bar and regaled his companions with risqué stories.*

Famous Five Any five individuals whose shared adventures or interests make them an identifiable group. The original Famous Five were the children Julian, Dick, Anne, and George, together with George's dog Timmy, whose adventures were recounted in a series of children's novels by ENID BLYTON. The formula is sometimes varied in number to apply to groups of four individuals, thus the equally alliterative ***Famous Four***. *Frank Sinatra, Dean Martin, Sammy Davis Jr., Peter Lawford, and Joey Bishop were the Famous Five who became known as the Rat Pack.*

famous for fifteen minutes The notion that in the modern media-driven age everyone will enjoy a brief moment of fame. The sentiment was first voiced in 1968 by U.S. avant-garde artist and filmmaker Andy Warhol (1928–87): "In the future everybody will be world famous for fifteen minutes." The phrase ***fifteen minutes of fame*** refers to this transitory period in the public eye. "You know, the 'Famous for fifteen minutes' type" (Shaun Hutson, *Heathen*, 1993).

farewell to arms, a A truce, a retreat from conflict. The allusion is to the novel *A Farewell to Arms* (1929) by Ernest Hemingway, which was based on the author's experiences as an ambulance driver in World War I. The novel itself relates the disillusionment of an American medical officer serving with the Italians and his subsequent desertion from the army. *His own farewell to arms took the form of a drunken party with his teammates after his last game with the side.*

far, far better thing, a *See* IT IS A FAR, FAR BETTER THING THAT I DO.

far from the madding crowd Away from the hustle and bustle of modern life. Most people assume the allusion is to the Thomas Hardy novel *Far From the Madding Crowd* (1874), although Hardy himself borrowed the phrase ultimately from Thomas Gray's *Elegy Written in a Country Churchyard* (1751): "Far from the madding crowd's ignoble strife, / Their sober wishes never learned to stray; / Along the cool sequestered vale of life / They kept the noiseless tenor of their way." "During the next ecstatic ten minutes, with my hand pressed against my wildly beating heart, I planned my wedding dress, selected with care and discrimination my trousseau, furnished the rose-embowered cottage far from the madding crowd—and wondered *why* Father did not send for me" (Eleanor H. Porter, *Mary Marie*, 1920).

fascism (fashizăm) Right-wing authoritarianism. The Fascist movement founded by Benito Mussolini in 1919 took its name from the *fasces* that were carried before the senior magistrates of ancient Rome as a symbol of their authority. These comprised a bundle of rods tied with a red thong, from which an ax projected. The *fasces* were subsequently adopted as a symbol by Mussolini's Fascists, who sought to make links between their movement and the glories of ancient Rome, and the term soon came to be applied more widely to other right-wing totalitarian organizations, political parties, policies, and regimes, including Nazi Germany. *The rise of fascism and communism in the 20th century was the greatest disfiguring phenomenon in international affairs.*

fasten your seatbelts Prepare for troubled times ahead. Originally an instruction to passengers on aircraft to secure their seatbelts before takeoff or landing or when flying into turbulence, the phrase featured memorably in the 1950 film *All About Eve*, in which Bette Davis delivers the line "Fasten your seat belts. It's going to be a bumpy night!" in anticipation of a blazing row she is about to have with an upstart actress seeking to steal her role. *If you're planning to go in there now before she's had a chance to calm down you'd better fasten your seatbelt.*

fast lane The most direct route to success, fame, wealth, etc. The allusion is to the lane on a highway or expressway that is reserved for vehicles overtaking slower traffic. The phrase is often encountered in the expression ***life in the fast lane***. "For them there was nothing tame about not living in the fast lane; nothing sanctimonious about unconsciously keeping clear of the edge of the cliff" (Hugh Barty-King, *The Worst Poverty*, 1991).

fatal attraction An obsessive or dangerous relationship. The allusion is to the 1987 film thriller *Fatal Attraction*, in which a deranged Glenn Close continues to pursue the married Michael Douglas after a short-lived affair. A woman who behaves in such a fashion may be called a ***bunnyboiler*** after a notorious scene in the film in which a pet rabbit is found in a pan of boiling water in the family home. *The police have had to deal with a number of fatal attraction cases in the last few weeks.*

Fat Controller A person in charge, especially if he or she is large in size and officious in character. The original Fat Controller (initially called the Fat Director) was the head of the railways featured in the *Thomas the Tank Engine* stories of the Rev. W. Awdry (1911–97) and his son, the first of which appeared in 1946. *There's room for only one Fat Controller in this organization.*

Fates (fayts) The implacable divinities who are commonly believed to control the lives of mortal men and women. The Fates (also called the ***Moirae*** by the Greeks or the ***Parcae*** by the Romans) were depicted in Greek and Roman mythology as three sisters—identified as daughters of Night—who handled the ***thread of destiny*** (a length of thread representing each individual life). Clotho spun the thread at birth, Lachesis measured its length and determined the amount of luck the person would enjoy, and Atropos cut it with her shears at the moment of death. "'Ah!' He shivered as one shivers at the thought of disaster narrowly averted. 'The fates were good that I only came near it!'" (Booth Tarkington, *His Own People,* 1907).

Father Christmas *See* SANTA CLAUS.

Father, forgive them Expression of exasperation at the nonsensical actions of others. The allusion is to the seven last sentences of Christ on the Cross, often referred to as the ***Seven Last Words***. The second of these, in which Christ requests forgiveness for those who have brought about his death, runs: "Father, forgive them; for they know not what they do" (Luke 23:34). "Lo! where the crucified Christ from his Cross is gazing upon you! See! in those sorrowful eyes what meekness and holy compassion! Hark! how those lips still repeat the prayer. 'O Father, forgive them!' Let us repeat it now, and say, 'O Father, forgive them'" (H. W. Longfellow, *Evangeline,* 1847). *See also* KNOW NOT WHAT THEY DO, THEY.

Father Time A very old person, or time itself. Time is often personified as an old man with a long white beard, bearing an hourglass and a scythe with which to "reap" lives when the allotted lifespans come to an end. The origins of this image are obscure, but it was certainly widely familiar by the 19th century at the latest. "Little Father Time is what they always called me. It is a nickname; because I look so aged, they say" (Thomas Hardy, *Jude the Obscure*, 1895). *See also* GRIM REAPER.

fat of the land A life of luxury. The expression comes from Genesis 45:18, in which Pharaoh offered the brethren of Joseph the best treatment: "I will give you the good of the land of Egypt, and ye shall eat the fat of the land." A person who is said to ***live off the fat of the land*** is one who enjoys the best of everything. "By—, those fellows, who haven't got a pound belonging to them, think that they're to live on the fat of the land out of the sweat of the brow of such men as me" (Anthony Trollope, *Ayala's Angel,* 1881).

fatted calf, kill the *See* KILL THE FATTED CALF.

fatwa (fatwă) An unarguable ruling passed down by someone in authority, especially one that calls for the punishment of a named individual on charges of heresy. The word is Arabic in origin and in its strictest sense refers to decisions made by Islamic religious leaders (*see* AYATOLLAH). Since the passing of a fatwa by Ayatollah Khomeini of Iran in 1989, in which he called for the death of the British writer Salman Rushdie in reaction to his controversial book *The Satanic Verses* (1988), it has been widely assumed that all such edicts demand the death sentence, although this is not always the case. *The state governor has delivered a fatwa forbidding any state employee indulging in such corrupt practices in the future.*

fat years and lean years Periods of prosperity and misfortune, which tend to alternate. The phrase comes from Genesis 41:25–27, in which Joseph interprets Pharaoh's dream about seven lean cows consuming seven fat cows as meaning that seven years of plenty would be followed by seven years of famine. *The family has known both fat years and lean years but has always held together until now.*

Faulknerian (fokneereeăn) In a manner reminiscent of the writing of the U.S. novelist and short-story writer William Faulkner (1897–1962). Faulkner's themes included the past, race relations, class conflict, sexual repression, and slavery. His style was typically elaborate, allegorical, and hallucinatory. *His prose was Faulknerian in its resonance and scope, rich in characterization and sometimes shocking in its violence.*

faun (fahn) A species of minor rural deity having the body of a man and the legs, tail, ears, and horns of a goat. Fauns (similar to the SATYRS of Greek tradition) were a feature of Roman mythology and were apparently derived from Faunus, the god of nature and fertility and the Roman equivalent of the Greek god Pan. They are generally depicted in art and literature as sprightly and mischievous. "As he stood there in the lamp-light, with dead leaves and bits of bramble clinging to his mud-spattered clothes, the scent of the night about him and its chill on his pale bright face, he really had the look of a young faun strayed in from the forest" (Edith Wharton, *The Reef,* 1912).

fauna (fahnă) The native or indigenous animal life of a particular place or period of time. The word comes from Fauna, the name of the sister of Faunus, the Roman god of nature and fertility. It was first used in its modern sense by the Swedish botanist Linneaus in 1746. "'You've never been to Kew?' Denham remarked. But it appeared that she had come once as a small child, when the geography of the place was entirely different, and the fauna included certainly flamingoes and, possibly, camels" (Virginia Woolf, *Night and Day,* 1919). *See also* FAUN; FLORA.

Fauntleroy, Little Lord *See* LITTLE LORD FAUNTLEROY.

Faustian bargain (fowsteeăn) A deal made for short-term gain, without regard to the costs in the long term. The allusion is to the bargain Faustus makes with the devil in Christopher Marlowe's play *Doctor Faustus* (1604), in which Faustus is granted his immediate desires in exchange for his immortal soul. The story was later reworked by various composers, notably Wagner, Berlioz, and Gounod. Also called a ***Faustian pact***, the term is usually applied today to anyone who appears to have sacrificed his or her morals for material benefit. *He made a Faustian bargain that appeased his enemies but lost him his friends.*

favonian (făvōneeăn) Of or relating to the west wind. Favonius (or Favonianus) was the Roman name for the west wind, which for its relatively gentle nature was considered favorable to living things. *A warm, favonian breeze ruffled the grasses on the hilltop and filled the sails of the ships in the bay.*

Fawkes, Guy *See* GUNPOWDER PLOT.

Fawlty Towers (foltee) A mismanaged organization or situation. The allusion is to the highly acclaimed 1970s BBC television comedy series *Fawlty Towers*, which revolved around the chaotic goings-on at a modest hotel run by a warring married couple named Fawlty in the English seaside resort of Torquay. In homage to the irascible, henpecked hotel manager played by John Cleese, anyone who behaves in a similarly manic fashion may be labeled a ***Basil Fawlty***. *This place is like Fawlty Towers—nothing works and nothing happens when it is supposed to.*

fear and trembling, in *See* IN FEAR AND TREMBLING.

fed with Saint Stephen's bread *See* SAINT STEPHEN'S LOAVES.

feeding the five thousand The providing of food or something else for a large number of people. The reference is to the miracle of the loaves and fishes related in Matthew 14:13–21, in which Christ miraculously fed a crowd of 5,000 people with just five loaves and two fish—and had several baskets of food left over after all had eaten. *It was like feeding the five thousand, trying to make sure every child had roughly the same amount and choice of food.*

feet of clay A fundamental character flaw, especially one that is not immediately obvious in someone or something that is otherwise greatly admired. The allusion is to Daniel 2:31–33, which relates a dream in which the Babylonian king Nebuchadnezzar dreamed of a huge figure with a head of gold, breast and arms of silver, belly and thighs of brass, legs of iron, and feet of iron and clay. When the feet are smashed by a stone, the whole statue falls. Daniel explained the image as a symbol of Nebuchadnezzar's empire and the feet of clay as a representation of the inherent weakness that would lead to its collapse. *For as long as anyone could remember the old man had been considered the ultimate authority on such matters, but now he was revealed to have feet of clay.*

Fell, I do not like thee, Doctor *See* I DO NOT LIKE THEE, DOCTOR FELL.

fell among thieves *See* FALL AMONG THIEVES.

fellow traveler A person who shares the same ideas or aims, but without necessarily being part of any official movement representing such notions. The term arose as a translation of the Russian word *poputchik*, which was first employed by Russian revolutionary Leon Trotsky to describe noncommunist writers who nonetheless supported the Russian Revolution of 1917. The term is often applied to communist sympathizers, typically with derogatory overtones. *We suspect a number of fellow travelers have infiltrated the organization over recent years.*

Fester, Uncle *See* ADDAMS FAMILY.

few are chosen *See* MANY ARE CALLED, BUT FEW ARE CHOSEN.

fiddle while Rome burns To occupy oneself with trivialities while ignoring a much more serious problem. The allusion is to the tradition that in the year A.D. 64 the emperor Nero (who considered himself a fine musician) played his fiddle rather than take action to prevent the city of Rome from being destroyed in a disastrous fire. Rumors that Nero had started the fire himself to clear a large area for his own ambitious building plans added to the resentment felt against him for this callousness (even though he was not apparently in the city at the time the fire broke out), and his reign only lasted another four years, despite his attempts to transfer the blame for the conflagration to the city's Christian population. "[Prime Minister Tony] Blair fiddles while Cumbria burns" (*Guardian,* April 2, 2001).

field of blood *See* ACELDAMA.

fiery furnace A punishment that rebounds on the persons inflicting it while leaving its intended victims unscathed. The allusion is to the biblical story of Shadrach, Meshach, and Abednego, who were hurled into a fiery furnace on the orders of King Nebuchadnezzar after they refused to worship a golden idol set up by him. According to the account given in Daniel 3, the three remained miraculously unharmed by the flames, although the people who threw them in were all scorched to death. "Tom stood silent; at length he said, 'Him that saved Daniel in the den of lions,—that saves the children in the fiery furnace,—Him that walked on the sea, and bade the winds be still,—He's alive yet; and I've faith to believe he can deliver you'" (Harriet Beecher Stowe, *Uncle Tom's Cabin,* 1852).

fifteen minutes of fame *See* FAMOUS FOR FIFTEEN MINUTES.

fifth, take the *See* TAKE THE FIFTH.

Fifth Avenue The epitome of elegance and wealth. Fifth Avenue in Manhattan is the location of New York's most fashionable and exclusive department stores, among them Cartier's and Tiffany's, as well as many of the city's finest houses and museums. *With her furs and diamonds, she reeked of the new American aristocracy and Fifth Avenue chic.*

fifth column A subversive organization operating secretly within a state. The original fifth column was that formed by the fascists in Spain to undermine the Republican forces occupying Madrid during the Spanish Civil War of the 1930s. Its name referred to the fact that there was a unit of so-called ***fifth columnists*** working in cooperation with the four military columns loyal to General Franco that were approaching the capital, as made clear in a broadcast by the fascist general Emilio Mola: "We have four columns on the battlefield against you and a fifth column inside your ranks." The expression became more widely known as the title of a 1938 play by Ernest Hemingway, who saw action during the war. *There is a fifth column in the Congress working against the interests of liberal democracy.*

fight like Kilkenny cats (kilkenee) To fight with great ferocity to the very end. The allusion is to an incident that occurred among Hessian troops serving in Kilkenny during the Irish Rebellion of 1798. The bored troops amused themselves by tying the tails of two cats together and then hanging them up to fight. When an officer approached, one of the soldiers quickly severed the cats' tails; when asked about the two tails he held in his hand the trooper explained that the cats had been fighting with such ferocity that they had consumed each other all but the tails. *When the women realized how they had been tricked they fought like Kilkenny cats.*

fight the good fight To pursue a goal (especially a religious one) with determination and courage. The expression comes from 1 Timothy 6:12: "Fight the good fight of faith, lay hold on eternal life, whereunto thou art also called, and hast professed a good profession before many witnesses." The phrase is commonly applied to the struggle of life itself, and Paul, foreseeing his own death, wrote, "I have fought the good fight, I have finished my course" (2 Timothy 4:7). "He did become member for East Barsetshire, but he was such a member—so lukewarm, so indifferent, so prone to associate with the enemies of the good cause, so little willing to fight the good fight, that he soon disgusted those who most dearly loved the memory of the old squire" (Anthony Trollope, *Doctor Thorne,* 1858).

fig leaf Something that serves, usually inadequately, to conceal a person's weaknesses or innermost feelings. The allusion is to the fig leaves with which Adam and Eve sought to conceal their nakedness after tasting the fruit of the tree of knowledge of good and evil and losing their innocence: "And the eyes of them both were opened, and they knew that they were naked; and they sewed fig leaves together, and made themselves aprons" (Genesis 3:7). *This gesture was not well received and was generally considered a very inadequate fig leaf to cover up for past indiscretions.*

filthy lucre Money; material wealth. The phrase appears in 1 Timothy 3:3, in which Timothy warns that leaders of the church should be "not greedy of filthy lucre." "Mrs. Dean was a very good woman, but she had aspirations in the direction of filthy lucre on behalf of her children, or at least on behalf of this special child, and she did think it would be very nice if Frank would marry an heiress" (Anthony Trollope, *The Eustace Diamonds,* 1873).

final solution An extreme measure taken to bring something to an end. The allusion is to the Final Solution devised in Nazi Germany to eradicate Europe's Jewish population through systematic persecution and a policy of genocide. The phrase was apparently first employed, on January 20, 1942, by Nazi official Reinhardt Heydrich when reporting to Adolf HITLER on the various ways in which the populations under German control might be purged of "undesirable" elements. The term remains highly contentious and is generally only employed in relation to the most extreme and inhuman schemes. *It has been suggested that the Serbs had in mind their own Final Solution to eliminate those parts of the population that came from a different ethnic background. See also* HOLOCAUST.

fin de siècle (fan(g) dă syeklă, fan dă seeekăl) A period of decadent excess. The term originally alluded specifically to the last decade of the 19th century, which witnessed something of a relaxation of the rules governing contemporary Western culture and society and a growing willingness to challenge conventional ideas and codes of behavior. In modern usage, the expression has been applied less restrictively to allude to any time in which accepted moral standards are perceived as having been ignored, not necessarily coinciding with the end of a century. *The occasion was celebrated with appropriate fin de siècle abandon.*

finest hour, their *See* THEIR FINEST HOUR.

finger in the dike An inadequate solution to a serious problem. The allusion is to an old story concerning the dikes that protected the Dutch lowlands from inundation by the sea and a tiny hole in the sea wall, which threatened a vast area of land if it was allowed to develop into a major breach. Legend has it that the hole was spotted by a small boy, who stuck his forefinger into it and thus kept the water back until help eventually arrived. Although the boy's action was sufficient to save the whole country from disaster, in modern usage the image of a finger in a dike usually emphasizes the apparent ineffectuality of measures being taken, or measures planned to be taken, to stave off trouble. *The unions applauded the decision, but many observers saw the move as simply putting a finger in the dike.*

finger of God Divine guidance, power, or authority. The phrase appears in Exodus 8:19 and elsewhere in the Old Testament. The image of God's pointing finger has been variously employed as a symbol of divine creativity, guidance, and punishment. The similar expression ***hand of God*** points to "God's sovereign power in creation and in his actions on his people's behalf, especially in redemption. Also used as a symbol of authority and in taking oaths" (*NIV Thematic Reference Bible,* p. 1,385), as in "Shall we receive good at the hand of God, and shall we not receive evil?" (Job 2:10). *Surely, if nowhere else, the finger of God may be detected in the great paintings of the Renaissance masters.*

fings ain't wot they used t'be Things were much better in the past. Although probably familiar long before the middle of the 20th century, the expression caught on after appearing as the title of a 1959 musical by Lionel Bart and Frank Norman, portraying life among London's poorer classes (hence the mock cockney spelling of the title). Nowadays, the phrase has the status of a cliché expressing any nostalgic sentiment about past times. *Years ago you could have stayed in the bar all night for just the price of a beer, but fings ain't wot they used t'be.*

Finn, Huckleberry *See* HUCKLEBERRY FINN.

fire and brimstone Zealotry threatening eternal damnation or other punishment by God. The phrase is biblical in origin, appearing in the Book of Revelation, where a ***lake of fire and brimstone*** represents the agonies that guilty souls will suffer in hell. In Genesis 19:24 the sinful cities of SODOM AND GOMORRAH are similarly punished with fire and brimstone (*brimstone* is an alternative name for sulfur). In modern usage the phrase is sometimes applied to the sermons of those preachers who threaten their congregations with eternal condemnation if they do not turn back to God. "'Deceit is, indeed, a sad fault in a child,' said Mr. Brocklehurst; 'it is akin to falsehood, and all liars will have their portion in the lake burning with fire and brimstone; she shall, however, be watched, Mrs. Reed'" (Charlotte Brontë, *Jane Eyre,* 1847).

fireside chat A broadcast made by a president or other public figure in a calculatedly informal manner. The allusion is ultimately to the fireside chats first delivered in this style via national radio by President Franklin D. Roosevelt in 1933. They have since become a favored ploy of politicians in many countries, enabling them to ingratiate themselves with the voting public by giving the appearance of speaking personally, even confidentially, with the listeners or viewers. *Tony Blair surpassed preceding prime ministers with his mastery of the soundbite and the fireside chat.*

fire that is not quenched *See* WORM THAT DIETH NOT.

first among equals A person who provides leadership for a group without being considered in any way superior to other members of it. Originally familiar in its Latin form *primus inter pares*, it was particularly associated with the knights of the ROUND TABLE in Arthurian legend, among whom KING ARTHUR himself sat as an equal. The title has sometimes been applied to the leading figures of Western democracies, such as the prime minister of the United Kingdom and the president of the United States. "At its best, the teaching situation takes on much of the character of the research process, with an open dialogue between the students and teacher, the teacher being the first among equals" (Ronald Barnett, *The Idea of Higher Education*, 1990).

first base, get to *See* GET TO FIRST BASE.

first catch your hare There is a difficult but essential first step to perform, or obstacle to overcome, before you can achieve your ultimate objective. Most people mistakenly believe this to be a piece of wisdom extracted from Mrs. Beeton's *Book of Household Management* (1851), but in fact it comes from a recipe described in *The Art of Cookery Made Plain and Easy* (1747) by Mrs. Hannah Glasse: "Take your hare when it is cased" ("cased" meaning "skinned"). In fact, similar sentiments had been expressed in variant forms for hundreds of years before this. *These are very grand plans, but remember that you must first catch your hare.*

firstest with the mostest The surest route to success is to get there quickest with the greatest force. The allusion is said to be to the military strategy favored by the Confederate general Nathan B. Forrest (1821–77) during the U.S. Civil War, who allegedly advised his fellow officers to ***git thar fustest with the mostest***. *If you lot want to have hot dogs at the party tonight, you will need to get there firstest with the mostest.*

first shall be last, the Those who are apparently least deserving shall not necessarily be the last to be rewarded. The expression is of biblical origin, coming from Matthew 20:16, in which Christ is questioned about who most deserves everlasting life and is quoted as replying, "So the last shall be first, and the first last." *The old rogue winked at me as he took his payment ahead of the captain, as if to remind the world that sometimes the last shall be first.*

fisher of men An evangelist. The phrase appears in Matthew 4:18–20 in references to Christ's recruitment of the disciples: "Jesus, walking by the sea of Galilee, saw two brethren, Simon called Peter, and Andrew his brother, casting a net into the sea: for they were fishers. And he saith unto them, Follow me, and I will make you fishers of men. And they straightway left their nets, and followed him." The pope, considered the heir of Peter as the chief fisher of men, wears a fisherman's ring at his investiture. This ring is used for sealing papal briefs and is destroyed at the pope's death. *The local populace soon tired of being berated by this offensive fisher of men and returned to their homes, grumbling at his insolence.*

five thousand, feeding the *See* FEEDING THE FIVE THOUSAND.

flak Criticism or complaints. The word originated during World War II as an acronym for the German *Fliegerabwehrkanone*, referring to antiaircraft fire. *We got a lot of flak about that advertisement featuring three naked women and a sports car.*

flaming sword A highly effective weapon of some kind, especially one used to keep a person at bay. The allusion is to the flaming sword wielded by God as he drove Adam and Eve out of the Garden of Eden and prevented their approaching the Tree of Life, as related at Genesis 3:24: "So he drove out the man; and he placed at the east of the garden of Eden Cherubims, and a flaming sword which turned every way, to keep the way of the tree of life." Some swords with a wavy edge are traditionally called flaming swords. "She had felt lonely enough when the flaming sword of Nick's indignation had shut her out from their Paradise; but there had been a cruel bliss in the pain" (Edith Wharton, *Glimpses of the Moon,* 1922).

Flanders (flanderz) The battlefields of the western front in World War I. Although land battles fought during the war took place as far away as Africa and the Middle East, those fought on the western front are often considered generic of the conflict as a whole. The region of Flanders in northwest Europe, where many of these battles took place, has become a synonym for the entire conflict. This region has a long history as a theater of war, and is sometimes referred to as the COCKPIT OF EUROPE. *An entire generation perished in Flanders. See also* PASSCHENDAELE; SOMME, THE; YPRES.

Flash Gordon Archetype of a space hero. Flash Gordon was the daredevil hero of a comic strip first published in 1934, whose adventures against such foes as ***Ming the Merciless*** were later brought to life both in the cinema and on television. His name today is chiefly used in gentle mockery of any man who behaves in an ostentatiously heroic or dashing manner or who clearly sees himself as being in a heroic mold. *I suspect he thinks he's Flash Gordon, with his shiny silver car and dazzling smile.*

Flash Harry An ostentatiously dressed man. The nickname became well known as that of the British conductor Sir Malcolm Sargent (1895–1967), who liked to dress fashionably, and subsequently as that of a comical cockney character in the SAINT TRINIAN'S film comedies of the 1950s. In modern usage, the term is sometimes extended to apply to anyone with an outspoken, boorish character. *He's a bit of a Flash Harry, with his kipper tie and check suits.*

Fleet Street The British press establishment. The allusion is to Fleet Street in London, which until the 1980s was the location for many of the country's leading newspaper publishers. *The blame fell on Fleet Street for distorting the story of the woman's disappearance.*

flesh is grass All living things soon perish, just as grass is mowed down as hay. The phrase appears in Isaiah 40:6–7: "And he said, What shall I cry? All flesh is grass, and all the goodliness thereof is as the flower of the field: The grass withereth, the flower fadeth: because the spirit of the LORD bloweth upon it: surely the people is grass." These verses are referred to in the New Testament in 1 Peter 1:24. "All flesh is grass—an' tesn't no bad thing—grass" (John Galsworthy, *The Forsyte Saga,* 1922).

flesh is weak, the Humans are physically frail and find temptations of the flesh hard to resist. The phrase comes from Matthew 26:40–41 and Mark 14:38, in which the disciples fall asleep in the Garden of Gethsemane despite Christ's entreaties that they remain awake with him: "What, could ye not watch with me one hour? Watch and pray, that ye enter not into temptation: the spirit indeed is willing, but the flesh is weak" (Matthew 26:40–41). "You must not mark me. I feel called to leave my kindred for a while; but it is a trial—the flesh is weak" (George Eliot, *Adam Bede,* 1859). *See also* SPIRIT IS WILLING, BUT THE FLESH IS WEAK, THE.

flesh of my flesh Offspring; children; one's own creation. The phrase comes from Genesis 2:23, where God presented Adam with his companion Eve, fashioned from one of his own ribs. Adam responds with the words: "This is now bone of my bones, and flesh of my flesh." "No woman was ever nearer to her mate than I am: ever more absolutely bone of his bone, flesh of his flesh" (Charlotte Brontë, *Jane Eyre,* 1847).

fleshpot Place where a person may indulge in sinful luxury or self-indulgence. The term appears in Exodus 16:3, in which the Israelites protest against Moses at the conditions they have to endure in the wilderness: "Would to God we had died by the hand of the LORD in the land of Egypt, when we sat by the fleshpots, and when we did eat bread to the full: for ye have brought us forth into the wilderness, to kill this whole assembly with hunger." *She did not like him to go on business trips abroad, fearing he might be lured to the fleshpots she had read about in magazines.*

Flood An overwhelming, extraordinary inundation of water. The original Flood was sent by God to punish the human race for the sinful ways it had fallen into. For 40 days and 40 nights the waters covered the entire face of the world, but God allowed Noah and his family to survive by building an ark, in which they preserved every species on earth (see Genesis 6–9). The Flood is recorded early in the Bible, and thus any reference to times ***before the Flood*** is understood to allude to the very earliest historical periods. *It was a phenomenon the like of which the world had not seen since before the Flood.*

flora (flo͟ră) The native or indigenous plant life of a particular place or period of time. The word comes from Flora, the Roman goddess of flowers, youth, and spring, as depicted in Sandro Botticelli's famous painting *Primavera.* Her name derived from the Latin *flos,* meaning "flower." "Nor less the place of curious plant he knows; / He both his Flora and his Fauna shows" (George Crabbe, *The Borough,* 1810). *See also* FAUNA.

Florence Nightingale (flo͟răns n͟ītingayl) A nurse or other woman who dedicates herself to caring for others. The historical Florence Nightingale (1820–1910) was a British nurse, otherwise known as the ***Lady with the Lamp***, who organized medical support for British troops fighting in the Crimean War in the 1850s, in the process doing much to promote standards in both military and, later, civilian hospitals. As founder of the nursing institute at St. Thomas's Hospital in London, she is revered in the United Kingdom as the founder of modern nursing. *For more than 20 years she played Florence Nightingale to her dying father.*

flotsam and jetsam Bits and pieces, a jumble of unsorted things. The allusion is to the law of salvage relating to shipwrecks, which makes a distinction between debris from a ship that is found floating in the sea (flotsam) and objects that are retrieved after having been deliberately thrown overboard in an attempt to save the vessel (jetsam). In modern usage, the phrase is often applied to people who find themselves members of the lowest ranks of society. "He sees man, especially 'primitive' man, as a rustic philosopher of great intellectual ingenuity and artistic brilliance, a wayward mentalistic beachcomber, endlessly improvising dazzling new patterns of culture from the flotsam and jetsam of other civilizations" (I. M. Lewis, *Social Anthropology in Perspective*, 1992).

flower child A person who embraces the idealistic notions associated with the HIPPIE movement of the 1960s. The ***flower power*** movement emerged during the summer of 1967, especially in San Francisco, with thousands of young people extolling the virtues of peace and love and wearing flowers in their hair. When confronted with armed troops sent to maintain public order, hippies famously spiked their guns with flowers. Today, the term may variously imply an innocent idealism or simply a lack of contact with the realities of modern life. *The leader of the protest group portrays herself as an innocent flower child but is actually a skilled and manipulative political activist.*

Flying Dutchman A cursed ship, or its captain. The legend of the *Flying Dutchman* relates how its captain, variously identified by the name Vanderdecken or Falkenberg, made a pact with the devil in order to save his ship from foundering during a storm off the Cape of Good Hope. Another version of the tale describes how God materialized on the ship's deck during the storm, only to be fired upon by the captain. As a result, the ghost ship was fated to wander the seas for ever. In the opera Richard Wagner later composed on the subject, the ship is allowed to land once every hundred years, and the captain himself can only be saved from his terrible curse by the love of a woman. Sightings of the *Flying Dutchman* are widely supposed by seafarers to be extremely unlucky, portending disaster. There are similar legends in other parts of the world. "If he had had his way we would have been beating up against the Nord-East monsoon, as long as he lived and afterward, too, for ages and ages. Acting the Flying Dutchman in the China Sea!" (Joseph Conrad, *The Shadow Line*, 1917). *See also* ANCIENT MARINER.

fly in the ointment A difficulty or flaw that constitutes a significant drawback in an otherwise ideal situation. The expression is biblical in origin, coming from Ecclesiastes 10:1: "Dead flies cause the ointment of the apothecary to send forth a stinking savour: so doth a little folly him that is in reputation for wisdom and honour." *The fete went very well. The only fly in the ointment was the poor weather.*

Flynn, Errol *See* ERROL FLYNN.

fold their tents like the Arabs To make a discreet, unnoticed exit. The allusion is to H. W. Longfellow's poem "The Day is Done" (1844): "The night shall be filled with music, / And the cares that infest the day / Shall fold their tents, like the Arabs, / And as silently steal away." *After this humiliation they had no option but to fold their tents like the Arabs.*

food of the gods *See* AMBROSIA; NECTAR.

foolish virgins *See* PARABLE OF THE WISE AND FOOLISH VIRGINS.

forbidden fruit Something that is especially desirable but prohibited. The phrase is commonly applied to the fruit of the Tree of Knowledge of Good and Evil described in Genesis 3:1–16, which Adam and Eve are forbidden to eat on God's command. When on the prompting of the serpent Adam and Eve disobey God's order and eat the fruit (commonly depicted as an apple or, in Islamic tradition, as a banyan, or Indian fig), they are expelled from the Garden of Eden. (See also Proverbs 9:17.) In the fuller proverbial form ***forbidden fruit tastes sweetest,*** the implication is that something becomes infinitely more desirable simply because it is prohibited. "Then this spring, three more newspapers—the *Independent,* the *Daily News* and the *Standard*—nibbled the forbidden fruit, and got a heavy legal case for their pains" (*Guardian,* July 13, 1987).

Forest of Arden (ahrdăn) A pastoral paradise, providing a refuge from the cares of the real world. The Forest of Arden was the setting of Shakespeare's comedy *As You Like It* (c. 1600). Shakespeare's Forest of Arden constituted an idealized version of the real forest of the same name, which was located north of his native Stratford-upon-Avon. "The next moment they were in the spacious shade of a sort of Forest of Arden, with great groups of bossy trees standing apart, and deer flashing by at the end of ferny glades" (Edith Wharton, *The Refugees*, 1919).

forlorn hope A force of men that is sent into action with little hope of survival. The allusion is to the groups of volunteers or picked men who were first to storm a breach in the walls of a besieged fortress: The chances of survival were slim, although honors were heaped upon any who did survive a successful attack. Today the phrase (which is ultimately derived from the Dutch *verloren hoop*, meaning "lost troop") is often extended to nonmilitary contexts. "Dreamers were for ever the vanguard, or maybe for ever the forlorn hope" (Kim Newman, *The Night Mayor*, 1990).

Forrest Gump A simpleminded innocent, typically a man who finds himself unintentionally or unwittingly involved in momentous events or who does great things by chance. The allusion is to the 1994 film of the same name starring Tom Hanks as a slow-witted Southerner who accidentally finds himself present at many of the most significant events of the 20th century. *He was a kind of Forrest Gump, floating through life without ever realising the amazing effect he had upon the people he met.*

for such a time as this At such a favorable opportunity, referring to the choice of a person who will have a widespread, significant influence. This phrase alludes to an episode recorded in the book of Esther. Mordecai, a Jewish captive from Judah, held a post at the palace of King Ahasuerus (Xerxes) of Persia at Shushan. When Queen Vashti disobeyed the king and was to be replaced, many young girls from all over the kingdom were brought to the palace to see whom the king would choose. Mordecai put forward his adopted daughter Esther (also known as Hadassah) for the honor. She was beautiful and was chosen by King Ahasuerus to become queen; the king did not know that she was a Jew. Haman, one of the king's high officials, was an anti-Semite and instigator of one of the first pogroms against the Jews. Mordecai heard about Haman's plot to have all the Jews killed and sent word to Esther, asking her to plead with the king to save the Jews: "For if thou altogether holdest thy peace at this time, then shall there enlargement and deliverance arise to the Jews from another place; but thou and thy father's house shall be destroyed: and who knoweth whether thou art come to the kingdom for such a time as this?" (Esther 4:14). This was a life-threatening petition, however, for one could only come into the king's presence at his request, and unless the king held out his golden scepter to Esther she would die in the undertaking. Esther asked that all the Jews fast for three days, and she went to the king, who spared her life. She invited him to several banquets at her palace and included Haman in the invitation. During these she exposed Haman's treachery, he was hanged, and the Jews were saved. *The young man was unexpectedly chosen out of all his peers to become leader. His background equipped him perfectly for the task: He had become a leader for such a time as this.*

Forth Bridge *See* PAINTING THE FORTH BRIDGE.

Fort Knox (noks) A place of great wealth, or one that is very securely guarded or protected. The allusion is to Fort Knox in north Kentucky, where the U.S. depository of gold bullion is located. *She fitted extra locks to all the doors after the burglary—the place is now like Fort Knox.*

Fort Sumter (sămtă) A place where conflict first breaks out. The allusion is to the federal garrison of this name in Charleston, South Carolina, where the first shots were fired in the U.S. Civil War on April 12, 1861. The fort surrendered after a brief siege, and three days later President Lincoln called for volunteers to go into battle against the rebellious South. *This incident, it was feared, would prove the Fort Sumter that would lead to a major war between the opposing factions.*

Fortuna (fortoonă) Personification of luck. Fortuna was identified as the goddess of fortune and good luck in Roman mythology, the equivalent of the Greek Tyche. *It seemed that Fortuna herself smiled on the party the next day, and they made better progress than they had done for many weeks past.*

Fortunate Islands/Isles *See* ISLANDS OF THE BLEST.

forty acres and a mule A promise that is never likely to be fulfilled. At the end of the U.S. Civil War, freed slaves were promised 40 acres and a mule with which to begin a new life as free citizens of the United States, but such compensation never actually materialized. The promise had originally been made by General Sherman in 1865, envisaging the division of land confiscated from Southern landowners, but it was later rescinded by President Andrew Johnson. *I opened the envelope and couldn't help wondering what had happened to the forty acres and a mule that I had been promised.*

forty days and forty nights *See* FLOOD.

forum (forăm) A place or opportunity for discussion of a particular issue or issues. The word alludes to the forum (meaning "public place") of ancient Roman society, a large open space in the center of a town or city that served as the marketplace. It was here that much financial and legal business was transacted, and meetings would also be held on matters of public interest or concern. The word itself comes ultimately from the Latin *foris,* meaning "outside." The ruins of the most famous forum of all, that of Rome, are preserved within the heart of the modern city. In modern usage the word may be applied much more widely, referring to any medium for discussion, such as a magazine or television program, or in computing to "virtual" meeting places on the World Wide Web, where people interested in a particular subject may air their views. "What is called eloquence in the forum is commonly found to be rhetoric in the study" (Henry David Thoreau, *Walden, or Life in the Woods,* 1854).

for whom the bell tolls All individuals are connected by their shared experiences and eventual fate. The phrase ultimately comes from John Donne's *Devotions* (1624): "Any man's death diminishes me, because I am involved in mankind; and therefore never send to know for whom the bell tolls; it tolls for thee." The expression is doubly familiar today as the title of a novel (1940) written by Ernest Hemingway about the Spanish Civil War. *His fate may seem bizarre, even funny, to us now, but we should remember for whom the bell tolls . . . See also* NO MAN IS AN ISLAND.

found wanting *See* WRITING ON THE WALL.

fountain of youth A source of perpetual youth. The notion of a fountain of youth dates back to classical times. Legend had it that Alexander the Great located the whereabouts of a fountain of youth and that both he and his soldiers enjoyed its benefits after bathing in its waters. Subsequently such fountains were a subject of great fascination to medieval scholars and explorers, and many expeditions were mounted in search of such a marvel (including, most notably, the exploration of the Florida Keys area by the Spanish explorer Juan Ponce de León in the early 16th century). In modern usage the phrase tends to be used metaphorically. "You'll never grow old, Teacher,' said Paul. 'You are one of the fortunate mortals who have found and drunk from the Fountain of Youth,—you and Mother Lavendar" (Lucy Maud Montgomery, *Anne's House of Dreams,* 1917).

Four Horsemen of the Apocalypse Personifications of war, famine, pestilence, and death. The Four Horsemen of the Apocalypse are described in the book of Revelation 6:1–8, in which John foresees the end of the world. According to this account, War rides a white horse, Pestilence (or strife) a red horse, Famine a black horse, and Death a pale horse. "Malnutrition, malaria, infant mortality, an AIDS epidemic, with more than half a million people HIV positive; some 3 million people driven out of their homes in a decades-long civil war with the country's large ethnic minorities; rampant corruption, drug abuse and the drugs trade, sexual exploitation, forced labour (you see the road gangs as you travel round the country), banditry; and most recently, allegations of the systematic use of rape by army units, as a weapon of war: every curse and plague of the world, every horseman of the Apocalypse, seems to be marching through Burma's jungles" (*Guardian,* July 11, 2002).

fourth estate The press. The phrase is attributed to Irish statesman and philosopher Edmund Burke (1729–97), who first used it to refer to British public opinion, as voiced by "the mob." The other three estates, according to Burke, were the monarch, the House of Lords, and the House of Commons, although other authorities identified them as the Lords Spiritual (the clergy), the Lords Temporal (the knights and barons), and the House of Commons. The French equivalents were the clergy, the nobility, and the rest of the people. In modern usage, the fourth estate is the press, representing public opinion. "For the press, the loosening of the relationship with politicians produced a dilemma: it aspired to greatness as the fourth estate and as an institution for political enlightenment yet it had to pursue the mass audience in order to survive commercially" (Ralph Negrine, *Politics and the Mass Media in Britain*, 1992).

Francis of Assisi (ăseesee) A person who behaves in a saintly manner, especially toward animals. The allusion is to Saint Francis of Assisi (1182–1226), the founder of the Franciscan monastic order, who was greatly revered for his holy ways and was canonized just two years after his death. He became particularly identified with nature and was said to have preached to the birds and beasts, hence the modern application to people who are known to be fond of animals. *He was a Francis of Assisi who devoted his life to the animals in his care.*

Frankenstein (frankănstīn) A monstrous creation, often one that turns on its own master, or its maker. The allusion is to Mary Shelley's classic horror story *Frankenstein; or, the Modern Prometheus* (1818), in which the scientist Victor Frankenstein constructs a living creature out of dead corpses, only for the monster to turn on him and kill first him and then itself. The name of the monster's creator is often confused with that of the creature itself, and allusions to Frankenstein may refer to a monstrous creation or the person responsible for creating it. The prefix "Franken-" is sometimes used to create new words, typically referring to freakish scientific innovations, as in ***Frankenfood*** (describing genetically modified foodstuffs). *He had created a Frankenstein that eventually destroyed his career. See also* IGOR.

frankincense, gold, and myrrh *See* MAGI.

frankly, my dear, I don't give a damn I don't care at all. The allusion is to one of the closing scenes of the classic 1939 film *GONE WITH THE WIND*, in which Rhett Butler finally rejects the self-absorbed Scarlett O'Hara's desperate appeals. Addressed in the film by Clark Gable to Vivien Leigh, the line differs from that in Margaret Mitchell's 1936 novel, on which the screenplay was based, which has it in the form: "My dear, I don't give a damn." Possibly the most famous quotation from any film, the line had particular power in its time through its inclusion of a swearword, defying contemporary rules about censorship in the film industry. *"Shall I wear my black dress to the party, or the outfit I bought for Carol's wedding?" "Frankly, my dear, I don't give a damn!"*

Fred Astaire (ăstair) A brilliant dancer. The U.S. film actor and singer Fred Astaire (1899–1987) achieved worldwide fame as the finest screen dancer of his (or arguably any other) generation, despite a notorious early audition notice that concluded "Can't act. Slightly bald. Also dances." His name may be applied today to any male who exhibits talent as a dancer, especially one with the same air of elegance and sophistication that Astaire himself exuded. The name of his dancing partner in many films, ***Ginger Rogers*** (1911–95), is sometimes similarly applied to gifted female dancers. *He's no Fred Astaire, but I need a partner for the dance and there's no one else available.*

Freddy Krueger *See* NIGHTMARE ON ELM STREET.

Fred Karno's Army An incompetent organization or group of people. The allusion is to a comedy troupe that enjoyed huge popularity on the British music-hall stage in the early part of the 20th century. Fred Karno was the pseudonym of Frederick John Westcott (1866–1941), leader of the troupe, which specialized in lively slapstick routines. During World War I the troupe's name was adopted as a jocular nickname for the British Army, the generalship of which was called into question by many people both inside and outside the armed forces. *Watching those people trying to sort out the computer was like watching Fred Karno's Army.*

Freudian (froideeăn) Relating to the ideas of Austrian neuropathologist Sigmund Freud (1876–1939), who established the basis for modern psychoanalysis. His theories about psychological problems, which placed great emphasis on childhood experiences and repressed sexuality, were in his day (and continue to be) very controversial. Freud's name is often invoked in discussion of psychological matters and more generally, often in the phrase ***Freudian slip***, which describes a slip of the tongue that may reveal underlying unconscious desires or preoccupations. "Perhaps not letting you know the party was off was a Freudian slip" (Robert Goddard, *Hand in Glove*, 1993).

Freyja (frayă) Personification of fertility. Freyja was identified in Norse mythology as the goddess of prosperity and peace as well as love and fertility. She was the wife of Odin and the Norse equivalent of Venus. *It was a valley ruled by Freyja, the trees heavy with fruit and everything blooming in profusion.*

Friar Tuck A fat, jolly person. Friar Tuck features prominently in the legends surrounding the English folk hero ROBIN HOOD, in which he appears as a jovial and generously proportioned friar. His name is also sometimes invoked in reference to people whose hairstyle recalls the tonsured haircut of the outlaw cleric. "His mature face was more likely to remind the observer of Friar Tuck's jollity than of Lord Brougham's long pointed nose" (Owen Chadwick, *Michael Ramsey: A Life*, 1991).

Friday The sixth day of the week. It was called Frigedaeg in Old English, having been named originally in honor of the Norse goddess Frig (or Frigga), who was identified as the wife of Woden (after whom Wednesday was named) and the mother of Thor (after whom Thursday was named). Venerated as the goddess of married love, she in turn was linked with FREYJA, the Norse goddess of love and fertility. *Some people fear Friday the 13th.*

Friday, Man *See* MAN FRIDAY.

friendly fire Criticism from a friendly source. Of military origin, the expression was introduced in the Vietnam War to describe accidental firing on troops fighting on the same side. *The president looked surprised and irritated to be subjected to friendly fire from someone he clearly expected to defend the official position.*

friend of Dorothy (dorăthee) A homosexual. This euphemistic allusion is to L. Frank Baum's children's story *The Wizard of Oz* (1900) and its famous film adaptation (1939), in which a young girl called Dorothy finds herself magically transported to the extraordinary land of Oz. The U.S. actress and singer Judy Garland (1922–69), who played Dorothy in the film, later became a favorite icon of the gay movement, hence this epithet for anyone who is, or is thought to be, homosexual. In the film, Dorothy's loyal friends are the

Tin Man, the ***Scarecrow***, and the ***Cowardly Lion***. "Charlie strolled past me, his arm around a girl who had her tits hanging out, and he said, to make her laugh, 'Hurry up, Karim, you great girl's blouse, you friend of Dorothy'" (Hanif Kureishi, *The Buddha of Suburbia*, 1990). *See also* WIZARD OF OZ.

frog prince A person who undergoes a transformation that reveals qualities not previously suggested by his or her appearance. The allusion is to the traditional fairy tale *The Frog Prince*, in which a prince is turned into a frog and can only regain his original form when kissed by a princess. *Her husband turned out to be something of a frog prince, defying expectations by proving good company and, even more impressively, useful around the house.*

from Dan to Beersheba *See* DAN TO BEERSHEBA, FROM.

from the mouths of babes come words of wisdom *See* OUT OF THE MOUTHS OF BABES AND SUCKLINGS.

fruit of one's labors The product of hard work. The expression comes from Philippians 1:22: "But if I live in the flesh, this is the fruit of my labour: yet what I shall choose I wot not." *It is a bitter thing to see the fruit of one's labors ignored in such a manner.*

fruits, know them by their *See* KNOW THEM BY THEIR FRUITS.

Führer (fyooră) A dictatorial person. The title (meaning "leader" in German) was adopted by Nazi dictator Adolf HITLER on replacing President Hindenburg as German leader in 1934. Such was the barbarity and inhumanity of the regime over which he presided that even now the term remains contentious, although it is not infrequently applied to any boss or other figure in authority who is perceived to act in a harsh or intolerant manner. *Her father was the office Führer, who insisted upon complete obedience from his underlings.*

full monty (montee) The complete version or full set of something. The origins of this term are obscure and much debated, though it appears to date from around the middle of the 20th century. The allusion may be to the British men's outfitters Montague and Burton, who were famous for their smart three-piece suits. Alternatively it may be a reference to the Spanish card game monte or to Field Marshal Bernard Montgomery (1887–1976), who was nicknamed Monty—hence, perhaps, the use of the term to describe the full English breakfast (which Monty used to enjoy every morning). The term gained new popularity (and other connotations) after it was used as the title of a 1997 film about a group of unemployed British workers who seek to raise money as striptease artists. In their case, the term refers to full-frontal nudity. *She had the full outfit on, cowboy hat, leather jacket, a pair of sixshooters, chaps—the full monty.*

Fu Manchu (foo manchoo) Archetype of a person from the East, especially one who is suspected of being a villain. The evil Chinese doctor Fu Manchu, complete with drooping ***Fu Manchu mustache*** and inscrutable manner, appeared as a criminal mastermind in stories by Sax Rohmer (Arthur Sarsfield Ward; c. 1883–1959) first published in the *Story-Teller Magazine* in 1912 and later in novel form and in films. Fu Manchu's plans to achieve world domination were thwarted time and time again by his English nemesis Dennis Nayland Smith. "He had a bald spot, under a straggle of brown hair, and a ratty Fu Manchu moustache" (Kim Newman, *Bad Dreams*, 1990).

Furies Avenging spirits. The Furies, also known as the ***Erinyes,*** were depicted in Greek mythology as three winged, snake-haired goddesses named Tisiphone, Alecto, and Megaera, who were merciless in their pursuit of unpunished criminals, especially those who had committed offenses against their own kin, blasphemed against the gods, or betrayed a guest or host. They were variously said to be the daughters of Gaea or to have sprung up from the blood of Uranus. Because it was thought unlucky to allude to the Furies by name, they were sometimes referred to euphemistically as the ***Eumenides,*** meaning "Kindly Ones." The story of how they pursued Orestes for having killed his mother Clytemnestra is related in the play *Eumenides* by Aeschylus (525–456 B.C.). "The Vengeance, uttering terrific shrieks, and flinging her arms about her head like the forty Furies at once, was tearing from house to house, rousing the women" (Charles Dickens, *A Tale of Two Cities,* 1859).

G

Gable, Clark *See* CLARK GABLE.

Gabler, Hedda *See* HEDDA GABLER.

Gabriel (gaybreeăl) A messenger of God. The archangel Gabriel appears four times in the Bible, each time bringing a message from God, such as that to Zechariah in Luke 1:19: "I am Gabriel, that stand in the presence of God; and am sent to speak unto thee, and to shew thee these glad tidings." His most notable appearance is in Luke 1:26–38, when he announces to Mary the forthcoming birth of Jesus: "The angel Gabriel was sent from God . . . Fear not, Mary: for thou hast found favour with God. And, behold, thou shalt conceive in thy womb, and bring forth a son, and shalt call his name JESUS" (Luke 1:26, 30–31). In Islamic tradition, it is Gabriel who reveals the Qur'an to Muhammad. "Alida Fischer calls him Archangel Gabriel, because his true self came out of its shell when her son was arrested" (Alan Paton, *Ah, but Your Land Is Beautiful,* 1981).

Gabriel's trumpet *See* LAST TRUMP.

Gadarene (gadăreen) Headlong; reckless; hasteful. The adjective alludes to the biblical story of the Gadarene swine to which, according to the account given in Mark 5:1–17 and Luke 8:26–37, Christ transferred demons that had possessed two men and made them mad. Under the influence of the demons the swine rushed madly down a steep slope into the Sea of Galilee and was drowned. *In his dream he was hurtling with Gadarene haste into a fire-brimmed pit, unable and even unwilling to stop. See also* MY NAME IS LEGION.

Gaea (jeeă) Personification of the Earth, especially with reference to its ecology. In Greek mythology Gaea (also called Gaia or Ge) gave birth to the sky, mountains, and sea and became the mother of Uranus, who united with him to create the Titans, the Cyclops, and the giants. The term Gaea has now acquired a much wider meaning, signifying a worldview of environmental issues.

Galahad (galăhad) A person of noble and virtuous character. Sir Galahad was renowned as the purest of the knights who formed the ROUND TABLE of KING ARTHUR. Only Sir Galahad was virtuous enough to find the HOLY GRAIL, a fact underlined by the fact that he alone could sit in the ***Siege Perilous***, a seat at the Round Table reserved for the knight who would complete the quest for the Grail. In modern usage, his name is usually bestowed upon someone who performs a heroic rescue, typically of a DAMSEL IN DISTRESS. "Neil, who never thought of himself as in any way a Galahad, or a knight errant in shining armour, saving virgins under attack, nevertheless felt compelled to investigate, particularly when the cry came again, more despairing than ever" (Paula Marshall, *An American Princess*, 1993).

Galatea (galăteeă) The archetype of a beautiful woman. In Greek myth Galatea was the stone statue of a perfect woman as created by the sculptor Pygmalion, who had been repulsed by the imperfections of mortal women. Aphrodite made Pygmalion fall in love with his creation but finally took pity on his misery and brought the statue to life. The concept of the artist constructing his ideal woman is familiar in modern times from the play *Pygmalion* (1913) by George Bernard Shaw, which provided the basis for the popular stage and motion-picture musicals *My Fair Lady* (1956 and 1964, respectively). ". . . with a sudden motion she shook her gauzy covering from her, and stood forth in her low kirtle and her snaky zone, in her glorious, radiant beauty and her imperial grace, rising from her wrappings, as it were, like Venus from the wave, or Galatea from her marble, or a beatified spirit from the tomb" (H. Rider Haggard, *She*, 1887).

galenical A medicine derived from plant or animal tissue. The word comes from the name of the Greek physician Galen (A.D. 129–199), whose ideas exerted a profound influence on the development of medicine for more than 1,000 years. Galen's name also appears alongside that of the equally renowned physician Hippocrates (c. 460–c. 377 B.C.) in the saying ***Galen says "Nay" and Hippocrates "Yea,"*** which patients have been known to quote wearily when their doctors disagree. *Some of the most interesting new medicines of recent years have been of galenical origin.*

gall and wormwood Spite; bitterness; feelings of mortification. The phrase is biblical in origin: "And I said, My strength and my hope is perished from the LORD: Remembering mine affliction and my misery, the wormwood and the gall" (Lamentations 3:18–19). "It was gall and wormwood to his soul to see that splendid, highly-accomplished woman, once so courted and admired, transformed into an active managing housewife, with hands and head continually occupied with household labours and household economy" (Anne Brontë, *Agnes Grey*, 1847).

Gallio (galeeō) A person who seems completely indifferent to something, especially a petty official who refuses to concern himself with matters outside his immediate province. The historical Gallio (c. 5 B.C.–A.D. 65) was the elder brother of the philosopher Seneca and was proconsul of the Roman province of Achaia in 51–52. While serving in this capacity he refused to listen to accusations made against the preaching of the apostle Paul because the charges against him related to Jewish, not Roman law (as related in Acts 18:12–13). "And ne'er was there mair need of poorfu' preachers than e'en now in these cauld Gallio days, when men's hearts are hardened like the nether millstone, till they come to regard none of these things" (Sir Walter Scott, *The Heart of Midlothian*, 1818).

Gallipoli (gălipălee) The Allied campaign in the Dardanelles during World War I. Gallipoli is the name of the peninsula on which the Allies landed in April 1915, only to find themselves under heavy fire from the Turkish defenders. After heavy losses the Allies finally withdrew in January 1916. Gallipoli is sometimes referred to in connection with other disastrous campaigns of various kinds. "Himself the son of a South Wales miner, Kinnock compared Scargill with a world war general who wanted 'another Gallipoli'" (Kenneth O. Morgan, *The People's Peace*, 1990).

Gamaliel (gămayleeăl) A teacher, especially a religious teacher. The biblical Gamaliel was a Pharisee rabbi, or doctor of law, and a mentor of Paul, who claimed to have studied sitting "at the feet of Gamaliel" (Acts 22:3). Gamaliel spoke up in defense of Paul and his companions when they were put on trial and is traditionally supposed to have subsequently converted to Christianity. "No man—that is, no gentleman—could possibly be attracted to Mr. Slope, or consent to sit at the feet of so abhorrent a Gamaliel" (Anthony Trollope, *Barchester Towers,* 1857).

game as Ned Kelly *See* NED KELLY.

gamesmanship The use of cunning, possibly illegal, strategies to achieve one's aims. The allusion is to the book *The Theory and Practice of Gamesmanship* (1947) by Stephen Potter, in which various methods of getting one's way without actually cheating are humorously described. "Let us say that, although not trapped in a fight for survival, we are all still caught up in the ordinary competitiveness of business, social gamesmanship, and marriage" (A. C. Graham, *Reason and Spontaneity*, 1985).

Gandalf (gandalf) A wise old wizard, or someone who has the appearance of one. Gandalf is the wizard who guides the heroes through their various adventures in the novels *The Hobbit* (1937) and *The Lord of the Rings* (1954–55) by J. R. R. Tolkien. In keeping with many other wizards of folklore and literature, Gandalf has a long white beard and wears a tall wizard's hat. *The old man raged with fury at their disobedience and shook his walking stick at them for all the world like a demented Gandalf.*

Gandhi (gahndee, gandee) A pacifist, especially one who is charismatic or inspirational. The allusion is to Mahatma Gandhi (Mohandas Karamchand Gandhi; 1869–1948), who advocated the use of peaceful methods when campaigning for Indian independence from Britain in the 1940s. He was finally assassinated by a Hindu nationalist. *He acted Gandhi to the hotheads who insisted that armed resistance was the only way forward.*

gang of four A group of four people acting together. The original Gang of Four were the leaders of a Chinese political faction who tried (and failed) to seize power in China on the death of Mao Zedong in 1976. They included Mao's widow Jiang Qing. The term was subsequently applied to the four founders of the Britain's Social Democratic Party in 1981. It is frequently employed in a critical fashion. *We do not want this country to come under the control of a U.S. Gang of Four.*

Gantry, Elmer *See* ELMER GANTRY.

Ganymede (ganimeed) An exceptionally beautiful youth. In Greek myth, Ganymede was a young man from Phrygia who was selected by Zeus as the most beautiful of mortals and on his command carried off by an eagle to serve as his cupbearer in heaven. Ganymede is also the name of one of the Galilean moons of Jupiter and is the largest satellite in the solar system. "I don't believe Ganymede cried when the eagle carried him away, and perhaps deposited him on Jove's shoulder at the end" (George Eliot, *Adam Bede,* 1859).

Garbo (gahrbō) An enigmatic, reclusive woman, especially a beautiful one. The Swedish-born U.S. film actress Greta Garbo (Greta Gustafsson; 1905–90) was famous both for her beauty and for her reluctance to accept the attentions of the world's media, which remained fascinated by her until her death after nearly 50 years in retirement. Impersonations of her almost invariably contain the quotation, delivered in heavily accented English, ***"I want to be alone"***—a line from her 1932 film *Grand Hotel. When it came to getting information out of her she turned out to be a second Garbo.*

Garden of Eden (eedăn) Paradise or some other unspoiled, idyllic place, or a state of perfect bliss or innocence. The biblical Garden of Eden, from which ADAM and EVE were expelled after disobeying God's command not to eat from the Tree of the Knowledge of Good and Evil, is described briefly in Genesis: "And the LORD God planted a garden eastward in Eden; and there he put the man whom he had formed. And out of the ground made the LORD God to grow every tree that is pleasant to the sight, and good for food; the tree of life also in the midst of the garden, and the tree of knowledge of good and evil. And a river went out of Eden to water the garden" (Genesis 2:8–10). The Hebrew word *eden,* incidentally, is usually translated as "pleasure" or "delight." Tradition variously places the historical site of the Garden of Eden as being in Mesopotamia, Armenia, or somewhere at the head of the Persian Gulf, possibly at Eridu, where clay tablets have been found telling of a garden with a sacred palm tree. "Versailles! It is wonderfully beautiful! You gaze, and stare, and try to understand that it is real, that it is on the earth, that it is not the Garden of Eden" (Mark Twain, *The Innocents Abroad,* 1869).

Gargantuan (gahrganchăwăn) Huge, on an enormous scale. The word is an allusion to a legendary giant called Gargantua, who was famed in Celtic or medieval mythology for his insatiable appetite. He is familiar today as a character in the 1534 satire *Gargantua* by the French writer François Rabelais (c. 1494–c. 1553). "It was not until 1960 that the gargantuan task of demolishing the attached asylum was undertaken and Forston Manor returned to its original self as though nothing had happened" (Lycett Green, *The Perfect English Country House*, 1991). *See also* RABELAISIAN.

Garibaldi (garăboldee) A revolutionary leader. Giuseppe Garibaldi (1807–82) led his army of Red Shirts to victory in the struggle for Italian independence and unification in the middle of the 19th century. His name today is also associated with a style of loose-fitting red blouse, called a Garibaldi, and with the ***Garibaldi biscuit***, a type of currant biscuit that the Italian revolutionary was said to be very fond of. *Like other South American countries, its history was transformed by the emergence of a homegrown Garibaldi figure.*

Garnett, Alf *See* ARCHIE BUNKER.

gasp, at the last *See* LAST GASP, AT THE.

-gate Suffix denoting a scandal of some kind. The origin lies in the WATERGATE political scandal of the 1970s, which precipitated the downfall of President Richard Nixon. The suffix is usually employed in referring to political, administrative, or financial scandals. *The Irangate scandal led to the premature destruction of several prominent political careers in 1986.*

Gates, Bill *See* BILL GATES.

Gath, tell it not in *See* TELL IT NOT IN GATH.

gather ye rosebuds Take advantage of opportunities when they present themselves, for they may not always be available. The expression is a quotation from the poem "To the Virgins, to Make Much of Time" by the English poet Robert Herrick (1591–1674): "Gather ye rosebuds while ye may, / Old Time is still a-flying; / And this same flower that smiles today / Tomorrow will be dying." *"Gather ye rosebuds," the old man was heard to mutter to his best man as he led his youthful bride up the aisle.*

Gatsbyesque (gatsbeeesk) In a manner reminiscent of the central character in F. Scott Fitzgerald's novel *The Great Gatsby* (1925). Fitzgerald's Jay Gatsby, who is at once a romantic innocent and a bootlegger with dubious underworld connections, is a rich but enigmatic Long Islander whose wealth proves insufficient compensation for loneliness and an unrespectable background. The term "Gatsbyesque" may refer to the corruption that often lies under apparently respectable appearances, to the attempts of a self-made man to escape his past, or merely to the superficial gloss and extravagance of the world in which the rich move. *She was well known for the Gatsbyesque parties she threw in her upstate mansion.*

gauntlet, run the *See* RUN THE GAUNTLET.

gauntlet, throw down the *See* THROW DOWN THE GAUNTLET.

gay Lothario *See* LOTHARIO.

Gaza, eyeless in *See* EYELESS IN GAZA.

Ge *See* GAEA. TELL IT NOT IN GATH.

geese that saved the Capitol The bearers of a timely warning that prevents disaster. The allusion is to the story of the sacred geese that warned of a Gaulish attack on the Capitoline Hill in 390 B.C. The Gauls had climbed unnoticed to the top of the hill before the cackling of the geese alerted Marcus Manlius, who roused the garrison just in time to drive off the attack. In gratitude, the Romans commemorated the event each year by carrying a golden goose in procession to the Capitol. *The two journalists were praised for their courage in pursuing the story, and their revelations were considered vital in staving off disaster. One paper even dubbed them the geese that saved the Capitol.*

Gehenna (gehenă) Hell or any wicked or unpleasant place. The name comes from the Hebrew *ge-hinnom,* meaning "valley of the son of Hinnom," which is identified in the Bible in Jeremiah 7:31–32 as the place where the followers of the god Molech sacrificed their children in fires at a "high place" called Tophet (or Topheth). This valley was located to the southwest of Jerusalem. It became associated with burning, especially as a site for the burning of the corpses of outcasts, which made it an effective analogy for the fires of hell and of everlasting judgment. ***Go to Gehenna*** is accordingly an alternative to *go to hell.* "Down to Gehenna or up to the Throne, / He travels fastest who travels alone" (Rudyard Kipling, *The Story of the Gadsbys,* 1890).

Gekko, Gordon *See* GORDON GEKKO.

generation of vipers A band of evil, untrustworthy people. The phrase appears in Matthew 3:7 ("O generation of vipers, who hath warned you to flee from the wrath to come?") and Luke 3:7, attributed to John the Baptist, and in Matthew 12:34 and 23:33, where it is credited to Christ in his condemnation of the Pharisees and Sadducees. *Eyeing the gun with growing unease, the young man began to suspect he had fallen in with a generation of vipers.*

genesis A beginning; the origin of something. The word comes from the Greek for "to be born" and is best known as the name of the first book of the Old Testament, which relates God's creation of the world. *The genesis of the project goes back to Duckworth's work in the late 1990s.*

Genghis Khan (gengis kahn) A person who behaves in a violent or barbaric manner. The Mongol leader Genghis Khan (c. 1162–1227) established an empire that extended from the Black Sea in the west to the Pacific Ocean in the east, in the process acquiring a reputation for ferocity and brutality. His real name was Temujin; "Genghis Khan" means "king of the ocean." People with extreme right-wing views are sometimes labeled as being ***to the right of Genghis Khan***. *The front room looked as if Genghis Khan had spent the night there. See also* ATTILA THE HUN; TARTAR.

genie (jeenee) A supernatural or magical being who will grant a person's wishes or carry out his or her commands and, by extension, a person who performs apparently impossible feats. The word comes from the Arabic *jinni,* a species of demon in Muslim mythology that inhabits the mountains since long before the birth of Adam. The jinn are credited with the power to change their appearance and assume the form of animals or humans; they play a leading role in numerous folktales. Some are good natured and beautiful, but others are hideously ugly and not to be trusted. "His closing exclamation is jerked out of the venerable gentleman by the suddenness with which Mr. Squod, like a genie, catches him up, chair and all, and deposits him on the hearth-stone" (Charles Dickens, *Bleak House,* 1852–53). *See also* ALADDIN'S LAMP.

genius loci (jeenyăs lōsī, jeeneeăs lōkee) The presiding spirit or deity of a particular place. The notion that there are supernatural entities that watch over specific locations and need to be honored and appeased was very familiar to the ancient Romans, who named them so. The modern notion of genius signifying intellectual brilliance is derived from the related belief that each individual has his or her personal guardian spirit who guides them through life. Another facet of the belief system suggests that each person has both a good genius and an evil genius who contend to influence the individual's thought and behavior. "His sudden appearance was to darkness what the sound of a trumpet is to silence. Gloom, the genius loci at all times hitherto, was now totally overthrown, less by the lantern-light than by what the lantern lighted" (Thomas Hardy, *Far from the Madding Crowd,* 1874).

gentian (jenshăn) A plant of the genus *Gentiana,* with attractive blue (but also sometimes yellow, white, or red) flowers. The name is thought to have come from the Illyrian king Gentius, who lived in the second century B.C. and is traditionally supposed to have been the first person to employ gentian flowers medicinally. The color of gentian flowers has also inspired the naming of a particular shade of purple-blue as ***gentian blue***. "'Bother the woman!' she thought. 'I do want that gentian dress got ready, but now I simply can't give it to her to do'" (John Galsworthy, *The Forsyte Saga,* 1922).

Geppetto *See* PINOCCHIO.

Geronimo (jăronimō) War cry commonly uttered on launching oneself into an exhilarating, even dangerous, activity. Geronimo (c. 1829–1909) was an Apache chieftain who carried out raids on white settlers in Arizona and Mexico before finally surrendering to the U.S. Army in 1886. Legend has it that when cornered by a U.S. cavalry patrol at Medicine Bluffs, Oklahoma, he yelled "Geronimo!" in defiance as he leaped on his horse into the river below. U.S. paratroops in World War II, many of whom trained near Medicine Bluffs, took to shouting the chief's name as they leaped from their aircraft into action. Geronimo's actual Native American name, however, was Goyathlay. *The youth ran to the water's edge and with an exuberant "Geronimo!" hurled himself into the water.*

gestalt (găstolt, găshtolt) A range of elements considered as part of a greater single context, such as a personality or a period of history. The word is German, meaning "form, shape, configuration." It was applied around 1950 to a new psychotherapeutic approach developed by Fritz Perls (1893–1970) and his wife Laura, though the term has since escaped its confined association with psychology. "A Gestalt is a mode of perception of a group of objects—say of the dots in a printed picture—so that they are seen as one thing" (Raymond Tallis and Howard Robinson, *The Pursuit of Mind*, 1991).

Gestapo (găstahpō) A ruthless, bullying police force or other authority. The allusion is to the *Geheime Staatspolizei* ("secret state police"), Gestapo for short, that served as the secret police of the German Nazi regime from 1933 to 1945. It acquired a notorious reputation for its brutal treatment of enemies of the state, among them political opponents and Jews. *The food Gestapo would never allow great stuff like that to be served up in school canteens.*

Geste, Beau *See* BEAU GESTE.

Gethsemane (gethsemănee) A painful ordeal; a place of anguish or suffering. The Garden of Gethsemane, at the foot of the Mount of Olives outside Jerusalem, was the place where Christ prayed after the Last Supper on the night of his betrayal and arrest: "Then cometh Jesus with them unto a place called Gethsemane, and saith unto the disciples, Sit ye here, while I go and pray yonder" (Matthew 26:36). According to one tradition, it was in Gethsemane that Mary was buried. The word itself means "oil press" in Greek. *That afternoon the stadium became the team's Gethsemane, their ultimate humiliation and yet the foundation of famous triumphs to come in the years ahead.*

get thee behind me, Satan (saytăn) Do not try to tempt me; I refuse to be tempted. This is a quotation from the Bible, appearing in Matthew 4:10 and Luke 4:1–8, which both recount Christ's reply to the devil in the wilderness when the latter tries to lure him with promises of power over all the kingdoms of the world in exchange for his allegiance: "Get thee behind me, Satan: for it is written, Thou shalt worship the Lord thy God, and him only shalt thou serve" (Luke 4:8). The phrase also appears in Matthew 16:23 as Christ's reply when Peter tries to persuade him against willingly going to crucifixion. *"Get thee behind me, Satan," said the colonel as he hurried past the beckoning open door of the saloon bar.*

get to first base To achieve the first stage of something. The allusion is to baseball, in which first base is the first of four points that a batter must reach in order to score a run. The expression is commonly associated with lovemaking, "first base" being kissing or other foreplay preceding full sexual intercourse. "Real shame our movie never got past first base" (J. Cartwright, *Masai Dreaming*, 1993).

Getty, Jean Paul *See* JEAN PAUL GETTY.

Gettysburg Address (getizberg) The ideal of a brilliant political speech. The Gettysburg Address was delivered by President ABRAHAM LINCOLN on November 19, 1863, just four months after the bloody Battle of Gettysburg, arguably the most decisive encounter of the U.S. Civil War. Only a few minutes long, Lincoln's speech in honor of the dead buried on the battlefield entered popular mythology and is still seen as a standard by which other political utterances may be measured: "We here highly resolve that these dead shall not have died in vain—that this nation, under God, shall have a new birth of freedom—and that government of the people, by the people, for the people, shall not perish from the earth." *The new governor's inaugural speech fell well short of the Gettysburg Address but it served to motivate the team around him.*

ghetto (getō) A neighborhood in which certain parts of the population are obliged to live, either by official order or because they cannot afford to live anywhere else. The origins of the word are uncertain. It may have come from the Italian for "cannon factory," there being a cannon factory beside the area of Venice in which the city's Jewish population settled, or it may be a reference to the Jewish quarter on the Venetian island of Il Geto. The term has since been applied to persecuted populations of many different kinds, as well as to other groups variously seen as being separated from the rest of society. *In her spare time she was studying for a law degree, anxious to escape from the financial-services ghetto.*

giant A person or thing of exceptional size, importance, etc. The huge ogres of European folklore are descended from a supernatural race in Greek myth, identified as the offspring of GAEA (representing the earth) and URANUS (representing the sky). According to legend, the giants, who had terrifying faces and serpents' tails for legs, rebelled against the gods on Olympus and waged war with them for 10 years before being defeated and killed or consigned by Zeus to Tartarus. One suggestion is that the story of the epic struggle between the gods and the giants was inspired by volcanic eruptions. *Stories about human-eating giants are common to many cultural traditions, and many are apparently of great antiquity.*

giants in the earth The heroes of a bygone age, when humans were far more glorious beings than they are today. The phrase is biblical, appearing in Genesis 6:4: "There were giants in the earth in those days." It is sometimes believed that after the time of Adam and Eve's expulsion from the Garden of Eden the world was populated by a race of magnificent giants called the Nephilim, who were produced by the union of various heavenly beings with human women. The terms *Nephilim* and *giants* are also applied to some of the pre-Israelite inhabitants of Canaan (Numbers 13:33), who were also referred to as the Rephaim/Rephaites and Anakim/Anakites (Deuteronomy 2:11; 3:11), and Goliath was one of their descendants, but they are not heard of after the time of David. The biblical references in Genesis 6:4 and Numbers 13:33 have also led to the expression ***land of giants***, "sometimes used figuratively to refer to areas of great opportunity that contain apparently formidable difficulties" (Manser, *King James Bible Word Book,* p. 253). *But things were different then, and there were giants in the earth.*

Gibson girl An elegant young woman of the early 20th century. The Gibson girl was named after her creator, U.S. artist and illustrator Charles Dana Gibson (1867–1944), who was well known for his drawings of wasp-waisted young beauties of the 1890s and 1900s, fashionably sporty and dressed in the latest styles. *Her mother was a Gibson girl who was often seen at fashionable Boston social gatherings.*

Gideons (gideeănz) An interdenominational Christian organization that works to make the Bible available to as many people as possible throughout the world. Founded in the United States in 1899 by three traveling businessmen—Samuel E. Hill, William J. Knights, and John H. Nicholson—the Gideon Society takes its name from Gideon, the great Israelite soldier and judge who led his people to victory over the Midianites, as recounted in Judges 6–7. *The room was sparsely furnished, the only extras being a jug of water and a Gideon Bible in the bedside cabinet.*

gift of tongues The ability to speak in many languages without having previously learned them. This ability, technically termed *glossolalia,* was a feature of early Christian worship and alludes to the biblical account of the apostles, who miraculously acquired the power to communicate in a variety of languages during the Feast of Pentecost (as related in Acts 2:4–12); the apostle Paul also refers to its use, with interpretation of tongues, in 1 Corinthians 12 and 14. "Ane wad hae needed the gift of tongues to ken preceesely what they said—but I pelieve the best end of it was, 'Long live MacCallummore and Knockdunder!'" (Sir Walter Scott, *The Heart of Midlothian,* 1818).

G.I. Joe An enlisted man in the U.S. Army. The nickname became widely known from 1942 after it appeared as the title of a comic strip in the U.S. Army magazine *Yank*. G.I. was understood to stand for "general issue" or "government issue," although it may well have been borrowed originally from an industrial context, in which it stood for "galvanized iron" (many articles made from galvanized iron being used by the military). Women serving in the U.S. Army were dubbed ***G.I. Janes***. In the 1960s G.I. Joe was also taken up as a brand name for a soldier doll figure widely sold to young boys (though retitled ***Action Man*** in the UK). *A couple of very drunk G. I. Joes rolled up at the bar around midnight, but were quickly removed by the military police.*

Gilded Age A time that is characterized by immorality and cynicism. The allusion is to an 1873 novel of the same title by Mark Twain and Charles Dudley, which was set in the period after the U.S. Civil War, when vulgarity, materialism, and corruption were seen as replacing more wholesome preoccupations and values. *The collapse of communism in Russia ushered in a gilded age in which billions were made by a greedy few.*

Gilderoy's kite *See* HIGHER THAN GILDEROY'S KITE.

gild the lily To add more than is necessary to something that is already beautiful or otherwise satisfactory. The expression comes from William Shakespeare's play *King John* (1595): "To gild refined gold, to paint the lily, / To throw perfume on the violet, / To smooth the ice, or add another hue / Unto the rainbow, or with taper-light / To seek the beauteous eye of heaven to garnish, / Is wasteful, and ridiculous excess." *Offering shareholders an extra dividend on top of the huge profits they had already made was just gilding the lily.*

Gilead, balm in *See* BALM IN GILEAD.

Ginger Rogers *See* FRED ASTAIRE.

Gin Lane A place or situation in which heavy drinking and the problems associated with it are rife. The allusion is to a 1751 print by the British artist William Hogarth (1697–1764), in which he depicted the social ills resulting from habitual drunkenness in contemporary London. Hogarth's model for his picture was the parish of St. Giles in London, where a quarter of all the residences were operating as gin shops by 1750. *The second duke, legend has it, took a stroll up Gin Lane as a young man and never returned. See also* HOGARTHIAN.

Ginnungagap (gin̲ăngăgap) A great void or abyss. In Norse mythology, Ginnungagap is the name given to the endless void that is said to separate NIFLHEIM, a region of intense cold, and Muspelheim, a region of intense heat. Having no beginning or end and no day or night, it was said to have existed long before the appearance of heaven and earth. *Into this purgatory, this spiritual Ginnungagap, vanished all his ideals and hopes for the future.*

Gioconda smile *See* MONA LISA SMILE.

Giovanni, Don *See* DON JUAN.

Gipper, win one for the *See* WIN ONE FOR THE GIPPER.

girdle of Venus *See* APHRODITE.

gird up thy loins To get ready for action; to prepare to apply oneself to a difficult task or to make a journey. The phrase appears several times in the Bible, such as in 1 Kings 18:46, where Elijah gathers up his long flowing robes and fastens ("girds") them with his belt ("girdle") in order to run freely: "And the hand of the LORD was on Elijah; and he girded up his loins, and ran before Ahab to the entrance of Jezreel." "'Yet,' said the Rabbi, 'take courage, for this grief availeth nothing. Gird up thy loins, and seek out this Wilfred, the son of Cedric'" (Sir Walter Scott, *Ivanhoe,* 1819).

Girl Friday A woman who takes on a range of duties, from housework to acting as a personal assistant. The expression represents a female equivalent of MAN FRIDAY, which was itself taken from the name of a character in Daniel Defoe's novel *Robinson Crusoe* (1719). The phrase furnished the title of the 1940 Cary Grant movie *His Girl Friday*, but has largely fallen into disfavor in recent years on the grounds of political incorrectness. "You were just a junior, a sort of Girl Friday with no qualifications, hoping to learn the ropes" (Jane Bauling, *Ransacked Heart*, 1993).

git thar fustest with the mostest *See* FIRSTEST WITH THE MOSTEST.

give up the ghost To die; to give in; to cease working. The phrase appears in various forms at several places in the Bible, as in Genesis 25:8, which describes how "Abraham gave up the ghost, and died in a good old age." "Why died I not from the womb? Why did I not give up the ghost when I came out of the belly?" (Thomas Hardy, *Jude the Obscure,* 1895).

give us this day our daily bread See DAILY BREAD.

gladiator A person who fights for or supports a particular cause or campaign. Derived from the Latin *gladius* (meaning "sword"), the term was applied to the combatants who fought to the death with a range of weapons as a form of public entertainment in the arenas of ancient Rome. Gladiatorial contests were eventually suppressed in the Eastern Empire in A.D. 325 and in the West in A.D. 500. *The two fighters squared up to each other like gladiators on the sands of the Colosseum.*

Gladstonian (gladstōneeăn) Relating to the policies or character of British prime minister William Gladstone (1809–98). Gladstone was well known for his rather stern and serious views as well as for his devout religious faith and undoubted talents as a statesman. Hence, a Gladstonian politician may be one who is regarded as a heavyweight, with strongly-held views. "'Perhaps then,' said Viola, whose lips were still set in a Gladstonian expression, 'you will find it possible to bring my grandchildren along for me to have a look at' (Robert Barnard, *Posthumous Papers*, 1992).

glad tidings of great joy See GOOD TIDINGS OF GREAT JOY.

glasnost (glaznost) Relaxation of rules and regulations. The term became widely familiar in the late 1980s as the official policy of the Soviet Communist Party under its general secretary Mikhail Gorbachev, who favored greater freedom from restraint in social and cultural affairs. The word *glasnost* (meaning "openness") was often used in conjunction with ***perestroika*** (meaning "restructuring"), which referred to economic and political reform. *He had declared a new policy of glasnost, which would allow every member of the family to have their say.*

glass ceiling A level beyond which an employee cannot hope to be promoted. The expression has its origins in the business world, in which context the term suggests the image of an invisible barrier that can be seen through, making promotion seem possible, but which impedes further upward progress. It is often applied in the world of work to female employees, who feel that their sex prevents them from reaching the highest levels. *There was a glass ceiling that she must break through if her dreams were to be realized.*

glass darkly, through a See SEE THROUGH A GLASS DARKLY.

glass jaw An inherent weakness that makes an individual vulnerable to defeat by an opponent. The phrase comes from boxing, in which it denotes a fighter who is easily knocked out by a blow to the chin. *His sensitivity to criticism turned out to be his glass jaw when he sought a career in public life.*

glass of wine with the Borgias See BORGIAS, THE.

Glaucus (glahkăs) A person who is destroyed by his passion for something. In Greek mythology, Glaucus was a son of Sisyphus. Glaucus was devoted to his horses but could not be persuaded to breed them. This provoked the anger of Venus, who made the horses tear their owner to pieces. *Like Glaucus, his passion for the turf proved his undoing.*

Glaucus swap *See* DIOMEDEAN EXCHANGE.

glory, in all one's *See* IN ALL ONE'S GLORY.

glory is departed, the The times are not what they were; the golden age has passed. The expression is biblical, appearing in 1 Samuel 4:21, where Phineas's wife names her new baby ***Ichabod*** (meaning "inglorious" or "no glory") after hearing that the Philistines have captured the Ark of the Covenant and that both the child's father and grandfather are dead. By the same token, the name Ichabod has in times past been used as an exclamation. "That pulpit would indeed be his own. Precentors, vicars, and choristers might hang up their harps on the willows. Ichabod! Ichabod! The glory of their house was departing from them" (Anthony Trollope, *Barchester Towers,* 1857). "And then, Ichabod! Ichabod! the glory will be departed from us" (T. H. Huxley, "A Liberal Education," 1899).

glory to God in the highest *See* GOODWILL TO ALL MEN.

gnashing of teeth *See* WEEPING AND GNASHING OF TEETH.

gnome (nōm) A diminutive creature resembling an old, deformed man: A familiar character of fairy tale and legend, conventionally described as living underground in mines or quarries, the gnome has obscure ancient roots and was probably named from the Greek *genomos* (meaning "earth dweller"). "Hitherto he had been treated very much as if he had been a useful gnome or brownie—a queer and unaccountable creature, who must necessarily be looked at with wondering curiosity and repulsion, and with whom one would be glad to make all greetings and bargains as brief as possible, but who must be dealt with in a propitiatory way" (George Eliot, *Silas Marner,* 1861).

go ahead, make my day I would be only too pleased to be challenged. The expression is a quotation from the 1983 movie *Sudden Impact*, in which it is delivered by Clint Eastwood in the character of tough San Francisco detective Harry Callaghan facing a suspected killer and daring him to raise his gun in an attempt to shoot it out. *If you want to fight me over this, then go ahead, make my day. See also* DIRTY HARRY.

go and do thou likewise Do the same thing; act in a similar fashion. The expression is biblical, appearing in Luke 10:37 in the parable of the Good Samaritan, where it is spoken by Christ and intended as encouragement to behave with the same charity. In modern usage it often appears in a rather more discouraging context in the form of an euphemistic admonition to someone to go away or otherwise refrain from interfering or some other action. *I told that jerk to get lost, and if you're sensible you'll go and do thou likewise before I get really angry.*

go and sin no more You will not be punished for what you have done but do not do wrong again. The expression comes from the biblical account of the ***woman taken in adultery*** in John 8:5–12, in which Christ forgives a woman who is faced with death by stoning on charges of adultery. When Christ challenges any member of the mob who is not guilty of sin himself to cast the first stone, no one comes forward. *The headmaster admonished them both for about an hour, then considered they had been punished enough and told them to go and sin no more. See also* LET HIM WHO IS WITHOUT SIN CAST THE FIRST STONE.

gobbledygook (gobăldeegook) Indecipherable nonsense. This word was coined in 1944 by Maury Maverick, a Texan lawyer and congressman who objected to the long-winded jargon used by bureaucrats, and thus (intentionally or not) likened it to the gobbling cry of turkeys. "The extract reads as gobbledygook if it is read as a speech by one individual" (G. Yule and G. Brown, *Discourse Analysis*, 1991).

God and mammon *See* MAMMON.

Godfather, The A person who exerts complete authority within a particular sphere. The term has strong associations with the criminal world, specifically with the MAFIA, as reflected in Mario Puzo's best-selling novel *The Godfather* (1969) and the celebrated trilogy of movies based on it, directed by Francis Ford Coppola. In modern usage, therefore, a Godfather is a criminal leader who expects unquestioning obedience and devotion from his underlings, who risk severe retribution for any act of rebellion. *The local godfathers are rumored to be planning to get together to carve up the gambling industry across the state. See also* OFFER YOU CAN'T REFUSE, AN.

God forbid May it never happen (used as a strong exclamation of dissent). The phrase appears in the Bible in Genesis 44:7 and in many subsequent passages, usually as a translation of the Hebrew *halilah,* from the verb *halal,* meaning "to defile or pollute." It was William Tyndale in his English translation of the Bible, begun in 1525, who settled on "God forbid" as his preferred English translation (in spite of the fact that God is not mentioned in corresponding Hebrew and Greek idioms). "If this cleaving distrust from which I cannot free myself should be in very truth the mute prophecy of evil to come—to come, I know not when—if it be so (which God forbid!), how soon she may want a friend, a protector near at hand, a ready refuge in the time of her trouble!" (Wilkie Collins, *After Dark,* 1856).

god from a machine *See* DEUS EX MACHINA.

Godiva, Lady *See* LADY GODIVA.

Godot *See* WAITING FOR GODOT.

go down to the sea in ships To journey across the sea by boat. The expression is biblical in origin, appearing in Psalm 107:23: "They that go down to the sea in ships, that do business in great waters; These see the works of the LORD, and his wonders in the deep." The phrase has become a cliché for the business of seafaring and was probably the inspiration for the famous opening lines of John Masefield's poem "Sea Fever" (1902): "I must go down to the seas again, to the lonely sea and sky."

God protect me from my friends The biggest threat comes from one's friends, not one's enemies. The allusion is to a 1956 book of the same title by Gavin Maxwell about the Sicilian bandit Salvatore Giuliano (1922–50). Similar sentiments can be dated back much earlier in various forms, often followed or preceded by "I can protect myself from my enemies." *"God protect me from my friends" muttered the gang's boss as he was led into the court.*

God save the king/queen Long live the king, or queen. This expression of loyalty to a reigning monarch is biblical in origin, appearing in 1 Samuel 10:24 as a shout of acclamation in honor of Saul. Elsewhere in the Bible it appears with reference to Absalom, Adonijah, Solomon, and Joash in such forms as "may the king live"—the word *God* being too sacred to use. Today it is perhaps best known as the title of the British national anthem. *With a shout of "God save the king!" the sergeant leapt into the throng of struggling bodies and was seen no more.*

God's in his heaven, all's right with the world An expression of satisfaction with the general state of affairs. It is a quotation from the long poem *Pippa Passes* (1841) by Robert Browning (1812–61): "The lark's on the wing; / The snail's on the thorn: / God's in his heaven— / All's right with the world!" In modern usage, the line is usually quoted sarcastically, condemning a person suspected of harboring an unduly optimistic view of the world. *She seems oblivious to her family's problems: as far as she's concerned, God's in his heaven, all's right with the world. See also* I'M ALRIGHT, JACK.

Godwin's oath (godwinz) A protestation of innocence that is immediately shown to be false. The expression alludes to an oath made by Godwin, earl of Wessex (d. 1053), who at the end of a long career of political double-dealing and treachery stood accused of murdering Edward the Confessor's brother Alfred. He swore he was innocent of the crime and added that heaven should strike him down at once if this was not so. Without further ado he choked to death on a piece of bread. *This promise proved to be like Godwin's oath, quickly revealed to be as hollow as a drum and the exact opposite of what was really intended.*

Godzilla (godzilă) A monstrous creature, person, or object. The original Godzilla was a ferocious dinosaur awoken by hydrogen bomb tests and transformed into a rampaging monster in a long series of low-budget Japanese-made movies, beginning with *Gojira* (1954), a U.S. version of which was released in 1956 under the title *Godzilla*. The name of the creature resulted from the combination of "gorilla" with the Japanese *kujira* (meaning "whale"). *This is the Godzilla of state-of-the-art trucks.*

Goebbels (gerbălz) A propagandist, especially a despicable one. The reference is to Joseph Goebbels (1897–1945), who in 1933 was appointed minister of propaganda in Adolf HITLER's Germany and subsequently used the various branches of the media to propagate the hateful ideals of the Nazi regime. He committed suicide with his wife and children shortly before Berlin fell to the Allies. *The press office was accused of acting Goebbels in its attempts to woo public favor on the issue of military intervention.*

go forth and multiply *See* BE FRUITFUL AND MULTIPLY.

go from strength to strength To become more and more successful. The phrase comes from the Bible, where it appears in Psalm 84:7: "They go from strength to strength, every one of them in Zion appeareth before God." *Under their new captain and coach the team is going from strength to strength.*

Gog and Magog (gog, maygog) Godless forces that threaten the end of the world through war. Gog and Magog are identified in Revelation 20:8 as the personification of nations at the farthest ends of the earth in the final apocalyptic conflict between good and evil. (See also Ezekiel 38–39.) Statues of Gog and Magog, depicted as giant warriors, stood for many years outside the Guildhall in London; these were destroyed by the Great Fire of 1666 but replaced in 1709 and once more in 1953 after their destruction during the bombing of London in 1940. ". . . it was shown that likeness in sound made them impossible: it was a method of interpretation which was not tested by the necessity of forming anything which had sharper collisions than an elaborate notion of Gog and Magog: it was as free from interruption as a plan for threading the stars together" (George Eliot, *Middlemarch,* 1871–72).

golden age A period of history considered to have been notably prosperous or creative. The golden age of myth was a legendary era that marked the beginnings of human history on earth, when humans lived in idyllic harmony with nature and one another. (It was followed by the legendary SILVER AGE and the historical Iron Age). Historical periods commonly referred to as golden ages include that of Egypt (c. 1312–1235 B.C.), of Assyria (c. 700–600 B.C.), of Athens (443–429 B.C.), and of Persia (c. A.D. 531–628). "'I have brought you a book for evening solace,' and he laid on the table a new publication—a poem: one of those genuine productions so often vouchsafed to the fortunate public of those days—the golden age of modern literature" (Charlotte Brontë, *Jane Eyre,* 1847).

golden apple *See* APPLE OF DISCORD.

golden bowl Life, youth, or anything else that is fragile or once lost cannot be regained. The image of life as a golden bowl comes from the Bible, where it appears in Ecclesiastes 12:1, 6–7: "Remember now thy Creator in the days of thy youth, while the evil days come not . . . or ever the silver cord be loosed, or the golden bowl be broken, or the pitcher be broken at the fountain, or the wheel broken at the cistern. Then shall the dust return to the earth as it was: and the spirit shall return unto God who gave it." The image of a broken bowl has long been a symbol of death: Its association here with a cord may suggest that the bowl in question is part of a lamp, which goes out when the cord breaks and the bowl falls. The phrase is perhaps best known today as the title of the Henry James novel *The Golden Bowl* (1904). *But the golden bowl had been broken, and there was no rousing the girl's lifeless body.*

golden calf Money, riches, or material values. The description of the golden calf comes from the biblical episode related in Exodus 32:1–14 in which the Israelites worshiped such an idol, made by Aaron from golden earrings, in the absence of Aaron's brother Moses. In modern usage people who place undue emphasis on the pursuit of material values may be accused of ***worshiping the golden calf.*** "The golden calf they worship at Boston is a pigmy compared with the giant effigies set up in other parts of that vast counting-house which lies beyond the Atlantic; and the almighty dollar sinks into something comparatively insignificant, amidst a whole Pantheon of better gods" (Charles Dickens, *American Notes,* 1842).

Golden Fleece Something of great value that is much sought after but very hard to obtain. In the Greek myth of Jason and the Argonauts, the Golden Fleece was a ram's fleece of pure gold that hung on an oak tree in a sacred grove in Colchis until Jason managed to carry it off. Australia is sometimes referred to as the "Land of the Golden Fleece" because of its extensive production of wool. ". . . a worn-out royal gun-brig condemned to sale, to be had dog-cheap: this he proposed that they two, or in fact Boyd with his five thousand pounds, should buy; that they should refit and arm and man it;—and sail a-privateering 'to the Eastern Archipelago,' Philippine Isles, or I know not where; and so conquer the golden fleece" (Thomas Carlyle, *The Life of John Sterling,* 1851).

golden rule The one principle or guideline that should be followed at all times. The original Golden Rule was the advice given by Christ during the Sermon on the Mount, as related in Matthew 7:12: "Therefore all things whatsoever ye would that men should do to you, do ye even so to them: for this is the law and the prophets." Christ's Golden Rule may be rendered in a variety of ways, among them "treat others as you would like to be treated yourself" and the succinct "do as you would be done by." "The golden rule is that there are no golden rules" (George Bernard Shaw, "Maxims for Revolutionists," *Man and Superman,* 1905).

golden shower Money, especially in the form of a bribe. The expression alludes to the Greek legend of Zeus and Danaë, in the course of which Zeus gained access to Danaë, the beautiful daughter of King Acrisius of Argos, by disguising himself as a shower of gold and subsequently foiled the king's attempts to protect his daughter's chastity. As a result of this union Danaë gave birth to Perseus. ". . . he folds his arms about him, and sits in expectation of some revolution in the state that shall raise him to greatness, or some golden shower that shall load him with wealth" (Samuel Johnson, "Idle Hope," *Essays,* 1753).

Goldilocks (gōldeeloks) A (generally sweet-natured) girl with flowing blonde locks. The allusion is the fairy tale *Goldilocks and the Three Bears*, in which a young girl called Goldilocks innocently stumbles upon the house of the ***three bears*** and there makes free with their porridge, chairs, and beds before the outraged occupants return home and she flees to safety. *You can tell Goldilocks over there that she's wasting her time if she thinks I'm going to tell her my brother's address.*

gold in them thar hills, there's *See* THERE'S GOLD IN THEM THAR HILLS.

gold of Ophir (ōfer) Something of the finest quality. In the Bible Ophir is the country from which fine gold is imported to decorate the Temple (1 Chronicles 29:4); thus, gold of Ophir was of the finest quality. *His opinions are like the gold of Ophir, and many admirers hang on his every word.*

gold of Tolosa *See* HE HAS GOT GOLD OF TOLOSA.

Goldwynism (gōldwinizăm) An unintentional and usually humorous misuse of language. The allusion is to the Polish-born U.S. movie mogul Samuel Goldwyn (1882–1974), who founded the MGM film studio and became well known for his (sometimes apocryphal) gaffes when using the English language, among them "A verbal contract isn't worth the paper it's written on," "In two words: im-possible," and "Include me out." *President Bush became celebrated among journalists for his Goldwynism-laden pronouncements at the microphone.*

Golgotha *See* CALVARY.

Goliath (gălīăth) A formidable opponent or obstacle. The allusion is to the Philistine giant Goliath, "six cubits and a span high," in the biblical tale of DAVID AND GOLIATH, as related in 1 Samuel

17. Such was Goliath's strength that the youthful David was the only Israelite prepared to answer his challenge to single combat. "Violent crime and AIDS are probably each of them individually bigger Goliaths than ever apartheid was" (*Christianity and Renewal,* September 2001).

Golightly, Holly *See* HOLLY GOLIGHTLY.

Gollum (golăm) A repulsive, slimy person or creature. Gollum appears as a character in J. R. R. Tolkien's novels *The Hobbit* (1937) and *The Lord of the Rings* (1954–55), in which he is depicted as a degenerate but pitiable creature who has been debased as a result of his long-term possession of the precious ring that is the object of the heroes' quest. His name has also been purloined to describe a wild throw in a game of frisbee. *The bar was usually peopled with a variety of gollums and other assorted white trash that rarely saw daylight.*

Gomez and Morticia *See* ADDAMS FAMILY.

Gomorrah *See* SODOM AND GOMORRAH.

Goneril *See* KING LEAR.

gone with the wind Disappeared completely. The phrase first appeared in the poem "Num sum qualis eram" (or "Cynara") written in the 1890s by the British poet Ernest Dowson (1867–1900): "I have forgot much, Cynara! Gone with the wind." The quotation is today best-known as the title of the classic 1939 movie *Gone With the Wind* (based on a 1936 novel of the same name by Margaret Mitchell), which starred Vivien Leigh as ***Scarlett O'Hara*** opposite Clark Gable as her lover ***Rhett Butler***. In modern usage, the phrase sometimes alludes to the film itself, suggesting that something is romantically overblown: *Her complaints about her boyfriend were all very Gone With the Wind as far as I was concerned. See also* FRANKLY, MY DEAR, I DON'T GIVE A DAMN; TOMORROW IS ANOTHER DAY.

Goodfellow, Robin *See* PUCK.

good fight, fight the *See* FIGHT THE GOOD FIGHT.

good for nothing *See* SALT OF THE EARTH.

good life, the A life of self-sustainability and environmental responsibility. The phrase is particularly associated with a 1970s BBC television sitcom of the same title, in which Richard Briers and Felicity Kendal played Tom and Barbara Good, a couple determined to abandon their former middle-class lifestyle and instead live a more self-sufficient existence, growing their own food and doing without many of the unnecessary and wasteful luxuries of the modern world. In nonallusive use the phrase has a very different meaning, referring to a life of luxury. *More and more people are opting out of the rat race in the hope of living the good life as smallholders.*

good neighbor policy Behaving well toward your neighbors. The original Good Neighbor Policy was that adopted by the U.S. government in the 1930s with the aim of appeasing the fear of South American states that the United States intended to expand its influence over the whole of the American continent, as made clear in the inaugural address of President Franklin D. Roosevelt in 1933: "In the field of world policy; I would dedicate this nation to the policy of the good neighbor." *The good neighbor policy observed by the two* *countries was set on one side when it became clear that only one of them could hope to attract significant UN backing.*

Good Samaritan (sămairităn) A person who kindly and selflessly helps a stranger in distress or difficulty. The expression alludes to the parable that Christ told, recorded in Luke 10:25–37, about a Jew who was brutally attacked while on his way from Jerusalem to Jericho and left for dead. His plight was ignored by a priest and a Levite who ***passed by on the other side*** without giving him any help at all. But later a Samaritan who happened by took compassion on the man, and in spite of the fact that the Samaritans were open enemies of the Jews, the Samaritan looked after him, paying an innkeeper to take care of him. The phrase Good Samaritan does not, incidentally, appear in the actual text of the King James Bible (1611) and appears not to have become an accepted translation until at least 1640. "No one would remember the Good Samaritan if he'd only had good intentions. He had money as well" (Margaret Thatcher, television interview, January 6, 1986). *See also* FALL AMONG THIEVES.

Good Shepherd Jesus Christ. Of many epithets by which Jesus is referred to in the Bible, this one appears in John 10:11 and alludes to the image of Christ as a shepherd tending his flock. It evokes the parable of the lost sheep related in Matthew 18:12–14, in which a shepherd goes to the aid of the single sheep that is lost, despite the fact that the other 99 sheep in his flock are all safely accounted for. The title is on occasion applied to anyone who assumes responsibility for the welfare of others. *I will put my faith in the Good Shepherd to see us safely home.*

good thing come out of Nazareth (nazărăth) Something good that comes from an unexpected source. The expression alludes to Christ, who spent his childhood in Nazareth. The phrase appears in John 1:46, where Nathanael expresses surprise upon learning that Jesus came from the insignificant town of Nazareth: "And Nathanael said unto him, Can there any good thing come out of Nazareth? Philip said unto him, Come and see." "She had almost fancied that a good thing could come out of Nazareth—a charming woman out of Tablothay's Dairy" (Thomas Hardy, *Tess of the D'Urbervilles,* 1891).

good tidings of great joy Good news. The phrase alludes to Luke 2:10, in which the angel of the Lord brings the good news of Christ's birth to shepherds tending their flocks in the field: "And the angel said unto them, Fear not: for, behold, I bring you good tidings of great joy, which shall be to all people." Sometimes this phrase is rendered as ***glad tidings of great joy,*** ". . . and though of the same religious sentiments as Mr. Treat, yet his attention was turned to those glad tidings of great joy, which a Savior came to publish" (Henry David Thoreau, *Cape Cod,* 1865).

goodwill to all men Charitable feeling to all of humanity. This exhortation to the faithful to behave with generosity toward their fellow humans (especially during the Christmas season) has its origins in Luke 2:14, in which the birth of Christ at Bethlehem is a cause of much rejoicing: "suddenly there was with the angel a multitude of the heavenly host praising God, and saying, Glory to God in the highest, and on earth peace, good will toward men." *After all, it's Christmas, the season of goodwill to all men.*

good works Charitable acts; actions carried out to help others. The phrase appears several times in the Bible, as in Acts 9:36: "Now there was at Joppa a certain disciple named Tabitha, which by interpretation is called Dorcas: this woman was full of good works and almsdeeds which she did." "'I like to hear your adventures and good works so much,' said Polly, ready to be amused by anything that made her forget herself" (Louisa May Alcott, *An Old Fashioned Girl,* 1870).

goody two-shoes A sickeningly well-behaved person, someone who never does wrong or at least gives the appearance of being saintly, despite suspicions that no one could be so perfect. The allusion is to a nursery story entitled *The History of Little Goody Two-Shoes* published in 1765 and often attributed to English playwright Oliver Goldsmith (c. 1730–74). The central character in the story is an orphan girl called Margery Meanwell, who acquires the nickname Little Goody Two-Shoes after a benefactor takes pity on her and gives her a pair of shoes. She goes on to enjoy a virtuous, rewarding life filled with good works and is greatly mourned at her death. "You say: Enough with these busybodies and goody two-shoes!" (Martin Amis, *Time's Arrow*, 1991).

go over the top To go into battle or otherwise enter the fray. The reference is to troops charging over the top of the trenches of World War I. The sense of the phrase ***over the top***, sometimes abbreviated to ***OTT***, has since expanded to mean "extreme, exaggerated, excessive, outrageous." *When it comes to decorating the Christmas tree, people are often tempted to go over the top with tinsel and baubles.*

Gordian knot *See* CUT THE GORDIAN KNOT.

Gordon, Flash *See* FLASH GORDON.

Gordon Gekko (gekō) Archetype of an unprincipled businessman. The original Gordon Gekko, played by Michael Douglas, was a greedy, amoral financial trader in the 1987 movie *Wall Street. She did not fancy the idea of trusting her modest inheritance to the Gordon Gekkos on Wall Street.*

gorgon A monstrously ugly or frightening woman. In Greek mythology, the Gorgons were three loathsome sisters, with wings, sharp tusklike teeth, brazen claws, and snakes for hair. The most famous of them was Medusa, whose ugliness was so extreme that anyone who saw her was immediately turned to stone. Medusa was beheaded by Perseus; her sisters were immortal. "Her mother is perfectly unbearable. Never met such a Gorgon . . . I don't really know what a Gorgon is like, but I am quite sure that Lady Bracknell is one" (Oscar Wilde, *The Importance of Being Earnest,* 1895).

Gormenghast (gormăngast) A gloomy, fantastical place, typically one with a labyrinthine layout or unfathomable character. The allusion is to the vast castle that provides the setting for the trilogy of novels by British writer Mervyn Peake (1911–68) comprising *Titus Groan* (1946), *Gormenghast* (1950) and *Titus Alone* (1959). The lives of the inhabitants of the castle are bound by stifling tradition, hence the application of the term Gormenghast to any place or situation that is similarly overburdened or otherwise detached from the real world. *The factory was a Gormenghast into which sunlight very rarely penetrated.*

gospel Something undeniably true or accepted as true; something strongly believed. The word derives from an Anglo-Saxon translation of the Latin *evangelium* as *godspell,* signifying "good tidings." The biblical Gospels are the New Testament books of the life of Christ, as written by Matthew, Mark, Luke, and John. The word is often used as a synonym for the actual teachings of Christ or, more specifically, the message of God's salvation of humanity through the life, death, and resurrection of Christ (as in Romans 1:16). In modern usage a ***gospel truth*** is something that is generally regarded as irrefutable, while any source or authority described as *gospel* is considered essential or reliable. ". . . the mere opportunity of venting a little ill-nature against the offending Miss Price, and affecting to compassionate her weaknesses and foibles, though only in the presence of a solitary dependant, was almost as great a relief to her spleen as if the whole had been gospel truth" (Charles Dickens, *Nicholas Nickleby,* 1838–39).

Gotham (gothăm) A village, town, or city of fools. The residents of the English village of Gotham in Nottinghamshire were traditionally considered to be the epitome of slow-witted peasants (medieval legend had it that they once tried to capture a cuckoo by building a wall around it, only for the bird to fly over the top). Another old tradition claims that the inhabitants of Gotham (sometimes called the ***Wise Men of Gotham***) were actually very cunning, only pretending to be fools in order to escape their public duties, such as paying tithes to the church. Washington Irving (1783–1859) used the same name to mock the follies of the residents of New York City, and in the 20th century the name reemerged in that of ***Gotham City***, home of the fictional superheroes BATMAN AND ROBIN and an allegory of the sinful, violent, and chaotic modern urban metropolis. *It was an act of folly that would not have looked out of place in Gotham.*

go the extra/second mile To make a special effort to do something beyond the norm; to go beyond the call of duty. The allusion is to Christ's saying in the Sermon on the Mount: "And whosoever shall compel thee to go a mile, go with him twain" (Matthew 5:41). "I was sort of lukewarm about the British before, but I'm more positive now they're willing to go the extra mile" (*The New York Observer,* October 12, 2001).

go the way of all flesh To die or disappear finally. The expression alludes to the biblical phrase "go the way of all the earth" in Joshua 23:14 and 1 Kings 2:2. "And yet—what could one do? Buy them and stick them in a lumber-room? No; they had to go the way of all flesh and furniture, and be worn out" (John Galsworthy, *The Forsyte Saga,* 1906–21).

Gothic An essentially medieval style of art and architecture whose characteristics include pointed arches, rich detail, and flamboyant decoration. The Gothic style was condemned by Renaissance artists and architects as primitive to the point of barbarism, hence the link with the warlike Goths, the Germanic people who destroyed many fine works of art as they laid waste to much of the Roman Empire between the third and fifth centuries A.D. The style nonetheless became popular again during the Gothic Revival of the late 18th and 19th centuries. The term *gothic* also came to be applied to a genre of literature characterized by gloom and the grotesque that enjoyed a considerable vogue during the Gothic Revival. Gothic writers wrote macabre stories of horror, passion and the supernatural against a backdrop of windswept moors, haunted castles, and other oppressive surroundings, and the term is used today in discussing novels, films, etc. that have a similarly brooding, melodramatic atmosphere. "Its whole visible exterior was ornamented with quaint figures, conceived in the grotesqueness of a Gothic fancy, and drawn or stamped in the glittering plaster, composed of lime, pebbles, and bits of glass, with which the woodwork of the walls was overspread" (Nathaniel Hawthorne, *The House of the Seven Gables,* 1851). *See also* AMERICAN GOTHIC.

go to Canossa (kanosă) To undergo humiliation, especially by subjection to a more powerful body. The allusion is to the Holy Roman Emperor Henry IV, who in January 1077, having been excommunicated by Pope Gregory VII (Hildebrand) for contesting the pope's power to create bishops, dressed as a penitent and stood for three days barefoot in the snow in the pope's palace at Canossa in order to obtain forgiveness. *The German chancellor Otto von Bismarck famously resisted the church's attempt to control secular affairs with the declaration "We will not go to Canossa!"*

go to Gehenna *See* GEHENNA.

go to the ant, thou sluggard Don't be lazy; stir yourself to action. This expression appears in Proverbs 6:6–9 as follows: "Go to the ant, thou sluggard; consider her ways, and be wise: Which having no guide, overseer, or ruler, Provideth her meat in the summer, and gathereth her food in the harvest. How long wilt thou sleep, O sluggard? when wilt thou arise out of thy sleep?" *The foreman tipped the boy out of his hammock. "Go to the ant, thou sluggard," he said. "There's work to be done."*

Götterdämmerung (gerterdemărung, gerterdamărung) The end of the world; any titanic clash or climactic disaster resulting in a universal cataclysm or the final destruction of a society or regime. From the German for "twilight of the gods," Götterdämmerung is described in detail in Norse mythology, which suggests that the world will come to an end after a dreadful battle between the good and evil gods in which all the good gods will die heroic deaths. A new world will then arise from the ashes of the old. Today the term is most familiar from *Götterdämmerung* (1876), the last of Richard Wagner's four operas in the *Ring* cycle. *If his life had been an opera he would have considered this last blow a prelude to his own personal Götterdämmerung. See also* RAGNAROK.

gourmand's prayer The wish of diners that they could savor the taste of good food for longer. It is rendered by Aristotle (384–322 B.C.) in his *Ethics* in the form "O Philoxenos, Philoxenos, why were you not Prometheus?" Philoxenos was an epicure who wished to have the neck of a crane so that he might enjoy longer the taste of his food as he swallowed it; Prometheus was the creator of humans, who sadly did not include a cranelike neck in his final design. *The meal that night was so good that I was not the only diner to close his eyes in ecstasy and mutter to himself the gourmand's prayer that it would never come to an end.*

go west, young man Go out to meet life's challenges. The expression alludes to the title of an editorial that appeared originally in the *Terre Haute Express* in 1851, in which the young were encouraged to travel west to meet the challenge of opening up unsettled parts of the country. The call was taken up by other newspapers and is often wrongly attributed to New York journalist Horace Greeley

(1811–72). *"Go west, young man," he slurred, waving the bottle in the general direction of the ocean, "you've nothing to lose and everything to gain!"*

Grable, Betty *See* BETTY GRABLE.

Grace Darling Archetype of a selfless young heroine. The historical Grace Darling (1815–42) was the daughter of a lighthouse-keeper off the northeast English coast who, in 1838, heroically assisted her father in rescuing survivors from the *Forfarshire* (which had run aground on the rocks of the Farne Islands in a storm) by rowing out to them in a small boat. She was widely honored for her courageous act, even by Queen Victoria, before dying a premature death of consumption. *Her status as a new Grace Darling came to an end after it was realized that there hadn't been any real danger at all.*

Graceland A palatial home, especially one that is expensively but tastelessly furnished. The allusion is to the home in Memphis, Tennessee of pop star Elvis Presley (*see* KING, THE), which was decorated at huge expense and with substantial vulgarity by its owner, and is now preserved in that state as a shrine to his memory. *Her home turned out to be a girly miniature Graceland, with pink pillars and a swimming pool in the shape of a poodle.*

Graces *See* THREE GRACES.

Gradgrind, Thomas *See* THOMAS GRADGRIND.

grail *See* HOLY GRAIL.

grain of mustard seed Anything that has small beginnings but grows into something much larger. This striking image is biblical in origin, being ascribed to Christ in Matthew 13:31–32, Mark 4:30–32, and Luke 13:18–19 and used as a metaphor for the kingdom of heaven, which like a mustard seed starts from the tiniest beginnings and blossoms into a huge tree, with birds nesting on its branches. "It is compared also to leaven, to sowing of seed, and to the multiplication of a grain of mustard-seed; by all which compulsion is excluded; and consequently there can in that time be no actual reigning" (Thomas Hobbes, *Leviathan,* 1651).

Grand Central Station A very busy place, especially one that is thronged with people. The allusion is to Grand Central Station in New York City, which is one of the busiest transport centers in the world. "The whole place was about as private as Grand Central Station on Glasgow Fair Saturday" (Liz Lochhead, *True Confessions and New Clichés*, 1985).

Grand Guignol (gron(g) geenyol) Bloodcurdling or gruesome in character. The reference is to a radical style of drama that became popular in the French theater in the late 19th century. Such dramas, which were named after the Théâtre de Grand-Guignol in Montmartre, Paris, where they were first staged in 1895, combined farce with scenes of brutal bloodletting, which included among other extreme acts eye-gougings and immersion in acid baths. "Under the glare of the fluorescent light the whole bizarre scene, Berowne's sprawled body and severed throat, the clotted blood, the tramp propped like a stringless marionette against the wall, looking for a moment unreal, a Grand Guignol tableau too overdone and too contrived to be convincing" (P. D. James, *A Taste for Death*, 1989).

Grandma Moses (grandmah mōziz) In a traditional rustic style. Grandma Moses (Anna Mary

Robertson; 1860–1961) was a self-taught artist who became famous at the advanced age of 80 for her nostalgic paintings executed in a characteristic naive, primitive style. *The fabrics on sale in the store had a rustic, Grandma Moses charm.*

grand slam The attaining of victory in every challenge contested. The expression comes from the game of bridge, in which a grand slam refers to the bidding and winning of all 13 tricks in a single game. The term is particularly associated today with the sporting world and is commonly used of the achievements of teams or individuals who win all the major events in their particular sport, such as tennis, golf, rugby, or soccer. *Victory for the team here today would complete a grand slam in all the trophy competitions at this level.*

Grant, Cary *See* CARY GRANT.

grassy knoll A source of perplexity or suspicion, especially one suggesting some hidden mystery or official cover-up. The allusion is to the assassination of President John F. Kennedy (1917–63) in Dallas on November 22, 1963 and the conspiracy theories that developed over the years. One of these suggests that he was killed not by Lee Harvey Oswald firing from the Texas School Book Depository but by a second unidentified assailant firing from a grassy knoll overlooking the presidential route. *The episode has turned into something of a grassy knoll, giving conspiracy theorists scope to suggest there may be more to the story than the government are admitting.*

graven image A statue or other object that is worshiped as a god or idol. The phrase appears several times in the Bible but is best known from the second of the Ten Commandments: "Thou shalt not make unto thee any graven image, or any likeness of any thing that is in heaven above, or that is in the earth beneath, or that is in the water under the earth" (Exodus 20:4). "'Still, he who would do justice,' she proceeded, 'will not forget that the cunning of our hands was bound by the prohibition, "Thou shalt not make unto thee any graven image, or any likeness of anything"; which the Sopherim wickedly extended beyond its purpose and time'" (Lew Wallace, *Ben Hur,* 1880).

Grave, where is thy victory? *See* DEATH, WHERE IS THY STING?

Gray, Dorian *See* DORIAN GRAY.

gray eminence *See* ÉMINENCE GRISE.

greasy pole The path to promotion or success. The allusion is to a popular sport dating back to the 19th century, in which two contestants mounted greased horizontal poles and attempted to knock each other off using pillows or other weapons. The modern allusive usage of the term, however, suggests that it is a vertical (not horizontal) pole up which people ascend with difficulty, or with the ever-present danger of slipping down again. "A friend of the Prince's youth, Benjamin Disraeli, was to explain with less elegance the reason for his own arrival in power: 'I have climbed to the top of the greasy pole'" (William H. C. Smith, *Napoleon III*, 1991).

Great Depression A period of prolonged economic gloom. The phrase is usually associated with the long-lasting economic depression that was triggered by the Wall Street Crash of 1929 (*see* WALL STREET), although it is sometimes applied to other similar periods or, more generally, to any period of low morale. *His Great Depression began in the 1950s and lasted the next 40 years. See also* BLACK MONDAY.

Great Divide A remote place, or a serious divide between two parties or things, especially the divide between life and death. The Great Divide is an alternative name for the Continental Divide or the Rocky Mountain range that runs down the western side of the United States from Canada to Mexico. "Like all the children born shortly after the Great War, we knew that to our parents, the war was the great divide" (Molly Horne, *Life, Love and Laughter*, 1989).

greater love hath no man The sacrifice of one's own life or interests for the good of others is the supreme virtue. The expression appears in the Bible in John 15:13, where Christ, in his last address to his disciples, teaches that "Greater love hath no man than this, that a man lay down his life for his friends." *"Greater love hath no man," quipped their friend as he stood up to accept the blame on their behalf.*

Great Escape An apparently miraculous escape in the face of overwhelming odds. The allusion is to the 1963 film *The Great Escape*, which depicted the mass escape of Allied prisoners-of-war from a German prison camp during World War II. "The journey represents the great escape from destruction; it is begun in time and ended beyond it" (Marion Glasscoe, *English Medieval Mystics: Games of Faith*, 1993).

Greatest, the A person who is unsurpassed in his or her field. The epithet is particularly associated with the U.S. boxer MUHAMMAD ALI (b. 1942), who famously boasted, with some justification within the boxing sphere, "I am the greatest." In fact, he may well have borrowed the line from a wrestler called George Raymond Wagner, who was also well known for his showmanship. *As far as disco-dancing goes, he's the Greatest.*

greatest of these is charity *See* FAITH, HOPE, AND CHARITY.

Greatest Show on Earth, The *See* P. T. BARNUM.

Great Leap Forward A substantial advance or great change of some kind. The original Great Leap Forward was a package of economic and social policies introduced by Chairman Mao Zedong of China in 1958 to improve the lives of Chinese peasants. In the event, the policy proved a complete failure and resulted only in a disastrous decline in the living standards of both the rural and the industrial populations. As a consequence, the term today is often employed facetiously of some measure that appears to be, or has actually turned out to be, doomed to failure. *The manager's Great Leap Forward consisted of hiring two new players and having the stadium repainted in garish colors.*

Great Train Robbery A robbery in which money or other valuables are taken from a train. There have been numerous robberies from trains over the years, many of which have been described as "great train robberies," but the most infamous is that which took place in England at Cheddington, Buckinghamshire, on August 8, 1963, when a gang stole £2.5 million from a mail train. The gang were eventually brought to justice, but much of the money was never recovered. The ultimate origin of the term is, however, probably a 1903 silent movie called *The Great Train Robbery*. *To hear him go on you would think he had pulled off the Great Train Robbery.*

Great Wall of China A formidable protective barrier. The Great Wall of China, or ***Chinese Wall***, was constructed along China's northern borders during the fourth century B.C., and was substantially rebuilt during the Ming dynasty (1368–1644). Up to 30 feet in height and some 4,000 miles in length, it is often referred to as the only man-made object that can be seen from the Moon (although this is a myth and no astronaut standing on the moon has ever claimed to have been able to make it out). The expression is sometimes employed today to refer to any barrier, real or illusory. "Her gaze fixed on her adversary, she had backed straight into what felt rather like a human version of the Great Wall of China" (Eleanor Rees, *Hunter's Harem*, 1992).

Great White Father A person who is perceived to exercise a fatherly, usually positive, influence over a country, organization, movement, field, etc. The term appears to have first emerged in the early 20th century in popular novels set in the Wild West, being introduced as an epithet describing the U.S. president in terms that might be understood by Native Americans. It has since come to be employed more widely, often facetiously. "And no one in the administration ever—such is the unfairness of life—quite achieved the renown achieved by Lord Delamere as a great white father to the Masai" (Kathryn Tidrick, *Empire and the English Character*, 1992).

Great White Hope A person or thing that is widely expected to succeed. The allusion is to boxing in the early 20th century, when boxing fans and promoters eagerly awaited the emergence of a white boxer who might defeat the all-conquering black world heavyweight titleholder Jack Johnson (1878–1946), a man who was much resented not only for his dominance in the sport but also for his arrogant manner and bad behavior outside the ring. The fact that several such contenders were roundly beaten by Johnson before he finally lost the title to Jess Willard in 1915 has lent the phrase (which is now applied without racist associations to people of any color) slightly pessimistic overtones. The survival of the expression long after the events it refers to owes much to its use as the title of a Pulitzer Prize-winning play by Howard Sackler about Johnson's career, first performed in 1967 and filmed in 1970. "For NIREX, the great white hope of the nuclear industry's waste management policy, this was hardly an auspicious start" (Crispin Aubrey, *Melt Down: Collapse of a Nuclear Dream*, 1991).

Great White Way The theater district of BROADWAY in New York City. The expression is often assumed to relate to the stunning displays of electric advertisements and street lighting in the region of Times Square, though in fact it was originally coined by journalists in December 1901 in reports about a heavy fall of snow in the city. The inspiration was a novel set at the South Pole published that year by Albert Bigelow Paine with the title *The Great White Way*. "Might I have seen you on the Great White Way?" (P. Falconer, *War in High Heels*, 1993).

Greek calends *See* AT THE GREEK CALENDS.

Greek chorus A group of singers or speakers who comment on the action taking place. In early Greek drama such a body of performers took a leading role as there were only one, two, or at most three individual actors on stage at any one time. The same device has been used by dramatists through the centuries, although since Shakespeare's time the role has often been fulfilled by one performer alone. ". . . it is always a source of pleasure and awe to me to remember that the ultimate survival of the Greek chorus, lost elsewhere to art, is to be found in the servitor answering the priest at Mass" (Oscar Wilde, *De Profundis,* 1905).

Greeks bearing gifts *See* BEWARE OF GREEKS BEARING GIFTS.

Greek to me, it's all *See* IT'S ALL GREEK TO ME.

green-eyed monster Jealousy. The phrase was coined by William Shakespeare in *Othello* (c. 1603), in which IAGO delivers the lines: "O! beware, my lord, of jealousy; / It is the green-ey'd monster which doth mock / The meat it feeds on." Green had been acknowledged as the color of envy long before Shakespeare's play, the action of which develops out of the jealous rage that Iago instils in his supposed friend OTHELLO. "Discontent, hatred, anger, doubt, inferiority complexes, suspicion, mistrust, envy, resentment, bitterness, animosity, vindictiveness, spite, irritation, annoyance, indignation, malice, prejudice—these are all part of the green-eyed monster called jealousy" (Stephanie Spindler, *Learn to Live*, 1991).

green pastures A place of ease and plenty, offering respite from the world. The image comes from Psalm 23:1–3, in which David writes of God: "The LORD is my shepherd; I shall not want. He maketh me to lie down in green pastures: he leadeth me beside the still waters; he restoreth my soul." In modern usage the phrase is most familiar from its inclusion in funeral services, in which it may be interpreted as representing heaven. Shakespeare's character Falstaff in *Henry V* (1598–1599) is reported to have "babbled of green fields" as he lay dying, and deathbed visions of pleasant fields have long been one of the subjects of popular novels and films. "But I've noticed that in these villages where the people lead a quiet life among the green pastures and the still waters, tilling the ground and tending the cattle, there's a strange deadness to the Word, as different as can be from the great towns, like Leeds, where I once went to visit a holy woman who preaches there" (George Eliot, *Adam Bede,* 1859).

Greenwich Village (grenich) Fashionably unconventional, creative, or bohemian in character. The allusion is to the Greenwich Village (or, simply, ***the Village***) area of Lower Manhattan in New York City, which became the home of many radical artists, writers, and other bohemians in the early 20th century and a focus of antiestablishment, liberal ideas in the 1950s and 1960s. Since then the area has also acquired a reputation as the home of a prominent gay community. *With so many leading American icons visiting, it was a little bit of Greenwich Village in the heart of old London town. See also* BEAT GENERATION.

Gregorian chant (grăgoreeăn) A style of vocal unaccompanied chant, best known as the official liturgical plainsong of the Roman Catholic Church. It was named after Pope Gregory I (c. 540–604), who promoted the use of plainsong in liturgical services during his papacy. *Recordings of Gregorian chant have been a surprising best-seller in the past year or two.*

gremlin A type of goblin or gnome that causes machinery to go wrong or makes plans go astray. Gremlins probably made their first appearance in the 1920s and 1930s, when they were humorously identified by RAF personnel serving in India and the Middle East as the culprits who caused aircraft to malfunction. Various explanations for the name of these mischievous creatures have been suggested, including one that links it to Fremlin's beer. *Gremlins in the electrical system meant that the car had to start the race from the back of the grid.*

Grendel (grendăl) A ferocious monster. In the epic Anglo-Saxon poem *Beowulf* (c. 700) Grendel is a fearsome underwater monster descended from Cain who repeatedly emerges from his lake at night to devour Danish warriors as they sleep in the banqueting hall of their king, Hrothgar. After 12 years of these ravages the hero Beowulf of the Geats arrives to fight Grendel, and after a long struggle Beowulf manages to kill him by tearing off his arm, to general rejoicing. Grendel's equally fearsome mother seeks to avenge her son, but Beowulf follows her into the lake and kills her, too. *Like some latterday Grendel he hauled himself out of the water and bore down upon his opponent, growling menacingly.*

Gresham's Law (greshămz) The theory that inferior goods or practices tend to drive out superior ones. The law is particularly associated with the world of finance, in which it relates to the replacement of "good" (intrinsically more valuable) money by "bad" (intrinsically less valuable) money as the better money is hoarded. Although the phenomenon had been observed at an earlier date by Copernicus among others, the law was named after English financier and merchant Sir Thomas Gresham (c. 1519–79), founder of the Royal Exchange. In modern usage, the law may be quoted in relation to a wide range of topics, from finance and trade to politics and art. *Gresham's Law insists that "bad drives out good" and this applies just as much in the world of fashion as it does anywhere else.*

Greta Garbo *See* GARBO.

Gretchen (grechăn) Stock name for a German girl or young woman. The name is well known as that of the tragic, innocent young heroine in Goethe's *Faust* (1808), since when it has been often employed in the context of young girls destroyed by love. "Kathy came downstairs with her long hair in what Helen called 'the Gretchen style': two plaits pinned neatly on top of her head" (Adele Geras, *The Green Behind the Glass*, 1989).

Gretna (gretnă) A runaway marriage, or the place where it is performed. The Scottish village of Gretna Green, close to the English border, was one of the nearest places to which, in former times, underage English couples lacking the consent of parents could travel in order to obtain marriages under Scottish law, which did not require a license, calling of the banns, or a priest. Marriages at Gretna were performed with a minimum of ceremony by the blacksmith (over his anvil), landlord, or other local official. The situation changed in 1856, when a new law insisted that at least one of the parties to the marriage had to have been resident in Scotland for 21 days beforehand, but Gretna remained attractive to eloping couples because minors still did not need to have parental consent. In 1969, however, Gretna finally fell into step with other places in the UK when the legal age of consent to marriage was set at 18. *Their parents refused to countenance the thought of marriage so they ran away to Gretna.*

Grimm's Fairy Tales A source of fantastical horror. The allusion is to the often gruesome fairy tales collected by the German folklorists and writers Jacob Grimm (1785–1863) and Wilhelm Grimm (1786–1859), known as the ***Brothers Grimm***. First published in 1812–15, the stories became the staple fare of nurseries throughout the Western world, despite the often terrifying witches, beasts, and giants depicted in them. *The sight that met her eyes as she opened the door was like something out of Grimm's Fairy Tales.*

Grim Reaper Death. Since medieval times, death has been personified as a terrifying skeletal figure in a black hooded cloak, carrying a scythe with which to "reap" men's lives. "Unfortunately, their penchant for the invention of bizarre new ways to tempt the grim reaper has filtered down to us, the lower orders, and we now follow their example" (Muriel Gray, *The First Fifty*, 1991).

grin like a Cheshire Cat *See* CHESHIRE CAT.

Griselda (grizeldă) The ideal of a patient, uncomplaining wife. The allusion is to the heroine called Griselda (or ***Patient Griselda***) who features in the final tale of the *Decameron* (1351–53) by the Italian writer Giovanni Boccaccio (1313–75) and also in "The Clerk's Tale" from *The Canterbury Tales* (c. 1387) by the English poet Geoffrey Chaucer (c. 1343–1400). Griselda is depicted as the wife of a rich nobleman, who tests her faithfulness to him by pretending that he has killed their children and is preparing to marry another woman: she patiently remains true to her vows and is ultimately rewarded when her husband admits his deception. *If he thinks he has married a Griselda who will put up with his infidelities, he will soon discover that he is sorely mistaken.*

Groucho Marx *See* MARX BROTHERS.

groundhog day The sensation of having to live through the same events over and over again. The allusion is to the 1993 movie *Groundhog Day*, which stars Bill Murray as a television weather presenter who finds himself having to relive the same day seemingly endlessly. The day in question is February 2, known as Groundhog Day, when according to tradition the groundhog emerges from its winter burrow to test whether spring has arrived: if the creature returns to its burrow this is read as a sign that winter will continue for another six weeks. *It was like groundhog day, with the same food and the same people and the same conversations being repeated every lunchtime.*

groves of academe (akădeem, akădeem) Academic circles in general or a college, university, or other place of study or research. Academe was the name of a public garden (with a grove) in Athens, in which the Greek philosopher Plato gave lessons. The garden itself had formerly been owned by a citizen of the city called Academus. *It seemed unlikely that the inspector, a diamond of the roughest kind, would be familiar with the rules of etiquette that governed this particular grove of academe.*

Grub Street Writing that is inferior in style and content. The allusion is to a former London street that in the 18th century was home to numerous impoverished "hack" writers seeking to make a precarious living from writing any kind of work that might sell a few copies. The expression was used in this sense by the lexicographer Samuel Johnson in his famous *Dictionary of the English Language* (1747–55) and by the writer George Gissing in the title of his novel *New Grub Street* (1891). "But, oh, dear me! oh, Osiris, Termagaunt, and Zeus! to think there are at least a dozen other ne'er-do-wells alive who would prefer to make a mess of living as a grand-duke rather than as a scribbler in Grub Street!" (James Branch Cabell, *The Certain Hour*, 1909).

Grundy, Mrs. *See* MRS. GRUNDY.

Guantánamo (gwantanămō) A high-security military prison. The allusion is to the controversial detention center that was established in 2002 at the U.S. naval base at Guantánamo Bay in Cuba to house al-Qaida and Taliban suspects taken during the so-called War against Terror declared after the attacks of September 11, 2001 (*see* 9/11). *Rumors that the government is planning to build a new Guantánamo to accommodate mafia bosses have been discounted by official sources.*

Gucci (goochee) Expensive and exclusive. Guccio Gucci (1881–1953) was an Italian designer whose Gucci company became one of the leading names in international fashion, selling expensive clothing and leather goods. The name of the company has been used in various contexts over the years to convey the notion of exclusivity and (sometimes) the sacrifice of content to superficial appearance. *We are witnessing the invasion of Washington by a new generation of Gucci warriors.*

Guernica (gernikă) A military atrocity, especially an instance of saturation bombing. The reference is to the village of Guernica, capital of the Basque region of Spain, which was devastated by German bombers on April 27, 1937 during the Spanish Civil War. The incident was memorably depicted by Pablo PICASSO in his painting *Guernica*. *It is probably an exaggeration to describe the incident as a second Guernica, but the episode could have serious implications for peace in the region.*

guillotine (gilăteen) A means of severing one thing from another. The word is chiefly associated with the device proposed by Joseph-Ignace Guillotin (1738–1814) for the convenient and painless dispatching of convicted criminals and enemies of the state at the time of the French Revolution. Ironically, Guillotin did not actually design the machine that bears his name, but merely suggested that the state adopt the device, which was originally designed by a French surgeon called Antoine Louis (1723–92). Louis's device, first used in 1792, comprised a heavy blade that descended rapidly upon the neck of the victim, severing the head from the body in a moment. The word "guillotine" has since been applied to less lethal devices, such as machines for cutting paper, and it has also been used more broadly in connection with any act of execution or with the curtailment of various kinds of activity. "This is usually done by a guillotine that cuts back a bundle of a dozen or so plants at a time, and it is not unusual to find the cut ends chopped and bruised rather roughly" (Bill Swain, *Roses: Questions and Answers*, 1990).

Guinevere, Queen *See* KING ARTHUR.

gulag (goolag) A prison camp, especially one that houses political prisoners. The word comes from the Russian *Glavnoye upravleniye ispravitel'no-trudovykh lagerey* (meaning "Chief Administration for Corrective Labor Camps"). Many thousands of prisoners died in the chain of such camps set up by the Soviet Union between 1930 and 1955. The word has since been applied to any grim place of confinement. *After this indiscretion he was confined to the gulag that is the mathematics department.*

Gulliver (guliver) A widely traveled person, especially one made wiser (or more cynical) by his or her travels. Lemuel Gulliver is the central character in the satirical novel *Gulliver's Travels* (1726) by Irish writer Jonathan Swift (1667–1745). Gulliver visits a series of exotic lands and marvels at the curious nature of their inhabitants who are variously smaller, taller, more absent-minded, and more bestial than he is himself, their bizarre nature forcing him to acknowledge the reality of mankind's own shortcomings. "I was a Gulliver, viewing a strange scene outside my experience" (Alfred Wainwright, *Wainwright in the Limestone Dales*, 1991). *See also* BROBDINGNAGIAN; LAPUTA; LILLIPUTIAN; YAHOO.

Gump, Forrest *See* FORREST GUMP.

gunfight at the OK Corral A climactic confrontation between opposing parties; a showdown. The allusion is to the fabled gunfight that took place between the notorious Clanton gang and the lawmen Virgil, Wyatt, and Morgan Earp and Doc Holliday at the OK Corral in Tombstone, Arizona, on October 26, 1881. When the smoke cleared, three of the Clanton gang were dead. The gunfight has long since entered the folklore of the Wild West and has been reenacted in numerous western movies. "At first I had visions of an OK Corral shoot-out at High Noon between dozens of different security forces who didn't know each other, but in fact we worked it out and there were no serious problems" (Harvey Thomas and Liz Gill, *Making an Impact*, 1989).

Gunga Din (gungă din) Stock name for a person of Indian descent. The allusion is to the central character in one of the poems from Rudyard Kipling's *Barrack Room Ballads* (1892), an Indian water-carrier who is killed performing heroic actions while serving with a British regiment in India, as acknowledged by the narrator of the poem: "Though I've belted you an' flayed you, / By the livin' Gawd that made you, / You're a better man than I am, Gunga Din!" Allusive use of the name is often in the context of this final line. "The cries of gratitude sounded from the car and heartfelt from Haverford, 'You're a better man than I am, Gunga Din' " (John Mortimer, *Summer's Lease*, 1988).

gung ho (gung hō) Very eager or enthusiastic. The phrase was picked up as a slogan by a battalion of U.S. Marines fighting in World War II. It was based on the Mandarin Chinese *king* ("work") and *ho* ("together") and had previously been used as a motivational slogan by the Chinese communists in the 1930s. It is sometimes used of rash or excessive enthusiasm in military contexts. "It also contains in the character of Colonel Calloway, the world-weary Englishman responsible for alerting the innocent American writer of pulp novels to his former friend's evil doings, a perfect symbol of Britain's position after World War II, standing in the middle between battered Europe and gung-ho America" (James Park, *British Cinema: The Lights that Failed*, 1990).

Gunn, Ben *See* BEN GUNN.

Gunpowder Plot A conspiracy to commit a major act of treason, or failure to carry it out. The allusion is to the 1605 plot to assassinate James I of England by blowing up the Houses of Parliament with gunpowder smuggled into the cellars of the building. The plot was conceived by leading Catholic radicals, including ***Guy Fawkes***, but failed after the plotters were discovered before they were ready to carry it out. The conspirators were all killed or captured and executed. *London's*

Metropolitan Police have foiled a modern-day Gunpowder Plot, thanks to information received from intelligence sources.

guns before butter Luxuries must be sacrificed to pay for what is necessary. The slogan dates back to 1936, when it was adopted by the German Nazi official Hermann Goering (1893–1946): "Guns will make us powerful; butter will only make us fat." *We would all like to spend our taxes on hospitals and the elderly, but in these difficult times when terrorists threaten our very existence it is clearly a case of guns before butter.*

guru (gooroo) A wise person, an expert. The word is Indian in origin, referring to a Hindu religious leader. In modern usage, the word is used more widely to refer to experts in a wide range of fields, from business to lifestyle. *Her brother is considered among the most influential of the modern generation of management gurus.*

Guy Fawkes *See* GUNPOWDER PLOT.

Gyges' ring (gījeez) The power of invisibility. According to Plato (c. 428–348/347 B.C.), Gyges was a Lydian shepherd of the seventh century B.C. who descended into a chasm in the earth, where he found a brazen horse. Inside the horse was the body of a giant, with a brazen ring on his finger. When Gyges slipped the ring on to his own finger he found it made him invisible. He went on to use the ring to make his fortune; usurp the reigning king; marry his wife, Candaules; and with her found a new dynasty. *As if he possessed some electronic Gyges' ring, he found he could roam wherever he liked on the Net without the slightest chance of his presence being detected.*

H

Hades (haydeez) The underworld or abode of the dead, according to Greek mythology. It took its name from Hades, the brother of Zeus who became the lord of the dead and was the equivalent of the Roman Pluto. Hades was said to be a sunless void separated from the mortal world by the waters of five rivers, the chief of these being the Styx. The most guilty souls were consigned to Tartarus, while those who were less guilty resided in the asphodel meadows. The entrance to Hades was guarded by the three-headed dog Cerberus. *"I'll see you in Hades first," quoth Sir Archibald defiantly.* *See also* ELYSIAN FIELDS.

Hagar *See* ISHMAEL.

halcyon days (halseeăn) Happy, prosperous times of peace and harmony. The word *halcyon* was the Greek name for the kingfisher (from *hals,* "the sea," and *kuo,* "to breed on"), a bird whose habits were shrouded in mystery in the classical era. It was believed that kingfishers nested far out to sea at the time of the winter solstice, when the seas remained calm for 14 days so that the birds could incubate their eggs on the waves. This notion harked back to the legend of Halcyon, the daughter of Aeolus, god of the winds, who married the mortal Ceyx and threw herself into the sea after her husband died in a shipwreck. Both were transformed into kingfishers. "He knew the world too well to risk the comfort of such halcyon moments, by prolonging them till they were disagreeable" (Anthony Trollope, *The Warden,* 1855). *Life in today's universities seems a far cry from the halcyon days of the 1970s and 1980s when money seemed no object.*

half is more than the whole It is better sometimes to settle for a share of something rather than spend a great deal in trying to gain more. This proverbial expression is supposed to have been first uttered by the ninth-century B.C. Greek poet Hesiod as advice to his brother Perseus when the latter was considering fighting a legal battle over an estate, thereby risking most of it being frittered away on lawyers' fees. *The lawyers conferred, then decided to settle on the grounds that half is sometimes more than the whole.*

Halicarnassus *See* EIGHTH WONDER OF THE WORLD.

halt and the blind *See* MAIMED, THE HALT, THE BLIND, THE.

hamadryad *See* NYMPH.

Haman, hang as high as *See* HANG AS HIGH AS HAMAN.

Hamlet A tortured, indecisive person. The allusion is to the central character in William Shakespeare's tragedy *Hamlet* (c. 1600), otherwise referred to as the ***prince of Denmark***, who wants to avenge his father's murder by killing the murderer, his uncle and stepfather Claudius, but agonizes and procrastinates over the performance and possible consequences of such action. Perhaps the most celebrated of all Shakespeare's tragic heroes, Hamlet's name has since been applied to various individuals who have exhibited similar qualities of self-doubt. "Had he been so, he would have hesitated, like Hamlet, and let irresolution mar his purpose" (Oscar Wilde, *Lord Arthur Savile's Crime*, 1909). *See also* OPHELIA; POLONIUS; SOMETHING IS ROTTEN IN THE STATE OF DENMARK.

Hancock, John *See* JOHN HANCOCK.

hand, left *See* LEFT HAND KNOW WHAT YOUR RIGHT HAND IS DOING, DO NOT LET YOUR.

hand, right *See* IF THY RIGHT EYE OFFEND THEE; LEFT HAND KNOW WHAT YOUR RIGHT HAND IS DOING, DO NOT LET YOUR.

hand against every man *See* ISHMAEL.

hand findeth to do, whatsoever thy *See* WHATSOEVER THY HAND FINDETH TO DO.

hand offend thee, if thy right *See* IF THY RIGHT EYE OFFEND THEE.

hand of God *See* FINGER OF GOD.

Hands, Israel *See* ISRAEL HANDS.

hands, wash one's *See* WASH ONE'S HANDS OF.

handwriting on the wall *See* WRITING ON THE WALL.

hang as high as Haman (haymăn) To suffer the fate that one has prepared for someone else. The phrase alludes to the biblical story of Haman, the favorite minister of King Ahasuerus (Xerxes) of Persia who was outmaneuvered by Esther and hanged on the very gallows he had built for the execution of his enemy Mordecai, Esther's father (Esther 7:9–10). Esther's triumph is commemorated by the Jewish festival of Purim, when celebrants eat triangular pastries called hamantaschen (meaning "Haman's purses" in Yiddish). "And they hanged Private Simmons—hanged him as high as Haman in hollow square of the regiment; and the Colonel said it was Drink; and the Chaplain was sure it was the Devil; and Simmons fancied it was both, but he didn't know, and only hoped his fate would be a warning to his companions" (Rudyard Kipling, "In the Matter of a Private," 1890).

Hanging Gardens of Babylon *See* EIGHTH WONDER OF THE WORLD.

Hannibal (hanibăl) A great military leader. Hannibal (247–182 B.C.) was a Carthaginian general who in 218 took the Romans by surprise, leading his army over the Alps and ravaging Italy, although he failed to take Rome itself. Ultimately he was defeated by Scipio Africanus at Zama in 202. *The general was revered by his troops and was ready to lead them, Hannibal-like, over the mountains.*

Hannibal Lecter (hanibăl lekter) A cannibalistic serial killer. Originally the creation of U.S. writer Thomas Harris (b. 1940), Dr. Hannibal Lecter—dubbed Hannibal the Cannibal—is the sadistic psychiatrist-turned-killer who likes to eat parts of his victims in the 1990 movie *The Silence of the Lambs*, in which he is consulted for information that might help in the detection of another serial killer. He was played on screen to chilling effect in this and various sequels by Anthony Hopkins, having previously been played by Brian Cox in the 1986 movie *Manhunter*. *We are searching for a killer who makes Hannibal Lecter look positively cuddly.*

Hans Christian Andersen (andersăn) A dreamy, unworldly, or otherwise distracted or ineffectual person. The allusion is to the Danish author Hans Christian Andersen (1805–75), who was greatly loved for his many classic fairy tales. In modern usage his name is often applied to people who are not only perceived as being out of touch with the real world but also suspected of having a fey, feminine character. *You won't get any help from the fire department—they are a real bunch of Hans Christian Andersens. See also* EMPEROR'S NEW CLOTHES; PRINCESS AND THE PEA; UGLY DUCKLING.

Hansel and Gretel (hansăl, gretăl) A brother and sister (or two other children) who appear to be lost or adrift in a hostile world. The allusion is to the central characters in a traditional fairy tale first published in the 19th century by the Brothers Grimm (*see* GRIMM'S FAIRY TALES), in which Hansel and Gretel narrowly escape the clutches of a wicked witch after being abandoned deep in the forest by their loving father on the insistence of his evil wife. The allusion is often specifically to the trail of breadcrumbs that the children leave behind them in the hope that this will guide them back out of the wood and show them the way home, or else to the picturesque cottage made of bread, cake, and candy into which the children are lured by the witch. "And beyond that, some fairy-tale kind of Hansel and Gretel cottage full of apple trees and roses and Alex herself stooping under a low lintel in a summery dress . . ." (Susannah James, *Love Over Gold*, 1993).

happiest days of your life A person's school years. The phrase was popularized as the title of a play (1948) by John Dighton, filmed in 1950, which charted the confusions arising from a boys' school and a girls' school having to share the same premises as a result of wartime upheavals. The expression may, however, be somewhat older. "I have never subscribed to the view that schooldays are the happiest days of your life, but I do think that student days are among the happiest" (Mairi Hedderwick, *Highland Journey*, 1992).

happy as Larry *See* AS HAPPY AS LARRY.

Happy Islands *See* ISLANDS OF THE BLEST.

hara-kiri (harăkeeree, harăkiree) Suicide, or some other self-damaging act. The phrase is Japanese in origin and alludes to the ritual suicide by disembowelment sometimes carried out by disgraced aristocrats and soldiers. The original Japanese term literally means "belly cut." The Japanese themselves, however, refer to the practice as *seppuku*. In modern English usage, the term is equally likely to be rendered as ***hari-kari*** or ***hari-kiri***. *He knew that by sending the letter exposing the scandal he had committed professional hara-kiri.*

hard day's night An exhausting time. The allusion is to the Beatles film *A Hard Day's Night*

(1964), the title of which supposedly originated as a remark made by drummer Ringo Starr after a particularly demanding filming session. According to some authorities, Starr was quoting from the Lennon–McCartney song of the same title, which had presumably already been written by the relatively late point in filming at which Starr delivered the line, or else from a poem by John Lennon. The ultimate origin may, however, lie in a sentence from a short story called "Sad Michael," which had been published in John Lennon's *In His Own Write* in March 1964: "He'd had a hard day's night that day, for Michael was a Cocky Watchtower." *With the amount of work we have to clear it looks like it's going to be a hard day's night.*

hard hat A person with conservative or reactionary views. The allusion is to the protective helmets worn by construction workers and other people working in hazardous environments. The phrase is of U.S. origin, and was inspired by the conservative attitudes that became associated with U.S. construction workers in the 1960s. *We don't think the hard hats in Congress will agree to support this measure.*

Hardy, Andy *See* ANDY HARDY.

Hardy, Oliver *See* LAUREL AND HARDY.

hare and the tortoise A patient, methodical approach may succeed better than a more hurried one. The allusion is to the fable of the hare and the tortoise attributed to the Greek writer AESOP (c. 620–560 B.C.). The tale relates how the hare lost a running race to the much slower tortoise because he was so confident of victory that he decided to take a short rest before completing the course. *When it comes to investment policies it is often a case of the hare and the tortoise as the more glamorous options often underperform compared to less exciting choices.*

Hari, Mata *See* MATA HARI.

hari-kari *See* HARA-KIRI.

harmless as doves *See* WISE AS SERPENTS AND HARMLESS AS DOVES.

Harmonia's necklace (hahrmōneeăz) A possession that brings bad luck to its owner. The allusion is to the necklace that King Cadmus gave to his bride, Harmonia, the daughter of Ares and Aphrodite. The necklace, which had been given to Cadmus by Hephaestus (Aphrodite's former husband), brought evil to all who owned it. After suffering many misfortunes Cadmus and Harmonia were changed into serpents by the gods, all of whom had attended the wedding. *Like Harmonia's necklace the property seemed to work like a curse on all who had possession of it.*

Harpagon (hahrpăgon) A miser. Harpagon is the name of the central character, a penny-pinching misanthrope, in the classic comedy *L'Avare* ("The Miser") by the French writer Molière (Jean-Baptiste Poquelin; 1622–73). When confronted with having to choose between his lover and his money, he chooses the money. *He was so mean with his money that his friends took to calling him Harpagon behind his back. See also* SCROOGE.

harpy (hahrpee) A predatory, grasping, shrewish woman. In Greek mythology, Harpies (meaning "snatchers" or "robbers") were loathsome monsters with the bodies of birds, the heads of women, and the claws of vultures. Variously given as one, two, or three in number, they were sometimes identified as personifications of the winds that could carry people off or as the souls of the dead who looked for opportunities to snatch the souls of the living. They are best known from the adventures of Jason and the Argonauts, in which they are depicted perpetually seizing food prepared for the blind king Phineus. "Nothing short of the twelve dollars and a half will satisfy this harpy, I perceive; and surely my reputation as judge is worth that trifle" (James Fenimore Cooper, *The Pioneers,* 1823).

hasta la vista, baby *See* TERMINATOR, THE.

Hastings, Battle of (haystingz) A decisive moment, or an event that happened so long ago that it is lost in the mists of time. The Battle of Hastings took place between an invading Norman army led by William the Conqueror and the Anglo-Saxon forces loyal to Harold I on Senlac Hill, near the town of Hastings on the southeast coast of England, on October 14, 1066. The death of Harold and eventual Norman victory resulted in a fundamental transfer of power in Britain and greatly influenced the subsequent course of European history. *The encounter was said by some to be a 20th-century Battle of Hastings.*

hath shall be given, to him that *See* WHOSOEVER HATH, TO HIM SHALL BE GIVEN.

hatter, mad as a *See* MAD AS A HATTER.

hat trick A sequence of three successes in a row. The allusion is to the now defunct custom among cricketers of rewarding a bowler who has taken three wickets in successive balls with a new cap, paid for by his club. The expression has long since escaped its origins and is now widely employed in other sports as well as in nonsporting contexts. *His success in the college poetry competition completed a hat trick of stiffly contested literary prizes.*

haughty spirit before a fall *See* PRIDE GOETH BEFORE A FALL.

have an ax to grind To have a grievance or an ulterior motive for doing something. The allusion is to a traditional story sometimes attributed to American statesman and scientist Benjamin Franklin (1706–90). According to this story, a young man (perhaps Franklin himself) was flattered by the compliments of another man into helping him sharpen his ax on a grindstone, with the result that he was made late for school. As soon as the ax was fully sharp, however, and the older man had no more use for the boy, he offered the lad no thanks and instead berated him for being late for school. The expression has since been applied to anyone who is suspected of pretending to be what he or she is not, or of saying what he or she does not mean, in order to achieve some secret purpose. "But then the Church came to the front, with an axe to grind; and she was wise, subtle, and knew more than one way to skin a cat—or a nation; she invented 'divine right of kings,' and propped it all around, brick by brick, with the Beatitudes" (Mark Twain, *A Connecticut Yankee in King Arthur's Court*, 1889).

Havisham, Miss *See* MISS HAVISHAM.

Haw-Haw, Lord *See* LORD HAW-HAW.

head off at the pass *See* CUT OFF AT THE PASS.

heap coals of fire To act with generosity or kindness to someone who has behaved badly, thereby causing the person to realize the wrongdoing and experience pangs of remorse. The expression appears in the Bible in Proverbs 25:22 in the form: "If thine enemy be hungry, give him bread to eat; and if be thirsty, give him water to drink: For thou shalt heap coals of fire upon his head, and the LORD shall reward thee." The same illustration is referred to in Romans 12:20: ". . . for in so doing thou shalt heap coals of fire on his head. Be not overcome of evil, but overcome evil with good." *These generous compliments were almost more than she could bear, each new expression of admiration heaping further coals of fire upon her head.*

heart of darkness The remotest depths of something, typically a place of death, horror, and depravity. The allusion is to the short novel *Heart of Darkness* (1902) by Joseph Conrad (1857–1924), which concerns a nightmarish journey made into the deepest jungles of the Congo by a man named Marlow in a bid to rescue a mysterious ailing ivory trader known as Mr. Kurtz, whom he eventually locates surrounded by horror and violence. The novel later provided the basis for the 1979 film *Apocalypse Now*. *I have looked into the heart of darkness that is the contemporary medical establishment, and I do not like what I found there. See also* HORROR, THE HORROR!, THE.

hearts and flowers Sentimentality. The allusion is to a heart-jerking tune of the same title written by Mary C. Brine in 1891, which was subsequently much used by pianists as an accompaniment for silent movies of the early 20th century. *She loved the show, but her husband hated it and said it was all hearts and flowers.*

Heathcliff (heethklif) Archetype of a brooding, passionate romantic hero. The allusion is to the fictional Heathcliff in Emily Brontë's novel *WUTHERING HEIGHTS* (1847), an unruly orphan whose obsessive love for the haughty Cathy Earnshaw ends in tragedy for all concerned. In modern usage, comparisons to the fictional Heathcliff and his unrealistic romantic ambitions are often disparaging in tone. They may, however, also be prompted by no more than a fancied physical resemblance to Emily Brontë's dark-complexioned, wild-haired hero. *He stood on the edge of the cliff and yelled his defiance like some demented Heathcliff.*

Heath Robinson (heeth robinsăn) Cobbled together in a makeshift, unnecessarily complicated fashion. The reference is to the British cartoonist William Heath Robinson (1872–1944) who was well known for his humorous pictures of absurd, intricate machines designed to carry out the simplest of tasks. "Ironically this Heath Robinson make-do also ended up contributing to the Dalek myth" (J. Bentham, *Doctor Who: The Early Years*, 1986).

heaven The Christian paradise; any ideal place or situation. The biblical heaven is depicted as the throne of God, accompanied by hosts of angels (as in Isaiah 6:1 and Revelation 4:1–11). The term is also used more widely to refer to the sky above or to the night sky with its stars and planets. "The Brahmin legends assert that this city is built on the site of the ancient Casi, which, like Mahomet's tomb, was once suspended between heaven and earth" (Jules Verne, *Around the World in Eighty Days,* 1873).

heaven's gate A place or situation in which a person faces the possibility of imminent death. The phrase alludes to the story of Jacob, who on waking from his dream about a ladder ascending to heaven exclaims, "Surely the LORD is in this place; and I knew it not. And he was afraid, and said, How dreadful is this place! this is none other but the house of God, and this is the gate of heaven" (Genesis 28:16–17). *The enemy brought up some cannon, and the general's confidence faltered as he realized, somewhat tardily, that they were trapped before heaven's gate.*

Hebe (heebee) Personification of youth. In Greek mythology she is identified as the daughter of Zeus and Hera and the cupbearer to the gods before being replaced by Ganymede. Another tradition has it that she lost her position after stumbling and falling while serving NECTAR to the gods. "Olivia, now about eighteen, had that luxuriancy of beauty with which painters generally draw Hebe; open, sprightly, and commanding" (Oliver Goldsmith, *The Vicar of Wakefield,* 1766).

Hecate (hekătee) Personification of witchcraft and sorcery. In Greek mythology Hecate was a moon goddess who ruled the underworld and by association the witches, ghosts, and world of magic. She is often depicted with three heads as she was identified with Selene in heaven, Artemis on earth, and Persephone in the underworld. *Drunken and screaming foul oaths, she erupted out of the shadows like Hecate from the underworld.*

hecatomb (hekătōm) A great sacrifice. The word comes from the Greek *hekaton,* meaning "a hundred," and *bous,* meaning "an ox," and referred originally to the sacrifice of 100 head of oxen in religious rituals. "Thirteen years later the Mahdi's empire was abolished forever in the gigantic hecatomb of Omdurman; after which it was thought proper that a religious ceremony in honour of General Gordon should be held at the palace at Khartoum" (Lytton Strachey, *Eminent Victorians,* 1918).

hector To badger, bully, or intimidate others. The word is an allusion to Hector, the hero of Homer's *Iliad* (c. eighth century B.C.), who led the Trojans against the besieging Greeks. The son of King Priam and Hecuba, he was a courageous warrior and the personification of every virtue. He died a hero's death in battle against Achilles, but the latter dishonored his corpse, dragging it behind his chariot and refusing it proper burial until the gods intervened. His name was invoked to describe brave and virtuous knights in medieval times, and it was only toward the end of the 17th century that it came to be applied in a negative sense, initially to gangs of wealthy young men who called themselves "Hectors" and terrorized the streets of London, frightening innocent passersby. ". . . several personages, who would otherwise have been admitted into the parlour and enlarged the opportunity of hectoring and condescension for their betters, being content this evening to vary their enjoyment by taking their spirits-and-water where they could themselves hector and condescend in company that called for beer" (George Eliot, *Silas Marner,* 1861).

Hecuba (hekyăbă) Personification of grief and misfortune. In Greek legend, Hecuba was the second wife of King Priam of Troy and saw many of her sons (who included Hector and Paris) slain one by one in the course of the Trojan War, as related by Homer in the *Iliad* (c. eighth century B.C.). After the fall of Troy Hecuba was claimed as a slave by the victorious Odysseus. Her grief was further intensified by the death of her daughter Polyxena (sacrificed on the demand of the ghost of Achilles) and of her grandson Astyanax (murdered at the hands of the Greeks). Ultimately she was turned into a dog and threw herself into the sea. *Grandmother took up her Hecuba pose of the mortally aggrieved innocent bystander.*

Hedda Gabler (hedă gahbler) A neurotic, vengeful, frenzied woman. The original Hedda Gabler was the central character in Henrick Ibsen's 1890 play *Hedda Gabler*, a restless, unfulfilled cynic who rejects marriage to the man she really loves and ultimately kills herself after she finds she is pregnant by the husband she despises. *When she heard that her sister had got much better reviews than she had she came over all Hedda Gabler and refused to speak to anyone for a week.*

hedonism The belief that the pursuit of pleasure or happiness is the aim of life. The word comes from the Greek *hedone,* meaning "pleasure," and the concept was first developed by the Greek philosopher Aristippus (c. 435–c. 356 B.C.). "Yes: there was to be, as Lord Henry had prophesied, a new Hedonism that was to recreate life and to save it from that harsh uncomely puritanism that is having, in our own day, its curious revival" (Oscar Wilde, *The Picture of Dorian Gray,* 1891).

Heep, Uriah *See* URIAH HEEP.

Hegelian (hegayleeăn) Relating to the concept of progress being achieved through the clash of opposing ideas. The allusion is to the German philosopher Georg Wilhelm Friedrich Hegel (1770–1831), who argued that only through the conflict of a proposition (thesis) and its antithesis could a synthesis be attained. His notion contributed to the development of the theory of dialectical evolution and formed part of the basis of the ideas of Marx and Engels, among others. "The reddish-haired young man contributed allusions to the Hegelian philosophy that momentarily confused the discussion" (H. G. Wells, *Ann Veronica: A Modern Love Story*, 1909).

hegira (hijīeră, hejără) An exodus or any flight to safety from oppression, especially from religious persecution, and by extension a change of policy or other move designed to put a person in a more favorable position. The term (meaning "departure") originally denoted the flight of Muhammad from Mecca to Medina in A.D. 622, the date marking the foundation of the Islamic faith. *The revolution prompted a hegira of refugees from the country under the threat of punitive action by the new regime.*

he has got gold of Tolosa (tolōsă) A person who obtains something by dubious means will not benefit from it. The allusion is to the sacking and looting of the Temple of Apollo at Tolosa (Toulouse) by the Roman consul Caepio. The gold and silver he looted was stolen from him in turn, and he and his men were defeated in battle in 106 B.C. with heavy losses. *It was truly said of Dobbs as he faced death at the hands of bandits that he had got gold of Tolosa.*

Heidi (hīdee) A young girl with a sunny, optimistic disposition, especially one of Swiss or central European descent or appearance. Heidi is the title character of a children's novel by Johanna Spyri, published in 1881. Undaunted by her orphan background, Heidi leads an idyllic life after settling in the Swiss Alps with her crusty old grandfather and her young companion Peter the goatherd. The name of Spyri's much-loved young heroine actually means, in German, "noble sort." "I had on this little dress, smock it was, with this pretty embroidery all over the bodice, sort of

Heidi, and Mum and I did my pigtails" (Johnathan Neale, *The Laughter of Heroes*, 1993).

heil Hitler (hīl <u>hit</u>ler) Salutation implying that someone is behaving in a dictatorial manner. The phrase (German for "hail Hitler") was routinely chanted by the Nazi hirelings of Adolf HITLER in the 1930s and 1940s, often with the right arm raised in the Nazi salute. Nowadays, the phrase is commonly addressed to anyone who is felt to be throwing his or her weight around in an unwarranted fashion. *As the managing director swept out with his entourage one of the junior secretaries was heard to breathe "Heil Hitler."*

Helen of Troy (<u>he</u>lăn, troi) Archetype of a beautiful woman, especially one whose beauty influences the course of events. The daughter of Zeus by Leda, Helen was the sister of Clytemnestra, Castor, and Pollux and won admiration as the most beautiful woman in the world. Many men competed for her hand, and it was agreed that whoever was successful would win the right to be defended by all the others. Menelaus of Sparta was the lucky suitor, but after a few years of marriage, she was abducted and carried off by Paris to Troy. The Greeks banded together to reclaim her and laid siege to Troy. After 10 years Troy fell, and Helen was restored to Menelaus in Sparta. Her beauty is legendary, and hers is often said to be ***"the face that launched a thousand ships,"*** a quotation from the play *Doctor Faustus* (1604) by Christopher Marlowe. *She may have looked like a real Helen of Troy, but she was the loneliest woman I ever met.*

Helicon (<u>he</u>likon) A source of artistic inspiration. According to Greek mythology, Mount Helicon in Boeotia was the home of the MUSES. Its features included the spring of Aganippe and the fountain of Hippocrene, whose waters are supposed to give poetic inspiration to those who drink from them. "O for a beaker full of the warm South, / Full of the true, the blushful Hippocrene" (John Keats, "Ode to a Nightingale," 1819).

Helios (<u>hee</u>leeăs, <u>hee</u>leeōs) Personification of the Sun. Helios was the sun god of Greek mythology, equivalent to the Roman Sol, and was conventionally depicted driving his chariot from east to west across the sky, pulled by four white horses. *Helios was directly overhead, and there was little shade from his blazing heat to be had anywhere.*

hell A place of suffering or other unpleasantness. According to Christian tradition, hell is the place of eternal punishment intended for Satan, his demons, and human beings who choose to reject God. It is conventionally depicted as a vast burning pit; in Revelation 19:20 it is described as "a lake of fire burning with brimstone." "For them Methodisses make folks believe as if they take a mug o' drink extry, an' make theirselves a bit comfortable, they'll have to go to hell for't as sure as they're born" (George Eliot, *Adam Bede*, 1859).

Hellespont (<u>he</u>lăspont) The strait (presently called the Dardanelles) that separates Europe from Asia in Turkey and connects the Sea of Marmora with the Aegean Sea. Its name (meaning "sea of Helle") is an allusion to an episode in the story of the Golden Fleece, in which a girl named Helle falls into this body of water from the back of an airborne golden ram as she flees from her mother-in-law, Ino, and is drowned. *I believe he would have swum the Hellespont to be with her, if only he had known what had happened. See also* HERO AND LEANDER.

Hellfire Club A group of people who are noted for their riotous and unfettered debauchery and other outrageous behavior. The original Hellfire Club comprised a group of English aristocrats led by Sir Francis Dashwood (1708–81) who held notorious orgiastic meetings at Medmenham Abbey in Buckinghamshire. *The students had their own Hellfire Club, at which they drank far too much and generally made idiots of themselves.*

Héloïse *See* ABELARD AND HÉLOÏSE.

Hemingway A person (often a writer) or a writing style of a tough, masculine character. The allusion is to the U.S. novelist and journalist Ernest Hemingway (1899–1961), whose life and writing reflected his own rugged personality. As well as being a keen big-game hunter and an aficionado of bullfighting and boxing, he was a heavy drinker and witnessed fighting at close quarters in the Spanish civil war and World War II. In his writing, he was characteristically blunt and direct, avoiding the use of long words and elaborate constructions. *With all those adjectives, and his tendency to use a hundred words when one would do, he's certainly no Hemingway. See also* LOST GENERATION.

hemlock *See* DRINK HEMLOCK.

hem of his garment, touch the To show great reverence for someone; to demonstrate one's faith in another's abilities or gifts. The image of touching or kissing the hem of a person's garment is biblical in origin, alluding to the story related in Matthew 9:20–22, Mark 5:25–34, and Luke 8:43–48 of the sick woman who dared to touch the hem of Christ's robe in the belief that he could perform miraculous cures by mere touch. "Considered from the point of view of a creator of character he ranks next to him who made Hamlet. Had he been articulate, he might have sat beside him. The only man who can touch the hem of his garment is George Meredith. Meredith is a prose Browning, and so is Browning" (Oscar Wilde, *Intentions*, 1891).

Henry VIII Archetype of a much-married man, especially one who disposes of his wives in a ruthless manner. Crowned king of England in 1509, Henry VIII ruled until 1574, during which time he had a fundamental impact upon English history, not least by breaking away from the Roman Catholic Church to create the Church of England. He is usually remembered, however, as a larger-than-life figure verging on a royal monster, who got through no less than six wives, two of whom (Anne Boleyn and Catherine Howard) he had beheaded. "He would be surrounded by his family and court just as Henry VIII might have been" (Patricia Holton, *Mother without a Mask*, 1991). *See also* BLUEBEARD.

Henry Morton Stanley *See* DARKEST AFRICA; DOCTOR LIVINGSTONE, I PRESUME?

Hephaestus (hefestăs, hefeestăs) Personification of skilled craftsmanship. In Greek mythology Hephaestus was the god of fire who served as blacksmith of the gods and made the armor of Achilles. He was the equivalent of the Roman god Vulcan. *The wrought ironwork of the gates marked their maker as a veritable Hephaestus.*

Hera (heeră) Archetype of a quarrelsome, vindictive, jealous wife. In Greek mythology, Hera was the wife and sister of Zeus and the equivalent of the Roman Juno. She was identified as the daughter of Cronos and Rhea and by Zeus gave birth to Ares, Hebe, Hephaestus, and Eileithyia. Several legends concern her revenge for the various love affairs of her husband. *Hera herself would have been proud of the way she nagged her husband about his indiscretions. See also* APPLE OF DISCORD.

Hercule Poirot (herkyool pwarō) An ace detective. The brilliant Belgian detective Hercule Poirot was the invention of British crime writer AGATHA CHRISTIE and appeared in an acclaimed series of murder mysteries, many of which were later adapted for television and the cinema. To detect the killer he routinely consults what he calls his ***little gray cells*** (that is, his brain). *It would take a Hercule Poirot to solve this enigma.*

Hercules (herkyooleez) A man who possesses great physical strength and courage. Hercules, or ***Heracles***, was one of the most celebrated figures in Greek mythology, a demigod who was the son of Zeus and the mortal Alcmena. He gave early notice of his remarkable powers when as a babe in arms he strangled two snakes placed in his crib by Zeus's jealous wife Hera, and went on to complete the formidable series of challenges now dubbed the LABORS OF HERCULES. When finally he died (*see* SHIRT OF NESSUS), his soul was taken to join the gods in heaven, where he was reconciled with Hera and married her daughter Hebe. The adjective ***Herculean*** denotes a task demanding a prodigious effort or great strength. *This Hercules of wrestling has captured a second world championship title in indefatigable style.*

here come the cavalry *See* U.S. CAVALRY.

hermaphrodite A plant or animal that possesses both male and female reproductive organs. The word alludes to the Greek god Hermaphroditus, who was the son of Hermes and Aphrodite. According to legend, Hermaphroditus rejected the suit of the nymph Salmacis when bathing in her pool. She embraced him nonetheless and petitioned the gods to keep them united permanently. The gods granted her request, and the couple became one entity incorporating both their genders. "Oh, it is pitiable to see him making of himself a thing that is neither male nor female, neither fish, flesh, nor fowl—a poor, miserable, hermaphrodite Frenchman!" (Mark Twain, *The Innocents Abroad*, 1869).

Hermes *See* HERMETIC; MERCURY.

hermetic Airtight, usually referring to a seal. The word has its origin in Hermes Trismegistus (meaning "Hermes, thrice-greatest"), which was the name by which Greeks knew Thoth, the Egyptian god of learning. It was also the name bestowed upon a celebrated third-century B.C. alchemist who was credited with using magic to invent the first airtight containers. *On inspection it was found that the hermetic seal on the canister had been broken and the contents contaminated.*

Hero and Leander (heerō, leeander,) Archetypal young lovers of Greek legend. Hero was a beautiful young priestess of Aphrodite who became the lover of Leander, a young man who lived on the opposite side of the HELLESPONT. Each night Leander swam across the strait to see Hero, guided by the lantern she held for him. Unfortunately, one night the light was extinguished by a storm, and Leander was drowned. Hero found his body on the shore and in her grief threw herself into the sea, faithful to her lover even in death. Lord Byron was among those subsequently inspired by the myth and famously re-created Hero's swim across the Dardanelles in 1810. *Their tragic story gave the two lovers the status of a modern Hero and Leander.*

Herod *See* OUT-HEROD HEROD.

Herodotus (herodătăs) Herodotus (480–425 B.C.) was a Greek historian who wrote some of the earliest chronicles and is remembered today for his systematic collection and arrangement of material and his testing of their accuracy. *He was the Herodotus of Napoleonic history, with scores of books and articles to his name.*

Hesperus, wreck of the *See* WRECK OF THE HESPERUS.

Hestia *See* VESTA.

he that hath, to him shall be given *See* WHOSOEVER HATH, TO HIM SHALL BE GIVEN.

he that is without sin *See* LET HIM WHO IS WITHOUT SIN CAST THE FIRST STONE.

he that runs may read The meaning is so clear that it may be taken in at once. The expression alludes to the Old Testament book of Habakkuk 2:2, in which God addresses the prophet Habakkuk as follows: "Write the vision, and make it plain upon tables, that he may run that readeth it." "But thieves from o'er the wall / Stole the seed by night. / Sow'd it far and wide / By every town and tower, / Till all the people cried / "Splendid is the flower." / Read my little fable: / He that runs may read" (Alfred, Lord Tennyson, *Enoch Arden,* 1864).

he that watereth Those who make the necessary effort are more likely to be rewarded. One of many parallel expressions of the same moral, it appears in the Bible in Proverbs 11:25: "The liberal soul shall be made fat: and he that watereth shall be watered also himself." "We have seen that the duties of bishop and pastor are to see and feed; and, of all who do so it is said, 'He that watereth, shall be also watered himself.' But the reverse is truth also. He that watereth not, shall be withered himself" (John Ruskin, *Sesame and Lilies*, 1865, 1871).

hewers of wood and drawers of water Those who do hard, menial jobs. The phrase is biblical in origin, appearing in a curse delivered by Joshua against the Gibeonites, who had attempted to deceive him into making terms with them by disguising themselves as strangers from a distant country: "Now therefore ye are cursed, and there shall none of you be freed from being bondmen, and hewers of wood and drawers of water for the house of my God . . . And Joshua made them that day hewers of wood and drawers of water for the congregation" (Joshua 9:23–27). ". . . what Roy Hattersley calls 'the modern hewers of wood and drawers of water'" (*Guardian,* June 30, 2001).

he who is not with me is against me Unless one supports a given person, cause, etc., one will be considered to be opposing the person, cause, etc. The phrase comes from the words of Jesus: "He that is not with me is against me" (Matthew 12:30). *Speaking at the election rally, the party leader tried to rally his supporters with the words, "He who is not with me is against me."*

hide one's light under a bushel To be modest about one's talents, abilities, virtues, etc. The phrase comes from Christ's Sermon on the Mount, in the course of which he compares the faithful to a lit candle: "Ye are the light of the world. A city that is set on a hill cannot be hid. Neither do men light a candle, and put it under a bushel, but on a candlestick; and it giveth light unto all that are in the house" (Matthew 5:14–15). A bushel is a unit of measurement traditionally gauged by using a wooden or earthenware container, thus, to be ***under a bushel*** signified being hidden from view. "Now did the Reverend Samuel Pentecost, whose light had hitherto been hidden under a bushel, prove at last that he could do something by proving that he could eat" (Wilkie Collins, *Armadale*, 1866).

Hieronymus Bosch (hăronămăs bosh) Of a bizarre, nightmarish character. The allusion is to the extraordinary paintings of Dutch artist Hieronymus Bosch (c. 1453–1516), whose works often depicted the torments of damned souls in hell. Even today his grotesque visions of weird animals and demons provoke fascination and astonishment. *Each night he descended into a dreamworld that seemed to have been designed by Hieronymus Bosch.*

higher than Gilderoy's kite (gildăroi) Punished more severely than anyone else. The allusion is to a Scottish highwayman called Gilderoy, who was said to have been hanged higher than other criminals to reflect the seriousness of his crimes. "She squandered millions of francs on a navy which she did not need, and the first time she took her new toy into action she got it knocked higher than Gilderoy's kite—to use the language of the Pilgrims" (Mark Twain, *Innocents Abroad*, 1869).

High Noon A climactic test or confrontation. The allusion is to the 1952 Western movie of the same title, in which a small-town marshal played by Gary Cooper ventures out to fight a deadly gun battle with four outlaws arriving on the noon train. The film in its turn was based on the short story "The Tin Star" (1947) by John W. Cunningham. "The auction ring of Ayr cattle market on 14th December, 1911, was arranged for the 'high noon' of the dispute" (Andrew Boyle, *Ayrshire Heritage*, 1990). Somewhat confusingly, drawing on the image of the sun being at its zenith at noon and entirely ignoring the subtext provided by the classic film, the phrase may also be used to describe a time when things are at their most flourishing: "For all that, the Thatcher high noon seemed to show the balance between state power and individual self-expression, in some key episodes, tilting against the individual or the dissenting minority" (Kenneth Morgan, *The People's Peace*, 1990).

hind of Arcadia *See* LABORS OF HERCULES.

hip and thigh, smite them *See* SMITE THEM HIP AND THIGH.

hippie A person who favors a relaxed, tolerant, and peace-loving attitude to life in preference to the hardheaded realities of the world around him or her. The original hippies emerged during the late 1960s, when a whole generation identified itself with antiestablishment ideas and indulged freely in rock music, drugs, and colorful fashions. The word itself probably had its roots in the slang "hip," meaning "fashionable." The term, often in the derogatory phrase ***long-haired hippie***, has since been applied more widely to anyone who is suspected of a dreamy, idealistic view of life or of espousing in some way the ideals of the hippie era. "Perdita, however, was deeply embarrassed to see her mother arriving in unsuitably colourful clothes and dripping wet hair, like a superannuated hippie" (Jilly Cooper, *Polo*, 1991). *See also* FLOWER CHILD; WOODSTOCK.

Hippocrates *See* GALENICAL; HIPPOCRATIC OATH.

Hippocratic oath (hipōkratik) The ritual promise traditionally made by doctors on qualifying for medical practice to the effect that they will observe the highest ethical standards and observe the confidentiality of their patients. Hippocrates (c. 460–c. 370 B.C.) was a Greek physician who for his 87 treatises on medical practice is remembered today as the father of medicine. Students under Hippocrates were believed to take such an oath. The name of Hippocrates is also preserved in ***Hippocrates' sleeve***, a square piece of flannel folded into a triangle and used to strain liquids. *Many doctors practicing today have only a hazy notion of what the Hippocratic oath really says, although they are aware of the seriousness that it has for patients.*

Hippocrene *See* HELICON.

hippogriff (hipōgrif) Symbol of love. In Greek mythology, the hippogriff was a winged horse, the offspring of a griffin and a filly. *Her head swam with emotion: The winged hippogriff of love had planted its hooves in her heart.*

Hippolyta *See* AMAZON; LABORS OF HERCULES.

Hiroshima (hirăsheemă, hărōshimă) A place that has been devastated by a nuclear explosion. The city of Hiroshima in Japan was largely obliterated when the U.S. Air Force dropped an atom bomb on it on August 6, 1945, the first instance of such a device being used in war. Over 160,000 people died and, after a second bomb was dropped on ***Nagasaki*** four days later, the Japanese government surrendered. Since then the name of Hiroshima has been widely understood to represent the dreadful threat of widespread nuclear destruction, though it may also be employed in a range of other contexts. "To limit poetry is a Hiroshima of the human spirit" (Edmund J. Smyth, *Postmodernism and Contemporary Fiction*, 1991).

his master's voice An authority that must be obeyed. The allusion has its roots in an advertisement for the Victor record company that featured a fox terrier listening to the sound coming from an old-fashioned phonograph horn (later updated as a gramophone horn), above the slogan "His master's voice." In real life the dog, named Nipper, had been owned by the brother of an English artist called Francis Barraud, the painter of the picture used in the original advertisement. When Nipper's master died, the terrier was handed over to Francis Barraud together with some wax cylinders on which his brother's voice had been recorded. Whenever these were played, Nipper focused hard on the horn from which his dead master's voice emanated, giving Barraud the idea for his famous painting. In modern usage, the phrase is typically muttered (with varying degrees of resentment) in apology when having to break off to do the bidding of someone else. The phrase (and dog logo) is still present in the record industry, albeit in truncated form, in the name of the HMV music and video stores. *I'd love to stop and chat but I'd better answer his master's voice.*

hit below the belt To act in an underhand manner against an opponent. The allusion is to prizefighting and the stipulation in the QUEENSBERRY RULES, which govern the sport of boxing, that it is illegal to punch an opponent below the waist belt. Something that is ***below the belt*** is thus something of an unfair or illicit nature. "That was below the belt, but instead of stopping there while she was still in one piece, she drove on in a high, hectoring voice, 'Don't you think your daughter deserves a little rest instead of going home to slave for you after she's been working all week?'" (Pamela Scobie, *A Twist of Fate*, 1990).

Hitchcockian (hichkokeeăn) After the style of British-born film director Alfred Hitchcock. Alfred Hitchcock (1899–1980) was well known for making hugely suspenseful thrillers in a distinctive personal style. Audiences learned to expect surprising twists in the plots of his films as well as fleeting appearances by Hitchcock himself in the guise of a passer-by or a member of the public. Some people, however, are more likely to be described as Hitchcockian in reference to their generous girth or imperturbable demeanor (both traits associated with the famous director) rather than to their grasp of macabre film-making. "The film recovers only in the brilliantly Hitchcockian scene when Michael, in a crowded theater, pretends to believe that the blowing, twisting red ribbons behind a vindictive ballerina (Tamara Toumanova) really are the fire that they represent" (D. Millar, *Special Effects: Cinema Secrets*, 1990). *See also* MACGUFFIN; PSYCHO.

Hitler An officious, ruthless, or vicious person; a tyrant. As head of Germany's Third Reich, Adolf Hitler (1889–1945) was responsible for crimes against humanity on a vast scale, for which his memory is almost universally vilified. Decades after his suicide as the Russians and the other Allies swept deep into a shattered Germany, Hitler's name is still likely to provoke strong reactions in those who find themselves being linked with his style of leadership, especially in countries that suffered particularly badly as a result of his policies. This has not prevented many far less significant bullies suspected of abusing positions of authority being routinely labeled a Hitler, or a ***little Hitler***. *I will not be pushed around by a little Hitler who has far less experience and fewer qualifications than I have. See also* BUNKER MENTALITY; FÜHRER; HEIL HITLER; HOLOCAUST; *MEIN KAMPF*.

Hobbesian (hobzeeăn) Relating to the philosophical ideas of English political philosopher Thomas Hobbes (1588–1679). Hobbes argued that men are naturally brutish and given to violence, and need to curb their natural impulses through good government. Life, he famously concluded, is otherwise "solitary, poor, nasty, brutish, and short." The term Hobbesian is usually employed in reference to underlying aggressive tendencies. "Trust, as such, is not an element in Hobbesian human nature" (R. S. Woolhouse, *The Empiricists*, 1988). *See also* NASTY, BRUTISH, AND SHORT.

Hobbit A small person. The Hobbits, a diminutive race of people with large, hairy feet who live in burrows underground, are the heroes of J. R. R. Tolkien's novels *The Hobbit* (1937) and *The Lord of the Rings* (1954–55). *He was sensitive about his height and found it difficult to forgive his friends when they referred to him as a Hobbit.*

Hobson's choice A nonexistent choice. The allusion is to Thomas (or Tobias) Hobson (1544–1631), the owner of a livery stable in Cambridge, England, who was reputed to deny his customers a free choice of horse, instead insisting that they took the one that had been longest in the stable. *Most people opt for this software by Hobson's choice, because it is the only package that is compatible with the operating system on the computer.*

Hoffa, Jimmy *See* JIMMY HOFFA.

Hogarthian (hōgahrtheeăn) After the style of British artist William Hogarth (1697–1764). The term is usually employed with reference to the satirical content of Hogarth's paintings and prints, which lampooned a range of contemporary vices. "The most unpleasant discoveries were made during the process of clearance: cupboards full of urine-encrusted chamber pots, of ancient patent medicine, of dead mice, of moth-infested garments, of fossilized scraps of 19th-century food: Hogarthian, Dickensian relics of an oppressed and squalid past" (Margaret Drabble, *The Radiant Way*, 1988). *See also* GIN LANE; RAKE'S PROGRESS.

hoist with one's own petard (pătahrd) Caught out by one's own cleverness or scheming. The phrase is based on a quotation from William Shakespeare's tragedy *Hamlet* (c. 1600): "For 'tis the sport to have the enginer \ Hoist with his own petar." The allusion is to medieval siege warfare and the use of a petard (a primitive explosive device) to blow up defensive works: the device was notoriously unpredictable and often exploded prematurely, blowing up the engineers who had set it. *She called for an inquiry in the hope of discrediting her colleague, only to find herself hoist with her own petard when it was discovered that the cause of the problem lay in an error she had made herself.*

Holden Caulfield (hōldăn kahlfeeld) Archetype of a confused, disaffected teenager. Holden Caulfield is the 16-year-old protagonist of J. D. Salinger's novel *The Catcher in the Rye* (1951). Holden's observations of the world around him lead him to conclude that he is surrounded by "phonies" and he accordingly rejects the adult world that he is about to enter, in the process becoming an icon for rebellious youth of his and succeeding generations. The role he gives himself, that of ***catcher in the rye***, is someone who seeks to catch children playing in a field of rye and thus save them from falling over the cliff at the edge of it. "It was like spending an evening with a character from *Catcher in the Rye*, one Holden Caulfield would have designated 'a phoney from some crummy place like Des Moines or somewhere'" (Tom Pow, *In the Palace of Serpents*, 1992).

hold the fort To keep things running smoothly, especially when others are absent. The phrase (in its fuller form "Hold the fort, I'm coming") became famous as a message sent in 1864, during the U.S. Civil War, by Federal General William Tecumseh Sherman to General John M. Corse when the latter found himself under threat from a Confederate advance at the Battle of Allatoona following the fall of Atlanta. Corse successfully held off the enemy until Sherman arrived. Sherman's actual message was somewhat different in form, the modern version of it dating from a religious song written around 1870 by Philip Paul Bliss: "'Hold the fort, for I am coming,' / Jesus signals still; / Wave the answer back to heaven, / 'By the grace we will.'" *I offered to stay at home and hold the fort while Michael and his brother went off in search of the missing teenagers.*

holier than thou Self-righteous; inclined to look down on others. The phrase appears in the Bible in Isaiah 65:5, where "a rebellious people" are condemned for their arrogance toward others: "Which say, Stand by thyself, come not near to me; for I am holier than thou. These are a smoke in my nose, a fire that burneth all the day." *His holier-than-thou attitude did not go down well with the troops, who began to murmur resentfully among themselves.*

hollow men People who lack any real substance or who lack intelligence, ideals, etc. The reference is to a 1925 poem entitled "The Hollow Men" by T. S. Eliot, the subject of which is the impossibility of redemption: "We are the hollow men / We are the stuffed men / Leaning together / Headpiece filled with straw. Alas!" *Wall Street is full of hollow men whose only interest is money.*

Holly Golightly (gōlītlee) Archetype of a carefree young socialite. Holly Golightly is the amoral central character in Truman Capote's novella *Breakfast at Tiffany's* (1958), and was memorably played on screen by Audrey Hepburn when the book was filmed in 1961. Restless and yearning, in the film she eventually finds contentment in a relatively conventional romance (although the ending in the book is left unresolved). *Like some Holly Golightly, she flitted from party to party without ever working out what it was she really wanted.*

Hollywood The U.S. cinema industry and the celebrity world connected with it. A district of the less glamorous Los Angeles, Hollywood was the location of the studios where the first motion pictures were made in the early 20th century and home to many of the leading stars. The area is said to have acquired its name in 1886, when it was laid out by Horace Wilcox. *She had sold her soul to Hollywood when she was still a young girl. See also* TINSELTOWN.

Holmes, Sherlock *See* SHERLOCK HOLMES.

holocaust (holăkost) An act of mass murder. The word is indelibly linked with the genocidal killing of much of Europe's Jewish population by the Nazis in the 1930s and 1940s. The word originally referred to destruction by burning, but since the 1940s the element of fire is no longer implied. "Loosely linked to it were the emerging environmentalist movements (the link being forged by a deep suspicion of advanced technology which had raised the spectre of nuclear holocaust and then manifested itself in the devastation inflicted on Vietnam)" (Bob Roshier, *Controlling Crime*, 1989). *See also* AUSCHWITZ; FINAL SOLUTION; HITLER; KRISTALLNACHT.

holy grail A final goal or destination achieved only with much difficulty; the object of a quest, especially one of a mystical or mythical character. The original Holy Grail was the cup or dish supposedly used at the Last Supper and also by Joseph of Arimathea to catch the blood dripping from the crucified Christ. Traditionally it is thought to have been brought in the first century A.D. to Glastonbury, England, by Joseph of Arimathea. The Grail became an object of great veneration in medieval times and remains best known today as a central icon of Arthurian legend (*see* KING ARTHUR), in pursuit of which many brave knights roamed far and wide. *A cure for cancer is the holy grail of modern medical research.*

holy of holies A very special or private place; an inner sanctum to which few are admitted. The allusion is to the sacred inner chamber of the Tabernacle in the wilderness and the Temple of Jerusalem, in which the ARK OF THE COVENANT was kept, according to Exodus 26:31–34 and 1 Kings 6:16–19. Only the high priest was permitted to enter the room, once a year, to make an animal sacrifice on behalf of the people. *It was only after much checking of credentials and letters of recommendation that he was finally admitted to the holy of holies, the Oval Office, in order to discuss his concerns with the president. See also* VEIL OF THE TEMPLE RENT.

home, James, and don't spare the horses! Take us home as quickly as possible. The expression comes from the title of a popular song written in 1934 by Fred Hillebrand, though it clearly harks back to an earlier era when people traveled around in horse-drawn carriages driven by their servants. *We need to get back before midnight, so home, James, and don't spare the horses!*

Homeric (hōmerik) Heroic, epic, mythic. The reference is to the celebrated eighth-century B.C. blind Greek poet Homer, traditionally credited with authorship of the *Iliad*, which recounts the latter stages of the Trojan War, and of the *Odyssey*, which describes the wanderings of Odysseus as he sails home after that war. ***Homeric laughter*** denotes unrestrained mirth of epic proportions, as heard at the feast of the gods according to the *Iliad*. "With a boy, trouble must be of Homeric dimensions to last overnight" (Booth Tarkington, *Penrod*, 1914).

Homer sometimes nods (hōmer) Even the wisest or most capable person can make a mistake. The reference is to the celebrated eighth-century B.C. blind Greek poet Homer, author of the *Iliad* and the *Odyssey*. The expression, also found in the form ***even Homer sometimes nods,*** is thought to have made its first appearance in *Ars Poetica* (359) by the Roman poet Horace, in which the author laments that Homer occasionally lapses from the highest standards in his writing, but quickly adds that such flaws are readily forgivable in one so great. *The final chapter of the book is a disappointment, as though the master had lost his concentration at the vital moment, but as they say "even Homer sometimes nods."*

Hood, Robin *See* ROBIN HOOD.

Hook, Captain *See* CAPTAIN HOOK.

Hooverville (hoovervil) A shanty town or other area of dilapidated or temporary housing. The term alludes to the shanty towns made largely of crates and other bits of scrap that sprang up in various parts of the United States during the GREAT DEPRESSION of the 1930s when Herbert Hoover (1874–1964) was president. Hoover himself was blamed for the existence of such areas by many of the destitute and otherwise homeless people who took up residence there. *The last the family heard of him was that he had been evicted from his home and forced to move to the Hooverville that had gradually built up between the interstate and the river.*

Hopalong Cassidy Archetype of a clean-cut cowboy hero. Hopalong Cassidy made his first appearance in a cowboy novel written in 1906 by Clarence E. Mulford, but enjoyed his heyday as a hero of the silver screen in a series of 66 low-budget movies made between 1935 and 1948, starring William Boyd. Comparisons to Hopalong Cassidy today are likely to be humorous in tone. *I'd pay you in cash and forget about the tax if it wasn't for Hopalong Cassidy over there.*

hope deferred makes the heart sick Delay or disappointment in realizing one's hopes can be the cause of great unhappiness. The saying has biblical origins: "Hope deferred maketh the heart sick: but when the desire cometh, it is a tree of life" (Proverbs 13:12). "She had not suffered so much from a want of food, however, as from a want of air and exercise; from unremitting, wasting toil at a sedentary occupation, from hope deferred and from sleepless nights" (James Fenimore Cooper, *Autobiography of a Pocket-Handkerchief*, 1843).

Horatian (hărayshăn) Of or relating to a balanced viewpoint, especially one that is satirical and respectful by turns. The adjective refers to the celebrated Roman lyric poet and satirist Horace (65–8 B.C.), who wrote relatively gentle satires during the reign of the emperor Augustus. He was renowned both for his wisdom and his sincerity. *The editorial comprised a subtly Horatian analysis of the situation that offered neither side much comfort.*

Horatius at the bridge (hă<u>ray</u>shăs, hă<u>ray</u>sheeăs) A person who behaves heroically in the face of vastly superior odds. The allusion is to the Roman legend of Horatius Cocles (530–500 B.C.), the heroic warrior who with two companions (Herminius and Lartius) kept the entire Etruscan army of Lars Porsena at bay by blocking their passage over a bridge on the Tiber River leading directly to Rome. By thus delaying the enemy the three heroes secured enough time to demolish the bridge behind them, thereby saving the city. Their task complete, Horatius sent his two companions back before following them to safety by swimming the Tiber in full armor. It has been suggested that the legend of Horatius and his companions may have been invented as propaganda to counter criticism of Roman aggression toward the Etruscans. The phrase *Horatius at the bridge* became widely familiar after the publication of Thomas Babington Macaulay's *Lays of Ancient Rome* (1842). *The secretary of state mounted a staunch defense of the government, but he looked increasingly like Horatius at the bridge, and few were convinced that he would manage to stem the tide of criticism for long.*

Horeb *See* MOUNT SINAI.

Horeb, rock in *See* SMITE THE ROCK.

horn of plenty *See* CORNUCOPIA.

horns of a dilemma A difficult choice between two alternatives, neither of which is ideal. The phrase is Greek in origin, referring to a "double lemma" (an ambiguous proposition) and coming ultimately from *lambanein* (meaning "to take"), in the sense of "something taken for granted." "Each had repeatedly hung the other on the horns of a dilemma, but neither seemed to be a whit the worse for the hanging; and so the war went on merrily" (Anthony Trollope, *Barchester Towers,* 1857).

horns of the altar, to the A loyal friend through thick and thin. This expression of devoted friendship alludes to the sacred horns that adorned altars in biblical times. According to Exodus 29:12 the altar at the Tabernacle had a projecting horn at each of its four corners, and these were ceremonially smeared with the blood of animal sacrifices (they may also have been used to tether the animals before sacrifice). These horns are referred to again in 1 Kings 1:50: "And Adonijah feared because of Solomon, and arose, and went, and caught hold on the horns of the altar." Ancient Romans similarly laid hold of the horns of the altar when swearing loyalty to their friends. "Thinkest thou, Waldemar, that the wily Archbishop will not suffer thee to be taken from the very horns of the altar, would it make his peace with King Richard?" (Sir Walter Scott, *Ivanhoe,* 1819).

horror, the horror!, the A complaint against something bad or unpleasant. The phrase is a quotation from the novel *HEART OF DARKNESS* (1902) by Joseph Conrad, in which these are the last words of Mr. Kurtz as he dies deep in the jungles of the Congo, tacitly acknowledging that he has become as barbarous and uncivilized as the natives he originally sought to redeem. In everyday usage, it is more likely to be delivered somewhat ironically in complaint against some minor annoyance. *Unfortunately the lad entered the room just as his grandmother was removing her dress to change into something cooler—oh, the horror, the horror!*

horse, wooden *See* TROJAN HORSE.

horse! A horse! My kingdom for a horse!, A An impassioned plea for help, at any price. The line is a quotation from William Shakespeare's play *Richard III* (c. 1592), spoken by the unhorsed king as he seeks the means to escape his enemies in the climactic Battle of Bosworth in which the historical Richard III was killed on August 23, 1485. There is evidence that in the real battle the king was brought a horse to carry him away from what was turning into a bloody defeat, though no suggestion that he actually delivered the line that features in Shakespeare's play. *We need to get to the Capitol at once—A horse! A horse! My kingdom for a horse!*

Hotspur A fiery-tempered person. The allusion is to Sir Henry "Harry" Percy (1364–1403), son of the first earl of Northumberland, who was so nicknamed. He is depicted in William Shakespeare's play *Henry IV, Part I* (1596) as a hotheaded, reckless knight, given to taking offense, who rebels against the Crown but is killed by Prince Hal during the Battle of Shrewsbury. *It's no good wading in like a Hotspur—the situation requires diplomacy.*

Hottentot (hotăntot) An uncivilized barbarian. The term was first bestowed upon the indigenous inhabitants of what was formerly known as Cape Colony or Cape Province in South Africa by Dutch colonists in the 17th century. The original meaning of the word itself is unknown. "He then took me into a saloon, and while I drank made me note that the floor was covered with coins sunk in cement. A Hottentot would not have been guilty of this sort of barbarism" (Rudyard Kipling, *American Notes*, 1891).

Houdini (hoodeenee) A person who has the reputation of being able to escape from difficult situations. The allusion is to the Hungarian-born U.S. escapologist and magician Harry Houdini (Ehrich Weiss; 1874–1926), who was well known for stage acts that involved escaping from an array of chains and padlocks, sometimes underwater or suspended from a rope and often at apparent risk of death. *That bird is a real Houdini when it comes to getting out of its pen.*

houri (hooree) A beautiful dark-eyed woman. In Muslim mythology, the houris are the perpetually young and beautiful maidens who tend the faithful in paradise, renewing their virginity at will. "That houri, appearing, shakes him up in the usual manner and is charged by the old gentleman to remain near him" (Charles Dickens, *Bleak House,* 1852–53).

house divided against itself, a Those who cannot agree among themselves cannot expect to succeed. The expression comes from Matthew 12:25, in which Christ responds to the accusations of the Pharisees that he had drawn on the powers of the Devil to achieve the miraculous healing of a deaf and mute man, pointing out that evil would hardly seek to destroy evil: "Every kingdom divided against itself is brought to desolation; and every city or house divided against itself shall not stand." Similar sentiments are expressed in Mark 3:25: "If a house be divided against itself, that house cannot stand." *The board of the company is at loggerheads over the issue, and you know what they say, a house divided against itself cannot stand.*

household gods *See* LARES AND PENATES.

house not made with hands Heaven; God's heavenly abode. The phrase comes from 2 Corinthians 5:1, in which Paul contrasts the physicality of the human body occupied by the soul on earth with the heavenly house that it may one day attain, "a building of God, an house not made with hands, eternal in the heavens." *His mother died last night at her huge old mansion in the hills and resides now in a house not made with hands.*

house of Atreus (aytreeăs) A family or other group who seem to be doomed to misfortune or under a dreadful curse. The allusion is to the cursed family of Atreus, king of Mycenae and father of Agamemnon and Menelaus. According to Greek mythology, the curse originated with Atreus's father, Pelops, who was slaughtered and served up by his own father, Tantalus, at a banquet to which all the gods had been invited (*see* IVORY SHOULDER OF PELOPS). *The company has become a house of Atreus, rocked by one misfortune after another.*

house of God A church or other place of worship. The phrase appears in the Bible in Genesis 28:17, in which Jacob awakes from his dream of a ladder reaching to heaven and exclaims, "How dreadful is this place! this is none other but the house of God, and this is the gate of heaven." "None of them, not even Dr Grantly, could close his ears, nor leave the house of God during the hours of service. They were under an obligation of listening, and that too without any immediate power of reply" (Anthony Trollope, *Barchester Towers,* 1857).

house of many mansions A spacious building or other place; any organization or other entity offering a wide range of aspects, possibilities, or opportunities. The phrase comes from Christ's farewell sermon to his disciples, in which it signifies heaven: "Let not your heart be troubled: ye believe in God, believe also in me. In my Father's house are many mansions: if it were not so, I would have told you. I go to prepare a place for you" (John 14:2). "There was, of course, a better world. 'In my Father's house are many mansions' was one of Aunt Juley's favourite sayings—it always comforted her, with its suggestion of house property, which had made the fortune of dear Roger" (John Galsworthy, *The Forsyte Saga,* 1922).

House of Usher (usher) A macabre, eerie place or situation. The allusion is to the story "The Fall of the House of Usher," one of Edgar Allan Poe's *Tales of Mystery and Imagination* (1839). The story revolves around the destruction of the last of the ancient Usher family in terrifying, supernatural circumstances. *The circumstances surrounding the party's fall from public favor created an atmosphere like the Fall of the House of Usher.*

Howard Hughes A very rich person, or a person who behaves as though he or she is very rich. Howard Hughes (1905–76) was a U.S. businessman and film producer who made a billion-dollar fortune and became one of the most familiar faces of his generation, despite his reputation in later years for being an obsessive recluse. *Look at Howard Hughes over there, buying everyone drinks when we all know he's about to be thrown out of his house for not keeping up the payments.*

How are the mighty fallen! An exclamation of amazement at how those who were once rich, successful, or otherwise considered superior to their fellows have been brought down to a much more humble level. The phrase is a quotation from

2 Samuel 1:19, in which David laments the deaths of Saul and Jonathan: "The beauty of Israel is slain upon thy high places: how are the mighty fallen!" "Once it took the head of my family a day's hard riding to make the circuit of his estates, but the mighty are fallen. Fast women and slow horses" (William Somerset Maugham, *Of Human Bondage,* 1915).

howling wilderness A wild, desolate place; a situation complete devoid of potential, style, or interest. The phrase comes from Deuteronomy 32:10, in which Moses recalls God finding the Israelites "in a desert land, and in the waste howling wilderness." Several 19th-century writers, including William Makepeace Thackeray, used the phrase to describe locations where unfashionable people lived. "In the old war, when I was out under Sir William, I travelled seventy miles alone in the howling wilderness, with a rifle bullet in my thigh, then cut it out with my own jack-knife" (James Fenimore Cooper, *The Pioneers,* 1823).

How long, O Lord? A rhetorical question expressing dismay at how long something is taking. The phrase has its origins in the Bible, as in Psalm 13:1, where it is a cry for deliverance from a life-threatening illness, and in Revelation 6:9–10, in which it is a cry for the martyrs who have died for their faith. "Now and then, as if to show the thoughts which were most poignant, he muttered—'Lepers, lepers! They—my mother and Tirzath—they lepers! How long, how long, O Lord!'" (Lew Wallace, *Ben Hur,* 1880).

Hoyle, according to *See* ACCORDING TO HOYLE.

hubris (hyoobris) Arrogant self-confidence or pride. The term is of Greek origin, referring to the refusal of characters to accept the authority of the gods in ancient Greek tragedy. This arrogance is invariably followed by the character concerned being punished by the gods for his impudence (usually at the hands of NEMESIS). *Hubris drove him to strike back at those who had sought to belittle him in the eyes of the public.*

Huckleberry Finn (hukălberee) Archetype of idealistic American youth. The central character in *The Adventures of Huckleberry Finn* (1885) by U.S. novelist Mark Twain, Huckleberry Finn is a spirited young lad who finds himself torn between friendship to a runaway slave called Jim and his legal duty to report him to the authorities. He eventually decides to protect his friend and with him seeks to escape the overbearing treatment of his drunken father by sailing on a raft down the Mississippi. "He had something of a Huckleberry Finn spirit, wanting to run away to sea" (Michael Munn, *Hollywood Rogues*, 1991). *See also* TOM SAWYER.

Hudson A butler, or other personal servant. Hudson, played by Gordon Jackson, was the family butler in the highly successful British television drama series *UPSTAIRS, DOWNSTAIRS* (1971–75), in which the lives of the wealthy Bellamy family were contrasted with those of the servants who kept their household running smoothly. *What we need in this household is our very own Hudson.*

Hughes, Howard *See* HOWARD HUGHES.

Hulk *See* INCREDIBLE HULK.

Humphrey, Sir (humfree) The embodiment of a political bureaucrat. Sir Humphrey Appleby, played by Nigel Hawthorne, was one of the two main characters in the acclaimed British television comedy series *Yes Minister* (1980–82) and *Yes Prime*

Minister (1986–88). As permanent undersecretary to politician Jim Hacker, Sir Humphrey spent most of his time trying to prevent politicians from interfering in the smooth running of the civil service, with varying degrees of success. At once comical and ludicrous, the series was praised by many political observers for the accuracy of its portrayal of the relationship between the political establishment and the bureaucracy supposed to serve it. The term is also sometimes used in reference to Sir Humphrey's characteristic circumlocution and equivocation. *Many ambitious plans have bitten the dust after a Sir Humphrey has got hold of them.*

Humpty Dumpty A person with an egg-shaped physique or, alternatively, something that is precariously balanced and risks being fatally broken. The allusion is to the nursery rhyme character, an egg perched on a wall who is broken to pieces when he falls off: "Humpty Dumpty sat on a wall, / Humpty Dumpty had a great fall. / All the king's horses and all the king's men / Couldn't put Humpty together again." There are various theories concerning the origins of Humpty Dumpty. Some say he originally represented Richard III, while others claim he had his beginnings in a riddle, the answer to which was "an egg." Alternatively, and perhaps significantly, a "Humpty Dumpty" was the name of an ale and brandy punch drunk in the late 17th century and, even more bizarrely, the nickname of a siege tower or cannon used during the siege of Gloucester in 1643. "Five feet high and weighing one hundred and seventy pounds, a veritable Humpty Dumpty of a woman, Mrs. Stych had no hope of ever being able to wear pants gracefully" (Helen Forrester, *The Latchkey Kid*, 1990).

Hunchback of Notre Dame (notră dahm, nōtră daym) A person of grotesque, misshapen appearance. The allusion is to the 1831 novel *The Hunchback of Notre Dame* by Victor Hugo (1802–85), in which the title character is an ugly, hunchbacked bellringer called ***Quasimodo***. "The shopkeeper was a Hunchback of Notre Dame, twisted, with grotesque growths protruding from his body" (Alison Leonard, *Gate-Crashing the Dream Party*, 1990).

hundred days The first hundred days of an administration, presidency, or other office. The original hundred days were those that began with the escape of NAPOLEON from ELBA on March 20, 1815, and ended on June 28, 1815, after his defeat at WATERLOO and the restoration of the French monarchy. The term has been applied to many periods in office since then and is especially associated with the presidency of Franklin Roosevelt and the three months in 1933 during which he laid the basis of his celebrated New Deal. By extension, the presidency of John F. Kennedy, which ended prematurely with his assassination in 1963, became known as the ***thousand days***, as that was how long his administration lasted. "His supporters talked of a new 'Hundred Days,' although the situation was far less serious than that of 1933 and the measures not as radical" (A. B. Lancaster, *The Americas*, 1984).

hyacinth A lily of the genus *Hyacinthus* with usually blue, pink, or white flowers. The name of the plant alludes to Hyacinthus, a youth whose beauty, according to Greek mythology, attracted the attention of the sun god Apollo and of Zephyrus, the god of the west wind. Hyacinthus favored Apollo, thus incurring the wrath of Zephyrus, who took his revenge by bringing about the accidental death of Hyacinthus as he and Apollo tossed an iron discus to each other in play. A sudden gust of wind blew the discus off course, and it hit Hyacinthus on the head, killing him instantly. The flower that the grieving Apollo caused to spring up from the young man's spilled blood has borne his name ever since. *The pool was fringed with hyacinths and rhododendron bushes.*

Hyde, Mr. See JEKYLL AND HYDE.

hydra-headed Many headed. In Greek mythology the Hydra was a fearsome monster faced by HERCULES in the course of the LABORS OF HERCULES. The Hydra had nine heads, each of which when severed was replaced by two more. Hercules overcame the Hydra by cutting off the heads and having his companion Iolaus scorch the wounds before they could grow back. In modern usage the term *hydra-headed* is usually applied to a troublesome, multifaceted problem or one that keeps recurring despite everything being done to solve it. *The club faces a hydra-headed conundrum: how to attract new supporters without offending long-standing members who are more than happy to keep things as they are.*

hygiene The science concerned with the safeguarding of health, especially through observing clean or healthy practices. The word comes from the name of the Greek goddess of health Hygeia, who was sometimes identified as the wife or daughter of Aesculapius, the god of medicine. *The link between hygiene and the outbreak of disease has been known for centuries.*

hymen A fold of membrane that partially covers the entrance to the vagina and is usually broken when sexual intercourse takes place for the first time. The word comes from Hymenaeus, the name of the Greek god of marriage. He was the son of Dionysus and Aphrodite and was traditionally depicted leading the revels at wedding feasts, often carrying a burning torch and crowned with a garland of flowers. *On inspection the girl's hymen was found to be unruptured and she was declared "virgo intacta."*

hyperborean Frigid; arctic; from the Far North. According to Greek mythology, the Hyperboreans were a race of people who lived in a remote sunny land in the extreme north (*hyper* meaning "beyond" and *Boreas* meaning "North Wind"). This faraway country was said to be protected by Apollo, and its inhabitants lived in a state of perpetual happiness. "It's the unnatural combat of the four primal elements.—It's a blasted health.—It's a Hyperborean winter scene" (Herman Melville, *Moby-Dick,* 1851).

Hyperion to a satyr (hipeereeăn, sayter) A contrast between two opposites. In Greek mythology, Hyperion was one of the Titans and the father of Helios (the Sun), Selene (the Moon), and Eos (the dawn). His name is sometimes employed as a synonym for the Sun itself. In contrast to the Titan satyrs were much more humble, sylvan gods, who were half human and half goat. This expression was popularized by William Shakespeare, who used it in *Hamlet* (c. 1600), in the course of Hamlet's first soliloquy: "So excellent a king; that was, to this, Hyperion to a satyr." *The author is a good storyteller, but to call him a modern-day Dickens is like comparing Hyperion to a satyr. See also* SATYR.

hypnosis An artificially induced state of relaxation revealing the subconscious self. The word was derived from the name of Hypnos, the Greek god of sleep and the equivalent of the Roman Somnus. *A course of hypnosis was suggested, but the doctors were inclined to dismiss such an approach as mere quackery.*

I

I accuse *See* J'ACCUSE.

Iago (yahgō) A person who pretends to be friendly and supportive, while actually behaving in a calculated and deceitful manner. The allusion is to the treacherous ensign in William Shakespeare's *Othello* (c. 1603), who by playing on the sexual jealousy of his commander OTHELLO cunningly brings about the latter's downfall and death. In modern use, the term is often applied more widely to anyone who conceals the pleasure he or she takes in causing trouble or pain to others. *Malcolm clearly enjoyed playing Iago to his superior's Othello, secretly relishing the latter's discomfort as he fed new revelations to the press.*

I am that I am I am as I appear to be, no more, no less. The expression is biblical in origin, appearing in Exodus 3:14 as God's reply to Moses when Moses asks his name during the episode of the burning bush. "I am" is one translation of God's Old Testament name Yahweh or Jehovah. This phrase has appeared in many guises throughout world literature, perhaps most notably in William Shakespeare's tragedy *Othello* (c. 1603), in which Iago misquotes it in the form "I am not what I am."

I came, I saw, I conquered I have achieved what I set out to do. These were the words (in Latin *veni, vidi, vici*) uttered by Julius Caesar (100–44 B.C.) as he looked back on his conquest in the Black Sea campaign of 47, according to Suetonius (c. A.D. 69–c. 140) in *Lives of the Caesars*. *"I came, I saw, I conquered," said the victor as he lay down his racket and reached for his jacket.*

I cannot tell a lie What I am telling you is the truth. This phrase famously alludes to the story of the young George Washington (1732–99) who, when accosted by his father after cutting down a cherry tree with his hatchet, resisted the temptation to conceal his guilt and said: "Father, I cannot tell a lie. I did it with my little hatchet." Often quoted to the young as an ideal of honest virtue, the story is apocryphal, making its first appearance in 1800 in *Life of Washington* by M. L. Weems. "So I do not say, 'Believe me, for I cannot tell a lie'" (Michael Dibdin, *Dirty Tricks*, 1991).

Icarus (ikărăs) A person who brings about his or her downfall through carelessness or recklessness. The allusion is to the Greek myth of Daedalus and his son Icarus who effected their escape from King Minos of Crete by constructing wings of wax and feathers and using them to fly off the island and over the ocean. Unfortunately, Icarus ignored his father's instructions not to fly too high as the heat of the sun would melt the wax;

consequently, Icarus fell to his death in the sea. The waters of the Aegean are still sometimes called the ***Icarian Sea.*** "He, like Icarus, had flown up towards the sun, hoping that his wings of wax would bear him steadily aloft among the gods" (Anthony Trollope, *Phineas Finn,* 1869). *See also* DAEDALIAN.

ice maiden A woman with a cold, detached manner. The reference is to a figure who appears in stories from Russian and Scandinavian folklore, as retold in the 19th century by HANS CHRISTIAN ANDERSEN (1805–75) and later used as the basis of Grieg's *Peer Gynt* suite. In these stories she is usually depicted as proud and malevolent, using her glacial beauty to attract young men, whom she then puts to death. Sometimes rendered in the form ***ice queen***, the epithet is typically applied to beautiful models, actresses, and other women who are perceived as having a reserved or unemotional nature. *Her lack of sympathy with her lover's plight earned her the reputation of an ice maiden.*

Ichabod *See* GLORY IS DEPARTED, THE.

Ichabod Crane (ikăbod) An awkward, gawky person, especially a tall, skinny one who wears ill-fitting clothes. The original Ichabod Crane was the central character in the Washington Irving story "The Legend of Sleepy Hollow" (1820), in which he figures as a timid village schoolteacher whose very appearance provokes mirth among his neighbors in ***Sleepy Hollow***, the archetypal old-world rural community. Ichabod competes for the hand of a local farmer's daughter, but meets with opposition from a rival suitor who frightens him with stories of a headless horseman—when the headless horseman duly "appears," Ichabod flees the area in fright and is never seen again. The 1999 film *Sleepy Hollow*, directed by Tim Burton and starring Johnny Depp as Ichabod Crane, is very loosely based on the original story. *She ridiculed him for his Ichabod Crane physique and his circus clown clothing sense.*

ichor (īkor) A watery, foul-smelling discharge from a wound or ulcer. In Greek mythology, *ichor* (meaning "juice") is the name given to the colorless blood of the gods. "The first indication of revival was afforded by a partial descent of the iris. It was observed, as especially remarkable, that this lowering of the pupil was accompanied by the profuse out-flowing of a yellowish ichor (from beneath the lids) of a pungent and highly offensive odor" (Edgar Allan Poe, *The Facts in the Case of M.Valdemar,* 1845).

I coulda been a contender I could have achieved something, given the opportunity. A quotation from the 1954 film *On the Waterfront*, the line was memorably delivered by Marlon Brando in the role of a former boxer who falls foul of racketeers in the docks of New York. Redolent of lost opportunities, it is usually employed ironically, due to its inevitable association with its iconic origins. *If it wasn't for my terminal lethargy and puny physique, I could have been a world champion too, I coulda been a contender.*

Ida, Mount (īdă) A place from which one can observe events without getting personally involved. In Greek mythology, Mount Ida was a "many-fountained" mountain or ridge in Asia Minor identified as the vantage point from which the gods followed the course of events during the Trojan War. This mountain (or one of the same name in Crete) was also said to be the birthplace of Zeus, the place where Ganymede was abducted, and the location for the JUDGMENT OF PARIS. "As Juno may have looked at Paris on Mount Ida, so did Mrs. Proudie look on Ethelbert Stanhope when he pushed the leg of the sofa into her lace train" (Anthony Trollope, *Barchester Towers,* 1857).

Identikit An identical copy of something that results from duplication of different elements in the original. The allusion is to the Identikit system first employed by the Los Angeles police in 1959 and since adopted by police forces worldwide to identify the faces of criminals, in which witnesses build up a composite image of a face through a selection of photographed facial features. *She lived in one of those identikit houses that comprise so many modern suburban estates.*

Ides of March (īdz) A day of reckoning, especially one that has been foretold. In ancient Rome, the Ides (from the verb *iduo,* meaning "to divide") marked the halfway point of a month. It was on the Ides of March (March 15) that Julius Caesar was murdered in the Capitol, as previously prophesied by a soothsayer with the doom-laden words "Beware the Ides of March." *On considering the alternatives left after this unexpected turn of events, the only conclusion one can reach is that the Ides of March would appear to have arrived for the Republican Party.*

I do not like thee, Doctor Fell Although I have no reason for it, I dislike this particular individual, however admirable he or she may otherwise be. This is an allusion to a poem by the satirical writer Thomas Brown (c. 1663–1704), a student at Oxford who was faced with expulsion on the order of Dr. John Fell (1625–86), dean of Christ Church and bishop of Oxford, unless he could prove capable of translating for him the 33rd Epigram of Martial. Brown's apparently spontaneous response was the following verse: "I do not love thee, Dr Fell, / The reason why I cannot tell; / But this I know, and know full well, / I do not love thee, Dr Fell." This amounted to a satisfactorily accurate translation of the original Latin, albeit with the insertion of Dr. Fell's name. In modern usage, the word "like" is generally used in the place of "love." "All the same; we do not like Mr. Bott—do we, Alice? He is Dr Fell to us; only I think we could tell why" (Anthony Trollope, *Can You Forgive Her?*, 1864).

if any would not work, neither should he eat Those who are not prepared to work do not deserve any reward. This saying comes from 2 Thessalonians 3:10, in which Paul advises the Thessalonians that only those who work for their bread actually deserve to have any. *The manager shrugged his shoulders and repeated the biblical injunction that if any would not work, neither should he eat.*

if the blind lead the blind, both shall fall into the ditch *See* BLIND LEADING THE BLIND.

if the mountain won't come to Muhammad If something requires some effort on the part of the speaker before it can be attained, then he or she must simply resign himself or herself to making that effort. A proverbial piece of wisdom that implies the fuller version "if the mountain won't come to Muhammad, Muhammad must go to the mountain," it refers to a story about MUHAMMAD (570–632), the founder of the Islamic faith. In the story, Muhammad (in front of a large crowd) commands a hill to come to him, only to find that the hill remains stubbornly where it is. Muhammad, reasoning that if the hill had indeed come to them he and his followers would all have been crushed, resigns himself to going to the hill and does so. In fact, the story appears to have made its first appearance in an essay by the English philosopher Francis Bacon (1561–1626), around a thousand years after the event described. "The child scrambled up to the top of the wall and called again and again; but finding this of no avail, apparently made up his mind, like Mahomet, to go to the mountain, since the mountain would not come to him" (Anne Brontë, *The Tenant of Wildfell Hall*, 1848).

if thy right eye offend thee If part of you tempts you to do wrong, then you need to take radical action to deal with it. This piece of proverbial advice comes from Christ's Sermon on the Mount, as recounted in Matthew 5:29: "And if thy right eye offend thee, pluck it out, and cast it from thee: for it is profitable for thee that one of thy members should perish, and not that thy whole body should be cast into hell." The line is sometimes quoted with reference to the expulsion of rebellious members of organizations or institutions. It is also found in the variant form ***if thy right hand offend thee.*** "If it chance your eye offend you, / Pluck it out, lad, and be sound" (A. E. Housman, *A Shropshire Lad,* 1896).

ignorant armies Forces that seem to act without any underlying understanding of what they are doing. The phrase comes from Matthew Arnold's poem "Dover Beach" (1867), which includes the lines "And we are here as on a darkling plain / Swept with confused alarms of struggle and flight, / Where ignorant armies clash by night." The phrase is typically used in reference to political disagreements. *The newspapers were, as usual, full of reports of the latest doings of Parliament's ignorant armies.*

Igor (e͟egor) A henchman or servant, especially one who is dim-witted and physically grotesque and is employed as a laboratory assistant by a mad scientist. The allusion is to the deformed servant called Igor who features in numerous horror films of the 20th century based upon Mary Shelley's original 1818 novel FRANKENSTEIN. *Every department head has his or her Igor, who does all the tedious, routine work considered beneath his boss's dignity.*

I have a dream I have a vision of an improved future. The phrase is most familiar as a refrain in the speeches of black civil rights activist Martin Luther King in the 1960s, specifically a speech he made to a vast audience in Washington on August 28, 1963: "I have a dream that one day this nation will rise up and live out the true meaning of its creed: 'We hold these truths to be self-evident, that all men are created equal.'" He repeated the phrase several times during the course of this and other speeches, and since his death it has acquired iconic status as a summary of his vision for a harmonious future in which all races could exist happily alongside each other. When not referring directly to Martin Luther King and his ideals, the phrase today tends to be used ironically. *'I have a dream,' Bob announced, 'that one day this company will rise up and get proper washroom facilities.'*

Iliad (i͟leeăd, i͟leead) A written work or other tale of epic proportions, especially one dealing with acts of heroism. The original *Iliad* was a celebrated epic poem of great length supposedly composed by the Greek poet Homer around 700 B.C. Its title comes from the Greek *Iliados* (meaning "of Ilium," Ilium being an alternative name for Troy), and it relates the events that took place toward the end of the Trojan War, which culminated in the death of Hector at the hands of Achilles. Only a very select number of great literary works have since been considered good enough to be ranked alongside Homer's *Iliad,* including the medieval *Romance of the Rose* (13th century), which came to be dubbed the French Iliad, and the *Nibelungenlied* (early 13th century), sometimes called the German Iliad. The series of disasters suffered by both sides during the war gave rise to the phrase ***an Iliad of woes*** to describe any series of setbacks or misfortunes. *This third film brings this Iliad of modern warfare and trilogy of Vietnam movies to a tragic and dispiriting close.*

I'll be back *See* TERMINATOR, THE.

I'm alright, Jack I don't care about anything else, as long as my interests are secure. The phrase has its origins in a traditional saying of unknown age, possibly ultimately of nautical origin ("Jack" being a nickname for a Royal Navy sailor). Today it is often associated with a 1959 film of the same title starring Peter Sellers as a militant shop steward who leads the staff of a factory in a strike against the management. *This callous and selfish behavior is yet another example of the "I'm alright Jack" attitude that prevails in modern society. See also* GOD'S IN HIS HEAVEN, ALL'S RIGHT WITH THE WORLD.

I'm going to make him an offer he can't refuse *See* OFFER YOU CAN'T REFUSE, AN.

immaculate conception Something that comes about in an unconventional or apparently inexplicable manner. The reference is to the conception of the Virgin Mary as defined in the dogma ("Ineffabilis Deus" of Pope Pius IX, December 8, 1854): "from the first moment of her conception the Blessed Virgin Mary was, by the singular grace and privilege of Almighty God, and in view of the merits of Jesus Christ, Saviour of mankind, kept free from all stain of original sin." Biblical allusions to this doctrine are held to be Genesis 3:15 and Luke 1:28, but this teaching is rejected by Protestants. The term is sometimes employed in modern usage in a somewhat sarcastic tone. *People tend to forget that such structures have been designed in detail by teams of engineers, preferring to believe they came about through some process of immaculate conception.*

impressionist Involving a fleeting impression of a reality or mood. The term alludes to the impressionist movement that caused a sensation in the art world in the second half of the 19th century. Championed by such artists as Claude Monet (1840–1926), Auguste Renoir (1841–1919), and Edgar Degas (1834–1917), impressionism depended upon capturing the essence of something without painting the actual details of it, typically through the handling of color and light. In modern parlance, the term impressionist, or ***impressionistic***, may be applied in a much wider range of contexts. "The backs of the other shops were an impressionistic picture of dirty grays, drained browns, writhing heaps of refuse" (Sinclair Lewis, *Main Street*, 1920).

in all one's glory In all one's beauty; having a beautiful appearance. The phrase comes from Matthew 6:29, which celebrates the beauty of the LILIES OF THE FIELD: "And yet I say unto you, That even Solomon in all his glory was not arrayed like one of these." In modern usage the phrase may sometimes appear in laconic references to a person who is entirely naked. *The girls squealed as the man emerged grinning from the pool in all his glory.*

Incredible Hulk A person with a large, imposing, and often ungainly physique. The original Incredible Hulk was the huge green creature into which the scientist Dr. David Bruce Banner was transformed whenever he became angry in the comic book stories originally published in Marvel Comics in 1962. The title, sometimes shortened to ***Hulk***, is also occasionally applied to inanimate objects of considerable bulk, such as large trucks or spacecraft. *I wouldn't call her fat, but her husband calls her the Incredible Hulk.*

Indiana Jones (indeeană) A dashing, even roguish adventurer, especially one with a seemingly unexciting academic background. The original Indiana Jones was the adventurer-archaeologist of the *Indiana Jones* films of the 1980s, played by Harrison Ford clad in distinctive slouch hat and carrying a long whip. *We had hoped for an Indiana Jones, but instead our professor turned out to be short, balding, and very, very dull. See also* ALLAN QUATERMAIN.

Indian summer A period of success or other good fortune enjoyed late in life or in the last stages of some process. The phrase is usually associated with a period of warm weather that occurs well into autumn, when colder weather might be expected. The phrase is of U.S. origin, referring originally to the warm, hazy weather common in regions once mostly inhabited by the country's Native American population. *Like many sportsmen, he enjoyed something of an Indian summer late in his career.*

in fear and trembling In an anxious, frightened way. The origin of the expression is Philippians 2:12: "Wherefore, my beloved, as ye have always obeyed, not as in my presence only, but now much more in my absence, work out your own salvation with fear and trembling." *The pupils waited outside the principal's office in fear and trembling.*

Inferno *See* DANTE'S INFERNO.

in harm's way In danger, at risk of suffering harm. The phrase has its origins in a famous letter written in 1778 by John Paul Jones, hero of the American Revolution, stating his intentions of finding a ship in which to sail against the British: "I wish to have no connection with any ship that does not sail *fast*; for I intend to go *in harm's way*." *We should respect the members of the armed forces who place themselves in harm's way every day on our behalf.*

inherit the wind To provoke trouble, especially to bring trouble down on one's own head. The phrase is a quotation from Proverbs 11:29: "He that troubleth his own house shall inherit the wind." *They had known prosperous times but had laid up little for the future and feared that in their old age they would find they had inherited the wind.*

in my father's house *See* HOUSE OF MANY MANSIONS.

inner man A person's soul or spiritual being, or more jocularly, his or her appetite. The phrase comes from Ephesians 3:16: "That he would grant you, according to the riches of his glory, to be strengthened with might by his Spirit in the inner man." "It is on the inner man, on his nature and disposition, that the happiness of a wife must depend." (Anthony Trollope, *Ayala's Angel,* 1881).

innocent as doves *See* WISE AS SERPENTS AND HARMLESS AS DOVES.

in Queer Street *See* CAREY STREET.

Inquisition Close questioning, especially in front of an investigating committee of some kind. The reference is to the system under which selected Franciscan and Dominican monks were ordered by papal decree to root out heretics within the Roman Catholic Church. Established in 1231 and at its height between the 15th and 17th centuries, the Inquisition became feared throughout Catholic Europe, using torture to extract confessions from suspected persons and executing those found guilty of crimes against the Church. Some of the Inquisition's worst excesses were carried out in Spain, home to the ***Spanish Inquisition*** (as depicted to comic effect in a famous MONTY PYTHON sketch of the 1970s). "For another hour the inquisition continued, almost, I felt, as though the 'judges' were scraping for any dirt they could find" (Noel Barber, *The Other Side of Paradise*, 1992).

Inspector Clouseau (kloozō) A policeman or detective, especially an incompetent one. The allusion is to the bungling central character in the *Pink Panther* film series, beginning with *The Pink Panther* (1963), in which he was played by British comedian Peter Sellers. "Max was a diplomat—a combination of Dr. Watson and Inspector Clouseau" (Arnold Goodman, *Tell Them I'm on My Way*, 1993).

Inspector Maigret (maygray) Archetype of an intuitive police detective. The patient, pipe-smoking Inspector Jules Maigret was the celebrated creation of Belgian crime writer Georges Simenon (1903–89). Maigret solves his cases through observation of the circumstances surrounding the crime as much as through examination of any material clues, and is usually ultimately successful in securing a confession from the guilty party. *The police officer who entered the room was smoking a pipe, just like Inspector Maigret.*

in the beginning was the Word Underlying everything else is the concept of divine order and reason. The phrase comes from John 1:1: "In the beginning was the Word, and the Word was with God, and the Word was God." The concept of the Word predated John but as used by him came to refer to Jesus Christ himself. These words reflect the opening words of the Bible "In the beginning" (Genesis 1:1). *"In the beginning was the Word," murmured the bishop, when his charges ventured to voice doubts. See also* WORD, THE.

in the right ballpark *See* BALLPARK FIGURE.

in the sweat of thy face *See* ADAM'S CURSE.

in vain the net is spread in the sight of the bird Setting a trap is futile if the proposed victim of it is allowed to see the trap being prepared. This advice comes from Proverbs 1:17: "Surely in vain the net is spread in the sight of any bird." "'If they come, we shall be ready,' said Bessas. 'In vain the net is spread in the sight of the bird.'" (L. Sprague De Camp, *The Dragon of the Ishtar Gate,* 1961).

Invasion of the Body-Snatchers A situation in which everything, or everyone, seems bizarrely altered. The allusion is to a 1956 film with the same title, in which an ordinary U.S. town is invaded by alien beings who have disguised themselves as the human inhabitants, but betray themselves by their oddly emotionless behavior. The film was remade in 1978 and 1993. *The way all the press were being so polite to the president, it was like Invasion of the Body-Snatchers.*

Invisible Man A person whose existence or influence upon events around him or her goes largely unnoticed. The allusion is to the 1897 novel *The Invisible Man* by H. G. Wells, which concerns the experiences of Dr. Griffin, a mad scientist who discovers how to make himself invisible (though his clothes and his footprints remain visible). In modern use, the phrase is often applied to underprivileged individuals or groups within society whose presence is often ignored (hence the title of Ralph Ellison's 1952 book *Invisible Man*, on the subject of racial oppression and identity). *If the children didn't turn the television on, maybe it was the Invisible Man.*

invita Minerva (inveetă minervă, inweetah minerwah) Uninspired, lackluster. Meaning in Latin "against the will of Minerva," the phrase, which first appeared in *Ars Poetica* by Horace (65–8 B.C.), has generally been reserved for literary or artistic works that do not meet expectations. Minerva was the goddess of wisdom and patroness of the arts and trades in Roman mythology, thus to proceed without her support doomed any artistic enterprise to failure. *Contemporaries were inclined to view her final book of poetry as misjudged and invita Minerva.*

in word and deed *See* WORD AND DEED, IN.

Io (īō) Archetype of a person who changes his or her shape or appearance. In Roman mythology Io was identified as a priestess of Juno who attracted the attentions of Jupiter. In order to prevent any liaison Juno transformed Io into a heifer, and in this form she wandered far and wide over the earth until finally restored to human form in Egypt. *Like some bewitched Io, once in costume, she instinctively assumed all the characteristics of the creature she portrayed.*

Ionic (īonik) Belonging to an order of architecture typified by capitals decorated with volutes. The order was named after Ionia, an ancient region of west central Asia Minor that was colonized by the Greeks around 1100 B.C. and where the style was first developed. "The State Bank, stucco masking wood. The Farmers' National Bank. An Ionic temple of marble. Pure, exquisite, solitary" (Sinclair Lewis, *Main Street,* 1920). *See also* CORINTHIAN; DORIC; TUSCAN.

I only am escaped I am the sole survivor. This expression is biblical in origin, coming from Job 1:15, in which Job's faith is tested by God by a series of catastrophes, news of which is brought to him by a series of single survivors who end their reports with more or less the same words. Herman Melville incorporates the line as the opening refrain in the epilogue of his novel *Moby-Dick* (1851), in which the reader learns that the narrator, Ishmael, was the only survivor of the sinking of the ship *Pequod.*

I only am left I am the only one remaining. The expression is biblical in origin: It reflects Elijah's self-pity after he flees to Horeb when Jezebel threatens his life following his success in defeating the prophets of Baal on Mount Carmel: "And he said, I have been very jealous for the LORD God of hosts: because the children of Israel have forsaken thy covenant, thrown down thine altars, and slain thy prophets with the sword; and I, *even* I only, am left; and they seek my life, to take it away" (1 Kings 19:14). In contemporary usage the expression ***only I am left*** is sometimes used. *"Only I am left," murmured the administrative assistant after all her colleagues had left early that afternoon.*

Irene (īreen, īreenee) Personification of peace and reconciliation. In Greek mythology, Irene was the goddess of peace and prosperity. She is conventionally depicted carrying PLUTUS (representing wealth) in her arms and sometimes with an OLIVE BRANCH or CORNUCOPIA. *The spirit of Irene reigned in the negotiating chamber that afternoon, though in the event this period of perfect harmony was to prove but short-lived.*

iris The colored part of the eye surrounding the pupil and, by extension, the area surrounding a source of illumination. The name comes from Iris, the Greek goddess of the rainbow who is reputed to have traveled between heaven and earth by means of a rainbow in order to fulfill her role as messenger of the gods. She was conventionally depicted with wings on her shoulders and a herald's staff in her left hand. The name has also been applied to a genus of plants notable for their showy, brightly colored blooms and, poetically, to the rainbow itself. "Filled with these thoughts—so filled that he had an unwholesome sense of growing larger, of being placed in some new and diseased relation towards the objects among which he passed, of seeing the iris round every misty light turn red—he went home for shelter" (Charles Dickens, *Hard Times,* 1854).

iron curtain An impenetrable barrier, especially one involving military hardware. The phrase is often attributed to British statesman Winston Churchill, specifically to a speech made by him at Fulton, Missouri, in 1946 in which he lamented the division of Europe into two distinct blocs: "From Stettin in the Baltic to Trieste in the Adriatic, an iron curtain has descended across the continent." In fact, the same phrase had been used the previous year by German propaganda minister Joseph Goebbels in a similar context: "If the German people lay down their arms, the agreement between Roosevelt, Churchill, and Stalin would allow the Soviets to occupy all eastern and southeastern Europe, together with the major part of the Reich. An iron curtain would at once descend on this territory." The expression also cropped up elsewhere considerably before the war years, the first instance being in the earl of Munster's journal as early as 1819. *They did their best, but there was no getting behind the iron curtain set in place by the authorities. See also* BERLIN WALL.

iron fist in a velvet glove, an Ruthlessness or tyrannical rule disguised by a polite, soothing manner. The phrase (sometimes also found in the form ***an iron hand in a velvet glove***) alludes to the policies of Napoleonic France concerning conquered territories in the early 19th century, and is often attributed to NAPOLEON himself, although something similar may have been uttered at an earlier date by the Holy Roman Emperor Charles V. "When she later read (at Clare's instigation) the Pankhursts' story, with the exhortation to suffragettes to be 'an iron fist in a velvet glove,' she immediately linked that image with the symbol of 'fist-in-a-bag'" (Jane Rogers, *Her Living Image*, 1990).

Isaac *See* ABRAHAM'S SUPREME TEST.

Isaiah (īzayă) Archetypal prophet. The prophecies of the biblical Isaiah are detailed in the Old Testament book that bears his name. It describes the threat of the Assyrian conquest and offers promise to the exiles in Babylon and later a message of hope to the Jews after they return from exile. *The old man stood at the doors of the theater like some Isaiah, exhorting the crowd not to go in to witness such a degrading spectacle.*

Ishmael (ishmayăl) A social outcast. Ishmael appears in the Bible as the son of Abraham and

Hagar, who was the Egyptian maidservant of Sarah. According to Genesis 16–25, Sarah allowed Hagar to become pregnant by Abraham as she believed herself barren, but the two women quarreled, and after Sarah gave birth to Isaac, Hagar and her son were thrown out of the house and sent into the desert, hence the adoption of Ishmael's name (or the term ***Ishmaelite***) for anyone who is expelled from society. God saved the pair from death from thirst by providing them with a well of water. Ishmael in his turn had 12 sons. The Ishmaelites were a tribal people who lived in Edom (Psalm 83:6); God's promise that Ishmael's descendants would become a great nation (Genesis 17:20; 21:17–18) has traditionally been thought to be fulfilled through the Arab peoples. If a person is described as having ***a hand against every man,*** this is a reference to a prophecy given by an angel at the time of Ishmael's birth to the effect that he was fated to become an outlaw: "his hand will be against every man, and every man's hand against him" (Genesis 16:12). "I am an Ishmael by instinct as much as by accident of circumstances, but if I keep out of society I shall be less vulnerable than Ishmaels generally are" (Samuel Butler, *The Way of All Flesh,* 1903).

Ishtar (ishtahr) Personification of love or fertility. Ishtar was the goddess of love in Babylonian and Assyrian mythology, equivalent to the Roman Venus. *In her sequined costume and veils she came down the stairs like Ishtar descending to earth.*

Isis *See* LIFT THE VEIL OF ISIS.

island race, the The British nation. The phrase echoes William Shakespeare's *Richard II* (1595), in which England is described as a "sceptr'd isle," but appears to have made its first appearance in its usual form as the title of a poem by Sir Henry Newbolt in 1898. "The aircraft was an enemy, and the two men who climbed down onto the concrete were enemies, also, two of the nameless killers who had tried to 'break this island race'" (Frank Kippax, *The Butcher's Bill*, 1992).

Islands of the Blest Heaven; paradise. The Greek epic poet Hesiod (eighth century B.C.) identified paradise by this name and placed the location of the islands in the far west, at the end of the known world. Elsewhere they were dubbed the ***Fortunate Islands,*** or ***Isles,*** or ***Happy Islands.*** Here chosen heroes could spend eternity relaxing in pleasant surroundings. *This part of the world is so beautiful and so peaceful it could be mistaken for an earthly paradise, and many call these isles the Islands of the Blest. See also* ELYSIAN FIELDS.

Isocrates (īsokrateez) Archetype of a great orator. Isocrates (436–338 B.C.) was a celebrated orator of ancient Athens and a famous teacher of the arts of eloquence. Among those to be likened to Isocrates was Esprit Fléchier (1632–1710), the bishop of Nîmes, who was well known for his funeral orations and dubbed the French Isocrates. *After his address to the Senate the young man was quickly recognized as a leading figure on the political stage, the Isocrates of his party.*

Isolde *See* TRISTAN AND ISOLDE.

Israel (izreeăl, izrayăl) The name of the Jewish state established in Palestine in 1948. The name means "God fights" and, according to Genesis 32:28, was bestowed upon Jacob after he wrestled with an angel. Jacob was the father of 12 sons, each of whom became the founder of one of the 12 tribes of Israel. The word Israel thus came to be applied to the Hebrew nation and subsequently the Jews and their state. *He is revered today as one of the patriarchs of Israel.*

Israel Hands (izreeăl, izrayăl) Archetype of an evil, bloodthirsty pirate. Israel Hands is the name of the villainous ship's mate on the sailing ship *Hispaniola* in Robert Louis Stevenson's adventure novel *Treasure Island* (1883). A murderous henchman of LONG JOHN SILVER, he was named after a real character who served as second mate under the fearsome pirate captain BLACKBEARD. *He advanced upon the boy with his blade between his teeth, the image of Israel Hands.*

Is Saul also among the prophets? *See* SAUL.

It Girl A vivacious young woman with irresistible sex appeal. The original It Girl was silent-movie star Clara Bow (1905–65), who enjoyed huge success in the central role of the 1927 film based on Elinor Glyn's provocative novel *It*, in which "it" was sex appeal. *Paris Hilton is perhaps the best-known of the current crop of It Girls.*

I think, therefore I am *See* CARTESIAN.

it is a far, far better thing that I do What I do now is a fine thing, though I am likely to suffer in doing it. The allusion is to the closing passage in *A Tale of Two Cities* (1859) by Charles Dickens, in which ***Sydney Carton*** bravely faces death on the guillotine in the place of the condemned aristocrat Charles Darnay (to whom he bears an uncanny resemblance), sacrificing himself in the knowledge that his death will preserve the happiness of Lucie Manette, Darnay's wife, and also the object of Sydney Carton's hopeless affection: "It is a far, far better thing that I do, than I have ever done. It is a far, far better rest that I go to, than I have ever known." In modern usage, the expression is only ever used in a self-consciously ironic context. *"It is a far, far better thing that I do, than I have ever done," muttered the professor as he followed her into the bedroom.*

it is better to give than to receive The act of giving is more noble and rewarding than that of receiving. The proverb is of biblical origin, appearing in Acts 20:35 in the form "It is more blessed to give than to receive." " 'Tis better to Give than to Receive, but yet 'tis Madness to give so much Charity to Others, as to become the Subject of it our Selves." (Samuel Palmer, *Moral Essays on some of the most Curious and Significant English, Scotch, and Foreign Proverbs,* 1710).

it is not for every man to go to Corinth *See* CORINTH, IT IS NOT FOR EVERY MAN TO GO TO.

it's all Greek to me The thing in question is completely incomprehensible to me. The allusion is to William Shakespeare's *Julius Caesar* (1599), in which Casca admits his failure to understand something Cicero had said in Greek: "Those that understood him smiled and shook their heads; for mine own part, it was Greek to me." Greek was the language of scholars and orators in ancient Rome, but not understood by the greater populace. "She leant across and said, 'This is all Greek to me' " (Robert Liddell, *Elizabeth and Ivy*, 1986).

Itt, Cousin *See* ADDAMS FAMILY.

it was the best of times, it was the worst of times The time in question witnessed both good things and bad. These are the opening words of *A Tale of Two Cities* (1859) by Charles Dickens, set against the backdrop of the French Revolution.

They had bittersweet memories of the war years, which for their family had been the best of times and the worst of times.

Ivan the Terrible (īvăn) A person who behaves in a tyrannical or vicious, overbearing manner. The original Ivan the Terrible was Ivan IV of Russia (1530–84), a ruler who became notorious for his many acts of cruelty. A more accurate translation of his name in Russian, however, would be "Ivan the Awesome." *The secretaries cowered whenever the managing director approached and routinely referred to him among themselves as Ivan the Terrible.*

ivory shoulder of Pelops (peelops) A person's distinguishing characteristic. The phrase alludes to the legend of Pelops, son of Tantalus, king of Lydia, who was killed by his father and served up as a meal to the gods in order to test the limits of their knowledge. The gods realized what Tantalus was offering them and restored Pelops to life. Unfortunately the goddess Demeter had already consumed the lad's shoulder, so a shoulder of ivory was fashioned to complete his restoration. Tantalus was consigned to hell for his presumption in challenging the wisdom of the gods, while in due course Pelops became the king of Elis. *This birthmark, as unique and striking as the ivory shoulder of Pelops, distinguished him from the mass of people around him.*

ivory tower A life of seclusion from the everyday world, typically dedicated to academic or indulgent pursuits. The allusion is of French origin and first appeared in 1911, when the critic and poet Charles Sainte-Beuve applied it to the poet Alfred de Vigny. In 1916 it became familiar in its English form through the title of the Henry James novel *The Ivory Tower*. The phrase has since come to be associated particularly with the exclusive lives of university scholars and students. *For three years she lived in an ivory tower, blissfully unaware of the problems facing her family.*

I want to be alone *See* GARBO.

I was a stranger, and ye took me in An expression of gratitude for an act of kindness shown toward a person in need. The line comes from Matthew 25:35: "For I was an hungred, and ye gave me meat: I was thirsty, and ye gave me drink: I was a stranger, and ye took me in: Naked, and ye clothed me." *"I was a stranger and ye took me in," quoted their unexpected guest as he lifted his glass in jovial salute to his hosts.*

Ixionian wheel (ikseeōneeăn) A source of endless torment. In Greek legend, Ixion was a king of Thessaly who murdered his father-in-law and sought to seduce Hera. Zeus fooled him by sending him a cloud in the form of Hera and then had him bound to a perpetually revolving wheel of fire as punishment. The cloud subsequently gave birth to the centaurs. "Round and round, then, and ever contracting towards the button-like black bubble at the axis of that slowly wheeling circle, like another Ixion I did revolve" (Herman Melville, *Moby-Dick,* 1851).

jabberwocky Nonsensical gibberish. The word was coined by Lewis Carroll in a mock medieval poem of the same name in *Through the Looking-Glass* (1872). According to Carroll, the Jabberwock is a monster with "jaws that bite" and "claws that catch." He derived the name through the combination of "jabber" (meaning "talk meaninglessly") and the Anglo-Saxon *wocer* (meaning "offspring"). *His nonsensical argument belonged to the school of jabberwocky enshrined by Lewis Carroll.*

j'accuse (zhakyooz) A serious accusation of wrongful or immoral behavior. The reference is to a letter by the French novelist Émile Zola that was published in the French newspaper *L'Aurore* on January 13, 1898 under the heading "J'accuse" (meaning "I accuse"). In it, Zola accused the French government of treating the French army captain Alfred Dreyfus (who was of Jewish origin) with inhuman indifference, resulting in his conviction on charges of selling military secrets to Germany and his transportation to the notorious DEVIL'S ISLAND prison colony. Zola's efforts to expose the government's attempts to cover up the scandal eventually led to Dreyfus's release, though not until after the novelist himself had been prosecuted and obliged to flee France for a time. The term is now used of any stalwart campaign against corrupt or illegal conduct. *It was brave of the media to stand up to Nixon and yell "J'accuse!"*

Jack Ketch The public hangman. The real Jack Ketch (d. 1686) was appointed executioner in London around 1663 and dispatched many notable victims, including Lord William Russell (in 1683) and the duke of Monmouth (in 1685). He later became the subject of many ballads and a character in PUNCH AND JUDY puppet shows. "At one time so many people from the area were hanged at Newgate it had been nicknamed Jack Ketch's Warren, and according to Paddy it had been known for as many as forty constables to march down with cutlasses to control disturbances" (Pamela Pope, *The Rich Pass By*, 1990).

Jackson Pollock (jaksăn polăk) Of or relating to the abstract paintings of U.S. artist Jackson Pollock (1912–56). Pollock was well known for his unconventional painting methods, the most famous of which involved dribbling paint onto a canvas laid flat on the ground. *Her paintings for this new exhibition are very Jackson Pollock, all splashy lines and big blobs of color.*

Jack the Giant-Killer A person who readily sets himself or herself against even the most formidable opposition. Folklore identifies Jack the

Giant-Killer as a peasant hero, specifically one from Cornwall in Arthurian times, who uses his wits to overwhelm a succession of fearsome giants and then helps himself to their gold or other treasures. *Switzerland hope to play the role of Jack the Giant-Killer in European football next season.*

Jack the Ripper A serial killer, or any person who behaves in a vicious or murderous manner. The original Jack the Ripper was an unidentified knife-wielding murderer who embarked on a reign of terror in the East End of London in 1888–89, during the course of which he savagely killed at least six prostitutes. "After that, I could have told her that you were Jack the Ripper and she'd have believed me" (Susan Gates, *The Lock*, 1990).

Jacobean (jakăbeeăn) Of a bloodthirsty, dark, and melodramatic nature. The allusion is to the gory tragedies that were presented to eager theater audiences in Jacobean England—the period that coincided with the reign of James I (1603–25). Such plays were notable for their memorable villains and themes of murder and revenge. *By the time the brawl was over the room looked like the set of a Jacobean revenge tragedy.*

Jacobin (jakăbăn) A political radical, especially one who behaves in an unforgiving, bloodthirsty manner. The original Jacobins were a group of political extremists who emerged as the dominant force during the French Revolution of 1789 under the leadership of Danton and ROBESPIERRE. Called Jacobins because they held their first meeting at a Jacobin monastery, they instituted the REIGN OF TERROR in which many prominent figures (including Danton and Robespierre themselves) were sent to the guillotine. *As a result of the Democratic resurgence, the Jacobin element in Congress has become quieter of late.*

Jacob's ladder (jaykobz) A ladder of rope or cable used to board a ship; a variety of plant *(Polemonium caeruleum)* with leaves positioned in a ladderlike arrangement. The original Jacob's ladder was a ladder connecting earth with heaven, envisaged in a dream by Jacob recounted in Genesis 28:12. The ladder itself was said to have 15 rungs, representing the virtues. The stone that Jacob used as a pillow when he had his dream was traditionally identified as the Stone of Scone, used in Scottish coronations. *The boys had rigged a serviceable Jacob's ladder to climb up to their treehouse.*

Jael (jayl) A treacherous, deadly woman. According to the Bible (Judges 4–5), Jael, whose name means "wild goat," was the wife of Heber the Kenite and feigned hospitality when her husband's enemy, the Canaanite general Sisera, arrived, giving him milk to drink and a tent to sleep in. While Sisera slept, Jael took a tent peg and drove it into his head with a hammer. Because this murder was committed in defense of Israel, Jael acquired the status of an Old Testament heroine, and her name is sometimes quoted as an archetype of feminine courage. "Bravo, Jael! The wife of Heber the Kenite was no braver woman than you!" (Dinah Craik, *John Halifax*, 1856).

James, Jesse *See* JESSE JAMES.

James Bond A secret agent, especially one of debonair and daring character. The allusion is to the fictional British agent of the name, otherwise known as *007*, introduced by British thriller writer Ian Fleming (1908–64) in *Casino Royale*

(1953). His adventures continued in a series of novels and were subsequently extended in a hugely popular series of action-packed movies in which he was played by Sean Connery, Roger Moore, and Pierce Brosnan, among other actors. Although many of Bond's adventures were suggested by those of real-life spies Sidney Reilly and Dusko Popov, he was named after someone quite unconnected with the world of espionage: British ornithologist James Bond, author of *Birds of the West Indies* and a neighbor of Fleming's in Jamaica. *He behaved like James Bond, ordering dry martinis and trying to pick up women with tales of bravado on behalf of British intelligence, when he was just a humble civil service bureaucrat.*

James Dean (deen) Archetype of a "cool" young man with attitude. The U.S. film actor James Dean (1931–55) became one of the biggest stars of his generation, specializing in the role of the hapless, discontented youth until his premature death in a car crash, which served only to confirm his semi-legendary status. *In his white T-shirt and faded jeans, he fancied himself a reincarnation of James Dean. See also* REBEL WITHOUT A CAUSE.

Jane *See* TARZAN.

Jane Eyre (air) A young, romantically-minded woman of reserved but inwardly passionate character, especially one who endures stoically when put upon by others. Such was the character of the fictional Jane Eyre created by Charlotte Brontë in the novel of the same name in 1847. *She put up with his callous behavior for years, like some suburban Jane Eyre. See also* MR. ROCHESTER.

Janet A hous keeper, especially one of a redoubtable, reliable nature. The original Janet was the housekeeper in the *Doctor Finlay* stories of Scottish writer A. J. Cronin (1896–1981). She was played by Barbara Mullen in the popular BBC television series based on Cronin's tales, *Dr. Finlay's Casebook* (1962–71), and by Annette Crosbie in a later television adaptation, *Doctor Finlay* (1993–96). *She played Janet to his Doctor Finlay, serving tea to his honored guests.*

January The first month of the year. January was named after Janus, the Roman god of doors, thresholds, bridges, and beginnings. Because he watched over doorways he was widely worshiped for his power to ward off evil influence. Like January itself, which marks the end of the old year and the beginning of the new, Janus was usually described as having two faces turned in opposite directions at the same time; thus, anyone today who is suspected of hypocrisy or double-dealing may be called ***Janus-faced*** or ***Janus-headed.*** The word ***janitor*** also originated with Janus, alluding to his role as a guardian or doorkeeper. *He gave her a look that was as chilly as January and strode down the steps and into the street without so much as a backward glance.*

Jarndyce and Jarndyce A prolonged court case. The allusion is to the seemingly endless legal case of Jarndyce and Jarndyce that is central to the plot of the Charles Dickens novel *Bleak House* (1852–53). As the case continues, the inheritance that is being disputed is whittled away to nothing due to legal fees. Dickens had in mind the real case of Jennens and Jennens, which lingered on for 80 years before being finally decided. *The case was threatening to turn into a real Jarndyce and Jarndyce that could go on for years.*

Jason *See* ARGONAUT.

Javert (zhavair) A merciless, relentless figure of authority. Inspector Javert is a character from Victor Hugo's *Les Miserables* (1862), in which he pursues his prey Jean Valjean without consideration to any humanitarian impulses. *His colleagues respected him for his dogged persistence, though his evident lack of sympathy led some to dub him a modern-day Javert.*

jawbone of an ass A weapon, especially a relatively humble one, that can nonetheless be used with great effectiveness. The reference is biblical, alluding to Samson's escape from the ropes binding him and his subsequent slaying of many of his Philistine enemies using the jawbone of an ass that he had snatched up: "With the jawbone of an ass, heaps upon heaps, with the jawbone of an ass have I slain a thousand men" (Judges 15:15). "Oh, the delicate mistiming of women! She has carefully / Snapped in half my jawbone of an ass" (Christopher Fry, *The Lady's Not for Burning*, 1949).

Jaws A shark, or anyone or anything with an impressive "bite." The 1975 film *Jaws*, about a man-eating great white shark terrorizing a seaside resort, captured the public imagination and soon anyone or anything that looked capable of swallowing someone up was likely to be labeled Jaws, even if only jokingly. *She called her goldfish Jaws.*

Jazz Age Unconventional, pleasure-loving, bohemian. The phrase, which was popularized by the novels and short stories of U.S. writer F. Scott Fitzgerald (1896–1940), is associated especially with the United States in the 1920s, a time when the irresponsible young rich filled their lives with jazz music and partying without worrying about more serious matters. *It was all very pleasant and relaxed, very Jazz Age.*

jealous God *See* SINS OF THE FATHERS.

Jean Brodie *See* MISS JEAN BRODIE.

Jean Paul Getty A very wealthy man, especially one from a business background. Jean Paul Getty (1892–1976) was a U.S. oil baron whose fortune made him one of the richest men on Earth. Despite his wealth, he was notorious for his parsimonious ways. His reputation as one of the richest tycoons on the planet passed after his death to his sons, of whom British-based Jean Paul Getty Jr. (1932–2003) became particularly well known for sharing his father's interest in the arts. *Okay, Jean Paul Getty, you can put your wallet away—we'll pay the check.*

Jedi knight (jedī) A hero figure with apparently superhuman gifts and intelligence. The allusion is to the Jedi knights of the *STAR WARS* films, a band of crusading guardian warriors with highly developed mental powers. *Furious to learn that such an important decision had been made in his absence, he stormed into the Senate like some avenging Jedi knight.*

Jeeves A manservant or butler, a gentleman's gentleman. In the comic novels of English-born writer P. G. Wodehouse (1881–1975), Jeeves is the supremely capable valet of the hapless ***Bertie Wooster***. He is discreet, resourceful, and coolly unruffled by his employer's misadventures, and these qualities are often implied in allusive use of his name. "My batman, who is a positive Jeeves, is with me and, truly, I am far less aware of being at war than I was in England" (Irene Young, *Enigma Variations*, 1990). *See also* ADMIRABLE CRICHTON.

Jeffreys, Judge A stern judge, especially one who hands down severe sentences. George Jeffreys (c. 1645–89) was the judge who presided over the so-called Bloody Assizes that followed the failed rebellion led by the duke of Monmouth in southwest England in 1685. Known as the Hanging Judge, he sentenced around 320 of the rebels brought before him to death on the gallows. *Every modern reality TV talent show has to have its own Judge Jeffreys.*

Jehoshaphat *See* JUMPING JEHOSHAPHAT; VALLEY OF JEHOSHAPHAT.

Jehovah (jăhōvă) God or a godlike figure. Jehovah is the personal name of God whose meaning was revealed to Moses (Exodus 3:14–15; 6:2–5). The name was arrived at as a means of referring to the Almighty, whose name was otherwise deemed too sacred to be uttered by mortal lips. Jehovah is an anglicization of ***YeHoWaH,*** or ***Yahweh,*** from the letters *YHWH,* which constitute the tetragrammaton, representing the Hebrew words *Elohim* ("God") and *Adonai* ("My Lord"). "It [Yahweh] emphasizes that God is the one who is eternal, unique, unchangeable and always actively present with his people. It expresses God's role as Israel's Redeemer and covenant Lord" (*NIV Thematic References Bible,* p. 1,383). "We shudder as we read the grim words of the Jehovah of the ancient Hebrews; and yet not all the learning of modern times has availed to deliver us from the cruel decree, that the sins of the fathers shall be visited upon the children" (Upton Sinclair, *Damaged Goods,* 1913).

jehu (jeehyoo) A coachman or driver, especially one who drives in a furious or dangerous manner. The biblical Jehu was the son of Nimshi and a king of Israel, as recounted in 2 Kings 9:20, in which a watchman comments on the approach of his chariot: "The driving is like the driving of Jehu the son of Nimshi; for he driveth furiously." The reason Jehu was driving his chariot so furiously (as was his custom) on this occasion was that he was on his way to kill King Jehoram and overthrow the dynasty of Ahab and Jezebel, thus ending worship of the pagan Baal. "A drunken postilion . . . who frightened her by driving like Jehu the son of Nimshi, and shouting hilarious remarks at her" (George Eliot, *Adam Bede,* 1859).

Jekyll and Hyde (jekăl) A person with a split personality, someone whose character changes abruptly from one extreme to another. Robert Louis Stevenson's novel *The Strange Case of Dr. Jekyll and Mr. Hyde* (1886) tells the story of a respected scientist called Jekyll who drinks a potion that transforms him into the hideous Mr. Hyde, in which unrecognizable guise he commits murder. Finding himself unable to return to his original identity as Hyde increasingly dominates his personality, the luckless scientist kills himself. "In one movement el Capitan swivelled round and sat on the edge of the table, all sympathy and charm, as if there had been no smudging between the polite and the brutal: Jekyll and Hyde, the line was easily crossed" (Tom Pow, *In the Palace of Serpents*, 1992).

Jenkins's Ear, War of A serious argument that arises over some minor, even trivial matter. The allusion is to an incident that led to war between Britain and Spain in 1739. A British vessel sailing in the West Indies was accosted by Spanish coastguards and the British captain Robert Jenkins's ear was cut off. The incensed Jenkins presented his pickled ear to the House of Commons, which responded by sanctioning war with Spain. *If we are not careful this incident could turn into a modern War of Jenkins's Ear.*

Jephthah's daughter (jepthăz) A chaste woman; a virgin. According to the account given in Judges

11:29–40, Jephthah was a judge of Israel who vowed to sacrifice the first living thing he met on returning home should he be victorious in battle against the Ammonites. He won the battle but on returning home was aghast to be greeted by his own unmarried daughter. The girl was allowed two months in which to go into the mountains and lament the fact that she would die a virgin and was duly sacrificed at the end of that time. *It appeared she had vowed to retain her virginity to the end of her days, like some reincarnated Jephthah's daughter.*

jeremiad (jerămīăd) A lengthy lamentation about life or a gloom-laden prophecy of disaster. The word is derived via French from the name of the Old Testament prophet Jeremiah, who is remembered for his stern warnings to Judah of God's judgment against idolatry, immorality, and false prophets (as in chapters 10, 14, and 16). Jeremiah became very unpopular (being thrown into prison and into a cistern) and was known as the Prophet of Doom. "Jeremiah also spoke about a fresh hope. He promised a new and lasting covenant which God would write on his people's hearts, characterized by the inwardness of genuine faith. . . . He also spoke of the restoration of Jerusalem, which Jeremiah symbolized by buying a plot of land as the Babylonians besieged the city . . . and of a new king in David's line to replace the corrupt monarchy of his own day" (Selman and Manser, *Hearthside Bible Dictionary,* p. 122). Even today any person who complains at length about the state of the world or who voices gloomy predictions about the future may be labeled a ***Jeremiah.*** "Since the world began there have been two Jeremys. The one wrote a Jeremiah about usury, and was called Jeremy Bentham" (Edgar Allan Poe, *Diddling,* 1850).

Jericho *See* WALLS OF JERICHO.

jeroboam (jerăbōăm) A very large wine bottle, with a capacity of three liters. Jeroboam (c. 931–910 B.C.) was a king of Israel who in 1 Kings 11:28 is described as "a mighty man of valour," hence the humorous adoption of his name as that of a large bottle in the 19th century. He promoted idol worship and "did sin, and . . . made Israel to sin." *By the end of the night the tables were laden with jeroboams.*

Jerry *See* TOM AND JERRY.

Jerusalem *See* NEW JERUSALEM.

Jesse James (jesee jaymz) A dashing, romantic rogue. The real Jesse James (1847–82) was a bank and train robber of Wild West fame, whose career was much glamorized in Hollywood films loosely based on his life. In reality, he was a vicious murderer, whose life ended when he was shot dead by a fellow gang member motivated by the reward on James's head. *With his mixture of charm and unprincipled ruthlessness, he earned himself the reputation of a latter-day Jesse James.*

Jesuitical (jezooitikăl) Using subtle, devious, or hairsplitting arguments. The Jesuits, members of the Roman Catholic Society of Jesus founded by Saint Ignatius of Loyola in 1534, acquired a reputation for secretiveness as well as for strict discipline and intellectual rigor. Their involvement in political affairs over the centuries means that the order is distrusted by many people outside the church. "The artist looked over Vincent's recent work and his comments were honest and constructive, not in the least 'Jesuitical'" (Philip Callow, *Van Gogh: A Life*, 1990).

Jesus wept! (jeezăs) An exclamation of exasperation. This is the shortest verse in the Bible, appearing in John 11:35. *The chief of the engineers surveyed the chaotic scene below and wiped a grimy hand across his brow. "Jesus wept! We'll be here all night."*

jethroization (jethrōizayshăn) The practice of delegating authority and responsibility to others. The allusion is to the biblical Jethro, who became concerned about the health of his son-in-law Moses and advised him to delegate some of his less important duties as a judge to others (as recorded in Exodus 18:1–27). *The new manager seemed to believe so wholeheartedly in the practice of jethroization that by the end of his first week people were wondering what there was left for him to do.*

jetsam *See* FLOTSAM AND JETSAM.

Jim Crow Racial discrimination, especially against black people. The name began as the title of a song with which Thomas Dartmouth Rice (a white performer who appeared in "blackface" makeup) had considerable success in the 1820s. It was later adopted as a pejorative term for any black person and was consequently applied to racial segregation as officially sanctioned under so-called Jim Crow laws in the southern United States up to the 1960s. "Jim Crow laws dictated that we all sit up in the coloured balcony, so we followed Earl up the stairs of the separate entrance, located to the right of the box office, and found ourselves in the highest tier of the auditorium" (Ian Breakwell and Paul Hammond, eds., *Seeing in the Dark*, 1990).

jezebel (jezăbel) A shameless, immoral woman. Jezebel was the daughter of Ethbaal, the king of Tyre and Sidon, and the wife of Ahab, king of Israel. Her evil deeds included the murder of the Lord's prophets and their replacement by the prophets of Baal and the attempted murder of Elijah. Elijah foretold a bad end for Jezebel with the words "The dogs shall eat Jezebel by the wall of Jezreel" (1 Kings 21:23), and she eventually met her death when she was hurled out of a palace window on the orders of King Jehu after she adorned herself with cosmetics and tried to seduce him: Her blood spattered the wall, as Elijah had predicted, and her body was torn apart by dogs (2 Kings 9:30–37). Any woman who is suspected of loose, immoral behavior may be dubbed a jezebel; if she wears heavy makeup she is likely to be condemned as a ***painted jezebel.*** "I have been a Jezebel, a London prostitute, and what not" (Samuel Richardson, *Pamela,* 1740).

Jimmy Hoffa (hofă) A person who disappears in suspicious circumstances, especially one with dubious connections. James "Jimmy" Hoffa (1913–c. 1975) was the controversial president of the Teamsters' Union of transport workers from 1957 to 1967, when he was imprisoned on charges of bribery. Released in 1971, he disappeared on July 30, 1975, when he was due to meet two mafia leaders. He is thought to have been murdered, although his body has never been discovered. *After his disappearance from public view the papers began to refer to him as another Jimmy Hoffa.*

Jimmy Porter *See* ANGRY YOUNG MAN.

jingoism (jingōizăm) Belligerent patriotism. The term, which made its first appearance in the 1870s, originally alluded to the wave of British nationalism that swept the country during the Crimean War, becoming familiar through a popular music-hall song of the period: "We don't want to fight, / But by Jingo, if we do, / We've got the ships, / We've got the men,

/ We've got the money, too." The word has since been applied to similar outbursts of patriotic fervour in various countries around the world. It has been suggested the word "Jingo" may have had its origins in the patter of 17th-century stage conjurers, who used it as a euphemism for "Jesus." "A mood of bellicose jingoism, unknown since the days of Suez in November 1956, swept the land, directed against 'the Argies'" (Kenneth O. Morgan, *The People's Peace*, 1990).

Joan of Arc A woman who heroically dedicates herself to a particular cause. Joan of Arc (c. 1412–31) was a young French peasant girl who devoted herself to throwing the English out of France, apparently on the instruction of "angelic voices." She won the confidence of the French dauphin and went on to inspire French soldiers to recapture many towns before being betrayed to the English, tried as a witch, and burned at the stake. "Who do you think you are, Joan of Arc?" (Kim Newman, *Bad Dreams*, 1990).

Job, patience of *See* PATIENCE OF JOB.

Job's comforter (jōbz) A person whose attempts to give comfort to another in distress only serve to intensify the other's misery. The allusion is to the biblical Job, who is visited by three sympathetic friends, Eliphaz, Bildad, and Zophar (described as "miserable comforters" in Job 16:2), who tactlessly attribute his current misfortunes to his disobedience to God. *As soon as news of his disappointment got abroad his front doorbell did not stop ringing with Job's comforters come to trawl through the ashes of his dream.*

Job's wife (jōbz) A wicked woman; a woman who offers evil advice to others. In the biblical story of Job and his multifarious sufferings, his wife does little to alleviate his agony, merely advising him to "curse God, and die" (Job 2:9–10). In some medieval versions of the story she actually exacerbates Job's pain by tossing water on his boils or by whipping him. *This Job's wife waged an unceasing campaign to have all aid to the refugees cut off and redirected to causes more to her liking.*

Jocasta *See* OEDIPUS COMPLEX.

Joe Palooka (pălookă) The plain-thinking, honest, man in the street. The character Joe Palooka, a simpleminded boxing champion with little education but an appealingly kindhearted nature, made his first appearance in a comic strip published in 1928 and quickly caught on as an archetype of the average American. In modern usage, his name has acquired a mildly pejorative tone, critical of the general public's lack of intelligence or imagination. A town of incompetents may, by the same token, be dubbed ***Palookaville***. *I don't expect every Joe Palooka to understand what we're trying to do.*

John Bircher (bercher) A right-wing extremist. John Birch was a U.S. military intelligence officer and Baptist missionary who was killed by Chinese communists in 1945. Extremists identified him as the first U.S. casualty of the COLD WAR and 13 years after his death founded the John Birch Society to oppose what they perceived as the communist threat to the U.S. Constitution. Critics of the John Birch Society have labeled its members ultraconservative and reactionary. *Her father is a real John Bircher and thinks all students are idle layabouts.*

John Brown A fanatical supporter of a particular cause. The abolitionist John Brown (1800–59) was determined to rid the United States of slavery and is remembered as one of the leaders of a raid made on a federal arsenal at Harper's Ferry in Virginia on October 16, 1859, with the aim of getting weapons with which to arm the slaves. The raid failed and Brown was tried and hanged, but he became an icon of the antislavery movement and is still remembered for his resolute (if misguided) zeal in an undubitably righteous cause, as celebrated in the marching song "John Brown's body lies a-moldering in the grave." *He thundered at them about the need to take up arms and act, like the ghost of John Brown himself.*

John Bull The archetype of an English squire and a symbol of England itself. Traditionally depicted as a plump, rosy-cheeked, middle-aged man in a Union Jack waistcoat and top hat, and often accompanied by a British bulldog, John Bull made his first appearance in John Arthuthnot's satire *The History of John Bull* (1712). He continued to appear in cartoons as a representation of English patriotism and traditionalism well into the 20th century, but is considered dated today. "He's a true John Bull" (Louisa May Alcott, *Little Women*, 1868–69).

John Dillinger *See* PUBLIC ENEMY NUMBER ONE.

John Hancock A person's signature. As president of the Continental Congress, John Hancock (1736–93) was one of the most prominent supporters of the American cause in the American Revolution and in 1776 became one of the signatories of the Declaration of Independence. His large, distinctive signature stood out among those of his fellows, hence the adoption of his name as an eponym for a signature. Legend has it that he deliberately wrote his name as large and clearly as he could so that King George III of England would be able to read it even without his reading glasses (although contemporaries observed that that was how he always signed his name). *Stick your John Hancock at the bottom of the page.*

Johnny Appleseed A person who shows others how to support themselves by understanding the ways of nature. The original Johnny Appleseed was the nomadic backwoodsman John Chapman (1774–1845), who became a folk hero for the help he gave pioneer settlers in the American West. His nickname reflects his reputation for scattering apple seeds throughout Illinois, Indiana, Ohio, and Pennsylvania to provide orchards for the benefit of pioneer families. He is also said to have warned settlers of imminent attack by Native American tribes. *His grandfather wore an old straw hat and spent his days contemplating the garden from his rocking chair like some superannuated Johnny Appleseed.*

John o' Groats (jon ō grōts) A remote, far-distant place. John o' Groats is the name of a village at the furthest northeastern point of mainland Scotland. Scottish folklore has it that the original John o' Groats (or Jan de Groot) was one of three Dutch brothers who settled hereabouts around 1500. When members of the eight branches of the family subsequently disagreed over who was most senior, John built an eight-sided room around an eight-sided table, so that all could sit at the head of the table. *You could have heard the groan of despair in John o' Groats.*

Johnsonian (jonsōneeăn) Written or said in a fine, erudite style or otherwise reminiscent of the lexicographer, essayist, and wit Dr. Samuel Johnson (1709–84). Johnson was justly revered in his own age and by later generations as a master of written and spoken English, and to be judged Johnsonian in writing style or conversation remains no small compliment. His name might also, however, be quoted less flatteringly in reference to the great man's portly frame. "With Johnsonian vigour, Eliot discussed the way to run a society; he surveyed with distanced irony 'The Literature of Fascism,' also printing MacDiarmid's 'Second Hymn to Lenin'" (Robert Crawford, *The Savage and the City in the Work of T. S. Eliot*, 1990).

John the Baptist (jon, baptist) A person who preaches or speaks out in defiance of hostile opinion, especially one who urges Christian repentance. John the Baptist was the prophet who foretold the coming of Christ and went on to baptize Jesus Christ in the Jordan River (Matthew 3:1–15; Mark 1:4–11; Luke 3:1–22). Jesus regarded him as the last and greatest prophet, fulfilling the promise of a second Elijah (Matthew 11:11–14). Despite a successful ministry, he was killed by Herod Antipas for criticizing Herod's marriage to his sister-in-law (Matthew 14:1–12). "He was a John the Baptist who took ennoblement rather than repentance for his text" (Thomas Hardy, *The Return of the Native,* 1880). *See also* VOICE CRYING IN THE WILDERNESS.

John Wayne The personification in the movies of the cowboy-hero of the Wild West. John Wayne (Marion Michael Morrison; 1907–79), the star of such iconic westerns as *Stagecoach* (1939) and *The Searchers* (1956), came to epitomize the rugged integrity and indomitable spirit of the colonial West as well as the old-fashioned patriotic, conservative values of the Republican establishment. *He walked into the bar like John Wayne looking for the man who had killed his best friend. See also* MAN'S GOTTA DO WHAT A MAN'S GOTTA DO, A.

Jonah (jōnă) A person who brings bad luck wherever he or she goes. The biblical Jonah was a prophet who was blamed for the storm that lashed the ship in which he was fleeing from God's command to go and preach repentance to the people of Nineveh (Jonah 1:4–12). To appease the storm and save the ship, Jonah readily agrees to be cast into the water "for I know that for my sake this great tempest is upon you." On being tossed into the sea he is swallowed by a "great fish" (often presumed to be a whale), inside which he spends three days and nights before being disgorged safely on land and subsequently making his way to Nineveh as commanded. To Jonah someone means to throw them overboard. "I felt some sentiment that it must be a judgment on us also. The Jonah, in my mind, was Mr. Earnshaw" (Emily Brontë, *Wuthering Heights,* 1847).

Jonathan *See* DAVID AND JONATHAN.

Jones, Casey *See* CASEY JONES.

Jones, Indiana *See* INDIANA JONES.

Jordan passed (jordăn) Death completed, heaven attained. The phrase refers to the Jordan River in the Holy Land and alludes to the miraculous dryfooted crossing of the river by the Israelites led by Joshua on their way to the Promised Land (located on the western side and often considered a metaphor for Heaven), as recounted in Joshua 3:7–17. *Her long struggle was over, Jordan passed and no more suffering to be borne. See also* CROSS OVER JORDAN.

jorum (jorăm) A large drinking bowl, especially one used to contain punch. The name may refer to the biblical king Joram of Hamath who offered "vessels of silver, and vessels of gold, and vessels of brass" (2 Samuel 8:10) as gifts to King David following the latter's victory over Hadadezer. "At the same table, with both her elbows upon it, was Mrs. Jiniwin; no longer sipping other people's punch feloniously with teaspoons, but taking deep draughts from a jorum of her own" (Charles Dickens, *The Old Curiosity Shop,* 1840–41).

Joseph (jōzef) A person who remains immune even to the most alluring sexual temptations. The allusion is to the biblical story of Joseph and POTIPHAR'S WIFE (Genesis 39), in which Joseph, an overseer in Potiphar's house, steadfastly resists seduction by her, resulting eventually in her falsely accusing him of making improper advances and having him thrown into prison. *For months he had been a veritable Joseph in the face of the most tempting of prospects, but the sight of her exposed thigh was too much.*

jot or tittle A tiny amount. The phrase comes from Christ's Sermon on the Mount, in which he denies that he comes to destroy the law but rather to fulfill it: "For verily I say unto you, Till heaven and earth pass, one jot or one tittle shall in no wise pass from the law, till all be fulfilled" (Matthew 5:18; Luke 16:17). Here *jot* signifies the Greek letter iota *(i),* the smallest letter in the Greek alphabet, while *tittle* is the slight extension of certain letters of the Hebrew alphabet that is used to distinguish one character from another. "Go ye back to London. We have nothing for you. By no jot or tittle do we abate our demands, nor will we until the whole of those demands are yielded" (John Galsworthy, *The Forsyte Saga,* 1922).

jovial *See* BY JOVE.

Joycean (joiseeăn) After the style of Irish novelist James Joyce (1882–1941). Joyce had a profound impact on modern fiction through his colorful and inventive writing, which was remarkable for the author's innovative experiments with grammar and vocabulary, in particular his "stream-of-consciousness" technique in which the narrative is seemingly allowed to flow without hindrance. In this regard, calling a person's writing "Joycean" would be considered a compliment, but some might be inclined to regard it a rather mixed compliment, bearing in mind Joyce's reputation for obscurity of meaning. *His speech was positively Joycean in its lack of coherence.*

J.R. *See* DALLAS.

Juan, Don *See* DON JUAN.

Jubal (joobăl) A musician or the muse of music and song. Jubal is identified in the Bible as the son of Lamech and Adah and described as the father of "all such as handle the harp and organ" (Genesis 4:21). *This Jubal played like a god, his fingers a blur upon the strings.*

jubilee A 50th anniversary and the festivities with which such an occasion may be celebrated. The word has biblical origins (Leviticus 25 and 27), harking back to the jubilees held after seven successive Sabbaths of years (49 years) to commemorate the deliverance of the Israelites from Egypt. Jubilee years, which were ushered in with the blowing of a *jobel* (Hebrew for a "ram's horn"), were marked by the fields being allowed to rest uncultivated, by the restoration of land to those to whom it originally belonged and by the release of Jewish slaves. "Wodger of the Purple Fawn and Mr. Jaggers the cobbler, who also sold second-hand ordinary bicycles, were stretching a string of union-jacks and royal ensigns (which had originally celebrated the Jubilee) across the road" (H. G. Wells, *The Invisible Man,* 1897).

Judas (joodăs) A traitor; a hypocrite. The allusion is to Judas Iscariot, who at Gethsemane betrayed Christ to the Romans for THIRTY PIECES OF SILVER (Matthew 26:14). He identified Christ to his captors by kissing him (Matthew 26:47–49), hence a ***Judas kiss*** signifies an act of betrayal disguised as a demonstration of friendship. Another adoption of the name of Judas may be found in the ***Judas slit*** or ***Judas hole,*** the name of the small peephole in a cell door through which a prisoner may be watched or inspected by his or her captors. The elder tree is sometimes known as the ***Judas tree*** because it was from an elder that Judas is supposed to have hanged himself in remorse for his actions (Matthew 27:5). A ***Judas goat,*** meanwhile, is someone who deceitfully leads others into danger (as one goat may lead others to slaughter). "What could you do? You could be Judas to yo' own mother to save yo' wuthless hide! Would anybody b'lieve it?" (Mark Twain, *Pudd'nhead Wilson,* 1894).

Judge Jeffreys *See* JEFFREYS, JUDGE.

judge not, that ye be not judged Do not be too hasty to condemn others, as you may invite unwelcome criticism of yourself. The sentiment comes originally from Christ's Sermon on the Mount (Matthew 7:1–5) and is usually quoted as a warning to keep one's unfavorable opinions of others to oneself. "It may seem strange that any men should fare to ask a just God's assistance in wringing their bread from the sweat of other men's faces; but let us judge not, that we be not judged" (Abraham Lincoln, "Gettysburg Address," 1863).

judgment day A day upon which something will be judged or decided once and for all. The biblical Day of Judgment, as described in the Book of Matthew (such as 11:22–24; 12:36; 13:49; 25:31–33), will come at the end of time. Following Christ's ***Last Judgment*** of all souls, from his throne on the ***judgment seat*** (Romans 14:10), the good will receive their eternal reward in heaven, while the ungodly will be punished in hell. "Davy at the first crash had howled, Anne, Anne, is it the Judgment Day? Anne, Anne, I never meant to be naughty, and then had buried his face in Anne's lap and kept it there, his little body quivering" (Lucy Maud Montgomery, *Anne of Avonlea,* 1909).

judgment of Paris (paris) A difficult case or argument to decide, especially one in which there is no solution that will satisfy all parties. The expression refers to an episode in Greek legend in which Paris, the handsome son of King Priam of Troy, was invited to decide which of the three goddesses Hera, Pallas Athene, and Aphrodite was the fairest. Faced with such a perilous decision, Paris awarded the prize to Aphrodite, who had bribed him with the promise of the most beautiful woman in the world. His decision made Hera and Pallas Athene his bitter enemies and led ultimately to the fall of Troy. "On the appointed afternoon, all Simla rode down to Annandale to witness the Judgment of Paris turned upside down" (Rudyard Kipling, *Cupid's Arrows,* 1888). *See also* APPLE OF DISCORD.

judgment of Solomon (solămăn) Great wisdom, as required to solve a particularly difficult dispute or problem. The allusion is to a biblical dispute (1 Kings 3:16–28) brought before King Solomon, who was widely respected for his wisdom and sense of justice, by two prostitutes who were both claiming possession of the same child. Having heard their cases, Solomon calmly proposed cutting the child in half so that the women could have equal shares; the woman who showed anxiety about this proposal proved she was the real mother and was accordingly awarded custody of the infant. The biblical account records Solomon's prayer for wisdom (1 Kings 3:5–15) and the giving by God to him of "a wise and understanding heart" (verse 12). "'The devil take all halves and quarters!' said the Captain; 'were it in my option, I could no more consent to the halving of that dollar, than the woman in the Judgment of Solomon to the disseverment of the child of her bowels'" (Sir Walter Scott, *A Legend of Montrose,* 1819).

judgment seat *See* JUDGMENT DAY.

Judy *See* PUNCH AND JUDY.

juggernaut (jugernot) A large, heavy truck; any immense object, force, or concept with seemingly unstoppable momentum. The word comes from Hindu mythology, specifically from the name Jagganath, which was one of the many titles adopted by the god Vishnu. Idols of Jagannath are traditionally borne on massive wheeled vehicles pulled by thousands of pilgrims at an annual festival held in the city of Puri in eastern India in his honor. Popular belief has it that extreme devotees of Jagganath regularly make sacrifices of themselves by lying down in front of the huge wheels carrying his image and being crushed to death, although the reality may be that these are simply unfortunates who have lost their footing in the press of worshipers. "It's as if he were some horrible old Juggernaut and I had to see my children's own father throwing them under the wheels to keep him satisfied" (Booth Tarkington, *Alice Adams,* 1921).

Julian calendar (jooleeăn) The calendar that preceded the present Gregorian calendar. The system was named after the Roman emperor Julius Caesar (100–44 B.C.), who introduced the system in 46 because the existing system (based on the lunar month rather than the solar year) had led to the Roman year being a full three months ahead of where it should have been. The fact that Caesar's own calendar meant that each year was longer by 11 minutes than it should have been eventually persuaded Pope Gregory XIII to replace it in 1582 with the so-called Gregorian calendar, which was subsequently adopted by Britain and its colonies in 1752, when 11 days (September 2–14) were omitted to correct the long-standing inaccuracy of the former system. People who did not understand the rationale behind this latest updating feared they were being robbed of the time and protested vigorously under the slogan "give us back our 11 days." Ethiopia ranks among the few countries that still retain the Julian calendar. *Such ideas belong to a different time, to the era of the Julian calendar and gladiatorial combat.*

Juliet *See* ROMEO AND JULIET.

July The seventh month of the year. July was named after the Roman emperor Julius Caesar (100–44 B.C.) on the command of Mark Antony (c. 82–30 B.C.); it was originally known as Quintilis. *Her smile was as sunny as July.*

Jumping Jehoshaphat! (jăhōshăfat) A mild oath. According to 1 Kings 22, Jehoshaphat, whose name means "Jehovah is judge," was one of the kings of Judah from 873 to 849 B.C. As king he promoted the religious education of his people and was renowned for his godly ways. The adjective *jumping* would appear have become attached purely for reasons of onomatopoeic appeal. *Jumping Jehoshaphat! The building's on fire!*

June The sixth month of the year. June was probably named after the moon goddess Juno, the wife and sister of Jupiter and the Roman equivalent of Hera in Greek mythology. Another theory suggests the month may have been named in honor of the Junius family of ancient Rome, from which came some of the murderers of Julius Caesar (100–44 B.C.). *In the conservatory it was as hot as June.*

Junoesque (joonōesk) Regally beautiful. The adjective alludes to Juno, the wife and sister of Jupiter, who was renowned for her great beauty and dignity. This stateliness was reflected in the adoption of her name as an epithet for the peacock, sometimes referred to as the ***Junonian bird.*** As Jupiter's queen she was identified as the guardian of mortal women and the protector of marriage. Juno was, however, also well known for her jealous anger at the faithless behavior of her husband, and many references to her name in literature relate to the ***anger of Juno.*** "She seldom ran—it did not suit her style, she thought, for being tall, the stately and Junoesque was more appropriate than the sportive or piquante" (Louisa May Alcott, *Little Women,* 1868–69). *See also* MONEY.

Jupiter (joopiter) The largest of the planets and the fifth from the Sun. In Roman mythology Jupiter was the king and ruler of the gods, equivalent of the Greek Zeus. His name literally means "bright heaven." *"By Jupiter!" exclaimed the colonel. "I see what you mean." See also* BY JOVE.

Jurassic Park (joorasik) Scientifically implausible or outlandish. The allusion is to the film *Jurassic Park* (1993) and its sequels, in which the central premise is that it would be possible to recreate living dinosaurs of the Jurassic period by isolating their DNA from mosquitos preserved in amber. Although the films were hugely successful, scientists dismissed the idea as wildly removed from reality. *The general opinion was that the whole theory was a bit "Jurassic Park."*

justified by works *See* FAITH WITHOUT WORKS.

Just William A mischievous or naughty little boy. The allusion is to William Brown, the rambunctious central character in the *Just William* stories (1922–70) of Richmal Crompton (1890–1969). Crompton's William is naturally rebellious and consequently often in trouble, though never seriously, with his parents and the authorities. The "Just William" tag is also applied more widely to anything that is reminiscent of Crompton's character or his now rather old-fashioned middle-class world. "He would stand there, with his Just William cap on and sing—no movements, just natural, and it made you forget the world" (Melvyn Bragg, *Rich: The Life of Richard Burton*, 1989).

Kafkaesque (kafkăesk) Nightmarish, defying logic, contradictory. The allusion is to the short stories and novels of the Czech-born writer Franz Kafka (1883–1924), which generally depict individuals overwhelmed by terrifying, surreal events of which they have little understanding and over which they have no control. The term "Kafkaesque" is often applied to the seemingly unfathomable or nonsensical actions of big bureaucracies or faceless state organizations. "Toiling up the slope from Falmer railway station, you had the Kafkaesque sensation of walking into an endlessly deep stage set where apparently three-dimensional objects turned out to be painted flats, and reality receded as fast as you pursued it" (David Lodge, *Nice Work*, 1988).

kalends *See* CALENDS.

kama sutra (kahmă sootră) An erotic sex manual detailing lovemaking techniques. Though today applied to virtually any sex guide, the term originally referred to an ancient Hindu text that gave advice on lovemaking and related matters, sometimes attributed to the first-century A.D. Indian sage Vatsyayana. Its name referred to Kama, an Indian love god (*kama* also being the Sanskrit word for "love"), and *sutra*, meaning "thread" or "way." The book became notorious in the West after its translation into English by Sir Richard Burton and F. F. Arbuthnot in 1883. *Geraldine was surprised to receive a lecture on the kama sutra from her aunt when she visited her in the retirement home.*

kamikaze (kamikahzee) A suicide attack or attacker. Derived from the Japanese for "divine wind," the term became widely familiar during the latter stages of World War II when it was adopted as a tactic by Japanese fighter pilots, who attempted to sink Allied warships by crashing their bomb-laden aircraft into them at the cost of their own lives. The original "divine wind" was a typhoon that removed the threat of an imminent Mongol invasion of Japan in August 1281 by destroying the Mongol invasion fleet. In modern usage, the term is commonly applied to anyone who behaves in a reckless manner apparently without regard to his or her own safety or interests. *The streets were being terrorized by kamikaze motorists who seemed oblivious of the danger they were putting themselves in.*

Kane, Citizen *See* CITIZEN KANE.

kangaroo court An improperly constituted court that has no legal validity. The expression would appear to be of U.S. (not Australian) origin, being first recorded in the American West around the middle of the 19th century, specifically to describe the impromptu legal proceedings set up to settle disputes among miners taking part in the 1849 gold rush (who happened to include many Australians). The name was probably inspired by the erratic bounds of the kangaroo. "They hold the odd kangaroo court to deal with those who have caused trouble but aren't what the state would consider criminals—people who con their own families out of earnings or land, that sort of thing" (David A. McIntee, *White Darkness*, 1993).

Kansas anymore, we're not in *See* WE'RE NOT IN KANSAS ANYMORE.

Karenina, Anna *See* ANNA KARENINA.

Karloff, Boris *See* BORIS KARLOFF.

karma (kahrmă) The essence of a person's spiritual being. The concept of karma is a central idea in both Hindu and Buddhist thought, and it is the state of a person's karma at the end of his or her life that decides the nature of the individual's next incarnation. In modern usage the word is often taken to refer generally to fate or to a person's soul or sense of spiritual well-being. *She resolutely refused to allow her karma to be disrupted by the disturbing news coming at her on the television and radio and settled down to spend the evening with a good book.*

Karno's Army *See* FRED KARNO'S ARMY.

Kate Archetype of a self-willed, nagging woman. The allusion is to the title character in William Shakespeare's comedy *The Taming of the Shrew* (c. 1594), in which Kate is depicted as an untamed, shrewish young woman who is eventually brought to heel by Petruchio, who cowes her after making her his wife. The play, with its somewhat misogynistic message, presents a problem for modern directors and audiences, although its comedy and characters remain as sparkling and effective as they were in Shakespeare's day. *He thought he had wed a Barbie, but it turned out he had married a Kate.*

Keaton, Buster *See* BUSTER KEATON.

Kedar's tents (keedahrz) The world of the human race. The expression is biblical in origin, alluding to Kedar, the son of Ishmael who is identified in Genesis 25:13 as the forbear of a tribe of nomadic Arabs. The phrase itself appears in Psalm 120:5: "Woe is me, that I sojourn in Mesech, that I dwell in the tents of Kedar!" *They found the old beggar's body the following day. Some time during the night he had made his escape from Kedar's tents.*

keep oneself unspotted from the world To keep oneself free of the corruptions of the world. The expression is biblical: "Pure religion and undefiled before God and the Father is this, To visit the fatherless and widows in their affliction, and to keep himself unspotted from the world" (James 1:27). "Then there was an interval and a scene with his people, who expected much from him. Next a year of living unspotted from the world in a third-rate depot battalion where all the juniors were children, and all the seniors old women; and lastly he came out to India, where he was cut off from the support of his parents, and had no one to fall back on in time of trouble except himself" (Rudyard Kipling, *Plain Tales from the Hills,* 1888).

keep the ball rolling To maintain momentum in something; to keep something going. The allusion here (though largely forgotten) is to the U.S.

presidential campaign of 1840, between William Henry Harrison and Martin Van Buren. One of the features of the ultimately successful campaign to get Harrison elected was the rolling of huge balls made of paper and buckskin and decorated with campaigning slogans substantial distances through cities and the countryside (for example, from Cleveland, Ohio, to Lexington, Kentucky, and from Kentucky to Baltimore, Maryland). Supporters propelling the balls onward were encouraged to "keep the ball rolling—on to Washington!" *I know we're all tired but we need to keep the ball rolling.*

keep up with the Joneses (jōnzăz) To keep level in status with one's neighbors. The allusion is to a comic strip called "Keeping up with the Joneses—by Pop" drawn by Arthur R. Momand for the *New York Globe* between 1913 and 1941, and allegedly inspired by the artist's own efforts to maintain his social standing with his real-life neighbors in an affluent New York suburb. "The adverts scold us and cajole us and wheedle us and fawn us to keep up with the Joneses" (Stewart Lamont, *In Good Faith*, 1989).

Kelly, Ned *See* NED KELLY.

Kemo Sabe *See* LONE RANGER.

Ken *See* BARBIE.

Kenobi, Obi-Wan *See* OBI-WAN KENOBI.

Kent, Clark *See* SUPERMAN.

Ketch, Jack *See* JACK KETCH.

Keynesian (keenzeeăn, kaynzeeăn) Of or relating to the theories of British economist John Maynard Keynes (1883–1946). Central to these was the idea that governments need to maintain control of monetary policy in order to control the economy. He also argued in favor of higher government spending to counter mass unemployment, a stance that was opposed by supporters of a free market. "Local government was a crucial element of the social-democratic or Keynesian welfare state so laboriously constructed after the war" (James Anderson and Allan Cochrane, eds., *Politics in Transition*, 1989).

keys of the kingdom The keys to heaven or more generally any means of access to authority or privilege. The phrase appears in Matthew 16:18–19, where Christ addresses Peter: "And I say also unto thee, That thou art Peter, and upon this rock I will build my church; and the gates of hell shall not prevail against it. And I will give unto thee the keys of the kingdom of heaven: and whatsoever thou shalt bind on earth shall be bound in heaven: and whatsoever thou shalt loose on earth shall be loosed in heaven." The symbol of crossed keys subsequently became an emblem of the papacy, and Peter is commonly depicted as the doorkeeper of heaven. *Winning a seat in the Senate seemed to him like being given the keys of the kingdom, but reality turned out to be very different.*

Keystone Cops (keestōn) A comically incompetent outfit of some kind, especially people in authority. The allusion is to the Keystone Comedies made in the silent movie era by Mack Sennett (1880–1960), the first of which appeared in 1913. The Keystone Cops themselves were a group of hilariously inept policemen in ill-fitting uniforms played by a talented cast of stunt performers who at one point included Charlie Chaplin (*see* CHAPLINESQUE). Highlights of the Keystone Comedies were the extended slapstick chase sequences. "It would have been like something out of the Keystone Cops" (Alastair MacNeill, *Time of the Assassins*, 1992).

KGB The state police, or some other secret police organization. The KGB, or Komitet Gosudárstvennoi Bezopásnosti (Committee for State Security), was the intelligence agency of the Soviet Union until the collapse of the Communist government in the late 1980s. It had an international reputation for brutality and oppression. *Being questioned by her parents was like being interrogated by the KGB.*

kick against the pricks To resist or protest against prevailing opinion or conditions. The expression comes from the biblical Book of Acts, in which Saul is struck by a bright light while on the road to Damascus and addressed by Christ himself: "And the Lord said, I am Jesus whom thou persecutest: it is hard for thee to kick against the pricks" (Acts 9:5). The phrase refers to the kicking of an ox or horse when goaded or spurred. "Paul was laid up with an attack of bronchitis. He did not mind much. What happened happened, and it was no good kicking against the pricks" (D. H. Lawrence, *Sons and Lovers*, 1913).

Kildare, Doctor *See* DOCTOR KILDARE.

Kilkenny cats, fight like *See* FIGHT LIKE KILKENNY CATS.

kill the fatted calf To offer a guest the finest food or other fare available; to arrange a lavish celebration. The phrase is biblical in origin, coming from the parable of the PRODIGAL SON in which the father welcomes his younger son home with a generous feast: "Bring hither the fatted calf, and kill it; and let us eat, and be merry" (Luke 15:23). "'Well, here I am. Kill the fatted calf, Warmson, let's have fizz'" (John Galsworthy, *The Forsyte Saga*, 1922).

kill the goose that laid the golden egg To cut off the supply of one's own wealth or other benefits. The allusion is to a folktale about a goose that laid golden eggs for its poor peasant owners. The peasants grew greedy and imagined they would find more gold if they cut the goose open; when they did so, however, they found no gold and the goose died. *By turning the event into a commercial tourist attraction, they risk killing the goose that lays the golden egg.*

kill the messenger To punish the bearer of bad news rather than tackle the source of it. The expression comes from the tragedy *Antigone* (c. 442 B.C.) by the Greek playwright Sophocles: "None love the messenger who brings bad tidings." Variants include ***shoot the messenger.*** *Political columnists agreed that the dismissal of the vice president's aide was a case of killing the messenger rather than going to the real source of the problem.*

killing field A place where slaughter on a massive scale takes place. The phrase was originally applied to the infamous killing fields of Cambodia where thousands of opponents of Pol Pot's Khmer Rouge regime and many more innocent victims were executed between 1975 and 1979. The actual location of Cambodia's killing fields was the paddy fields around Phnom Penh. The grim events of the period were presented before a worldwide audience in the film *The Killing Fields* (1984). "The stadium chosen for the game was literally the killing fields, a place where supporters of the deposed Allende government had been tortured and assassinated" (Stuart Cosgrove, *Hampden Babylon*, 1991). *See also* YEAR ZERO.

Kilroy was here (kilroi) Ubiquitous graffiti slogan. The origins of this familiar graffiti tag are unclear, although there are suggestions that the original Kilroy was a shipyard inspector at Quincy, Massachusetts, who chalked up these words on pieces of material he had inspected. Whatever the origin, the phrase became well known during World War II, when it was scrawled on walls all over the world by U.S. troops, especially members of Air Transport Command. *No one should expect great cultural awareness from this "Kilroy was here" generation, whose chief artistic expression seems to be defacing rolling stock with garish tags.*

kindness of strangers, the *See* BLANCHE DUBOIS.

King, the The nickname by which U.S. pop star Elvis Presley (1935–77) became universally known. The nickname, otherwise rendered as the ***King of Rock 'n' Roll***, reflects Presley's preeminence among the pop stars of his generation. Another nickname, ***Elvis the Pelvis***, reflects the sexual allure of his stage performances. *He had a large collection of singles by the King and other giants of the early rock 'n' roll era. See also* GRACELAND.

King Arthur The ideal of a chivalric ruler. A lengthy cycle of legends describes the adventures of King Arthur and his knights, from his pulling the sword from the stone (thereby proving his claim to the throne of England), through the formation of the ROUND TABLE and the search for the HOLY GRAIL, to his betrayal by Queen ***Guinevere*** and Sir ***Lancelot*** and eventual death. Historically, the legends are hazily placed somewhere between the departure of the Romans from Britain and the Saxon invasion. The stories are widely familiar, and the term ***Arthurian*** is immediately understood to represent such knightly qualities as courage, loyalty, honor, and Christian fidelity. *Like some modern King Arthur, he believed implicitly in the righteousness of his presidential court. See also* AVALON; CAMELOT; EXCALIBUR; MERLIN.

King Canute (kănoot) A person who makes fanciful claims far beyond his or her real influence or importance. The historical King Canute (d. 1035) was the Danish-born king of England who, in order to demonstrate to his flattering courtiers the limits of his earthly powers, led his court to the seashore and there ordered the incoming tide to retreat. Perversely, despite the intent behind the gesture, Canute's name is today usually invoked as an illustration of overweening ambition, not humility. "Having proved myself incapable of holding back an irresistible force, I now know exactly how Canute felt" (Lee Wilkinson, *Joy Bringer*, 1992).

King Kong A person or thing of large, even monstrous proportions. The allusion is to the classic 1933 movie *King Kong*, since remade several times, in which King Kong is a terrifying giant gorilla who is brought low by his weakness for a pretty human woman, played in 1933 by Fay Wray, in 1976 by Jessica Lange, and in 2005 by Naomi Watts. "So there they stood, five feet apart: the monstrous stranger and the pure-beef hooligan, both ready for battle and roaring their jungle challenges into the night air like Godzilla and King Kong" (Helen Forrester, *The Latchkey Kid*, 1990).

King Lear (leer) Archetype of a foolish and tragic old man, especially one who becomes deranged when stripped of his illusions and brought face to face with harsh realities. As told by William Shakespeare in his tragedy *King Lear* (1605), the story of Lear begins with the king deciding to divide his kingdom between his three daughters, ***Goneril***, ***Regan***, and CORDELIA, on condition that each profess her love for him. When Cordelia refuses to match the insincere adoration of her two elder sisters, she is cut off from her inheritance. Cordelia's honesty, combined with the ensuing contempt of Goneril and Regan, triggers Lear's descent into madness and, after the death of Cordelia, his own broken-hearted demise. There was a legendary early king of Britain called Lir (or Lear), who was reputed to have been married to Fingula and, after Fingula's death, to the wicked Aoife, who turned Lir's children into swans. In modern usage, Lear's name is often quoted in discussions about problematic relations between parents and children. *He looked like King Lear, ranting at his daughter from the top step in the pouring rain, his long white hair billowing in the wind.*

King Log (log) A peace-loving ruler who rules with a gentle hand. The allusion is to a Greek fable about some frogs who petition Zeus for a king. When the god provides them with a log as their monarch, the frogs complain, and Zeus sends them a stork instead, which immediately sets about eating them. "We have all heard of King Log; but, in these jostling times, one of that royal kindred will hardly win the race for an elective chief-magistracy" (Nathaniel Hawthorne, *The House of the Seven Gables,* 1851).

king of kings A supremely powerful king or other authority. The phrase comes from the Bible, in which it is one of the titles used to describe God (as in Ezekiel 26:7 and 1 Timothy 6:15) and Jesus Christ (as in Revelation 17:14). It has been borne formally by some Eastern monarchs over the centuries and was adopted as a title by several rulers of Ethiopia. *The managing director likes to remind other directors that he is the king of kings. Contrary opinions are not encouraged.*

Kiplingesque (kiplingesk) Reminiscent of the writings of Rudyard Kipling (1865–1936), especially with regard to the imperialistic associations of his work. Many of Kipling's stories were set in British-controlled India, in which country Kipling himself was born. *Tony tried to interrupt, but his aunt was lost in visions of her Kiplingesque past. See also* GUNGA DIN; WHITE MAN'S BURDEN.

kirche, küche, kinder (kerkă, kookă, kinder) The limitation of women's interests to religious and domestic duties. The German for "church, kitchen, children," the phrase was adopted by the Nazis to delineate what they insisted was the proper place for the woman in the modern world. *His grandmother was not one of those women for whom life was going to be confined to kirche, küche, kinder.*

Kirk, Captain *See* STAR TREK.

kiss me, Hardy Farewell, I am dying (used facetiously). These are reputed to have been the last words of Admiral NELSON to Captain Thomas Masterman Hardy during the Battle of Trafalgar in October 1805, the admiral having been shot by a French sniper and carried below decks on board his flagship HMS *Victory*. There has been much discussion of the possibility that his actual last words, misheard by witnesses, were "Kismet, Hardy" ("kismet" meaning "fate"), although the fact that Hardy did then kiss Nelson on the cheek casts some doubt over this suggestion. *"'Kiss me, Hardy,' giggled Colin as Rod tried to help him up from the bar-room floor.*

kiss of Judas *See* JUDAS.

kiss the Blarney stone To be endowed with the gift of eloquence. The allusion is to the Irish folk belief that anyone who kisses the Blarney stone (a limestone block set in the wall of Blarney Castle near Cork) will become silver-tongued. Kissing the stone, a tradition that dates from the 18th century, is no easy feat, as it involves hanging precariously over a sheer drop. The legend has its origins in the story of Cormac MacDermot MacCarthy, lord of Blarney, who by making glib promises and hollow assurances for many years managed to talk his way out of transferring his allegiance to the English Crown. ***Blarney*** has also entered the language as a word for smooth-talking nonsense. "'And didn't we all know you kissed the blarney stone?' she whispered back" (Emma Richmond, *Love of My Heart*, 1993).

kiss the hem of his garment *See* HEM OF HIS GARMENT, TOUCH THE.

Kit Carson Archetype of a pioneer frontiersman. Christopher (or Kit) Carson (1809–68) had an adventurous life as a frontier guide, hunter, trapper, and explorer. He also participated in the conquest of California, served as agent of Indian affairs, and fought on the Confederate side in the U.S. Civil War. *What we need now is a Kit Carson to show us the way out of these woods.*

kitchen cabinet An informal group of advisers, who may well have more influence than their official counterparts. The expression was first used in the 19th century in reference to the advisers (including newspapermen and Treasury officials) who contributed to the decisions made by U.S. president Andrew Jackson, apart from his official staff. *According to inside sources, top-level policy decisions are being strongly influenced by the views of an unelected kitchen cabinet.*

Kitchener, Lord *See* YOUR COUNTRY NEEDS YOU.

kitchen-sink Denoting a genre of drama, art, movie-making, etc., that deals with the harsh realities of ordinary life among the working class. The term itself first appeared in a review written by David Sylvester in 1954 and was soon being applied across the cultural landscape. The kitchen-sink drama emerged as a major new force in British and U.S. cultural life in the mid-1950s with such plays as John Osborne's *Look Back in Anger* (1956) and Arnold Wesker's *The Kitchen* (1959). *We were fed up with the kitchen-sink dramas that every management in London was putting on. See also* ANGRY YOUNG MAN; ASHCAN SCHOOL.

Klondike (klondīk) A source of fabulous, easily attained wealth. The Klondike region of the Yukon, Canada, was the scene of a gold rush that began after George Cormack found gold in Bonanza Creek there on August 17, 1896. Thousands hurried to the Klondike to make their fortunes panning gold in the streams of the area; some succeeded, many did not. The Klondike has since remained synonymous with the achievement of overnight wealth. "The Klondike and Hollywood had much in common" (John Parker, *The Joker's Wild: Biography of Jack Nicholson*, 1991).

knight in shining armor A person who rescues someone from peril or other difficulty. The allusion is to medieval legends in which the rescuers were literally knights in shining armor, often depicted rushing to the aid of a DAMSEL IN DISTRESS. "She was convinced that if only she could find 'a knight in shining armour,' her life would be transformed" (Gill Edwards, *Living Magically*, 1991).

knights of the Round Table *See* ROUND TABLE.

knock and it shall be opened *See* SEEK AND YE SHALL FIND.

know-nothing A bigoted, anti-intellectual, reactionary, or xenophobic person. The allusion is to an anti-Catholic, anti-immigrant movment, nicknamed the "Know-Nothing" movement, that enjoyed a brief spell in the limelight in the United States in the 1850s, when concerted efforts were made to ensure that important public offices went only to native-born Americans. The nickname of this secret political organization referred to the usual reply given by its supporters to any query into the party's activities: "I know nothing." *The campaign lost support among the liberal intelligentsia after some of the candidates made a blatant appeal to the know-nothings who feared their jobs might go to recently arrived foreign immigrants.*

know not what they do, they Said of those who act without realizing the significance of their actions or the consequences that may follow. The phrase is a quotation from Christ on the Cross, when he requests divine forgiveness for those who have put him to death: "Father, forgive them; for they know not what they do" (Luke 23:34). "'Yes, Mrs. Reed, to you I owe some fearful pangs of mental suffering. But I ought to forgive you, for you knew not what you did . . .'" (Charlotte Brontë, *Jane Eyre,* 1847). *See also* FATHER, FORGIVE THEM.

know someone from Adam, not to To be entirely ignorant of someone's identity. The expression alludes to the biblical Adam (Genesis 2:19), who as the first man ever to live, should surely be familiar to everyone. *This grizzled old veteran claimed to know my grandfather, but Grandpa protested that he did not know him from Adam.*

know them by their fruits To make judgments about a person's character based on his or her behavior or actions. The phrase is biblical in origin, coming from Matthew 7:16–20, in which Christ warns against FALSE PROPHETS: "Ye shall know them by their fruits. Do men gather grapes of thorns, or figs of thistles? Even so every good tree bringeth forth good fruit; but a corrupt tree bringeth forth evil fruit . . . Wherefore by their fruits ye shall know them." *We'll see if his claims to be a reformed person are backed up by his actions. As the good book says, "You will know them by their fruits."*

Kojak (kōjak) A bald-headed person. The allusion is to the fictional New York police detective Theo Kojak, played by Telly Savalas (1924–94) in the U.S. television series *Kojak* (1973–77). His trademarks were his lollipops and his famously bald head. *He went in with a mop of dark curls and came out looking like Kojak.*

Kong, King *See* KING KONG.

K.P. Domestic duties. The allusion is to U.S. Army slang, in which "K.P." was an abbreviation for "kitchen police." *Richard explained that he could not come out with them as he had to stay at home to do some K.P.*

Krakatoa (krakătōă) A volcanic eruption or a similarly destructive explosion or outburst of some kind. The volcanic island of Krakatoa in Indonesia erupted with devastating power in 1883, resulting in the destruction of most of the island itself and widespread damage and loss of life. The island has since reformed as pressure builds up below for a future eruption. *The scandal erupted like Krakatoa, prompting many leading figures to run for cover.*

Kramer vs. Kramer (kraymăr) Archetype of a painful, legally protracted divorce. The allusion is to the 1979 movie *Kramer vs. Kramer*, which starred Dustin Hoffman and Meryl Streep as a divorcing couple fighting over the custody of their son. *They had hoped they could disentangle their lives without their divorce becoming Kramer vs. Kramer, but this proved impossible.*

K-ration A meal consisting of basic or emergency foodstuffs. The first K-rations were those provided to U.S. soldiers fighting in World War II. They were named after the U.S. physiologist Ancel B. Keys (1904–2004) who devised them. *We were on K-rations for ten days until supplies could be flown out to our base camp.*

Kristallnacht (kristalnakt) An outburst of mob violence against a particular section of society. The allusion is to the original Kristallnacht (German for "night of glass") that took place during the night of November 9–10, 1938. German Brownshirts led mobs against Jewish shops and houses in many German towns and cities, breaking windows as well as looting and then setting fire to the premises. Many Jews fled Germany in the wake of the outrages, which had led to the deaths of over 300 Jews and the destruction of hundreds of synagogues. Today the term is often used not so much with reference to the violence committed during the original Kristallnacht but in horror at the subsequent lack of protest by the rest of the world at the events that had taken place. *The authorities are worried that this might prove to be a Kristallnacht leading to much worse victimization of the Kurdish minority. See also* HOLOCAUST.

Kronos *See* CRONOS.

Krueger, Freddy *See* NIGHTMARE ON ELM STREET.

kryptonite (kriptonīt) Something that may have a powerfully negative effect on something else. The fictitious green-colored substance kryptonite, from the equally fictitious planet Krypton, is identified as the one thing that can deprive the comic-strip and movie hero SUPERMAN of his superhuman powers. In November 2006 it was announced that a chemical substance with a remarkably similar formula to that of the fictitious kryptonite (though white, not green in color) had been discovered in drill holes made in Serbia, leading to suggestions that the new substance be called kryptonite in Superman's honor (though it is properly identified as jadarite). *Magnolia paint is like kryptonite to most contemporary interior designers.*

Ku Klux Klan (koo kluks klan) A secret society based on racist bigotry. The Ku Klux Klan was formed by white supremacists in Tennessee in 1865 following the abolition of slavery at the end of the Civil War and its influence quickly spread throughout the Confederate southern states. Klan members disguised their identity with long white robes and hoods and terrorized their black neighbors, who were threatened, beaten up, and even lynched. Other victims included the Catholic and

Jewish populations of the southern states. The authorities have taken repeated steps to suppress the organization over the years and by the end of the 20th century it had been greatly reduced. The name of the organization was derived from the Greek word *kuklos* (meaning "circle"). *Being critical of government policy toward immigration does not automatically mean someone is a fully paid-up member of the Ku Klux Klan, at least not yet.*

Kulturkampf (kuultuurkamf) The battle for control of civilization, especially that waged between the state and the church. The word was originally applied to the political conflict in the 1870s between Chancellor Otto von Bismarck and the Roman Catholic establishment. "Even the Jesuits, who were called upon in 1573 to lead the Kulturkampf against the Protestant heresy, were forced to provide devotional literature and hymns in Slovene" (F. Singleton, *A Short History of the Yugoslav Peoples*, 1993).

Kurtz, Mr. *See* HEART OF DARKNESS; HORROR, THE HORROR!, THE.

L

la belle dame sans merci (la bel dam son mairsee) Archetype of an unattainable lover. The allusion is to the poem "La belle dame sans merci" (1820) by the British poet John Keats, in which a knight falls hopelessly in love with an unattainable fairy woman. Keats himself drew on an older tradition, notably a 1424 poem of the same title by the French poet Alain Chartier. *She was fated to remain his belle dame sans merci, ever out of his reach.*

la belle époque (la bel aypok) A period of easy living, elegance, and high culture, especially the period that began in Europe at the close of the Franco-Prussian War in 1871 and ended with the outbreak of World War I in 1914. The phrase is French for "the beautiful era." In modern usage, it often implies a glossy appearance masking less attractive realities beneath. *The 1950s were la belle époque for the club, when they were the equal of any team in the world.*

laborer is worthy of his hire, the A person who does work for others deserves to be paid. The proverb comes from Luke 10:7, which quotes Christ as saying, "And in the same house remain, eating and drinking such things as they give: for the labourer is worthy of his hire." (See also 1 Timothy 5:18.) Variants include the Roman proverb ***the dog must be bad indeed that is not worth a bone.*** "Your service will not be altogether gratuitous, my old friend—the labourer is worthy of his hire" (Sir Walter Scott, *St Ronan's Well,* 1824).

labor of love Work undertaken voluntarily, for the love of doing it, rather than for payment. The phrase is biblical in origin, appearing at 1 Thessalonians 1:3: "Remembering without ceasing your work of faith, and labour of love, and patience of hope in our Lord Jesus Christ, in the sight of God and our Father." "Her willing feet were never tired of taking steps for those who had smoothed her way; her skilful hands were always busy in some labour of love for them" (Louisa May Alcott, *Eight Cousins,* 1874).

labor of Sisyphus *See* SISYPHEAN.

labors of Hercules (herkyooleez) A series of daunting, almost impossibly demanding tasks. The allusion is to the 12 challenges that were imposed on the Greek hero HERCULES by his cousin King Eurystheus of Tiryns. In order, they were killing the terrible Nemean lion; vanquishing the many-headed serpent called the Hydra; capturing the formidable Erymanthean boar; taking possession of the Sacred Hind of Arcadia; destroying the Stymphalian birds; cleaning out the Augean stables;

capturing the human-eating mares of King Diomedes of Thrace; acquiring the girdle of Hippolyta, queen of the Amazons; capturing the Cretan bull; taking the oxen of Geryon; killing the dragon Ladon and bringing back the Golden Apples of the Hesperides; and, finally, taking the three-headed dog Cerberus from his station in Hades. Hercules successfully performed all of these tasks. *By the end of the week the team felt as if they had completed the labors of Hercules.*

labyrinth (labărinth, labrinth) A mazelike arrangement of paths, rooms, passages, concepts, etc., in which it is easy to get lost. In Greek mythology the original labyrinth was the system of tunnels and chambers constructed by Daedalus for King Minos of Crete to house the terrible Minotaur, described as half man and half bull. Each year, as punishment for the murder in Athens of Androgeos, the son of King Minos, the Athenians were obliged to give up 14 youths to be fed to the Minotaur as a sacrifice. This continued until THESEUS succeeded in killing the monster, armed with a sword given to him by the king's daughter, Ariadne, and with a ball of thread that he had unraveled in order to find his way out by retracing his steps. It has been suggested that the legend of the labyrinth of Crete may have been inspired by the complex ground plan of the huge royal palace at Knossos, built around 1700 B.C. and unearthed by Arthur John Evans, a British archaeologist, in A.D. 1900. By extension, anything that is considered complicated or convoluted may be described as ***labyrinthine.*** "Such an elaborately developed, perplexing, exciting dream was certainly never dreamed by a girl in Eustacia's situation before. It had as many ramifications as the Cretan labyrinth, as many fluctuations as the Northern Lights, as much colour as a parterre in June, and was as crowded with figures as a coronation" (Thomas Hardy, *The Return of the Native,* 1878).

Lachesis *See* FATES.

laconic (lăkonik) Terse; concise; pithy; using a minimum of words. The word alludes to Laconia, the Greek district of which Sparta was the capital in classical times. The inhabitants of Laconia pursued a spare, simple lifestyle and were renowned for their abruptness and terseness of speech, hence the modern meaning of the word. "Jude did not pause to remember that, in the laconic words of the historian, 'insulted Nature sometimes vindicated her rights' in such circumstances" (Thomas Hardy, *Jude the Obscure,* 1895).

la dolce vita (la dolchay veetă) The easy life; a life of pleasure and idleness. An Italian phrase meaning "the sweet life," it provided the title for the 1960 Federico Fellini movie *La Dolce Vita*, which depicted the decadent and meaningless lives of bored, wealthy Roman socialites. *I've been working so hard lately I need a holiday and a bit of la dolce vita.*

Ladon *See* LABORS OF HERCULES.

Lady Bountiful (bowntifăl) A generous, charitable woman, especially one who tends to the sick. Lady Bountiful was a memorable character in the stage comedy *The Beaux' Stratagem* (1707) by the Irish playwright George Farquhar (1678–1707). She is admired in the play for her care of the sick and is credited with curing large numbers of her patients. *After her retirement she earned a reputation as a Lady Bountiful, using her wealth to support a number of worthy local causes.*

Lady Bracknell (braknăl) Archetype of a stern, elderly female relative. Lady Bracknell is one of the characters in the comedy *The Importance of Being Earnest* (1895) by the Irish playwright Oscar Wilde (1854–1900). She is the epitome of Victorian respectability and reacts with predictable horror to the news that her daughter's suitor, Jack Worthing, was found as a baby in a handbag on a railway platform, having lost both his parents: "To lose one parent, Mr. Worthing, may be regarded as a misfortune . . . to lose both looks like carelessness." This famous line is often adapted for allusive use in a variety of circumstances. *As Lady Bracknell would have told you, losing your passport was simply unfortunate, but losing your birth certificate as well was sheer carelessness.*

Lady Chatterley (chaterlee) A woman, especially one with aristocratic connections, who engages in a passionate sexual affair. The novel *Lady Chatterley's Lover* (1928) by British novelist D. H. Lawrence (1885–1930) remained unpublished in its unexpurgated form in the United Kingdom and the United States until 1960, when it became the subject of a famous obscenity trial that was seen as a test throughout the literary world of the law on censorship. The acquittal of the publishers on charges of obscenity is now viewed as a major legal landmark. Lady Chatterley in Lawrence's novel is a repressed aristocratic married woman who finds sexual fulfilment with her gamekeeper, ***Oliver Mellors***. Lawrence is said to have based his character loosely upon Lady Cynthia Asquith (1887–1960). *He panicked when he realized he was locked in the bedroom with this slavering Lady Chatterley.*

Lady Godiva (gădīvă) A woman who goes about in the nude. According to medieval legend, Lady Godiva was the wife of Leofric, earl of Mercia (d. 1057). When her husband imposed new taxes on his tenants, Lady Godiva begged him to lift them, in return promising to ride naked through the town of Coventry. The earl agreed to her request and Lady Godiva performed her famous unclothed ride, her nakedness concealed only by her long golden hair. The people of Coventry were ordered to stay indoors so that she should not be embarrassed, and in gratitude all obeyed—with the single exception of a local tailor (*see* PEEPING TOM). "You're not suggesting I turn up like Lady Godiva?" (Kristy McCallum, *Driven by Love*, 1993).

Lady in Red *See* PUBLIC ENEMY NUMBER ONE.

Lady in the Lake *See* EXCALIBUR.

Lady Macbeth (măkbeth) A coldhearted, murderous woman, especially one who urges her husband to commit evil. The allusion is to the wife of the central character in William Shakespeare's tragedy *MACBETH* (1606), who urges her husband on when he hesitates to murder the Scottish king Duncan and claim the throne for himself. Later in the play, she is driven mad by guilt and is last seen sleepwalking, trying desperately to rid her hands of Duncan's imaginary blood. *In her steely ambition and lack of sympathy for weakness in others she was a veritable Lady Macbeth. See also* OUT, DAMNED SPOT!

Lady with the Lamp *See* FLORENCE NIGHTINGALE.

Laelaps (laylaps) Personification of speed. In Greek mythology Laelaps was the name of a hound that could outrun any quarry. *The hound leapt like Laelaps from the shadows, straight for the duke's unprotected throat.*

Laestrygonians (līstrigōneeănz) Cannibals. The Laestrygonians, or ***Lestrigons,*** were a legendary tribe of cannibal giants who, according to Homer, came into contact with ODYSSEUS and his companions when they landed in Sicily in the course of their long journey home. *Local rumor had it that the missing tourists must have fallen prey to a tribe of old-fashioned Laestrygonians high up in the mountains.*

Lais (layis) Archetype of a beautiful prostitute. Lais was born in Sicily in the fifth century B.C. and became one of the most famous of all Greek courtesans after being carried off to Corinth after an Athenian raid. Admired by Demosthenes, Xenocrates, and Diogenes, she moved to Thessally and eventually met her end at the hands of a mob of jealous women, who pricked her to death with their bodkins. *This Lais of the Waterfront was a familiar sight among the dockyard bars, but no one had an unkind word to say about her.*

laissez-faire (lesayfair) The principle of leaving others to act free of outside interference. The term, literally meaning "let do" in French, is commonly associated with the Scottish economist Adam Smith (1723–90), who used it in his book *The Wealth of Nations* (1776) when advocating that governments should restrain themselves from interfering too directly in economic matters. The slogan may date to the reign of the French king Louis XV (1715–74) and was later adopted by French politicians of the 18th century who argued strongly against the imposition of customs duties. It has since been applied in many noneconomic spheres. "Beneath this irascible veneer was a man of cultivation and taste, whose priorities contrasted sharply with his son's laissez-faire approach to life and amiable enjoyment of the traditional outdoor pursuits of an English country gentleman" (Andrew Morton, *Diana: Her True Story*, 1993).

lake of fire and brimstone *See* FIRE AND BRIMSTONE.

Lamb of God Jesus Christ as a symbol of meekness and the perfect sacrifice for sin. The epithet is applied to Christ in John 1:29: "The next day John seeth Jesus coming unto him, and saith, Behold the Lamb of God, which taketh away the sin of the world." *In his daily existence and dealings with others he strove manfully, but with little success, to imitate the example set by the Lamb of God.*

lamb to the slaughter A defenseless victim; someone who is apparently too naive or powerless to defend his or her interests, especially one who ventures into danger without complaining or protesting. The expression is biblical in origin, appearing in Isaiah 53:7 as "He was oppressed, and he was afflicted, yet he opened not his mouth: he is brought as a lamb to the slaughter, and as a sheep before her shearers is dumb, so he openeth not his mouth," and in similar form in Acts 8:32. In Isaiah the lamb is understood to be the suffering servant, identified in Acts as Jesus Christ. "Brother, brother: let them rage and kill: let us be brave and suffer. You must go: as a lamb to the slaughter" (George Bernard Shaw, *Androcles and the Lion,* 1912).

lame, the halt, the blind, the *See* MAIMED, THE HALT, AND THE BLIND, THE.

lamia (laymeeă) A female demon; a witch. According to Greek mythology, the Lamia was a hideous monster with the head and breasts of a woman and the body of a serpent. Originally a queen of Libya and a lover of Jupiter, she was transformed into a child-eating monster after her children were abducted by the jealous Juno. "Lamia is a serpent transformed by magic into a woman. The idea of both is mythological, and not in any sense physiological. Some women unquestionably suggest the image of serpents; men rarely or never" (Oliver Wendell Holmes, *Elsie Venner,* 1859–60).

lamp of Phoebus (feebăs) The Sun. *The lamp of Phoebus had risen high in the sky, and there was barely a shadow in sight. See also* PHOEBUS.

Lancelot, Sir *See* KING ARTHUR.

land flowing with milk and honey A real or imaginary place where life is easy and all good things are readily available. The phrase appears in the Bible in a description of the PROMISED LAND to which the Israelites aspired: "I am come down to deliver them out of the hand of the Egyptians, and to bring them up out of that land unto a good land and a large, unto a land flowing with milk and honey; unto the place of Canaanites, and the Hittites, and the Amorites, and the Perizzites, and the Hivites, and the Jebusites" (Exodus 3:8). *Refugees continue to pour into the country, expecting to find it a land flowing with milk and honey.*

land of Beulah (byoolă) A land of ease and plenty; the PROMISED LAND. In its original biblical context (Isaiah 62:4) Beulah, meaning "married," stands in contrast to "Desolate." In John Bunyan's *PILGRIM'S PROGRESS* (1678, 1684) it is depicted as a pleasant land where pilgrims pass their time until summoned to the CELESTIAL CITY. *The preacher depicted California, with its orchards and vineyards, as a new land of Beulah, where all would live a life of contentment and harmony.*

Land of Cockaigne (kokayn) A fool's paradise; a state of illusory happiness. The Land of Cockaigne (or Cockayne) featured in medieval legend as an imaginary land where everything a person could desire was in plentiful supply. According to a 13th-century French poem of the same title, it was a place where "the houses were made of barley sugar cakes, the streets were paved with pastry, and the shops supplied goods for nothing." The name came via French ultimately from the Middle Low German *kokenje*, meaning "little cake." *His return to reality from the Land of Cockaigne was sudden and painful.*

land of giants *See* GIANTS IN THE EARTH.

land of Goshen (gōshăn) A place where inhabitants can enjoy conditions of peace and plenty. The original land of Goshen was the fertile territory in which the Israelites were allowed to settle in Egypt during their captivity (Genesis 47:6). While the rest of the country was ravaged by the plagues of Egypt, the land of Goshen remained unharmed (Exodus 8:22 and 9:26). *They were reluctant to leave the peaceful valleys where they had spent so many years in peace and safety, like the Israelites in the land of Goshen.*

land of Nod The realm of sleep or sleep itself. The land of Nod is identified in Genesis 4:16 as an area EAST OF EDEN to which Cain was exiled after murdering his brother Abel: "And Cain went out from the presence of the LORD, and dwelt in the land of Nod, on the east of Eden." In its original context Nod denoted "wandering" rather than "sleep." The term became a popular name for sleep after Jonathan Swift used it for such in *A Complete Collection of Genteel and Ingenious Conversation* (1731). It has been suggested that Nod has its origins in the nodding of the head when a person is drowsy. "At last I slid off into a light doze, and had pretty nearly made a good offing towards the land of Nod, when I heard a heavy footfall in the passage, and saw a glimmer of light come into the room from under the door" (Herman Melville, *Moby-Dick,* 1851).

land of promise *See* PROMISED LAND.

land of the living The realm of the living; alive. The expression appears several times in the Bible, for example in Isaiah 53:8: "He was taken from prison and from judgment: and who shall declare his generation? for he was cut off out of the land of the living: for the transgression of my people was he stricken." "He had spoken of it as yet to no one, and he thought that he was resolved not to do so while Sir Louis should yet be in the land of the living" (Anthony Trollope, *Doctor Thorne,* 1858).

Lane, Lois *See* SUPERMAN.

Laocoön (layahkăwahn) Archetype of a prophet who suffers for telling the truth. In Greek legend Laocoön was a priest of Apollo who warned his fellow Trojans against bringing the TROJAN HORSE within the walls of Troy. As he prepared to sacrifice a bull to Poseidon, he and his two sons were set upon and killed by two sea serpents (an event memorably depicted by a huge statue by an unknown sculptor of classical times found in Rome in 1506 and today known simply as *The Laocoön*). "'I don't know what to do,' cried Scrooge, laughing and crying in the same breath; and making a perfect Laocoon of himself with his stockings. 'I am as light as a feather, I am as happy as an angel, I am as merry as a schoolboy'" (Charles Dickens, *A Christmas Carol,* 1843).

Laodamia (layōdaymeeă) Archetype of a loving, devoted wife. According to Greek legend Laodamia was the wife of King Protesilaus of Thessaly, who despite knowing from the oracle at Delphi that the first of the Greeks to set foot on the Trojan shore was doomed to death, became the first of the invading Greeks to land at the start of the Trojan War. Protesilaus was duly slain by Hector. The grieving Laodamia begged the gods to grant her an audience with her dead husband. The gods allowed Protesilaus to return to the mortal world for three hours, and when the time was up, Laodamia voluntarily accompanied him to Hades. The episode subsequently furnished the English poet William Wordsworth with the material for his celebrated poem "Laodamia" (1815). *Like Laodamia, she refused to leave her husband's side, even accompanying him to the guillotine.*

Laodicean (layōdiseeăn) Lukewarm; timid; indecisive, especially with regard to religious matters. The allusion is to the early Christian inhabitants of "lukewarm" Laodicea, who are described as half hearted in their attitude toward religion in Revelation 3:15–16: "I know thy works, that thou art neither cold not hot; I would thou wert cold or hot. So then because thou art lukewarm, and neither cold not hot; I will spue thee out of my mouth." "He felt himself to occupy morally that vast middle space of Laodicean neutrality which lay between the Communion people of the parish and the drunken section" (Thomas Hardy, *Far from the Madding Crowd,* 1874).

Laputa (lapootă) A society of intellectuals who are completely incompetent in practical matters. The flying island of Laputa and its population of absent-minded scientists was an invention of the Irish satirist Jonathan Swift (1667–1745) in his book *Gulliver's Travels* (1726). Because of the impracticality of its inhabitants, the island has a ruined economy and its people live in conditions of poverty and hunger. *The household was full of professors and theoreticians, but like Swift's Laputa it was the last place a sensible person would go to for practical advice.* See also BROBDINGNAGIAN; GULLIVER; LILLIPUTIAN; YAHOO.

lares and penates (lahreez, penayteez) Home or cherished domestic or personal possessions that are essential to a home. In ancient Roman society the Lares and Penates ***(dii penates)*** were the household gods who influenced domestic matters (although they were originally spirits who presided over crossroads). The *lar familiaris* was the protective spirit of the founder of the house. The Penates guarded the inner spaces and storerooms. Each family had its own guardian spirits, which were venerated at special shrines in the home that went with the family when it moved. The phrase in time came to represent domestic matters in general and ultimately cherished personal belongings or household effects. "He said a man was not to be dictated to. I said a man was. He said a man was not to be insulted, then. I said he was right there—never under my roof, where the Lares were sacred, and the laws of hospitality paramount" (Charles Dickens, *David Copperfield,* 1849–50).

Larry, as happy as See AS HAPPY AS LARRY.

lash of scorpions See SCOURGE OF SCORPIONS.

last Adam See ADAM.

last gasp, at the At the point of death; at the very last moment. The phrase appears in the apocryphal book of 2 Maccabees 7:9. "None of them at all except such Roman Catholics as should have the luck to have a priest handy to sandpaper their souls at the last gasp, and here and there a presbyterian. No others savable. All the others damned" (Mark Twain, *Letters from the Earth,* 1909).

Last Judgment See JUDGMENT DAY.

last of the Mohicans (mōheekănz) The last of a particular race or other group of people. The phrase is best known as the title of the novel *The Last of the Mohicans* (1826) by the U.S. writer James Fenimore Cooper (1789–1851), in which the last of the Mohican tribe is identified as ***Chingachgook***, who lives to see his only son and heir, ***Uncas***, killed in the war being waged for control of Canada between Britain and France and their various Native American allies. In reality, it seems that Fenimore Cooper's Mohicans actually combined elements of the historical Mohican (or Mahican) tribe, originally from the Hudson Valley area and still in existence in Wisconsin, and the Mohegan tribe of New England. *To hear him talk about the importance of carrying on the family line you would think he was the last of the Mohicans.*

last shall be first and the first last, the See FIRST SHALL BE LAST, THE.

Last Supper A last meal eaten before facing an ordeal of some kind or the unfolding of some event. The allusion is to the meal taken by Christ and his disciples the night before his Crucifixion and during which he instituted the ***Eucharist.*** The occasion, also referred to as the ***Lord's Supper,*** is described in the Bible in Matthew 26:26–28; Mark 14:22–25; Luke 22:17–20; and 1 Corinthians 11:23–26. "It was over a chicken vindaloo supper prepared by Ffion in their Yorkshire home that

Mr. Hague came to the grim realisation that it was all over. . . . Only two friends, who shared their 'last supper,' had been informed in advance" (*Times*, June 9, 2001).

Last Trump The end of the world; JUDGMENT DAY. The signal for the end of the world will be a blast on Gabriel's trumpet, when the dead will rise for judgment: "We shall not all sleep, but we shall all be changed, in a moment, in the twinkling of an eye, at the last trump" (1 Corinthians 15:51–52). " 'How like a first night at the Opera!' he thought, recognising all the same faces in the same boxes (no, pews), and wondering if, when the Last Trump sounded, Mrs. Selfridge Merry would be there with the same towering ostrich feathers in her bonnet, and Mrs. Beaufort with the same diamond earrings and the same smile" (Edith Wharton, *The Age of Innocence,* 1920).

Las Vegas (vaygăs) A place offering brash entertainment, especially gambling. Las Vegas in the Mojave Desert of Nevada was a fairly insignificant Mormon town until the legalization of gambling throughout Nevada in 1931 and, with the opening of the Flamingo in 1946, the arrival of the first luxury casino. It subsequently developed into the biggest city in the state, with huge hotels, neon-lit casinos, nightclubs and other attractions. In the process its name has also become a byword for glitzy vulgarity. Las Vegas means "the meadows" in Spanish. *The town has ambitions to become the Las Vegas of the south coast.*

Laurel and Hardy (lorăl) An incompetent duo. British comedian Stan Laurel (1891–1965) and U.S. comedian Oliver Hardy (1892–1957) were among the most popular comedy stars of the early silent cinema, appearing in numerous short and full-length movies in the 1920s and 1930s. Their brand of slapstick humor continues to delight audiences several decades after their deaths, and such catchphrases as ***this is another fine mess you've got me into*** remain well known. "Our suave heroes were transformed into Laurel and Hardy: suburban life speeded up into some manic, coronary inducing rush hour" Ian Breakwell and Paul Hammond, (eds., *Seeing in the Dark*, 1990). *See also* ABBOTT AND COSTELLO.

laurels (lorălz) Honor; distinction; fame. The ancient Greeks crowned the champion at the Pythian Games with a wreath of laurels, the evergreen laurel having long held sacred status. Subsequently many athletic champions as well as prominent poets and military leaders of the ancient world were honored with laurel crowns, and since medieval times winners of certain accolades and high offices have been termed ***laureates.*** By extension to ***rest on one's laurels*** means to rely on past successes rather than trying to achieve new ones and to ***look to one's laurels*** means to need to make a new effort to maintain one's lead over others. " 'I never heard your Grace / So much in the vein for preaching; let the Cardinal / Look to his laurels, sir' " (Oscar Wilde, *The Duchess of Padua,* 1891).

law is an ass, the The law is not always based on what is sensible or realistic. This is usually identified as a quotation from the novel *OLIVER TWIST* (1837–38) by the British novelist Charles Dickens (1812–70), specifically the reaction of Mr. Bumble to the news that the law presumes his wife to act under his direction: "If the law supposes that . . . the law is a ass–a idiot." The phrase is actually much older, appearing in other works as early as the 17th century. *Having lost his driver's license for* *what he regarded as a trivial offense, the earl's son was convinced that the law is an ass, and did not hesitate to tell everyone so.*

law of the jungle *See* SURVIVAL OF THE FITTEST.

law of the Medes and Persians (meedz, perzhuns) A rule or practice that is followed with great strictness or rigidity and is to all appearances unalterable. The phrase appears in a passage in Daniel 6:8, in which a group of advisers suggests that King Darius issue a decree under the terms of which any person praying to anyone other than the king should be thrown into the lions' den: "Now, O King, establish the decree, and sign the writing, that it be not changed, according to the law of the Medes and Persians, which altereth not."The laws of the Medes and Persians had been merged since 550 B.C. when the Persian king Cyrus the Great gained control of Media. "'I am laying down good intentions, which I believe durable as flint. . . . and at this moment I pass a law, unalterable as that of the Medes and Persians'" (Charlotte Brontë, *Jane Eyre,* 1847).

Lawrence of Arabia (lorăns, ăraybeeă) A person who demonstrates expertise in some way with life in the desert. The title was originally bestowed upon the British soldier and writer T. E. Lawrence (1888–1935), an unconventional adventurer who led Arab forces against the Turks in the Arabian region during World War I with considerable success. A complex and private man, he shunned publicity after the war and enlisted under a different name in the RAF before dying in a motorbike accident. The story of his war years was spectacularly retold in the 1962 movie *Lawrence of Arabia*, starring Peter O'Toole as the enigmatic Lawrence. *He had himself photographed on a camel in full Arab dress, looking like Lawrence of Arabia.*

Lawrencian (lorenseeăn) Reminiscent of the style, subjects, or characters of the writings of the British novelist D. H. Lawrence (1885–1930). Though he took up a variety of themes in his novels, including class tensions and the effects of industrialization, Lawrence earned a somewhat notorious reputation for his treatment of such earthy themes as adultery and sexuality, and the term Lawrencian is sometimes applied to men who exude elemental, sexual passion. *Her husband was a Lawrencian brute with few manners.*

law unto oneself, a Disregarding the wishes and conventions of others in favor of what one wants or believes. The phrase is biblical in origin, appearing in Romans 2:14: "For when the Gentiles, which have not the law, do by nature the things contained in the law, these, having not the law, are a law unto themselves." In the original context the meaning is that the moral nature of the Gentiles serves in place of the law of Moses to show God's demands. In this sense, the Gentiles are "a law unto themselves." "The wind, which had hauled round, rose at sundown and blew steadily. There was not enough sea, though, to disturb even a dory's tackle, but the Carrie Pitman was a law unto herself" (Rudyard Kipling, *Captains Courageous,* 1897).

lay hands on the ark *See* ARK OF THE COVENANT.

lay not up treasures upon earth It is futile devoting one's life to the hoarding of worldly riches. The sentiment is voiced by Christ in his Sermon on the Mount, as recounted in Matthew 6:19–20:

"Lay not up for yourselves treasures upon earth, where moth and rust doth corrupt, and where thieves break through and steal: But lay up for yourselves treasures in heaven, where neither moth nor rust doth corrupt, and where thieves do not break through nor steal." *Walking through the huge house cluttered with paintings and valuable furniture while its owner lay dead in his bed reminded her forcibly of the old adage lay not up treasures upon earth.*

lazaretto lazăretō A hospital where people with contagious diseases, especially leprosy, may be treated in quarantine. The term *lazaretto,* or ***lazaret,*** was arrived at through the combination of the names of the beggar Lazarus (see DIVES) and Nazaret (from Santa Maria di Nazaret), the name of a church in Venice that housed a hospital. Lepers have oftentimes been referred to as ***lazars*** in Lazarus's memory. "The Lieutenant-Governor had arranged that he should not be driven to the ordinary lazaretto, but to Fort Mannel, where apartments were ready for him and his party" (J. G. Lockhart, *The Life of Sir Walter Scott,* 1839).

Lazarus (lazărăs, lazrăs) A person who unexpectedly emerges revived after dying or renewed after apparently ceasing to have anything further to offer. The allusion is to the ***raising of Lazarus*** as described in the New Testament in John 11:1–44. Lazarus was raised from the dead by Christ upon the entreaties of his sisters Mary and Martha. Christ recited the words "I am the resurrection, and the life: he that believeth in me, though he were dead, yet shall he live, and whosoever liveth and believeth in me shall never die" (John 11:25–26), and when the stone that sealed the tomb of Lazarus was rolled away, the dead man rose and emerged at Christ's command. ". . . the former chancellor used his Lazarus-like return from a four-year exile on the back benches to appeal for tolerance and a search for the centre ground" (*Guardian,* July 18, 2001). *See also* DIVES; LAZARETTO.

lead on, Macduff (măkduf) Lead the way. This is based on a quotation from William Shakespeare's tragedy *Macbeth* (1606), although the line does not appear as such in the play itself but as: "Lay on, Macduff; / And damn'd be he that first cries, 'Hold enough!' " In fact, in its original form, the phrase was not an invitation to Macduff (Macbeth's enemy) to lead the way, but to open the fight. *"Lead on, Macduff," said the archbishop with a broad grin, stepping aside so that his aide could get through the door.*

lead us not into temptation A plea not to be tempted into doing something one should not. The phrase is a quotation from the Lord's Prayer, as given in Matthew 6:13. In modern usage it is usually voiced whenever a person is faced with some tempting, mildly illicit opportunity. " 'Lead us not into temptation but deliver us from evil.' But what is temptation? What is evil? Is this evil—is this temptation?" (Anthony Trollope, *Barchester Towers,* 1857).

lean and hungry look An appearance that suggests a willingness to fight or to act in one's own interest. The phrase comes from William Shakespeare's play *Julius Caesar* (1599), in which Caesar delivers the following speech to Antony: "Let me have men about me that are fat; / Sleek-headed men, and such as sleep o'nights. / Yond Cassius has a lean and hungry look; / He thinks too much. Such men are dangerous." *His son had a lean and hungry look that suggested he was not to be trusted.*

Leander *See* HERO AND LEANDER.

lean years *See* FAT YEARS AND LEAN YEARS.

Lear *See* KING LEAR.

leaven the lump To redeem something much larger by introducing a smaller element of good. The metaphor, which alludes to the small amount of yeast (leaven) that is required for a whole lump of dough to be raised for baking, comes from 1 Corinthians 5:6: "Your glorying is not good. Know ye not that a little leaven leaveneth the whole lump?" "Except for literary men and painters, present in small quantities to leaven the lump, Becket was, in fact, a rallying point for the advanced spirits of Land Reform" (John Galsworthy, *The Forsyte Saga,* 1922).

lebensraum (laybănzrowm) Room to grow or pursue one's aims. The need for *lebensraum* (German for "living space") to provide homes for the expanding population of Germany was the argument used by the Nazis to justify their territorial ambitions in the 1930s. The term was originally coined by German geographer and ethnologist Friedrich Ratzel (1844–1904) to describe the concept of relating human societies to their geographical locations. "The back door of the kitchen led out onto a slate-paved path at the foot of three steep terraces giving much lebensraum to many varieties of voracious weeds and scrubby elder bushes" (Jane Spottiswoode, *Undertaken with Love*, 1991).

Lecter, Hannibal *See* HANNIBAL LECTER.

Leda (leedă) The 13th satellite of Jupiter, discovered in 1979. In Greek mythology Leda was the daughter of Thestius and the wife of Tyndareus, king of Sparta. She attracted the amorous attentions of Zeus, who seduced her in the form of a swan while she was bathing. As a consequence of this she laid eggs from which hatched HELEN OF TROY and the twins CASTOR AND POLLUX. *She took the goose everywhere with her, looking for all the world like Leda and the swan.*

left hand know what your right hand is doing, do not let your Do not make an ostentatious show of your good deeds. The expression comes from Matthew 6:3–4, in which Christ in his Sermon on the Mount advises that those who give alms should keep it as much as possible a secret, even, as it were, from themselves: "But when thou doest alms, let not thy left hand know what thy right hand doeth: That thine alms may be in secret: and thy Father which seeth in secret himself shall reward thee openly." In modern usage the phrase is more often a symbol of a failure in communication between two parts of the same organization. *This confusion seems to illustrate that as far as this administration is concerned, the left hand does not know what the right hand is doing.*

legion, my name is *See* MY NAME IS LEGION.

Legree, Simon *See* UNCLE TOM.

Lemnian actions (lemneeăn) Barbaric or inhuman behavior. The phrase alludes to Roman legend, specifically to the island of Lemnos, which was the scene of two infamous massacres. In the first of these the men of Lemnos killed the children of the Athenian women they had abducted. In the second massacre the men were slain by their outraged wives. Fortunately, the troubled and severely depopulated island was then visited by the Argonauts, whose couplings with the women of Lemnos resulted in a compensatory boost in the birthrate. *Such Lemnian actions are increasingly leading to the perpetrators making appearances before international courts of justice.*

Lenten (lentăn) Frugal; meager, especially in relation to food. The adjective comes from Lent, the period of fasting between Ash Wednesday and Easter in the Christian calendar. The tradition of Lent is itself a commemoration of the 40 days and 40 nights spent by Christ in the wilderness, as described in Matthew 4:1–2. "But none can say / That Lenten fare makes Lenten thought" (Alfred Tennyson, *Tiresias,* 1885).

Leonardo da Vinci (leeănahdō dă vinchee) A genius whose skills extend across science and the arts. The Tuscan-born Leonardo da Vinci (1452–1519) was preeminent among the artists and thinkers of the RENAISSANCE, famed as the creator of artistic masterpieces such as the *Mona Lisa* as well as for his many scientific and technological ideas, which included numerous inventions that were hundreds of years before their time. *In the modern era of specialization it is unlikely we will ever encounter another Leonardo da Vinci. See also* MONA LISA SMILE.

Leonidas *See* THERMOPYLAE.

leopard cannot change its spots, a It is impossible for a person to change his or her essential character or nature. The proverb comes from the Bible, appearing in Jeremiah 13:23: "Can the Ethiopian change his skin, or the leopard his spots? then may ye also do good, that are accustomed to do evil." *His parents hoped he would mend his ways once he went to college, but a leopard cannot change its spots.*

Leopold and Loeb (leeăpōld, lōb) Archetype of murderers who kill for sadistic amusement. In 1924 Nathan Leopold (aged 19) and Richard Loeb (aged 18), both highly gifted college students from wealthy Chicago families, kidnapped and murdered 14-year-old Bobby Franks purely for their own entertainment. Their subsequent trial resulted in both being found guilty of murder but insane: they were sentenced to life imprisonment, with 99 years added on for kidnapping. *The way the pair cooperated in their killing spree reminded experts strongly of the Leopold and Loeb affair.*

lesbian (lesbeeăn) A female homosexual. The word (a late-19th-century coinage) has its origins ultimately in the island of Lesbos in the eastern Aegean, where the Greek poetess Sappho (fl. 580 B.C.) was born. Sappho's passionate verse celebrated love between women, hence lesbian, or ***sapphic,*** came to describe such relationships. Sappho was married to a wealthy man named Cercolas and according to one legend threw herself into the sea in despair over her unrequited love for the boatman Phaon. The belief that she was herself a lesbian is speculative, although the tone of her poetry does suggest at least an ardent attachment to her female friends. *All her friends knew she was a lesbian, but her parents had never suspected a thing.*

les-Deux-Églises (laydăzaygleez) A place to which a person who is out of favor retreats to await a revival in his or her fortunes. French president Charles de Gaulle (1890–1970) retired to his home at Colombey-les-Deux-Églises on two occasions during his career when out of office: on the first occasion he was duly begged to come back. *The governor has gone back to Miami-les-Deux-Églises to sulk until he is summoned back to Washington.*

less is more Simplicity is preferable to complexity. This well-known slogan, commonly applied in all manner of contexts, is generally attributed to the German-born U.S. modernist architect Ludwig Mies van der Rohe (1886–1969), whose work exemplified this notion. In fact, the sentiment had been expressed in this way long before, by the British poet Robert Browning (1812–89) in *Andrea del Sarto* (1855): "Yet do much less, so much less, Someone says, / (I know his name, no matter)—so much less! / Well, less is more, Lucrezia: I am judged." *I was going to add more detail to the design, but remembered just in time that less is more.*

Lestrigons *See* LAESTRYGONIANS.

l'état c'est moi (layta say mwa) The state is vested in me. This French phrase, meaning "I am the state," is associated primarily with the French king Louis XIV (1638–1715), who at the age of just 17 thus responded to parliament's objections to his demands for funds, on the grounds that they were contrary to the interests of the state. Since Louis, the phrase has not been confined to discussions of absolute monarchy. *The secretary of state appears to believe l'état c'est moi.*

lethe (leethee) Forgetfulness; oblivion; death. In Greek mythology Lethe was the name of one of the rivers over which the dead crossed on their way to HADES. When they drank from its waters they immediately forgot all their deeds and actions in the mortal world. "Minds that have been unhinged from their old faith and love, have perhaps sought this Lethean influence of exile, in which the past becomes dreamy because its symbols have all vanished, and the present too is dreamy because it is linked with no memories" (George Eliot, *Silas Marner,* 1861).

let him who is without sin cast the first stone People should not criticize or punish others when they may be equally guilty of wrongdoing themselves. The proverb is of biblical origin, appearing in John 8:7, in which Christ admonishes the mob threatening to stone the woman taken in adultery: "He that is without sin among you, let him first cast a stone at her." "Thou knowest who said, 'Let him who is without sin among you cast the first stone at her!' There have been plenty to do that. Thou art not the man to cast the last stone, Stephen, when she is brought so low" (Charles Dickens, *Hard Times,* 1854). *See also* GO AND SIN NO MORE.

let my people go A plea for mercy, especially to one who imposes his or her will on others. The expression comes from the Bible, appearing in Exodus, when Moses and Aaron ask Pharaoh to release the Israelites from their captivity: "And afterward Moses and Aaron went in, and told Pharaoh, Thus saith the LORD God of Israel, Let my people go" (Exodus 5:1). In modern usage the phrase is sometimes used ironically. *When it became clear how late they would have to work, the foreman flung his arms up in mock horror with a cry of "Let my people go!"*

let not your left hand know *See* LEFT HAND KNOW WHAT YOUR RIGHT HAND IS DOING, DO NOT LET YOUR.

letter killeth, the *See* LETTER OF THE LAW, THE.

letter of Bellerophon (bălerăfăn, bălerăfon) A letter or other message that poses a threat to the person who delivers it. The allusion is to the Greek legend of Bellerophon, who was seduced by Proteus's wife, Antaea. Antaea then told her husband that she had been raped by Bellerophon. Proteus asked Bellerophon to carry a letter to his wife's father, Iobates, king of Lycia, in which (unbeknownst to Bellerophon) he repeated Antaea's accusation and requested that Bellerophon be put to death. Iobates was fond of Bellerophon and declined to kill him himself, instead dispatching him on a series of hazardous missions. When Bellerophon succeeded in all these tasks, Iobates relented and made him his heir. *The secretary carried the message to the head of the department, little realizing that it was a letter of Bellerophon and she was taking him instructions for her own dismissal.*

letter of the law, the Rigid adherence to the rules, especially when seen as negating the spirit behind them. The expression alludes to 2 Corinthians 3:5–6, in which Paul writes, "Not that we are sufficient of ourselves to think any thing as of ourselves; but our sufficiency is of God; Who also hath made us able ministers of the new testament; not of the letter, but of the spirit: for the letter killeth, but the spirit giveth life." "'I was going to explain that although I am aware you have infringed the letter of the law, and made yourself liable to proceedings which may, perhaps, be unpleasant—' 'I ain't liable to anything unpleasant at all, Mr. Emilius'" (Anthony Trollope, *The Eustace Diamonds,* 1873).

letter of Uriah (yoorīă) A treacherous letter, especially one in which the writer feigns friendship. The reference is to 2 Samuel 11:15, which relates how DAVID gave his lover Bathsheba's husband, Uriah, secret orders to carry to Joab. These orders instructed Joab to leave Uriah in the thick of the fighting so that he would be killed, leaving David free to pursue his relationship with Bathsheba and eventually marry her. *He delivered the message himself, unaware that, like the letter of Uriah, it contained instructions for his own downfall.*

let the day perish *See* CURSE THE DAY I WAS BORN.

let the dead bury the dead Do not grieve over people who are dead or things that are past but concentrate on the present. The expression is biblical in origin, appearing in Matthew 8:21–22: "And another of his disciples said unto him, Lord, suffer me first to go and bury my father. But Jesus said unto him, Follow me; and let the dead bury their dead." "March 21, night. Free. Soul free and fancy free. Let the dead bury the dead. Ay. And let the dead marry the dead" (James Joyce, *Portrait of the Artist as a Young Man,* 1914–15).

let them eat cake Let the poor look after themselves. This cynical expression is usually attributed to MARIE ANTOINETTE, wife of the French king Louis XVI, and is reputed to show her lack of understanding or sympathy when told that the poor had no bread to eat. Though she was undoubtedly extravagant well beyond the point of folly, Marie Antoinette never actually said these words, however. The true origin of the phrase is to be found in the *Confessions* (1767) of Jean-Jacques Rousseau (1712–78), where he writes about a princess who made this remark in similar circumstances. *As for the shareholders who will lose out because of this, it seems the directors have decided to let them eat cake.*

let there be light An exclamation upon a sudden revelation, a moment of comprehension, or any act shedding light upon a scene or matter. The phrase is a quotation from Genesis 1:3: "God said,

Let there be light: and there was light." "Does like join itself to like; does the spirit of method stir in that confusion, so that its embroilment becomes order? Can the man say, Fiat lux, Let there be light; and out of chaos make a world?" (Thomas Carlyle, *On Heroes and Hero Worship and the Heroic in History,* 1841).

let thou thy servant depart in peace *See* NUNC DIMITTIS.

let us now praise famous men Let us give praise where it is due. The expression comes from the apocryphal book of Ecclesiasticus (Sirach) 44:1 and is often used in memorial services. *The two professors have always been very modest about their achievements, but with the presentation of this award the time has come for us to praise famous men.*

let us reason together *See* SINS BE AS SCARLET.

leviathan (lăvīăthăn) A vast or immensely powerful force or thing, especially a massive organization, state bureaucracy, etc. The name comes from that of a monstrous beast mentioned at several points in the Bible, for example, "Canst thou draw out Leviathan with a hook?" (Job 41:1). Other examples are Psalm 74:14, Psalm 104:26, and Isaiah 27:1. The legend of Leviathan has its origins in a much older myth in which God overcomes a terrible sea monster (possibly inspired by a crocodile, whale, or python) representing chaos. "The fog seemed to break away as though split by a wedge, and the bow of a steamboat emerged, trailing fog-wreaths on either side like seaweed on the snout of Leviathan" (Jack London, *The Sea Wolf,* 1904). *See also* BEHEMOTH.

Lex Luthor *See* SUPERMAN.

Liar, Billy *See* BILLY LIAR.

Lidice (lideechay) A community that is ruthlessly destroyed in an act of revenge. The mining village of Lidice in the former Czechoslovakia was demolished by the Nazis on June 10, 1942, in retaliation for the assassination of Reinhard Heydrich, the Reich Protector of Bohemia and Moravia, by the Czech resistance: All the inhabitants were either shot or transported to the concentration camps. A new village was established on a site nearby in 1947, and the site of the original settlement became a memorial garden. *The destruction of Muslim communities in the former Yugoslavia evoked chilling memories of Lidice.*

life begins at forty After the age of 40 people have more opportunities for leisure and time to take up new projects, as their children are now more or less grown up. This questionable theory was proposed by U.S. writer Walter B. Pitkin (1878–1953) in a 1932 book with the same title. *On her birthday she tried to cheer herself up by reminding herself that "life begins at 40." See also* DANGEROUS AGE, A.

life in the fast lane *See* FAST LANE.

life of Riley (rīlee) A life of indulgence and luxury. There was a U.S. television comedy series starring Jackie Gleason called *The Life of Riley* (1949–50); otherwise, the phrase is probably connected with an 1882 vaudeville song that referred to a Mr. Reilly. "I've been leading the life of Riley since I got away from the place" (Rachel Elliot, *Lover's Charade*, 1992).

lift the veil of Isis (īsis) To go to the heart of a great mystery. The allusion is to the inscription on a statue of Isis, the principal goddess of ancient

Egypt, which read: "I am that which is, has been, and shall be. My veil no one has lifted. The fruit I bore was the Sun." *With this scientific breakthrough scientists in this field are just beginning to lift the veil of Isis as regards the cloning of humans.*

light of the world Jesus Christ. This appellation appears in John 8:12: "Then spake Jesus again unto them, saying, I am the light of the world: he that followeth me shall not walk in darkness, but shall have the light of life." *There are several celebrated paintings of Christ as the light of the world.*

light under a bushel *See* HIDE ONE'S LIGHT UNDER A BUSHEL.

like a lamb to the slaughter *See* LAMB TO THE SLAUGHTER.

like a thief in the night *See* THIEF IN THE NIGHT, LIKE A.

like a vestal virgin *See* VESTA.

like Caesar's wife *See* CAESAR'S WIFE MUST BE ABOVE SUSPICION.

like mother, like daughter A woman's character and behavior tend to reflect her mother's character and behavior. The sentiment comes from Ezekiel 16:44: "Behold, every one that useth proverbs shall use this proverb against thee, saying, As is the mother, so is her daughter." Related proverbs include ***like father, like son.*** *She was a pretty little girl but inherited an acerbic sense of humor. Like mother, like daughter, as they say.*

like people, like priest The way a spiritual leader's followers behave reveals that leader's true character. The proverb comes from the Bible, appearing in Hosea 4:9: "And there shall be, like people, like priest: and I will punish them for their ways, and reward them their doings." The saying is also encountered in the form ***like priest, like people.*** *The congregation—like people, like priest—showed considerable reluctance to voice their true feelings.*

like the walls of Jericho *See* WALLS OF JERICHO.

lilies of the field Spiritual matters, especially as considered superior to earthly things. The phrase comes from Matthew 6:28–29, in which Christ, in his Sermon on the Mount, chooses the lilies of the field as an emblem of the spirit: "And why take thee thought for raiment? Consider the lilies of the field, how they grow; they toil not, neither, do they spin; And yet I say unto you, That even Solomon in all his glory was not arrayed like one of these." Various attempts have been made to identify lilies of the field with a particular plant, suggestions including the white daisy *Anthemis palaestina,* the poppy anemone *Anemone coronaria,* and the crown marguerite *Chrysanthemum coronarium.* To ***consider the lilies*** means do not worry and do not strive to provide oneself with material benefits, but trust to providence for what is needed" *(Oxford Dictionary of Current Idiomatic English,* vol. 2, p. 115). "Solomon's court fool would have scoffed at the thought of the young Galilean who dared compare the lilies of the field to his august master" (Oliver Wendell Holmes, *Over the Tea-Cups,* 1891).

Lilith Archetype of a female demon or monstrous woman. Although she is not actually named in the Bible, Lilith features in Christian legend as the first wife of ADAM, who was exiled from Eden after making Adam's life a misery. By him she was supposed to have given birth to a swarm of devils.

After her banishment she became a demon haunting various remote places at night and attacking women in childbirth. She is sometimes identified as the "screech-owl" mentioned in Isaiah 34:14. *Mad with rage, with her long hair tangled and matted, she hurtled through the ruined house, screaming like some demented Lilith.*

Lilliputian (lilăpyooshăn) On a miniature scale. The Lilliputians were a race of tiny people encountered by GULLIVER in Jonathan Swift's satire *Gulliver's Travels* (1726). Only six inches tall, they have a sense of self-importance quite unmatched by their stature, making them ridiculous to the towering Gulliver. "For this was the season when at every doorway and table the locals were noisily betting on the lilliputian battles of fighting cicadas" (Lorne Blair, *Ring of Fire*, 1988). *See also* BROBDINGNAGIAN; LAPUTA; YAHOO.

lily of the valleys *See* ROSE OF SHARON.

Lincoln, Abraham *See* ABRAHAM LINCOLN.

lion in the way A contrived excuse for not doing something one does not feel like doing. The expression comes from Proverbs 26:13: "The slothful man saith, There is a lion in the way; a lion in the streets." It may also be encountered in the variant forms ***lion in the path*** and ***lion in the streets.*** ". . . but it was three miles off, and there was a lion in the way: they must pass in sight of Squire Raby's house" (Charles Reade, *Put Yourself in His Place,* 1870).

lion in winter A man whose great strength and resolution is in gradual decline because of advancing age. The phrase is best known as the title of a 1966 play (filmed in 1968) by James Goldman about King Henry II of England and his struggle to maintain control of the country as his mental and physical powers weaken. The lion is one of the most familiar emblems of British royalty. *The prime minister retained his powers of rhetoric into advanced old age, proving time and again he was a lion in winter who still knew how to roar.*

lions' den *See* DANIEL IN THE LIONS' DEN.

lion shall lie down with the lamb Idyllic view of a future in which natural enemies will be reconciled and live in peace. The expression appears in Isaiah 11:6–7, which contains a prophecy of peace and safety in the future messianic age: "The wolf also shall dwell with the lamb and the leopard shall lie down with the kid; and the calf and the young lion and the fatling together; and a little child shall lead them. And the cow and the bear shall feed; their young ones shall lie down together: and the lion shall eat straw like the ox." ". . . the time is come when the past should be buried in oblivion; when my family should take Mr. Micawber by the hand, and Mr. Micawber should take my family by the hand; when the lion should lie down with the lamb, and my family be on terms with Mr. Micawber" (Charles Dickens, *David Copperfield,* 1849–50).

Little Bighorn *See* CUSTER'S LAST STAND.

little cloud no bigger than a man's hand *See* CLOUD NO BIGGER THAN A MAN'S HAND.

Little Corporal *See* NAPOLEON.

little gray cells *See* HERCULE POIROT.

little Hitler *See* HITLER.

Little John *See* ROBIN HOOD.

Little Lord Fauntleroy (fontlăroy) A young male member of the aristocracy, or a boy who dresses like one. The allusion is to the children's novel *Little Lord Fauntleroy* (1886) by Frances Hodgson Burnett (1849–1924), in which the central character is seven-year-old Cedric Errol, the angelic golden-haired heir to the seat of an ill-tempered English earl. He is described as wearing a black velvet suit with lace collar, known ever since as a Fauntleroy suit. Calling someone a Little Lord Fauntleroy usually implies that he is an effeminate "sissy." "Little as he wanted to do anything about it, the boy's babyishness, his Fauntleroy air, embarrassed and distantly annoyed him: it seemed to reflect on his own manhood" (Nina Bawden, *Tortoise by Candlelight*, 1989).

Little Nell A sweet-hearted, ultimately tragic little orphan girl. Little Nell, properly Nell Trent, is one of the characters in the novel *The Old Curiosity Shop* (1840–41) by British novelist Charles Dickens (1812–70). Nell does her best to comfort her indigent grandfather, maintaining a cheerful disposition even as their fortunes decline and, worn out, she succumbs to the hardships she has suffered and dies. The death of Little Nell was one of the most traumatic of all the events depicted in Victorian fiction and the story was told of U.S. readers crowding the docks of New York to find out from newly arrived English passengers whether or not Little Nell survived in the latest episode of the serialized novel. Nowadays the fate of Little Nell tends to be quoted as a prime example of Victorian sentimentality. *Most people quickly tired of the small girl's sickly-sweet Little Nell act.*

Little Orphan Annie A self-reliant young girl, especially one with curly red hair or one who is ill-dressed. The allusion is to the 11-year-old central character in the U.S. comic strip *Little Orphan Annie*, first published in 1925 by Harold Gray. It seems that her name came originally from an 1885 poem with the title "Little Orphant Annie" by James W. Riley. Her story later became the subject of the highly successful musical *Annie* (1977). "When Maire Carroll's mother said thoughtfully to Eve, 'Do you know I always ask myself why a sensible woman like Mother Francis would let you out on the street looking like Little Orphan Annie' Benny's brow darkened" (Maeve Binchey, *Circle of Friends*, 1991).

little red book A publication purporting to be a source of authority on something. The allusion is to the *Little Red Book*, otherwise known as the *Thoughts of Chairman Mao*, published in 1964 in huge numbers for the benefit of his followers by Chinese leader Mao Zedong (1893–1976). Comprising quotations from the leader on a range of subjects, the booklet became an unquestionable source of communist ideology and an icon of Chinese communism, some 800 million copies being sold or distributed between 1966 and 1971. "He did not hand out sayings of Jesus in a little red book, or give them Christmas presents" (George Carey, *I Believe*, 1991).

Little Rock Emblem of the struggle against school segregation. Little Rock in Arkansas attracted international attention in September 1957, when federal troops were called in to ensure that nine black children could attend classes at the Central High School, in line with a recent change in the law designed to promote school integration. Angry white segregationists protested loudly, but were eventually obliged to back down. *For the first time since Little Rock the use of troops to get black children into school seems a possibility.*

live by bread alone *See* MAN CANNOT LIVE BY BREAD ALONE.

live by the sword shall die by the sword, those who Those who employ violence to their own ends will eventually fall victim to violence themselves. The proverb is of biblical origin, appearing in Matthew 26:52: "Then said Jesus unto him, Put up again thy sword into his place: for all they that take the sword shall perish with the sword." " 'Had He wished help,' he said, 'He could have summoned legions of archangels from heaven, so what need had He of your poor bow and arrow? Besides, bethink you of His own words—that those who live by the sword shall perish by the sword' " (Sir Arthur Conan Doyle, *The White Company,* 1891).

live dog is better than a dead lion, a *See* LIVING DOG IS BETTER THAN A DEAD LION, A.

live off the fat of the land *See* FAT OF THE LAND.

living dog is better than a dead lion, a It is better to compromise and thus survive than perish through one's refusal to adapt. The proverb is found in Ecclesiastes 9:4: "To him that is joined to all the living there is hope: for a living dog is better than a dead lion." It is also found in the form ***a live dog is better than a dead lion.*** "When the lion is shot, the dog gets the spoil. So he had come in for Katherine, Alan's lioness. A live dog is better than a dead lion" (D. H. Lawrence, *The Woman, Who Rode Away,* 1928).

Lizzie Borden (lizee bordăn) A female murderer, especially one who murders her parents. The original Lizzie Borden (1860–1927) was tried in 1893 for the murder of her father and stepmother in Fall River, Massachusetts, after they were found dead in the family home from multiple ax wounds. Lizzie was acquitted, although a rhyme composed at the time made no bones about her guilt: "Lizzie Borden took an ax / And gave her mother forty whacks; / When she saw what she had done / She gave her father forty-one." In fact, the stepmother received 19 ax blows and Lizzie's father 10. Although many neighbors in Fall River remained convinced of Lizzie Borden's guilt, the crime was never solved. *The police reserved their opinions about the case, but the papers were quick to label the grieving daughter a Lizzie Borden.*

loaves and fishes *See* FEEDING THE FIVE THOUSAND.

Lochinvar (lokinvahr) A young, heroic knight. Lochinvar features in the poem *Marmion* (1808) by Sir Walter Scott (1771–1832), in which he arrives at a marriage feast and carries the bride away on his horse: "O, young Lochinvar is come out of the west, / Through all the wide Border his steed was the best; / And save his good broadsword he weapons had none, / He rode all unarm'd, and he rode all alone. / So faithful in love, and so dauntless in war, / There never was knight like the young Lochinvar." In modern usage, the name is usually applied sarcastically. *"Look out, here comes young Lochinvar," the mayor quipped as the old man shuffled into the hall, coughing and sneezing into a grubby handkerchief.*

Locusta (lōkăstă) Archetype of a woman who murders someone she is supposed to be nursing. The allusion is to the imperial nurse who poisoned the emperor Claudius on the instructions of his wife, Agrippina, and his son Britannicus on the instructions of Agrippina's son Nero. She was rewarded by Nero but put to death by his successor, Galba. *The midwife has been arrested on suspicion of acting Locusta to her defenseless charges.*

locusts, plague of *See* PLAGUE OF LOCUSTS.

Log *See* KING LOG.

loins, gird up thy *See* GIRD UP THY LOINS.

Lois Lane *See* SUPERMAN.

Loki (lōkee) Personification of mischief and evil. In Norse mythology Loki was identified as the god of mischief and destruction. He was the sworn enemy of the good gods and caused the death of Odin's son Balder after tricking the blind god Hod into striking Balder with a bough of mistletoe, the one thing to which Balder was fatally vulnerable. As punishment he was chained to a rock, sentenced to remain there until the gods are overthrown. *The more the jury heard, the more the defendant began to seem a truly evil man, the equal of any Loki or Lucifer.*

Lolita (lōleetă) A young, sexually alluring girl, especially one who is under the age of consent. The highly controversial 1958 novel *Lolita*, by Vladimir Nabokov (1899–1977), describes how a middle-aged professor called Humbert Humbert falls disastrously in love with a 12-year-old girl, whose real name is Dolores Haze. Stanley Kubrick's famous 1962 film version of the book became one of the most discussed movies of the era. *People said he made a complete fool of himself when he abandoned his wife of 35 years for a Lolita younger than his granddaughter.*

Loman, Willy *See* WILLY LOMAN.

Lon Chaney (chaynee) A man with a menacing appearance or personality. The U.S. actor Lon Chaney (Leonidas Frank Chaney; 1883–1930) established a reputation in silent horror movies of the 1920s, being dubbed the ***Man of a Thousand Faces*** for his ability to transform his appearance with makeup. His son Lon Chaney Jr. (1906–73) continued the family tradition by appearing in similar roles. *It's very off-putting to get in a cab and find your driver looks like Lon Chaney.*

Lone Ranger A hero who pits himself against the evils of the world. The *Lone Ranger* was a popular Western radio and television series, first broadcast in 1933, that featured a masked cowboy with a white hat who enforced the law aided by his Native American friend ***Tonto***, who addresses him as ***Kemo Sabe*** (supposedly meaning "faithful friend" but not actually from any real Native American language), and his white stallion ***Silver***, who gallops off with him on the command "Hi-ho, Silver, away!" "Let's just get everyone safe, and then you can go out there and do your Lone Ranger impression if you still want to" (Stephen Laws, *Darkfall*, 1993).

longest day A day in which a great many things happen. The phrase is particularly associated with D-DAY (June 6, 1944), which witnessed the Allied landings in Normandy and was a landmark in the final defeat of Nazi Germany. It was used as the title of an ambitious 1962 movie retelling the events that took place on the first day of the invasion. *Thousands of lives were changed forever on the Longest Day.*

long-haired hippie *See* HIPPIE.

Long John Silver A piratical rascal, or a person with one leg. Long John Silver, complete with wooden leg and parrot on his shoulder, is the archetypal pirate in the classic adventure novel *Treasure Island* (1883) by Scottish novelist Robert Louis Stevenson (1850–94). At once villainous and charming, he is very much the center of the story, which was originally to have been entitled *The Sea Cook* (Silver serves as cook on board the *Hispaniola*). He was loosely based upon a friend of Stevenson's, the writer W. E. Henley (1849–1903), who had a foot amputated as a boy. *He stumped up the ward on his crutches, like Long John Silver.*

long march A long and arduous journey on foot. The allusion is to the Long March of some 6,000 miles that was undertaken by Chinese communists through nationalist lines in 1934–35 to reestablish their base in northwest China. Of the 100,000 who began the march, considerably less than half completed it. "Students set out on a 'Long March' across Paris from the Sorbonne to the Renault works" (B. M. Gill, *Dying to Meet You*, 1989).

looking-glass *See* THROUGH THE LOOKING-GLASS.

look to one's laurels *See* LAURELS.

Lord Fauntleroy, Little *See* LITTLE LORD FAUNTLEROY.

Lord giveth and the Lord taketh away, the Things provided by God can just as easily be taken away by him. The proverb is of biblical origin, appearing in Job 1:21 as "Naked came I out of my mother's womb, and naked shall I return thither: the Lord gave, and the Lord hath taken away." *The minister shook his head sadly over the child's body and murmured, "The Lord giveth and the Lord taketh away."*

Lord Haw-Haw A man who makes propaganda broadcasts on behalf of his country's enemies. The original Lord Haw-Haw was the U.S.-born William Joyce (1906–46), who broadcast Nazi propaganda during World War II. Of Irish descent, he was a figure of scorn to the Allies, who mocked his exaggerated, sneering, upper-class Oxford accent (hence his nickname, Lord Haw-Haw, originally bestowed by *Daily Express* journalist Jonah Barrington). After the war ended he was hanged for treason. *He was about as effective as a propagandist as Lord Haw-Haw was. See also* TOKYO ROSE.

Lord, how long? *See* HOW LONG, O LORD?

Lord is my shepherd, the *See* GREEN PASTURES.

Lord Jim A man who cannot accept his own human failings. The allusion is to the central character in the Joseph Conrad novel *Lord Jim* (1900), a tragic figure who struggles to come to terms with an act of cowardice in his youth, when he abandoned the passengers of a ship in which he was an officer. *Her grandfather was a Lord Jim who never came to terms with his disgrace in the war.*

Lord Kitchener *See* YOUR COUNTRY NEEDS YOU.

lord of the flies *See* BEELZEBUB.

Lord's Supper *See* LAST SUPPER.

Lorelei (lorălī) A fatally fascinating woman; a siren. The Lorelei is a rocky promontory on the River Rhine on which, according to German folklore, a golden-haired siren lived, luring boatmen to their deaths on the rocks with her bewitchingly lovely singing. Legend had it that she was a woman who drowned herself after an unhappy love affair. The name Lorelei means "peeping cliff." *He was not the first successful man to ruin himself over some Lorelei and he was unlikely to be the last.*

Lost Boys *See* PETER PAN.

Lost Generation A generation that goes through some vast traumatizing experience and emerges from it greatly changed. The term was first applied to the generation of young men that was decimated in World War I: Those who survived the war were left traumatized and doubting the values they had hitherto taken for granted. The term came to be particularly associated with certain writers (including Rupert Brooke, Ernest HEMINGWAY, F. Scott Fitzgerald, and Ezra Pound) who witnessed the war or similarly challenged the attitudes of the prewar generation. "Nearly as many women died too, in a sense, as spinsters and widows of the lost generation in the decades that were to follow" (K. M. Peyton, *Who, Sir? Me, Sir?*, 1988).

lost tribes of Israel Something that is irretrievably lost, leaving no trace. The biblical account of the flight from Egypt (in the books of Exodus through Joshua) describes how the Jewish people settled in the PROMISED LAND, where the sons and grandsons of JACOB founded the 12 tribes of Israel. Upon the death of Solomon (1 Kings 11:41) the tribes separated into two kingdoms, the southern kingdom which was called Judah (formed by the tribes of Judah, Simeon, and part of Benjamin) and the northern kingdom which was called Israel (formed by the tribes of Asher, part of Benjamin, Dan, Ephraim, Gad, Issachar, Manasseh, Naphtali, Reuben, and Zebulun). The northern kingdom was overrun by the Assyrians in 722 B.C. and was sent into exile, subsequently vanishing from history as an identifiable group. Over the centuries they became known as "the (10) lost tribes," and various communities around the world have claimed descent from them. *Trying to track the family down after all these years was like trying to trace one of the lost tribes of Israel.*

lost weekend A dissolute or drunken weekend, the events of which cannot later be recalled by those taking part. Although the term may be older, it is usually associated with the 1945 movie *The Lost Weekend*, based on a 1944 novel by Charles Jackson, which starred Ray Milland as an alcoholic writer. So vivid was its portrayal of the perils of alcohol, leaders of the liquor industry tried to buy the movie negatives to prevent it being released in case it damaged sales of their products. "One day when Modi finally turned up he was penniless, unable to account for his lost weekend, hungry and dirty" (June Rose, *Modigliani*, 1990).

Lothario (lothahreeō) A womanizer, a libertine, a rake. The allusion is to a character in the play *The Fair Penitent* (1703) by the English poet and playwright Nicholas Rowe (1674–1718). A callous seducer whose lecherous behavior eventually proves his undoing, he is described as "haughty, gallant, gay"—hence references to a ***gay Lothario***. "You shan't be shamed for she'll think you a great lover, a real Lothario, a dandy Don Juan" (Will Self, *My Idea of Fun*, 1993). *See also* CASANOVA; DON JUAN.

Lotophagi *See* LOTUS-EATER.

Lot's wife Archetype of an individual who brings about his or her own downfall through disobedience. The reference is to Genesis 19:26 and the story of Lot and his wife and family who, on account of Lot's goodness, were forewarned by angels of the destruction of SODOM AND GOMORRAH and given time to leave on condition that they did not look back as the cities were laid waste with FIRE AND BRIMSTONE: "Escape for thy life; look not behind thee, neither stay thou in the plain" (Genesis 19:17). Lot's wife disobeyed this command, perhaps regretting the loss of the worldly pleasures Sodom and Gomorrah represented, and was turned into a pillar of salt as punishment. (See also Luke 17:32.) In modern usage the tale is often evoked as a warning both to eschew worldly things and never to look back. The area around the Dead Sea, where the cities of Sodom and Gomorrah are said to have been located, is well known for its unusual salt formations. "Very well; I hope you feel the content you express: at any rate, your good sense will tell you that it is too soon yet to yield to the vacillating fears of Lot's wife" (Charlotte Brontë, *Jane Eyre,* 1847).

lotus-eater (lōtăs) A daydreamer; a person who lives in a state of blissful indolence and forgetfulness, especially one induced by drugs. The phrase alludes to an episode in Homer's *Odyssey* (c. 700 B.C.), which described how Odysseus and his men arrived at the land of the lotus-eaters, or ***Lotophagi,*** in North Africa. When some of the heroes ate the honeyed fruit of the lotus (also spelled ***lotos***) they fell into such a state of dreamy torpor that they lost all will to continue their journey home and had to be carried back to the ships by their leader. The episode was rendered in verse form by Alfred, Lord Tennyson as "The Lotos-Eaters" (1833). The lotus of the original story has been tentatively identified as the date, the jujube, or one of various other trees and plants. "Her presence brought memories of such things as Bourbon roses, rubies, and tropical midnights; her moods recalled lotus-eaters and the march in 'Athalie'; her motions, the ebb and flow of the sea; her voice, the viola" (Thomas Hardy, *The Return of the Native,* 1880).

love of money is the root of all evil, the *See* MONEY IS THE ROOT OF ALL EVIL.

love passing the love of women A friendship that is so intense it surpasses any ordinary attraction between a man and a woman. The phrase appears in David's lament for his companion Jonathan, as recorded in 2 Samuel 1:26: "I am distressed for thee, my brother Jonathan: very pleasant hast thou been unto me: thy love to me was wonderful, passing the love of women." In modern usage the term is usually used in reference to male friendship, sometimes as a circumlocution for homosexual love. "He was an older brother to Paul Riesling, swift to defend him, admiring him with a proud and credulous love passing the love of women" (Sinclair Lewis, *Babbitt,* 1922). *See also* DAVID AND JONATHAN.

love that dare not speak its name, the Homosexual love, or any forbidden or frowned-upon relationship. This is an allusion to a poem entitled "The Two Loves" by Lord Alfred Douglas (1870–1945), the lover of Irish writer and wit Oscar Wilde (1854–1900), which includes the line: "I am the love that dare not speak its name." Wilde's homosexual relationship with Douglas triggered the infamous libel trial that led ultimately to Wilde's imprisonment in Reading Gaol. *It was only years afterward that he felt able to talk about his brush with the love that dare not speak its name.*

love thy neighbor Treat others with charity, respect, and tolerance. The proverb is of biblical origin, appearing in Leviticus 19:18: "Thou shalt not avenge, nor bear any grudge against the children of thy people, but thou shalt love thy neighbour as thyself: I am the LORD." It is quoted by Jesus in Matthew 5:43, 19:19, 22:38 and Mark 12:31 and by Paul in Romans 13:9 and Galatians 5:15. It is also found in James 2:8. Contemporary extensions of the proverb include "Love your neighbor, but don't pull down the fence" and "Love your neighbor, but leave his wife alone." *The group of youngsters were discussing current events, and one of them pointed out that loving thy neighbor seemed to have gone out of style among world leaders.*

love your enemies Forgive your enemies rather than retaliate against them. The sentiment was expressed by Christ in the course of his Sermon on the Mount, as recorded in Matthew 5:44–45: "But I say unto you, Love your enemies, bless them that curse you, do good to them that hate you, and pray for them that despitefully use you, and persecute you; That ye may be the children of your Father which is in heaven: for he maketh his sun rise on the evil and on the good, and sendeth rain on the just and on the unjust." "That was love. 'Love your enemies as yourself!' was a divine word, entirely free from any church or creed" (Zane Grey, *Riders of the Purple Sage,* 1912).

Lubianka (loobeeankă) A forbidding building, especially a state prison in which inmates are likely to be subjected to torture and execution. Lubianka was the prison in Moscow where important enemies of the former communist state were confined and interrogated; many were murdered there. It was notable for its grim architecture. *He hated his job in finance and considered the bleak office building in which he spent his days a Lubianka.*

Lucian (looshăn) Personification of the follies and vices of a given age. Lucian is the central character in what is usually called *The Golden Ass,* a satirical romance of the second century A.D. written by Apuleius. Lucian is a young man who is accidentally turned into a donkey and in this guise has a series of adventures, in the course of which he is much abused before returning to his human form. *In Don Quixote, Cervantes provided his contemporaries with a Lucian for the age of chivalry.*

Lucifer (loosifer) Personification of evil. Lucifer is identified in the Bible as the leader of the angels who rose in rebellion against God and consequently fell, as described in Isaiah 14:12: "How art thou fallen from heaven, O Lucifer, son of the morning!" Lucifer became the devil of Christian tradition, also going by the name SATAN. The name Lucifer means "light-bearer" in Latin and as a result was for a time adopted as a name for a friction match in the 19th century. "'O Rebecca, Rebecca, for shame!' cried Miss Sedley; for this was the greatest blasphemy Rebecca had as yet uttered; and in those days, in England, to say, 'Long live Bonaparte!' was as much as to say, 'Long live Lucifer!'" (William Makepeace Thackeray, *Vanity Fair,* 1847–48).

Lucrezia Borgia *See* BORGIAS, THE.

Lucullan (lookălăn) Lavish; luxurious; opulent. Lucius Licinius Lucullus (c. 110–56 B.C.) was a Roman general and consul who acquired great wealth as a result of his success on the battlefield in Asia against Mithridates VI, king of Pontus. Lucullus became famous for his lavish lifestyle, especially his fabulous banquets, after his retirement to Rome around 66. He spent enormous sums on entertaining his guests and was credited with being the first to introduce cherries to Italy. Any sumptuous feast or other display of opulence may now be dubbed a ***Lucullan banquet.*** The word is sometimes encountered in the forms ***Lucullian*** or ***Lucullean.*** When a person dines well alone it may be said on such an occasion that ***Lucullus sups with Lucullus,*** in reference to the reply that Lucullus gave when asked who his guests would be one evening when a particularly fine meal was being prepared. *Guests at the castle were treated to a Lucullan banquet, with the finest wines and choicest meats.*

Lucy Stoner (stōner) A woman who keeps her maiden name after getting married. Lucy Stone (1818–93) was a U.S. suffragist who refused to change her surname on her marriage, with the support of her husband. She went on to found the American Woman Suffrage Association in 1869. *The minister was not best pleased when his new daughter-in-law declared she was a Lucy Stoner and would be keeping her own name.*

Luddite (ludīt) A person who opposes the use of new technology or other innovations. The original Luddites were textile workers in England who feared the loss of their jobs when newly invented machines threatened to take over the work of hand-loom weavers. They attacked many factories between 1799 and 1816, destroying the hated machinery, but failed to stop the inevitable spread of improved industrial technology. They named themselves after one Ned Ludd, who was reputed to have destroyed machines in a Leicestershire factory 30 years earlier. "I'm just a senile old Luddite, I suppose" (Ian Maitland, *Cathedral*, 1993).

Luke Skywalker *See* STAR WARS.

lukewarm Laodicea *See* LAODICEAN.

Lurch (lerch) A tall, ungainly person. The allusion is to the towering butler in the ADDAMS FAMILY comic strip, television series, and films. *Uncle Joe was a huge man with a deep voice and a shambling gait, like Lurch.*

Lusitania (loositayneeă) Emblem of a tragic nautical disaster. During World War I, the British Cunard passenger liner *Lusitania* was sailing from Liverpool to New York when it was torpedoed off Ireland by a German submarine on May 7, 1915; 1,198 people drowned, including 128 Americans (among them the millionaire Alfred Vanderbilt and the theater producer Carl Frohman). The loss of the *Lusitania* provoked a strong reaction on both sides of the Atlantic and proved a significant step toward the United States entering the war in 1917 (it has even been suggested that the British Admiralty realized the danger the ship was in but deliberately put it at risk so that the United States would be persuaded to enter the war). *It was a maritime crime on the scale of the sinking of the* Lusitania.

Luthor, Lex *See* SUPERMAN.

lyceum (līseeăm) A school; a public concert or lecture hall. The original Lyceum was the open-air school in a grove on the banks of the Ilissus River in Athens where Aristotle engaged his pupils in discussions of philosophy. "I did not see why the schoolmaster should be taxed to support the priest, and not the priest the schoolmaster; for I was not the State's schoolmaster, but I supported myself by voluntary subscription. I did not see why the lyceum should not present its tax bill, and have the

State to back its demand, as well as the Church" (Henry David Thoreau, *Civil Disobedience,* 1849).

lyncean (linseeăn) Having exceptionally keen eyesight. The allusion is to Lynceus, the Argonaut who was renowned for sharpsightedness. He was reputed to able to see right through the Earth and to be able to make things out many miles away. *You would need to have eyesight of truly lyncean brilliance to be able to read the words on that board from a mile away.*

Lysistrata (līsisstrătă) Archetype of a woman who uses her sexuality to get her own way. Lysistrata is the central character in a comedy of the same name by the Greek playwright Aristophanes, first produced in 411 B.C. When she suspects the men of Athens and Sparta of not working hard enough to end the long war between their countries, Lysistrata and the other wives of both sides agree to withdraw all sexual favors from their spouses until the latter come to some agreement. The men rapidly agree to a peace treaty and normal marital relations are resumed, to the relief of all. *The local womenfolk threatened to adopt Lysistrata-style tactics unless their demands were agreed to by the end of the day.*

M

Macbeth (măkbeth) A hypocrite who is prepared to betray or sacrifice anyone in the pursuit of power. The title character of William Shakespeare's tragedy *Macbeth* (1606) was based upon a historical figure, who ruled Scotland from 1040 to 1057. There is little evidence, however, that he was the murderous, conscience-stricken usurper depicted by Shakespeare, as the real king actually killed his predecessor Duncan in open battle, not while he was an honored guest in his home. *That man would do anything to get what he wants and is about as trustworthy as Macbeth.*

Macbeth, Lady *See* LADY MACBETH.

McCarthyism (măkahrtheeizăm) Political witch-hunting, especially where the victims are communists. The allusion is to the systematic rooting out of people with supposed communist sympathies conducted in the 1950s by U.S. Republican Senator Joseph McCarthy (1908–57). As a result of McCarthy's campaign, many notable writers and other prominent citizens found themselves hauled before official committees and interrogated on their political views; many found their subsequent careers blighted by political prejudice against them, regardless of their innocence or guilt. *This witch-hunt against the left smacks of a new form of McCarthyism.*

McCoy, real *See* REAL MCCOY.

Macduff *See* LEAD ON, MACDUFF.

MacGuffin (măgufin) A means of keeping a narrative moving by introducing a detail that later turns out to be insignificant or irrelevant. The word was coined by British-born U.S. movie director Alfred Hitchcock (1899–1980), who frequently employed such devices to trigger the action in his films, which he always considered secondary to the characters he created. According to Hitchcock himself, he got the name from the story of a Scottish train passenger who, when asked about a parcel he was carrying, replied that it was a MacGuffin—that is, a device for catching lions in the Highlands. When someone else observed that there were no lions in the Highlands, he replied that there were no MacGuffins either. *This turned out to be a MacGuffin designed to distract us from the real issue behind the dispute.*

Machiavellian (makeeăveleeăn) Unscrupulous, calculated, amoral. Niccolò Machiavelli (1469–1527) was a Florentine statesman who set out his often cynical views on the art of government in his treatise *The Prince* (1513). In this work he defended the use of deceit and violence in the pursuit of peace and prosperity. In reality, Machiavelli was a proponent of republicanism and an enemy of senseless brutality, but history remembers him for his cold-blooded pragmatism and readiness to employ dubious methods to achieve his aims. "He had his little peccadilloes, the quaint and rather Machiavellian ways to gain his little ends, but he knew me and I knew him, and in essentials he made good" (Kathryn Tidrick, *Empire and the English Character*, 1992).

Madame Arcati (ahrkahtee) The archetype of an eccentric spiritualist medium, especially one who is middle-aged and full-figured. Madame Arcati appears in the stage comedy *Blithe Spirit* (1941) by Noël Coward and provided a memorable role for Margaret Rutherford in this and the 1945 film version. *The lady who turned up for the séance was small and wiry, not a bit like the Madame Arcati we expected.*

Madame Bovary (bōvăree) A dissatisfied young woman who yearns for a better life. Emma Bovary is the title character in *Madame Bovary* (1857) by the French novelist Gustave Flaubert (1821–80). Having married a dull local doctor, she becomes restless with her quiet provincial existence and longs for a life of romance and luxury. Her yearnings lead her into adulterous affairs and debt, with disastrous consequences. *Like Madame Bovary, she found marriage something of an anticlimax and longed to escape from her humdrum life.*

Madame Defarge (dăfahrj) A vengeful woman who rejoices in the misfortunes of others. The allusion is to a character in *A Tale of Two Cities* (1859) by the British novelist Charles Dickens (1812–70). Madame Defarge is a fanatic revolutionary who sits knitting gleefully at the foot of the guillotine as French aristocrats are executed. She is implacable in her hostility to the victims of the Revolution and knits the names of those who are killed into a long scarf. Her name is sometimes applied more innocently to a woman who is forever knitting. "The needles of that one clicking like Madame Defarge, her soiled yellow hair piled up on her head and red lipstick like a gaping wound" (Tanith Lee, *Dark Dance*, 1993).

mad as a hatter Completely mad, or furious. In most people's minds the allusion is to the Mad Hatter character in Lewis Carroll's *Alice's Adventures in Wonderland* (1865), whose behavior is particularly eccentric. The phrase "mad as a hatter" is, however, considerably older, referring to people involved in the hat-making industry. The exposure of these hatters to the chemical mercury, with which they came into contact on a daily basis, led many of them to suffer uncontrollable fits or even to go insane, hence the phrase. The simile is also sometimes attached to one Robert Crab, a 17th-century hatter who became well known for giving away everything he had to the poor and living on a diet of grass and dock leaves. Carroll, meanwhile, is thought to have drawn inspiration from a furniture dealer named Theophilus Carter, whose nickname "the Mad Hatter" reflected both his eccentric behavior and his customary wearing of a top hat. *His father is as mad as a hatter.*

mad, bad, and dangerous to know A person who is thoroughly reckless or amoral and likely to cause trouble to everyone he or she encounters. The phrase was first applied, in her journal, by the British novelist and aristocrat Lady Caroline Lamb (1785–1828) to the poet Lord Byron (1788–1824), with whom she embarked on a turbulent nine-month affair in 1812. This description of the BYRONIC personality has stuck and has remained closely associated with the poet ever since.

"Nonconformists are often regarded as mad, bad and dangerous to know" (Philippa Davies, *Status: What It Is and How to Achieve It*, 1991).

madding crowd *See* FAR FROM THE MADDING CROWD.

madeleine (madălayn) An object that triggers vivid memories of the otherwise forgotten past. A madeleine is a small French cake, possibly named after a 19th-century French pastry cook called Madeleine Paulmier. The allusion is to the novel cycle *À la recherche du temps perdu* (*Remembrance of Things Past*; 1913–27) by the French writer Marcel Proust (1871–1922), in which the narrator tastes one of these cakes and is instantly reminded of the minutest details of his childhood. *That small toy car was like Proust's madeleine to me, reminding me vividly of many happy days spent in the playroom with my brothers. See also* PROUSTIAN.

Madison Avenue (madisăn) The world of advertising. The allusion is to Madison Avenue in Manhattan, New York, where many of the world's best-known designers have boutiques, and which has been home to some of the biggest advertising agencies since the 1920s. Madison Avenue takes its name from Madison Square, which was itself named after James Madison (1751–1836), the fourth president of the United States. *This is one of the most expensive publicity campaigns ever devised by Madison Avenue.*

Maecenas (miseenăs) A generous patron of the arts, especially literature. Gaius Cilnius Maecenas (c. 70–8 B.C.) was a wealthy Roman noble and a favorite of the Emperor Augustus until he was obliged to go into seclusion later in life. He was celebrated as a patron of literature and included Horace and Virgil among the writers to whom he lent his support. *The literati were nothing if not sycophantic in their response to the great man's generosity, hailing him as a veritable Maecenas for the new century.*

maenads *See* BACCHANTE.

Mae West (may west) An inflatable life vest. The U.S. stage and movie actress Mae West (1892–1980) was famous both for her buxom figure and for her explicitly sexual performances, hence the application of her name to life vests by airmen in World War II. Mae West herself was delighted with this act of homage, remarking in a letter to members of the RAF: "I've been in *Who's Who*, and I know what's what, but it'll be the first time I ever made the dictionary." *You'll find your Mae Wests in the locker over there. See also* BEULAH, PEEL ME A GRAPE; COME UP AND SEE ME SOMETIME.

mafia (mafeeă) A group of criminals or other people, organizations, etc., who cooperate in imposing their will on others. The term is most commonly applied to Cosa Nostra (Italian for "our thing"), the U.S. criminal network based around families of ultimately Sicilian extraction. Mafia families are notorious for their involvement in drugs, gambling, prostitution, extortion, and protection rackets as well as for enforcing discipline on their own members and for bloodily avenging slights from outside the family. The word "mafia" means "boldness" in Sicilian, and itself may come from the Arabic *mahyah*, meaning "bragging," or else from an Arabic word for a place of refuge. *The business is controlled by a mafia of crooked operators. See also* GODFATHER, THE.

magdalen (magdălăn) A reformed prostitute; a house for reformed prostitutes. The name alludes to the biblical Mary Magdalene (or Magdalen), a woman from whom Christ had cast "seven devils" (Luke 8:2). She has traditionally been thought to be the unnamed woman of Luke 7:36–50, though the biblical narrative does not warrant this. The woman, who according to the biblical account was "a sinner" (possibly a prostitute) now reformed, wept with remorse over her past sins when Jesus came to the house of the Pharisee. She washed his feet with her tears, drying them with her hair. Mary Magdalene was the first person to see Christ after the Resurrection (Mark 16:9). In art Mary Magdalene is conventionally depicted as weeping. *With great reluctance she allowed herself to be persuaded into the local magdalen, where she was scrubbed, scolded, and entreated not to return to her old ways. See also* MAUDLIN.

magi (mayjī) Astrologers. The original Magi are traditionally thought of as the three wise men from the East who, according to Matthew 2:1, came to Bethlehem with gifts of gold, frankincense, and myrrh to celebrate the birth of Christ. Later traditions presented the Magi as the kings ***Caspar***, ***Melchior***, and ***Balthazar***, but this suggestion is not supported by the Gospels. It is thought that the biblical Magi may have come from Persia or southern Arabia. *When the young woman had finished, the three professors nodded sagely, for all the world like three bearded and bespectacled magi.*

Maginot Line (mazhinō) A seemingly impregnable static line of defense, especially one that is not as effective as it looks. The Maginot Line was the impressive system of defenses constructed between 1929 and 1934 on the border between France and Germany to defend French-held territory from possible German attack. Such was the confidence of the French in the Maginot Line that French generals became complacent and were totally outwitted when the Germans outflanked the line by attacking through Belgium in 1940. The line was named after the French minister of war, André Maginot (1877–1932). "They were much more likely to stick to the 'maginot line' of municipal antiracism and therefore, paradoxically, to experience any shift away from that defensive position as a retreat" (J. Donald and A. Rattansi, *Race, Culture and Difference*, 1993).

Magna Carta (magnă kahrtă) A document that guarantees legal rights or defends the civil liberties of individuals. The original Magna Carta (Latin for "great charter") was signed by King John at Runnymede on the River Thames in 1215 under pressure from his barons, who wished to curb royal abuses of power. It was actually very limited in what it guaranteed in terms of individual rights, but is remembered nonetheless as a statement of fundamental liberties. *This country needs a Magna Carta to establish the limits of government interference in the lives of citizens.*

Magnificat (magnifikat) A hymn of praise and by extension any instance of praise. In its strictest sense the term refers to Mary's joy at the news that she was to bear Christ, as related in Luke 1:46–55. Her words "Magnificat anima mea Dominum" ("My soul doth magnify the Lord") form an important part of Roman Catholic vespers and also appear in the liturgy of the Anglican and Orthodox Churches. "There is the lesson of 'Cinderella,' which is the same as that of the Magnificat—exaltavit humiles. There is the great lesson of 'Beauty and the Beast'; that a thing must be loved before it is loveable" (G. K. Chesterton, *Orthodoxy*, 1909).

Magog *See* GOG AND MAGOG.

Magoo, Mr. *See* MR. MAGOO.

Mahomet *See* MUHAMMAD.

Maid Marian *See* ROBIN HOOD.

Maigret *See* INSPECTOR MAIGRET.

maimed, the halt, and the blind, the Those members of society who suffer from some physical disability. The phrase, used often in the context of charity giving, is a quotation from Luke 14:13, in which Christ advises the wealthy that they should invite the poor, the maimed, the lame, and the blind to their houses rather than other rich friends and neighbors. "Some of them did us no great honour by these claims of kindred; as we had the blind, the maimed, and the halt amongst the number" (Oliver Goldsmith, *The Vicar of Wakefield,* 1766).

Main Street Provincial, materialistic, and mediocre, or a place with these characteristics. The allusion is to the novel *Main Street* (1920) by U.S. writer Sinclair Lewis (1885–1951), in which the author lampoons the complacency and parochialism of the fictional Gopher Prairie, Minnesota. Lewis based the town upon a real place, his own hometown of Sauk Centre, Minnesota: the residents of the real town were not flattered by the book and harbored a grievance against the writer for many years. *The company's aim was to bring culture to the people of Main Street.*

major league The top level in sport, business, or some other pursuit. The reference is to major league baseball, which comprises the National and American professional leagues. *We are talking major league crime here.*

make my day *See* GO AHEAD, MAKE MY DAY.

malapropism (malăpropizăm) The accidental replacement of one word with another similar word, usually through a confusion of their respective meanings. The allusion is to Mrs. Malaprop, a character in the stage comedy *The Rivals* (1775) by the Irish playwright Richard Brinsley Sheridan (1751–1816), who often mistakenly substitutes one word for another (such as "allegory" for "alligator" or "epitaph" for "epithet") in her misguided attempts to impress other people with her eloquence. Her name is based on the French for "not to the purpose." "Whether his comment is taken as a malapropism or a keen insight, the view of one charge nurse that the hospital had become 'an archival thing' was apposite" (D. Tomlinson, *Utopia, Community Care and Retreat*, 1991). *See also* DOGBERRY.

male chauvinism *See* CHAUVINISM.

Malthusian (malthoozeeăn) Of or relating to the theories of the British economist Thomas Robert Malthus (1766–1834). The word usually refers to theories of population growth, which Malthus discussed in *An Essay on the Principle of Population* (1798), in particular to his contention that poverty can never be overcome and that war, disease, and famine are nature's way of restricting population growth. "By the end of the century industrialization uncoupled fertility and population growth from its Malthusian connection with the price of grain and real wages" (J. Salt and D. Coleman, *The British Population: Patterns, Trends*, 1992).

Malvolio (malvōleeō) A pompous killjoy, especially one who finds himself humiliated by others. The allusion is to the arrogant steward in William

Shakespeare's comedy *Twelfth Night* (1600), who disapproves of frivolous behavior in others, but is then outraged when made to look ridiculous himself as the result of a practical joke. *He stormed off the stage like Malvolio, red in the face and swearing revenge on the whole pack of them.*

mammon (mamăn) Money or the desire for material wealth. An Aramaic word meaning "riches," it appears in Matthew 6:24 and Luke 16:9–13 in the course of warnings that excessive interest in worldly riches is incompatible with devotion to God. "Ye cannot serve God and mammon." Several later writers, including Edmund Spenser (1552/53–99) and John Milton (1608–74), chose to personalize material greed in the form of an avaricious pagan god or devil called Mammon. Material wealth that has been acquired by dubious means may sometimes be referred to as ***mammon of unrighteousness*** (as in Luke 16:9). "Mr. Crimsworth . . . frequented no place of worship, and owned no God but Mammon" (Charlotte Brontë, *The Professor,* 1857). *See also* NO MAN CAN SERVE TWO MASTERS.

man after his own heart, a A person who shares the same opinions, enthusiasms, or interests as another. The expression comes from 1 Samuel 13:14, in which Samuel rebukes Saul: "But now thy kingdom shall not continue: the LORD hath sought him a man after his own heart, and the LORD hath commanded him to be captain over his people, because thou hast not kept that which the LORD commanded thee." "As for Passepartout, he was a true Parisian of Paris. Since he had abandoned his own country for England, taking service as a valet, he had in vain searched for a master after his own heart" (Jules Verne, *Around the World in Eighty Days,* 1873). *The leader of the community association spent several years grooming his successor, wanting a man after his own heart.*

man born of woman The human race, especially with regard to the shortlived nature of human existence. The phrase comes from Job 14:1–2, in which Job laments, "Man that is born of a woman is of few days, and full of trouble. He cometh forth like a flower, and is cut down: he fleeth also as a shadow, and continueth not." "Well-a-well, man that is born of woman is of few days and full of trouble, as the Scripture says, and I reckon it's so" (Mark Twain, *The Adventures of Tom Sawyer,* 1876).

man cannot live by bread alone It takes more than such basic necessities as food to constitute a full human life. The proverb comes from the Bible, appearing at Deuteronomy 8:3: "Man doth not live by bread only, but by every word that proceedeth out of the mouth of the LORD." It is quoted by Jesus Christ in his temptation (Matthew 4:4). "Man, we know, cannot live by bread alone but hang me if I don't believe that some women could live by love alone" (Joseph Conrad, *Chance,* 1913).

man cannot serve two masters *See* NO MAN CAN SERVE TWO MASTERS.

mandarin (mandărin) A senior official, especially one with a pompous, arrogant manner. The word was first applied by Portuguese visitors to China to an important Chinese official otherwise known as the *kuan*. The word "mandarin" comes from the Sanskrit *mantrin*, meaning "counsellor." *The government mandarins got hold of the project and that was the last anyone heard of it.*

Manderley *See* REBECCA.

manes *See* APPEASE HIS MANES.

man for all seasons, a A person with an impressive range of talents, which enables him or her to be equal to virtually any challenge. The allusion is to the play *A Man for All Seasons* (1960) by the British playwright Robert Bolt (1924–95), about the Tudor statesman, writer, and philosopher Sir Thomas More (1478–1535). More employed his many talents to rise to the position of Lord Chancellor of England, but eventually even his great gifts were insufficient to save him from the executioner's ax after he fell foul of his master, Henry VIII, having opposed the latter's assumption of the role of head of the Church of England and his decision to divorce Catherine of Aragon and marry Anne Boleyn. Bolt was not actually the first person to apply the phrase to More, as it was thus employed many years earlier by More's contemporary Robert Whittington (c. 1480–c. 1530) and, before that, by More's friend Erasmus (c. 1466–1536). *With his many interests and skills, he was truly a man for all seasons.*

Man Friday A faithful servant or personal assistant. The allusion is to the young savage recruited as a servant by the castaway ROBINSON CRUSOE in the 1719 novel of the same name by the English writer Daniel Defoe (1660–1731). Crusoe calls him ***my man Friday*** because it was on a Friday that he found him. *He sent his Man Friday to get coffee and doughnuts for everyone. See also* GIRL FRIDAY.

Manichaean (manăkeeăn) Holding a dualistic view of the universe based on the perceived primordial conflict between light and dark and good and evil. Manichaeism, which incorporated elements of several religious doctrines, among them Gnosticism, Buddhism, Christianity, and Zoroastrianism, was named after the Persian prophet Manes (or Mani or Manichaeus), who promulgated such a philosophy in the third century A.D. *The government's policy has a Manichaean quality, drawing a clear distinction between good practice and bad and making no allowance for anything in between.*

Manlius *See* GEESE THAT SAVED THE CAPITOL.

manna from heaven (mană) A welcome gift, discovery, or otherwise much-needed source of relief. The phrase appears in Exodus 16:14–15, in which "manna" miraculously raining down from heaven provides the Israelites with sustenance during their 40-year sojourn in the wilderness: "And when the dew that lay was gone up, behold, upon the face of the wilderness there lay a small round thing, as small as the hoar frost on the ground. And when the children of Israel saw it, they said to one another, It is manna: for they wist not what it was." It is described as looking like coriander seed and tasting like honey. Speculation about what form of food manna actually was has suggested that it may have come from the tamarisk tree. "Brian Sedgemore, the leftwing Labour MP, spoke for dozens in Blunkett's own party when he called the proposed legislation 'manna from heaven for any future or present home secretary who wants to establish a police state'" (*Guardian,* November 23, 2001).

Man of a Thousand Faces *See* LON CHANEY.

man of lawlessness *See* ANTICHRIST.

man of sorrows Jesus Christ, especially an artistic depiction of Christ at the Crucifixion. The traditional image of the man of sorrows depicts Christ wearing his crown of thorns and with the wounds in his palms and side clearly visible. The title comes from Isaiah 53:3, in which it is prophesied that the Messiah would be "a man of sorrows, and acquainted with grief." "It seems to me as if you were stretching out your arms to me, and beckoning me to come and take my ease and live for my own delight, and Jesus, the Man of Sorrows, was standing looking towards me, and pointing to the sinful, and suffering, and afflicted" (George Eliot, *Adam Bede,* 1859).

man's gotta do what a man's gotta do, a Sometimes there is no escaping difficult and dangerous tasks in life. This is a quotation from the classic 1939 Western movie *Stagecoach*, in which it is delivered in more or less this form by a young JOHN WAYNE. Overfamiliarity with the phrase means that today it is only ever used facetiously. *The bathroom was in such a state after the party that I didn't really want to go in, but a man's gotta do what a man's gotta do.*

Manson, Charles *See* CHARLES MANSON.

mantle of Elijah (ălījă) Authority or leadership. In the Bible the phrase alludes to the mantle worn by the Hebrew prophet Elijah, known especially for his contest with the prophets of Baal on Mount Carmel (1 Kings 18:18–46). When Elijah was carried up to heaven by a whirlwind, his mantle was taken up by his chosen successor Elisha as a symbol of the authority he thus assumed (1 Kings 19:19; 2 Kings 2:13–14). Any person who succeeds to a position of authority or leadership is thereby said to ***assume the mantle of Elijah.*** "But like the prophet in the chariot disappearing in heaven and dropping his mantle to Elisha, the withdrawing night transferred its pale robe to the breaking day" (Herman Melville, *Billy Budd,* 1891).

man who came to dinner, the A guest who outstays his or her welcome. The 1939 stage comedy *The Man Who Came to Dinner* by George S. Kaufman (1889–1961) and Moss Hart (1904–61), filmed in 1941, relates how a suburban family is obliged to play host for several weeks to Sheridan Whiteside, a radio presenter with very decided opinions, after he breaks his leg while there for dinner. The venomous Sheridan Whiteside was based on a real person, the waspish theater critic Alexander Woollcott (1887–1943), who was delighted to be so immortalized and even played the part himself when the play went on tour. *He feared he was in danger of becoming the man who came to dinner, but his hosts seemed happy for him to stay as long as he liked.*

man who would be king, the A person who has ambitions to rise to the very top. The allusion is to a short story by the British writer Rudyard Kipling (1865–1936), in which he describes how two British adventurers gain the throne of a distant part of Afghanistan and there rule in glory until they fall out and are overthrown. *The governor tonight revealed himself as the man who would be king when he announced his candidature for the presidency.*

man without a country, a A person who lives in exile from his or her country. The allusion is to the title of a short story by the U.S. writer and minister Edward Everett Hale (1822–1909) about a young naval officer who finds himself implicated in a treasonous plot and is sentenced to sail with the navy for the rest of his life without returning home or even hearing the United States being mentioned. *Having left the party he is now truly a man without a country.*

man with the golden arm, the A heroin user. The allusion is to the title of a 1949 novel by the U.S. writer Nelson Algren (1909–81), filmed in 1955 with Frank Sinatra in the role of heroin addict

Frankie Machine. *Over the years he had spent a fortune on heroin and other drugs, and was known on the street as the man with the golden arm.*

many are called, but few are chosen Though many people may think themselves capable of doing something or be considered as candidates for something, only a few are actually likely to receive the opportunity to do so. The proverb first appears in the Bible in Matthew 20:16, in which Christ tells the parable of the laborers in the vineyard and emphasizes the challenge faced by all those who seek admission to heaven: "So the last shall be first, and the first last: for many be called, but few chosen." "There must also be the recollection which seeks to transform and transcend intelligence. Many are called, but few are chosen—because few even know in what salvation consists" (Aldous Huxley, *After Many A Summer,* 1939).

many mansions *See* HOUSE OF MANY MANSIONS.

man you love to hate, the A villain or rogue who nonetheless has a certain appeal. The description was originally applied to the Austrian-born U.S. movie actor and director Erich von Stroheim (1885–1957), who with his masterly portrayals of Teutonic arrogance was usually cast as a villain, his roles including callous murderers and sneering German soldiers. *Here comes her father, the man we all love to hate.*

many waters cannot quench love True love will not be extinguished by disappointment or setbacks. This proverbial observation comes from Song of Solomon 8:7, where it reads, "Many waters cannot quench love, neither can the floods drown it." The British novelist Thomas Hardy adopted the phrase in *Far From the Madding Crowd* (1874) to distinguish between profound love and more superficial attraction: "Where, however, happy circumstances permit its development, the compounded feeling proves itself to be the only love which is as strong as death—that love which many waters cannot quench, nor the floods drown, beside which the passion usually called by the name is evanescent as steam."

Marah (mahrah) A source or cause of bitterness. Marah, which means "bitterness" in Hebrew (see Ruth 1:20), was the name of an oasis some three days' journey from the Red Sea where the Israelites sought to slake their thirst. The waters proved bitter, however, and it was not until God had shown Moses a plant whose foliage would sweeten the water that they were able to drink (Exodus 15:23–25). "In his petition for a blessing on the meal, the poor old man added to his supplication, a prayer that the bread eaten in sadness of heart, and the bitter waters of Marah, might be made as nourishing as those which had been poured forth from a full cup and a plentiful basket and store" (Sir Walter Scott, *The Heart of Midlothian,* 1818).

maranatha *See* ANATHEMA.

marathon A long-distance cross-country running race and by extension any lengthy or arduous struggle or effort. Marathon was the name of a village northeast of Athens, and the plains nearby were the site of a climactic battle between the Greeks and a much larger invading Persian army in 490 B.C. Defeat in the battle would have left the way open to Athens, but the vastly outnumbered Greeks triumphed and the Persians were routed. In order to prevent the Persians from launching a new attack on Athens from a different direction, a runner was ordered to take the news and warning to the citizens before the enemy could regroup. The messenger ran the 26 miles, 385 yards as fast as he could and successfully got word to the city in time. His remarkable feat is still commemorated in the running of the marathon over a similar distance to that covered by the original messenger in the modern OLYMPIC GAMES. The ancient Greek runner is sometimes identified by name as Pheidippides, although the latter actually ran from Athens to Sparta to seek help before the battle. *After this marathon effort few members of the task force had the physical or mental stamina to offer further resistance to the proposals.*

March The third month of the year. It was named after MARS, the Roman god of war, and before the introduction of the JULIAN CALENDAR marked the beginning (first month) of the year. It also marked the period of the year when generals could launch new battle campaigns, hence the link with the warlike Mars. *March is a time of signals and alarms and the true beginning of the year, as far as nature is concerned.*

march to the beat of a different drummer To act or think in an independent way; to part from the majority. The allusion is to a passage in "Where I Lived and What I Lived For" by the U.S. essayist Henry David Thoreau (1817–62): "If a man does not keep pace with his companions, perhaps it is because he hears a different drummer. Let him step to the music which he hears, however measured or far away." *It was clear from a very young age that the great man marched to the beat of a different drummer.*

Marian, Maid *See* ROBIN HOOD.

Marie Antoinette (maree ontwănet) A frivolous, luxury-loving woman, especially one who disregards the suffering of others. The Austrian-born Josèphe Jeanne Marie Antoinette (1755–93) was notorious for the decadent, self-indulgent life she led at the court of her husband Louis XVI of France. She spent money extravagantly and showed little interest in the welfare of the poorer members of society (*see* LET THEM EAT CAKE), earning the hatred of the Paris mob, which ultimately had the satisfaction of seeing her guillotined in the turmoil following the French Revolution. *Once she had married her millionaire she lived like Marie Antoinette.*

Marie Celeste (maree sălest) A boat that is found inexplicably abandoned by its crew, or any other similarly deserted place. The U.S. brigantine *Marie Celeste* (properly, *Mary Celeste*) was found abandoned at sea between Portugal and the Azores on December 5, 1872. Apart from a few missing items, such as a sextant and chronometer, everything was as it should be, except that the crew had completely vanished. The riddle has never been solved and the crew's disappearance remains one of the great mysteries of the sea. "In a ghost town, silent and deserted as the *Marie Celeste*, I gave myself a history lesson" (Bette Howell, *Dandelion Days*, 1991).

Marilyn Monroe (marilin mănrō) A voluptuous blonde. Marilyn Monroe (Norma Jean Mortenson; 1926–62) achieved fame as a model and movie actress, combining the elemental appeal of a sexy screen goddess with a natural talent for comedy. She became an icon of the 1950s with highly acclaimed appearances in such movies as *Gentlemen Prefer Blondes* (1953), *Bus Stop* (1956), and *The Misfits* (1961). Her premature death, apparently from an overdose of sleeping pills, was a cause of lasting international regret. *She's not unattractive but she's no Marilyn Monroe.*

mark of Cain (kayn) A brand or other distinguishing mark that bears witness to some past crime or misdeed. According to the biblical account of Abel's murder at the hands of his brother Cain, Cain was branded by God with a special mark so that those who met him would refrain from killing him out of vengeance: "And the LORD set a mark upon Cain, lest any finding him should kill him" (Genesis 4:15). Tradition has it that the mark took the form of a bloodstained brand on Cain's brow. In modern usage a mark of Cain, or ***curse of Cain,*** is generally understood to be a mark of punishment rather than protection. "The commitment is total and to opt out of the system is a mark of Cain" (*Guardian,* July 19, 1991). *See also* CAIN AND ABEL.

mark of the beast A physical mark or something else that indicates a person's association with evil. In the book of Revelation (13:16–17, 16:2, and 19:20) an angel punishes those who bear the mark of the beast, a brand on the right hand or forehead signifying those who, at the behest of a creature risen up from the earth, worship a seven-headed beast from the sea. Those who criticize a person or activity as evil are said to ***set the mark of the beast*** on the object of their condemnation. In the Royal Navy the lapel flashes of midshipmen are traditionally nicknamed marks of the beast. "Each of these creatures, despite its human form, its rag of clothing, and the rough humanity of its bodily form, had woven into it—into its movements, into the expression of its countenance, into its whole presence—some now irresistible suggestion of a hog, a swinish taint, the unmistakable mark of the beast" (H. G. Wells, *The Island of Doctor Moreau,* 1896).

Marlboro man (mahrlbărō) Archetype of a rugged, masculine cowboy. The allusion is to a long-running advertising campaign for Marlboro cigarettes, which was launched in 1954. The campaign featured the stirring image of a cowboy contentedly smoking a Marlboro cigarette as he surveyed an expansive Wild West landscape. The campaign was apparently conceived to popularize filter cigarettes, which until then had been considered feminine. It was hugely successful and over the years many actors and male models appeared in the role of the Marlboro man; two of them, it must be added, later died of lung cancer. The quintessential wild country in which the Marlboro man supposedly thrived was dubbed ***Marlboro country***, though the cigarettes themselves were actually named after Great Marlborough Street in the West End of London, where the manufacturers of the cigarettes were originally based. *The guide clearly thought of himself as a Marlboro man, with his white stetson and faded blue jeans.*

Marlene Dietrich (mahrlaynă deetrik) Archetypal femme fatale. The German-born movie actress and singer Marlene Dietrich (Magdalena von Losch; 1901–92) sprang to fame in *The Blue Angel* (1930) and acquired iconic status as a vampish sex symbol whose husky voice came to be widely imitated by admirers and impersonators. *In his high heels, fishnet stockings, and top hat he looked like a nightmarish version of Marlene Dietrich.*

Marley's ghost *See* SCROOGE.

Marlowe, Philip *See* PHILIP MARLOWE.

Marner, Silas *See* SILAS MARNER.

Marple, Miss *See* MISS MARPLE.

Marquess of Queensberry rules *See* QUEENSBERRY RULES.

marriage in Cana *See* WATER INTO WINE.

Mars (mahrz) The personification of war. Though generally identified as the god of war in Roman mythology, Mars began as a god of spring growth who was venerated for keeping livestock safe from threat. Later he became strongly associated with the warlike instinct, and the area in Rome where soldiers trained was dubbed the Field of Mars. He was also identified as the father of ROMULUS AND REMUS. *The king assumed the guise of Mars himself, personally ordering his battalions forward and ranging his magisterial eye over the entire field of battle. See also* MARCH.

Marshall Plan (mahrshăl) An economic aid package to relieve a whole region or nation under pressure. The allusion is to the plan proposed in 1947 by U.S. secretary of state George C. Marshall (1880–1959) to deliver aid to assist in the economic recovery of Europe after World War II. The ensuing European Recovery Program did much to restore the industries of various western European states. *We need to organize a new Marshall Plan to help the ailing nations of central Africa.*

Martha (mahrthă) A woman who is constantly occupied with domestic chores. According to Luke 10:38–42, when Christ visited the home in Bethany of the sisters Martha and MARY, Martha carried on preparing a meal while Mary broke off to listen to Christ's words. When Martha complained that her sister was leaving her to do all the work, she was gently rebuked by Christ: "Martha, Martha, thou art careful and troubled about many things: But one thing is needful: and Mary hath chosen that good part, which shall not be taken away from her" (Luke 10:41–42). Martha is now honored as the patron saint of homemakers. "Her paradise was not a tranquil one, for the little woman fussed, was over-anxious to please, and bustled about like a true Martha, cumbered with many cares" (Louisa May Alcott, *Little Women,* 1868–69).

martinet (mahrtinet) A strict disciplinarian. The reference is to the marquis de Martinet, a colonel in the French infantry during the reign of Louis XIV. It was into Martinet's regiment, which was renowned for its strict discipline, that young aristocrats were obliged, at the king's command, to do military service. He was killed "accidentally" by his own troops at the siege of Duisberg in 1762. *The captain was a real martinet who would tolerate no misbehavior in his crew.*

Marvel, Captain *See* CAPTAIN MARVEL.

Marx Brothers (mahrks) A team of comical incompetents. The Marx Brothers were among the most popular comedy stars of the 1930s, starring in such movies as *The Cocoanuts* (1929) and *A Night at the Opera* (1935). They comprised Leonard Marx (Chico; 1886–1961), Adolph Marx (Harpo; 1888–1964), Julius Marx (Groucho; 1890–1977), Herbert Marx (Zeppo; 1901–79), and Milton Marx (Gummo; 1892–1977), although Gummo left the team relatively early in their career. *Watching that team of builders putting up a wall was like watching the Marx Brothers.*

Mary (mairee) A quiet, contemplative woman. According to Luke 10:38–42, Mary, the sister of MARTHA, listened attentively to Christ's words while her sister carried on with her domestic chores. *Unlike her sister, who busied herself in the connecting room, the other girl sat like Mary quietly in the corner mulling unhappily over her father's words. See also* VIRGIN MARY.

Mary Magdalene *See* MAGDALEN; MAUDLIN.

Mary Poppins (popinz) A children's nanny, or a woman who seems particularly gifted at domestic and other chores. Mary Poppins, a likable nanny with a magical touch, was introduced to the world in the stories of P. L. Travers (1899–1996), making her first appearance in 1934. She was later brought to life on the cinema screen by Julie Andrews in the musical *Mary Poppins* (1964). *Her house is so tidy she must be Mary Poppins.*

Mason, Perry *See* PERRY MASON.

massacre of the innocents A complete rout or comprehensive annihilation of a defenseless enemy. The phrase refers to the systematic killing of all male children two years old and younger that according to Matthew 2:1–16 took place in Bethlehem on the orders of Herod the Great in an attempt to stop the prophecy from coming true that one of these boys was destined to become king of the Jews. In modern usage the phrase is not limited to acts of murderous slaughter but may also be applied to any seemingly merciless action against innocent or defenseless parties. "Herod reigns in France, and over all the earth, and begins each year his massacre of the innocents; and if it be not blasphemy against the sacredness of life, I say that the most happy are those who have disappeared" (Upton Sinclair, *Damaged Goods,* 1913).

Mata Hari (mahtă hahree) A beautiful female spy. Mata Hari was the stage name of the Dutch dancer Margaretha Geertruida Zelle (1876–1917), whose notorious career ended with her being shot by a French firing squad on charges of spying for the Germans during World War I. Her pseudonym came from a Malay name for the sun, and meant "eye of the day." *She seemed so innocent that no one thought she could possibly turn out to be a Mata Hari.*

Mather, Cotton *See* COTTON MATHER.

Matilda (mătildă) A congenital liar. This is an allusion to one of the *Cautionary Tales* (1907) of Hilaire Belloc (1870–1953). The story concerns a small girl called Matilda who is in the habit of playing the practical joke of shouting "Fire!", only to be disbelieved (and consequently burned to death) when a real fire breaks out. *His daughter was a Matilda whose every other sentence was a blatant untruth.*

maudlin Foolishly tearful, sentimental, or rambling. The word comes from the name of Mary Magdalene (or Magdalen), conventionally depicted in art as weeping. (See MAGDALEN.) "I hurried back to that door and glanced in. Alas, there was small room for hope—Backus's eyes were heavy and bloodshot, his sweaty face was crimson, his speech maudlin and thick, his body sawed drunkenly about with the weaving motion of the ship" (Mark Twain, *Life on the Mississippi,* 1883).

Maundy Thursday (mahndee) The Thursday before Easter, commemorating the Last Supper. *Maundy* comes from the Old French *mandé* (meaning "commanded"), a translation of the Latin *mandatum* ("commandment"), which appears in a quotation of Christ's: "Mandatum novum do vobis," meaning "A new commandment I give unto you" (John 13:34). The commandment in question is "That ye love one another; as I have loved you." The day is marked by special services, and in Britain the monarch presents specially minted coins called ***Maundy money*** to a small number of elderly people (one for each year of the present reign). This custom recalls the former tradition of monarchs and bishops honoring Christ, who showed his humility by washing the feet of his disciples and of a few select poor people and by handing out food and clothes. *The Maundy Thursday service will be broadcast from the cathedral at an earlier hour this year.*

mausoleum (mahzōleeăm) A tomb, especially one of imposing dimensions, or a place that is as lifeless or gloomy as a tomb. The term is an allusion to the magnificent tomb of Mausolus, king of Caria (d. 353 B.C.), which was constructed at Halicarnassus in the fourth century B.C. and was included among the seven wonders of the ancient world. Some 140 feet high and complete with huge statues of Mausolus and his wife, it is thought to have been destroyed by an earthquake in medieval times. "Of course, Aunt Myra could not be neglected, and, with secret despair, Rose went to the 'Mausoleum,' as the boys called her gloomy abode" (Louisa May Alcott, *Eight Cousins,* 1874).

maverick (mavărik) A person who behaves with cavalier disregard for convention. The allusion is to Samuel August Maverick (1803–70), a Texan rancher who rejected the usual practice of branding his cattle and let them roam freely. Consequently, any unbranded steer became known as a "maverick," and it was only a matter of time before the term was applied to unfettered humans as well, initially to politicians who had no allegiance to their party leadership. "In his own time he had been a maverick, and for being a maverick his grateful sovereign had pinned on his chest the gallantry medal of the Military Cross" (Gerald Seymour, *Condition Black*, 1991).

May The fifth month of the year. It was named after Maia, the Roman goddess of spring and fertility. *She was in the May of her life, fresh and young and blooming.*

Mayflower Symbol of the fundamental, egalitarian spirit of the founders of the United States. The *Mayflower* was the sailing ship that brought the 102 Pilgrim fathers across the Atlantic from Plymouth in England in 1620. These colonists agreed the so-called "Mayflower Compact," under the terms of which they dedicated themselves to founding a community in which the majority will would prevail, thus providing a model for modern western democracy. The *Mayflower* subsequently returned to England, and timbers from the ship are said to have been used to build a barn at Jordans, Buckinghamshire. *The crowd applauded this demonstration of the true Mayflower spirit.*

meander To follow a winding, twisting course; to ramble aimlessly. The word is an allusion to the Meander River in Phrygia, whose many windings are supposed to have inspired Daedalus to build the LABYRINTH. "She always returned, with greater emphasis and with an instinctive knowledge of the strength of her objection, 'Let us have no meandering.' Not to meander myself, at present, I will go back to my birth" (Charles Dickens, *David Copperfield,* 1849–50).

measure for measure A matching response, revenge, or other return; tit for tat. The expression is best known as the title of a tragicomedy by William Shakespeare (1604) but is actually biblical in origin, appearing in Matthew 7:2: "For with what judgment ye judge, ye shall be judged: and with what measure ye mete, it shall be measured to you again." "All things are double, one against another—Tit for tat; an eye for an eye; a tooth for a tooth; blood for blood; measure for measure; love for love" (Ralph Waldo Emerson, "Compensation," 1841).

meat that ye know not of A private source of solace, sustenance, or other support, especially of a spiritual nature. The expression comes from John 4:32 in which the disciples entreat Christ to eat something but receive the reply that "I have meat to eat that ye know not of." *When asked how he supported himself, the wizard cryptically replied to his followers, "I have meat you know not of."*

mecca (meka) An ultimate goal or ambition, a place that attracts many visitors or tourists. The term comes from Mecca, a city in modern Saudi Arabia that has special significance in Islamic lore as the birthplace of MUHAMMAD and as a result is the destination for Muslims taking the hajj, or pilgrimage that all the faithful are supposed to take at least once in their lifetime. "East Grafton was the ancient habitat of the race, and Penhallow Grange, where 'old' John Penhallow lived, was a Mecca to them" (Lucy Maud Montgomery, *Chronicles of Avonlea,* 1912).

Medea (medeeă) A vengeful, jealous, and cruel woman, especially one believed to be a sorceress. In Greek legend Medea was the daughter of the king of Colchis, an enchantress who helped her lover Jason and the Argonauts in their quest for the GOLDEN FLEECE. The victims of her cruelty included her own brother Absyrtus (whom she cut into pieces to delay pursuit by her father), Jason's uncle Pelias, and ultimately the princess Glauce and her father King Creon of Corinth after Jason decided to abandon Medea and marry Glauce. She also killed the children she had borne Jason and, after seeking shelter at the court of King Aegeus, sought to poison the king's son Theseus. When this plot failed she fled to Colchis. *The rest of the family were jaundiced in their opinion of the old lady, generally agreeing she had behaved like a Medea over her husband's relatively innocuous lapse.*

Medes and Persians, law of the *See* LAW OF THE MEDES AND PERSIANS.

Medici (medeechee) Patrons of culture and the arts. The Medici family, notably Cosimo de' Medici (1389–1464), towered over the Italian RENAISSANCE of the 14th and 15th centuries, using their great wealth to foster the talents of such luminaries as Botticelli, LEONARDO DA VINCI, and MICHELANGELO. *Toward the end of the 19th century several prominent East Coast families vied to become the Medicis of their day.*

medium is the message, the Sometimes the means by which communication is made is more significant than the message itself. This is a quotation from *Understanding Media* (1964) by the Canadian philosopher Marshall McLuhan (1911–80), in which the author argues that the changing pace of technology represented by computers and other electronic media is a dominant influence upon modern life, outweighing anything actually communicated using such media. "The medium is the message because the message, the culture and ideology of consumerism, has engulfed the medium" (Leslie Sklair, *Sociology of the Global System*, 1991).

medusa (medoosă) Alternative name for a jellyfish. The creature received its name through a fancied resemblance between its tentacles and the snake hair of the fearsome Medusa, one of the GORGONS. According to legend, she acquired her loathsome appearance as punishment for offending the goddess Athena by consorting with Poseidon in the temple of Athena. Medusa was finally slain by Perseus when he cut off her head. *It rapidly emerged that the affair was more complicated than first imagined, with as many tentacles as a medusa.*

meek as Moses (mōziz) Long suffering; uncomplaining; quietly accepting. In the Bible meekness is interpreted not as weakness but rather in terms of humility or gentleness of spirit. It is because of the devoutness and restraint of the biblical prophet Moses under the taunts of Aaron and Miriam that God actively defends him from his enemies and helps him to deliver his people from slavery (Numbers 12:3). By the same token, Christ is also described as "meek" (Matthew 11:29; 21:5). In modern usage meekness is more likely to be understood to signify an inclination to accept one's lot and may just as readily be interpreted as a sign of weakness as praiseworthy restraint. "He wasn't the able seaman you see now. He was meek as Moses" (Lucy Maud Montgomery, *Anne's House of Dreams,* 1915).

meek shall inherit the earth, the Those who are humble in heart will receive their just reward in the end. The proverb comes from the Bible, appearing in Matthew 5:5: "Blessed are the meek: for they shall inherit the earth." Modern variants on the theme have included J. Paul Getty's quip "The meek shall inherit the earth, but not its mineral rights." "Blessed are the meek, blessed are the failures, blessed are the stupid, for they, unknown to themselves, have a grace which is denied to the haughty, the successful, and the wise" (Arnold Bennett, *Anna of the Five Towns,* 1902). *See also* BEATITUDE.

meet one's Waterloo *See* WATERLOO.

Megaera *See* FURIES.

Mein Kampf (mīn kampf) An autobiography, especially one that contains highly controversial political views. *Mein Kampf* ("My Struggle") was written by Adolf HITLER while he was serving a prison sentence following the Munich PUTSCH of 1923 and published in two parts, in 1925 and 1927. It summarized the deranged political theories that led to the formation of the Nazi movement and became the "bible" of Hitler's followers. Publication of the book has been officially suppressed since World War II, although occasional editions have been released from time to time. *He found this lengthy political statement of intent about as readable as Mein Kampf, and about as forgivable.*

Mekon *See* DAN DARE

Melchior *See* MAGI.

Melchizedek (melkizădek) A person without parents; a priest whose service to God is without end. Melchizedek is identified in Genesis 14:18–20 and elsewhere as a high priest of Salem who was "without father, without mother, without descent, having neither beginning of days, nor end of life; but made like unto the Son of God; abiding a priest continually." Melchizedek, whose name means "king of righteousness," blessed Abraham and is depicted as an Old Testament precursor of Jesus Christ (Hebrews 7). "He would hold his secret knowledge and secret power, being as sinless as the innocent; and he would be a priest forever according to the order of Melchisedec" (James Joyce, *A Portrait of the Artist as a Young Man,* 1915).

Meleager *See* CALYDONIAN BOAR HUNT.

Mellors, Oliver *See* LADY CHATTERLEY.

Melpomene *See* MUSES.

meltdown A situation in which events move irrevocably toward total disaster. The reference is to nuclear reactions, specifically to what happens if a radioactive core becomes overheated and melts, releasing radioactivity: In theory there would be nothing to stop the molten core burning its way right through the earth, with even more catastrophic effects. Meltdowns of varying degrees became reality as a result of the nuclear accidents that occurred at THREE MILE ISLAND in 1979 and, more seriously, at CHERNOBYL in 1986. *The organization has been in meltdown since the resignation of the entire board of directors. See also* CHINA SYNDROME.

Menalcas (menalkas) A shepherd or other rural character. The allusion is to a minor character in Virgil's *Eclogues* (42–37 B.C.) and also in the *Idylls* of Theocritus (c. 310–250 B.C.). *The crew eventually found what they wanted in the local bar, a withered old Menalcas who knew everything about the hills and forests and, even better, all there was to know about the folklore of the region.*

men are from Mars, women are from Venus Men and women have fundamentally different outlooks on the world. The notion that men and women are so different that they might seem to come from different planets was the premise of a best-selling book of the same title, published in 1992 by U.S. family therapist Dr. John Gray (b. 1951). *Many a marriage has faltered when one or both partners have forgotten the basic reality that while men are from Mars, women are from Venus.*

mend one's fences To repair damaged relationships. The allusion here is to the U.S. statesman John Sherman (1823–1900), brother of the celebrated Civil War general William Tecumseh Sherman, who when planning his next political advance in Washington made a strategic visit to his farm in Ohio to renew connections with, and thus regain the support of, local voters. When asked by reporters what he was doing back at his farm in Ohio, Sherman replied that he was mending fences, hence the modern meaning of the expression. *She had not spoken with her mother for years, but now the time had come to mend some fences.*

mene, mene, tekel, upharsin *See* WRITING ON THE WALL.

Menechmians (menekmeeănz) People who resemble one another closely. The word originated in reference to the comedy *Menaechmi* by Plautus (c. 254–184 B.C.), the plot of which depends on the confusions of identity resulting from the striking similarity between the central characters. Centuries later it provided the basis for *The Comedy of Errors* (c. 1594) by William Shakespeare. *When they were dressed similarly, few people could tell these two Menechmians apart, and many were the confusions and embarrassments that ensued.*

men in black Secret agents, especially ones who work for the government in an attempt to suppress the truth about contact with aliens. The notion that such extraterrestrial contacts were being kept quiet by various governments through the agency of their "men in black" became current during the 1950s and has been a theme of various best-selling science-fiction books and big-budget Hollywood movies, such as *Close Encounters of the Third Kind* (1977) and *Men in Black* (1997). The success of the latter gave more currency to the phrase, as did its use in the X-FILES television series. The term reflects the popular idea that such agents dress in dark suits, wear dark glasses, and drive in black cars. *She refused to tell us about the incident, saying she feared she might be silenced by the men in black.*

mentor A wise and faithful adviser or teacher, especially one who gives advice to someone younger or less experienced. In Greek mythology, Mentor was identified by Homer as the trusted friend of ODYSSEUS and, in the absence of Odysseus during the Trojan War, the tutor of his son Telemachus. When Telemachus went in search of his father, the goddess Athena took the guise of Mentor to accompany him. "He did not think it expedient to receive her alone. He consulted his mentor, Mr. Dove, and his client, John Eustace, and the latter consented to be present" (Anthony Trollope, *The Eustace Diamonds,* 1873).

Mercury (merkyăree) Epithet for a messenger or, alternatively, a thief. In Roman mythology Mercury was the god of commerce, thieves, and traffic, equivalent to the Greek Hermes. He remains best known as the messenger of the gods and is conventionally depicted wearing the pair of winged sandals that gave him great speed. The adjective ***mercurial*** (meaning "lighthearted" or "volatile") was originally applied by astrologers to people born under the influence of the planet Mercury and were thereby supposed to have fanciful, changeable natures. *Like her mother, she had a mercurial character, melancholy one moment but laughing the next as if she didn't have a care in the world.*

Mercutio *See* PLAGUE ON BOTH YOUR HOUSES, A; ROMEO AND JULIET.

mercy seat *See* THRONE OF GRACE.

Merlin (merlin) A person who appears to have magical powers at his disposal. Merlin is one of the main characters in the various myths and legends surrounding KING ARTHUR and the knights of the ROUND TABLE. Merlin plays an important role in most of the key events of Arthur's life, and the Round Table was said to have been his own creation. It has been suggested that the character was based upon a real historical figure, a bard who lived around the end of the fifth century A.D., perhaps in Wales. *He played Merlin in the court of John F. Kennedy.*

Merops's son (meropsiz) A person who mistakenly thinks he or she can put everything right. The reference is to the legendary PHAETON, reputedly the son of King Merops of Ethiopia, who thought he could steer the car of PHOEBUS (actually the Sun itself) safely through the sky and only narrowly avoided setting the Earth on fire. In modern usage the term is usually applied to agitators or demagogues. *The butler murmured darkly something about Merops's son but oozed out of the room before he could be questioned more closely, leaving us all wondering to whom he had been referring.*

merry men *See* ROBIN HOOD.

Meshach *See* FIERY FURNACE.

mesmerism (mezmărizăm) The use of hypnotism as a therapeutic treatment. The practice is named after the Austrian physician Franz Anton Mesmer (1734–1815), who first experimented with such therapies in Vienna. *There was no way they would get her to agree to it short of resorting to mesmerism.*

Messalina (mesăleenă) A lustful, sexually voracious woman. Valeria Messalina (c. A.D. 22–48) married the future emperor Claudius at the age of 15 and after he achieved power three years later, wielded immense influence through him, controlling imperial appointments and ordering the deaths of political opponents. Although faithful in the early years of her marriage in order to forestall any doubts about the paternity of her son Britannicus, she subsequently became notorious for her many sexual conquests, who included notable political and military figures. She was eventually undone when rumors of a mock wedding she had gone through with the consul designate Gaius Silius reached Claudius, who had her executed for treason in her own garden. The name has been applied to several individuals since classical times, notably to Catherine the Great (1729–96), who was dubbed the Modern Messalina. *"My god," cried the director, clutching his temple. "I asked for a Goldilocks, and they've sent me Messalina!"*

messiah (măsīă) Someone who is hailed as a savior, especially one who has been long awaited. Derived from the Hebrew word *masiah,* meaning "anointed," it is one of the titles by which Jesus Christ is often referred to (for example, in Matthew 16:16 and 26:63 and in John 1:41). The name *Christ* is a translation into Greek of *Messiah.* The coming of a messiah was predicted by such Old Testament prophets as Isaiah, Jeremiah, and Ezekiel, and since biblical times the title has often been applied to leaders who are expected to restore the fortunes of a particular people or other group. "For a year Vida . . . was healthily vexed by Carol's assumption that she was a sociological messiah come to save Gopher Prairie" (Sinclair Lewis, *Main Street,* 1920).

mess of pottage *See* SELL ONE'S BIRTHRIGHT FOR A MESS OF POTTAGE.

me Tarzan, you Jane *See* TARZAN.

Methuselah *See* AS OLD AS METHUSELAH.

Micawber, Wilkins *See* WILKINS MICAWBER.

Michaelmas (mikălmăs) September 29, marking the feast of St. Michael the Archangel. Michael is identified in the Bible as the prince of the angels, who protected the Jewish people (Daniel 12:1) and led the celestial army against Satan (Jude 9). Traditionally Michaelmas Day was one of the four quarter-days upon which various rents and other payments became due; some British universities still have a Michaelmas term in the autumn. *The Michaelmas term is relatively short this year.*

Michelangelo (mīkălanjălō) A brilliantly gifted artist or sculptor. Michelangelo di Lodovico Buonarroti Simoni (1475–1564) was hugely admired in his own time for his unsurpassed artistic creations and is remembered today as one of the giants of cultural history. His masterpieces include the statue of *David* (1501–04) and the stunning ceiling of the Sistine Chapel at the Vatican in Rome (1508–12). *He has been called Spain's Michelangelo.* *See also* PAINTING THE SISTINE CHAPEL.

mickey finn (mikee fin) A drugged or doctored drink, the effect of which is to render the drinker unconscious. The original Mickey Finn is said to have worked as a bartender at the Lone Star and Palm saloons in Chicago around 1900. He was proficient at making up a potion that would have such an effect, using it to rob customers. An essential ingredient of a mickey finn is allegedly chlorine. In modern usage the term may also be applied to anything else that delivers a debilitating, "knockout" blow. *They slipped him a mickey finn and then went through his pockets looking for anything of value.*

Mickey Mouse (mikee mows) Something that is deemed to be on a derisorily small or insignificant scale. The cartoon character Mickey Mouse was the most famous creation of U.S. filmmaker Walt Disney (1901–66). The fact that Mickey Mouse was a staggering success and the foundation stone of what became the Disney empire has not prevented the character's name from coming to represent what is trivial and not to be taken seriously—an association that may have arisen through reference to the thousands of cheaply-made, unreliable watches and other products bearing Mickey Mouse's image that were subsequently manufactured to cash in on the character's immense popularity. *Their grand plan was eventually exposed as a Mickey Mouse project that lacked any proper funding.*

Mickey Spillane (mikee spilayn) Archetype of a writer of hard-boiled detective fiction. Mickey Spillane (b. 1918) became a best-selling author with his combination of sex and violence, notably in the novels featuring the tough detective ***Mike Hammer***. *He was a crime novelist in the hard-hitting Mickey Spillane tradition.*

Midas touch (mīdăs) The ability to turn virtually any project into a success; a golden touch. The reference is to King Midas of Phrygia, who was granted his wish to be able to turn anything he touched to gold. His newfound talent backfired, however, when he found that his food and drink (and even his daughter, according to one version of the tale) turned to gold at his touch, and soon he was begging to be returned to his original condition. This was eventually achieved by his bathing in the waters of the Pactolus, from which time the river has always been edged by golden sand. "So twenty years, with their hopes and fears and smiles and tears and such, / Went by and left me long bereft of hope of the Midas touch" (Robert Service, *Ballads of a Cheechako,* 1909).

mighty fallen, how are the *See* HOW ARE THE MIGHTY FALLEN!

mighty hunter *See* NIMROD.

Mike Hammer *See* MICKEY SPILLANE.

Milesian tales (mīleezheăn) Short stories of a characteristically obscene nature. The original collection of such stories was compiled by and named after the Greek writer Aristides of Miletus, who lived in the second century B.C. The tales, which have not survived to modern times, were ultimately the work of one Antonius Diogenes. *The group at the bar was swapping Milesian tales in subdued tones, broken every now and then by unsuppressible gusts of delighted laughter.*

milk and honey *See* LAND FLOWING WITH MILK AND HONEY.

millennium A period of 1,000 years, often referring to the period before Satan's final overthrow (Revelation 20) when Satan is bound and believers are resurrected and reign with Christ. It has been interpreted in different ways: "as a symbol of the present time between Christ's first and second comings (***amillennialism***), of a time when Christ will return and reign on earth before the final resurrection (***premillennialism***), and of a period of great success for the church and the gospel before

Christ's second coming (***postmillennialism***)" (Selman and Manser, *Hearthside Bible Dictionary,* p. 162). The millennium was expected by some to begin in the year 1000, but when this did not happen various theories based on different readings of the biblical text were put forward as to the possible date. Similar expectations were raised, and disappointed, in 2000. "You hear talk, sometimes, 'd make you think the millennium had come—but right the next breath you'll hear somebody hollerin' about "the great unrest." You BET there's a 'great unrest'!" (Booth Tarkington, *The Turmoil,* 1915).

Mills and Boon Of or relating to a strongly romantic, sentimental type of fiction. The Mills and Boon publishing company was founded by Gerald Mills (1877–1928) and Charles Boon (1877–1943) and from the 1930s became a byword for popular escapist romantic fiction. Interestingly, the company did not initially start out with such books, but included among its early output novels by distinguished writers such as Hugh Walpole and P. G. Wodehouse. *The wedding was all very Mills and Boon, with half a dozen sweet young children acting as bridesmaids amid a sea of flowers.*

millstone around one's neck An inescapable and onerous obligation or duty that tends to handicap a person's efforts. The expression comes from Matthew 18:6, which delivers a warning against those who would lead a child astray: "But whoso shall offend one of these little ones which believe in me, it were better for him that a millstone were hanged about his neck, and that he were drowned in the depth of the sea." *His obligations to his family are a real millstone around his neck.*

Milo (mīlō) Personification of great physical strength. Milo was a famous Greek athlete who lived in Crotona toward the end of the sixth century B.C. Legend has it that he once carried a four-year-old heifer through the stadium at Olympia before eating the entire animal, and also that he met his death after attempting to pull apart a partially riven oak tree, becoming trapped by the hands and in this helpless condition being devoured by wolves. *This new Milo seemed not to know the limits of his strength and looked about him for a new way to impress the growing crowd with his prodigious muscle power.*

Milquetoast, Caspar See CASPAR MILQUETOAST.

Miltonic (miltonik) Of or relating to the writings of the English poet John Milton (1608–74). The author of the masterpieces *Paradise Lost* (1667) and *Paradise Regained* (1671), among other works, John Milton dealt with such profound, lofty, "Miltonic" themes as the fall of man, the rights of the people against the monarchy, the shortcomings of the Church of England, and the greatness of God. *He condemned the failings of the contemporary cultural establishment in ringing, Miltonic tones.*

Minerva See ATHENA; INVITA MINERVA.

Ming the Merciless See FLASH GORDON.

Minotaur See LABYRINTH.

mint A place where money is manufactured. The word comes from the Latin *moneta* (meaning "money"), which was in turn a reference to an alternative title (meaning "the admonisher") for the Roman goddess Juno. It was next to the temple of Juno in Rome that the city's money was coined. *All the new coins will have to be returned to the mint and replaced by a new issue. See also* MONEY.

minuteman (minitman) A person who is ready to respond at a moment's notice. The allusion is to the militiamen called "minute men" who volunteered to be ready to turn out at short notice to fight the British army at the start of the American Revolution in 1776. During the cold war era, the term was also applied to members of extremist right-wing U.S. organizations dedicated to opposing communist infiltration into the United States. "Two booklets said that the president of the USA was a Communist and suggested that I should . . . buy a gun now and form a secret minuteman team" (Len Deighton, *Billion-Dollar Brain*, 1991).

Miranda (mirandă) A beautiful young woman, especially one who is curious about but largely innocent of the ways of the world. Miranda is the daughter of the magician PROSPERO in William Shakespeare's *The Tempest* (1611), an innocent young girl who has been brought up in seclusion from the real world of men (*see* BRAVE NEW WORLD). It is thought that Shakespeare actually invented the name, deriving it from the Latin *mirandum*, meaning "fit to be admired." *She was as wide-eyed as Miranda but appeared to know nothing of the fate that awaited her.*

Miriam (mireeăm) A person who sings, especially one who sings with joy. The allusion is to the biblical Miriam, a prophetess and the elder sister of Moses and Aaron, who urged the Israelites to sing with joy to celebrate their safe crossing of the Red Sea: "Sing ye to the LORD, for he hath triumphed gloriously" (Exodus 15:20–21). *The news she received on the telephone was evidently good, for she is now dancing with her handkerchief and singing like the biblical Miriam in a spirit of reckless gaiety.*

miserable comforters *See* JOB'S COMFORTER.

Miss Havisham (havishăm) Archetype of an elderly spinster, especially one embittered by past romantic disappointments. Miss Havisham is an aged jilted bride in the Charles Dickens novel *Great Expectations* (1860–61). Unable to get over the fact that she was deserted on her wedding day, she has spent the rest of her life living in her decaying house amid the ruins of her wedding feast, still wearing her wedding dress. *Her aunt was a Miss Havisham who loathed all men because of some unspoken disappointment in her youth.*

missing link A person with Neanderthal characteristics, such as limited intelligence or an overhanging brow. For many years evolutionists sought the missing link—a supposed intermediate form between *Homo sapiens* and the apes. Various finds were identified as providing evidence of the existence of such a creature, but most have since been discounted (*see* PILTDOWN MAN). *When he heard the news he lost his temper completely and stamped about the apartment like he was the missing link.*

mission impossible An impossibly difficult task. The allusion is to the popular U.S. spy thriller television series *Mission Impossible* (1966–73), which was later revived as a successful movie franchise. It revolved around the adventures of members of a sophisticated espionage agency, called the Impossible Missions Force, and episodes memorably began with instructions delivered by means of a tape recording that self-destructed five seconds after being played. *Getting to the top of the mountain before dusk was beginning to look like a mission impossible.*

Miss Jean Brodie (jeen brōdee) A challenging, unconventional teacher. Miss Jean Brodie is the Scottish schoolteacher in the 1961 novel *The Prime* *of Miss Jean Brodie* by Muriel Spark (1918–2006), a powerful character who urges her young charges to achieve their potential, regardless of convention. In the 1969 film version of the novel she was memorably played by British actress Maggie Smith. *Like Miss Jean Brodie, she believed in free expression and getting the best out of her pupils.*

Miss Marple (mahrpăl) Archetypal shrewd spinster-detective. Miss Jane Marple was one of the most celebrated creations of the British crime writer AGATHA CHRISTIE, making her first appearance in *Murder at the Vicarage* (1930). The village in which she lives, ***Saint Mary Mead***, is the setting for numerous tales of murder and mayhem, all of which are solved through Miss Marple's patient deductions and acute understanding of human nature. *The murderer was unmasked by his own aunt, a real-life Miss Marple.*

Miss Piggy A fat woman, or a woman with a volatile temper or squeaky voice. The allusion is to a puppet character of the name in Jim Henson's highly successful television series *The Muppet Show* (1976–81). A large pig with long blonde hair and a high-pitched voice, Miss Piggy is both temperamental and immensely vain. "'You're skating on thin ice,' she yelled in her Miss Piggy voice as she skied dangerously close behind members of the group" (Andrew Morton, *Diana: Her True Story*, 1993).

Miss World A very attractive, shapely woman. The allusion is to the Miss World beauty contest, first held in the United Kingdom in 1951, and still televised annually in many parts of the world, despite the fact that it has long been lampooned for its artificiality and outmoded sexist premise. A Mr. World competition inaugurated in 1996 has failed to capture the public imagination to the same degree. *His sister is a Miss World type, with long legs, flashing teeth, and vacant smile.*

mite *See* WIDOW'S MITE.

Mithras (mithrăs) The Sun or a personification of light. Mithras was a Persian god of light and truth and was also venerated by the Romans. The word itself means "friend." *"Mithras reveals all," whispered the archaeologist as the sun's rays entered the tomb, lighting the way ahead.*

mithridatism (mithridaytizăm) Immunity to a poison acquired through the consumption of gradually increased doses of it over a long period. The term is a reference to Mithridates VI, king of Pontus (c. 132–63 B.C.), who became famous for his supposed immunity to poison acquired in this manner. Ultimately Mithridates tried to commit suicide after being defeated by Pompey the Great, only to find no poison would kill him. In the end he had to resort to ordering a soldier to put him to death with his sword. *The emperor's survival when all around him perished was a cause of much conjecture, and suggestions that the solution lay in mithridatism have never been fully discounted.*

Mitty, Walter *See* WALTER MITTY.

Mnemosyne *See* MUSES.

Moby Dick (mōbee) A whale, or some other large aquatic creature. The 1851 novel *Moby-Dick* by the U.S. writer Herman Melville (1819–91) tells the story of a whaling captain's obsession with catching a great white whale called Moby-Dick, which in the past has cost him his leg. His insane pursuit of the creature results in the loss of his ship, the ***Pequod***, and the deaths of both pursuer and pursued. Melville's creation was apparently based on a real whale, called Mocha Dick, which was blamed for damaging whaling ships and causing the deaths of many whalers during the 1830s and 1840s. *The downed zeppelin wallowed in the surf like a flabby Moby Dick. See also* CAPTAIN AHAB.

modest proposal, a An outrageous proposal suggested as a possible solution to a problem. In 1729 the Irish satirist Jonathan Swift (1667–1745) suggested in his pamphlet "A Modest Proposal for preventing the Children of poor People in Ireland, from being a Burden to their Parents or Country, and for making them beneficial to the Publick" that the children of poor families should be fed to the rich, thus solving the problems of both famine and poverty in Ireland. *This was a modest proposal guaranteed to offend anyone with allegiance to the church.*

Mohammed *See* MUHAMMAD.

Moirae *See* FATES.

Moloch (mahlăk, mōlok) A god or other power who demands the sacrifice of what a person holds most dear. According to Leviticus 18:21, Moloch (or Molech) was an Ammonite god to whom followers sacrificed their children in the Valley of Hinnom outside Jerusalem. Over the centuries the name has been applied to various dreadful rulers and instruments of death, including war and, during the French Revolution, the guillotine. "Artists are the high priests of the modern Moloch" (George Bernard Shaw, *An Unsocial Socialist,* 1887).

Molotov cocktail (molătof) A homemade grenade consisting of an inflammable liquid poured into a bottle, fitted with a burning rag or wick, and thrown at an enemy, igniting on impact. Such devices were first employed against tanks during the Spanish Civil War of the 1930s. They were named after the Soviet minister of foreign affairs Vyacheslav Molotov (1890–1986), a reference to their use during the "Winter War" that broke out between the Soviet Union and Finland in 1939. "Before Adam could react with his weapons, the passenger in the BMW, a young blond skinhead, set light to a glass bottle half-filled with petrol with a piece of rag stuffed in the top, and hurled the Molotov cocktail through Billie's open window into the Quattro" (Eddy Shah, *The Lucy Ghosts*, 1993).

moly (mōlee) An herb with magical properties. This mysterious herb was allegedly given by Hermes to Odysseus to make him immune from spells cast by the sorceress Circe. It was described as having a black root and a milk-white flower. The name has since been associated with several plants, including wild garlic. *She could not describe the medicine the shaman had administered to her but concluded that it was some modern equivalent of the magical moly that Odysseus had used to protect himself from the witchcraft of Circe.*

moment of truth The time when the final outcome is revealed or when someone or something is put to the test. The expression comes from bullfighting, specifically from the Spanish *el momento de la verdad*, which describes the moment when a bullfighter makes the sword-thrust that finally kills the bull. *He stood on the diving platform, knowing that this was going to be his moment of truth.*

Momus (mōmăs) A person who complains about everything. In Greek mythology Momus was the god of ridicule who was obliged to flee heaven after incurring the wrath of the other gods. Even Venus, renowned for the flawless perfection of her beauty, was mocked by Momus for the sound her feet made when she walked. "I do not think, I will tell you candidly, that Wickham is a person of very cheerful spirit, or what one would call a—' 'A daughter of Momus,' Miss Tox softly suggested" (Charles Dickens, *Dombey and Son,* 1848).

Mona Lisa smile (mōnă leesă) An enigmatic smile. The allusion is to LEONARDO DA VINCI's masterpiece *Mona Lisa*, painted around 1504 and otherwise known as *La Gioconda* (hence references also to a ***Gioconda smile***). The woman in the painting, tentatively identified as Lisa Gerhardini, the wife of a merchant called Francesco di Zanobi del Giocondo, gazes at the viewer with a slight smile playing on her lips: what she is smiling about remains one of art's greatest secrets. *He remembered the Mona Lisa smile she had given him that morning and now wondered what she had been thinking about.*

Monday morning quarterback A sports enthusiast who criticizes a team's or an individual's performance with the benefit of hindsight. The allusion is to the aftermath of American football games played over the weekend. *The bar was full of Monday morning quarterbacks who all knew what the team should have done.*

money Currency in the form of banknotes, coins, etc. The word has its origin in the Latin *moneta* (meaning "money"), which was in turn an alternative title, in this case (meaning "the admonisher"), for the Roman goddess Juno (see JUNOESQUE). It was beside the temple of Juno in Rome that the city's money was coined. *In these surroundings people tend to be judged by how much money they earn. See also* MINT.

money changers in the temple *See* CAST MONEY CHANGERS OUT OF THE TEMPLE.

money is the root of all evil The desire for material wealth will lead people to commit all manner of crimes and other misdeeds. The saying is a misquotation from 1 Timothy 6:10: "For the love of money is the root of all evil: which while some coveted after, they have erred from the faith, and pierced themselves through with many sorrows." "The urbane activity with which a man receives money is really marvelous, considering that we so earnestly believe money to be the root of all earthly ills. . . . Ah! how cheerfully we consign ourselves to perdition!" (Herman Melville, *Moby-Dick*, 1851).

Monroe, Marilyn *See* MARILYN MONROE.

Montagu *See* PLAGUE ON BOTH YOUR HOUSES, A.

Monte Cristo, the Count of *See* COUNT OF MONTE CRISTO, THE.

Monty Python (montee pīthăn) Humorously surreal. The allusion is to the popular British television comedy series *Monty Python's Flying Circus*, first broadcast in 1969. Comprising John Cleese, Michael Palin, Terry Jones, Eric Idle, Graham Chapman, and Terry Gilliam, the Monty Python team broke many conventions of television comedy, linking sketches that ranged from the satirical to the nonsensical, and inspired numerous imitators on both sides of the Atlantic. They also made a number of highly successful and equally anarchic ***pythonesque*** films. *The whole evening had a Monty Python air about it.*

Mordecai at your gate, a (mordăkī) An irritatingly persistent or nagging person. The biblical Mordecai is described in the book of Esther as a devout Jew who serves at the court of King Ahasuerus (Xerxes) of Persia. He warns the king of a plot to assassinate him, incurring the wrath of Haman, who frames Mordecai and persuades Ahasuerus to order his hanging (see HANG AS HIGH AS HAMAN). Haman is denounced by Mordecai's cousin Esther, however, and is himself hanged in Mordecai's place, and Mordecai is rewarded by being made second only to the king in status. The phrase *a Mordecai at your gate* alludes to Mordecai's stubborn habit of going every day to the house where Esther had been kept as a concubine to demand news about her. *You might as well give in because I don't tend to let this drop: I will be a veritable Mordecai at your gate.*

Morgan le Fay *See* AVALON.

Morgiana *See* OPEN SESAME.

Moriarty, Professor *See* NAPOLEON OF CRIME; SHERLOCK HOLMES.

morphine Alkaloid extracted from opium and used as an anesthetic and sedative in medicine. The name is an allusion to Morpheus, the god of dreams in Greek mythology and the son of the god of sleep, Somnus. *Soldiers routinely carried ampoules of morphine to provide immediate pain relief to casualties in the field.*

mosaic A decoration made up of small pieces of colored glass or stone. The word comes from the Greek *mouseios* (meaning "of the Muses") and is thus an allusion to the MUSES, who were believed to provide all manner of artistic inspiration as patrons of the arts and sciences. *The sun's rays pouring through the stained glass were split into a kind of mosaic.*

Moses (mōziz) The archetype of a wise old (and probably bearded) man. The biblical Moses was the prophet who with God's help led the Israelites out of captivity in Egypt; the accounts of his life are related in the books of Exodus, Leviticus, Numbers, and Deuteronomy. Outstanding leaders who have successfully led their people in times of trouble are sometimes compared to the biblical patriarch, although the name is also applied to any venerable old man. *The old man sat like Moses on a block of marble and waited patiently for the crowd to gather round him. See also* MOSES BASKET; MOSES' ROD.

Moses, Grandma *See* GRANDMA MOSES.

Moses basket (mōziz) A portable basket for babies. The name alludes to the cradle made of papyrus in which, according to Exodus 2:3, the infant Moses was placed by his mother among the reeds of the Nile to conceal him from Pharaoh's soldiers, who had orders to kill all male children of Jewish parentage: "And when she could not longer hide him, she took for him an ark of bulrushes, and daubed it with slime and with pitch, and put the child therein; and she laid it in the flags by the river's brink." Moses was found by Pharaoh's daughter when she came down to the river to bathe and was entrusted to the safekeeping of her nurse. *In the end we bought them a Moses basket for their new baby.*

Moses' rod (mōziz) A divining rod. The name alludes to the rod with which, according to Exodus 7:9, Moses performed miracles before

Pharaoh. It was also with this rod or one similar to it that Moses struck water from a rock, as related at Exodus 17:6. *He held the Moses' rod loosely in his outstretched hands and began to pace down the garden, watching it intently. See also* SMITE THE ROCK.

most unkindest cut of all, the *See* UNKINDEST CUT OF ALL, THE.

mote and beam An insignificant fault and a more major one. The origins of the phrase lie in Christ's Sermon on the Mount, in which he warns those who seek to tackle the minor faults of others to consider first their own failings: "Why beholdest thou the mote that is in thy brother's eye, but considerest not the beam that is in thine own eye?" (Matthew 7:3). *Mote* relates to a tiny particle of dust or a chip of wood, while *beam* signifies a more substantial piece of timber. References to ***motes in thy brother's eye*** are usually heard when a person is suspected of hypocrisy. *He was tackling things in entirely the wrong order, failing to deal with the mote in his own eye before wrestling with the beam in his brother's.*

moth and rust corrupt *See* LAY NOT UP TREASURES UPON EARTH.

motherhood and apple pie *See* APPLE PIE.

Mother Hubbard *See* OLD MOTHER HUBBARD.

Mother Teresa (tăreeză, tărayză) A person with a strong charitable nature. Mother Teresa (Agnes Gonxha Bojaxhiu; 1910–97) was an Albanian Roman Catholic missionary who dedicated her life to helping the destitute and dying in Calcutta. She acquired an international reputation and received the Nobel Peace Prize in 1979. *To hear her go on about how much she does for charity you'd think she was Mother Teresa.*

Mount Everest (evărăst) A peak that is dauntingly high. At 29,028 feet, Mount Everest is the highest mountain peak in the world and the ultimate challenge for climbers. *The walk up the hill would be easy for most people, but a Mount Everest for disabled visitors. See also* BECAUSE IT'S THERE.

Mount Olympus *See* OLYMPIAN.

Mount Parnassus *See* PARNASSIAN.

mount Pegasus *See* PEGASUS.

Mount Pisgah (pizgah) A place or point that affords optimism about or foresight into the future. According to Deuteronomy 34:1, Moses ascended Mount Pisgah in order to get a glimpse of the Promised Land in the distance just before he died. *His account of the view from Mount Pisgah left us all feeling very buoyant.*

Mount Sinai (sīnī) A place or situation where a person comes face to face with some revelation or challenge. In the Bible, Mount Sinai, or ***Horeb,*** is identified as the hill where Moses received the Ten Commandments from God (Exodus 20 and 31:18 and Deuteronomy 5). *Feeling like Moses on Mount Sinai he struggled to take in the import of this new revelation.*

mouths of babes and sucklings, out of the *See* OUT OF THE MOUTHS OF BABES AND SUCKLINGS.

Mozart (mōtzahrt) The embodiment of musical genius. The Austrian composer Wolfgang Amadeus Mozart (1756–91) was recognized as a musical prodigy while still a young child and over the course of his relatively short life wrote some of the world's best-loved classical music. Consequently, his name is only applied to musicians and composers of singular talent. *It is probably too early to be sure, but some are saying we have another Mozart in our midst.*

Mr. Bean A person who demonstrates great incompetence or an inability to understand the world around him or her. Mr. Bean was the comic invention of British comedian Rowan Atkinson (b. 1955) and made his first appearance on television in 1990, later making the transition to movies and cartoons. He rarely speaks and through his ungainly movements and misunderstandings of the surrounding world causes chaos everywhere he goes. *Tall and awkward, he floundered about like Mr. Bean.*

Mr. Clean A person whose reputation is unbesmirched by scandal, wrongdoing, etc. The allusion is ultimately to a brand of household cleaning fluid. In politics, the nickname became particularly associated with U.S. secretary of state James Baker (b. 1930), although others dubbed Mr. Clean have included U.S. pop singer Pat Boone (b. 1934). *The party needs a Mr. Clean to be its public face in these troubled times.*

Mr. Darcy (dahrsee) A dashing, handsome lover. Fitzwilliam Darcy is the name of the stern young man who eventually becomes engaged to the Elizabeth Bennet in the romantic novel *Pride and Prejudice* (1796) by British writer Jane Austen (1775–1817). A man of great good sense, he is initially rejected as a suitor by Elizabeth, who finds his manner haughty and aloof. *That night she dreamt of a black-haired Darcy scooping her up and whisking her away to his mansion in the countryside.*

Mr. Kurtz *See* HEART OF DARKNESS; HORROR, THE HORROR!, THE.

Mr. Magoo (măgoo) A person with very poor eyesight. The allusion is to a bald-headed, bad-tempered cartoon character and the scrapes he gets into as a result of his severe myopia. The first Mr. Magoo cartoon was screened in 1949 and he became a great favorite, although he has made fewer appearances since the advent of political correctness. *He blundered about the darkened room like Mr. Magoo, bumping into the furniture and cursing it for getting in his way.*

Mr. Micawber *See* WILKINS MICAWBER.

Mr. Rochester Archetype of a dark, brooding, romantic lover. The forbidding but attractive Edward Rochester is the object of the heroine's affections in the classic romantic novel *JANE EYRE* (1847) by Charlotte Brontë. Rochester's great secret is that his mad first wife is still alive, as Jane discovers on her wedding day. "Mrs. Fleming's . . . well, she's quite fat, and she looks a lot older than Mr. Fleming—not that I think he's about to do a Mr. Rochester, stick her up the Loft nor nothing!" (Liz Lochhead, *True Confessions and New Cliches*, 1985).

Mrs. Danvers (danverz) A stern, hostile woman. The allusion is to the menacing housekeeper Mrs. Danvers in the 1938 novel *REBECCA* by Daphne du Maurier (1907–89), who resents the arrival of the second Mrs. de Winter and treats her cruelly. *She appeared at the top of the stairs and stared down at them with a cold expression on her face, reminding him forcibly of Mrs. Danvers.*

Mrs. Grundy (grundee) A narrow-minded, prudish person who is instinctively opposed to unconventional behavior in others. Mrs. Grundy is an unseen character referred to in Thomas Morton's play *Speed the Plough* (1798), in which other characters repeatedly worry "What will Mrs. Grundy say?" *This novel is sure to outrage the Mrs. Grundys of this world.*

Mrs. O'Leary's cow (ōleereez) An unsuspecting cause of disaster. A cow belonging to the widowed Mrs. Catherine O'Leary was blamed for igniting the Great Chicago Fire of 1871 by accidentally kicking over a kerosene lantern in a barn in DeKoven Street. Most of old Chicago was destroyed in the ensuing conflagration and some 250 people lost their lives. Mrs. O'Leary always denied any responsibility for the fire, and some observers have instead identified one of her neighbors, Daniel "Peg Leg" Sullivan, as the culprit. *Like Mrs. O'Leary's cow, he little knew the disastrous chain of events he had set in motion by making that telephone call.*

Mr. Spock *See STAR TREK.*

much study is a weariness of the flesh *See* OF MAKING MANY BOOKS.

muckraker A person who dredges up scandal and exposes uncomfortable truths. The term has its origins in John Bunyan's *PILGRIM'S PROGRESS* (1678, 1684), in which the Muck Rake is identified as man so busy with raking up filth that he fails to notice the vision of a celestial crown above him. President Theodore Roosevelt later used the term to denigrate his opponents, and subsequently it became identified (not altogether negatively) with investigative reporters, whose job it is to delve into corruption in order to expose wrongdoing in society. *The muckrakers in the city newspapers have got hold of the story and there's no telling where it will end.*

Mudville, there is no joy in *See* CASEY AT THE BAT.

mugwump (mugwămp) A person who changes his or her party allegiance. The word has its origins in the Algonquin *mugquomp*, meaning "big chief." It was later used to describe those members of the Republican Party who opted to support the Democratic presidential candidate Grover Cleveland instead of the Republican James Blaine, who was tainted with charges of corruption, in 1884. The term is also sometimes encountered in a more general sense, referring to a gullible fool or an idiot. "Like bread-making, any mugwump can do it" (Elizabeth David, *An Omelette and a Glass of Wine*, 1987).

Muhammad (mōhamăd, mōhahmăd, măhamăd) The founder of Islam, whose teachings form the basis of modern Islamic faith. Muhammad (570–632), also called ***Mohammed*** or ***Mahomet***, was forced to leave MECCA because of his teachings in 610; he fled to Medina with his followers but returned as conqueror of Mecca in 630. He is venerated today as the prophet of God, whose beliefs are enshrined in the Qur'an, or Koran. *See also* IF THE MOUNTAIN WON'T COME TO MUHAMMAD.

Muhammad Ali (măhamăd alee) A formidable boxer. Born Cassius Clay in 1942, the U.S. heavyweight boxer Muhammad Ali won the world title in 1964 and recaptured it in 1974 and 1978. He was almost as well known for his eloquence outside the ring as he was for his skill as a fighter in it. *He was as light on his feet as Muhammad Ali. See also* GREATEST, THE.

Mulder, Fox *See* X-FILES.

Munchausen (muunchhowzăn) A teller of tall tales, an outrageous liar. The allusion is to Baron Munchausen, whose many far-fetched adventures are described in *Baron Munchausen's Narrative of his Marvellous Travels and Campaigns in Russia* (1785), by the German writer Rudolf Erich Raspe (1736–94). Raspe based his fictional character on the real Karl Friedrich Hieronymus, Freiherr von Münchhausen (1720–97), a German baron who served with the Russian army against the Turks and later told exaggerated stories about his escapades, which included flying on a cannonball and pulling himself out of a swamp by his own hair. The term has also entered the field of medicine: patients with Munchausen syndrome lie about their nonexistent symptoms in order to gain medical treatment. *It was a tall story worthy of Baron Munchausen himself.*

Munchkin (munchkin) A small person or child, or someone who is otherwise insignificant. The allusion is to Frank L. Baum's novel *The Wizard Of Oz* (1900), in which the Munchkins appear as a race of diminutive beings who live in the land of Oz. "Jo looked like a Munchkin in anything that showed her legs" (Celia Brayfield, *The Prince*, 1990). *See also* WIZARD OF OZ.

Munich Agreement *See* PEACE IN OUR TIME; PIECE OF PAPER.

Munich Putsch *See* PUTSCH.

Munsters, The (munsterz) A family or other group of people who share a grotesque, monstrous appearance. The allusion is to the classic 1960s U.S. television series *The Munsters*, which comically depicted the home life of a family of assorted ghoulish characters, namely FRANKENSTEIN-lookalike Herman Munster and his vampire wife Lily Munster, father-in-law Grandpa, and son Eddie, as well as the weirdly very ordinary all-American niece Marilyn. *The house was old and creepy, like something out of The Munsters. See also* ADDAMS FAMILY.

Murder, Inc. A crime syndicate that provides hired hitmen to carry out contract killings. Murder, Inc. was formed in the 1930s and its so-called ***enforcers*** are believed to have been responsible for several hundred murders, almost exclusively of rival gangsters. The organization disintegrated in the 1940s under pressure from the authorities. *The FBI are not Murder, Inc. and do not execute suspects out of hand. See also* MAFIA.

Muses Personifications of artistic and creative inspiration. In Greek mythology the Muses were nine in number, namely Clio (the muse of history), Euterpe (of lyric poetry), Thalia (of comedy), Melpomene (of tragedy), Terpsichore (of choral dance and song), Erato (of love songs), Polyhymnia (of songs to the gods), Urania (of astronomy), and Calliope (of epic poetry). They were identified as the daughters of Zeus and Mnemosyne (the goddess of memory) and had a temple on Mount HELICON in Boeotia. Related words include ***music*** and ***museum.*** *He tottered on the edge of the cliff, bottle in hand, lamenting loudly that the Muses had deserted him and there was nothing left to live for. See also* MOSAIC; TENTH MUSE.

music of the spheres A type of celestial music supposedly created by the movements of the spheres, which in the Ptolemaic system of cosmology carried the planets and stars around the Earth.

The concept of the sublime harmony of the universe being expressed in the form of music was devised by the Greek philosopher and mathematician Pythagoras. "He said that, the people of their island had their ears adapted to hear 'the music of the spheres', which always played at certain periods, and the court was now prepared to bear their part, in whatever instrument they most excelled" (Jonathan Swift, *Gulliver's Travels,* 1726).

mustard seed *See* GRAIN OF MUSTARD SEED.

Mutt and Jeff (mut, jef) A pair comprising a tall and a short person. The allusion is to a once-popular U.S. comic strip, first published in 1907, about two comical characters—Mutt, the tall and lanky one, and Jeff, the short and bald one. *Father and son were so different in stature they looked like Mutt and Jeff when they stood next to each other.*

Muttley *See* DICK DASTARDLY.

my brother's keeper Someone who has responsibility for another person and should know where he or she is and what he or she is doing. The phrase alludes to the biblical story of CAIN AND ABEL and the former's indignant reply when asked by God where Abel is: "I know not: Am I my brother's keeper?" (Genesis 4:9). In fact, Cain has murdered Abel and is trying to deny any knowledge of the crime. "I am not my brother's keeper. I cannot bring myself to judge my fellows; I am content to observe them" (William Somerset Maugham, *The Summing Up,* 1938).

my cup runneth over Good things are coming in abundance. The expression comes from Psalm 23:5–6, in which the blessings of God are described: "Thou preparest a table before me in the presence of mine enemies: thy anointest my head with oil; my cup runneth over. Surely goodness and mercy shall follow me all the days of my life." In the translation in the *Book of Common Prayer,* the phrase is ***my cup shall be full.*** *A new job, a new home, getting married all in one year . . . Louise felt that her cup was indeed running over.* "Her in-box runneth over with new mail" (*Guardian,* August 13, 2001).

My God, why hast thou forsaken me? A cry of desperation or despair at one's abandonment by God or others. According to Matthew 27:46 and Mark 15:34 these were the words of Christ at the time of the Crucifixion: "And about the ninth hour Jesus cried with a loud voice, saying Eli, Eli, lama sabachtani? That is to say, My God, my God, why hast thou forsaken me?" *That evening nothing went right for him at the casino, and by eleven o'clock he was reduced to glaring forlornly up at the fan on the ceiling and mentally intoning, My God, why hast thou forsaken me? See also* SEVEN LAST WORDS.

My Lai (mī lī) An atrocity in which soldiers massacre helpless civilians. The allusion is to the village of My Lai in South Vietnam, which on March 16, 1968, was the scene of a notorious atrocity, when U.S. troops under Lieutenant William Calley Jr. murdered 22 old men, women, and children. Calley was tried and convicted of the crime, but was later acquitted, with the blame for the incident being placed on the stress of battle. *Army chiefs are anxious to avoid Iraq witnessing another My Lai.*

my man Friday *See* MAN FRIDAY.

my name is legion We are many in number, usually referring to evil spirits or other undesirable persons or phenomena. The phrase comes from Mark 5:9, in which Christ encounters a man possessed by a host of demons, the first of which explains, "My name is Legion." Roman legions comprised between 4,000 and 6,000 soldiers. Christ expelled the demons and transferred them to a herd of swine, who promptly drowned themselves in deep water. "And there I found what appalled me; a zoo of lusts, a bedlam of ambitions, a nursery of fears, a hareem of fondled hatreds. My name was legion" (C. S. Lewis, *Surprised by Joy,* 1955). *See also* GADARENE.

myrmidon (mermidon) A devoted follower or henchman; a servant or other person who follows orders without question or scruple. According to Greek mythology the original Myrmidons were a race of people from Thessaly who were created by Zeus from ants (***murmex*** in Greek means "ant") after the previous inhabitants of the country had been wiped out by plague. The Myrmidons were famed for their loyalty to Achilles during the Trojan War, although they were also notorious for their brutality. The term *myrmidon* is often quoted today in relation to gangs of ruffians or thugs but may on occasion also be applied to the forces of law and order, with the police sometimes being referred to as ***myrmidons of the law.*** "Within eight days she was to enter an appearance, or go through some preliminary ceremony, towards showing why she should not surrender her diamonds to the Lord Chancellor, or to one of those satraps of his, the Vice-Chancellors, or to some other terrible myrmidon" (Anthony Trollope, *The Eustace Diamonds,* 1873).

my yoke is easy I can bear my burden or responsibility with ease. The phrase appears in Matthew 11:28–30, in which Christ says to his followers, "Come unto me, all ye that labour and are heavy laden, and I will give you rest. Take my yoke upon you, and learn of me; for I am meek and lowly in heart: and ye shall find rest unto your souls. For my yoke is easy, and my burden is light." "It was easy to be good. God's yoke was sweet and light. It was better never to have sinned" (James Joyce, *Portrait of the Artist as a Young Man,* 1914–15).

N

nabob (naybob) A wealthy or powerful person. The term, meaning "viceroy," is of Hindi origin, and was originally applied in the 16th century to the governors and rulers of the Mogul Empire, who built up substantial fortunes and became princes. When India became part of the British Empire the term came to be applied informally and somewhat irreverently to India's colonial rulers, who similarly amassed great wealth to finance a comfortable life for themselves back in the home country. *However loudly the locals protest, the nabobs of Washington will decide the fate of this and other small Latin American countries.*

Naboth's vineyard (nayboths) Something of value that is coveted and obtained from its rightful owner by another, stronger person using dishonest or extreme means. The phrase alludes to the biblical tale of Naboth, whose vineyard neighboring the royal grounds in Jezreel attracted the avaricious attention of AHAB, king of Israel, and his wicked wife, Jezebel. According to 1 Kings 21, Naboth refused to sell his land and was subsequently made the target of trumped-up charges of blasphemy and was stoned to death, together with his children. The vineyard duly passed to Ahab. *The estate, like Naboth's vineyard, went to the relative with the most money and thus the greatest influence with the lawyers rather than to the relative with the strongest moral right to the inheritance.*

Nagasaki *See* HIROSHIMA.

naiad *See* NYMPH.

naked and ye clothed me, I was *See* I WAS A STRANGER, AND YE TOOK ME IN.

naked city The harsh modern urban environment. The tag comes from the title of a 1948 crime thriller, filmed in New York City, which concludes with the narration: "There are eight million stories in the naked city. This has been one of them." The movie spawned a popular television series of the same title in the 1960s. "After all, there are eleven million people in the Naked City and only some of them are honest" (Mike Ripley, *Just Another Angel*, 1989).

namby-pamby (nambeepambee) Weak, ineffectual, wishy-washy, or sentimental. The term was coined by English playwright Henry Carey (c. 1687–1743) as an insulting nickname for the poet Ambrose Philips (c. 1675–1749), who was a rival of Carey's friend Alexander Pope and whose works included nauseatingly sweet verses on babies and the like. The name Ambrose was commonly abbreviated to Amby, facilitating Carey's conversion of it into the "baby-talk" version: "Namby-Pamby's doubly mild / Once a man and twice a child." The nickname is remembered; Philips's more infantile poems are not. "He's not a whining, namby-pamby little git like most men are" (Frank Kippax, *Other People's Blood*, 1993).

name is legion, my *See* MY NAME IS LEGION.

name is mud, one's *See* ONE'S NAME IS MUD.

name of God in vain, take the *See* TAKE THE NAME OF GOD IN VAIN.

Nancy Archetype of a prostitute with a heart of gold. Nancy is the name of the prostitute who shows kindness to the young hero in the novel *OLIVER TWIST* (1837–38) by Charles Dickens. She is eventually murdered by her lover, the brutal ***Bill Sikes***, who mistakenly believes she has informed on his criminal activities. *With her haunted eyes and brittle gaiety, she reminded him a little of Nancy in Oliver Twist.*

naphtha (nafthă, napthă) A bituminous distillation obtained by boiling coal tar (although it also occurs naturally in certain places). It appears in Greek legend in the story of Medea, in which it is identified as the magical substance smeared by a sorceress upon the wedding robe of Glauce, daughter of King Creon, causing her to be burned to death just before her marriage to Jason. "Masses of the slimy and sulphurous substance called naphtha, which floated idly on the sluggish and sullen waves, supplied those rolling clouds with new vapours, and afforded awful testimony to the truth of the Mosaic history" (Sir Walter Scott, *The Talisman,* 1825).

Napoleon (năpōleeăn) A dictatorial leader, or anyone who behaves in a megalomaniacal or overbearing manner. The Corsican-born Napoleon Bonaparte (1769–1821) rose rapidly through the ranks of the French Revolutionary Army to become, in 1804, the emperor of the French and the most feared man in Europe. Adored by his soldiers, who called him the ***Little Corporal***, Napoleon extended French rule over much of continental Europe until temporarily exiled to ELBA and finally defeated by Britain and her allies at WATERLOO in 1815, after which he lived out his last years in exile on SAINT HELENA. His name is also sometimes invoked to describe someone who exhibits brilliance as a military leader or other strategist. *Who does he think he is, ordering us all about like that—Napoleon? See also* HUNDRED DAYS; OLD GUARD; RETREAT FROM MOSCOW.

Napoleon of crime (năpōleeăn) A criminal mastermind. The title comes from the SHERLOCK HOLMES stories of Arthur Conan Doyle (1859–1930), who bestowed it upon Holmes's archenemy Professor James Moriarty. The poet T. S. Eliot subsequently borrowed it for Macavity, one of the feline characters in his *Old Possum's Book of Practical Cats* (1939). *The police were anxious to detain this Napoleon of crime before people started accusing them of incompetence.*

narcissism Obsessive interest in or love of oneself. The allusion is to the Greek legend of Narcissus, a beautiful young man who rejected all suitors and was punished by falling in love with his own reflection in a pool of water. Unable to fulfill his desire, he wasted away at the water's edge until the gods finally relented and turned him into a flower, known ever since as a ***narcissus.*** A variation of the story has Narcissus falling in love with his reflection and in trying to embrace it being drowned and then resurrected as the flower. "It was Narcissism in him to love the city so well; he saw his reflection in it; and, like it, he was grimy, big, careless, rich, strong, and unquenchably optimistic" (Booth Tarkington, *The Turmoil,* 1915). *See also* ECHO.

Narnia (nahrneeă) A beguiling but also menacing fantasy world peopled by witches and creatures from folklore and mythology. Narnia, ruled over by the beneficent Christlike lion ***Aslan*** (when not deposed), was the creation of British novelist C. S. Lewis (1898–1963), providing the setting for seven books beginning with *The Lion, the Witch and the Wardrobe* (1950). Lewis gave no particular reason for choosing this name for his imaginary land, beyond liking the sound, although he may have been influenced by various Roman towns bearing the name. *This is no Narnia to be reached through the back of a wardrobe but a reality that must be faced.*

narrow way *See* STRAIGHT AND NARROW.

nasty, brutish, and short Referring to the brevity and essential unpleasantness of life. This pessimistic view of human existence was first voiced by the English writer Thomas Hobbes (1588–1679) in his book *Leviathan* (1651): "No arts; no letters; no society; and which is worst of all, continual fear and danger of violent death; and the life of man, solitary, poor, nasty, brutish, and short." *His career in national politics proved nasty, brutish, and short. See also* HOBBESIAN.

Nathan *See* EWE LAMB.

Nation, Carry *See* CARRY NATION.

nation of shopkeepers The British. It was the French emperor NAPOLEON who thus famously dismissed the nation of his enemies, the British, scorning their commercial preoccupations in comparison with the military glories of France. This was not, however, his own conception, as he knew it already from Adam Smith's *The Wealth of Nations* (1776): "To found a great empire for the sole purpose of raising up a people of customers, may at first sight appear a project fit only for a nation of shopkeepers." "To sum up: in a time of unprecedented expansion of world trade Britain, the nation of shopkeepers, paid itself higher wages for producing very little more, while putting up its prices much faster than its competitors" (Peter Lewis, *The Fifties: Portrait of a Period*, 1989).

Nativity, the The birth of Jesus Christ (Matthew 1:18–2:12; Luke 2:1–40); commemorations of this event held during the Christmas period. The original Cave of the Nativity, where Christ is thought to have been born (although there is no definite suggestion in the Bible that the birth took place in a cave), is traditionally located under the chancel of the basilica of the Church of the Nativity in Bethlehem. "Attached to the bolster by a towel, under his father's bayonet and the oleograph depicting the Nativity, sat the baby" (John Galsworthy, *The Forsyte Saga,* 1922).

Nazarene (nazăreen) Someone who comes from the town of Nazareth in Israel. The term is usually reserved for Christ, who spent his childhood there (Matthew 2:23). "'Let not your heart be troubled, neither let it be afraid,' said the Nazarene. Clare chimed in cordially; but his heart was troubled all the same" (Thomas Hardy, *Tess of the D'Urbervilles,* 1891).

Nazareth, good thing come out of *See* GOOD THING COME OUT OF NAZARETH.

Nazirite (nazărīt) A person who is set apart from the rest of the population because of his or her religious beliefs. The Nazirites, or ***Nazarites,*** are described in the Bible (Numbers 6:2–6) as individuals who demonstrate their devotion to God by abstaining from wine, never cutting their hair, and avoiding contact with dead bodies. Samson and probably Samuel and John the Baptist were Nazirites. Today the term may be applied to those who attempt to keep themselves separate from the world for religious reasons, especially if they have an unkempt appearance or long, untrimmed hair. *The valley was a refuge for Nazirites and other outcasts whose presence would not be tolerated in the surrounding towns and villages.*

Neaera (nieeră) A female lover; a sweetheart. Neaera, a Greek nymph, appears in the writings of Horace, Tibullus, and Virgil. "Were it not better done as other use, / To sport with Amaryllis in the shade, / Or with the tangles of Neaera's hair?" (John Milton, *Lycidas,* 1637).

nebuchadnezzar (nebăkădnezer, nebyăkădnezer) A wine bottle with a capacity equivalent to that of 20 standard bottles (approximately 15 liters). Nebuchadnezzar II (605–562 B.C.) was the evil king of Babylon who took the Israelites into captivity in Babylon, as described in Daniel 1–4 and 2 Kings 24–25. He was punished for his wickedness by going insane and ended his days grazing in a field like an animal. The adoption of his name for the wine bottle, the huge size of which reflects his own inflated arrogance, seems to date from the early 20th century. *The old gentleman generously offered to host the occasion, making a note to himself to ask the wine merchants to provide a nebuchadnezzar of wine, if such a thing could still be had in this day and age.*

nectar A sugary fluid produced by flowers and, by extension, any exceptionally delicious drink. In Greek mythology nectar was identified as the drink of the gods on Olympus and was believed to confer immortality on those who tasted it. "He was back in a minute with a big dipperful of stale brown water which tasted like nectar, and loosed the jaws of Disko and Tom Platt" (Rudyard Kipling, *Captains Courageous,* 1897). *See also* AMBROSIA.

Ned Kelly Archetype of an Australian criminal or criminally-minded rogue. Ned Kelly (1855–80) was an Australian bushranger and bandit who was famous for the suit of homemade armor he wore. Having killed three policemen in 1878, he was eventually captured and hanged at Melbourne; his courage on the scaffold inspired the expression ***as game as Ned Kelly***. *Your father looks like Ned Kelly in that gray balaclava.*

Nefertiti (neferteetee) An archetype of feminine beauty. Nefertiti was queen of Egypt in the 14th century B.C. and the wife of Akhenaton. Her beauty is preserved in a celebrated portrait bust. *Her profile was striking, imperious yet sensual, like some pale-skinned Nefertiti.*

Nelson A brilliant naval commander. The British admiral Horatio Lord Nelson (1758–1805) became a great national hero when, after many earlier triumphs, he led the British fleet to a crushing victory over the combined French and Spanish fleets at Trafalgar in 1805, though losing his own life to a sniper's bullet at the height of the conflict. He was also well known for his distinctive appearance, having lost an eye and an arm in battle, and for his scandalous affair with Lady Emma Hamilton, wife of a British diplomat. *It was a well-executed affair, but* *the commodore is no Nelson. See also* ENGLAND EXPECTS; KISS ME, HARDY.

Nemean lion *See* LABORS OF HERCULES.

nemesis (nemăsis) Retribution or an agent of it. In Greek mythology Nemesis was identified as the goddess of retribution, described by the poet Hesiod (c. 800 B.C.) as the daughter of Erebus (hell) and Nyx (night). Nemesis enacted the revenge of the gods upon mortals who had offended them through such sins as pride and insolence. In modern usage the term is usually taken to refer to a person's inescapable doom, especially to any stubborn rival or hindrance that seems fated to bring about his or her downfall or failure. "It was one of the most cynical political decisions in recent memory and, unsurprisingly, Nemesis has come back to haunt the railways" (*Guardian,* May 26, 2001).

nepenthe (nipenthee) A drug or other agent that induces sleep or serves to make a person forget his or her griefs or troubles. The word comes from the Greek *ne* ("not") and *penthos* ("grief"). It is mentioned in Homer's *Odyssey* (c. 700 B.C.) as a drug given to Helen by Polydamna to make her forget her cares. "'I know not Lethe nor Nepenthe,' remarked he; 'but I have learned many new secrets in the wilderness'" (Nathaniel Hawthorne, *The Scarlet Letter,* 1850).

Neptune (neptoon) A personification of the sea itself and nautical matters in general. In Roman mythology, Neptune was the god of the sea, the equivalent of the Greek POSEIDON. *They gave up trying to save the ship and threw themselves into the waves, putting their trust in Neptune to bring them to shore.*

nereid *See* NYMPH.

Nero (neerō) An archetype of despotic cruelty and depravity. Nero, originally Lucius Domitius Ahenobarbus (A.D. 37–68), was brought up under the protection of the Emperor Claudius, but as emperor himself (54–68), Nero was infamous for his irrational behavior and cruelty. Contemporaries murdered on his orders included his mother, Agrippina; his first wife, Octavia; his second wife, Poppaea (whom he kicked to death while pregnant); and his rival Britannicus, while those obliged to commit suicide for opposing him included the philosopher Seneca and the poet Lucan. *Power seems to have gone to his head: Colleagues who used to be his admirers have accused him publicly of behaving like Nero. See also* FIDDLE WHILE ROME BURNS.

Ness, Eliot *See* UNTOUCHABLE.

Nessus, shirt of *See* SHIRT OF NESSUS.

nestor (nester) A wise old man; the most experienced and wise member of a particular group or company. Nestor was a legendary king of Pylos and the oldest of the Greek commanders in the Trojan War. Renowned for his eloquence, Nestor was widely respected for the wisdom of his counsel and did much to alleviate tensions between other Greek leaders when they fell out with each other. His contemporaries even considered him the equal of the gods as an adviser because of his prudence and experience. "The Nestor of the Hebrew camp, in him the words of the Psalmist were anticipated, that he bore fruit in old age, and to the last was fat and flourishing" (F. B. Meyer, *Joshua,* 1893).

never in the field of human conflict was so much owed by so many to so few Rarely has so much been accomplished by so few. This familiar sentiment is a quotation from a speech delivered by British prime minister Winston Churchill in August 1940 in tribute to the RAF's defense of the United Kingdom during the Battle of Britain. It has since been applied, often in the truncated form "never was so much owed by so many to so few," to a wide variety of other contexts, often ironically. *When it came to their finances it was a case of never was so much owed by so many to so few.*

Never-Never Land An unattainable, unrealistic paradise or other ideal place far removed from the harsh realities of ordinary life. Never-Never Land (originally simply Never Land) is the name of the imaginary land that is home to PETER PAN and his companions in J. M. Barrie's play *Peter Pan* (1904). The name has since been applied specifically to the Australian outback. *If he thinks I'm going to pay him back then he's living in Never-Never Land.*

new Adam *See* ADAM.

New Deal A fresh economic or political program, especially one offering hopes of recovery or relief. The allusion is to the original New Deal announced by Franklin D. Roosevelt during the presidential campaign of 1932 with the words "I pledge you, I pledge myself, to a new deal for the American people." He went on to introduce three separate New Deals (1933, 1935, and 1938) and many other political leaders have since imitated his example with New Deals of their own. *The government have promised a New Deal designed to reinvigorate the country's heavy industry.*

new Jerusalem (jăroosălăm) Heaven, paradise, or some other kind of perfect community. The phrase comes from the Bible (Revelation 21:2): "And I John saw the holy city, new Jerusalem, coming down from God out of heaven, prepared as a bride adorned for her husband." In its biblical context the phrase refers specifically to heaven, but it has since been applied to many other kinds of utopia: "It may not have been a new Jerusalem, but the Lansbury estate in London's east end was designed to capture the post-war mood of optimism generated by the Festival of Britain" (*Guardian,* July 11, 2001).

newspeak A simplified, deceitful form of English in which the meaning of words is subtly changed to suit the views of the state or other authority. The concept of newspeak was introduced by British novelist George Orwell (1903–50) in his novel *Nineteen Eighty-Four* (1949) as a tool wielded by a totalitarian state to control the population and limit the ability of individuals to voice subversive ideas (*see* BIG BROTHER). "On pricing, the conclusions which could be generally agreed were so flabby and meaningless that they might have made even the most brazen practitioner of newspeak blush" (Leslie Hannah, *Engineers, Managers and Politicians*, 1993). *See also* DOUBLESPEAK; DOUBLETHINK.

Newtonian (nootōneeăn) Of or relating to the theories of the distinguished English mathematician and physicist Sir Isaac Newton (1642–1727). Newton, who believed in a rational universe set in motion by God, made significant advances in a number of scientific fields, including the understanding of gravity, astronomy, and other branches of physics. "Instead of the clarity and precision of Newtonian mechanics, we have to be content with a more fuzzy account of affairs" (J. C. Polkinghorne, *The Quantum World*, 1984).

new wine in old bottles New ideas, materials, etc., are wasted if not accompanied by new practices, methods, and so forth. The phrase comes from Christ, who advised his followers that his new teachings demanded new practices to go with them: "Neither do men put new wine into old bottles: else the bottles break, and the wine runneth out, and the bottles perish: but they put new wine into new bottles, and both are preserved" (Matthew 9:16–17). The image alludes to the fact that the tanned animal skins used as bottles in Christ's time tended to be much less elastic and therefore prone to splitting if used more than once. *Many experts felt that the tweaked version of the railroad-safety system was not sufficient—it was a case of new wine in old bottles.*

nice guys finish last Victory goes to those with the necessary aggression and ruthlessness. A favorite maxim of sportsmen and -women over the decades, the slogan has its roots in a quotation by U.S. baseball coach Leo Durocher (1906–91), delivered in 1946 about the New York Giants: "All nice guys. They'll finish last. Nice guys. Finish last." *The crowd loved him for his cheerful manner on court, but you know what they say, nice guys finish last.*

Nick Carter Archetype of an ace detective. Nick Carter made his first appearance in print as early as 1886 and has continued to pursue villains ever since, though he has become distinctly more hard-boiled in character since the 1960s. The first story, *The Old Detective's Pupil; or, The Mysterious Crime of Madison Square* (1886) was written by John R. Coryell, but many of his later adventures (which also transferred to radio and the movies), often related in the first person, were published without author credits or under pseudonyms. *As a boy he had dreamed of growing up to become a Nick Carter.*

Nicodemused into nothing (nikădeemăst) Wrecked or ruined (as in one's prospects) through rumor and insinuation. The phrase alludes to the biblical Nicodemus, who attempted to defend Christ before the authorities on the grounds that he should not be tried in his absence (John 3 and 7:50–52). "How many Caesars and Pompeys . . . might have done . . . well in the world . . . had they not been Nicodemused into nothing" (Laurence Sterne, *The Life and Opinions of Tristram Shandy, Gentleman,* 1759–67).

Nietzschean (neecheeăn) Of or relating to the ideas of German philosopher Friedrich Wilhelm Nietzsche (1844–1900). Certain aspects of Nietzsche's ideas, which included the rejection of the concept of God and notions of the supremacy of the "superman" over lesser mortals, influenced the ideology of the Nazis and have thus remained controversial. "This striding, Nietzschean self, 'bigger' as opposed to 'better,' couldn't be accommodated in any kind of social order, would never really be happy" (Simon Reynolds, *Blissed Out*, 1990).

Niflheim (nifălhīm) The underworld. This Norse version of the underworld was believed to be cold, dark, and misty and very different in character to VALHALLA, where chosen heroes feasted with Odin. It comprised nine worlds to which those who died of old age or disease were consigned after death. The word itself means "mist home." *When the mist rolls in from the sea the Danish marshes become menacing and are peopled with ghosts, taking on the character of some dread Niflheim.*

night cometh, when no man can work An injunction to undertake things while the opportunity is there, for it will soon pass. The sentiment is biblical in origin, appearing as a quotation of

Christ: "I must work the works of him that sent me, while it is day: the night cometh, when no man can work" (John 9:4). "Repent—resolve, while yet there is time. Remember, we are bid to work while it is day—warned that 'the night cometh when no man shall work'" (Charlotte Brontë, *Jane Eyre,* 1847). "'Still there are works which, with God's permission, I would do before the night cometh.' Dr Arnold was thinking of his great work on Church and State" (Lytton Strachey, *Eminent Victorians,* 1918).

Nightingale, Florence *See* FLORENCE NIGHTINGALE.

nightmare on Elm Street A nightmarish situation. The allusion is to a blood-soaked horror movie of the same title released in 1984. The plot revolves around the demonic Freddy Krueger, who stalks and murders a succession of middle-class American teenagers as they sleep, savaging them with his long steel-tipped fingernails. The success of the original movie spawned several sequels. *With people collapsing all around it was like being caught up in a nightmare on Elm Street.*

night of the long knives A period of sackings, dismissals, and demotions of staff or other personnel. The original Night of the Long Knives took place throughout Germany on June 30, 1934, when Adolf HITLER had numerous opponents and rivals for power murdered by his supporters in the SS, thus allowing him to establish unchallenged personal control of an emergent Nazi state. Casualties (the number of which has been estimated at somewhere between 60 and 400) included several senior figures who had thought Hitler their ally or friend. Hitler himself made little secret of the purge he had initiated, as evidenced by an address he subsequently made to the Reichstag: "It was no secret that this time the revolution would have to bloody . . . When we spoke of it, we called it 'The Night of the Long Knives.'" It appears that Hitler may have borrowed the phrase from an early Nazi marching song. Later nights of the long knives, such as that instituted by British prime minister Harold Macmillan in 1962, have not necessarily entailed the murder of those removed from office. *It is only six months since the last night of the long knives, and already those at the top are considering another purge of middle management.*

Nijinsky (nijinskee) A superbly talented male classical ballet dancer. The Russian ballet dancer Vaslav Nijinsky (1890–1950) won acclaim as a star of the celebrated Ballet Russe company in the early years of the 20th century, creating many of the great parts in the modern ballet repertoire and dancing to the music of Debussy, Stravinsky, and others. He made his final appearance as early as 1917, having fallen victim to paranoid schizophrenia, but is remembered as a paragon of the classical dance tradition, famed for his prodigious leaps. *You might be okay at the jive, but let's face it, you're no Nijinsky. See also* NUREYEV.

Nike (nīkee) The personification of victory. Nike was the goddess of victory in Greek mythology and was usually depicted with wings and carrying a palm or wreath. Her name is best known today as a trade name for a brand of sportswear. *The spirit of Nike hovers over the stadium as the victors come forward for the presentation.*

nil admirari (neel admirahree) Unimpressed; indifferent. The expression, which in Latin literally means "to admire nothing," comes from the *Epistles* of the Roman poet Horace (65–8 B.C.).

"Very many men nowadays besides the archdeacon adopt or affect to adopt the nil admirari doctrine; but nevertheless, to judge from their appearance, they are just as subject to sudden emotions as their grandfathers and grandmothers were before them" (Anthony Trollope, *Barchester Towers,* 1857).

nil desperandum (neel despărahndăm) Never give in to despair. This nugget of proverbial advice comes from the writings of the Roman poet Horace (65–8 B.C.). "This hitch in the mainspring of the domestic machinery had a bad effect upon the whole concern, but Amy's motto was 'Nil desperandum,' and having made up her mind what to do, she proceeded to do it in spite of all obstacles" (Louisa May Alcott, *Little Women,* 1868–69).

Nimrod (nimrod) A daring or skillful hunter of animals. Nimrod, the grandson of Ham, is identified in Genesis 10:9 as a "mighty hunter before the LORD." His kingdom included Babylon, Erech, and Akkad. According to legend, he acquired the link with hunting because he wore the animal skins that God had given to Adam for clothing, and it was through the divine influence of these that he could subdue any beast he encountered. Medieval tradition named Nimrod as the builder of the tower of Babel, and in former times his name was often applied to tyrants. The epithet is more often applied today to hunters of big game or to outstanding figures in sports. "You may think that Herr Doctor Kennicott is a Nimrod, but you ought to have seen me daring him to strip to his B. V. D.'s and go swimming in an icy mountain brook" (Sinclair Lewis, *Main Street,* 1920).

911 (nīn wăn wăn) The emergency services. The numbers 911 are those dedicated for calling assistance on the U.S. telephone system and have thus become synonymous with emergencies of one kind or another. *His weird behavior soon had his mother shrieking for 911.*

9/11 (nīn ilevăn) Of or relating to the terrorist attacks that took place on U.S. targets on September 11, 2001. The horror surrounding the destruction of the Twin Towers of the World Trade Center in New York City and the damage caused to the Pentagon in Washington using hijacked aircraft has made the date (otherwise referred to as ***September 11***) synonymous with terrorist atrocity. It also profoundly affected Western attitudes toward terrorist organizations around the world: Awareness of the threat posed by international terrorism was greatly promoted and subsequently influenced the foreign policies of the United States and various allies with relation to states accused of sponsoring such activity. *Memories of 9/11 have not faded in the years that have passed since that fateful day. See also* GUANTÁNAMO.

Nineveh and Tyre (ninăvă, tīr) Great cities that face ruination through the evil ways of their inhabitants. According to Nahum 3:7 and Ezekiel 25–26, the wealthy cities of Nineveh and Tyre were both destroyed as a result of the indulgent lifestyles of their citizens, who had ignored warnings of the fate they risked. Nineveh was a capital of Assyria and now lies in ruins on the opposite bank of the Tigris to modern Mosul in Iraq; the site of Tyre, once an important port in Syria and later the capital of Phoenicia, is occupied by a small fishing village called Sur in southern Lebanon. Their names are usually invoked as a warning against the wicked or conceited: "Lo, all our pomp of yesterday / Is one with Nineveh and Tyre" (Rudyard Kipling, "Recessional," 1897). To John Masefield, in his poem "Cargoes" (1903), however, Nineveh represented not the threat of ruin but rather a distant exoticism: "Quinquireme of Nineveh from distant Ophir / Rowing home to haven in sunny Palestine."

ninth plague of Egypt (eejipt) Impenetrable darkness. According to the Old Testament book of Exodus, God sent 10 plagues to punish the Egyptians for oppressing the Israelites and failing to acknowledge God's power. The ninth of these took the form of "a thick darkness in all the land of Egypt three days" (Exodus 10:22). "By reason of the density of the interwoven foliage overhead, it was gloomy there at cloudless noontide, twilight in the evening, dark as midnight at dusk, and black as the ninth plague of Egypt at midnight" (Thomas Hardy, *Far from the Madding Crowd,* 1874). *See also* EGYPTIAN DARKNESS; PLAGUES OF EGYPT.

Niobe (nīōbee) The archetype of the inconsolable grieving mother. In Greek mythology Niobe was the daughter of Tantalus and wife of Amphion, king of Thebes, with whom she had 12 children. When she arrogantly boasted herself superior to the goddess Leto, who had only two children (Apollo and Artemis), Leto's offspring punished her by killing all 12 of her children with arrows. The inconsolable Niobe was herself turned into a stone on Mount Sipylus in Lydia but even in this petrified form was said still to weep tears for her children. In canto 4 of *Childe Harold* (1819) Lord Byron subsequently dubbed Rome after the fall of the empire the ***Niobe of nations.*** "Like Niobe, all tears" (William Shakespeare, *Hamlet,* c. 1600).

nirvana (nervahnă) A state of euphoric bliss or spiritual ecstasy. Nirvana is the aim of both the Buddhist and Hindu religions, a state achieved by transcending such ordinary human preoccupations as pain, passion, and anxiety and through this extinguishing any sense of personal identity. "And then gradually my mind drifted away into strange vague dreams, always with that black face and red tongue coming back into them, and so I lost myself in the nirvana of delirium, the blessed relief of those who are too sorely tried" (Sir Arthur Conan Doyle, *Tales of Terror and Mystery,* 1923).

Nisus and Euryalus (nīsăs, yooreealăs) An archetype of perfect friendship. Nisus and Euryalus were two Trojans who journeyed to Italy with Aeneas and died during night attack on the camp of the Rutulians while the enemy was deep in drunken sleep. Unfortunately Euryalus lost his life in the fight, and when Nisus tried to avenge his friend, he too was killed. The friendship of Nisus and Euryalus has long since become proverbial. *The boys vowed to escape or die together in the attempt, faithful to the end like Nisus and Euryalus.*

Noah's ark *See* ARK.

Noah's wife (nōăz) A quarrelsome, obstreperous wife. Tradition has it that when Noah tried to usher his family into the ark to escape the Flood (Genesis 7:13), his wife refused. The quarrel between Noah and his wife was one of the stock scenes of medieval mystery plays. *She was a regular Noah's wife, always shrieking abuse at her hapless mate, and few men relished the prospect of crossing her threshold.*

noble savage The fundamental goodness of human nature, especially as seen in the uneducated savage untainted by the debatable advantages of civilization. The term is particularly associated with the French writer and philosopher Jean-Jacques Rousseau (1712–78), specifically with his novel *Émile* (1762), which describes the rearing of a child kept apart from other children. Rousseau did not, however, coin the phrase, which appeared elsewhere as early as 1672, in John Dryden's play *The Conquest of Granada*: "I am as free as Nature first made man, / Ere the base laws of servitude began, / When wild in woods the noble savage ran." "He was the noble savage, the Negro in chains, the archetype of exploited humanity, quintessential victim of the capitalist-imperialist-industrial system" (David Lodge, *Nice Work*, 1988).

Nod, land of *See* LAND OF NOD.

noise of many waters *See* VOICE OF MANY WATERS.

no jot or tittle *See* JOT OR TITTLE.

no joy in Mudville *See* CASEY AT THE BAT.

noli me tangere (nolee mee tanjăree) Latin for "touch me not." The phrase is spoken by Jesus Christ after the Resurrection, when he appears to Mary Magdalene as she is weeping at his empty tomb: "Touch me not; for I am not yet ascended to my Father" (John 20:17). "This precious aunt of yours is become insensibly a part of my constitution—Damn her! She's a *noli me tangere* in my flesh which I cannot bear to be touched or tampered with" (Tobias George Smollett, *The Expedition of Humphry Clinker,* 1771).

no man can serve two masters It is impossible to be faithful to two different causes, organizations, employers, etc., at the same time. This proverb has biblical origins, appearing in the form, "No man can serve two masters: for either he will hate the one, and love the other; or else he will hold to the one, and despise the other. Ye cannot serve God and mammon" (Matthew 6:24). "Not serve two masters?—Here's a youth will try it—Would fain serve God, yet give the devil his due" (Sir Walter Scott, *Kenilworth,* 1821). *See also* MAMMON.

no man is an island No individual can live entirely independently of his or her fellow creatures. The phrase comes from the works of English poet John Donne (c. 1572–1631), whose devotional writings include the lines: "No man is an island, entire of itself; every man is a piece of the continent, a part of the main . . . any man's death diminishes me, because I am involved in mankind; and therefore never send to know for whom the bell tolls; it tolls for thee." *Like many other tycoons, he sought to hide from the world in his palatial home, only to find that no man is an island and that even the immensely rich must depend from time to time upon the kindness of their fellow men. See also* FOR WHOM THE BELL TOLLS.

no man's land The area between warring armies or other factions that is controlled by neither side. The term is particularly associated with the trench warfare of World War I, when no man's land was a clearly delineated stretch of contested earth between the two front lines, in places only hundreds of yards wide. It does have an older history, however, being one of various terms used since medieval times to describe patches of land over which no one claimed ownership. *He found himself trapped in a no man's land between the two ideologies.*

no more spirit in her *See* QUEEN OF SHEBA.

no new thing under the sun *See* NOTHING NEW UNDER THE SUN.

noonday demon Indolence, vanity, or some other sin to which a person may be most susceptible when all is going well. The phrase is biblical in origin, appearing in Psalm 91:4–6, where it warns against dangers that can arise when least expected: "His truth shall be thy shield and buckler. Thou shalt not be afraid for the terror by night; Nor for the arrow that flieth by day; nor for the pestilence that walketh in darkness; nor for the destruction that wasteth at noonday." It is usually applied nowadays to threats that come in disguise or, specifically, to the temptations to laziness that come with middle age. *Financially secure and comfortable in his surroundings, he no longer resisted the lures of his noonday demons and began to spend his evenings slumped in front of the television, humming softly to himself.*

no other gods before me *See* THOU SHALT HAVE NO OTHER GODS BEFORE ME.

no peace for the wicked There is always some task to be done, considering the interruptions and disturbances of daily life. The phrase comes from Isaiah 57:21, where it implies that those who are given to evil can expect no respite from anxiety and fear: "There is no peace, saith my God, to the wicked." In modern parlance the expression is usually applied ironically, typically when a person feels obliged to cut short a rest in order to meet the demands of others or return to work that needs to be done. *But there is no peace for the wicked, and hardly had she sat down but there was a knock at the front door and she had to get up again.*

no respecter of persons The treatment of others without favor or prejudice, regardless of their status, wealth, etc. The phrase is biblical in origin, for example, "Then Peter opened his mouth, and said, Of a truth I perceive that God is no respecter of persons" (Acts 10:34). In Deuteronomy 1:17 Moses instructs those who are to sit as judges as follows: "Ye shall not respect persons in judgment; but ye shall hear the small as well as the great; ye shall not be afraid of the face of man; for the judgment is God's." "The law, gentlemen, is no respecter of persons in a free country" (James Fenimore Cooper, *The Pioneers,* 1823).

Norman Bates *See* BATES MOTEL; PSYCHO.

Norman Rockwell Representative of idealized small-town America. The artist Norman Rockwell (1894–1978) became famous for his depictions of ordinary life in homely small-town settings during the 1950s and 1960s, many of which appeared on the covers of popular magazines of the era. *Her parents still lived in a Norman Rockwell world, where everything was neat and tidy and crime was something you only read about in the racier newspapers.*

Norns (nornz) The fates. In Norse mythology, the Norns were three goddesses (Urd, Verdandi, and Skuld) who spun the threads of destiny and exercised supreme control over the fates of both mortals and gods. *The three controllers of the company were like the Fates, or the Norns of the Vikings, cutting the threads of life as they thought fit and thus closing down entire networks and departments without warning.*

no room at the inn No vacancy; no space available. The expression comes from the Bible, where it appears in Luke 2:7, which relates how Joseph and the pregnant Mary arrived at Bethlehem only to find the rooms in the local inn were all taken, obliging them to sleep in the stable: "No room for them in the inn." *We had hoped to stay at the hotel overlooking the town square, but the place was packed for the carnival and there was no room at the inn.*

Nostradamus (nostrădahmăs) A person who prophecies future events. Michel de Nostredame (1503–66), otherwise known as Nostradamus, was a French astrologer and physician whose *Centuries* (1555) contained a series of enigmatic prophecies about events that he said would happen in future centuries. Though derided by many, he is said to have predicted, among other things, air warfare, the rise of HITLER in Nazi Germany, and the atom bomb. *If he carries on predicting the results of future games so accurately people will start calling him Nostradamus.*

not by bread alone *See* MAN CANNOT LIVE BY BREAD ALONE.

nothing new under the sun What appears to be new often turns out to be nothing more than a revival or reintroduction of an old idea. This familiar comment on the changeless nature of things is biblical in origin, appearing in Ecclesiastes 1:9: "The thing that hath been, it is that which shall be; and that which is done is that which shall be done: and there is no new thing under the sun." "'They're after something quite new—something that's never been heard of before.' 'My dear fellow! There is nothing new under the sun'" (George Orwell, *Coming Up for Air,* 1939).

not peace but a sword A threat of violence or other stern action, as opposed to a pacific approach. The phrase appears in Matthew and Luke, where it is attributed to Christ: "Think not that I am come to send peace on earth: I came not to send peace, but a sword. For I am come to set a man at variance against his father, and the daughter against her mother, and the daughter in law against her mother in law" (Matthew 10:34–35). Critics usually defend the militaristic tone of the passage by interpreting it as a metaphorical comment directed toward Christ's followers, warning them that their commitment to God might bring them on occasion into conflict with their own families. "He had brought not peace to the city, but a sword" (W. Somerset Maugham, *Catalina,* 1948).

Nottingham, Sheriff of *See* SHERIFF OF NOTTINGHAM.

not tonight, Josephine (jōzăfeen) Mocking rejection of a sexual or other advance. The suggestion is that this is what the French emperor NAPOLEON said to his wife Josephine when she sought to distract him from affairs of state, although there is absolutely no historical evidence that he ever said any such thing. It is more likely to have been an invention of music-hall comedians later in the 19th century. *Wearing that bikini, she is unlikely ever to hear the words "not tonight, Josephine."*

not waving but drowning In a state of desperation or needing help, often despite appearances to the contrary. The allusion is to a 1953 poem of the same title, which was possibly the most famous creation of British poet Stevie Smith (1902–71): "Nobody heard him, the dead man, / But still he lay moaning: / He was much further out than you thought / And not waving but drowning." *They tried to look cheerful as they set off for the court, but you had the feeling they were not waving but drowning.*

not with a bang but a whimper Describing something that does not end dramatically but instead just fizzles out anticlimactically. This is a quotation from the 1925 poem "The Hollow Men" by the Anglo-American poet T. S. Eliot (1888–1965): "This is the way the world ends / Not with a bang but a whimper." "This is how careers end, Adjudicator: not with a bang, but with a whimper" (J. Mortimore and A. Lane, *Lucifer Rising*, 1993).

not worth a bone, the dog must be bad indeed that is *See* LABORER IS WORTHY OF HIS HIRE, THE.

now is the winter of our discontent Now things are at their worst. This is the first line of William Shakespeare's play *Richard III* (c. 1592), spoken by the malevolent future king as he contemplates the long-awaited chance to claim the throne of England for himself: "Now is the winter of our discontent / Made glorious summer by this sun of York; / And all the clouds that lowered upon our house / In the deep bosom of the ocean buried." *With the closure of the last theater staging challenging drama in town, it would seem that for serious actors this really is the winter of our discontent.*

number of the beast The devil's number; 666. The mystical reputation of the number depends on its appearance in Revelation 13:18: "Let him that hath understanding count the number of the beast: for it is the number of a man; and his number is Six hundred threescore and six." Various explanations have been put forward for the origins of the number, most of them based on the numerical values given to the letters of certain names, such as that of the wicked Roman emperor Nero, among others. Over the centuries the number has been associated with many other figures accused by their enemies of being the Antichrist, including Martin Luther, Napoleon Bonaparte, and Kaiser Wilhelm II. *He noticed that his new telephone number ended with the number of the beast, but he quickly shrugged off the momentary unease that welled up in his mind.*

Nunc Dimittis (nunk di<u>mi</u>tis) A canticle granting permission to leave, especially to depart this life. The words appear in the opening line of the prayer of Simeon, which is sung in evensong in the Anglican Church: "Nunc dimittis servum tuum Domine" ("Lord, now lettest thou thy servant depart in peace"), taken from Luke 2:29–35. By extension, if people are said to ***receive their Nunc Dimittis*** they are understood to have permission to depart; if they ***sing their Nunc Dimittis*** they are understood to be happy to be going. "I shall finish my artist's life with your face; but I shall want a bit of those shoulders, too . . . If they aren't divine I will eat my hat. Yes, I will do your head and then—nunc dimittis" (Joseph Conrad, *The Arrow of Gold,* 1919).

Nuremberg defense (<u>nyoor</u>ămberg) A defendant's plea that in committing a crime he or she was only "following orders." Such defenses were presented at several of the notorious trials of leading German Nazis at Nuremberg following the close of World War II. These excuses were largely ignored by the courts, reinforcing the principle that simply obeying someone else's orders does not render a person blameless for any crime he or she commits. *The youth's resort to the Nuremberg defense, that he was only doing what he had been told to do, cut little ice with the judges.*

Nureyev (nyoo<u>ray</u>ef) A brilliantly talented male ballet dancer. The Russian ballet dancer and choreographer Rudolph Nureyev (1939–93) was hugely admired for his performances in the great ballet roles, both with Russian companies and after defecting to the West in 1961, earning him a reputation as the greatest male dancer since NIJINSKY. *He is so young it is far too soon to say whether he is destined to be the next Nureyev.*

Nurse Ratched (rached) Archetype of a disciplinarian nurse. Nurse Ratched is a character in the 1962 Ken Kesey novel *One Flew Over the Cuckoo's Nest*, later filmed with Louise Fletcher as the hatchet-faced nurse who seeks to subdue the rebellious spirit of mental patient Randle McMurphy, played by Jack Nicholson. *She had all the charm and patience of Nurse Ratched, and when she administered the injection he felt as if he had been jabbed to the heart with a sharpened stick.*

nymph A young woman or girl, especially one with a lithe, youthful figure. The nymphs of Greek and Roman mythology were minor female deities of nature associated with specific locations, including rivers, trees, and mountains. They were said to remain perpetually young (though not actually immortal themselves) and to be very beautiful and generally friendly toward mortals. Several mortal heroes, including Achilles, had mothers who were nymphs. They could be subdivided into five broad types: the ***dryads*** and ***hamadryads*** lived in trees and groves; the ***naiads,*** in freshwater; the ***nereids*** inhabited the waters of the Mediterranean; the ***oceanids*** lived in the outer oceans; and the ***oreads,*** in grottoes and mountains. "When not engaged in reading Virgil, Homer, or Mistral, in parks, restaurants, streets, and suchlike public places, he indited sonnets (in French) to the eyes, ears, chin, hair, and other visible perfections of a nymph called Therese" (Joseph Conrad, *The Mirror of the Sea,* 1906).

O

Oakley, Annie *See* ANNIE OAKLEY.

Oates, Captain *See* CAPTAIN OATES.

Obi-Wan Kenobi (ōbee won kănōbee) A wise, elderly man. The allusion is to the character of the name in the *STAR WARS* films who helps the young hero Luke Skywalker develop his skills as a JEDI KNIGHT. He was played in the original trilogy of films by Alec Guinness and in the second trilogy, as a younger man, by Ewan McGregor. *The children regarded him as an Obi-Wan Kenobi who could explain to them the secrets of an alien adult world.*

Oblomov (oblomov) An extremely lazy, inactive person. Oblomov is the central character in the celebrated novel *Oblomov* (1859) by Ivan Goncharov (1812–91). Unable to stir himself into action, he spends his days in bed, dreaming about his childhood and resisting the attempts of others to make him change his indolent, passive ways. *It is much easier to live as an Oblomov than it is to live the life of an all-action hero.*

obsidian (obsideeăn) Glassy volcanic rock formed by rapid solidification of lava. The name comes from the Latin *obsianus lapis* (meaning "stone of Obsius") and is thought to have acquired the *d* through an inaccurate rendering of Obsius, the name of the person who first discovered the rock in Ethiopia, according to Pliny the Elder (A.D. 23–79). "At my side hung one of the Indian weapons that serve them instead of swords, a club of wood set on both sides with spikes of obsidian, like the teeth in the bill of a swordfish" (H. Rider Haggard, *Montezuma's Daughter,* 1899).

oceanid *See* NYMPH.

Oceanus (ōseeănăs) Alternative name for the Atlantic Ocean. In Greek mythology the Titan Oceanus was the god of the river that was supposed to flow around the Earth and was identified as the father of all the deities and nymphs of the world's waters. As the Greeks learned more about the world around them, Oceanus came to signify only the furthermost seas and oceans and the Atlantic in particular. *In her dreams she sailed with him upon the waters of Oceanus.*

Ockham's razor (okămz) The principle, also rendered as ***Occam's razor***, that the simplest explanation is usually the right one. The principle was established by the English philosopher William of Ockham (*c.*1280–*c.*1349) and is sometimes expressed in the form of the maxim "No more things should be presumed to exist than are absolutely necessary." Ockham was the philosopher's birthplace in Surrey, while the word "razor" is presumed to refer to the shaving away of unnecessary detail implicit in the principle itself. *A lot of scientific research would benefit from the application of Ockham's razor.*

Odd Couple, the An apparently mismatched pair of people. The allusion is to the stage comedy (1965) and film (1968) *The Odd Couple* by U.S. playwright Neil Simon. The comedy of the piece arises from the clash of lifestyles between the slovenly Oscar (played on screen by Walter Matthau) and the fastidious Felix (played by Jack Lemmon) when they opt to share an apartment. "'Talk about the odd couple,' Cy McCray was saying" (John Francombe, *Stone Cold*, 1990).

O death, where is thy sting? *See* DEATH, WHERE IS THY STING?

Odessa steps (ōdesă) A scene of slaughter, especially of innocents. The allusion is to the classic 1925 silent movie *Potemkin* directed by the Russian director Sergei Eisenstein, the most famous scene of which depicts the massacring of men, women, and children on a long flight of harbor steps during the events surrounding the rebellion that took place on the battleship *Potemkin* at Odessa in 1905. *With so many shots being fired the staircase soon looked like the Odessa steps.*

Odin (ōdin) The king of the gods in Scandinavian mythology and a personification of wisdom. According to legend Odin (known elsewhere as ***Woden, Wodin,*** or ***Wotan***) achieved his great wisdom by drinking from the giant Mimir's well, a privilege he obtained in exchange for one of his eyes. Also venerated as the god of war, poetry, and the dead, he became the husband of Frigga and the father of Thor and Balder. *Her grandfather presided over the family like some dreadful Odin, dispensing rewards and punishments according to his own unchallenged will.*

Odysseus (ōdiseeăs) Archetype of the heroic adventurer. According to Greek legend Odysseus, also known as ***Ulysses,*** was the son of King Laertes of Ithaca and one of those who sought the hand of the beautiful Helen and swore to protect her. This oath led ultimately to the Trojan War, in which Odysseus played a prominent role. Having helped in the final victory over the Trojans as one of the warriors concealed in the wooden horse, he set off back home to be reunited with his wife, Penelope. However, having offended the gods, he was not allowed to complete his journey for a full 10 years (see ODYSSEY). On his return he slaughtered the various suitors who were trying to claim Penelope and was reunited with his son, Telemachus. It was not long, however, before he embarked on further wanderings. His name is now synonymous with the courageous adventurer, although the Greek poet Homer and others tended to emphasize his cunning and even depicted him as wiley and scheming rather than simply brave. *If she was in trouble, he would be her Odysseus, negotiating all obstacles and traversing all chasms to rescue her from the dangers that pressed her on all sides.*

odyssey (ahdăsee) A lengthy journey or quest, typically one in which the person concerned has to overcome many obstacles. The word comes from Homer's epic poem the *Odyssey* (c. 700 B.C.), in which he relates the adventures of the Greek hero ODYSSEUS during the course of the perilous 10-year journey he undertook to return home after the fall of Troy. ". . . Nick could imagine how disconcerting his departure must be on the eve of their Grecian cruise which Mrs. Hicks would certainly call an Odyssey" (Edith Wharton, *Glimpses of the Moon,* 1922).

Oedipus complex (edăpăs) The unconscious sexual attraction of a boy for his mother and associated hostility toward his father (and more rarely the same attraction of a daughter for her father). The term, coined by the Austrian psychoanalyst Sigmund Freud (1856–1939), is an allusion to the Greek legend of Oedipus, the son of King Laius and Queen Jocasta of Thebes, who was brought up in ignorance of his parentage and ultimately killed his own father in a quarrel and married his own mother before realizing he was their son. When the truth came out, Oedipus put out his own eyes and went into exile, eventually dying at Colonus near Athens, while Jocasta committed suicide. Related words include the adjective ***oedipal.*** *The only motivation the detective could suggest to explain the crime was some kind of extra-twisted Oedipus complex. See also* ELECTRA COMPLEX.

off base Off target; mistaken. The allusion is to the game of baseball, in which a player on the batting side who is not touching one of the four "bases" may be deemed to be out and forced to leave the field. *Their conclusion was well off base.*

offending Adam *See* WHIP THE OFFENDING ADAM.

offer you can't refuse, an A proposition that is accompanied by a threat of violence or other "persuasion" that makes it impossible to turn down. The reference is to the 1969 Mario Puzo novel *The Godfather*, filmed in 1971, in which an aspiring movie actor is assured that he will get the part he wants after the director of the movie has been made "an offer he can't refuse." *He didn't want to vote against his conscience, but someone made him an offer he couldn't refuse. See also* GODFATHER, THE.

of making many books The human appetite for books can never be satisfied and thus the business of making them will never come to an end. The sentiment was first voiced in the Bible in Ecclesiastes 12:12: "Of making many books there is no end; and much study is a weariness of the flesh." It is often delivered as also a warning against excessive intellectualism. "Solomon saith truly, 'Of making many books there is no end,' so insatiable is the thirst of men therein: as also endless is the desire of many in buying and reading them" (Thomas Fuller, *The Holy and the Profane State,* 1642).

of such is the kingdom of heaven *See* SUFFER THE LITTLE CHILDREN.

Og of Bashan *See* BULL OF BASHAN.

O'Hara, Scarlett *See* GONE WITH THE WIND.

Oh, for the wings of a dove! *See* WINGS OF A DOVE.

OK Corral *See* GUNFIGHT AT THE OK CORRAL.

old Adam *See* WHIP THE OFFENDING ADAM.

old as Methuselah *See* AS OLD AS METHUSELAH.

Old Contemptibles Nickname of the British Expeditionary Force at the start of World War I in 1914. The nickname had its origins in an army order supposedly issued by Kaiser Wilhelm II of Germany on August 19, 1914: "It is my royal and imperial command that you exterminate the treacherous English, and walk over General French's contemptible little army." The soldiers of the BEF, who proved less easy to overwhelm than the kaiser had envisaged, assumed the nickname Old Contemptibles themselves. "The Old Contemptibles had become a compulsory and unwilling army" (John Cairney, *Worlds Apart*, 1991).

old guard A body of individuals representing established values and typically old-fashioned, conservative thinking. The reference is to the imperial Old Guard of veteran soldiers who constituted the most revered elite regiments of NAPOLEON's French armies. Members of the Old Guard, many of whom were of relatively advanced years, were selected from other regiments for their courage and imposing physical appearance, which was enhanced by tall bearskin hats and long, flowing mustaches. The Old Guard was resolute in its loyalty to the emperor, a dedication reflected in its refusal to surrender at the Battle of WATERLOO in 1815, even when all was clearly lost. "Colborne conceded that he was fighting a losing battle; a battle against the entire social structure within the palace and the snobbery and jealousy of the Old Guard that surrounded the Prince" (Penny Junor, *Charles and Diana*, 1991).

Old Man of the Sea A heavy burden, especially one that is virtually impossible to lay down. The allusion is to the tales of the *ARABIAN NIGHTS*, specifically to that of SINBAD the Sailor and an episode in which Sinbad offers to carry an old man, only to find that the old man refuses to dismount for many days and nights. Sinbad finally frees himself of his burden after getting the old man drunk, so that he falls off. "She fastened on to the person whose house it was like the Old Man of the Sea in 'Sinbad the Sailor'" (Winifred Beechey, *The Reluctant Samaritan*, 1991).

old men dream dreams Even the old may harbor dreams about the future. The expression comes from Joel 2:28, which looks forward to the messianic age when all, young and old, will share in the Spirit of God: "Your old men shall dream dreams, your young men shall see visions." Some later writers suggested that another reading may be that young men's visions are clearer—and hence more reliable—than old men's dreams. In modern usage the phrase is usually quoted in discussions of idealism and ambition. *Her grandfather grinned ruefully and noted, "Old men dream dreams, you know."*

Old Mother Hubbard (huberd) A very poor old woman. The allusion is to a nursery rhyme, first published in 1805, in which Old Mother Hubbard is described as a poor old lady whose cupboard is so bare she lacks even a bone to offer her dog. The nursery rhyme was written by Sarah Catherine Martin (1768–1826) on a visit to Kitley, east of Plymouth in Devon, England, possibly about a poor lady who lived in a cottage at nearby Yealmpton. *Her situation resembled that of Old Mother Hubbard, and she had nothing she could offer her visitors.*

Old Nick *See* SATAN.

old school tie A notional network linking people who have been to the same school or university, enabling them to gain access to privileged information, assistance, promotion, etc. The allusion is to the distinguishing ties worn by pupils at particular schools. The earliest record of the phrase is in Rudyard Kipling's *Limits and Renewals* (1932). "The whole squirearchy, old school tie, old boy network was a recipe for disaster" (Jeremy Paxman, *Friends in High Places*, 1990).

Old Testament Sometimes used to describe stern, retributive justice or thinking. The Old Testament is that part of the Bible describing the history of Israel. It is divided into the five books of the Pentateuch (Genesis through Deuteronomy); the historical books of Joshua through Esther; the books of poetry and wisdom, Job through Song of Solomon, including Psalms; and the books of the prophets Isaiah to Malachi. In particular thinking the God of the Old Testament is sometimes seen as less forgiving than that of the New Testament, but closer reading of the Bible shows that both testaments describe God as holy, yet also kind and loving. *He was a believer in Old Testament justice—short, sharp, and entirely merciless.*

olive branch A peace offering or symbol of peace. The olive branch has had special significance as a peace symbol since classical times. A Greek myth relates how Poseidon and Athena both competed to be chosen patron of the city of Athens. Poseidon tried to bribe the citizens with the offer of a horse, which represented his strength and courage, while Athena presented them with an olive tree, representing peace and prosperity. Athena won and the new city was named in her honor. The olive branch also has significance in Christian and Jewish iconography as it was an olive leaf that the dove brought back to Noah as a sign that the waters of the Flood were finally receding (Genesis 8:11). "We are now not armed for war, but approach the reverend towers of the old cathedral with an olive branch in our hands." (Anthony Trollope, *Barchester Towers,* 1857).

Olive Oyl *See* POPEYE.

Oliver *See* ROLAND.

Oliver Twist A foundling or orphan. Oliver Twist is the central character in the novel (1837–38) bearing his name published to great acclaim by the British novelist Charles Dickens (1812–70). Oliver is a young pauper who endures the harsh realities of life in the workhouse and becomes part of a gang of pickpockets led by the rascally FAGIN before being rescued and taken in by the kindly Mr. Brownlow. In the most famous scene from the novel, the hapless and hungry Oliver causes consternation in the workhouse when he innocently asks for more food. *Like Oliver Twist, many children even now go the whole school day without a meal. See also* ARTFUL DODGER; NANCY.

Olympia; Olympiad *See* OLYMPIC GAMES.

Olympian (ălimpeeăn) Godlike; majestic; superior; aloof. According to Greek mythology the home of the gods (sometimes called the Twelve Olympians) was located on the snowy summit of ***Mount Olympus*** in northern Greece, hidden from human sight by clouds. Here the gods lived in wonderful palaces and held meetings in a great council chamber or were entertained by the Muses with the lyre and song. "I think I shall have a lofty throne for you, godmamma, or rather two, one on the lawn and another in the ballroom, that you may sit and look down upon us like an Olympian goddess" (George Eliot, *Adam Bede,* 1859). *See also* OLYMPIC GAMES.

Olympic Games (ălimpik) International athletics competition held every two years, alternating for summer sports and winter sports. The modern Olympic Games, first held in Athens in 1896, were modeled on the famous competitions held in ancient Greece, in which competitors from all over the Greek world participated in foot races, wrestling, boxing, and chariot racing, among other events. These contests took place on a plain on the west coast of the Peloponnesus, which included the sacred grove of Olympian Zeus, hence the region's name, ***Olympia.*** The victor was presented with a garland of wild olive branches taken from a sacred olive tree, and special privileges were confirmed upon the winners and their families. The four-year period between the ancient games was called an ***Olympiad,*** although this term is now taken to mean the whole festival of the games themselves. The modern games are now the most important event in the worldwide sporting calendar. Competitors and especially medalists are often referred to as ***Olympians.*** *Do you have to get up at five o'clock in the morning to train? After all, it's only a village fun run, not the Olympic Games! See also* MARATHON.

Olympus, Mount *See* OLYMPIAN.

omega *See* ALPHA AND OMEGA.

omphalos (omfălăs) A central point or source. The word means "navel" in Greek and in ancient times was the name of the oval stone in the temple of Apollo at Delphi that was supposed to mark the center of the earth. *As far as the professor was concerned his desk was the omphalos of his world, the place where his ideas became crystal, or, on bad days, burned to ashes.*

onanism (ōnănizăm) Coitus interruptus; masturbation. The word originated through reference to the biblical character Onan, who according to Genesis 38:1–10 found himself expected to take his brother's widow, Tamar, after the former died. This was in observance of the ruling that a man should support his brother's widow as a matter of duty if his brother had died without children. Reluctant to consummate the union out of respect for his brother, Onan "spilled his seed on the ground," hence the adoption of his name for the practice of coitus interruptus (and occasionally any other form of birth control) or masturbation. *The minister muttered something dark about the evils of onanism and excused himself hurriedly.*

Onassis, Aristotle *See* ARISTOTLE ONASSIS.

on a wing and a prayer *See* COMIN' IN ON A WING AND A PRAYER.

on cloud nine Deliriously happy. The phrase has its origins in the descriptions given to cloud formations by the U.S. Weather Bureau. Cloud nine refers to a towering form of cumulonimbus. "I recognised it right away, and I was on Cloud Nine" (Sasha Stone, *Kylie Minogue: The Superstar Next Door*, 1989).

on earth peace *See* GOODWILL TO ALL MEN.

one jot or tittle *See* JOT OR TITTLE.

one little ewe lamb *See* EWE LAMB.

one's name is mud One's reputation is in tatters. This expression is said to allude to the assassination of ABRAHAM LINCOLN at Ford's Theater in Washington in April 14, 1865, specifically to Dr. Samuel Mudd of Bryantown, Maryland, who unwittingly set the broken leg of Lincoln's assassin, actor John Wilkes Booth (*see* BREAK A LEG!), thus enabling him to continue to evade capture. When the identity of the doctor's patient became known, Mudd himself was charged with being involved in the assassination plot. Despite a lack of any real evidence against him, Mudd was sentenced to life imprisonment and (though he was pardoned in 1869) ever since then his name has been associated with loss of reputation. *If they find out what really happened to the food parcels, my name will be mud.*

one-two A quick succession of blows, metaphorical or otherwise. The allusion is to boxing, in which the expression describes a combination of two quick punches, the first to the stomach and the second to the jaw. *The change in rosters gave the old one-two to his plans for the weekend.*

only I am left *See* I ONLY AM LEFT.

on skid row Destitute; penniless. Skid row is a notional place where only the poorest people live, in thoroughly dilapidated and impoverished surroundings. The name came originally from the lumber industry, in which newly felled timber is sometimes slid down a row of logs, and in due course it came to be applied to the run-down parts of town in which loggers lived. *After years of squandering the fortune he had inherited from his parents he finally found himself on skid row.*

on the ball Alert; wide awake. The phrase comes from baseball, in which it refers to the application by the pitcher of spin or added speed to a ball. "It certainly keeps the teacher on the ball when the pupils are not prepared to accept everything you say or do without questioning" (David Pimm, *Mathematics, Teachers and Children*, 1988).

on the horns of a dilemma *See* HORNS OF A DILEMMA.

on the ropes Under pressure; up against it; on the verge of defeat. The expression comes from boxing, in which a fighter pinned against the ropes by his opponent is deemed to be losing the contest. "Even in the worst hours she never gave any public impression that she was on the ropes" (Norman Fowler, *Ministers Decide*, 1991).

on the shoulders of giants Profiting from the knowledge, discoveries, and insights of illustrious predecessors to make further progress, particularly in relation to scholarship. This expression comes from the epic poem *Pharsalia* by the Roman poet Lucan (A.D. 39–65): "Pygmies placed on the shoulders of giants see more than the giants themselves." Today the phrase is often associated with the English scientist Sir Isaac Newton (1642–1727), who quoted the line when praised for his achievements. *It must be remembered in this moment of triumph that this new young team has only gotten this far by climbing on the shoulders of giants.*

007 *See* JAMES BOND.

open sesame (sesămee) A supposedly magical formula to open something or achieve a desired end. The words appear in the *ARABIAN NIGHTS*, being the charm that is spoken by the poor woodcutter ***Ali Baba*** to open the door of a secret cave in the tale of "Ali Baba and the Forty Thieves." Having gained access to the cave and the riches hidden within, and having put to death the 40 thieves with the help of the slave girl ***Morgiana***, Ali Baba is assured of a comfortable future as a wealthy man. "'Open sesame,' she said, slipping into the car" (Jack Yeovil, *Krokodil Tears*, 1990).

opera's not over till the fat lady sings, the The eventual outcome of something is not certain until the very end. A favorite expression of sports commentators with relation to a wide variety of games and contests in which a last-minute breakthrough may easily change the final result, it appears to have been first used in a sporting context by U.S. sports commentator Dan Cook in 1978. Its ultimate origins are usually traced to the appearance of a typically sturdily-built diva to sing the final aria in Wagner's opera *Die Walküre* or similar works. *It looks like nothing can stop the Giants winning the title this year, though we must remember the opera's not over till the fat lady sings.*

Ophelia (ōfeeleeă) Archetype of a tragic, trusting young woman. Ophelia, the daughter of POLONIUS, is the lover of the Danish prince HAMLET in William Shakespeare's tragedy *Hamlet* (c. 1600). After Hamlet kills her father, Ophelia slips into madness, hastened by Hamlet's apparent rejection of her, and eventually drowns in a river while gathering flowers. *They found her sister in the lake, drifting among the lilies like the drowned Ophelia.*

Ophir *See* GOLD OF OPHIR.

opiate of the people (ōpeeăt) Religion. Religious belief was thus described, albeit in the form ***opium of the people***, by the German political philosopher Karl Marx (1818–83) in his *Critique of the Hegelian Philosophy of Right* (1843–44): "Religion is the sigh of suppressed creatures, the feeling of the heartless world, just as it is the spirit of unspiritual conditions. It is the opium of the people." The underlying notion is that religion serves to suppress the natural fears and desires of the common people. "The new opiate of the people, she jeered; now that religion had failed, TV had taken its place: the gods and goddesses of the new world were the stars and staresses of soap: the bosses' latest plot to keep the minds of the proletariat addled" (Fay Weldon, *Darcy's Utopia*, 1991).

oracle A source of authoritative information, especially about the future. The concept of the oracle goes back to classical mythology and to the celebrated oracles at Delphi, Dodona, Oympia, and elsewhere. These shrines were consulted by pilgrims over the course of many centuries in the hope of receiving revelations from the gods about the future, usually delivered through the priestesses who attended these sites. The advice offered was typically obscure in content and capable of being interpreted in several different ways. Today the term *oracle* is variously applied to places, people, and branches of the media. Those who succeed against the odds in influencing the future in their favor, meanwhile, are people who ***work the oracle.*** *The man frowned and turned to consult the oracle, his wife. See also* DELPHIC.

orc (ork) An uncivilized, barbaric brute. The orcs are the ugly, savage creatures that are unleashed in huge armies by the evil wizard Sauron in J. R. R. Tolkien's fantasy novel *The Lord of the Rings* (1954–55). Tolkien was not, however, the first writer to describe monstrous creatures called orcs: Michael Drayton (1563–1631) gave the name to a fearsome sea monster capable of consuming men, while John Milton wrote of "seals, orcs, and sea-mews" in his *Paradise Lost* (1667). *Rugby forwards resemble orcs in their muscle-bound physiques and aggressive determination to wreak havoc on their opponents.*

order of Melchizedek *See* MELCHIZEDEK.

oread *See* NYMPH.

original sin A state of sin considered to be the innate condition of the whole human race since the FALL of Adam. In modern usage the phrase is sometimes used more loosely and may refer to a range of either fundamental or relatively trivial failings. "'Some people are naturally good, you know, and others are not. I'm one of the others. Mrs. Lynde says I'm full of original sin.'" (Lucy Maud Montgomery, *Anne of Green Gables,* 1908).

Orion (ărīon) A constellation of stars near Canis Major. Supposedly resembling the figure of a giant with a belt of three stars representing a sword, a lion's skin, and a club, it takes its name from that of a Boeotian giant who was renowned as a hunter and according to Greek legend was raised to the stars after his death (in some accounts, slain by the goddess Artemis). *The alcohol had gone straight to her head, and she had to lie down in the grass, gazing up with bewilderment at distant Orion.*

Orphan Annie *See* LITTLE ORPHAN ANNIE.

Orpheus (orfeeăs) An archetype of a master musician. Orpheus, the son of Apollo and Calliope, was a Thracian lyre player who was instructed in music by the Muses and became so fine a musician he could enchant wild beasts and even rocks and trees with his playing. He sailed with the Argonauts but faced his sternest test when he attempted to retrieve his wife, ***Eurydice,*** from the underworld after she died from a snakebite. Having played his lyre to Hades, it was agreed that he could have Eurydice providing he did not look back to see her as they returned to the world above. Unfortunately Orpheus could not resist the temptation to see if this wife was following him, and Eurydice was promptly returned to the underworld. Grief at this loss left Orpheus embittered toward other women, and ultimately he met his own end when he was torn to pieces by the women of Thrace in a Bacchanalian frenzy after he offended them. His skill as a musician is still remembered, and the adjective ***orphean*** denotes anything melodious or enchanting. *After the concert the critics hailed him as a veritable Orpheus.*

Orwellian (orweleeăn) Of or relating to the works of British novelist George Orwell (1903–50) or reminiscent of the nightmarish future he depicted in such novels as *ANIMAL FARM* (1945) and *Nineteen Eighty-Four* (1949). Originally named Eric Blair, the author called himself Orwell after the River Orwell in Suffolk, where he lived at one time. "The cult of sport sometimes seems to take on the quality of an Orwellian nightmare" (Richard Holt, *Sport and the British*, 1989). *See also* BIG BROTHER; DOUBLETHINK; NEWSPEAK; ROOM 101; THOUGHT POLICE.

ostracism The practice of deliberately excluding someone from a particular group, society, etc., after he or she has committed a perceived offense of some kind. The word has its origins in the customs of the ancient Greeks. In order to protect their democratic system from tyrants it was possible once a year for Greek citizens to name the one person they wished to see exiled from Athens for being too powerful or ambitious. The "ballots" were written on shards of broken pottery (in Greek, *ostrakon*) and then counted. The person with the most votes was obliged to go into exile for at least 10 years. The custom fell into disuse after 417 B.C., when two mistrusted politicians, Alcibiades and Nicias, combined to avoid being ostracized and instead secured the ostracism of their harshest critic, Hyperbolus. Persons thus exiled were not considered disgraced, but the word in its modern usage necessarily casts a pall of shame over the person concerned. "He said to himself that she was too light and childish, too uncultivated and unreasoning, too provincial, to have reflected upon her ostracism, or even to have perceived it" (Henry James, *Daisy Miller,* 1879).

Othello (ōthelō) Archetype of a jealous lover. The central character in William Shakespeare's tragedy *Othello* (c. 1603), Othello the Moor becomes convinced (falsely) of his wife DESDEMONA's infidelity and kills her before realizing his mistake and committing suicide. *Jealousy turned him from a meek little rabbit into a raging Othello. See also* IAGO.

OTT *See* GO OVER THE TOP.

our daily bread *See* DAILY BREAD.

Our Father *See* PATERNOSTER.

ours not to reason why It is not up to us to question our orders, but just to obey them. This weary acceptance of the authority of others has its roots in a quotation from Alfred, Lord Tennyson's poem "The Charge of the Light Brigade": "Theirs not to make reply, / Theirs not to reason why, / Theirs but to do and die." *Personally I think it's a mad decision, but ours not to reason why. See also* CHARGE OF THE LIGHT BRIGADE.

out, damned spot! An expression of remorse at some past misdeed that refuses to be forgotten. The exclamation is a quotation from William Shakespeare's tragedy *MACBETH* (1606), in which it is delivered by LADY MACBETH as she tries to clean her hands of the (imaginary) blood of King Duncan, murdered by her husband with her encouragement. In modern usage, with its inevitable suggestion of melodrama, the line is usually quoted in a humorous or mocking tone, or in such everyday contexts as the cleaning of clothes. *"Out, damned spot!" he roared as he held the door open for the dog to go out.*

outer darkness The most distant darkness, as a judgment for those who reject the light of God's truth. The phrase is biblical in origin, appearing in Matthew 8:12 in the words of Christ himself: "But the children of the kingdom shall be cast into outer darkness." (See also Matthew 22:13 and 25:30.) ". . . and the Chief priest of Corporate Affairs demanded of the Lord High Editor that the poor scribe who inhabiteth the back page be cast into the outer darkness" (Alan Williams, *Modern Railways,* May 2001). *See also* WEEPING AND GNASHING OF TEETH.

Outer Mongolia (mongōleeă) A very remote place. The use of the term was undoubtedly suggested by the remoteness and inaccessibility of Outer Mongolia, which is situated between Russia and China. *When they posted her boyfriend to the offshore oil rig, they might as well have sent him to Outer Mongolia, for there was absolutely no way she could get to him.*

out for the count *See* DOWN FOR THE COUNT.

out-Herod Herod (herăd) To outmatch someone in something, especially in cruelty. The allusion is to Herod the Great (c. 37–4 B.C.), the ruler of Judaea who ordered all the male infants of Bethlehem put to death in an attempt to secure the death of the newly born Christ (Matthew 2:16–18). It was William Shakespeare, in his play *Hamlet* (c. 1600), who first employed the phrase: "I would have such a fellow whipped for o'erdoing Termagant: it out-herods Herod: pray you, avoid it." It sometimes occurs with another name in place of Herod (*see* TIMON). "James' wish to learn as many languages as possible may well have been fired by the desire to out-Leyden Leyden" (K. M. Elisabeth Murray, *Caught in the Web of Words,* 1979).

out of left field Coming from an unexpected, unlikely quarter or direction. The allusion is to baseball, the left field being the area to the left of the outfield beyond third base. *His next suggestion for the way forward really came out of left field, something we had never even considered before.*

out of the abundance of the heart the mouth speaks People cannot resist talking about the things that most preoccupy them. The proverb has biblical origins, appearing at Matthew 12:34: "O generation of vipers, how can ye, being evil, speak good things? for out of the abundance of the heart the mouth speaketh." Also encountered in the variant form.

out of the ark *See* ARK.

out of the eater came forth meat *See* OUT OF THE STRONG CAME FORTH SWEETNESS.

out of the fullness of the heart the mouth speaks. *She guessed her mother had promised not to say anything, but out of the fullness of the heart the mouth speaks.*

out of the mouths of babes and sucklings Children often recognize—and voice—truths that older, more experienced people do not perceive. The proverb is biblical in origin, appearing at Psalm 8:2 as "Out of the mouth of babes and sucklings hath thou ordained strength" and at Matthew 21:16 as "Yea; have ye never read, Out of the mouth of babes and sucklings thou hast perfected praise?" The fuller version of the phrase is usually given as ***out of the mouths of babes and sucklings come great truths.*** A variant runs ***from the mouths of babes come words of wisdom.*** "There was something fantastic to him in this sudden philosophising by one whom he had watched grow up from a tiny thing. Out of the mouths of babes and sucklings—sometimes!" (John Galsworthy, *The Forsyte Saga,* 1922).

out of the strong came forth sweetness Sweet and gentle things can come from the unlikeliest sources. The allusion is to the riddle posed by Samson and related at Judges 14:5–10. Having killed a lion with his own hands and subsequently seeing a swarm of bees in the carcass, Samson challenged the Philistine guests at a wedding feast to solve the riddle implicit in the statement "Out of the eater came forth meat, and out of the strong came forth sweetness" (Judges 14:14). The solution (given to the Philistines by Samson's wife) lies in the eater being the lion and the sweetness being the honey produced by the bees. *It was a surprise when the author of this tender love poem turned out to be the grizzled old cowboy in the corner, but then out of the strong came forth sweetness.*

out-Timon Timon *See* TIMON.

over the top *See* GO OVER THE TOP.

oxen of Geryon *See* LABORS OF HERCULES.

O ye of little faith Expression of lamentation at another's lack of confidence in something, especially when his or her doubts have been proved groundless. The phrase is biblical in origin, appearing in Matthew 6:30, which reads: "Wherefore, if God so clothe the grass of the field, which to day is, and to morrow is cast into the oven, shall he not much more clothe you, O ye of little faith?" *You didn't think we would get here on time, did you, O ye of little faith.*

Oz *See* WIZARD OF OZ.

Ozymandian (ozeemandeeăn) Grandiose but ultimately devoid of any real, lasting significance. In his 1818 poem "Ozymandias" the English poet Percy Bysshe Shelley (1792–1822) gave the name Ozymandias to an imaginary ancient king, whom he identified as the subject of a huge statue in the desert reduced over the years to a mere fragment: "My name is Ozymandias, king of kings: / Look on my works, ye Mighty, and despair!" The statue in question, at Thebes, actually depicted the Egyptian pharaoh Ramses II (1304–1237 B.C.). The adjective Ozymandian has thus come to refer to any ambitious but inevitably futile flaunting of earthly power or other display of vanity. *His pride in his children's trifling achievements was positively Ozymandian.*

P

paean (peeăn) A song or other expression of praise. The original paeans were composed in honor of the Greek god Apollo, whose alternative titles included Paian, a name denoting his status as physician to the gods. Other words from the same root include the flower name ***peony,*** the blooms of which were formerly prized for their medicinal properties. "This quickly took us out of range of Red-Eye, and the last we saw of him was far out on a point of land, where he was jumping up and down and chanting a paean of victory" (Jack London, *Before Adam,* 1907).

Paine, Tom *See* TOM PAINE.

painted Jezebel *See* JEZEBEL.

painting the Forth Bridge Undertaking an apparently never-ending task. The cantilevered railway bridge over the Firth of Forth in southeast Scotland was built in 1890 and according to legend takes four years to paint, at which point it is necessary to begin painting all over again from the beginning. In fact, this is not (and probably never has been) true of the Forth Bridge, although it is true that it has a permanent maintenance staff. The paint used on the bridge today needs reapplying every ten years. "After Melanie shopped, she helped her aunt, either serving in their own shop or writing out price tags or performing the endless task of polishing the woodwork of counter and drawers, a Forth Bridge of polishing that was no sooner completed than the messy fingers of small customers meant it must be started again" (Angela Carter, *The Magic Toyshop*, 1993).

painting the Sistine Chapel (sisteen) Undertaking a demanding and seemingly endless task, especially one of a creative nature. The allusion is to the painting of the ceiling of the Sistine Chapel at the Vatican in Rome by the great Italian Renaissance artist MICHELANGELO (1475–1564). This masterpiece of Western art famously took Michelangelo years to complete, to the exasperation of Pope Julius II (1443–1513), who had commissioned the work. *You'd think she was painting the Sistine Chapel the way she moans about decorating her house.*

paint the town red To celebrate with gusto. The phrase is said to allude to a memorable night of roistering in the town of Waterford, Ireland, on April 5, 1837, during the course of which the marquis of Waterford and his friends made liberal use of pots of red paint. Alternative origins include references to the red-light district of certain towns or to the convivial gatherings of huntsmen in the English town of Melton Mowbray. "By the time they were ready to leave she was having to use every ounce of effort to convince André that no, she didn't want to paint the town red, or any other colour, for that matter, and no, she didn't want to have any candlelit dinners with him" (Cathy Williams, *A French Encounter*, 1992).

palace guard *See* PRAETORIAN GUARD.

paladin (paladin) A defender or champion of a particular cause. The original paladins were the 12 legendary heroes who fought for the emperor CHARLEMAGNE (742–814), ruler of the Franks and Holy Roman Emperor. They represented the highest ideals of chivalry and were prepared to die in the struggle against wrong. "Edricson and Terlake rode behind him in little better case, while Ford, a careless and light-hearted youth, grinned at the melancholy of his companions, and flourished his lord's heavy spear, making a point to right and a point to left, as though he were a paladin contending against a host of assailants" (Sir Arthur Conan Doyle, *The White Company,* 1891). *See also* ROLAND.

Palamedes (palămeedeez) An ingenious person. According to Greek legend Palamedes was a Greek commander who persuaded the reluctant ODYSSEUS to join the campaign against Troy. Odysseus had feigned madness in order to excuse himself from going, demonstrating his insanity by yoking an ox and a horse to his plow and using them to plow the sand with salt. Palamedes cleverly tricked him into betraying his true state of mind by placing Odysseus's son, Telemachus, in the path of the plow, obliging Odysseus to change course and thus reveal his mastery of his senses. Odysseus eventually got his revenge by framing Palamedes for treachery and having him stoned to death. Other alleged proofs of the ingenuity of Palamedes included his invention of four letters of the Greek alphabet as well as of the lighthouse, scales, measures, discus, and dice. *Even as a research student he established a reputation of being quite a Palamedes.*

pale, beyond the *See* BEYOND THE PALE.

Palinurus (palinoorăs) A pilot, especially one who is careless or irresponsible. In Roman myth and Virgil's *Aeneid,* Palinurus served as helmsman under Aeneas but was washed overboard after he fell asleep and was murdered when he reached land three days later. *Like Palinurus, our pilot was more concerned with his own comfort than he seemed to be with the safety of the vessel.*

Pal Joey A calculating, worldly-wise opportunist. The allusion is to the central character of the book *Pal Joey* (1940) by the U.S. writer John O'Hara (1905–70); the character was brought to life in the 1940 Rodgers and Hart musical of the same title based on the book. The 1957 film version starred Frank Sinatra in the title role. *He had all the cynicism of Pal Joey.*

palladium (pălaydeeăm) A safeguard; something that gives protection. The original Palladium was a wooden statue of Pallas Athena supposedly thrown out of heaven by Zeus and retrieved by the Trojans. Tradition had it that the safety of Troy depended on the protection of this statue. It was eventually stolen by Odysseus and Diomedes, and the city fell to the Greeks. In modern usage the term is typically applied to freedom of speech or something else that is considered a guarantee of the safety of a country or constitution. *This measure will act to some degree as a palladium against further encroachments.*

Palooka, Joe *See* JOE PALOOKA.

Pan (pan) Personification of disorder and licentiousness. According to Greek mythology, Pan was a nature god who protected flocks and the shepherds who tended them but who also enjoyed tormenting wanderers in the forests and woods where he roamed (see PANIC). He was usually depicted with horns and goats' feet, attributes that were subsequently passed on to the devil of Christian lore. "Of the rushing couples there could barely be discerned more than the high lights—the indistinctness shaping them to satyrs clasping nymphs—a multiplicity of Pans whirling a multiplicity of Syrinxes" (Thomas Hardy, *Tess of the D'Urbervilles,* 1891). *See also* PANPIPES.

Pan, Peter *See* PETER PAN.

panacea (panăseeă) A universal remedy or cure. The word alludes to Panacea, the daughter of Aesculapius, the Greek god of medicine and healing. "This was a relief to Mrs. Peniston, who could give herself up to her own symptoms, and Lily was advised to go and lie down, her aunt's panacea for all physical and moral disorders" (Edith Wharton, *The House of Mirth,* 1905).

pandemonium (pandămōneeăm) Uproar; tumult; confusion. The origin of this word appears to be Greek, in which it would mean "all the demons," but it was in fact invented by the English poet John Milton (1608–74) in *Paradise Lost* (1667), in which it is identified as the capital city in hell: "The rest were all / Far to the inland retired, about the walls / Of Pandemonium, city and proud seat / Of Lucifer." "On descending, I found the kitchen on the brink of pandemonium, and in general, an extremely tense atmosphere amongst all levels of staff" (Kazuo Ishiguro, *The Remains of the Day*, 1989).

Pandora's box (pandorăz) A source of manifold unforeseen difficulties that once released are hard to bring back under control. The phrase alludes to Greek mythology and the legend of the beautiful Pandora, the first woman, and the box or jar she possessed containing all the problems that if unleashed would lead to the downfall of humanity. She was instructed to entrust this box to the man she married. One legend has it that Pandora (whose name means "all gifts") opened the box out of curiosity to see what was inside, while another has her eventual husband, Epimetheus, opening it against her advice. In either event the box was opened, and the human race has since been beset by a multiplicity of sorrows and problems. Only hope remained within. "We unlock the genetic code and open a Pandora's box of ethics" (Philip Yancey, *Reaching for the Invisible God,* 2000).

panem et circenses *See* BREAD AND CIRCUSES.

Panglossian (pangloseeăn) Unrealistically optimistic. The word is an allusion to the fictitious Dr. Pangloss in Voltaire's *CANDIDE* (1759), in which he is depicted as a pedantic old tutor who stubbornly believes, despite all evidence to the contrary, that ***all is for the best in this best of all possible worlds***. *The old man's Panglossian optimism in the face of repeated setbacks and disasters grew to be infuriating. See also* BEST OF ALL POSSIBLE WORLDS, THE.

panic A feeling of terror, anxiety, and confusion. The word is Greek in origin, referring to the god PAN, the lecherous god of forests and shepherds who was notorious for playing tricks on travelers in valleys and mountains, typically by springing out on them unexpectedly or by making menacing noises in the undergrowth. Any sensation of fear welling up for no apparent reason came to be dubbed *panikos,* hence the modern word, which completed its journey to English via the French *panique* around the early 18th century. *Panic spread quickly through the crowd as news of the executions passed from one person to another.*

Panoptes *See* ARGUS.

panpipes A musical wind instrument consisting of various reeds of different lengths bound together. It was named after the Greek nature god Pan, who is supposed to have devised the instrument. The legend goes that Pan pursued the nymph Syrinx, but she escaped from him by hiding in the earth and being turned into reeds, from which the thwarted Pan made his set of pipes. Panpipes may also be known as ***pipes of Pan*** or as a ***syrinx.*** *He sat on the ground blowing softly into a set of panpipes and eyeing her quizzically.*

Pantagruel *See* RABELAISIAN.

pantheon (pantheeon, pantheeăn) A group of distinguished or revered individuals. In ancient Greece and Rome the Pantheon (from the Greek meaning "all of the gods") was a temple dedicated to the gods collectively. The famous pantheon in Rome was built by the emperor Hadrian in the second century A.D., incorporating an older structure built by Agrippa in 27 B.C., and became a Christian church in 609. In due course the term came to be applied to all the gods collectively of any religion and thus to any group of outstanding individuals, especially to national heroes and memorials built in their honor. "How will the demi-gods in your Pantheon—I mean those legendary persons you call saints—intercede for you after this?" (Thomas Hardy, *Jude the Obscure,* 1895).

pantisocracy (pantisokrasee) An ideal, communistic society. The word, derived from the Greek "all of equal power," was devised around 1794 by the English poet Samuel Taylor Coleridge (1772–1834) as the name of the perfect society he and fellow poet Robert Southey and others planned to found on the banks of the Susquehannah River in New England. Lack of funds meant that the envisaged community never came into being. *Idealists in the party envisaged a pantisocracy where decisions were made directly by the electorate.*

Panza, Sancho *See* DON QUIXOTE.

panzer (panzer) A tank, especially one belonging to a highly mobile tactical unit. The original panzers were the tanks of the German armored divisions—the *Panzerdivisionen*—that spearheaded the Nazi invasion of western Europe and Russia during World War II. The German word *panzer* means simply "armor." Although primarily associated with the tanks of Nazi Germany, the term is occasionally applied to tanks generally. *We told the Russians in no uncertain terms to get their panzers off our lawn.*

Paolo and Francesca (powlō, francheskă) Archetype of a pair of tragic lovers. The story of Paolo and Francesca, which featured in Dante's *Inferno,* described how Francesca da Rimini married Giovanni Malatesta but then fell in love with Giovanni's brother Paolo, with the result that the lovers were both executed in 1289. *Like Paolo and Francesca, everything went wrong when she fell for his* *brother—only it wasn't his brother, it was his sister. See also* PELLÉAS AND MÉLISANDE.

paparazzi (papăratsee) Press photographers who pursue celebrities to take their photographs. The singular form of the word, used less frequently, is an allusion to a photographer called Paparazzo in the 1960 movie *LA DOLCE VITA* directed by Federico Fellini (1920–93). The name came ultimately from *Sulle rive dello Ionio* (1957), Margherita Gandacci's translation of George Gissing's travel book *By the Ionian Sea* (1901), in which it was borne by an Italian hotel owner who took exception to his guests dining at other establishments. "They have been spied on by the paparazzi, betrayed by trusted servants, embarrassed by indiscreet friends, and have had to endure a constant torrent of innuendo, gossip, lies and half-truths in newspapers, magazines and books—none of which are they able to repudiate" (Penny Junor, *Charles and Diana*, 1991).

paper tiger Something that appears much more formidable or impressive than it is actually revealed to be. The phrase was first heard in the 1940s, when it was used (as *zhĭ lăohŭ* in the original Chinese) by the Chinese leader Mao Zedong, talking about the United States: "The atom bomb is a paper tiger which the United States reactionaries use to scare people. It looks terrible, but in fact it isn't . . . All reactionaries are paper tigers." "Is it only a paper tiger, or does it really have teeth?" (H. McVea, *Financial Conglomerates and the Chinese Wall*, 1993).

Paphian (payfeeăn) A prostitute. The word originally meant "relating to Venus" and came about as an allusion to the city of Paphos on Cyprus, where Venus, the Roman goddess of love, was worshiped. *A Paphian by trade, she became a popular figure in high society, though heartily disliked by other women.*

parable of the sower Story illustrating the point that there are various responses to God's word. The parable is related in Mark 4:3–9: "Hearken; Behold, there went out a sower to sow; And it came to pass, as he sowed, some fell by the way side, and the fowls of the air came and devoured it up. And some fell on stony ground, where it had not much earth; and immediately it sprang up, because it had no depth of earth: But when the sun was up, it was scorched; and because it had no root, it withered away. And some fell among thorns, and the thorns grew up, and choked it, and it yielded no fruit. And other fell on good ground, and did yield fruit that sprang up and increased; and brought forth, some thirty, and some sixty, and some an hundred. And he said unto them, He that hath ears to hear, let him hear." Jesus explains the parable in verses 13–20. Perhaps a better name would be the parable of the soils: The same seed is sown in different soils. Some seed ***falls by the wayside,*** analogous to the word immediately being taken away by Satan. Some seed falls on stony ground and so does not take root, like those who receive the word gladly but quickly fall away when times become difficult. Other seed falls among thorns, which choke the growth of the plants, much like those for whom "the cares of this world, and the deceitfulness of riches, and the lusts of other things" (verse 19) come in and kill off the growth. But in the final case seed falls on good ground where people hear and receive the word and are greatly fruitful and productive. *The story graphically illustrated the truth behind the biblical parable of the sower. See also* FALL BY THE WAYSIDE; FALL ON STONY GROUND.

parable of the talents Story emphasizing the belief that all people will be judged at the Last Judgment according to the life each has led. The parable is related by Christ in Matthew 25:14–30, which compares the behavior of three servants after their master entrusts to each a sum of money. (A talent was originally a measure of weight and later a unit of coinage.) Two of the men invest the money sensibly, earning a considerable amount of interest, while the third hides the money in the ground and returns no more than the sum that was entrusted to him in the first place. On his return the master congratulates the two who have used the money wisely and rebukes the third for doing nothing with it, the moral being that God-given opportunities and talents should be faithfully used. *Then began the usual secular imitation of the parable of the talents with each of the candidates being questioned in detail about their previous employment history.*

parable of the wheat and tares Story illustrating the point that God allows good and evil to coexist. The parable is related in Matthew 13:25–30 and 13:36–43, where workers are told not to remove tares, or weeds, sown by the enemy. Jesus explains that the field is the world and the wheat, or "good seeds," are the children of the kingdom. The enemy is the devil, and the weeds are the children of the evil one. This parable illustrates the point that God allows good and evil to coexist, although eventually justice will be done and evil will be destroyed. "'I hope there will be more wheat and fewer tares every year,' said Amy softly" (Louisa May Alcott, *Little Women,* 1868–69).

parable of the wise and foolish virgins Story illustrating the difference between those who are farsighted and prepared and those who are improvident and unprepared. This parable, recorded in the Bible in Matthew 25:1–13, describes the wedding custom of the day. The bridegroom went in the evening to the bride's home to collect her, followed by a procession to his home, lit by torchbearing friends. In the story, the bridegroom was late and the torchbearers, all virgins, fell asleep. When the groom arrived, five foolish virgins did not have enough oil to relight their lamps and went to buy more, later being refused entry to the celebrations. Five wise virgins were prepared, however: They had brought extra oil. Jesus explained that people should be alert and ready for him when he returns at the end of the age. ". . . a little food, enough to keep us for three or four days if necessary, together with some matches and a good supply of oil, since, as Bastin put it, he was determined not to be caught like the foolish virgins in the parable" (H. Rider Haggard, *When the World Shook,* 1919).

paradise Heaven or any idyllic place or condition in which a person's desires or aspirations are fully realized. The word comes from the Greek *paradeisos,* meaning "garden" or "park," and appears in the Old Testament in descriptions of the GARDEN OF EDEN (Genesis 2:8) and in the New Testament as a synonym for the Christian heaven (Luke 23:43; 2 Corinthians 12:4; and Revelation 2:7). *The new mall is a paradise for shoppers.*

paradise lost A state or place of innocence, perfection, or happiness that has been irretrievably lost or is no longer attainable. The phrase is usually associated with the epic poem *Paradise Lost* (1667) by the English poet John Milton (1608–74), in which he describes the FALL of man and the expulsion of Adam and Eve from the GARDEN OF EDEN. Milton's version of paradise owed much to the earlier epic *La Semaine* ("The First Week of

Creation") by Guillaume de Salluste du Bartas (1544–90), who in turn borrowed from *The Creation*, *The Fall*, and *The Expulsion from Paradise* by St. Avitus (d. 523). Milton's epic had a sequel, *Paradise Regained* (1671), but this phrase has not entered the language to the extent that "paradise lost" has. *In the great man's autobiography, he tended to view the world of his youth as a paradise lost.*

Parcae *See* FATES.

pariah (părīă) A person, nation, organization, etc., that is shunned by other people and considered outside decent society. The allusion is to the Pariahs, one of the lowest of Hindu castes, from southern India. The word itself means "drummer" in Tamil, a reference to the fact that Pariahs often beat the drums at Hindu festivals. It was the Europeans who extended the term to encompass people who belonged to no caste at all and thus all outcasts. "Of course architects are human and it must be seen that such an approach is liable to make the architect a pariah figure, unbeloved of the society in which his creations are set" (Stewart Lamont, *In Good Faith*, 1989).

Paris (paris) Archetype of a beautiful young man. Paris, the second son of King Priam of Troy, played a pivotal role in bringing about the Trojan War by carrying off Helen, the wife of Menelaus, and thus causing the Greeks to lay siege to the city. When Troy finally fell, Paris was wounded by Philoctetes, who returned him to his wife, Oenone. She refused to heal Paris's grievous wound, so he returned to Troy, where he died before a repentant Oenone could reach him. Overcome with grief, Oenone hanged herself. *The general's son was as beautiful as Paris and as cantankerous as Donald Duck.* *See also* JUDGMENT OF PARIS.

Paris is well worth a mass (paris) Principles should be sacrificed where the reward is great enough. This cynical observation was first voiced by Henri of Navarre (1553–1610), who was destined to rule France as Henri IV. During his struggle to gain the French throne, Henri demonstrated a willingness to abandon religious allegiance for the sake of expediency on more than one occasion, switching from Protestantism to Catholicism in 1572, then recanting, and finally, after a long siege of Paris, declaring himself a Catholic once again in order to be allowed into the city unopposed to claim the crown of all France. As king, he introduced the Edict of Nantes, which guaranteed freedom of worship, only to be assassinated by a Catholic priest in 1610. *Winston Churchill was not the only politician to change sides, excusing himself with the thought that "Paris is well worth a mass."*

Park Avenue A street that is lined with the homes of the very rich. Park Avenue in Manhattan is lined with the homes of some of the wealthiest families in the United States. *She was evidently impressed by his elegant suit and his Park Avenue chic.*

Parkinson's Law The proposition that "work expands so as to fill the time available for its completion." One of the most familiar of all the tenets of business life, it was first suggested by the British writer and historian Cyril Northcote Parkinson (1909–93) in his satirical book *Parkinson's Law* (1958), which explored the various ways in which the "law" applied: "The rise in the total of those employed is governed by Parkinson's Law and would be much the same whether the volume of work was to increase, diminish or even disappear." *If you ever need proof of the reality of Parkinson's Law, just watch a road-mending team at work on overtime.* *See also* PETER PRINCIPLE.

Parks, Rosa *See* ROSA PARKS.

Parnassian (pahrnaseeăn) Of or relating to literature, especially poetry. The term alludes to ***Mount Parnassus,*** the mountain in central Greece that was held sacred to Apollo and the MUSES, who inspired artistic and creative enterprise. The term came to be particularly associated with a school of French poets, headed by Charles-Marie-René Leconte de Lisle, that flourished toward the end of the 19th century. The phrase to ***climb Parnassus*** means to write poetry. "Such a concert of treble voices uttering accents like these had not been heard since the great Temperance Festival with the celebrated 'colation' in the open air under the trees of the Parnassian Grove,—as the place was christened by the young ladies of the Institute" (Oliver Wendell Holmes, *Elsie Venner,* 1861).

Parthian shot (pahrtheeăn) A parting shot; a final hostile remark, glance, or gesture made on departure. The expression alludes to the practice of Parthian archers, who carried on firing arrows behind them even as they retreated. The Parthians were a nomadic Persian race. They developed the tactic of avoiding a direct confrontation when outnumbered, instead relying on their skill as mounted archers to make an impression on their enemy. *As he left he could not resist firing one last Parthian shot at his rival in the form of a taunt about the latter's sense of humor.*

parting of the Red Sea *See* CROSSING OF THE RED SEA.

pas de deux (pa dă doo) A relationship in which the acts of two individuals or parties are intricately connected. The allusion is to ballet, in which the phrase (which literally means "step for two" in French) refers to a dance or sequence of steps for two performers, usually a male and female dancer. *As the elections approached the two sides performed a pas de deux in the polls, first one party gaining the lead by a few points, then the other.*

pass all understanding To be difficult to understand. The phrase is a quotation from Philippians 4:7: "And the peace of God, which passeth all understanding, shall keep your hearts and minds through Christ Jesus." *The professor's explanation of the theory of relativity passed all understanding, and we understood little more about the subject when he had finished than we did when we came in.*

pass by on the other side *See* GOOD SAMARITAN.

Passchendaele (pashăndayl) A battle in which the slaughter is on an appalling scale. The village of Passchendaele in western Belgium became, from July to November 1917, the scene of some of the bitterest fighting on the western front during World War I. Soldiers involved in the fighting had to endure life and death in a morass of mud; at the end of the battle (also known as the Third Battle of YPRES) the British, Canadians, and Australians had lost over 350,000 men, while the Germans had lost a similar number. *The battle was bloody but in the final analysis it was no Passchendaele. See also* FLANDERS; SOMME, THE.

paternoster A set form of words recited as a prayer or charm. The word comes from the Latin *pater noster* (meaning "Our Father"), the opening words of the Lord's Prayer and an alternate name for the recitation, which appears in Matthew 6:9 and Luke 11:2. *She recited the rhyme every morning, a personal paternoster of her own invention.*

paths of glory The route to greatness. This is a quotation from *Elegy Written in a Country Churchyard* (1751) by the British poet Thomas Gray (1716–71), in which the author contemplates the lives of the people buried in a country churchyard and the ultimate futility of the pursuit of glory. It later became doubly familiar as the title of a Humphrey Cobb novel dwelling on the terrible nature of war, which was made into the acclaimed 1957 movie *Paths of Glory*, directed by Stanley Kubrick and starring Kirk Douglas. *Those who follow the paths of glory should remember that there is little glory in the grave.*

patience of Job (jōb) Endless patience in the face of great difficulty or suffering. Job's patience despite the manifold disasters that God inflicted on him in order to test his faith (as related in the book of Job) is proverbial and is referred to in James 5:11. *These threads are so tangled that whoever unravels them will need the patience of Job.*

Patient Griselda *See* GRISELDA.

patrician Aristocratic; fatherly. The word comes from the Latin *patres,* meaning "fathers," a title reserved for the senators of Rome and their families to distinguish them from the more humble populace (see PLEBEIAN). "Sir Leicester receives the gout as a troublesome demon, but still a demon of the patrician order" (Charles Dickens, *Bleak House,* 1852–53).

Patroclus *See* ACHILLES AND PATROCLUS.

Paul *See* ROAD TO DAMASCUS.

Paul Bunyan (bunyăn) A person of huge size and strength. Paul Bunyan was a folk hero of the American West, described as a gargantuan lumberjack whose strength and appetite inspired numerous myths that were swapped at the firesides of the lumber camps of the northwestern United States. Among other things, he was said to have created the Grand Canyon by dragging his pick behind him, and to have kept as his companion a gigantic blue ox called Babe. *The team's attack was spearheaded by three Paul Bunyans who were as wide as they were tall.*

Paul Revere (răveer) A patriot who brings a timely warning. Paul Revere (1735–1818) was an American silversmith and patriot who was present at the Boston Tea Party of 1773. On April 18, 1775, on the outbreak of the American Revolution, he undertook a celebrated night ride from Boston to Lexington to warn the American troops there that the British were coming. Because of Revere's warning, the American forces had time to prepare to defend themselves against the British assault at the Battle of Lexington. Revere's ride was later immortalized by Henry Wadsworth Longfellow in his poem "Paul Revere's Ride" (1861). *He rode that bike home faster than Paul Revere galloping from Boston to Lexington.*

pavlova (pavlōvă) A dessert comprising a meringue covered with fruit and whipped cream. The dessert was named in honor of the celebrated Russian-born ballerina Anna Matveyevna Pavlova (1881–1931), who was admired for her lightness and grace of movement, during a tour she made of Australia and New Zealand in 1926. The ruffles on the edge of the meringue are traditionally supposed to represent the tutu of a ballet dancer. *We finished with a pavlova that was as light and enchanting as the ballerina after whom it was named.*

Pavlovian (pavlōveeăn) Automatic; conditioned; reflex. The allusion is to the Russian physiologist Ivan Petrovich Pavlov (1849–1936), whose observations of the reaction of hungry dogs trained to associate the sound of a bell with the arrival of food led him to develop the theory of the conditioned reflex. Such unthinking, knee-jerk reactions in humans and animals have since been known as ***Pavlovian responses***. Pavlov's other work on digestion earned him a Nobel Prize in 1904. "The object of this sort of propaganda was to produce a Pavlovian state of dumb obedience" (Mark Almond, *The Rise and Fall of Nicolae and Elena Ceausescu*, 1992).

pax (paks) Peace; truce. In Roman mythology Pax was the goddess of peace, equivalent to the Greek IRENE. She was often depicted by the Romans holding an olive branch, a symbol of peace or reconciliation still familiar today. *The younger lad called out "Pax," and the fight came to an abrupt end.*

peace for the wicked, no *See* NO PEACE FOR THE WICKED.

peace, goodwill toward men *See* GOODWILL TO ALL MEN.

peace in our time A guarantee of peace, especially a dubious one. The allusion is to British prime minister Neville Chamberlain (1869–1940) and an address he gave to a large crowd in Downing Street on his arrival back from Nazi Germany on September 30, 1938, reassuring them about the peace agreement he had just negotiated with Adolf HITLER in Munich: "My good friends, this is the second time in our history that there has come back from Germany to Downing Street peace with honor. I believe it is peace for our time." Chamberlain's choice of words was clearly influenced by the versicle in Morning Prayer from the Church of England's *Book of Common Prayer*: "Give peace in our time, O Lord"—and Chamberlain's words are almost invariably rendered as "peace in our time" not "peace for our time." The hollowness of the so-called ***Munich Agreement*** was quickly exposed, and within 12 months Britain was at war with Hitler's Germany. *If the union accept the proposal it could mean peace in our time. See also* PIECE OF PAPER.

peacemakers, blessed are the *See* BEATITUDE.

peace of God which passeth all understanding *See* PASS ALL UNDERSTANDING.

Pearl Harbor Epitome of a treacherous and catastrophic surprise attack. The U.S. naval base at Pearl Harbor on the island of Oahu, Hawaii, was the unsuspecting target of a massed raid by Japanese carrier-borne aircraft on Sunday, December 7, 1941. Many major U.S. warships were sunk or damaged during the raid, although the carriers the Japanese had hoped to find there were at sea at the time of the attack. The raid shocked U.S. public opinion and was a key factor in bringing the United States into World War II. U.S. troops were subsequently reported going into battle shouting ***remember Pearl Harbor!*** and Pearl Harbor is still remembered as a prime example of a disastrous setback. "It will take a second Pearl Harbor for the Americans to realise how inefficient the NSA really is, just as it took the Falklands War of 1982 to reveal the deficiencies at GCHQ" (James Rusbridger, *The Intelligence Game*, 1991). *See also* DAY OF INFAMY.

pearl of great price Something of great value or importance. The phrase is biblical in origin, appearing in Matthew 13:45–46 in one of Christ's parables describing the value of spiritual riches: "Again, the kingdom of heaven is like unto a merchant man, seeking goodly pearls: Who, when he had found one pearl of great price, went and sold all that he had, and bought it." *Government contracts are pearls of great price, and competition for them is usually intense.*

pearls before swine Something good or valuable that is offered to or in the possession of a person who cannot appreciate it. The expression comes from Matthew 7:6: "Give not that which is holy unto the dogs, neither cast ye your pearls before swine, lest they trample them under their feet, and turn again and rend you." "Against establishment predictions—polite variants on the theme 'pearls before swine'—the project worked, and still flourishes" (*Guardian,* September 12, 2001).

pearly gates The entrance to heaven or, more loosely, heaven itself. The gates of the Christian heaven are described in Revelation 21:21: "And the twelve gates were twelve pearls; every several gate was of one pearl: and the street of the city was pure gold, as it were transparent glass." *She expressed the hope that by the time she came to appear before the pearly gates of heaven, she would be reconciled with her daughter.*

Pecksniff (peksnif) An oily, fawning hypocrite. Seth Pecksniff is an unctuous hypocrite in the 1844 novel *Martin Chuzzlewit* by British novelist Charles Dickens (1812–70). He attempts to smooth-talk Chuzzlewit into leaving him his fortune, but is eventually exposed as the hypocrite he really is. His name has also given rise to the adjective ***Pecksniffian.*** *Pecksniff himself couldn't have done a better job than this young salesman with his flattering manner and greasy smile.*

pedagogue (pedăgog) A teacher, especially one that is pedantic or dogmatic. In ancient Greece a *pedagogos* (meaning "boy leader") was a slave who was required to accompany the children of his master whenever they left their home. "Their children from earliest childhood / Grew up together as brother and sister; and Father Felician / Priest and pedagogue both in the village, had taught them their letters / Out of the selfsame book, with the hymns of the church and the plain-song" (Henry Longfellow, *Evangeline,* 1849).

peel me a grape, Beulah *See* BEULAH, PEEL ME A GRAPE.

Peeping Tom Someone who looks at something forbidden; a voyeur. According to a 17th-century addition to the much older legend of LADY GODIVA, the original Peeping Tom was a tailor called Tom who disobeyed the order not to look upon the naked Lady Godiva as she rode through Coventry in a bid to dissuade her husband Leofric from imposing new taxes on the local population. Tradition has it that the moment the tailor peeped through a knothole in his shutters, he was struck blind. "This Peeping Tom has put his eye to the nick or cranny in our walls and peers shamelessly in" (A. S. Byatt, *Possession*, 1990).

Pegasus (pegăsăs) Archetypal flying horse; any speedy mount, animate or mechanized. In Greek mythology Pegasus was a winged horse that arose from the blood of MEDUSA when Perseus cut off her head. The Corinthian hero Bellerophon, with the aid of Athena, managed to catch Pegasus, mount him, and kill the CHIMERA, but when Bellerophon tried to fly on Pegasus to heaven, he fell off and was lamed. Pegasus carried on upward, however, and became a constellation. Another tradition has it that the spring of the Hippocrene on Mount Helicon poured forth where Pegasus had struck a hoof, and hence Pegasus has always been linked with the MUSES, who dwelled on Mount Helicon. Thus to ***mount Pegasus*** means to embark on creative or artistic work. *He bestrode the motorbike as if it was Pegasus and the front wheel reared up in the air as he twisted the throttle.*

Pelé (pelay) A supremely gifted soccer player. Edson Arantes do Nascimento (b. 1940), otherwise known as Pelé, became a star player for the Brazilian club Santos (1955–74) and later played for the New York Cosmos (1975–77). He also enjoyed huge success as the leading star with Brazil's national side, winning World Cup winner's medals in 1958 and 1970. By 1969 he had notched up over 1,000 goals in first-class football and was widely acknowledged the most talented footballer in the world. *Thousands of youngsters in the slums of the city still dream of becoming a new Pelé.*

Peleus *See* APPLE OF DISCORD.

Pelion *See* PILE PELION ON OSSA.

Pelléas and Mélisande (pelayas, melisond) Archetype of a pair of tragic lovers. The story of the doomed love of Pelléas and Mélisande was first told by the Belgian playwright Maurice Maeterlinck (1862–1949) in a poetic drama of the same title (1892) and later provided the basis for an opera by Claude Debussy (1902). Maeterlinck's story tells how the beautiful Mélisande marries the king's grandson Golaud, only to fall in love with his younger half-brother Pelléas. Golaud is consumed with jealousy, although it remains unclear whether the lovers have ever behaved inappropriately. Finding Pelléas and Mélisande alone together, Golaud stabs them both to death. Before she finally dies Mélisande gives birth to a child. *Like Pelléas and Mélisande, no one knew for sure if their friendship had been purely platonic or guilty as hell. See also* PAOLO AND FRANCESCA.

Pelops *See* IVORY SHOULDER OF PELOPS.

Pelvis, Elvis the *See* KING, THE.

penalty of Adam *See* ADAM'S CURSE.

penates *See* LARES AND PENATES.

Penelope (penelăpee) Archetype of the dutiful, loyal wife and the personification of patience. In Greek mythology Penelope is the wife of ODYSSEUS, king of Ithaca, who waited patiently at home while he was absent fighting in the Trojan War. After 10 years of warfare Odysseus set off for home but was delayed by the gods, and it was another decade before husband and wife were reunited. In the meantime Penelope had to resist the advances of more than 100 suitors and their insistent demands that she marry one of them. In order to appease them she promised to marry one of them once she had finished weaving a shroud for her father-in-law. The suitors reluctantly agreed to this proposal, unaware of the fact that each night Penelope unwove the threads she had worked on during the day so that the shroud was no nearer being complete. A ***web of Penelope*** is therefore a metaphor for a task that has no end. Fortunately for Penelope, just as the patience of the 100 suitors was wearing out, Odysseus arrived home and slaughtered all rivals for his wife's hand. "Whatever I see you doing, you're not really there: you are waiting—like Penelope when she did her weaving" (D.H. Lawrence, *Sons and Lovers,* 1913).

Penthesilea (penthăsileeă) A strong, commanding woman. According to Greek mythology Penthesilea was the daughter of Ares and the queen of the AMAZONS, whom she led to the aid of the Trojans after the death of Hector. She died in combat with Achilles, who lamented over the death of such a good-looking, courageous woman. *She is the Penthesilea of the Democratic Party.*

peony *See* PAEAN.

Peoria *See* PLAY IN PEORIA.

Pepys (peeps) A diarist, especially one whose diary present, a vivid and informative depiction of his or her life and times. The allusion is to the English diarist Samuel Pepys (1633–1703), whose diary provides a uniquely colorful insight into life in early Restoration London and an invaluable record of such important historical events as the Great Plague and the Fire of London. Pepys eventually became concerned that the hours he spent writing his diary were harming his eyesight and so, after nine years (1660–69), he abandoned it (although modern medical diagnosis suggests he could have kept on writing it without the least damage to his eyes). The lively style of the diary, which covered his private life as well as events of national importance, have maintained to this day Pepys's reputation as one of the most celebrated Englishmen of his era and provided a ***Pepysian*** standard beside which most other diarists have since been measured. His not infrequent way of ending a day's entry, ***and so to bed***, has also entered the annals of familiar allusions. *As a diarist he noted down the chief events of his time, but he lacked humor and was no Pepys.*

Pequod *See* MOBY DICK.

perestroika *See* GLASNOST.

perfidious Albion (albeeăn) Treacherous England. The name ALBION was applied to England as early as the Romans, but it was the French who labeled the country "perfidious Albion," in protest against its persistent interference in European affairs. The phrase is usually attributed to the French poet the marquis de Ximenès (1726–1817), who used it in a poem in 1793, although it was not until the early 19th century that the phrase became widely familiar in Napoleon's France, when English interference played havoc with the emperor's territorial ambitions. "During the 19th and 20th centuries, this came to be known as the policy of the balance of power, and was principally associated with perfidious Albion" (William Cash, *Against a Federal Europe*, 1991).

peri (peeree) A beautiful girl. In Persian mythology a peri was a malevolent spirit who attacked crops and caused eclipses, among other disastrous acts. They were subsequently depicted in the Qur'an and elsewhere as gentle creatures resembling fairies. ". . . and then, how delightfully refreshing is the sight, when, perhaps, some ex-member, hurled from his paradise like a fallen peri, reveals the secret of that pure heaven" (Anthony Trollope, *Doctor Thorne,* 1858).

Periclean (perikleeăn) Wise; eloquent; honest. The word refers to the respected Athenian statesman and soldier Pericles (c. 500–429 B.C.), who assumed the reins of power in 460 and oversaw a golden era in Athenian democracy and the arts. Important achievements under his leadership included the building of the Parthenon. Typical of the stories about his integrity, on his death it was reported that he had not enriched himself beyond what he had inherited by a single drachma. *His last speech to the Senate was typically Periclean.*

Perils of Pauline (pahleen) A series of breathtakingly hazardous adventures. The allusion is to a thrilling silent-movie serial first screened in 1914 and called *The Perils of Pauline.* It starred Pearl White as a heroine who finds herself in all manner of life-threatening situations from which she is only rescued in the nick of time. "Spooner picked up on this idea and thought the best way to do it would be as an extended Perils of Pauline-type adventure, complete with 'How are they going to get out of that?' endings" (J. Bentham, *Doctor Who: The Early Years*, 1986).

Perry Mason (peree maysăn) A brilliant lawyer-detective. The *Perry Mason* radio and television detective series, based on the best-selling novels of Erle Stanley Gardner (1889–1970), were a mainstay of broadcast schedules on both sides of the Atlantic for many years. The television series, featuring Raymond Burr as Perry Mason, ran from 1957 to 1966, and Burr reprised the role in a further series of television movies from 1985. Mason appeared for the defense and always proved his client's innocence, usually in a tense courtroom finale. In the last episode of the original television series, Gardner himself made a cameo appearance as the judge in the case. "It was a classic Perry Mason prisoner-and-jury setting" (Norman Fowler, *Ministers Decide*, 1991).

Persephone (persefănee) Personification of the cycle of the seasons. In Greek mythology Persephone (***Proserpina*** to the Romans) was identified as the daughter of Zeus and Demeter and was snatched away to the underworld to be the wife of Hades, the lord of the dead. Zeus eventually gave in to the distraught Demeter's requests for her return, but Persephone had disregarded the instruction not to eat anything while in the underworld (as this would bind her there forever) and eaten the seeds of a pomegranate. As a compromise it was agreed that Persephone would be allowed back to the living world for part of the year but would have to return to Hades for the remaining months. Her arrival in the upper world is heralded by the coming of spring, while her return to Hades marks the beginning of winter. *Persephone had scattered spring flowers through the meadow.*

Perseus (perseeăs) Archetype of the classical hero. In Greek mythology Perseus is the central character in a number of heroic episodes, including the killing and cutting off the head of MEDUSA and the rescue of ANDROMEDA, who became his wife. He was also a model ruler of Argos and Tiryns and was credited with the foundation of Mycenae. *He felt like Perseus facing Medusa, undaunted but unable to look directly at the danger that threatened him.*

person from Porlock (porlok) An interruption in the creative flow. The British poet Samuel Taylor Coleridge (1772–1834) was staying in the village of Nether Stowey in Somerset in 1797, the year he wrote the fantastical poem "Kubla Khan," destined to become one of the most celebrated of all poems written in the English language. According to Coleridge himself, he had composed the poem while in a drugged sleep and found on waking that he could still remember every word of the remarkable work. He wrote down several hundred lines of the poem in a feverish, inspired rush but was then, according to his own account, interrupted by a "person from Porlock" (a nearby village) calling on a business matter. When Coleridge finally got rid of the visitor he returned to his work, only to find that he could remember no more of the masterpiece he had composed in his dream. Over the years, many critics have speculated that the person from Porlock was invented by Coleridge to cover the failure of his own inspiration. "At least no person from Porlock was likely to interrupt me today" (Mary Stewart, *Stormy Petrel*, 1992).

petard, hoist with one's own *See* HOIST WITH ONE'S OWN PETARD.

Peter Pan A person who never seems to grow old. The allusion is to the central character in the play *Peter Pan* (1904) by the Scottish playwright J. M. Barrie (1860–1937), which was later published in book form (1911) and subsequently provided the foundation for various popular movies and cartoons. Barrie's Peter Pan is a young lad who lives a life of perpetual boyhood with his gang of friends, the ***Lost Boys***, fighting pirates and pursuing an existence blissfully free of the pressures of adult responsibility. In creating his famous fictional character, Barrie drew on the characters of the five young sons of his friends Arthur and Sylvia Llewelyn Davies, although it was their son Peter who was the chief inspiration. Sadly, several of the Llewelyn Davies brothers met unfortunate ends, George dying fighting in World War I, Michael drowning while at Oxford, and Peter committing suicide on the London Underground in 1960. Michael was the model upon whom the statue of Peter Pan in Kensington Gardens, London, was based. *Cliff Richard, with his youthful good looks, is often described as pop music's Peter Pan. See also* NEVER-NEVER LAND.

Peter Principle The rule that all people within an organization tend to rise to the level of their own incompetence. It was named after the Canadian-born U.S. educationist Dr. Laurence J. Peter (1919–90), who devised it alongside Raymond Hull in *The Peter Principle: Why Things Always Go Wrong* (1969). *The disastrously low caliber of most of the company's senior management was an ample demonstration of the Peter Principle in action. See also* PARKINSON'S LAW.

Petrarch and Laura (petrahk) Archetype of unfulfilled, idealized love. In 1327, while living in exile in Avignon, France, the Italian Renaissance poet Petrarch (1304–74) fell passionately in love with a woman now known to us only as Laura. Petrarch immortalized Laura in his celebrated love poetry, although it appears she did not return the love he felt for her. *She became his muse, although their relationship was more like that of Petrarch and Laura than Romeo and Juliet.*

Peyton Place (paytăn) A seemingly respectable community that is actually a hotbed of sex, violence, and intrigue. The allusion is to the highly successful television SOAP OPERA *Peyton Place* (1964–69), which was in turn based upon a 1956 best-selling novel by Grace Metalious (1924–64). The original book, which was apparently inspired by the actual New England town of Gilmanton Iron Works, New Hampshire, caused a sensation with its exposure of illicit relationships and racy goings-on in small-town America. *With all these rumors of adultery and betrayal the town was beginning to feel like Peyton Place.*

phaeton (fayătăn) A light, four-wheeled horse-drawn carriage with two seats. In Greek mythology Phaëthon (or Phaëton) was identified as the son of the sun god Helios (or Apollo), although elsewhere he was also described as MEROPS'S SON (referring to King Merops of Ethiopia). Phaëthon decided to try his hand at steering his father's chariot—the Sun—across the sky and very nearly set fire to the Earth by flying too close. As it was, Libya was reduced to a parched desert while the rest of Africa was similarly scorched. The Earth was saved from further damage when Zeus killed Phaëthon with a thunderbolt. The swan is sometimes called ***Phaeton's bird*** in commemoration of Cycnus, son of Neptune, who was inconsolable after the death of his friend Phaëthon and was eventually transformed into a swan by Apollo and placed among the constellations. "From the drawing room they could distinguish nothing in the lane, and were indebted to Mr. Collins for the knowledge of what carriages went along, and how often especially Miss De Bourgh drove by in her phaeton, which he never failed coming to inform them of, though it happened almost every day" (Jane Austen, *Pride and Prejudice,* 1813).

phalanx (faylanks) A closely ranked, unyielding mass of people; a body of people united in a common cause. The name was originally given to an ancient Greek and Macedonian battle formation in which spearsmen sheltered behind a wall of shields. "I feel that I can face an army with banners—or all the professors of Redmond in one fell phalanx—with a chum like Priscilla by my side" (Lucy Maud Montgomery, *Anne of the Island,* 1915).

Pharisee (fairăsee) A self-righteous or hypocritical person, especially one who insists on legalistically and slavishly observing rules, regardless of the intent behind them. The Pharisees (a name meaning "separated") were members of a Jewish sect that emerged in the second century B.C. "Despite their original emphasis on God's law, or Torah, their insistence on equal prominence for oral law and their emphasis on human behavior rather than God's work brought them into conflict with Jesus. Jesus accused some Pharisees of being hypocrites because their teaching was inconsistent with their actions" (Selman and Manser, *The Hearthside Bible Dictionary,* p. 184). Jesus denounced them in the "seven woes" (Matthew 23:1–36). "Woe unto you, scribes and Pharisees, hypocrites! For ye are like unto whited sepulchres, which indeed appear beautiful outward, but are within full of dead men's bones, and of all uncleanness. Even so you also outwardly appear righteous unto men, but within ye are full of hypocrisy and iniquity" (Matthew 23:27). "But he's got tongue enough to speak disrespectful about's neebors, for he said as I was a blind Pharisee—a-usin' the Bible i' that way to find nick-names for folks as are his elders an' betters!—and what's worse, he's been heard to say very unbecomin' words about Your Reverence" (George Eliot, *Adam Bede,* 1859).

pharos (fairăs) A lighthouse or beacon. The name comes from that of the small island off the Egyptian coast where Ptolemy II (308–246 B.C.) built a lighthouse made of white marble, subsequently included among the seven wonders of the ancient world. The lighthouse was destroyed in an earthquake in 1375. *The fleet was guided by the light of a pharos marking the entrance to the bay. See also* EIGHTH WONDER OF THE WORLD.

pheasant A long-tailed bird of the family Phasianidae, the males of which have brightly colored plumage. The bird's name means "bird of the Phasis," the Phasis being the classical name for a river of Colchis, the present-day Rioni River, which flows into the Black Sea. Legend has it that pheasants originated from that area and were brought elsewhere by the Argonauts. *A white pheasant stalked imperiously back and forth in front of the house.*

Pheidippides *See* MARATHON.

Philadelphia lawyer (filădelfeeă) A particularly gifted, cunning lawyer. The phrase is an allusion to a 1735 legal case of criminal libel that looked so unpromising that only one barrister, a lawyer from Philadelphia called Andrew Hamilton, would agree to take on the defense. Against all expectations, Hamilton rebutted the accusations and secured his client's acquittal. To be called a "Philadelphia lawyer" was thus originally the highest of compliments to make to a lawyer, but it has since acquired a derogatory tone, signifying a lawyer who is far too clever for his or her own good. *The defendant is going to need a clutch of Philadelphia lawyers if he is going to wriggle out of this one.*

Philemon and Baucis (făleemăn, fileemăn; bahsis) Archetypes of the generous, welcoming host. According to Greek legend Philemon and Baucis were an aged and impoverished Phrygian couple who welcomed the disguised Zeus and Hermes into their home after other richer people had turned the gods away. In gratitude the two deities saved the couple from a flood, turned their home into a temple, and granted their desire that neither of them should outlive the other. When the couple died, the gods transformed Philemon into an oak and Baucis into a linden tree, and their branches entwined. *Like Philemon and Baucis, the couple threw their door open to the strangers, beckoning them to come inside without delay.*

Philip Marlowe (mahrlō) The epitome of a hard-boiled private detective. Philip Marlowe, who made his first appearance in the novel *The Big Sleep* in 1939, was the creation of U.S. crime writer Raymond Chandler (1888–1959). A cynical anti-hero, he has a laconic sense of humor and a sense of honor that made him a great favorite of both readers and cinema audiences, especially when played on screen by Humphrey Bogart. "She talked as if she had taken on the mantle of Philip Marlowe, a female arch sleuth for whom the teeming underworld held no secrets" (Lisa Appignanesi, *Memory and Desire*, 1992). *See also* BIG SLEEP, THE; CHANDLERESQUE.

philippic (făl**i**pik) An impassioned denunciation of an enemy; a bitter tirade. The word refers to the three scathing speeches made by the celebrated Athenian orator Demosthenes (384–322 B.C.) to bolster resistance against the threats posed to Athenian democracy by Philip II of Macedon (hence the "Philippics"). Philip intended to absorb Athens into his kingdom and, despite the efforts of Demosthenes, eventually succeeded in this ambition after defeating the Greeks at the Battle of Chaeronea in 338. In 322 the Macedonian ruler Antipater planned to kidnap Demosthenes but was thwarted when his quarry escaped to the island of Calauria and committed suicide there before another attempt to capture him could be made. The word was subsequently applied to Cicero's attacks *(Philippics)* on Mark Antony in 44 and 43 B.C. and thereby entered into general usage. "The talk, as usual, had veered around to the Beauforts, and even Mr. van der Luyden and Mr. Selfridge Merry, installed in the honorary arm-chairs tacitly reserved for them, paused to listen to the younger man's philippic" (Edith Wharton, *The Age of Innocence,* 1920). *See also* APPEAL FROM PHILIP DRUNK TO PHILIP SOBER; DEMOSTHENIC.

philistine (fi̲lăstīn) An uncultured, ignorant person. The original Philistines were a warlike non-Semitic people who in biblical times inhabited ancient Philistia in close and often hostile proximity to the Hebrews. Individual Philistines to attract special criticism included the giant GOLIATH (1 Samuel 17) and the seductive DELILAH (Judges 16). The term was subsequently taken up as a reference to any enemy and ultimately to individuals or societies perceived as lacking any cultural sophistication or intellectual enthusiasm. It was first used in its modern sense by university students in 17th-century Germany, who applied it to townsfolk who lacked a similar education, calling them "Philisters." It was transmitted to English through the writings of Matthew Arnold (1822–88), who applied it specifically to bourgeois opponents of art and literature. Archaeological finds suggest, however, that ancient Philistine society was not as brutish and materialistic as Hebrew writings suggest, and Philistine pottery in particular has been much admired. They were also skilled architects and metalworkers and apparently had well-developed political and commercial structures. "But clearly Anthony was no diplomatist. His brother-in-law must have appeared to him, to use the language of shore people, a perfect philistine with a heart like a flint" (Joseph Conrad, *Chance,* 1913).

philosopher's stone A stone or other object that has the power to turn base metals into gold. The quest for the philosopher's stone occupied generations of alchemists over the centuries. Although no such magical stone was ever found, discoveries made in the search for it provided the basis for modern chemistry. The term has since been applied to anything, real or intangible, that constitutes the key to happiness or other benefits. *Confidence is the philosopher's stone for the successful athlete.*

Phintias *See* DAMON AND PYTHIAS.

phobia (fō̲beeă) An obsessive, often irrational fear of something. The word is Greek in origin and alludes to Phobos, a son of Ares and Aphrodite and the Greek god of dread and alarm. Somewhat ironically he was conventionally depicted with the head of a lion. *His sister developed a phobia of snakes and ever after refused to go anywhere near the reptile house at the zoo.*

Phoebe (fe̲e̲bee) Personification of the Moon. Phoebe was identified in Greek mythology as the goddess of the moon and as one of the Titans, by whom Zeus sired Apollo and Artemis. *She uttered a brief prayer to Phoebe before slipping down into the moonlit street.*

Phoebus (fe̲e̲băs) Literary name for the Sun. In Greek mythology the sun god Apollo was sometimes referred to by the name Phoebus (meaning "bright" or "shining one"). "He must have passed Mr. Rugg on his way out, for, a minute or two afterwards, that ruddy-headed gentleman shone in at the door, like an elderly Phoebus" (Charles Dickens, *Little Dorrit,* 1855–57).

phoenix (fe̲e̲niks) Something that rises anew in the face of defeat or adversity. This legendary bird appears in the mythology of ancient Egypt, ancient Greece, and early Christianity and was widely considered a symbol of immortality and life after death. According to most traditions the phoenix resembled an eagle, with gold and scarlet feathers, and lived for about 500 years. When the time came for it to die, it lay down on a pyre and allowed itself to be burned in the flames. It then emerged renewed from the ashes, hence the expression a ***phoenix rising from the ashes.*** ". . . and there she is with her plumage unruffled, as glossy as ever, unable to get old:—a sort of Phoenix free from the slightest signs of ashes and dust, all complacent amongst those inanities as if there had been nothing else in the world" (Joseph Conrad, *The Arrow of Gold,* 1919).

phone home *See* E.T. PHONE HOME.

Phrynean (frīneeăn) Of or relating to a prostitute. Phryne was a famous and very wealthy Greek courtesan who lived in the fourth century B.C. Her beauty was widely admired, and she is supposed to have been the model for many celebrated statues. It is said she made so much money that she offered to pay for the rebuilding of the walls of Thebes. "Her underclothes are positively Phrynean" (Aldous Huxley, *Point Counter Point,* 1928).

physician, heal thyself Do not criticize others when you are guilty of the same failings; refrain from tackling the problems of others before you have dealt with your own difficulties first. The proverb is of biblical origin and is spoken by Christ to the people in the synagogue in Nazareth: "Ye will surely say unto me this proverb, Physician, heal thyself: whatsoever we have heard done in Capernaum, do also here in thy country" (Luke 4:23). "How can a man . . . teach sobriety or cleanliness, if he be himself drunken or foul? 'Physician, heal thyself,' is the answer of his neighbours" (Samuel Smiles, *Thrift,* 1875).

Picasso (pikasō) A brilliant, controversial artist, especially one who paints in a challenging, modernistic style. The Spanish artist Pablo Picasso (1881–1974) earned a reputation as perhaps the most daring and talented artist of the 20th century, developing the concept of cubism and painting some of the best-known masterpieces of his generation, among them the iconic *Les Demoiselles d'Avignon* (1907), *Three Dancers* (1925), and GUERNICA. His experimental, abstract style won him many admirers as well as many detractors, who were perplexed by his trademark distortion of features and figures. *The college has trained hundreds of students but has yet to produce its first Picasso.*

Pickett's charge (pikit) A heroic but doomed effort. The reference is to an incident that took place on July 3, 1863, during the Battle of Gettysburg, the climactic battle of the U.S. Civil War. Under severe pressure from the Federal forces, the Confederate major general George Edward Pickett (1825–75) ordered his 15,000 men into a last-ditch attack on the Union lines on Cemetery Ridge. Pickett's force was attacked by artillery fire as it crossed the open ground in front of the ridge and was finally ordered to retreat by General Robert E. Lee. Pickett's gallant but futile gesture resulted in the loss of three-quarters of his men. The defeat at Gettysburg was widely seen as a final blow from which the Confederate cause never recovered. *The team made a Pickett's charge down the field, but the final result was never in doubt.*

Pickwickian (pikwikeeăn) Jovial; benevolent; full of curiosity and zest for life. The allusion is to the central character in *The Pickwick Papers* (1837) by the British novelist Charles Dickens (1812–70). The novel follows Mr. Pickwick and his friends as they make a tour of the English countryside, getting involved in various comical escapades and adventures along the way. The term "Pickwickian" can also be used to describe words that are not meant to be taken literally, a reference to Mr. Pickwick's teasing way of phrasing a compliment in the form of insult in the first chapter of the book. His name may also be applied to anyone who is similar in appearance to Dickens's character, who is described as short, rotund, and bespectacled. *He had a truly Pickwickian sense of humor and loved a good practical joke. See also* SAM WELLER.

piece of paper An agreement that is not worth the paper it is written on. The allusion is to the ***Munich Agreement*** made between British prime minister Neville Chamberlain and Nazi Germany's leader Adolf HITLER in Munich on September 30, 1938 (*see* PEACE IN OUR TIME). When Chamberlain arrived back in Britain he waved a piece of paper at the waiting crowds after emerging from his aircraft. Many believed that this precious agreement would ensure lasting peace in Europe; when war broke out the following year, however, Chamberlain's treaty was revealed to be worthless. Hitler himself had a low opinion of Chamberlain and after the agreement was signed is said to have told an aide: "If ever that silly old man comes interfering here again with his umbrella, I'll kick him downstairs and jump on his stomach in front of the photographers." *That contract is just a piece of paper that will change nothing.*

pied piper A person who entices others with delusive promises. The allusion is to a German folktale of the 15th century or earlier that provided the basis for the poem "The Pied Piper of Hamelin" (1842) by the British poet Robert Browning (1812–89). Browning's poem describes how the rat-infested town of Hamelin in Westphalia is cleared of its thousands of rats by the curiously-dressed Pied Piper, whose pipe charms all living things into following it. Having led the town's rats to the river to drown, the Pied Piper demands payment; when this is refused he leads all the town's children, except one crippled child, away from the town and into a hillside, never to be seen again. It has been suggested that the original folktale, which purported to describe events in Hamelin in 1284, was inspired by the Children's Crusade of 1212, which saw thousands of French and German children join an ill-fated crusade to take back the Holy Land from the Muslims. "Some fall in behind her, and follow her to the lecture theatre, so that she appears to be leading a little procession, a female Pied Piper" (David Lodge, *Nice Work*, 1988).

Pierian spring (pīereeăn) Inspiration or learning. According to Greek mythology the Pierian spring lay on the slopes of Mount Olympus and was sacred to the MUSES. It was said that anyone who drank from the spring would enjoy wisdom or inspiration. "A little learning is a dangerous thing; / Drink deep, or taste not the Pierian spring" (Alexander Pope, *Essay on Criticism,* 1711).

pigmy *See* PYGMY.

Pilate's wife (pīlătz) A person who claims to have learned something important from a dream. In the New Testament the wife of PONTIUS PILATE discussed with her husband a distressing dream she had just had, warning him that he should avoid any involvement with the trial of Christ, who was about to be brought before his court: "Have thou nothing to do with that just man: for I have suffered many things this day in a dream because of him" (Matthew 27:19). *Like Pilate's wife, she urged him not to take this journey. She had dreamed that he lay in a white coffin.*

Pilate washed his hands *See* PONTIUS PILATE; WASH ONE'S HANDS OF.

pile Pelion on Ossa (peeleeăn, ahsă) To heap difficulty upon difficulty or embarrassment upon embarrassment. The expression has its roots in Greek mythology and the legend of the GIANTS who tried to climb up to heaven by piling the mountain Pelion on top of Mount Ossa, in eastern Thessaly. *Then, piling Pelion on Ossa, the news came through that the date for the completion of the project had been moved forward by two weeks.*

Pilgrim's Progress A Christian's progress through life. The allusion is to the epic moral allegory *The Pilgrim's Progress* (1678, 1684) by the English writer and Baptist preacher John Bunyan (1628–88). The poem follows ***Christian*** as he makes the long and difficult journey to the DELECTABLE MOUNTAINS and the CELESTIAL CITY. Bunyan himself was no stranger to the difficulties of life, writing *The Pilgrim's Progress* while in prison after defying a royal edict forbidding him from preaching. *He made a Pilgrim's Progress through the ranks before finally making it to commander-in-chief. See also* LAND OF BEULAH; MUCKRAKER; SLOUGH OF DESPOND; VALLEY OF THE SHADOW OF DEATH; VANITY FAIR.

Piltdown Man A scientific hoax. In 1912 the fossil remains of an early man found in a gravel pit at Piltdown in Sussex, England, was thought to prove the MISSING LINK between apes and the development of the first humans. However, closer examination of the find in 1953 revealed that it comprised the skull of a human and the jaw of an orangutan. It remains uncertain who was responsible for this deliberate fraud, although suspicion has rested upon rival palaeontologists seeking to discredit Sir Arthur Smith Woodward (1864–1944), Keeper of Geology at the British Museum (Natural History). *Personally, I think his account of events is about as reliable as the Piltdown Man.*

pillar of fire A revelatory sign that serves as a guide to show the way. The allusion is to the biblical story of the pillar of fire—a ***pillar of cloud*** by day—set up by God to guide the Israelites out of the wilderness on their flight from Egypt, as related in Exodus 13:21–22. "You are unjust to women in England. And till you count what is a shame in a woman to be an infamy in a man, you will always be unjust, and Right, that pillar of fire, and Wrong, that pillar of cloud, will be made dim to your eyes, or be not seen at all, or if seen, not regarded" (Oscar Wilde, *A Woman of No Importance,* 1893). *See also* CLOUD BY DAY, PILLAR OF FIRE BY NIGHT.

pillar of salt *See* LOT'S WIFE.

pillar of society A person or institution seen as part of the establishment. The phrase is closely associated with the 1877 play *The Pillars of Society* by the Norwegian playwright Henrik Ibsen (1828–1906). Entitled *Samfundets støtter* in the original Norwegian, it was first produced in English in 1888 under the title *Quicksands*. In Ibsen's play the pillars in question are the spirit of truth and the spirit of freedom rather than particular individuals. "In fact, he was the archetypal 'pillar of society': flour-miller, magistrate and county councillor" (Philip Heselton, *The Elements of Earth Mysteries*, 1991).

pillars of Hercules (herkyooleez) The limits of the known world. In classical times the rocks on opposite sides of the entrance to the Mediterranean were called the Pillars of Hercules in allusion to the legend that Hercules separated them in order to reach Gades (modern Cádiz, in Spain). *Those two constellations are our pillars of Hercules, marking the extremes of the known universe.*

Pindaric verse (pindarik) A form of irregular verse characterized by its high-flown style. Such poetry, written in a variety of meters, was popularized by the English poet Abraham Cowley in the 17th century. Cowley mistakenly believed he was re-creating a form of verse composed by the celebrated Theban lyric poet Pindar (c. 522–443 B.C.). *There are few writers today who excel in the field of Pindaric verse.*

Pinkerton A private detective. The Scottish-born Allan Pinkerton (1819–84) made a living smuggling runaway slaves into Canada after immigrating to the United States in 1850, but then became the first detective of the Chicago Police Department. He opened what became the famous Pinkerton Detective Agency in 1852 and subsequently made many high-profile arrests, although he also earned a reputation for ruthlessness and crooked tactics. *They weren't satisfied with the efforts of the local police to find their daughter and decided to hire their own Pinkerton.*

Pinocchio (pinōkeeō) A liar, especially a child who tells lies. The allusion is to the wooden puppet Pinocchio who is the central character in the children's story *The Adventures of Pinocchio* (1883) by the Italian writer Carlo Collodi (Carlo Lorenzini; 1826–90). Pinocchio is a puppet boy who comes magically to life after his maker, ***Geppetto***, wishes for a child of his own. He has a number of bizarre adventures and finds that if he tells a lie his nose grows mysteriously longer, thus revealing his guilt. Having proved his essential goodness, he is transformed into a real boy at the end of the story. Pinocchio in Italian means "pine seed." A ***Pinocchio's nose*** is something that indicates that a lie is being told. *Watergate turned Nixon into Pinocchio.*

Pinteresque (pintăresk) Reminiscent of the subject matter and style of writing in the plays of British playwright Harold Pinter (b. 1930). Pinter's much-admired early plays were notable, among other things, for their use of deliberately long pauses, which the author insisted should be observed exactly during performance. *His conversation was peppered with Pinteresque pauses, suggesting he didn't really know what he was talking about.*

pipes of Pan *See* PANPIPES.

Pisgah *See* MOUNT PISGAH.

Piso's justice (pīsōz) Strictly correct but not in the spirit of justice, especially in relation to legal decisions. The phrase alludes to a story related by the Roman philosopher Seneca the Younger (c. 4 B.C.–A.D. 65) about a judge called Piso. Piso had condemned a prisoner to death on a charge of murder and delivered the man to a centurion for execution; however, the murder victim then appeared, and the centurion returned the prisoner to Piso. Piso responded by sentencing all three men to death, the prisoner on the grounds that he had already been sentenced, the centurion on the grounds that he had disobeyed his orders, and the supposed murder victim for causing the death of two innocent men. *It was generally agreed that this decision was harsh in the extreme, a good example of Piso's justice.*

pitch defiles *See* TOUCH PITCH AND BE DEFILED.

pit of the dragon *See* BOTTOMLESS PIT.

place of skulls *See* CALVARY.

plague of locusts A mob of people who eat or strip everything in sight. The allusion is to the biblical plague of locusts (Exodus 10:4–19), which was the eighth plague inflicted by God upon the Pharaoh of Egypt and led ultimately to the Exodus of the Jews. The locusts consumed all the food they could find. *The children descended upon the meal like a plague of locusts, and soon there was not a crumb remaining. See also* PLAGUES OF EGYPT.

plague on both your houses, a Both sides in a dispute are deserving of equal blame. The allusion is to William Shakespeare's tragedy ***ROMEO AND JULIET*** (1594), in which Mercutio thus curses the rival ***Montagu*** and ***Capulet*** families, whose disputes have indirectly led to his own death in a duel: "I am hurt. A plague o' both your houses!" *Neither party has said anything to win my vote and I can only wish a plague on both their houses.*

plagues of Egypt (eejipt) The 10 disasters by which God punished the Egyptians for oppressing the Israelites and failing to acknowledge God's power (Exodus 7–12): the plague of water turned to blood, the plague of frogs, the plague of gnats, the plague of flies, the plague on livestock, the plague of boils, the plague of hail, the PLAGUE OF LOCUSTS, the plague of darkness (see EGYPTIAN DARKNESS; NINTH PLAGUE OF EGYPT), and the plague of the death of the firstborn. After the last plague, Pharaoh released the Israelites from bondage.

platonic (plătonik) Of or relating to a close, nonsexual relationship or more generally to any perfect, idealized vision or idea. Such a relationship, in which spiritual communion between individuals is believed superior to physical union, was first described by and thus named after the Greek philosopher Plato (c. 427–c.347 B.C.) in his *Symposium* when he discussed the ideal relationship that his teacher Socrates had with the young men who studied under him. "The intimacy between them had been kept so abstract, such a matter of the soul, all thought and weary struggle into consciousness, that he saw it only as a platonic friendship" (D. H. Lawrence, *Sons and Lovers,* 1913). *See also* PLATO'S CAVE.

Plato's cave (playtōz) An image of the limits of human knowledge and perception. The phrase alludes to an allegory employed by the Greek philosopher Plato (c. 427–c. 347 B.C.) to illustrate how far removed ordinary perception is from a vision of ultimate reality. Plato propounded the image of some men chained in a cave in front of a fire so that all they could see were the shadows cast against the firelight: Knowing no better, they assumed the shadows were real. *For her it was like emerging into the sunlight of reality after years of being trapped in Plato's cave.*

play Cupid *See* CUPID.

play hardball To adopt a serious, hardheaded approach to something. The allusion is to baseball, which is played with a harder ball than that used in the junior version of the game, softball. *The government have decided to play hardball with the Chinese over this issue.*

play in Peoria (peeoreeă) To win acceptance among the ordinary population. In the heyday of vaudeville in the 1930s, the city of Peoria in Illinois was one of the places where new stage acts were tried out to see how popular they were before going on to the bigger venues in the big cities. Peoria has since become a testing ground in other fields, notably business and politics, giving rise to the metaphorical question ***will it play in Peoria?*** (meaning "how will this go down with the average person?")—also remembered as a catchphrase of the Nixon administration (1969–74). *It sounds like a good move, but will it play in Peoria?*

plead the Fifth *See* TAKE THE FIFTH.

plebeian (plebeeăn) Of or relating to the common people, the masses. The term was first adopted in ancient Rome to describe ordinary citizens, as opposed to slaves and citizens who made up the aristocracy (see PATRICIAN). "I believe you know how very much I dislike what are called family affairs, which are only fit for plebeian Christmas days, and have no manner of business with people of our condition" (Charles Dickens, *Barnaby Rudge,* 1841).

pleiad (pleeăd) A group of seven distinguished persons. The word comes from Greek mythology, specifically from the seven daughters of ATLAS, who were known as the Pleiades. The sisters were transformed into stars to protect them from pursuit by Orion or (according to another version) after they killed themselves in grief over the demise of their half sisters, the Hyades. The cluster of stars in the constellation of Taurus known as the Pleiades may, however, have gotten its name from the Greek *plein,* meaning "to sail," as sea conditions were generally calmer when this constellation was visible. *This pleiad of scientists has become the dominant influence in the field and threatens to revolutionize both theory and practice.*

plowshares *See* BEAT SWORDS INTO PLOWSHARES.

Pluto *See* HADES.

Plutus (plootăs) Personification of wealth. In Greek mythology Plutus was the son of Demeter and was usually depicted as blind, dispensing wealth indiscriminately. He was also described as being lame, to represent the fact that rewards are slow to come, and with wings, because his gifts rapidly vanished. *She had become accustomed to spending much of her time in the realms of Plutus, eating at the Savoy and being driven everywhere in a chauffeured Rolls-Royce.*

Pluvius policy (plooveeăs) An insurance policy that offers coverage against a holiday being spoiled by wet weather. Pluvius was a surname sometimes given to JUPITER, the ruler of the gods in Roman mythology. Jupiter was routinely worshiped as the giver of rain, upon which life depended. *The weather was so bad they promised that before they went away again they would check to see whether they could take out a Pluvius policy to compensate them if it happened again.*

Pocahontas (pōkăhontăs) A Native American girl or woman. Pocahontas (c. 1595–1617) was a real historical character, the daughter of a Native American chief of Virginia called Powhatan. Legend has it that she saved the life of the English Captain John Smith (1580–1631) and subsequently became the wife of the English tobacco-grower John Rolfe. She sailed to England in 1616 and was presented at the court of James I, but died off Gravesend the following year soon after setting sail back to Virginia. "Is that why you're creeping about looking like Pocahontas?" (Emma Richmond, *A Stranger's Trust*, 1991).

Podunk (pōdănk) A small, sleepy town where the inhabitants are typically narrow-minded or culturally unaware. The allusion is to a small town of the name near Hartford, Connecticut. *Liberal ideas like this do not usually go down well in Podunk.*

pogrom (pōgrăm, pogrom) A campaign of extermination aimed at a particular ethnic group. From the Russian for "devastation" or "destruction," the term was applied originally to the systematic persecution of the Jews and other minority groups in Czarist Russia, but has since been applied to similar campaigns elsewhere in the world, particularly where the victims are Jewish. *Many thousands of Polish Jews were arrested and executed in concentration camps as a result of Nazi pogroms during the war.*

point man A person who goes ahead, leading the way forward and in so doing risking the greatest danger. The allusion is of military origin, referring to the man sent ahead of a patrol to draw any enemy's fire, but the term is also often encountered in the political sphere. *The White House spokesman appears to have become the president's point man on this contentious issue.*

Poirot, Hercule *See* HERCULE POIROT.

Pollock, Jackson *See* JACKSON POLLOCK.

Pollux *See* CASTOR AND POLLUX.

Polly Adler (adler) A "madam" who runs a brothel. Polly Adler (1900–62) was the notorious owner of a high-class bordello in New York, where her customers included gangsters, politicians, and many other public figures. She retired from the profession in 1944 and recorded the sensational events of her life in an autobiography. *He thought she was just a very nice woman and did not suspect she was a budding Polly Adler until he was shown into a room full of half-naked women.*

Pollyanna (poleeana) A tireless optimist. The 11-year-old Pollyanna Whittier was introduced to the world in the novel *Pollyanna* (1913) by the U.S. writer Eleanor Hodgman Porter (1868–1920) and was subsequently brought to life in plays and movies. She is portrayed as irrepressibly optimistic and always capable of finding the bright side in any depressing situation. Although the book was hugely successful, the name of its central character has since come to be used mockingly of anyone who expresses a persistently and unrealistically rosy view of the world. "I am aware that much of what I am saying makes me sound like some ageing Pollyanna who just wants to pretend that all is sweetness and light" (Molly Horne, *Life, Love and Laughter*, 1989).

Polonius (pălōneeăs) A long-winded, meddlesome old man. Polonius appears in William Shakespeare's tragedy *HAMLET* (c. 1600) as the father of Laertes and OPHELIA and adviser to King Claudius. Hamlet mocks Polonius for his sententious manner and ultimately kills him while he is hiding in the room of Queen Gertrude (Hamlet's mother), hoping to spy on an interview between mother and son. *His uncle was a garrulous old man who, like Shakespeare's Polonius, was only too happy to share his views of how others should lead their lives.*

Polyhymnia *See* MUSES.

Polyphemus (pahlifeemăs) Archetype of a dimwitted brute; a Cyclops. In Greek mythology Polyphemus was a Sicilian Cyclops (see CYCLOPEAN) who fell in love with the nymph Galatea and, when she rejected him, killed her lover, Acis. According to Homer's ODYSSEY (c. 700 B.C.) Polyphemus took Odysseus and his men prisoner when they landed on Sicily and kept them in his cave with his sheep. In order to escape Odysseus put out Polyphemus's one eye with a sharpened stake and dressed his men in sheepskins so the blinded monster could not recognize them by touch. *The story of Odysseus and Polyphemus is a classic parable of superior intelligence and cunning outwitting brute force and stupidity.*

Pontius Pilate (ponshăs pīlăt) A person who is indifferent to cruelty or injustice as long as his or her own interests remain untouched; a person who refuses to take responsibility for his or her own actions; a hypocrite. Pontius Pilate was the Roman governor of Judaea (A.D. 26–36) who remained unconvinced of Christ's guilt at his trial but ultimately allowed him to be crucified in order to avoid provoking a riot (Matthew 27, Mark 15, Luke 23, and John 18). The expression ***Pilate washed his hands*** alludes to the biblical account of Pilate washing his hands in public as an expression of the fact that he refused to accept any blame for Christ's death. Legend has it that after the Crucifixion Pilate was overcome with remorse and committed suicide. *The district attorney, like some latter-day Pontius Pilate, refused point blank to accept that he was to blame for this miscarriage of justice. See also* PILATE'S WIFE; WASH ONE'S HANDS OF.

Pony Express A mail delivery company, especially one that offers speedy delivery of messages. The original Pony Express was started by the U.S. government in 1860 and covered the 1,800 miles between St. Joseph, Missouri, and Sacramento, California. To ensure the mail got there in the shortest time possible (at its fastest, just seven days, 17 hours) riders changed horses at prearranged posts along the route. It operated for less than two years, being superseded by the electric telegraph network in 1862. *The proofs left by Pony Express an hour ago.*

Pooh-Bah An overbearing, pompous, self-important official, especially one who holds more than one post. The allusion is to the light opera *The Mikado* (1885) by W. S. Gilbert (1836–1911) and Sir Arthur Sullivan (1842–1900), in which Pooh-Bah, the Lord-High-Everything-Else and holder of many senior positions, is a prominent character. He admits to being an insufferable snob and is impossible to work with, so when others give up their posts he simply adds them to those he already holds. "Not that this Pooh-Bah of a person let his duties worry him, even though they were within his sight at all hours" (Miss Read, *The World of Thrush Green*, 1990).

poor are always with us, the There will always be those who live in poverty and in need of assistance. The expression appears in Matthew 26:11, Mark 14:7, and John 12:8, which recount an incident in which a woman used expensive ointment to anoint Christ. The disciples rebuke the woman for her extravagance, but Christ protests, "Why trouble ye the woman? for she hath wrought a good work upon me. For ye have the poor always with you; but me ye have not always" (Matthew 26:10–11). "Still, with [the almshouse's] gateway and wicket Meek, in the midst of splendour, its humble walls seem to echo Softly the words of the Lord:—'The poor ye always have with you'" (Henry Wadsworth Longfellow, *Evangeline*, 1849).

Popeye (popī) A man with superhuman strength. The cartoon character Popeye made his first appearance in the comic strip *Thimble Theater* in 1929 and went on to star in movie and television cartoons and even live-action movies. He owes his extraordinary strength to his prodigious consumption of tinned spinach, wears the bell-bottomed uniform of a sailor, and is rarely seen without his pipe. He has a girlfriend called ***Olive Oyl*** and an archenemy called ***Bluto***. "A deep-voiced character with five o'clock shadow all over his face and fists like Popeye the Sailor grabbed the girl by her Indian beads and slammed her up against the mantelpiece" (Kim Newman, *Bad Dreams*, 1990).

Poppins, Mary *See* MARY POPPINS.

pork barrel Legislation that directs federal funds to local projects that just happen to benefit the district of the member of Congress who promoted the measure in the first place. The term dates back to the custom of presenting slaves on southern plantations with their allowance of pork in a barrel. "Without close supervision the suggested cuts, in particular, would fall victim to the machinations of interest groups and the pork barrel orientations of members of Congress" (David Mervin, *Ronald Reagan and the American Presidency*, 1990).

Porlock, person from *See* PERSON FROM PORLOCK.

Porter, Jimmy *See* ANGRY YOUNG MAN.

Porthos *See* THREE MUSKETEERS.

Portia *See* QUALITY OF MERCY IS NOT STRAINED, THE; SHYLOCK.

Poseidon (păsīdăn) The god of the sea. In Greek mythology Poseidon was one of the 12 gods of Olympus and a brother of Zeus. As the ruler of the oceans he was usually depicted with a trident and usually described as being violent and ill tempered. He was also feared as the god of earthquakes. *As far as anyone knows, both men were lost in the realm of Poseidon when their ship foundered. See also* NEPTUNE.

postmillennialism *See* MILLENNIUM.

Potemkin village (pōtemkin) A showy facade that conceals an unattractive reality. The allusion is to the Russian statesman Grigory Aleksandrovich Potemkin (1739–91), who is said to have had cardboard villages constructed to impress Catherine the Great, during a royal visit to the Ukraine in 1787, with the improvements he had apparently made. Sad to relate, the story is untrue. "They built manyattas, but were not to be found in them; they were Potemkin manyattas, the real ones flourishing in inaccessible places" (Kathryn Tidrick, *Empire and the English Character*, 1992).

Potiphar's wife (potifarz) A woman who gets revenge on a man who has rejected her advances by falsely accusing him of rape. Potiphar is described in Genesis 37:36 as one of Pharaoh's officers who bought JOSEPH as a slave and made him overseer of his household. Potiphar's wife tried to seduce Joseph, but he refused her, so in a rage she snatched some of his clothing and went to her husband to complain that Joseph had raped her, offering his clothing as corroborating evidence. Potiphar believed his wife's accusations, and Joseph was thrown into prison (Genesis 39:7–20). "A good housewife is of necessity a humbug; and Cornelia's husband was hoodwinked, as Potiphar was—only in a different way" (William Makepeace Thackeray, *Vanity Fair,* 1847).

potter's field A burial ground for paupers and unclaimed bodies. The original Potter's Field was, according to Matthew 27:7, a patch of ground outside Jerusalem that was purchased by the priests of the Temple as a burial place for the poor. The area was bought with the THIRTY PIECES OF SILVER that a remorseful Judas Iscariot had received as payment for betraying Christ and had returned to the Temple shortly before taking his own life. The cemetery's name referred to the land's former use as a source of clay for local potters. Subsequently the name was borrowed for pauper burial grounds at many locations throughout the Christian world. Another version claims that Judas himself bought the field with the thirty pieces of silver and died there (see ACELDAMA). "She is whimsical, and may really like to have the truth. It's quite clear her heart is as insensible to eloquence and poetry, as a Potter's Field wall, and it might answer to try her with a little truth" (James Fenimore Cooper, *Autobiography of a Pocket-Handkerchief,* 1843).

pound of flesh *See* SHYLOCK.

pour encourager les autres (por onkoorahzhay layz ōtră) To make an example of someone as a warning or incentive to others. The reference is to the British admiral John Byng, who was executed by firing squad in 1757 after his admittedly fairly modest naval force failed to press home an attack on the French-held island of Minorca during the Seven Years' War (1750–57). The incident prompted the French writer Voltaire to observe of England in *Candide* (1759): "*Dans ce pays-ci il est bon de tuer de temps en temps un amiral pour encourager les autres.*" ("In this country, it is good to kill an admiral from time to time to encourage the others.") "Twelve of their heads were impaled on the Charles Bridge pour encourager les autres and remained there for more than a decade" (Walter Perrie, *Roads that Move*, 1991).

pour out the vials of wrath *See* VIALS OF WRATH.

powers that be, the The government or those in authority; the establishment. The phrase comes from Romans 13:1: "Let every soul be subject unto the higher powers. For there is no power but of God: the powers that be are ordained of God." *The powers that be have ordered that there should be no review of department policy.*

praetorian guard (preetōreeăn) The protectors or closest confederates of an individual or government in power. In ancient Rome the Praetorian Guard, instituted during the reign of Augustus, around 27 B.C., served as the bodyguards of the emperor. The very first such guards were a small body of elite soldiers chosen to protect a commanding officer on campaign and took their name from that of a commanding officer's tent, his *praetorium.* Members of the imperial Praetorian Guard, which numbered some 9,000 men under Augustus, wielded considerable power in their own right and on many occasions played a prominent role in installing or deposing the emperor. It is thought that at least nine emperors were murdered by the Praetorian Guard between the years A.D. 41 and 282. The Praetorian Guard was finally disbanded in 312, having lost its role to the army generals, upon whom emperors had come to rely directly for support. The term, sometimes rendered in the form ***palace guard,*** is still used today to refer to the cohorts of aides and confidants who attach themselves to those in power. The adjective ***praetorian*** may also be applied to regimes of a strong military, authoritarian character. *In times of trouble it is the duty of aides to gather around the president as a form of praetorian guard, sheltering him from further hostile attentions.*

Praxitelean (praksiteleeăn) Of the highest standard in sculpture. Praxiteles was an Athenian sculptor who flourished in the fourth century B.C. and was regarded as the finest sculptor Greece had ever known. His few surviving works include a statue of Hermes carrying the infant Dionysus. "She had bared her plump neck, shoulders, and arms to the moonshine, under which they looked as luminous and beautiful as some Praxitelean creation" (Thomas Hardy, *Tess of the D'Urbervilles,* 1891).

premillennialism *See* MILLENNIUM.

Presley, Elvis *See* KING, THE.

priapic (prīapik) Of or relating to the sexual urge in males; phallic. The word alludes to Priapus, the son of Dionysus and Aphrodite and the god of gardens and vineyards and of male reproductive power. *He was not too old to feel the need to satisfy the odd priapic urge, although he rarely did anything about it.*

price of wisdom is above rubies, the Nothing is more valuable than wisdom. This proverb is of biblical origin, appearing in Job 28:18: "No mention shall be made of coral, or of pearls: for the price of wisdom is above rubies." (See also Proverbs 3:15 and 8:11.) "Who can find a virtuous woman? for her price is far above rubies" (Thomas Hardy, *Tess of the D'Urbervilles,* 1891).

pricks, kick against the *See* KICK AGAINST THE PRICKS.

pride goeth before a fall Overconfidence and arrogance often result in humiliation or disaster. The proverb is of biblical origin: "Pride goeth before destruction, and an haughty spirit before a fall" (Proverbs 16:18). It is also encountered in the form ***pride comes before a fall.*** "'I suppose he thinks he'd be mayor himself,' said the people of Blackstable. They pursed their lips. 'Pride goeth before a fall'" (W. Somerset Maugham, *Cakes and Ale,* 1930).

priests of Bacchus *See* BACCHUS.

primrose path An easy path of indulgence and pleasure, especially one that leads to ruin. The expression appears in two of William Shakespeare's plays, ***HAMLET*** (c. 1600) and ***MACBETH*** (1606). *He was a long way down the primrose path of wine, women, and song before he realized how it might end.*

Prince Charming A male lover, especially one who has various ideal qualities, such as charm, good looks, and a lot of money. The allusion is to the fairy tale CINDERELLA, which ends with Cinderella finally being united with her Prince Charming, although similar idealized lovers—sometimes identified by the same name—appear in other fairy tales, such as SLEEPING BEAUTY and SNOW WHITE. *She's been on hundreds of blind dates, but she's still looking for her Prince Charming.*

Prince of Darkness *See* SATAN.

prince of Denmark *See* HAMLET.

princes in the Tower Innocent victims of political murder. Edward, Prince of Wales (b. 1470), who reigned briefly as Edward V, and Richard, duke of York (b. 1472) were the heirs of the English king Edward IV, but after their father's death in 1483 both were incarcerated in the feared TOWER OF LONDON on the orders of their uncle, the future Richard III. The two boys then vanished and are generally believed to have been murdered on their uncle's orders. Skeletons found in the Tower in 1674 were said to be those of the two boys. "I thought of us as the little princes in the Tower, and of the city of London as the cruel torturer Hubert who at any moment might come and put out our poetic eyes" (James Kirkup, *A Poet could not but be Gay*, 1991).

princess and the pea A person who is considered unreasonably fussy or sensitive. The allusion is to the fairy tale *The Princess and the Pea* (1836) by the Danish writer HANS CHRISTIAN ANDERSEN (1805–75), in which an unknown young woman who claims she is a princess is tested by being offered a bed comprising 20 mattresses and 20 eiderdowns. She is unaware that a single pea has been concealed deep in the pile, but complains in the morning that she has not been able to get a moment's sleep because of a lump in the bed, thus proving that she has had a truly luxurious, royal upbringing. *His teenage daughter complains at the slightest thing, like the princess and the pea.*

Priscian *See* BREAK PRISCIAN'S HEAD.

Procris *See* UNERRING AS THE DART OF PROCRIS.

procrustean (prăkrăsteeăn, prōkrăsteeăn) Achieving conformity through the arbitrary use of violent or ruthless means, regardless of individual rights or circumstances. In Greek mythology Procrustes was a cruel, villainous highwayman who forced his victims to lie on an iron bed, stretching their bodies or lopping off their limbs to make them fit it perfectly. His name literally means "the stretcher." His notorious career came to a premature end when he was killed by Theseus. A ***bed of Procrustes*** or ***procrustean bed*** denotes a system, scheme, or standard to which others are obliged to conform. "A certain set of highly ingenious resources are, with the Prefect, a sort of Procrustean bed, to which he forcibly adapts his designs" (Edgar Allan Poe, "The Purloined Letter," 1845).

prodigal son A person who returns after a lengthy absence, having squandered his or her money. The allusion is to Christ's parable of the prodigal son related in Luke 15:11–32, in which a young man returns home after recklessly frittering away his inheritance. Instead of rebuking him for his profligacy, and braving the protests of his other son, who had stayed at home, the father welcomes him back and holds a lavish celebration in honor of the event. By much the same token a ***prodigal*** is someone who squanders his or her money. "Then he looked at the highly-coloured scripture pieces on the walls, in little black frames like common shaving-glasses, and saw how the Wise Men (with a strong family likeness among them) worshipped in a pink manager; and how the Prodigal Son came home in red rags to a purple father, and already feasted his imagination on a sea-green calf" (Charles Dickens, *Martin Chuzzlewit,* 1843–44). *See also* KILL THE FATTED CALF.

Professor Moriarty *See* NAPOLEON OF CRIME; SHERLOCK HOLMES.

Promethean (prămeetheeăn) Exceptionally creative, inventive, or original. The word alludes to the Greek demigod Prometheus (whose name means "forethought"), who was credited with making the first man from clay. He later stole fire from Olympus and presented it to the human race and also taught mortals many artistic, medical, and agricultural skills. Because of his defiance of the gods in stealing fire from Olympus, Zeus had Prometheus chained to a rock so that an eagle (or vulture) could feed on his liver, which was magically restored each day. He was eventually rescued from this agony by HERCULES. Inspiration, creativity, or life itself is sometimes referred to as ***Promethean fire.*** "Now, don't you suppose, my inexperienced girl, that I cannot rebel, in high Promethean fashion, against the gods and fate as well as you" (Thomas Hardy, *The Return of the Native,* 1878).

promised land A place or situation believed to offer great happiness, fulfillment, and security. In the Old Testament the land of Canaan was promised by God to Abraham and his descendants, and thus Canaan came to be referred to as the Promised Land: "And the LORD appeared unto Abram and said, Unto thy seed will I give this land" (Genesis 12:7). In other contexts the same title is sometimes applied to heaven: "I just want to do God's will. And He's allowed me to go up to the mountain. And I've looked over. And I've seen the promised land" (Martin Luther King, speech, April 3, 1968). *See also* LAND FLOWING WITH MILK AND HONEY.

prophet is not without honor, save in his own country, a A person who issues warnings or advice is often taken least seriously by those closest to him or her. The proverb comes from Matthew 13:57, which describes how Christ was ill received in his home town of Nazareth and quotes him as saying: "A prophet is not without honour, save in his own country, and in his own house." Also encountered in the form ***a prophet is without honor in his own country.*** "In Florence the signori thought him an amusing fellow and his letters often made them laugh, but they had no great confidence in his judgment and never followed his advice. 'A prophet is not without honor save in his own country,' he sighed" (W. Somerset Maugham, *Then and Now,* 1946).

Proserpina *See* PERSEPHONE.

Prospero (prospărō) A person with powerful magical powers. Prospero is the central character in William Shakespeare's play *The Tempest* (1611), a nobleman of Milan exiled to a desert island who has mastered the magical arts and uses them to overcome his former enemies, achieve a reconciliation with them, and secure a better future for his daughter MIRANDA. He finally renounces his magic and returns to Milan. *He seemed to control the destinies of all those around him, like Prospero with his magic staff. See also* ARIEL; BRAVE NEW WORLD; CALIBAN.

protean (prōteeăn, prōteeăn) Versatile; variable; changeable. The word comes from the name of the Greek sea god, Proteus, who tended the flocks of Poseidon and could change his shape at will. "Donald appeared not to see her at all, and answered her wise little remarks with curtly indifferent monosyllables, his looks and faculties hanging on the woman who could boast of a more Protean variety in her phases, moods, opinions, and also principles, than could Elizabeth" (Thomas Hardy, *The Mayor of Casterbridge,* 1886).

Proustian (<u>proo</u>steeăn) Reminiscent of the psychology or style of the writings of the French novelist Marcel Proust (1871–1922). The subjects of Proust's novels, which are typically long and highly detailed, include memory, heartbreak, sickness, and the passage of time. The term Proustian may allude to any of these, although it is equally likely to be employed in relation to his technique of using a simple sensation to evoke detailed memories of times long past (*see* MADELEINE). *The smell of her perfume had a Proustian effect, bringing back memories of his childhood in Africa.*

psyche (<u>sī</u>kee) The human mind or soul. The word alludes to Greek mythology and the beautiful Psyche, a mortal who was loved by Eros, the god of love, and visited by him each night on the condition that she did not ask his name or look at his face. Eventually Psyche, tricked by her sisters into thinking her secret lover was a monster, succumbed to temptation and looked on Eros's face in the lamplight. Eros fled but Psyche sought him out, and after lengthy wandering and many adventures they were reunited. Psyche was granted immortality and became the personification of the soul. *Somewhere deep in his psyche was a niggling desire to make himself heard, but he suppressed it with a deliberate effort.*

Psycho (<u>sī</u>kō) A situation reminiscent of the 1960 movie *Psycho*, about a deranged serial killer. The movie was directed by Alfred Hitchcock (1899–1980) and starred Anthony Perkins (1932–92) as the psychopathic ***Norman Bates***. In the most memorable and shocking scene in the movie, the unsuspecting Janet Leigh is stabbed to death in the shower. "No one of the post-Psycho generation likes being surprised in the shower, so I closed the bathroom door loudly behind me" (Michael Dibdin, *Dirty Tricks*, 1991). *See also* BATES MOTEL.

P. T. Barnum (<u>bahr</u>năm) A person who presents spectacular large-scale shows. Phineas Taylor Barnum (1810–91) staged ambitious public entertainments from the 1840s onward, his many famed attractions ranging from TOM THUMB to the ELEPHANT MAN. He also opened a Museum of Curiosities on Broadway in New York City. Most celebrated of all was his renowned circus, cofounded with James H. Bailey in 1870, which toured the United States and Europe under the slogan "The Greatest Show on Earth." He is remembered both for his resourcefulness and for his lack of principles when it came to exploiting the fee-paying public. *The city had seen nothing like it since the last visit by Barnum's circus.*

Ptolemaic (tolă<u>may</u>ik) Of or relating to the theories of the Greco-Egyptian astronomer and mathematician Claudius Ptolemaeus, who flourished in the second century A.D. His theory that the universe revolved around the Earth remained unchallenged until the 16th century, when it was discredited by Nicolaus Copernicus. Since then *Ptolemaic* has been variously applied to theories or attitudes based on an assumption that the universe revolves around the Earth and human affairs. "Geology has initiated us into the secularity of nature, and taught us to disuse our dame-school measures, and exchange our Mosaic and Ptolemaic schemes for her large style" (Ralph Waldo Emerson, *Nature,* 1836).

public enemy number one A criminal whose crimes are especially heinous, or anything that is seen to pose a serious threat to the general public. The title was first bestowed, in 1925, upon the bank robber and murderer ***John Dillinger*** (1903–34), who (with his companion Anna Sage, the ***Lady in Red***) carved his bloody way through the Midwest until finally shot to death by the FBI in 1934, by which time he had killed 10 people. The title has since been applied to many other murderers and terrorists. "Since 1980 a new environmental public enemy number one has replaced nuclear power" (Don Hedley, *World Energy*, 1986).

Puck A mischievous sprite. Otherwise known as ***Robin Goodfellow***, Puck has his roots in English folklore. He is depicted as an evil spirit in Edmund Spenser's *Epithalamion* (1595) but is best known from his more innocently provocative appearances in William Shakespeare's play *A Midsummer Night's Dream* (1595). Shakespeare's Puck uses his magic to confound mortals on the orders of his master Oberon, king of the fairies. Someone who is ***puckish*** behaves in an impish, mischievous manner. *Guests quickly tired of his puckish pranks at the Christmas party.*

Punch and Judy A married couple or two other parties who have a knockabout, even violent, relationship. The allusion is to the Punch and July puppet shows, distantly descended from the Italian commedia dell'arte, that were once a common feature of the English seaside. Punch was a hunchbacked rogue who strangled his baby, beat his wife Judy, and was eventually sentenced to the gallows, while Judy was almost equally violent; other characters included a crocodile and a policeman. *Modern politics seems to have descended to the level of a Punch and Judy show.*

Punic faith (pyoonik) Dishonest, deceitful, treacherous behavior; faithlessness. The Latin word for a Carthaginian was *Punicus* (a reference to their Phoenician origins), and the concept of Punic faith alludes to the hostility that existed between Carthage and ancient Rome during the Punic Wars of the third and second centuries B.C. Conscious that the influence of Carthage represented a serious threat to their own republic, Romans accused their Carthaginian enemies of all manner of dishonest, treacherous behavior, and the statesman Cato the Elder spoke for many when he took to ending each speech he made in the Senate with "Carthage must be destroyed." This was finally achieved with victory in the Third Punic War in 146 B.C. *As a further demonstration of his Punic faith he gave the authorities full details of his former employer's bank accounts. See also* CARTHAGINIAN PEACE.

pure all things are pure, to the *See* UNTO THE PURE ALL THINGS ARE PURE.

purgatory (pergătoree) A state or place of suffering or torment. In Catholic tradition purgatory is the temporary abode of those spirits who are obliged to spend a period of time being purged of their sins before they can enter heaven. Scriptures that are alluded to in support of this teaching include 2 Maccabees 12:44–45 of the Apocrypha, Matthew 12:32, John 14:2, and 1 Corinthians 3:11–15. The name itself comes from the Latin *purgatorium* ("place of cleansing"). "From the surface of the water rose a dense cloud of steam. Alphonse groaned out that we were already in purgatory, which indeed we were, though not in the sense that he meant it" (H. Rider Haggard, *Allan Quatermain,* 1887).

puritanical Stern, austere, or unforgiving; opposed to indulgence and excess. The Puritans emerged within the Church of England in the late 16th and early 17th centuries as a group of religious dissenters who were determined to rid the church of any practices left over from Roman Catholicism. They were also opposed to the absolute power of the monarchy (which was suspected of harboring Catholic sympathies) and, having achieved considerable political influence with the overthrow and execution of Charles I and the rule of Oliver Cromwell, sought to repress what they saw as sinful behavior in society, such as going to the theater and many other forms of frivolity. The Puritans lost favor in England after the Restoration of Charles II and many emigrated to America to found new Puritan colonies, thus exercising a profound and lasting influence upon the formation of the national character. Nowadays, however, the term "puritanical" is usually employed to condemn attitudes that are seen as overly rigid and narrow-minded. "He had, of course, given up cigarettes by the time he had gone into the clinic, but as a result he had abandoned the puritanical principles inculcated into him in youth and had started eating sweets instead; and this meant that he was putting on weight" (Peter Ackroyd, *T. S. Eliot*, 1988).

push the envelope To go beyond normal limits. The phrase, which was first heard in the 1940s, comes from aviation, specifically from graphs illustrating an aircraft's known range and powers, the lines on the graph suggesting the shape of an envelope. To "push the envelope" is thus to exceed these limits, for instance, in breaking the sound barrier. *We need to push the envelope if this company is to get ahead of the opposition.*

putsch (puuch) A political uprising. Meaning "push" in German, the word is best known from the ***Munich Putsch*** staged by the Nazis in November 1923, during which HITLER and his followers recruited the support of right-wingers meeting in a Munich beer hall to march on the center of Munich. The rising failed and Hitler was imprisoned for five months, but his leadership of the burgeoning Nazi movement was thus confirmed. "In this he was to be sadly mistaken, and the collapse of his position in the face of what was initially little more than a putsch organized by the queen shows how shallowly based his authority was, resting on fear and coercion rather than genuine loyalty" (Anthony Tuck, *Crown and Nobility 1272–1461*, 1986).

Pygmalion (pigmaylyăn, pigmayleeăn) A person who creates or re-creates another individual and then becomes obsessed with the creation. In Greek mythology Pygmalion was a sculptor who, repelled by the flaws of mortal women, fashioned a statue of the perfect woman, calling her GALATEA. This act angered Aphrodite, the goddess of love, who punished Pygmalion by making him fall in love with his creation. Driven to distraction by the fact that he could not consummate his love, Pygmalion begged the gods to breath life into the figure. Eventually Aphrodite agreed to his request, and Galatea became a real, living woman. The central theme of the myth, a warning to those who obsessively pursue an artistic ideal, provided the basis for George Bernard Shaw's play *Pygmalion* (1913), in which a linguist sets himself the intellectual challenge of passing off a common flower vendor as an aristocratic lady (*see* ELIZA DOOLITTLE) and in the process neglects his own emotional attachment toward her until it is too late. The play was subsequently turned into the musical *My Fair Lady* (1956), which in turn became a movie (1964). *As her manager he assumed the role of her Pygmalion, transforming her from a talented hopeful into a fully rounded professional.*

pygmy Something or someone very small or insignificant. Pygmies, or ***pigmies,*** were featured in classical lore as a legendary race of dwarfs living in central Asia and were first recorded in the writings of Homer (c. eighth century B.C.). The word itself comes from the Greek *pygme,* a measure of length equivalent to the distance from a person's elbow to the knuckles. When HERCULES went into battle with the pygmies he overcame them by rolling them up in his lion skin. The name was subsequently applied to certain peoples of equatorial Africa characterized by their small stature, although they are considerably larger than the pygmies of classical legend, who used miniature hatchets to cut individual ears of corn and had to wage war annually against the cranes that fed on them. *Although a significant player in the home market, the company is a pygmy on the international stage.*

Pylades and Orestes (pīlaydeez, oresteez) Archetypes of devoted friendship. Pylades and Orestes appear in the writings of Homer (c. eighth century B.C.) as a model of perfect friendship. Orestes was the son of Agamemnon, while Pylades was Agamemnon's nephew. *Like Pylades and Orestes, they would have done anything for each other.*

pylon A steel structure supporting high-tension electrical cables or other equipment. The original pylons were the monumental gateways that were a chief feature of ancient Egyptian temples. *Most electrical companies today try to put their cables underground rather than hoist them up in the air on long chains of pylons running across the countryside.*

Pyramids *See* EIGHTH WONDER OF THE WORLD.

Pyramus and Thisbe (pirămăs, thizbee) Archetypal tragic lovers of classical legend. Pyramus and Thisbe were two lovers who defied their parents' opposition to their match and arranged to meet in a remote place where Thisbe, arriving first, was attacked by a lion. Thisbe fled, and when Pyramus arrived, all he found was her bloody scarf. Assuming she was dead, he killed himself, only for Thisbe to find his body and commit suicide in turn. *When she found his apparently lifeless body, the young woman swooned on the spot, a virtual modern reenactment of Pyramus and Thisbe.*

Pyrrhic victory (pirik) A hollow victory; a victory so costly that its benefits are relatively insignificant. Pyrrhus (312–272 B.C.) was a king of Epirus, in western Greece, who waged a lengthy campaign against Rome. Following the battle of Asculum (279), which he won narrowly and only at the cost of many of his men, he is said to have exclaimed, "One more such victory and we are undone!" By the time he returned to Epirus he had lost two-thirds of his army. Such a victory may also be called a ***Cadmean victory*** in allusion to the Greek legend of Prince Cadmus, who fought and killed a dragon, but a host of armed men subsequently sprang up from the dragon's teeth, which Cadmus had planted in the ground. Cadmus threw a stone into their midst and all but five died in the ensuing mayhem (hence the phrase). *Pleased though they were to secure the house after such a long struggle, it was a Pyrrhic victory, for there would be very little left in the kitty after they had met the dramatically inflated purchase price. See also* SOW DRAGON'S TEETH.

Pythagorean theorem (păthagăreeăn) Mathematical rule that the square of the length of the hypotenuse is equal to the sum of the squares of the lengths of the other two sides of a right triangle. Pythagoras (c. 580–c. 500 B.C.) was a Greek philosopher and mathematician. It seems that this theorem was familiar to ancient Egyptian surveyors and the Babylonians at least 100 years before Pythagoras. *Children are expected to have mastered the* *basic laws of mathematics, such as the Pythagorean theorem, by the time they take their first major set of examinations.*

pythonesque *See* MONTY PYTHON.

Pythias *See* DAMON AND PYTHIAS.

python A family of large, nonvenomous snakes native to Africa, southern Asia, and Australia that kill their prey by constriction. They are named after a monstrous snake of Greek mythology called the Python. Legend had it that this serpent arose from the mud following the flood sent by Zeus that drowned everyone except Deucalion and his wife, Pyrrha. The Python became the guardian of Delphi until killed by Apollo, who set up his oracle there and established the ***Pythian Games*** to celebrate his victory. *The feather boa curled like a python round her generous figure.*

Q

quality of mercy is not strained, the Mercy, which is free, is always an option. The source of this oft-repeated sentiment is William Shakespeare's play *The Merchant of Venice* (1596), in which the giving and withholding of mercy is a primary theme. Among the best-known quotations from Shakespeare, it is voiced by SHYLOCK's nemesis ***Portia***. *He was tempted to humiliate his enemies in his hour of triumph, but reminded himself just in time that the quality of mercy is not strained.*

Quasimodo *See* HUNCHBACK OF NOTRE DAME.

Quatermain, Allan *See* ALLAN QUATERMAIN.

Queeg, Captain *See* CAPTAIN QUEEG.

Queen Anne is dead That is old news. The Queen Anne referred to, the daughter of James II and his first wife Anne Hyde, ruled Great Britain and Ireland from 1702 to 1714. Queen Anne suffered from ill health for many years before her eventual death on August 1, 1714, at the age of 49. Rumors that she had died were circulating two days before her actual death, so that by the time the reports became official it was already stale news. *"Yes, and Queen Anne's dead" was his dismissive comment when they told him the plant was going to close.*

Queen of Heaven Title traditionally bestowed upon the VIRGIN MARY in the Catholic and Orthodox liturgies. Mary was crowned Queen of Heaven on her Assumption, and a Feast of Mary the Queen was subsequently instituted by Pope Pius XII (1876–1958). Her other titles include ***Queen of Angels, Queen of Apostles, Queen of Confessors, Queen of Patriarchs, Queen of Peace, Queen of Prophets, Queen of Saints,*** and ***Queen of Virgins.*** "But he believed in his mother and sisters as though they were heaven-born; and he was one who could believe in his wife as though she were the queen of heaven" (Anthony Trollope, *The Eustace Diamonds,* 1873). *See also* ASHTORETH.

Queen of Sheba (sheebă) Legendary queen whose name is sometimes applied pejoratively to woman who is suspected of dressing or otherwise behaving in an inappropriately grand manner. The biblical Queen of Sheba, described in 1 Kings 10:1–13, 2 Chronicles 9:1–9 and 12, and elsewhere, is a shadowy figure, supposedly the proud ruler of an area equating to modern Ethiopia and Yemen. She visited Solomon in Jerusalem in order to confirm for herself the tales she had heard of both his wisdom and of the magnificence of his palaces. She was greatly humbled when these tales were proved accurate, and "there was no more spirit in her" (1 Kings 10:4–5). According to some accounts she and Solomon became lovers. Her name is usually invoked as a criticism of women who are guilty of pretensions of grandeur or haughty behavior, but it may also sometimes symbolize vanquished pride, as in Thomas Hardy's *Tess of the D'Urbervilles* (1891), in which Tess laments, "I'm like the poor Queen of Sheba who lives in the Bible. There is no more spirit in me." "'You ought'—'Ought what, sir?' demanded the lady, gazing at her husband with the air of a Queen of Sheba" (Honoré de Balzac, *Cousin Pons,* 1847).

Queensberry Rules (kweenzbăree) The rules of fair play. John Sholto Douglas, the marquess of Queensberry (1844–1900), was an enthusiastic sportsman who, in 1867, oversaw the establishment of a new set of rules intended to make boxing a safer sport. The so-called "Queensberry Rules" prohibited (among other tactics) biting, kicking, and hitting below the belt. Nowadays, anyone who does not play fairly in any sporting or nonsporting context may be accused of not playing by the Queensberry Rules. "Not exactly the Queensberry Rules, but it worked" (Simon Romain, *How to Live Safely in a Dangerous World*, 1989). *See also* HIT BELOW THE BELT.

queer as a clockwork orange *See* CLOCKWORK ORANGE.

Queer Street *See* CAREY STREET.

que sera, sera *See* CHE SARÀ, SARÀ.

quick and the dead, the The living and the dead. The phrase appears in the Apostles' Creed (in the *Book of Common Prayer*), in which Christ is identified as the judge of the living and the dead: "From thence he shall come to judge the quick and the dead." It appears in the Bible in similar form in Acts 10:42, 2 Timothy 4:1, and 1 Peter 4:5. In modern usage it is usually quoted with parodic intent. *Local tradition insisted that the old churchyard was a place of macabre happenings, where the quick and the dead came face to face.*

quick on the draw Quick to respond to an opportunity or threat. The allusion is the gunfighters of the Wild West and the cliché of the duel with guns fought in the streets of Dodge City and other towns, although these were largely the stuff of legend somewhat removed from reality. Survival in such a duel depended upon being the first to draw the revolver from the holster. An early variant was ***quick on the trigger***. "But Goldie, quick on the draw, intervenes" (Ellen Galford, *The Dyke and the Dybbuk*, 1993).

Quis custodiet ipsos custodes? (kwis kăstōdeeăt ipsos kăstōdayz) Who will guard the guards themselves? This proverbial word of warning emphasizing the need for those in authority to be themselves accountable to others comes from the writings of the Roman satirist Juvenal (c. A.D. 55–c. 140), specifically Satire VI. Juvenal addressed it originally to nervous husbands who hired others to guard the chastity of their wives. The line continues to be quoted today whenever doubt is cast about the trustworthiness of people occupying posts of considerable power, authority, or opportunity. "The bad measures or bad appointments of a minister may be checked by Parliament; and the interest of ministers in defending, and of rival partisans in attacking, secures a tolerably equal discussion: but quis custodiet custodes? who shall check the Parliament?" (John Stuart Mill, *Considerations on Representative Government,* 1861).

quisling (kwizling) A collaborator or traitor. Vidkun Quisling (1887–1945) was a Norwegian fascist politician who sided with Adolf Hitler's Germany prior to the German invasion of Norway in 1940 and as a reward was made Germany's puppet president while the country remained under German occupation. Reviled by most Norwegians, he gave himself up in 1945 after the defeat of the Nazis; he was tried by a Norwegian court and shot later the same year. Winston Churchill was the first person to use Quisling's name as a synonym for treason. "While setting up the calm surface of village life in a realistic manner, the film does so only as a contrast to the savagery that ensues: a priest is shot while making a stand against 'the enemies and oppressors of mankind,' the Post Office lady kills a German with an axe and is promptly bayonetted herself, and the vicar's daughter disposes of the Quisling squire, to whom she had been amorously linked" (James Park, *British Cinema: the Lights that Failed*, 1990).

quixotic *See* DON QUIXOTE.

Quo vadis? (kwō vahdis) Whither goest thou? This formal challenge comes directly from the Vulgate version of John 13:36, in which the words are addressed by Peter to Christ at the Last Supper. (See also John 16:5.) According to one legend, a variant origin of the phrase is when Christ appears in a vision during Peter's flight from Rome to escape martyrdom. When Christ replies "To Rome to be crucified again," a chastened Peter turns back to the capital to face his own execution. The quotation was subsequently used as a title for several major religious paintings depicting the episode. A novel of the same title (1895) by the Polish writer Henryk Sienkiewicz, who depicted Rome during the reign of Nero, has been staged and filmed several times. *The sentry leveled his rifle and uttered the time-honored quo vadis as instructed by his sergeant.*

R

rabbit hole *See* DOWN THE RABBIT HOLE.

Rabelaisian (rabălayzeeăn) Coarse, licentious, or ribald; concerned with bodily functions and the pleasures of the flesh. The allusion is to the works of the French writer François Rabelais (c. 1494–c. 1553), who is usually remembered for the outrageous comic satires *Gargantua* and *Pantagruel*, about the extravagant and grotesque behavior of two giants (Pantagruel being Gargantua's son). Rabelais himself turned to writing only after abandoning life in a monastery, his attacks on both religious and secular authorities making him one of the most controversial figures of his age. "It could be a bit vulgar, I grant you, but Rabelaisian, nothing nasty" (Ruth Dudley Edwards, *Clubbed to Death*, 1993). *See also* GARGANTUAN.

race is not to the swift nor the battle to the strong, the It is not always the stronger or faster side that wins the contest. This proverbial observation has biblical origins: "The race is not to the swift, nor the battle to the strong, neither yet bread to the wise, nor yet riches to men of understanding, nor yet favour to men of skill; but time and chance happeneth to them all" (Ecclesiastes 9:11). "Poor child! she lay . . . trying to work out . . . why the race is not to the swift, nor the battle to the strong" (Charlotte Mary Yonge, *Pillars of House,* 1873).

Rachel weeping for her children A woman in the throes of grief, especially one mourning her dead child. According to Genesis 29–35, Rachel was the second wife of Jacob and the mother of Joseph and Benjamin. She died giving birth to Benjamin but subsequently is described as weeping over the fate of her descendants when they were about to be carried off into captivity in Babylon: "Rachel weeping for her children refused to be comforted for her children, because they were not" (Jeremiah 31:15). (See also Matthew 2:17–18.) "But by her halting course and winding, woeful way, you plainly saw that this ship that so wept with spray, still remained without comfort. She was Rachel, weeping for her children, because they were not" (Herman Melville, *Moby-Dick,* 1851).

radical chic (sheek) The espousal of leftist causes by members of the fashionable elite. The term was coined by U.S. journalist and novelist Tom Wolfe (b. 1931) in his book *Radical Chic (Mau-Mauing the Flak Catchers)* (1970) to describe a contemporary fad for members of high society to identify with various political radicals, holding fund-raising events and the like to promote their causes (though usually in order to appear modish rather than because of any real political conviction). "In the liberated world of radical chic, we may be intended to think, favours could be done for the right person" (Karl Miller, *Authors*, 1989).

Raffles (rafălz) A gentleman thief. The reference is to the central character in the Raffles stories of E. W. Hornung (1866–1921). Introduced in *The Amateur Cracksman* (1899), A. J. Raffles is a dashing English gentleman and sportsman with a sideline in burglary (usually from unappealing rich victims), who commits his crimes as much for the challenge they present as for any pecuniary interest. He shared his name with the historical Sir Ernest Stamford Raffles (1781–1826), who founded the celebrated Raffles Hotel in Singapore. *He clearly thought of himself as some sort of modern Raffles, but his shareholders now realized he was just a common thief.*

raft of the *Medusa* (mădoosă) A harrowing scene of human suffering, typically one depicting survivors from a shipwreck. The allusion is to a painting of the same title by the French artist Théodore Géricault (1791–1824), in which he depicted a group of stricken survivors on board a raft from the *Medusa*, a French naval frigate bound for Senegal in 1816. The vessel foundered on reefs off the coast of Africa, and the officers set 154 of their men adrift on a raft. Just 15 of them managed to survive, allegedly resorting to cannibalism before being rescued. Géricault's painting attracted notoriety for its unromantic realistic depiction of the raft and its occupants after 13 days at sea. *By the time they managed to get the yacht and its occupants back to harbor it looked like the raft of the* Medusa.

Ragnarok (ragnărok) A cataclysmic struggle resulting in universal disaster. In Norse mythology the world will end in a climactic battle between the good and evil gods. *The impact of the two armies was so titanic it seemed for a moment he was witnessing the fighting of some Ragnarok in which all creation would be destroyed. See also* GÖTTERDÄMMERUNG.

rainbow *See* END OF THE RAINBOW.

rain check The postponement of something. The term comes from baseball, which, being an outdoor game, is sometimes postponed due to bad weather; spectators who have bought tickets can use the counterfoil or a receipt to attend a later game without having to pay again. The phrase has since been applied to many other kinds of sport and entertainment and beyond that in many other contexts, often in the form ***take a rain check***, used in polite response to an invitation made at an inconvenient time. *I'm afraid I'll have to take a rain check on your invitation as I have to get home before the children go to bed.*

rain falls on the just and the unjust, the Some things affect the good and the bad regardless of their virtues or lack of them. The phrase comes from Christ's Sermon on the Mount: "That ye may be the children of your Father which is in heaven: for he maketh his sun to rise on the evil and on the good, and sendeth rain on the just and on the unjust" (Matthew 5:45). The passage is sometimes quoted as a reminder to leave retribution against one's enemies to God. *The rain falls on the just and on the unjust fella, but chiefly on the just because the unjust has stolen his umbrella.*

raise Cain (kayn) To stir up a fuss; to cause a noisy disturbance. The phrase alludes to the story of CAIN AND ABEL, specifically to Cain's violent temper, which was the underlying cause of his murdering his brother (Genesis 4:5). In centuries past Cain's name was adopted as a euphemism for the devil, as most people hesitated to mention the latter's name for fear of summoning him. "And look at Charles Second, and Louis Fourteen, and Louis Fifteen, and James Second, and Edward Second, and Richard Third, and forty more; besides all them Saxon heptarchies that used to rip around so in old times and raise Cain" (Mark Twain, *The Adventures of Huckleberry Finn,* 1884).

raising of Lazarus *See* LAZARUS.

rake's progress The downward passage through life of a dissolute young man or other reprobate. The allusion is to a famous set of pictures painted and engraved under this title in 1735 by the English artist William Hogarth (1697–1764), in which he satirized the foibles of contemporary society through the immorality and ultimate downfall of a reckless young man-about-town. *As a young man with money in his pocket he followed a rake's progress through high society until the cash ran out. See also* GIN LANE; HOGARTHIAN.

Rambo (rambō) A man who relies on physical strength or force of arms to achieve his purpose. The allusion is to the muscle-bound hero of a series of adventure films, beginning with *First Blood* (1982), starring U.S. actor ***Sylvester Stallone*** as misfit Vietnam veteran John Rambo, who single-handedly overwhelms his foes using a range of heavy weaponry. The films were inspired by a 1971 novel entitled *First Blood* by David Morrell. The term later became a nickname of U.S. president Ronald Reagan, who referred approvingly to the films in one of his speeches, but has otherwise come to symbolize an unthinking resort to extreme violence. "Of course, there are other situations when the toughness that accompanies the Rambo self-image is useful in disarming trouble-makers and preventing further crime, as happened more than once during field-work" (John Brewer and Kathleen Magee, *Inside the RUC*, 1991).

rape of the Sabine women (saybīn) Archetype of a mass abduction of women. The allusion is to a legendary episode of early Roman history, according to which the first Romans, under the leadership of Romulus, finding themselves short of females, invited their male Sabine neighbors to a festival and meanwhile invaded Sabine territory and carried off their womenfolk by force. War subsequently broke out between the two sides, but they were eventually reconciled. *It was like the rape of the Sabine women, terrified girls seeking to elude the clutches of their grinning partners.*

Rapunzel (rapănzăl) A girl or woman with very long hair. The allusion is to a story collected in GRIMM'S FAIRY TALES by the 19th-century German folklorists the Brothers Grimm. The story decribes how the girl Rapunzel, imprisoned by a witch in a high tower, lets down her hair for a prince to climb up and rescue her. "'What the hell?' said Lydia, leaning indignantly out of the window over the door, like Rapunzel with a haircut" (Alice T. Ellis, *Unexplained Laughter*, 1985).

Raskolnikov (raskolnikov) An alienated, angry young man, especially one who commits murder, believing himself to be above the law. Rodion Romanovich Raskolnikov is a central character in the novel *Crime and Punishment* (1866) by Russian writer Fyodor Dostoevsky (1821–81), in which he appears as an impoverished student who falls victim to his own conscience after murdering a woman pawnbroker and her sister. *The dictates of his conscience forced this sorry Texan Raskolnikov to admit to a crime that no one knew had even been committed.*

Rasputin (raspyootin) A person who exercises a baleful influence on someone else, especially someone in a position of power. Grigory Yefimovich Rasputin (1872–1916) was a notoriously dissolute and debauched Russian mystic and healer who gained influence over the royal family in prerevolutionary Russia by appearing to be able to exert a beneficial effect upon the czar's hemophiliac son, heir to the imperial throne. Jealousy of growing power of this "mad monk" led a group of courtiers to plot and carry out Rasputin's murder, though they had to poison him, shoot him twice, and throw him in the River Neva before he finally died. *According to the press, the secretary of state's chief adviser was behaving like some latter-day Rasputin.*

read my lips Mark my words; I mean what I say. Though not coined by him (it was current in rock music in the 1970s), the phrase is usually associated with U.S. president George H. W. Bush (b. 1924), having been used by him as a campaigning slogan in 1988 to underline his determination not to introduce new taxes: "Read my lips: no new taxes!" The slogan later came to haunt Bush in office, when he went on to raise taxes, and it undoubtedly contributed to his failure to secure a second presidential term in 1992. "So, if you're out there spying on me, read my lips, little cheat: big brother is not going screwy, young lady, and your thin-ended wedges stop right here!" (Ian Maitland, *Cathedral*, 1993).

read the riot act To make it clear that further misbehavior, incompetence, etc. will not be tolerated. Under former British law, if 12 or more people threatened to commit a riot, it was the duty of magistrates to order them to disperse by reading them the relevant part of the Riot Act of 1715 before sanctioning the use of force to break up the gathering: "Our Sovereign Lord the King chargeth and commandeth all persons assembled immediately to disperse themselves and peacefully to depart to their habitations or to their lawful business." The Riot Act was replaced by the Public Order Act of 1986, but people still talk of "reading the riot act" to restore peace and order or reprimand someone for behaving badly. "Every now and again, Albert's digestive system revolted, and his hard-pressed medical advisers were called in, prescribed tablets, and read the riot act yet again" (Miss Read, *The World of Thrush Green*, 1990).

real McCoy (măkoy) The genuine article; the real thing. The allusion is generally said to be to a celebrated U.S. welterweight boxer, Norman Selby (1873–1940), who had a long and highly successful career in the 1890s fighting under the name Kid McCoy, becoming world champion in 1896. Various other aspiring champions took the name Kid McCoy for themselves, but any possible confusion was settled in 1899 when Selby achieved his most impressive victory yet, beating the renowned Joe Choynski and prompting one sports journalist to write "Now you've seen the Real McCoy," hence the modern phrase. An alternative derivation links the phrase to whiskey, being used in reference to Scottish whiskey as distinct from the less highly regarded whiskey made in Canada and the United States. "Walter stayed in the North, felt at home there, so his books are authentic—the real McCoy" (Robert Barnard, *Posthumous Papers*, 1992).

Realpolitik (rayahlpoliteek, rayahlpōliteek) Pragmatic politics. A German term, it is usually applied to politics based on national interests or practical (not theoretical or ethical) considerations. It was coined in 1853 by Ludwig von

Rochau in criticism of the unrealistic policies advocated by German liberals of the period and was later applied to Otto von Bismarck's hard-headed and ultimately successful attempts to unify Germany. *In its dealings with some of the more dubious regimes in sub-Saharan Africa the government has clearly bowed to the demands of Realpolitik.*

reap the whirlwind *See* SOW THE WIND AND REAP THE WHIRLWIND.

reap what you sow The benefit you receive depends on what you have put in. The phrase comes from Paul's letter to the Galatians: "God is not mocked: for whatsoever a man soweth, that shall he also reap" (Galatians 6:7). (See also 2 Corinthians 9:6.) The same image of reaping and sowing is evoked at Matthew 25:24, where it appears in the parable of the talents: "Lord, I knew thee that thou art an hard man, reaping where thou hast not sown, and gathering where thou hast not strawed." *As children they had been brought up with the maxim that you reaped what you sowed, so the qualities of respect, honesty, and hard work stood them in good stead throughout their lives.*

rearrange the deck chairs on the Titanic *See* TITANIC.

Rebecca (răbekă) Archetype of a first wife or lover whose baleful influence blights any later relationship. The allusion is to Daphne du Maurier's 1938 novel *Rebecca*, in which the shadow of the deceased first wife of Maxim de Winter, owner of the forbidding mansion of ***Manderley***, hangs heavily over the happiness of de Winter's new bride. Du Maurier apparently based her story on her own feelings of jealousy concerning an ex-fiancée of her husband Lieutenant-General Frederick Browning. *The memory of his previous girlfriend lingered Rebecca-like in her thoughts as the wedding day approached. See also* MRS. DANVERS.

rebel without a cause A person, usually a teenager, who rebels instinctively against the adult world. The allusion is to the 1955 film of the same title starring JAMES DEAN as Jim Stark, a troubled young man who became an icon for disaffected youth everywhere. After Dean's premature death in a road accident before the film had even opened the actor became synonymous with the role he had played and himself the archetypal rebel without a cause. "He was a rebel without a cause, a born mutineer" (Jack Caplan, *Memories of the Gorbals*, 1991). *See also* ANGRY YOUNG MAN.

receive one's Nunc Dimittis *See* NUNC DIMITTIS.

Rechabite (rekăbīt) A teetotaler, especially one who is a member of the Independent Order of Rechabites (founded 1835) or another similar temperance society. Rechab was a biblical character who encouraged his family and his descendants to abstain from alcoholic drink and live strict, moderate lives (Jeremiah 35:1–19). *His uncle was a Rechabite who would not allow alcohol of any kind in the house.*

redeem the time Do not waste time. The origins of the phrase are biblical, being a quotation from Paul's letter to the Ephesians: "See then that ye walk circumspectly, not as fools, but as wise. Redeeming the time, because the days are evil" (Ephesians 5:15–16). "'Therefore,' urged the good man, his voice trembling with emotion, 'redeem the time, my unhappy brethren, which is yet left'" (Sir Walter Scott, *The Heart of Midlothian*, 1818).

red herring A false trail; something that is irrelevant to the issue under consideration. The allusion is to smoked herrings, which turn red and release a strong odor in the process of being dried, smoked, and salted. Trails made by smelly red herrings were traditionally created in order to train police dogs to follow the scent of a fugitive criminal, and one ruse used by fleeing felons was to trick the dogs by creating a false trail in this way. "On the other hand, the 'hero' label seemed a red herring, something the media themselves had dreamed up" (Ann Wroe, *Lives, Lies and the Iran-Contra Affair*, 1991).

red-letter day A special or auspicious day. The reference is to ecclesiastical calendars in which important festivals and saints' days were printed in red to mark them out from the rest, which were printed in black. "Finally the couple may be celebrating a birthday, a wedding anniversary or some other red-letter day" (M. Holborn and M. Haralambos, *Sociology: Themes and Perspectives*, 1991).

redneck An ill-educated, narrow-minded, reactionary bigot. The term was first applied to the impoverished rural poor of the Deep South with reference to the sunburnt necks of farm laborers toiling in the fields, but it has since been applied much more widely. "The Maggot, Ellen insisted, was an untoilet-trained redneck jerk whose only expertise was as a player of the most brutal and mindless sport to be devised since the lions took on the Christians" (Bernard Cornwell, *Crackdown*, 1990).

Red Sea *See* CROSSING OF THE RED SEA.

Regan *See* KING LEAR.

rehoboam (reeă<u>bō</u>ăm) A large wine bottle, equivalent to six standard-sized bottles. It takes its name from Rehoboam (10th century B.C.), a son of Solomon, the last king of the united Israel, and the first king of Judah (1 Kings 11:43). His name means "expansion of the people." *It has been many years since anyone ordered a rehoboam of claret at this particular restaurant.*

Reign of Terror A period when a government or other organization institutes a clampdown on dissent. The term alludes to a historical episode during the French Revolution when thousands of real or imagined enemies of the new French state were executed. Extending from April 1793 to July 1794, the Reign of Terror saw some 2,300 people sent to the guillotine in Paris alone on the orders of the Committee of Public Safety under the leadership of ROBESPIERRE. "They instigated a reign of terror in London's East End, controlling their manor with a ruthless disregard for others" (Stuart Cosgrove, *Hampden Babylon*, 1991).

Rembrandt (<u>rem</u>brant) Archetype of a great artist. The Dutch artist Rembrandt Harmenszoon van Rijn (1606–69) is ranked among the finest painters in the history of Western art, being acclaimed for his varied output of portraits, self-portraits, and landscapes. He handled light and shade with great inventiveness and dexterity, and his name is associated with the very greatest achievements in painted art. *I like some of his paintings, but let's face it, he's no Rembrandt.*

remember Pearl Harbor *See* PEARL HARBOR.

remember the Alamo (<u>a</u>lămō) A rallying cry, especially when faced by overwhelming odds. The allusion is to the siege by the Mexican army of the former Christian mission building called the Alamo in San Antonio in 1836 during the struggle for Texan independence from Mexico. Although the Alamo eventually fell and all of the 187 defenders (including DAVY CROCKETT and Jim Bowie) were killed, their resistance became a symbol of heroism in the face of a probable defeat. The slogan "remember the Alamo!" was taken up by the army of Texas when it successfully avenged itself upon the Mexicans at San Jacinto six weeks later. *The coach tried to restore some enthusiasm during the break, encouraging his squad to "Remember the Alamo!", but the final result was never in doubt.*

remnant *See* SAVING REMNANT.

Remus *See* ROMULUS AND REMUS.

Renaissance (renăsons) A resurgence of vitality in a particular field, originally the arts. From the French word meaning "rebirth," the term is primarily associated with the period of religious, cultural, and artistic development that took place in various European countries in the 14th, 15th, and 16th centuries, marking the end of the medieval era and the start of the modern age. The works of classical authors were rediscovered, laying the foundations of modern scholasticism and triggering a revival of interest in such fields as science, philosophy, and literature. "Deep well-springs of ideas were tapped and a new Renaissance set in motion by men who were unafraid to let their spirits roam in the new universe of science and invention" (Edward Chisnall, *Bell in the Tree: The Glasgow Story*, 1989).

Renaissance man (renăsons) A person who excels in not just one but several fields. The term harks back to the historical RENAISSANCE era, when courtiers throughout Europe sought to master a range of scholarly and other pursuits, from learning foreign languages and reading the classics to playing musical instruments and learning how to dance, ride, fence, and conduct a conversation. In modern usage, the term may be applied to anyone who demonstrates skill in more than one field, not necessarily confined to the arts and cultural pursuits. *Having demonstrated his abilities not only as a diplomat and writer but also as an artist and amateur opera singer on numerous occasions, his admirers commonly described him as a Renaissance man.*

render unto Caesar (seezer) Surrender to your masters the things that they are entitled to demand. The phrase appears in the Bible in Matthew 22:21 and Luke 20:25, where it is given as Christ's reply to the Pharisees' question as to whether it was lawful to pay tribute to Caesar (hoping to trick Jesus into a confession of open disloyalty to the emperor): "Then saith he unto them, Render therefore unto Caesar the things which are Caesar's; and unto God the things that are God's." The implication in Christ's reply is that there are some things that Caesar is not entitled to ask for and that his authority is limited. *When it comes to taxes, there is little alternative but to bite the bullet and render unto Caesar what is Caesar's.*

respecter of persons, no *See* NO RESPECTER OF PERSONS.

rest on one's laurels *See* LAURELS.

retreat from Moscow A costly, full-scale retreat in the face of overwhelming defeat. The allusion is to the retreat of NAPOLEON's invading army from Russia in 1812 when defeated by the combined onslaught of the Russian winter and the evasive tactics of Russian generals. Thousands of French soldiers died in the course of the retreat, Napoleon's costliest setback. History repeated itself in the latter stages of World War II, when Germany's invading armies were forced into retreat after being similarly beaten into submission by the Russian winter and by their inability to inflict a final crushing defeat on the Red Army. *This was a limited tactical withdrawal for strategic reasons, not a retreat from Moscow.*

retreat? Hell, no! We just got here! Rejection of a suggestion that the best plan might be to abandon an apparently lost cause. This is a quotation from World War I, and is usually attributed to a U.S. army officer called Lloyd S. William as his response when advised by retreating French soldiers to retire, shortly after arriving on the western front. It has since been repeated in many other contexts, not necessarily military. *You say we should give up this campaign before it's even started. Retreat? Hell, no! We just got here!*

Revere, Paul *See* PAUL REVERE.

rhadamanthine (radămanthin, radămanthīn) Stern and incorruptible in judgment. In Greek mythology Rhadamanthus was the son of Zeus and Europa and brother of King Minos of Crete. Having established his reputation as a wise and incorruptible judge in life, he became one of the judges of the dead in the underworld, alongside Minos and Aeacus. "He accordingly addressed a carefully considered epistle to Sue, and, knowing her emotional temperament, threw a Rhadamanthine strictness into the lines here and there, carefully hiding his heterodox feelings, not to frighten her" (Thomas Hardy, *Jude the Obscure,* 1896).

rhesus factor (reesăs) Protein found in the red blood cells of most people. The rhesus factor, or ***Rh factor,*** was named after the rhesus monkey, a macaque from southern Asia that is widely used in medical research and in whose blood this protein was first discovered. The monkey in turn was named after Rhesus, king of Thrace and an ally of Troy, who according to Greek myth was killed by Odysseus and Diomedes as they stole his horses. Legend had it that if the horses fed on the grass of the Trojan plain and drank from the Xanthus River, Troy would never fall. *The presence of the rhesus factor in a person's blood is not normally a problem but can cause a hemolytic reaction, especially during pregnancy or following a blood transfusion that lacks this agglutinogen.*

Rhett Butler *See* GONE WITH THE WIND.

rich man enter heaven *See* CAMEL: GO THROUGH AN EYE OF A NEEDLE.

Richter scale (rikter) A measure of the magnitude of something. The Richter scale was devised in 1935 by the U.S. seismologist Charles Richter (1900–85) to measure the severity of earthquakes, but the term has since been applied metaphorically to events in many other contexts. Richter himself disapproved of his name being used for his scale, as it ignored the contribution made in its development by his colleague Beno Gutenberg (1889–1960): he would have preferred it to be called the "magnitude scale." *His sister was average-looking, but her scantily-clad best friend hit nine on the Richter scale.*

riddle of the Sphinx (sfinks) The legendary riddle posed by the Sphinx or any particularly challenging riddle, puzzle, or problem. According to Greek mythology the Sphinx prevented anyone from entering the city of Thebes unless he could solve the riddle What creature goes on four legs in the morning, two legs at noon, and three in the evening? Those who got the answer wrong suffered instant death, but if someone answered correctly, the Sphinx's power would be destroyed. Oedipus correctly identified the answer as "man," because he crawls as a child, walks as an adult, and proceeds with the aid of a staff in old age. Oedipus thus saved the city and won the hand of Queen Jocasta, at the time ignorant of the fact that she was his mother (see OEDIPUS COMPLEX). "The Interviewer had attempted the riddle of the Sphinx, and had failed to get the first hint of its solution" (Oliver Wendell Holmes, *A Moral Antipathy,* 1885).

riddle wrapped in a mystery inside an enigma An impenetrable mystery. This is a quotation from a speech by British statesman Winston Churchill (1874–1965) broadcast on October 1, 1939, referring specifically to the unknowable nature of Russian policy in the early stages of World War II. The term has continued to be applied to Russia ever since, although it has also been used in many other contexts. *Why your father ever married your mother remains a riddle wrapped in a mystery inside an enigma.*

ride off into the sunset To leave the scene; to depart. The allusion is to Western movies of the 1930s and 1940s, which not infrequently ended with just such an image of the hero riding away into a glorious sunset. *The news is that the old man has ridden off into the sunset for the last time.*

ride shotgun To act as guard over something as is being taken from one place to another. The allusion is to the days when people and valuables being carried in stagecoaches were protected from any threat by an armed guard, who typically occupied the seat next to the coachman. In modern usage, the term is sometimes applied to any person who sits next to the driver of a vehicle. *The army has provided men to ride shotgun with UN convoys bringing humanitarian aid to the refugee camps on the border.*

right hand offend thee *See* IF THY RIGHT EYE OFFEND THEE.

right stuff, the Courage; reliability; toughness. This was originally army slang, dating from at least the 1930s and possibly ultimately of 19th-century origin, but it became more widely familiar after it appeared as the title of a 1979 book by U.S. writer Tom Wolfe (b. 1931) about the first U.S. astronauts. "If you all get on well and are prepared to make the same sacrifices to succeed, you might just be 'the right stuff' " (Norton York, *The Rock File*, 1991).

Riley, life of *See* LIFE OF RILEY.

Ripper *See* JACK THE RIPPER.

Rip Van Winkle (winkăl) Archetype of a person who is evidently completely out of touch with the surrounding world or contemporary events. The allusion is to a story by U.S. writer Washington Irving (1783–1859), first published in *The Sketch Book* (1819–20). Irving's Rip Van Winkle is the henpecked husband of a nagging wife, who goes to sleep for 20 years after sharing a drink with gnomes in the Catskill Mountains. When he wakes up, having slept right through the death of his wife and the fighting of the American Revolution, he is astonished to find the world greatly changed. "In 1958 Harold Macmillan called him Rip Van Winkle, because he talked about the 'Concert of

Europe' and 'seemed not to have quite realized what had happened to the world since the end of the Second War'" (Andrew Shennan, *De Gaulle*, 1993).

rise from the ashes *See* PHOENIX.

rise, take up thy bed, and walk Get out about your business (usually said after the removal of some impediment). The phrase is a quotation from John 5:1–9, which relates the story of the crippled man at the Pool of Bethesda who was cured and "made whole" by Jesus with these same words. (See also Mark 2:9.) *The doctor took one look at the malingerer, snorted and ordered him to rise, take up his bed, and walk.*

river, sell down the *See* SELL DOWN THE RIVER.

river, send up the *See* SEND UP THE RIVER.

rivers of Babylon *See* BY THE RIVERS OF BABYLON.

road less traveled, the A path that is different from that chosen by the majority of people. The phrase is a quotation from the poem "The Road Not Taken" by the U.S. poet Robert Frost (1874–1963), in which the author describes choosing between two roads in the woods: "Two roads diverged in a wood, and I—/ I took the one less traveled by, / And that has made all the difference." The phrase is often quoted in contemplation of the choices individuals make when deciding the future course of their lives. "Understanding recovery is itself a progressive and unending process that brings immeasurable rewards to all who share 'the road less travelled'" (Robert Lefever, *How to Combat Alcoholism and Addiction*, 1988).

roads lead to Rome, all *See* ALL ROADS LEAD TO ROME.

road to Damascus (dămaskăs) A process of revelation resulting in a fundamental change of viewpoint or opinion (typically the result of a sudden, even miraculous insight). The allusion is to the episode in the New Testament (recounted in Acts 9:1–19, 22:1–21, and 26:1–23), in which Saul of Tarsus has a vision of the risen Christ while on his way to Damascus to persecute Christians there. Saul immediately declares himself a Christian and, as Paul, in due course becomes one of the apostles and a great Christian missionary. A ***road-to-Damascus experience*** is a sudden, dramatic revelation resulting in a fundamental change of view or way of life. "You don't reach Downing Street by pretending you've travelled the road to Damascus when you haven't even left home" (*Guardian*, October 14, 1989).

roar like a bull of Bashan *See* BULL OF BASHAN.

robbed, we wuz *See* WE WUZ ROBBED.

Robben Island (robăn) A prison in which political prisoners are confined for long periods. Robben Island off the coast of South Africa was the prison in which Nelson Mandela and other black activists were imprisoned for many years under the country's former apartheid regime. The release of Mandela in 1990, after 27 years, was seen as a key moment in the ending of the apartheid era. *The authorities did not want Guantánamo Bay to get the reputation of another Robben Island, but perhaps this was inevitable.*

robber baron An unscrupulous business tycoon. The name was first applied to the speculative businessmen who amassed vast fortunes in various capitalist enterprises in the second half of the 19th century by Matthew Josephson in his book *The Robber Barons: The Great American Capitalists 1861–1901* (1934). These tycoons acquired notorious reputations for their grasping ways and they remain today archetypal examples of the greedy capitalist making his fortune off the backs of his toiling employees. *In those days the very presidency of the United States remained largely in the gift of America's robber barons.*

Robert the Bruce (broos) A person who perseveres after initial failure. The allusion is to the tale of Robert I (1274–1329), king of Scotland, who at one point early in his reign is said to have gone into hiding from his English enemies on the island of Rathlin. There he noticed a spider struggling to fix its web to a beam in the ceiling; after six failed attempts, the spider finally succeeded, inspiring Bruce himself to make renewed efforts to rally his followers and lead them to victory at the Battle of Bannockburn in 1314. *Like Robert the Bruce, he kept on trying until he eventually passed the examination.*

Robespierre (rōbzpyair) A tyrannical despot. Maximilian Marie Isidore de Robespierre (1758–94) emerged as one of the radical leaders of the French Revolution that swept away the French aristocracy in 1789. It was Robespierre who instituted the bloody REIGN OF TERROR that led to the deaths of thousands of people on the guillotine including, after his rivals became jealous of his growing power, Robespierre himself. *The mob had created its own Robespierre, who had no hesitation in engineering the arrest and execution of anyone who opposed his policies. See also* JACOBIN.

Robin *See* BATMAN AND ROBIN.

Robin Goodfellow *See* PUCK.

Robin Hood A person who takes from the rich and gives to the poor. Robin Hood was an English folk hero whose historical existence, allegedly during the reign of King John (1167–1216), has been a subject of heated discussion for centuries. He is variously claimed to have been a dispossessed nobleman who lived in Yorkshire or in ***Sherwood Forest*** near Nottingham and there to have gathered round him a ***band of merry men***—including FRIAR TUCK and ***Little John***—with whom he waylaid wealthy men traveling through the forest, later sharing among the poor any wealth they had seized. Numerous tales of his life and death, and his love for the beautiful ***Maid Marian***, were recorded in ballads and poems, and various locations in northeast England bear his name. "Backless Hill, to the north of the loch, was the 18th-century lair of a Caithness 'Robin Hood' said to have robbed the rich and given to the poor" (Bruce Sandison, *Tales of the Loch*, 1990). *See also* SHERIFF OF NOTTINGHAM.

Robinson, Heath *See* HEATH ROBINSON.

Robinson Crusoe (robinsăn kroosō) A person who lives in either voluntary or enforced isolation, especially on a desert island or in some other remote spot. Robinson Crusoe is the eponymous central character, a castaway on a remote desert island, in the classic best-selling novel *The Life and Strange Adventures of Robinson Crusoe* (1719) by Daniel Defoe (1660–1731). Defoe based his famous character upon a real person, Alexander Selkirk (1676–1721), who was marooned on the island of Más a Tierra in the South Pacific after falling foul of his shipmates, though only for four years compared to the 24 endured by the fictional Crusoe.

"From time to time, generally during long, cold winter months, suffering from wander-lust, I descend upon my local library like some latter-day Robinson Crusoe, anxious to return to desert island life" (Bruce Sandison, *Tales of the Loch*, 1990). *See also* MAN FRIDAY.

Rochester, Mr. *See* MR. ROCHESTER.

Rockefeller (rokăfeler) A fabulously rich tycoon. John D. Rockefeller (1839–1937) made his fortune from oil and became one of the richest men in the world. He used his wealth to endow various worthy causes, as did other members of the family who succeeded to the family fortune in subsequent years. *What we need is a Rockefeller to give us a million or two to get the project started.*

Rockwell, Norman *See* NORMAN ROCKWELL.

rococo (răkōkō) Decorated in a flamboyant, overblown style. The rococo style of architecture and design was perfected in France during the reign of Louis XV (1715–74) and was subsequently taken up by architects and artists throughout Europe. In many respects it was essentially an embellishment of the earlier BAROQUE style. In modern usage, the term is sometimes applied metaphorically to describe things that are grandly convoluted or exaggerated in some way. "Then in June the honours scandal passed from the baroque to the rococo stage" (Roy Jenkins, *Baldwin*, 1988).

Rogers, Buck *See* BUCK ROGERS.

Rogers, Ginger *See* FRED ASTAIRE.

Rogers, Roy *See* ROY ROGERS.

Roland (rōlănd) A hero of exemplary virtue and courage. Roland and Oliver were two of the 12 paladins who served at the court of the emperor CHARLEMAGNE. Roland was Charlemagne's nephew and became Oliver's inseparable friend after the two fought an evenly matched duel that lasted for five consecutive days with each matching the other's blow, hence the saying ***a Roland for an Oliver*** for "tit for tat" or "a blow for a blow." The names of ***Roland and Oliver*** as a combination are still sometimes evoked as archetypes of perfect friends. Both knights died celebrated deaths in battle after being betrayed to the Saracens at Roncesvalles in Spain in 778, a last stand immortalized in the 11th-century French epic poem *La Chanson de Roland.* Although faced with vastly superior odds, Roland, who was also known as "the Christian Theseus" and "the Achilles of the West," stoutly refused to blow his horn Olivant to summon help from Charlemagne until it was almost too late. When he did finally blow the horn, Ganelon persuaded Charlemagne that Roland was merely hunting deer, and the warriors' fate was sealed. A variation of the legend claims that Roland survived the battle but died some time later of starvation or thirst while trying to cross the Pyrenees; hence, if a person is doomed to ***die like Roland,*** he or she faces a similar end. *His chivalrous behavior on this occasion earned him the reputation of a latter-day Roland, although those who knew him better were inclined to scoff at this. See also* CHILDE ROLAND TO THE DARK TOWER CAME; ROUNCEVAL.

Rolls-Royce Of the highest quality; the best in its field. The Rolls-Royce company, founded in the United Kingdom in 1906 by Charles Stuart Rolls (1877–1910) and Frederick Henry Royce (1863–1933), became celebrated for its expensive, luxurious, and well-made vehicles, which became a favorite choice of the rich and famous all over the world. *This is the Rolls-Royce of fountain pens.*

Roman holiday A public performance that features extravagant acts of barbarity and debauchery. The entertainments that took place in the arenas of ancient Rome were notorious for their cruelty, which included gladiatorial combats to the death and the throwing of captives to wild animals. Such bloodthirsty extravaganzas were prohibited by Emperor Constantine I in A.D. 325 but were soon revived and carried on until 405. "For I have written about the Coliseum, and the gladiators, the martyrs, and the lions, and yet have never once used the phrase 'butchered to make a Roman holiday.' I am the only free white man of mature age, who has accomplished this since Byron originated the expression" (Mark Twain, *The Innocents Abroad,* 1869).

Rome *See* ALL ROADS LEAD TO ROME; FIDDLE WHILE ROME BURNS; ROMULUS AND REMUS; WHEN IN ROME, DO AS THE ROMANS DO.

Romeo and Juliet (rōmeeō, jooleeet) Archetypal pair of tragic lovers. William Shakespeare's tragedy *Romeo and Juliet* (1594) told the story of two young lovers of Verona, whose love was doomed from the outset by the enmity between their warring families. The play ends with the death of both lovers among various others, including Romeo's best friend ***Mercutio***. Shakespeare based his tale on a poem by Arthur Brooke entitled *The Tragicall History of Romeo and Juliet* (1562), which itself drew ultimately upon an earlier Italian version by Luigi da Porto, written in 1535. Somewhat perversely, a man who has the reputation of being a slick womanizer is often dubbed a ***Romeo***. *This was no Romeo and Juliet love story, but a sordid tale of lust and betrayal. See also* PLAGUE ON BOTH YOUR HOUSES, A.

Romulus and Remus (romyălăs, reemăs) The legendary founders of Rome, whose names are still frequently invoked in references to the city. Romulus and Remus were variously identified as the twin sons of Mars and Rhea Silvia or of Aeneas' daughter Ilia. Because Rhea Silvia was a vestal virgin, obliged to maintain her virginity on pain of death, the twins seemed doomed but were saved by the gods and suckled by a she-wolf. Romulus killed Remus during an argument over where they should site their city and in due course became the first king of Rome. *The company the two brothers built around their initial idea has become one of the biggest conglomerates in the world, and they are still honored as the Romulus and Remus upon whom this huge empire was constructed.*

Roncesvalles *See* ROLAND; ROUNCEVAL.

room at the inn, no *See* NO ROOM AT THE INN.

room of one's own, a A private place or a retreat from the world. The phrase was selected by the British novelist Virginia Woolf for the title of a 1929 essay examining contemporary prejudices against women. *To survive the stresses of modern urban life it is more important than ever to have a room of one's own in which to escape the constant pressure.*

Room 101 A place in which people are brought face to face with what they fear most as a form of torture. The allusion is to the George Orwell novel *Nineteen Eighty-Four* (1949), in which Room 101 is the room in which Winston Smith is tormented by his fear of rats. The story goes that the author had undergone many tedious discussions in a Room 101 at London's Broadcasting House as an employee of the BBC, hence his choice of the number for his own infamous room. *Bearing in mind the team's dismal run of results so far this season, their stadium has become a Room 101 for their fans. See also* BIG BROTHER.

room to swing a cat Adequate space. The allusion is to nautical jargon and the use of the cat o' nine tails (a whip with nine lashes) to punish sailors who were guilty of breaking naval rules. Space between decks on sailing ships was obviously restricted, and a certain amount of room was needed to administer the punishment effectively. The phrase is commonly used in the negative to describe a cramped space, as in "no room to swing a cat." *They called it a spare bedroom but there wasn't room to swing a cat.*

root of all evil *See* MONEY IS THE ROOT OF ALL EVIL.

Rosa Parks (rōză) A committed campaigner against racism. Rosa Parks (1913–2005) was a black woman who, on December 1, 1956, in Montgomery, Alabama, defied the state's race laws by refusing to vacate the seat she had taken in the white-only section of a bus, thus triggering the Montgomery bus boycott and rallying opposition to racial segregation. For her act of defiance, Rosa Parks came to be considered the mother of the modern civil rights movement. *The old woman looked set to become South Africa's Rosa Parks.*

Roscius (roshăs) An outstanding actor. This epithet alludes to Quintus Roscius Gallus (c. 126–62 B.C.), who was a celebrated comic actor on the Roman stage and a friend of Cicero. Likewise, the adjective ***Roscian*** describes a theatrical performance of great skill. Among later performers compared with Roscius were Shakespeare's contemporary Richard Burbage (c. 1567–1619), who was described as "another Roscius"; Thomas Betterton (1635–1710), who was known as the "British Roscius"; and William Betty (1791–1874), who was called the "Young Roscius." "The celebrated provincial amateur of Roscian renown" (Charles Dickens, *Great Expectations,* 1860).

Rosebud Something that serves to remind a person vividly of their youth, or of their unrealized dreams. The allusion is to the classic 1941 movie *CITIZEN KANE*, in which "Rosebud" is the mysterious final utterance of the dying tycoon, played by Orson Welles. Everyone wonders what it could have meant, and it is only the final shot of a child's sled labeled "Rosebud" that reveals that the dead man was thinking back to his early childhood. *This child's toy was his Rosebud, the key to a thousand distant happy memories.*

rose of Sharon (sharăn) An unidentified flower whose beauty is variously taken to represent love or loveliness, especially as a description of Jesus Christ. The image of the rose of Sharon occurs in the biblical Song of Solomon 2:1–2, in which it is put into the mouth of the bride: "I am the rose of Sharon, and the lily of the valleys." The flower in question has been tentatively identified as the autumn crocus, asphodel, or narcissus, which flourished on the plain of Sharon, a fertile area on the coast of ancient Palestine. " 'The Rose of Sharon and the Lily of the Valley,'—answered the Prior, in a sort of snuffling tone; 'but your Grace must remember she is still but a Jewess' " (Sir Walter Scott, *Ivanhoe,* 1819).

Rosetta stone (rōzetă) The key to unraveling a code or mystery of some kind. The Rosetta Stone is a slab of basalt that was unearthed in Egypt during Napoleon's military campaign in the country in 1799. Because it bore the same script in both Greek and hieroglyphics, the French scholar Jean François Champillon (1790–1832) was able (after many years' work) to translate the hitherto unknown hieroglyphic characters. The stone itself is now preserved in the British Museum. "Perhaps we shall be lucky and discover another 'dictionary' like the Rosetta Stone" (John Grant, *The Great Unsolved Mysteries of Science*, 1990).

Rosinante *See* DON QUIXOTE.

Rose Without a Thorn An epithet of the Virgin Mary. The name alludes to the fact that according to Catholic tradition Mary is deemed to be without the taint of Original Sin, just as the rose lacked thorns when it first grew in Paradise; it acquired its thorns (sins) when planted on Earth after the expulsion of Adam and Eve from the Garden of Eden, thus coming to represent the moral imperfections of the human race. *To the other villagers she was a perfect example of innocence and virtue, a Rose Without a Thorn.*

Rothschild (rothschīld) A fabulously wealthy person. The fortune of the Rothschild banking family was founded during the Napoleonic Wars by Meyer Amschel Rothschild (1743–1812) and was subsequently substantially consolidated by his sons and their successors. Over the years the family has used some of its vast wealth to benefit a range of Jewish and non-Jewish causes. *Unfortunately, like many third world countries, there are no native Rothschilds to whom to make appeals for additional local finance.*

rounceval (rownsival) Very large or strong. Also spelled ***rouncival,*** the word is probably an anglicization of Roncesvalles, in Spain, where ROLAND and his colleagues fell in their final battle. Years later various large bones found at the site were rumored to belong to these great heroes. Large marrowfat peas are sometimes called ***rounceval peas,*** and substantially built women may sometimes be dubbed ***rouncevals.*** *The abbess was of such imposing proportions that Rounceval, nay, Gargantuan, would not have been misplaced.*

round table A meeting at which all attending are considered equal, with no one having precedence over the others. The allusion is to the fabled circular table that KING ARTHUR provided for his knights, the so-called ***knights of the Round Table***: because of its shape no one could sit at its head and thus claim seniority over all present. A round table (allegedly made by the wizard MERLIN) kept on permanent display inside Castle Hall in the English city of Winchester was formerly claimed to be that of King Arthur, but has since been proved to have been made in the 13th century, probably on the orders of King Edward I, who wished to link his kingship with that of the legendary Arthur (Henry VIII later had it repainted to show it off to Francis I of France). *The two leaders first met at a round table organized to bring together many of the most influential political figures of the developed world. See also* FIRST AMONG EQUALS; GALAHAD.

round up the usual suspects To make a show of investigating a problem or wrongdoing without any real intention of finding out who or what is actually to blame. The phrase is a quotation from the 1942 Humphrey Bogart movie *Casablanca*, in which it is delivered by slippery French policeman Captain Reynaud (played by Claude Rains), making it plain to Bogart's Rick that there will be no thorough police investigation into who (actually

Rick himself) shot the Nazi officer Major Strasser. The phrase is also used in more general contexts, with "the usual suspects" referring to things (or people) that are always found in a particular situation, items that are always mentioned when a particular subject comes up, and so on. "Excise duties are taxes on specific home-produced or imported goods, with 'cigarettes, booze and petrol' being the usual suspects to be rounded up on each Budget day" (Philip Jones and John Cullis, *Public Finance and Public Choice*, 1992).

Roy Rogers Archetype of a wholesome cowboy hero. Roy Rogers (1912–98) was an actor and country-and-western singer who starred in a series of films and in his own television Western series, *The Roy Rogers Show* (1955–57). Aided by Dale Evans and mounted on a palomino horse called ***Trigger***, he maintained law and order in between singing songs about the Old West. *He looked like Roy Rogers in his check shirt and big white hat.*

Rubenesque (roobănesk) Describing a woman who is curvaceous, voluptuous, or generously fleshed. The allusion is the somewhat corpulent women who featured in substantial numbers in the paintings of the Flemish artist Peter Paul Rubens (1577–1640). *The first woman he was introduced to at the party was a Rubenesque matriarch with bright red hair.*

Rubicon *See* CROSS THE RUBICON.

ruby slippers *See* WICKED WITCH OF THE WEST.

Rudolph Nureyev *See* NUREYEV.

Rudolph Valentino *See* VALENTINO.

rule, golden *See* GOLDEN RULE.

rule with a rod of iron To rule harshly; to exercise authority with severity. The expression comes from the Bible, occurring in Revelation 2:27, 12:5, and 19:15 and in Psalm 2:9. "Emmeline took after her father; she was big and dark and homely, and she was the most domineering creature that ever stepped on shoe leather. She simply ruled poor Prissy with a rod of iron" (Lucy Maud Montgomery, *Chronicles of Avonlea,* 1912).

Rumpelstiltskin (rumpălstiltskin) A person who easily flies into a temper, especially one of relatively small stature. The allusion is to a story collected in GRIMM'S FAIRY TALES about a malevolent gnome who challenges a princess to guess his name in order to save her firstborn child from him. When she successfully finds out what his name is, the little man flies into a rage and stamps his foot through the floor; when he tries to pull it free he only succeeds in tearing himself apart. *No one liked the boss, a vindictive little man whose nickname was Rumpelstiltskin.*

run the gauntlet To risk or undergo a demanding ordeal or trial. In this phrase the word "gauntlet" comes from the Swedish *gatlopp*, meaning "passageway," and relates to a punishment commonly inflicted upon soldiers and sailors at the time of the Thirty Years' War (1618–48). It involved guilty men being forced to run between two files of men who beat them with rope ends. "However, such trust is not shown towards relatives and friends who assist suffering people in this way: they must run the gauntlet of a legal process which accords no formal recognition to the circumstances under which they killed" (Andrew Ashworth, *Principles of Criminal Law*, 1991).

Runyonesque (runyonesk) After the style of journalist and short-story writer Alfred Damon Runyon (1884–1946). Runyon's stories vividly brought to life the street life of New York City in the first half of the 20th century, and were characterized by his colorful use of authentic street slang, which itself became known as "Runyonesque." *The dockworkers had their own Runyonesque words for just about everything, and it took some time to work out what they were saying.*

Ruritania (rooritayneeă) A fictitious mid-European country, especially one in which there is much hollow pageantry. Ruritania was the setting for the romantic adventure novels *The Prisoner of Zenda* (1894) and *Rupert of Hentzau* (1898) by the British novelist Anthony Hope (1863–1933). "On the face of it, in asserting that Ruritania does not exist we seem to be asserting something about Ruritania" (Edo Pivcevic, *The Concept of Reality*, 1986).

Russian roulette A dangerous activity in which those participating take risks in turn, or in which death is a random possibility. The allusion is to the "game" in which a gun loaded with a single bullet is passed from one person to another, each pointing it at his own head and pulling the trigger until the bullet is actually fired. This hazardous pastime was apparently popular among officers at the court of the czar in prerevolutionary Russia. "Contrary to popular belief, it was not merely by chance, or even more crudely, by a game of Russian Roulette, that our ancestors singled out the edible and medicinal plants from those that were poisonous" (Christine Wildwood, *Aromatherapy Massage with Essential Oils*, 1992).

Ruth (rooth) The archetype of a devoted, loyal woman. A Moabite widow, Ruth promised never to desert her mother-in-law: "Intreat me not to leave thee, or to return from following after thee: for whither thou goest, I will go; and where thou lodgest, I will lodge: thy people shall be my people, and thy God my God" (Ruth 1:16). Her kindness to her mother-in-law impressed the wealthy Boaz, and in due course he and Ruth were married and Ruth subsequently appeared in the genealogy of Matthew 1:5 as the great-grandmother of King David. "Perhaps the selfsame song that found a path / Through the sad heart of Ruth, when, sick for home, / She stood in tears amid the alien corn" (John Keats, "Ode to a Nightingale," 1819). *See also* AMID THE ALIEN CORN; WHITHER THOU GOEST, I WILL GO.

S

Sabbath A period of rest. The allusion is to the Jewish Sabbath, which is traditionally reserved for religious worship rather than work (Exodus 20:8–11 and Deuteronomy 5:12–15). According to the book of Genesis (2:2), God rested from creating the Earth on the seventh day, dictating that it become a day of rest and worship for the faithful. The word comes from the Hebrew *shabbath* (meaning "rest"). A ***Sabbath day's journey*** (Acts 1:12) is a short and easy journey, an allusion to the Law of Moses, which forbade Jews to travel any further than the distance between the Ark of the Covenant and the edge of their camp (about two-thirds of a mile). "Not even Lizzie Eustace, on behalf of her cousin Frank, would have dared to disturb Mr. Gowran with considerations respecting a pony on the Sabbath" (Anthony Trollope, *The Eustace Diamonds,* 1873).

Sabine women *See* RAPE OF THE SABINE WOMEN.

sackcloth and ashes A public display of grief or remorse. The tradition of donning clothing made of sackcloth and scattering ashes over one's head as a sign of mourning or repentance dates back at least to biblical times, as described in the book of Esther: "And in every province, whithersoever the king's commandment and his decree came, there was great mourning among the Jews, and fasting, and weeping, and wailing; and many lay in sackcloth and ashes" (Esther 4:3). (See also Esther 4:1, Jonah 3:6, Matthew 11:21, and Luke 11:13.) "She felt that she might yet recover her lost ground, that she might yet hurl Mr. Slope down to the dust from which she had picked him and force her sinning lord to sue for pardon in sackcloth and ashes" (Anthony Trollope, *Barchester Towers,* 1857).

sacred cow Something that is considered above criticism and immune from interference. The allusion is to the sacred cows of Hinduism, which are traditionally associated with certain deities and believed to house the souls of the dead. Even today they are allowed to wander freely in the streets of India without being molested. The term has been applied more generally since the early 20th century. *This administration's foreign policy is a sacred cow as far as the president is concerned.*

sacrificial lamb Someone or something sacrificed to appease an enemy and thus avert a greater disaster. The allusion is to the Old Testament practice of sacrificing lambs and other animals at the altar in order to give thanks to God, obtain atonement and forgiveness, and restore a right relationship between the people and God (see, for example, Genesis 8:20, Exodus 29:38–41, and

Leviticus 4:1–3). "A dreadful performance could see Mr. Byers offered up as a sacrificial lamb" (*Guardian,* February 20, 2002).

Sadducee (sajăsee, sadyăsee) A person who stubbornly refuses to believe a commonly accepted truth. The allusion is to the Sadducee sect of the time of Christ who accepted the authority only of the written Law and rejected a belief in the Resurrection and angels and demons. Supposedly named after the high priest Sadoq, who was reputed to have founded the sect, they, like the Pharisees, were hostile toward Jesus Christ and his teachings (Matthew 22:23–33, Mark 12:18–27, and Luke 20:27–38). They lost influence after the fall of Jerusalem in A.D. 70. "I was quite drawn out to speak to him; I hardly know how, for I had always thought of him as a worldly Sadducee. But his countenance is as pleasant as the morning sunshine" (George Eliot, *Adam Bede,* 1859).

sadism (saydizăm) The infliction of pain or suffering on another for the sake of one's own pleasure (often specifically sexual gratification). The origin of the term lies in the scandalous reputation of Comte Donatien Alphonse François, marquis de Sade (1740–1814), a French writer and soldier whose sexual exploits and pornographic writings were the source of much controversy during and after his own lifetime. He was imprisoned on several occasions for sexual crimes and in all spent some 30 years behind bars. "Then one day the mask had slipped, and beneath the apparent loving concern she had glimpsed spite and sadism" (Dana James, *Bay of Rainbows*, 1993).

Saint Helena (hăleenă) A place of exile, especially one from which there is no possibility of return. The tiny island of Saint Helena in the South Atlantic was the place of exile chosen for the French emperor NAPOLEON after his final defeat at WATERLOO in 1815. Napoleon remained there until his death in 1821—according to some he died as the result of arsenic poisoning (perhaps from the arsenic in the wallpaper at Longwood, the house he occupied), although a more recent suggestion is that he probably died of stomach cancer. Napoleon was not the only person to be incarcerated on the remote island: in 1890 the son of the Zulu chief Cetshwayo began a seven-year term there, following which the island was used by the British to accommodate 5,000 Boer prisoners during the Boer War. *His wife liked the peace and quiet of the island, but to him it was a Saint Helena far removed from the urban surroundings he loved. See also* ELBA.

Saint Mary Mead *See* MISS MARPLES.

Saint Stephen's loaves Rocks. The reference is to the stoning to death of Saint Stephen, the first Christian martyr, who died C. A.D. 35 after being accused of blasphemy (as described in Acts 6:1–8:2). By the same token to be ***fed with Saint Stephen's bread*** is a euphemism for being stoned to death. *At this unwelcome news she feared the mob would start to toss Saint Stephen's loaves at her, in time-honored fashion.*

Saint Trinian's (trineeănz) Archetype of an old-fashioned girls' school, especially a badly-run one where discipline has gone to pieces and the ill-dressed pupils do as they please. The allusion is to the notorious fictional girls' school created by the British cartoonist Ronald Searle (b. 1920) and immortalized not only in his cartoons and books but also in various movies, the first of which was *The Belles of Saint Trinian's* (1954). Searle got the name of his famous school from the real Saint

Trinnean's girls' school in Edinburgh, having become friends with two of the pupils there. He drew his first Saint Trinian's cartoon to tease them; the second followed in very different circumstances, while he was a Japanese prisoner-of-war during World War II and forced to work on the infamous "Death Railway" from Siam to Burma. *Her mother went to a very strict Catholic school where beatings were a daily feature of life, not a bit like Saint Trinian's.*

Saint Valentine's Day massacre (valăntīnz) An act of mass murder, especially one with gangland associations, or some other ruthless act of extermination or purging. The original Saint Valentine's Day massacre took place on Saint Valentine's Day (February 14), 1929, in a garage on North Clark Street, Chicago. Seven members of George "Bugsy" Moran's North Side gang were put up against a wall and machine-gunned to death by men loyal to the notorious Chicago mobster AL CAPONE. Moran happened to be late arriving at the garage and escaped being murdered, but his power in the city was broken. Capone had a cast-iron alibi on the day of the killings, but the slaughter created such a public outcry that the authorities redoubled efforts to ensnare Capone and eventually had the satisfaction of seeing him imprisoned for tax evasion. *The management decided to replace at least half their junior staff in a Saint Valentine's Day massacre.*

Salamis (salămis) Archetype of a great naval victory. The Battle of Salamis took place between the Greek and Persian fleets in 480 B.C. in the waters of the Saronic Gulf, between the island of Salamis and the Greek mainland. The Greeks achieved a famous victory over their Persian enemies, the whole battle being witnessed by the Persian leader Xerxes from Mount Aegaleos. *The staff had planned this Salamis for months, hoping to lure the enemy's chief vessels away from the relative safety of the coastal waters.*

salary (salăree) A set payment received for employment. The word comes ultimately from the Latin *sal* (meaning "salt") and alludes to the ancient practice of paying Roman soldiers stationed inland (away from the sea, the usual source of salt in the ancient world) a *salarium* with which to purchase salt, at that time a valuable commodity. The connection with salt had been forgotten by medieval times, but the word remained current. Related phrases include ***worth one's salt*** (meaning "worth the salary one is paid"). "Her husband was a retired tradesman, who had realized a very comfortable fortune; but could not be prevailed upon to give a greater salary than twenty-five pounds to the instructress of his children" (Anne Brontë, *Agnes Grey,* 1845).

Salem (saylăm) An outbreak of hysteria leading to the mass trial of suspects, regardless of any evidence available. The allusion is to the infamous witchcraft trials that took place in New England in 1692, arising from accusations of witchcraft leveled at various local people by two young girls living in Salem, Massachusetts. Dozens of suspects were arrested and 19 people were convicted and hanged before the hysteria (which provided the basis of Arthur Miller's 1953 play *The Crucible*) finally died down. The resulting backlash led to witchcraft trials being ended once and for all in New England and elsewhere. *Recent terrorist outrages have created a Salem-like atmosphere in which any suspicious behavior may provoke instant arrest and detention.*

salmanazar (salmănazăr) A large wine bottle, equivalent to 12 standard bottles. It is named after eighth-century B.C. Assyrian king Shalmaneser V, who appears in the Bible (2 Kings 17:3). *The company stopped providing salmanazars for the hotels of New York several decades ago.*

Salome (sălōmee, salōmay) A seductive, deceitful temptress. The allusion is to the biblical Salome, the stepdaughter of Herod Antipas, who (at the prompting of her mother) demanded the head of JOHN THE BAPTIST; she had been promised whatever she wanted in payment for her dancing before her stepfather (Matthew 14:1–12 and Mark 6:16–29). *This Salome, in a figure-hugging red gown and long black gloves, advanced slowly toward their table with a predatory look in her half-closed eyes.*

salt of the earth A person or group of people admired for their sterling qualities. The phrase comes from Christ's Sermon on the Mount, as related in Matthew 5:13: "Ye are the salt of the earth: but if the salt have lost its savour, wherewith shall it be salted? It is thenceforth good for nothing, but to be cast out, and to be trodden under foot of men." The reference is to the use of salt as a preservative, preventing food from going rotten. "Retired sea-captains, in easy circumstances, who talked of farming as sea-captains are wont; an erect, respectable, and trustworthy looking man, in his wrapper, some of the salt of the earth, who had formerly been the salt of the sea" (Henry David Thoreau, *Cape Cod,* 1865).

Sam, Uncle *See* UNCLE SAM.

Samaritan *See* GOOD SAMARITAN.

Samian letter (saymeeăn) The letter *y*. The allusion is to Pythagoras, who was born on Samos in the sixth century B.C. and who used the Greek upsilon (equivalent to the modern *y*) as a symbol of the divergence between vice and virtue. Pythagoras himself is sometimes referred to as the ***Samian sage.*** "When reason doubtful like the Samian letter, / Points him two ways, the narrower the better" (Alexander Pope, *The Dunciad,* 1728).

Samson (samsăn) A person of exceptional physical strength. The allusion is to the biblical Samson, a judge of Israel, who was renowned for his great strength. His feats included tearing a lion apart with his bare hands, catching 300 foxes, and knocking down 1,000 men with the jawbone of a donkey (as related in Judges 13–16). He was brought low, however, by the wiles of DELILAH, who cut off the long hair on which his strength depended and had his eyes gouged out. Once his hair grew back, however, his strength returned. When his Philistine enemies amassed in the temple of Dagon, Samson gripped the two central pillars of the temple and pushed them down, causing the whole building to collapse, killing everyone inside (Judges 16:30). "He passed the remainder of the afternoon in a curious high-strung condition, unable to do much but think of the approaching meeting with her, and sadly satirize himself for his emotions thereon, as a Samson shorn" (Thomas Hardy, *The Mayor of Casterbridge,* 1886). *See also* EYELESS IN GAZA; SAMSON, BLIND, GRINDS IN PRISON.

Samson, blind, grinds in prison (samsăn) Reference to a worker who is obliged to work long and hard under terrible conditions. The allusion is to the fate of the biblical SAMSON, who was betrayed by Delilah, subsequently blinded, then forced to work in the mills of the Philistines (Judges 16:21). *A cursory examination of the maquiladora reminded the* *inspector forcibly of Samson, blind, grinds in prison. See also* EYELESS IN GAZA.

Sam Spade (spayd) Archetype of a tough, shrewd private detective. Sam Spade was created by U.S. crime writer Dashiell Hammett (1894–1961) in his novel *The Maltese Falcon* (1930) and memorably brought to life in the cinema by Humphrey Bogart. *The inspector is no fool, I grant you, but he's not Sam Spade.*

Samuel (samyăwăl, samyăl) Archetype of a prophet whose prophecies always come true. The allusion is to the biblical Samuel, the prophet and judge who anointed Saul and David (as related in 1 Samuel 9–10 and 16). *By this time the old man had acquired a reputation as the party's Samuel, divining long before any others which way the political wind was likely to blow.*

Sam Weller (weler) A constant, devoted companion, especially a personal servant of some kind. Sam Weller is the cheerful cockney manservant of the bumbling Mr. Pickwick in *The Pickwick Papers* (1837) by British novelist Charles Dickens (*see* PICKWICKIAN). Though comically unable to pronounce the letter "v," he is more worldly-wise than his master and helps get the latter out of more than one embarrassing mess as he conducts his famous tour round the countryside. *The archbishop was very accident-prone and needed his own Sam Weller to keep him out of trouble.*

Sancho Panza *See* DON QUIXOTE.

sanctum sanctorum *See* HOLY OF HOLIES.

sandals of Theramenes *See* WEAR THE SANDALS OF THERAMENES.

Sandhurst (sandherst) The officer class of the British army. Since 1802 the town of Sandhurst, near Camberley in Surrey, has been home to the British army's officer-training establishment, originally called the Royal Military College but renamed the Royal Military Academy Sandhurst in 1947. The term is now synonymous with the training of the army's commanders. *Her father was a Sandhurst type, with a bristling mustache and barking parade-ground voice but also a developed eye for a good claret. See also* ALDERSHOT.

sansculottes (sonskoolot) Political extremists, especially ones hailing from a working-class background. The original sansculottes were radical French Republicans who formed the core of the Paris mob duing the French Revolution of 1789. They were so named with reference to the fact that they wore trousers or pantaloons as opposed to the knee breeches (*culottes*) of the wealthy upper classes—*sans* being the French for "without." "By this time I was thoroughly disgusted with these fat cats taking food from the mouths of the sansculottes" (Bette Howell, *Dandelion Days*, 1991).

Santa Claus (santă klahz) A jovial, gift-giving Christmas character. The name Santa Claus comes from the Dutch *Sante Klaas*, identifying him as the patron saint of Dutch and German children (elsewhere called Saint Nicholas). Although his feast day actually falls on December 6, Santa Claus eventually merged with the British character ***Father Christmas*** in the English-speaking world. He now has a developed mythology, supposedly being a white-bearded, fat old man dressed in a bright red suit lined with white fur and delivering sacks of presents to well-behaved children around the world by means of a sleigh drawn by reindeer, gaining access to houses via the chimney. "Mostly she quizzed me about the burglars and I said they'd tried to get in through the bathroom window and one of them had put a foot through it, probably coming from the roof next door, and I generally made out that there was a whole gang of footpads up there lying in wait for Santa Claus" (Mike Ripley, *Angel Hunt*, 1991).

sapphic *See* LESBIAN.

Sapphira *See* ANANIAS CLUB.

Sarah (sairă) Archetype of an older mother. The allusion is to Sarah, the elderly but childless wife of ABRAHAM, who in Genesis 17:15–22 prayed to God for a child and later gave birth to Isaac. *Like the biblical Sarah, she bore her first child at an age when most women are nearly grandmothers.*

Sarajevo (sarăyayvō) A key event that precipitates a war. The allusion is to the assassination of Archduke Franz Ferdinand of the Austro-Hungarian Empire in Sarajevo on June 28, 1914, which triggered the outbreak of World War I. Fired by a Bosnian Serb terrorist called Gavrilo Princip, the fatal shot became known as the SHOT HEARD ROUND THE WORLD and was considered indirectly responsible for the millions of deaths that were to follow in the next four years: Germany sided with Austria-Hungary against Serbia and its ally Russia, France became involved when it refused Germany's demand that it remain neutral, and thus Britain and ultimately the United States (among many other countries) became embroiled in the conflict. Some eight decades later the word Sarajevo became once again synonymous with continent-shaking events when it was besieged (1992–94) by Bosnian Serb forces in the wake of the breakup of the former Yugoslavia, threatening the stability of the whole region before a United Nations ultimatum finally restored some kind of peace. *This assassination could prove to be the Middle East's Sarajevo.*

Sardanapalus (sahrdănapălăs) Archetype of an extravagant, luxury-loving tyrant, especially one given to effeminate pleasures. Sardanapalus was probably a fictional character resulting from the combination of three kings of ancient Assyria—Ashurbanipal, Shamash-shum-ukin, and Sin-shar-ishkun—who reigned around the seventh century B.C. Sardanapalus whiled away much of his time wearing women's clothing and enjoying such activities as spinning and making clothes. He gave up his self-indulgent ways, however, when threatened by invasion and inflicted several heavy defeats on his enemies until after a long siege at Nineveh, he set fire to everything he owned, including his concubines and himself, on a funeral pyre. "Pleasure shall preside at my last moments, as it has presided at my whole life! I will die like Sardanapalus, with my loves and my treasures around me; and the last of my guests who remains proof against our festivity, shall set fire to my palace, as the kingly Assyrian set fire to his!" (Wilkie Collins, *Antonina,* 1850).

sardonic (sahrdonik) Scornful; mocking; derisive. The word derives ultimately from Greek legend about a poisonous herb that was supposed to grow on the island of Sardinia. Tradition had it that those who ate some of this acrid herb found themselves subject to uncontrollable spasms, their face being contorted into a rigid, unnatural smile. "I had started, on entering the room, at the skeleton, and I started once more at the dog. The old servant noticed me each time with a sardonic grin" (Wilkie Collins, *After Dark,* 1856).

Satan (saytăn) The devil. The word is a Hebrew term that actually means "the enemy" or "the accuser" (Job 1:6). In the New Testament Satan is described as a tempter (Matthew 4:1–11, Mark 1:11–13, and Luke 4:4–13), "the prince of this world" (John 12:31), and "the prince of the power of the air" (Ephesians 2:2). He seeks to undermine the kingdom of God, and he opposes and tests believers. The New Testament also presents the death of Jesus Christ on the cross as the decisive moment of Satan's defeat (John 12:31), which will be confirmed when Jesus Christ returns and Satan is punished and his work destroyed (Revelation 20:10). In the works of John Milton, he is identified as the fallen angel who challenges the rule of God in heaven and is exiled to hell as punishment for the rebellion he leads. His many other titles include ***Prince of Darkness*** and ***Old Nick.*** *He sat on top of the company like Satan presiding over hell. See also* BEELZEBUB; LUCIFER.

Saturday The seventh day of the week. It was named after Saturn, the Roman god of agriculture. *Tradition has it that weddings take place on Saturday.*

Saturn (satern) The sixth planet from the Sun. It was named after the Roman god of agriculture and vegetation, equivalent to the Greek Cronos and thus also representing time. According to legend Saturn was once a king of Italy who presided over a golden age of peace and plenty. "Thus, in reviewing the horoscope which your Lordship subjected to my skill, you will observe that Saturn, being in the sixth House in opposition to Mars, retrograde in the House of Life, cannot but denote long and dangerous sickness, the issue whereof is in the will of Heaven, though death may probably be inferred" (Sir Walter Scott, *Kenilworth,* 1821). *See also* SATURDAY; SATURNALIAN; SATURNINE.

saturnalian (saternayleeăn) Of or relating to wild, unrestrained revelry. The allusion is to the Roman festival of Saturnalia, during which the harvest was celebrated—reputedly an occasion of much licentiousness and debauchery. All the schools and law courts were closed, and slaves were temporarily released from the strict rules that governed their lives to enjoy feasts at which they dressed up in the clothes of their masters. The festival was named after Saturn, the god of agriculture. "Altogether this time of trouble was rather a Saturnalian time to Kezia; she could scold her betters with unreproved freedom" (George Eliot, *The Mill on the Floss,* 1860).

saturnine (saternīn) Having a gloomy, taciturn temperament. The word is an allusion to the planet SATURN, which was traditionally supposed to exert a depressive influence. "He stands for a moment, saturnine in the ruddy light, to see who is present, looking in a singular and rather deadly way at Sir Howard; then with some surprise and uneasiness at Lady Cicely" (George Bernard Shaw, *Captain Brassbound's Conversion,* 1900).

satyr (sayter) A lecher; a man who exhibits abnormally strong sexual desire. According to Greek mythology satyrs were minor deities of the forest, depicted as having the bodies of unusually hairy men, the legs and feet of goats and short horns on their head. Representing the raw power of nature, they attended upon the god Dionysus and were notorious for their lustful ways. "'This is the face of a satyr.' 'It is the face of my soul'" (Oscar Wilde, *The Picture of Dorian Gray,* 1891). *See also* HYPERION TO A SATYR.

Saul (sahl) Archetype of a troubled, melancholy ruler. Saul is identified in the Old Testament as the first king of Israel (1 Samuel 11:15), who led the Israelites to victory against the Philistines but clashed with the high priest Samuel and ultimately went mad and took his own life, upon which he was succeeded by David. The expression of surprise ***Is Saul also among the prophets?*** was uttered by those who knew Saul's character and then saw him prophesying (1 Samuel 10:11–12). Saul was also the name of the apostle Paul prior to his revelatory experience on the ROAD TO DAMASCUS and his subsequent conversion to Christianity (Acts 9:1–22). "'Many learned and great men have thought otherwise,' said Varney; 'and, not to flatter your lordship, my own opinion leans that way.' 'Ay, Saul among the prophets?' said Leicester. 'I thought thou wert sceptical in all such matters as thou couldst neither see, hear, smell, taste, or touch, and that thy belief was limited by thy senses'" (Sir Walter Scott, *Kenilworth,* 1821).

saved by the bell Prevented in the nick of time by some outside intervention from suffering defeat, damage, or a setback of some kind. The allusion is to the ringing of a bell to signal the end of a round in a boxing match. *The attorney was about to ask me where the money had come from, but I was saved by the bell when the judge announced a recess.*

saving remnant A small group of survivors of a larger assembly who serve to redeem the whole. The phrase comes from Isaiah 10:20–23, in which Isaiah describes how the remaining Israelites would be brought back to the Promised Land after being defeated and exiled by the Assyrians. The Old Testament idea of a "remnant" is about people who have been saved or delivered from disaster rather than those who bring about the salvation of a larger group. The saving remnant is the group with which God can begin again and whose members will preserve the existence of Israel. "The remnant shall return, even the remnant of Jacob, unto the mighty God. For though thy people Israel be as the sand of the sea, yet a remnant of them shall return: the consumption decreed shall overflow with righteousness" (Isaiah 10:21–22). *The team will have to rely on a saving remnant of established stars if they are to remain at this level next season.*

Savonarola *See* BONFIRE OF THE VANITIES.

Sawyer, Tom *See* TOM SAWYER.

say it ain't so, Joe Please tell me this piece of bad news is not true. This is an allusion to the notorious Black Sox baseball scandal of 1919, which arose with the revelation that eight members of the team had accepted bribes to lose the World Series that year to the underdogs, the Cincinnati Reds. The words were originally directed by a tearful young fan to "Shoeless Joe" Jackson, one of the eight accused men, as he left a grand jury session. The men were acquitted through lack of evidence, but were banned from the sport for life. *The game is off? Say it ain't so, Joe!*

say the word To give the go-ahead for something to be done. The expression derives from Matthew 8:8, when Christ is speaking to the Roman centurion whose servant lay paralyzed and suffering at home: "The centurion answered and said, Lord, I am not worthy that thou shouldest come under my roof: but speak the word only, and my servant shall be healed." The incident is also reported in Luke 7:1–10. "'I'll have it done, I will, by heavens! if you'll only say the word,' protested Sir Roger. But the doctor did not say the word, and so the idea was passed off" (Anthony Trollope, *Doctor Thorne,* 1858).

Scaevola (skeevălă) Archetype of a person who endures suffering without complaint. According to Roman legend Scaevola (meaning "left handed") was the nickname bestowed on one Gaius Mucius, who entered the camp of the invading Etruscan leader Lars Porsena with the intention of assassinating him during his siege of Rome. Unfortunately Gaius Mucius killed the king's secretary by mistake and was apprehended. Having been sentenced to death by burning, Gaius Mucius voluntarily held his right hand in the flames to show his indifference to his fate, keeping it there without flinching until it was quite burned away. Duly impressed, the Etruscans allowed him to go free and agreed to peace with the Romans. *Like Scaevola under torture, he endured the most severe physical abuse without a murmur.*

scales fell from his eyes This expression is used to describe a person who has been stripped of a former illusion and now recognizes the real truth of something. The expression comes from Acts 9:18, which describes the conversion of Paul on the ROAD TO DAMASCUS: "And immediately there fell from his eyes as it had been scales: and he received sight forthwith, and arose, and was baptized." "Then the scales fell from the eyes of the Seven, and one said, Alas, that we drank of the curious liquors. They have made us weary, and in dreamless sleep these two long centuries have we lain" (Mark Twain, *The Innocents Abroad,* 1869).

scapegoat A person who is made to take the blame for others. According to Leviticus 16, the Day of Atonement included a ceremony in which two goats were brought to the altar of the Tabernacle and lots were drawn to decide which would be sacrificed. The second goat was then symbolically laden with the sins of the Israelites and led into the wilderness and allowed to escape. The term *scapegoat* may be derived from the Hebrew *azazel* (which may have been the name of a demon believed to haunt desolate regions). "Madame Merle defended the luckless lady with a great deal of zeal and wit. She couldn't see why Mrs. Touchett should make a scapegoat of a woman who had really done no harm, who had only done good in the wrong way" (Henry James, *Portrait of a Lady,* 1881).

Scarecrow *See* FRIEND OF DOROTHY.

scarlet letter A mark of shame. The allusion is to the custom among the early Puritans of New England of forcing a woman guilty of adultery to wear a scarlet letter A (for "adulteress") on her dress as a public acknowledgment of her misbehavior. The practice was famously described by U.S. novelist Nathaniel Hawthorne (1804–64) in his novel *The Scarlet Letter* (1850), in which Hester Prynne is punished in this way. *If you think any wife today is going to go round with a scarlet letter on her coat you're very much mistaken.*

Scarlet Pimpernel (pimpernel) An elusive person. The adventure novel *The Scarlet Pimpernel* (1905), by the Hungarian-born novelist Baroness Orczy (1865–1947), featured the escapades of an English aristocrat called Sir Percy Blakeney, who at the time of the French Revolution rescued intended victims of the guillotine under the pseudonym "The Scarlet Pimpernel" (an allusion to the small red flowers he left behind as his calling card). His assumed foppishness and frivolity as Sir Percy fooled his enemies into thinking he was the most unlikely person to be the Pimpernel, thus making him very difficult to unmask and inspiring him to taunt his pursuers with the rhyme: "We seek him here, we seek him there, / Those Frenchies seek him everywhere. / Is he in heaven?—Is he in hell? / That demned, elusive Pimpernel." "He's like the Scarlet Pimpernel—totally elusive" (Jenny Ashe, *Sweet Deceiver*, 1993).

Scarlett O'Hara *See* GONE WITH THE WIND.

Scarlet Whore of Babylon *See* WHORE OF BABYLON.

scarlet woman A woman with a reputation for sexual promiscuity; a prostitute. The allusion is to the WHORE OF BABYLON, a sinful woman described as wearing scarlet in Revelation 17. "Nay, we might have judged that such a child's mother must needs be a scarlet woman, and a worthy type of her of Babylon!" (Nathaniel Hawthorne, *The Scarlet Letter*, 1850).

Scarpia (skahrpeeă) A malevolent police chief. Scarpia is the menacing chief of police in the opera *Tosca* (1900) by the Italian composer Giacomo Puccini (1858–1924). He lusts after the singer Tosca and has her lover Mario Cavaradossi arrested in the hope that she will agree to sleep with him in exchange for his sparing Cavaradossi from execution, but by the end of the opera all three are dead. *The Italian prime minister did not attempt to defend his chief of police, who was behaving more and more like Puccini's Scarpia.*

Schwarzenegger, Arnold *See* ARNOLD SCHWARZENEGGER.

Scipio *See* CONTINENCE OF A SCIPIO.

Sciron (sīrăn) Archetype of a vicious robber. According to Greek legend Sciron waylaid travelers on the Scironian rock in Megara and made them wash his feet before he kicked them into the sea, where they were devoured by a sea monster. Sciron met his death at the hands of THESEUS. *He showed his enemies the mercy of a Sciron, taking pleasure in humiliating his victims before putting them out of their misery on a permanent basis.*

Scotland Yard The headquarters of London's police force, or the police themselves. Great Scotland Yard, Whitehall, was the headquarters of the Metropolitan Police from around 1842 to 1890. The force then moved to New Scotland Yard on Victoria Embankment and remained there until 1967 when the headquarters was transferred to Broadway, Westminster, which was again dubbed "New Scotland Yard." The original Scotland Yard was a piece of land granted in the 10th century to the kings of Scotland to be used by them on their annual visits to London, and was technically considered to be part of Scotland, hence the name. In modern usage, the Metropolitan Police, or even the British police in general, may be referred to variously as "Scotland Yard," "New Scotland Yard," or just "the Yard." "Gathering his wits, the potman said, 'The constable and a man from Scotland Yard in London came to Dore's Lodge today'" (E. V. Thompson, *Wychwood*, 1992).

Scott of the Antarctic An intrepid explorer, especially one of polar regions. The British explorer Captain Robert Falcon Scott (1868–1912) is remembered primarily for his heroic but ultimately tragic expedition to the South Pole, which resulted in the deaths of the whole party. The resolution and self-sacrifice of the expedition members enshrined Scott and his companions as ideals of the courageous exploring spirit. *You'd have to be Scott of the Antarctic to get to town through this snow. See also* CAPTAIN OATES.

scourge of scorpions A particularly severe punishment. The phrase, also encountered as ***lash of scorpions,*** alludes to 1 Kings 12:11: "My father hath chastised you with whips, but I will chastise you with scorpions." *The rebels have threatened to unleash a scourge of scorpions, and the government is more nervous today than it has been for years.*

scrip and staff Wallet and stick, as symbols of earthly possessions, usually in the context of relinquishing them. The phrase appears in Mark 6:7–10, Luke 9:3, and Matthew 10:10, in which Christ urges his disciples to forsake all possessions when embarking on their travels: "Take nothing for your journey, neither staves, nor scrip, neither brand, neither money; neither have two coats apiece." In medieval times the faithful often carried a staff as a sign that they were on pilgrimage, and somewhat perversely, a purse and staff became recognized emblems of pilgrimage. ". . . from that moment until the closing of the curtain it was music, just music—music to make one drunk with pleasure, music to make one take scrip and staff and beg his way round the globe to hear it" (Mark Twain, *What Is Man and Other Essays,* 1906).

Scrooge (skrooj) A person who is mean with his or her money; a parsimonious skinflint. The allusion is to Ebenezer Scrooge, the penny-pinching miser who is the central character in *A Christmas Carol* (1843) by the British novelist Charles Dickens (1812–70). After being visited by the spirits of Christmas Past, Christmas Present, and Christmas Yet to Come, and by ***Marley's ghost*** (the ghost of his deceased partner Jacob Marley), he mends his ways and determines to be more generous in the future. *Her husband is such a Scrooge he doesn't even buy her a birthday present. See also* BOB CRATCHIT; HARPAGON.

Scully, Dana *See* X-FILES.

Scylla and Charybdis *See* BETWEEN SCYLLA AND CHARYBDIS.

Scythian defiance (sitheeăn) A threat or gesture of resistance, especially one tersely delivered. The allusion is to the message the nomadic peoples of Scythia sent to Darius I, when he approached with an invading Persian army in 512 B.C. The Scythian ambassador arrived at the king's tent and without a word produced a bird, a frog, a mouse, and five arrows. It was explained to the king that the Scythians were warning him to fly away like a bird, hide in a hole like a mouse, or swim across the river like a frog or else suffer death by Scythian arrows five days later. The attempted Persian conquest failed. *This gesture of Scythian defiance did nothing in the long run to alter the inevitability of defeat.*

season, to every thing there is a; season for all things *See* TIME AND PLACE FOR EVERYTHING.

second Adam *See* ADAM.

second coming A triumphant return from obscurity. The reference is to the Second Coming, or ***Second Advent,*** of Jesus Christ, when he will visibly return at the end of history to judge the world, destroy evil, and consummate his kingdom (Matthew 16:27 and 24:30, Acts 1:11, 2 Thessalonians 1:3–10, and Revelation 1:7). *The star's return to the silver screen in this movie was greeted as a second coming, although he had never really been away.*

second front Activities begun on a new front to divide an enemy's forces. The phrase is particularly associated with the long-awaited Allied invasion of France in 1944 during World War II, which meant that Nazi Germany was faced with attacks on two fronts, in the east against Russia and now also in the west. *The government opened up a second front on poverty by shaking up the welfare system.*

second mile *See* GO THE EXTRA/SECOND MILE.

seek and ye shall find Those who make some effort to get what they want are more likely to succeed. The proverb is of biblical origin, coming from Matthew 7:7–8, which commends the power of prayer: "Ask, and it shall be given you; seek, and ye shall find; knock, and it shall be opened unto you: For every one that asketh receiveth; and he that seeketh findeth; and to him that knocketh it shall be opened." It can also be found in Luke 11:9–13. *Finding the solution to this puzzle will not be easy, but seek and ye shall find.*

see the light To experience a significant revelation; to realize the truth. The allusion is to the revelation undergone by Saul on the ROAD TO DAMASCUS when he was suddenly bathed in a light from heaven and converted to a follower of Jesus Christ (Acts 9:1–22). *He claimed he saw the light at college: Before this he was a hardened atheist, but afterwards he was a devout Christian.* "Stonehenge solstice revellers see the light" (*Guardian,* June 22, 2001).

see through a glass darkly To glimpse the truth despite limitations of the senses. The quotation is from 1 Corinthians 13:12: "Now we see through a glass, darkly; but then face to face." In its original biblical context the phrase refers to the imperfect human understanding of God's purpose. *One day all knowledge will be complete, but for now we see through a glass darkly.* "Britain seen through a glass darkly" (*Guardian,* June 6, 2001).

Seian horse (seeăn) A possession that brings its owner bad luck. The allusion is to a fine horse that belonged to the Roman nobleman Cneius Seius. Seius was put to death on the orders of Mark Antony, and the horse's next owner, Cornelius Dolabella, similarly met a premature end, dying in battle in Syria. The horse then passed to Caius Cassius, who died a violent death after the Battle of Philippi (42 B.C.), and it ultimately became the property of Mark Antony himself, who committed suicide in 30 B.C. after defeat at Actium. *Like the Seian horse, the jewel seemed to bring its owners nothing but bad luck and in some cases even death itself.*

seize the day *See* CARPE DIEM.

Selene (săleenee) Personification of the Moon. Selene, the daughter of the Titans Hyperion and Theia and the sister of Helios and Eos, was identified as the moon goddess in Greek mythology. When she fell in love with Endymion, a handsome shepherd boy, Endymion was cast into an eternal sleep so that Selene would always be able to visit him in his dreams. *Selene cast an eerie glow over the scene, bathing the dead and the living alike in her cool light.*

sell down the river To sacrifice someone else's interests for the sake of one's own advantage. The allusion is to the slave trade that once flourished on the Mississippi, which involved slaves being sent down the river to plantations where conditions were often much worse. *He was a respected broker until he sold his clients down the river when he saw the chance of making a killing on the stock market for himself.*

sell one's birthright for a mess of pottage To give up one's rights in something for a paltry sum or other reward. According to Genesis 25:29–34 ESAU foolishly sold his birthright to his treacherous twin brother, Jacob, in exchange for a bowl of soup or stew. "And Jacob sod pottage: and Esau came from the field, and he was faint: And Esau said to Jacob, Feed me, I pray thee, with that same red pottage; for I am faint: therefore was his name called Edom. And Jacob said, Sell me this day thy birthright. And Esau said, Behold, I am at the point to die: and what profit shall this birthright do to me? And Jacob said, Swear to me this day; and he sware unto him: and he sold his birthright unto Jacob. Then Jacob gave Esau bread and pottage of lentils; and he did eat and drink, and rose up, and went his way: thus Esau despised his birthright." "But he who sold his birthright for a mess of pottage existed, and Judas Iscariot existed, and Castlereagh existed, and this man exists!" (Charles Dickens, *Hard Times,* 1854).

Semiramis (să<u>mir</u>ămis) Archetype of a powerful female ruler. Semiramis was the legendary founder of Babylon, a mortal Assyrian sometimes described as the daughter of the goddess Derceto. She married King Ninus of Assyria and persuaded him to hand over the crown to her, upon which she had him put to death. An immensely capable queen, she was herself murdered by her son Ninyas. Various queens and empresses have since aspired to her name, including Catherine II of Russia, who was dubbed the "Semiramis of the North." "'Have you completed all the necessary preparations incident to Miss Sedley's departure, Miss Jemima?' asked Miss Pinkerton herself, that majestic lady; the Semiramis of Hammersmith, the friend of Doctor Johnson, the correspondent of Mrs. Chapone herself" (William Makepeace Thackeray, *Vanity Fair,* 1847–48).

Semite; Semitic *See* SHEM.

send a sow to Minerva (mi<u>ner</u>vă) To attempt to teach something to a person who is already thoroughly familiar with the subject. The source of the image is a Latin proverb, which likens such behavior to a pig attempting to educate Minerva, the goddess of wisdom. *Lecturing a banker in ways in which to fleece customers is rather like sending a sow to Minerva.*

send in the clowns Even in times of catastrophe, ordinary life (or the appearances of ordinary life) must go on. The phrase was originally associated with the circus, where the stock response when things went wrong was to amuse the audience with a clown act. It became more familiar as the title of a popular song from the Stephen Sondheim musical *A Little Night Music* (1973), recorded by Judy Collins in 1975. *It looks like there will be a short delay so we'd better send in the clowns until the band are ready.*

send to Coventry To ostracize or ignore someone. The story goes that the residents of the English city of Coventry were once so hostile to the army that they shunned any soldiers who were stationed among them. Alternatively, the phrase may have its roots in the English Civil War, when Royalist prisoners taken in Birmingham were sent to Coventry, a Parliamentarian city, where they were less than welcome guests. *The young man was sent to Coventry by his friends until he apologized for what he had said.*

send up the river To send someone to prison. The allusion is to Sing Sing, the notorious prison that is located at Ossining, which lies up the Hudson River from New York City. *If the cops think they're sending me up the river for this, then they're mistaken.*

separate the sheep from the goats To cull the good or useful from the bad or useless. The expression originated from Matthew 25:31–33: "The Son of Man . . . shall separate them one from another, as a shepherd divideth his sheep from the goats: And he shall set the sheep on his right hand, but the goats on the left." It is also encountered in the form ***divide the sheep from the goats.*** "The political feelings of the country are, as a rule, so well marked that it is easy, as to almost every question, to separate the sheep from the goats" (Anthony Trollope, *Phineas Redux,* 1869). *See also* SEPARATE THE WHEAT FROM THE CHAFF.

separate the wheat from the chaff To divide what is valuable from what is worthless. The expression comes from Matthew 3:12, in which John the Baptist describes how Christ will judge the good and the bad on JUDGMENT DAY. *Chaff* describes the husks and other outer material of seed, which is separated from the good grain, in this case wheat, during threshing or winnowing. "Everything is most carefully gone into; we endeavour to sift the wheat from the chaff" (John Galsworthy, *The Forsyte Saga,* 1922). *See also* SEPARATE THE SHEEP FROM THE GOATS.

September 11 *See* 9/11.

seraphic (sărafik) Serene; rapt. The word alludes to the seraphim, or seraphs, the highest of the nine orders of angels. According to the account in Isaiah 6:1–7 the seraphim are God's fiery six-winged attendants, who sing his praises around his throne. The word comes from *saraph* (meaning "to burn" in Hebrew). "There was a beggar in the street, when I went down; and as I turned my head towards the window, thinking of her calm seraphic eyes, he made me start by muttering, as if he were an echo of the morning: 'Blind! Blind! Blind!'" (Charles Dickens, *David Copperfield,* 1849–50).

Serbonian bog (serbōneeăn) A situation from which it is impossible to extricate oneself. The allusion is to a vast area of marshland of the same name that stretched from the isthmus of Suez to the Nile delta in ancient times and in which many armies were said to have been lost. It is now covered in sand. "The lingering twilight served to show them through this Serbonian bog, but deserted them almost totally at the bottom of a steep and very stony hill, which it was the traveller's next toilsome task to ascend" (Sir Walter Scott, *Waverley,* 1814).

Sermon on the Mount A lengthy and authoritative statement of principle, policy, etc. The allusion is to the Sermon on the Mount given by Jesus Christ to his disciples, as described in Matthew 5–7. The passage begins with the BEATITUDES and contains the Lord's Prayer. "This was the first of a series of moral lectures or Sermons on the Mount, which were to be delivered from the same place every Sunday afternoon as long as the fine weather lasted" (Thomas Hardy, *The Return of the Native,* 1880). *See also* CITY ON A HILL; DELIVER US FROM EVIL; ENTER INTO ONE'S CLOSET; GO THE EXTRA/SECOND MILE; HIDE ONE'S LIGHT UNDER A BUSHEL; IF THY RIGHT EYE OFFEND THEE; JOT OR TITTLE; JUDGE NOT, THAT YE BE NOT JUDGED; LAY NOT UP TREASURES UPON EARTH; LEAD US NOT INTO TEMPTATION; LEFT HAND KNOW WHAT YOUR RIGHT HAND IS DOING, DO NOT LET YOUR; LILIES OF THE FIELD; LOVE YOUR ENEMIES; MOTE AND BEAM; RAIN FALLS ON THE JUST AND THE UNJUST, THE; SALT OF THE EARTH; SUFFICIENT UNTO THE DAY IS THE EVIL THEREOF; TOMORROW WILL TAKE CARE OF ITSELF; TURN THE OTHER CHEEK; WOLF IN SHEEP'S CLOTHING.

serpent A source of trouble; an evil influence. The allusion is to the Serpent in the GARDEN OF EDEN, which is described as "more subtil than any beast of the field which the LORD God had made" (Genesis 3:1) and which tempts Eve into tasting the FORBIDDEN FRUIT of the Tree of Knowledge of Good and Evil, telling her that "in the day ye eat thereof, then your eyes shall be opened, and ye shall be as gods, knowing good and evil" (Genesis 3:5). The identification of the Serpent with the devil is based on Revelation 20:2: "And he laid hold on the dragon, that old serpent, which is the Devil, and Satan, and bound him a thousand years." *The serpent of international terrorism has reared its head, and suddenly no one is safe.*

serve God and mammon *See* NO MAN CAN SERVE TWO MASTERS.

serve two masters *See* NO MAN CAN SERVE TWO MASTERS.

Set (set) Incarnation of evil. Set, or ***Seth,*** featured in ancient Egyptian mythology as the god of fertility, warfare, and storms. He was usually depicted in the form of a dog and was described as the implacable foe of his brothers Horus and Osiris. *The sorcerer called upon Set to help him in his unearthly quest for revenge.*

set the mark of the beast *See* MARK OF THE BEAST.

seven deadly sins The seven chief sins upon which all the crimes of mankind can allegedly be blamed. According to the Roman Catholic religious writer Saint Thomas Aquinas (1227–75), in his *Summa Theologica* (1265–74), the seven deadly sins are pride, lust, wrath, envy, gluttony, avarice, and sloth. Pride he rated as the most serious of all. "It was only because she was a Christian woman, with a clear view of the seven deadly sins, that she pushed the bedclothes back firmly" (Susan Hill, *Gentleman and Ladies*, 1969).

seven last words The seven last sentences of Christ on the cross. They are as follows: "Eli, Eli, lama sabachthani? . . . My God, my God, why hast thou forsaken me?" (Matthew 27:46; *see* MY GOD, WHY HAST THOU FORSAKEN ME?), "Father, forgive them; for they know not what they do" (Luke 23:34; *see* FATHER, FORGIVE THEM; KNOW NOT WHAT THEY DO, THEY), "Today shalt thou be with me in paradise" (Luke 23:43), "Father, into thy hands I commend my spirit" (Luke 23:46), "Woman, behold thy son! . . . Behold thy mother!" (John 19:26–27), "I thirst" (John 19:28), and "It is finished" (John 19:30).

seven pillars of wisdom The fundamental truths upon which life depends. The phrase appears in Proverbs 9:1: "Wisdom hath builded her house, she hath hewn out her seven pillars." Various authorities have identified the seven pillars with the seven patriarchs—Adam, Enoch, Noah, Abraham, Isaac, Jacob, and Moses—while Augustine linked them to the seven churches that united to form the one true church. *These beliefs constitute the seven pillars of wisdom upon which the city has burgeoned over the last 20 years.*

seventy times seven Many times; ad infinitum. The phrase alludes to Matthew 18:21–22, in which Peter asks Christ, "Lord, how oft shall my brother sin against me, and I forgive him? till seven times? Jesus saith unto him, I say not unto thee, Until seven times: but, Until seventy times seven." "'Sir,' I exclaimed, 'sitting here, within these four walls, at one stretch, I have endured and forgiven the four hundred and ninety heads of your discourse. Seventy times seven times have I plucked up my hat and been about to depart—Seventy times seven times have you preposterously forced me to resume my seat" (Emily Brontë, *Wuthering Heights,* 1847).

seven wonders of the world *See* EIGHTH WONDER OF THE WORLD.

seven-year itch The notion that after a marriage or other relationship has lasted seven years one or both partners are tempted to be unfaithful. The phrase became widely familiar when it was used as the title of a George Axelrod comedy (1952), filmed in 1955 with MARILYN MONROE providing the temptation. Before Axelrod's play the phrase was associated with various medical ailments, such as scabies, which were believed to need seven years' treatment before they were fully cured. *He never thought he would drive anything except a Mustang, but he fell victim to a seven-year itch and exchanged it for a Porsche. See also* DANGEROUS AGE, A.

seven years of plenty A period of prosperity, especially one that is likely to be followed by a corresponding period of want. The phrase comes from the biblical episode of Pharaoh's dream of "seven well favoured kine and fatfleshed" being devoured by seven "ill favoured and leanfleshed kine" and seven withered ears of corn being consumed by seven good ears (Genesis 41:1–7). Joseph interpreted Pharaoh's dream as a prophecy of seven years of plenty being followed by seven years of famine (Genesis 41:25–32). *The market confidently expects at least seven years of plenty without having to worry about foreign debt.*

shadow of death *See* VALLEY OF THE SHADOW OF DEATH.

Shadrach, Meshach, and Abednego *See* FIERY FURNACE.

shake off the dust from/on one's feet To leave somewhere or disassociate oneself from someone as a result of the treatment one has received. The expression comes from Matthew 10:14, in which Christ advises his disciples what to do when they find themselves in places where their preaching receives a hostile reception: "And whosoever shall not receive you, nor hear your words, when ye depart out of that house or city, shake off the dust of your feet." "The message had been delivered, and Captain Batsby with a frown of anger on his brow was about to shake the dust off from his feet on the uncourteous threshold when there came another message, saying that Captain Batsby could go in and see Sir Thomas if he wished it" (Anthony Trollope, *Ayala's Angel,* 1881).

Shakespearean (shayk<u>speer</u>iăn) Of or relating to the writings of the English playwright William Shakespeare (1564–1616). Commonly described as the greatest writer in the English language, Shakespeare covered a wide range of themes and genres in his plays and poetry. The term "Shakespearean" typically suggests the epic scale and poetic intensity of his best-known tragedies, though it may equally evoke his comic sense, his profound understanding of human nature, or his unrivaled eye for character. "The picture that thus emerges of the tensions and jealousies in the Imperial family has a grand, almost Shakespearean feel to it: the Emperor Shah Jehan governs the Mughal Empire through its period of greatest magnificence" (William Dalrymple, *City of Djinns*, 1993).

shanghai (shanghī) To appropriate someone's services against their will. The allusion is to the former practice among naval captains of various Western nations of kidnapping young men and forcing them to serve in their ships' crews, often by the means of "press gangs" who roamed the streets and taverns of port towns looking for likely candidates. Many merchant vessels manned by such crews carried cargoes to the Chinese port of Shanghai, hence the term. In modern usage the word is sometimes applied to projects and other inanimate things that are deemed to have been summarily taken over. *The idea of opening up relations with potential clients has been shanghaied by our competitors.*

Shangri-La (shangreelah) A paradise far removed from the troubles of the world. Shangri-La was the name given by British writer James Hilton (1900–54) to an imaginary utopian retreat in the mountains of Tibet in his novel *Lost Horizon* (1933), later filmed with Ronald Colman in the leading role. The inhabitants of Shangri-La, living in such beautiful, peaceful surroundings, never grow old unless they leave their secluded valley, in which case their great age catches up with them and they shrivel to dust. *The family used their great wealth to create a Shangri-La in the distant hills, to which only their closest friends were ever invited. See also* CAMP DAVID.

Sharon, rose of *See* ROSE OF SHARON.

Sharp, Becky *See* BECKY SHARP.

Shavian (shayveeăn) Reminiscent in some way of the writings, philosophy, or character of the Irish writer and critic George Bernard Shaw (1856–1950). Shaw is remembered for his many lively, intelligent plays for the theater and as a brilliant, controversial observer of the culture and society of his time, preserved in essays, letters, novels, and other writings as well as in his drama. A person who is described as "Shavian" is likely to be witty, clever, and playfully biting in his or her criticisms of others. *He had a perverse, Shavian wit that delighted as much as it hurt its victims.*

shazam *See* CAPTAIN MARVEL.

Sheba, Queen of *See* QUEEN OF SHEBA.

sheep from goats *See* SEPARATE THE SHEEP FROM THE GOATS.

sheep to the slaughter *See* LAMB TO THE SLAUGHTER.

Sheherezade *See* ARABIAN NIGHTS.

Shem (shem) Archetype of a homeless wanderer or vagrant. The allusion is to the biblical Shem, the eldest son of Noah, who according to the Book of Genesis received Noah's blessing after he and his brother Japheth showed respect to their father when he was drunk. Noah promised his son that God "shall dwell in the tents of Shem" (Genesis 9:24–27), hence his association with wandering peoples and vagrants and his identification as the ancestor of the Hebrews. His name has also given rise to the words ***Semite*** and ***Semitic***. *Like a latter-day Shem he spent years wandering with his family.*

Sheriff of Nottingham (notingham, notingăm) An evil, grasping local official. The allusion is to the archenemy of the English folk hero ROBIN HOOD, who makes himself rich at the expense of the city's population. Several of the Robin Hood adventures revolve around the sheriff's attempts to capture the famous outlaw and disperse his band of merry men. *Like the Sheriff of Nottingham, the state believes itself to be entitled to a generous share of everyone else's personal wealth.*

Sherlock Holmes (sherlok hōmz) An ace detective. The brilliant, eccentric private detective Sherlock Holmes was the creation of the British novelist and short-story writer Sir Arthur Conan Doyle (1859–1930). He made his first appearance in *A Study in Scarlet* in 1887, together with his devoted friend and biographer DOCTOR WATSON, and his adventures quickly attracted a huge readership. Doyle's attempt to kill Holmes off in 1902 by throwing him off the Reichenbach Falls in the clutches of his archenemy ***Professor Moriarty*** led only to concerted calls for his revival, and Doyle felt obliged to resurrect him for a further series of cases. Holmes has been brought to life in numerous movies as well as on radio, television, and the stage and his methods of deduction through minute observation of details continue to fascinate and beguile. Holmes himself professes to think little of his talents, modestly informing Watson that his deductions are "elementary." Doyle is said to have modeled his detective's techniques upon those of Dr. Joseph Bell of the Edinburgh Infirmary. *The police have so little to go on that even Sherlock Holmes would find it difficult to know what conclusions to draw. See also* ELEMENTARY, MY DEAR WATSON; THREE-PIPE PROBLEM.

Sherwood Forest *See* ROBIN HOOD.

She Who Must Be Obeyed A wife or other woman whose orders are always followed. The term is an allusion to the 1887 novel *She* by the British writer H. Rider Haggard (1856–1925), in which he describes a fictional lost African city ruled by Ayesha, a 2,000-year-old beauty possessed of eternal youth and an iron will. The phrase was later adopted by British novelist John Mortimer in his Horace Rumpole stories as the means by which the lawyer Rumpole refers to his reportedly ferocious wife. "Simon Draper took to calling her 'She who must be obeyed'—if not to her face" (M. Brown, *Richard Branson: The Inside Story*, 1989).

shibboleth (shibăleth) A watchword or a generally accepted rule or fundamental precept; a phrase that is difficult to pronounce or a peculiarity of behavior, dress, etc., that is difficult to master and thus may be used to test whether a person belongs to a particular class, profession, or other group. In its original biblical context (Judges 12:1–16) the word (meaning "stream in flood" in Hebrew) was used by Jephthah to tell the Gileadites from their enemies the Ephraimites, who pronounced the word *sibboleth* and thus betrayed their identity and were summarily put to death. "If it works, then some of the old shibboleths about Saturday night being family entertainment night will be buried alongside Noel's House Party" (*Guardian,* July 2, 2001).

Shiloah (shīlōă) A place of heavenly peace and rest. The allusion is to Isaiah 8:6–7, in which Isaiah refers to the "waters of Shiloah that go softly," and also to John 9:1–11, in which Christ heals a blind man by sending him to wash his eyes in the pool of Shiloah, or ***Siloam,*** just outside Jerusalem. (*Shiloah* comes from the Hebrew word *shalah,* "to send"; *Siloam* is the Greek form used in the Book of John.) *After a lifetime of trouble and misfortune he found himself able to enjoy a brief respite beside the softly flowing waters of Shiloah.*

shining light A person who is recognized as one of the foremost figures in a particular field; a person who shows the way forward. The phrase comes from John 5:35, which describes John the Baptist: "He was a burning and a shining light: and ye were willing for a season to rejoice in his light." It also appears in Proverbs 4:18: "But the path of the just is as the shining light, that shineth more and more unto the perfect day." "She's a capital girl, and she ought to marry a missionary, or one of your reformer fellows, and be a shining light of some sort" (Louisa May Alcott, *An Old Fashioned Girl,* 1870).

Shirley Temple A sweet-natured young girl, especially one with curly golden hair. The original Shirley Temple (b. 1928) became famous throughout the world as a child star in 1930s movies, among them *Little Miss Marker* (1934), *Curly Top* (1935), and *Dimples* (1936). The movies projected her as the ideal child—loving, innocent, and cheerful—though many found her performances saccharine. She retired from movies at a fairly early age and later in life found a new career as a diplomat. *She behaved like Shirley Temple but was really about as innocent as Mae West.*

shirt of Nessus (<u>ne</u>săs) A misfortune from which it is impossible to escape. The allusion is to the death of HERCULES, which came about after he put on a shirt soaked in the poisonous blood of the centaur Nessus, offered to him by his own wife, Deianeira. According to the legend Deianeira had become jealous after the dying Nessus told her Hercules had fallen in love with the beautiful Iole. Nessus also told her that by making her husband wear a shirt soaked in the centaur's blood her husband would be restored to her, so Deianeira dipped the shirt in Nessus's blood and sent it to her husband. The pain inflicted by the centaur's blood was so agonizing that ultimately Hercules sought relief from it by throwing himself onto a funeral pyre. "The words stuck to him like the shirt of Nessus, lacerating his very spirit" (Anthony Trollope, *Doctor Wortle's School,* 1881).

shoot the messenger *See* KILL THE MESSENGER.

shot heard round the world The shooting of a bullet or some other event that proves to have momentous international significance. The phrase has been applied to more than one such shot in history, but is particularly associated with the first shot of the American Revolution. It was fired on the morning of April 19, 1775, when a force of farmers and minutemen confronted British troops across a bridge at Concord, Massachusetts. An unidentified man fired the first shot without any order being given, and the first of many battles was joined. The phrase was later incorporated by Ralph Waldo Emerson (1803–82) in his "Concord Hymn" (1836): "By the rude bridge that arched the flood, / Their flag to April's breeze unfurled, / Here once the embattled farmers stood, / And fired the shot heard 'round the world." In 1914 another "shot heard round the world" was fired by Gavrilo Princip at SARAJEVO, triggering World War I. *In 1963 Lee Harvey Oswald fired a shot that was heard round the world.*

shoulders of giants *See* ON THE SHOULDERS OF GIANTS.

show the cloven hoof *See* CLOVEN HOOF.

Shulamite (<u>shoo</u>lămīt) A remarkably beautiful woman. According to the Song of Solomon 6:13, the Shulamite is the beloved. The word could be a variant form of *Shunammite,* which means "a girl from Shunem," or a feminine form of *Solomon,* in which instance the word would signify "Solomon's girl." "Love her, Esther! She was to me more than the Shulamite to the singing king, fairer, more spotless; a fountain of gardens, a well of living waters, and streams from Lebanon" (Lew Wallace, *Ben Hur,* 1880).

shut up the bowels of compassion *See* BOWELS OF COMPASSION.

Shylock (shīlok) A heartless, avaricious, money-grasping individual. The allusion is to the Jewish moneylender Shylock who is a central character in William Shakespeare's play *The Merchant of Venice* (1596). Shylock is highly resentful of the prejudice he has endured from the Christians of Venice and sees his opportunity to exact revenge against a respected Christian merchant called Antonio after the latter unwisely agrees to provide security for Shylock's loan to his friend Bassanio, jokingly agreeing to allow the moneylender to take a ***pound of flesh*** from his body if Bassanio defaults. When Bassanio fails to repay the money, Shylock insists upon his rights to his pound of flesh, though he is finally outwitted in this demand by Bassanio's lover Portia, who argues that though Shylock is entitled to his pound of flesh he is not entitled to the blood that will inevitably be spilled when it is removed (*see also* QUALITY OF MERCY IS NOT STRAINED, THE). *When it came to negotiating the contract her father revealed himself to be a Shylock who put money before all other considerations.*

Siamese twins (sīămeez) Physically joined twins, or two other people who act, speak, or think in a noticeably similar way. Chang and Eng were conjoined identical twins born in Bangkok, Thailand, in 1811, when the country of their birth was called Siam. They became internationally famous and toured the world before settling in North Carolina, finally dying in 1874. They remain history's best-known conjoined twins, hence the term "Siamese twins," which has only recently fallen from favor in this literal sense. " 'Just because you're married doesn't mean you've got to be Siamese twins,' I said loftily" (Bette Howell, *Dandelion Days*, 1991).

Siberia (sībeereeă) A cold, inhospitable place, especially one to which outcasts are sent. Siberia in northern Russia is a frozen wasteland in which life for most people is a matter of grim survival. For many years, notably under Communist rule, Siberia was a dreaded place of exile and imprisonment for individuals who had offended the state. *It was like Siberia in the apartment after the heating system broke down.*

sibyl (sibăl) A witch, sorceress, or fortune-teller. The word was originally applied in ancient Greece and Rome to the prophetesses (between four and 10 in number) who attended the oracles of the ancient world and delivered messages from the gods. The most famous of them was the sibyl of Cumae, who advised Aeneas on his journey to the underworld and was the supposed fount of the ***sibylline books,*** a set of prophetic sayings offering guidance in matters of policy and religion. These were kept in the temple of Jupiter on Capitoline Hill in Rome until they were lost in a fire in 83 B.C. "Poor Jotham, whose life paid the forfeiture of his folly, acknowledged, before he died, that his reasons for believing in a mine were extracted from the lips of a sibyl, who, by looking in a magic glass, was enabled to discover the hidden treasures of the earth" (James Fenimore Cooper, *The Pioneers,* 1823).

sick as a parrot Fed up; disappointed; dejected. The origin of the phrase is somewhat obscure. Suggestions concerning its origin range from the traditional melancholy Pierrot character to the parrot disease psittacosis. Whatever the case, the phrase is strongly associated with a famous MONTY PYTHON comedy sketch featuring a disgruntled customer's attempts to return a DEAD PARROT to a pet store. *When he heard what the stock he had sold was now worth he felt sick as a parrot.*

sick man of Europe A European country or institution that is seen to be in serious decline. The description was first bestowed upon what was then the ailing Ottoman Empire by Czar Nicholas I of Russia in 1853. It has since been applied to modern Turkey, among other European countries. "The strength of the British economy in the mid-1980s, the signs of growth and rising prosperity, helped dispel the old image of 'the sick man of Europe'" (Kenneth O. Morgan, *The People's Peace*, 1990).

Siege Perilous *See* GALAHAD.

sign of the times Something that is viewed as symptomatic of present attitudes, fortunes, etc. The phrase comes from Matthew 16:3: "And in the morning, It will be foul weather to day: for the sky is red and lowring. O ye hypocrites, ye can discern the face of the sky; but can ye not discern the signs of the times?" There follows a list of signs of the times that will herald the Second Coming of Christ, such as the appearance of false prophets, wars and rumors of wars, nation rising against nation, famines, pestilences, and earthquakes. ". . . a special financial article in a hostile tone beginning with the words 'We have always feared' and a guarded, half-column leader, opening with the phrase: 'It is a deplorable sign of the times' what was, in effect, an austere, general rebuke to the absurd infatuations of the investing public" (Joseph Conrad, *Chance,* 1913).

Sikes, Bill *See* NANCY.

Silas Marner (sīlăs mahrner) Archetype of an unhappy miser. In the novel *Silas Marner* (1861) by George Eliot (Mary Ann Evans; 1819–80), the title character is an embittered weaver who hoards his wealth and never spends anything on creature comforts. His attitude slowly changes, however, after a generous-hearted young girl called Eppie comes to live with him. *He was so mean with his money that he made Silas Marner look like Santa Claus.*

Silenus (sīleenăs) Personification of a jovial, pleasure-loving man. Silenus was identified in Greek mythology as the foster father and teacher of Dionysus and considered the god of springs and running water. He shared many of the same characteristics as the SATYRS and was commonly depicted as a fat man riding drunkenly on a donkey or astride a wineskin, wearing a crown of flowers. "I will invite my friends to a last feast; a saturnalia in a city of famine; a banquet of death, spread by the jovial labors of Silenus and his fauns!" (Wilkie Collins, *Antonina,* 1850).

Silicon Valley (silikăn) A place where modern technological manufacture is concentrated, or such technologies themselves. The name was originally bestowed upon Santa Clara Valley, south of San Francisco, California, which became a heartland of the burgeoning electronics industry in the 1980s. Silicon is a material widely used in the manufacture of semiconductors. Variants on the theme include Scotland's Silicon Glen between Glasgow and Edinbugh and England's Silicon Fen at Cambridge. *He plans to make his fortune in Silicon Valley and spend the rest of his life on the Riviera.*

Siloam *See* SHILOAH.

Silvanus (silvaynăs) Personification of the countryside. Silvanus was identified in Roman mythology as the god of woodlands, fields, and flocks, the equivalent of the Greek god Pan. He was reputed to keep wolves away from livestock. *They spent the rest of the afternoon enjoying all the pleasures that Silvanus offered to visitors in that delightful glade.*

Silver *See* LONE RANGER.

Silver, Long John *See* LONG JOHN SILVER.

silver age A period of history considered inferior to a GOLDEN AGE. According to Hesiod (fl. c. 800 B.C.) and other poets of the classical era, the original silver age was the second of the ages of the world, when humans abandoned themselves to voluptuous and godless ways. *Commercialism has entirely replaced the artistic impulse in what has been termed a second silver age.*

silver cord *See* GOLDEN BOWL.

Simon Legree *See* UNCLE TOM.

simony (sīmănee) The practice of buying and selling spiritual or church benefits such as pardons, relics, and ecclesiastical offices. The word comes from the name of Simon Magus, a sorcerer who lived in the first century A.D. and who, having converted to Christianity, sought to buy spiritual power from the apostles until rebuked by Peter (as related in Acts 8): "And when Simon saw that through laying on of the apostles' hands the Holy Spirit was given, he offered them money, saying, Give me also this power" (Acts 8:18–19). The word has also produced the verb ***simonize*** to describe such activity. *Some modern people could be accused of simony. They think they can buy their way into the kingdom of God.*

Simple Simon A slow-witted person, a fool. The allusion is to a nursery rhyme character who, among other nonsensical activities, goes fishing for a whale in a bucket of water. *He pretended to be Simple Simon but was really a brilliant thinker.*

Sinai *See* MOUNT SINAI.

Sinbad A sailor or adventurer of some kind. The adventures of Sinbad the Sailor were featured in one of the tales of the *ARABIAN NIGHTS*, which described his seven voyages to exotic distant lands. *He was a regular Sinbad the Sailor, with his own sailboat and everything. See also* OLD MAN OF THE SEA.

sing one's Nunc Dimittis *See* NUNC DIMITTIS.

sinister Ominous; threatening evil or harm. The word comes from the Latin *sinister* (meaning "left handed") and alludes to the ancient notion that in divination, portents that appeared toward the west (on the left of the augur, who traditionally faced north) were negative, while those that appeared toward the east (on the augur's right) were positive. "The hand he gave me was the hand I had bitten. I could not restrain my eye from resting for an instant on a red spot upon it; but it was not so red as I turned, when I met that sinister expression in his face" (Charles Dickens, *David Copperfield,* 1849–50).

Sinon (sīnon) Personification of a person who betrays others by deceit. Sinon was the Greek who convinced the Trojans that there was no danger in dragging the TROJAN HORSE, and the Greek warriors hidden inside it, within the city's walls. *He agreed to act as Sinon, volunteering to go to the meeting and tell anyone who would listen that management was now ready to negotiate.*

sins be as scarlet Even those who are guiltiest of the worst crimes may be forgiven. The phrase comes from Isaiah 1:18, in which sinners are reassured of the possibility of divine forgiveness: "Come now, and let us reason together, saith the LORD: Though your sins be as scarlet, they shall be as white as snow; though they be red like crimson, they shall be as wool." "What if this cursed hand / Were thicker than itself with brother's blood / Is there not rain enough in the sweet heavens / To wash it white as snow?" (William Shakespeare, *Hamlet,* c. 1600).

sins of the fathers The misdeeds of one generation may have to be atoned for by the generations that follow. The phrase comes from the second of the Ten Commandments, as rendered in Exodus 20:5, which warns that those who offend God may find their descendants must pay for their offenses: "Thou shalt not bow down thyself to them, nor serve them: for I the LORD thy God am a jealous God, visiting the iniquity of the fathers upon the children unto the third and fourth generation of them that hate me." "Do you believe in the sins of the father being revisited on the son?" (*Times,* January 8, 2002).

sin will find you out Crimes and other misdeeds invariably reveal themselves in time. The phrase comes from Numbers 32:23, in which Moses commands the reluctant Reubenites and the Gadites to cross the Jordan, warning them that if they refuse to do so they will have committed a crime against God: "But if ye will not do so, behold, ye have sinned against the LORD: and be sure your sin will find you out." "It sounds horrible and wicked enough, but he cannot be blamed too much, and be sure his sin will find him out" (H. Rider Haggard, *She,* 1887).

Sion *See* ZION.

siren (sīrăn) A seductive or beguiling woman; a temptress. According to Homer's *Odyssey* (c. 700 B.C.) the Sirens were sea nymphs (part women, part bird) who lured sailors and their ships to destruction with their enchanting singing; hence, a ***siren song*** signifies an extremely attractive and tempting but highly dangerous offer or invitation. Odysseus was curious to hear the song of the sirens and had himself tied to the mast of his ship while the rest of his crew plugged their ears with wax. When the Argonauts sailed past the Sirens, they kept themselves safe by listening instead to the superior singing of Orpheus, upon which the Sirens threw themselves into the sea and were turned into rocks. "Of course such a marriage was only what Newland was entitled to; but young men are so foolish and incalculable—and some women so ensnaring and unscrupulous—that it was nothing short of a miracle to see one's only son safe past the Siren Isle and in the haven of a blameless domesticity" (Edith Wharton, *The Age of Innocence,* 1920).

Sirius (sireeăs) The brightest star in the sky, situated in the constellation of Canis Major. Also called the dog star, it was named Sirius by the Romans, who believed that dogs were most likely to go mad when the star was at its height (the so-called DOG DAYS of mid-summer). The word itself comes from the Greek *seirios* (meaning "scorching"). "The sky was still thick, but looking straight up he saw a single star, and tried vaguely to reckon whether it were Sirius, or—or—The effort tired him too much, and he closed his heavy lids and thought that he would sleep" (Edith Wharton, *Ethan Frome,* 1911).

Sisera *See* STARS IN THEIR COURSES.

Sistine Chapel *See* PAINTING THE SISTINE CHAPEL.

Sisyphean (sisăfeeăn) Of or relating to a seemingly endless or futile effort. The allusion is to the punishment that was imposed by Tartarus upon Sisyphus, king of Corinth, for various misdemeanors. Sisyphus was condemned for eternity to push a large rock up a hill, only to find that when he reached the summit the rock tumbled all the way back to the bottom, so he had to begin all over again. By the same token any fruitless or never-ending task may be called a ***burden*** or ***labor of Sisyphus.*** *For years he had engaged in an apparently Sisyphean effort to persuade the government to change its mind.*

sit at the feet of Gamaliel *See* GAMALIEL.

six million dollar man *See* BIONIC MAN.

sixty-four thousand dollar question An all-important, deciding question, especially one that is difficult to answer. The allusion is to a U.S. radio and television quiz of the 1950s in which the prize money gradually escalated until it reached the maximum total of $64,000. *The sixty-four thousand dollar question is who's got the key?*

skeleton at the feast A somber or melancholy note in otherwise joyous surroundings. This colorful image is of ancient origin, its earliest mention being in the *Moralia* of the Greek historian Plutarch (A.D. 46–120). According to Plutarch, who had traveled widely, the Egyptians were in the habit of placing a mummy among the diners at their feasts and celebrations as a reminder of their own mortality. In modern usage the term is often applied to a person who remains depressed and gloomy while those around him or her are throwing themselves into the festivities. "Blunt noticed this and remarked that I seemed to be attracted by the Empress. 'It's disagreeable,' I said. 'It seems to lurk there like a shy skeleton at the feast. But why do you give the name of Empress to that dummy?'" (Joseph Conrad, *The Arrow of Gold,* 1919).

skeptic A person who refuses to accept what he or she is told. The word comes from the Greek *skeptesthai* (meaning "to examine") and was adopted in the fourth century B.C. by the followers of Pyrrho as a name to describe their philosophical movement, otherwise known as Pyrrhonism. Essential to their beliefs were the notions that nothing could be proved beyond doubt and that only the reality of the sensations could be trusted. "'Am I a liar in your eyes?' he asked passionately. 'Little sceptic, you shall be convinced'" (Charlotte Brontë, *Jane Eyre,* 1847).

skid row *See* ON SKID ROW.

skin of one's teeth, by the By the narrowest of margins. The expression comes from Job 19:20: "My bone cleaveth to my skin and to my flesh, and I am escaped with the skin of my teeth." *He escaped serious injury only by the skin of his teeth.*

Skywalker, Luke *See* STAR WARS.

slam dunk An impressive success. The term comes from basketball, in which it describes a shot in which a player leaps high in the air before slamming the ball down into the basket. *The party's slam dunk in the primaries was a surprise to everyone.*

slaughter of the innocents *See* MASSACRE OF THE INNOCENTS.

Sleeping Beauty A person who is sleeping soundly. The allusion is to a fairy tale collected by the French folklorist Charles Perrault (1628–1703) in 1697, which relates how a princess falls into a magic sleep for 100 years until she is woken by the kiss of a handsome young prince. *You'd better go and wake up Sleeping Beauty over there or he'll be late for school. See also* PRINCE CHARMING.

Sleepy Hollow *See* ICHABOD CRANE.

Sleipnir (sleepneer) Archetype of a fast horse or other animal or vessel. Sleipnir was identified in Norse mythology as the eight-legged horse belonging to Odin. It was reputed to be able to outstrip the wind while running on land or water or in the air. *He patted his mount lovingly, as though convinced it would prove a new Sleipnir in the right conditions.*

slings and arrows Setbacks; adversity. The phrase comes from William Shakespeare's tragedy *Hamlet* (c. 1600), in which Hamlet muses on the foibles of fate: "To be, or not to be—that is the question; / Whether 'tis nobler in the mind to suffer / The slings and arrows of outrageous fortune, / Or to take arms against a sea of troubles, / And by opposing end them?" "One of the reasons why play is so absorbing is that it is self-initiated, in a way that is not available to us in the process of combating, enduring or avoiding the slings and arrows of day-to-day living" (Gavin Bolton, *Drama as Education*, 1988).

slough of despond (slow) A state of hopeless despair or despondency. The allusion is to the allegorical *PILGRIM'S PROGRESS* (1678, 1684) by the English preacher and poet John Bunyan (1628–88), in which the Slough of Despond is a bog into which Christian and his companion Pliable become stuck on their journey to the CELESTIAL CITY. Christian fights his way out, but Pliable gives up and turns back. "It was while I was in this slough of despond that my publisher rang to ask if I would like to read a manuscript that needed transforming into a readable book before it could be published" (Raymond Hitchcock, *Fighting Cancer: A Personal Story*, 1989).

small is beautiful Sometimes things on a smaller scale are more satisfactory. The allusion is to the title of the book *Small is Beautiful* (1973) by German-born British economist E. F. Schumacher (1911–77), although it was actually coined by his publishers Anthony Blond and Desmond Briggs. The slogan became a favorite of businessmen and politicians, but has since been applied in many other contexts. *The company's survival through turbulent times only goes to show that small is beautiful.*

smile like a Cheshire Cat *See* CHESHIRE CAT.

smite them hip and thigh To beat someone thoroughly. The phrase comes from Judges 15:8, which describes how Samson exacted his revenge on the Philistines after they burned his wife and father-in-law, smiting them "hip and thigh with a great slaughter." ". . . the old Jew could for some time only answer by invoking the protection of all the patriarchs of the Old Testament successively against the sons of Ishmael, who were coming to smite them, hip and thigh, with the edge of the sword" (Sir Walter Scott, *Ivanhoe,* 1819).

smite the rock To perform a miraculous act. The reference is to Exodus 17:6 and Numbers 20:11, which relate how God instructed Moses to provide water for his people journeying in the wilderness: "Behold, I will stand before thee there upon the rock in Horeb; and thou shalt smite the rock, and there shall come water out of it, that the people may drink." When Moses struck the rock water poured forth. *This time there were no resources left to save them; the rock had been smitten one too many times. See also* MOSES' ROD.

smoke-filled room A room in which hard bargaining or other intense negotiations take place. The allusion is to the tobacco smoke that tends to fill the room during long hours of discussion. The term was first applied to a suite in Chicago's Blackstone Hotel, the scene of negotiations leading to the selection of Warren Harding as the Republican presidential candidate in 1920. *Her destiny was decided in a smoke-filled room by a bunch of elderly relatives and their lawyers.*

smoking gun Irrefutable evidence that places the guilt for a crime or other act at a particular person's door. The phrase alludes to a gun from which a bullet has just been fired. The search for a "smoking gun" was famously undertaken by journalists investigating the WATERGATE scandal of 1973, which led ultimately to the downfall of Richard Nixon as U.S. president. The evidence that sealed the president's fate was a tape recording in which Nixon was heard sanctioning the cover-up into the Watergate burglary. The phrase was in frequent use once more in 2003 in relation to the search for the alleged "weapons of mass destruction" thought to have been developed in Iraq under Saddam Hussein. *This could be the smoking gun that sends the defendants to prison.*

Snow White A girl or woman of stainless virtue, or one who at least appears to be entirely innocent. The allusion is to the fairy tale *Snow White and the Seven Dwarfs*, which tells how the lovely Snow White becomes housekeeper to some kindly dwarfs but then falls victim to the scheming guiles of her stepmother, an evil queen who is jealous of Snow White's beauty and feeds her a piece of poisoned apple. Snow White falls into a deep sleep, from which she is eventually awakened by the kiss of a young prince. *She may look as if butter wouldn't melt in her mouth, but she's no Snow White. See also* PRINCE CHARMING.

soap opera A long-running radio or television drama series, usually with a domestic setting and a melodramatic tone. The first such series were sponsored by soap manufacturers, hence the name, which is often shortened to simply ***soap***. "The demand for a little something to take the mind off the day's troubles is now much more fulfilled by a soap opera or a half-hour crime story on the telly" (H. R. F. Keating, *Writing Crime Fiction*, 1986).

sock A symbol of comic drama. The sock (in Latin *soccus*) was a low loose-fitting slipper commonly worn about the house in the ancient world and also worn on stage by comic actors. "Then to the well-trod stage anon / If Jonson's learned sock be on, / Or sweetest Shakespeare, fancy's child, / Warble his native wood-notes wild" (John Milton, *L'Allegro,* 1631). *See also* BUSKIN.

Socratic (săkratik) Of or relating to the philosophical approach of the Greek philosopher Socrates (c. 470–399 B.C.) or more generally to anyone who adopts unconventional philosophical ideas. Transmitted through his pupils Plato and Xenophon, as Socrates left no written account of his thinking, the ***Socratic method*** recommends the use of questions and answers to reach the truth. By employing ***Socratic irony*** (feigning ignorance in an argument) the interrogator may quickly reveal the greater ignorance of an opponent in a philosophical debate or encourage students to develop their own ideas about something. Socrates' own use of such tactics made him many enemies in Athens, and ultimately he was forced to commit suicide by drinking hemlock. "Mr. Craig paused a moment with an emphatic stare after this triumphant specimen of Socratic argument" (George Eliot, *Adam Bede,* 1859).

Sodom and Gomorrah (sodăm, gămoră) A place that is notorious for depravity and vice, especially of a sexual nature. Sodom and Gomorrah are described in the book of Genesis as cities of corruption, and for this reason they are both destroyed by FIRE AND BRIMSTONE sent by God: "Then the LORD rained upon Sodom and upon Gomorrah brimstone and fire from the LORD out of heaven; And he overthrew those cities, and all the plain, and all the inhabitants of the cities, and that which grew upon the ground" (Genesis 19:24–25). The term ***sodomy,*** for anal intercourse, comes from the name of Sodom, whose inhabitants were infamous for such practices (Genesis 19:5). *The preacher warned his congregation in the strongest possible terms against following the sexual sins of Sodom and Gomorrah.*

soft answer turns away wrath, a A gentle response to an insult or other provocation will reduce tension and soothe the anger of others. This advice comes from Proverbs 15:1: "A soft answer turneth away wrath: but grievous words stir up anger." *The situation could easily have gotten out of hand, but the teacher, clearly knowing that a soft answer turns away wrath, calmed down both parties with a quiet word.*

Sol Personification of the Sun. Sol was identified in Roman mythology as the sun god, equivalent to the Greek Helios. In Norse mythology Sol was identified as the maiden who steered the chariot of the Sun. *The beach was crowded with scantily clad tourists making their annual obeisance to the great god Sol.*

sold his birthright for a mess of pottage *See* SELL ONE'S BIRTHRIGHT FOR A MESS OF POTTAGE.

solecism (solăsizăm) A grammatical mistake; a violation of etiquette or good manners. The word, from the Greek *soiloikos* (meaning "speaking incorrectly"), alludes to the ancient Athenian colony of Soli (or Soloi) on the coast of Cilicia in Asia Minor, whose inhabitants spoke a form of Greek considered degenerate in comparison to Greek as spoken in Athens. "It often is so felt, but we are inclined to say that it never produces half the discomfort or half the feeling of implied inferiority that is shown by a great man who desires his visitor to be seated while he himself speaks from his legs. Such a solecism in good breeding, when construed into English, means this: 'The accepted rules of courtesy in the world require that I should offer you a seat; if I did not do so, you would bring a charge against me in the world of being arrogant and ill-mannered; I will obey the world, but, nevertheless, I will not put myself on an equality with you'" (Anthony Trollope, *Barchester Towers,* 1857).

solitary, poor, nasty, brutish, and short *See* HOBBESIAN; NASTY, BRUTISH, AND SHORT.

Solomon *See* JUDGMENT OF SOLOMON; SOLOMON'S SEAL; SOLOMON'S TEMPLE.

Solomon's seal (solămănz) A flowering plant of the genus *Polygonatum* and a member of the lily family. The plant owes its name to the shape of the prominent leaf scars on its stem that supposedly resemble seals. Another suggestion has it that it is so called because its roots may be used medicinally to seal wounds. The STAR OF DAVID emblem has always been closely associated with Solomon himself and is sometimes referred to as Solomon's seal. *Celandine and Solomon's seal were growing by the side of the road.*

Solomon's temple (solămănz) A lavish building or other structure notable for its extravagance. The allusion is to the great Temple in Jerusalem built on the command of King Solomon. The Temple, as described in 1 Kings 5–8 and 2 Chronicles 3–7, was remarkable for the magnificence of its decoration, which included rich cedar wood panels and gold ornamentation. "In this process the chamber and its furniture grew more and more dignified and luxurious; the shawl hanging at the window took upon itself the richness of tapestry; the brass handles of the chest of drawers were as golden knockers; and the carved bed-posts seemed to have some kinship with the magnificent pillars of Solomon's temple" (Thomas Hardy, *Tess of the D'Urbervilles,* 1891).

solon (sōlăn) A wise lawgiver; any member of a legislative body. The allusion is to the Athenian statesman Solon, who in the sixth century B.C. repealed most of the unfeasibly severe laws imposed by the DRACONIAN code. His reforms did much to give power back to the Athenian people and helped to lay the foundation for Athenian democracy. "I saw thee once give a penny to a man with a long beard, who, from the dignity of his exterior, might have represented Solon" (Sir Walter Scott, *Redgauntlet,* 1824).

some are more equal than others *See* ALL ANIMALS ARE EQUAL, BUT SOME ANIMALS ARE MORE EQUAL THAN OTHERS.

something is rotten in the state of Denmark Something is wrong. This is a quotation from William Shakespeare's tragedy *HAMLET* (c. 1600), in which it is voiced by Marcellus, an officer of the Danish palace guard, after the ghost of the dead king has appeared. In modern usage, it tends to be employed facetiously. *A government spokesman denied there was anything in the rumors, but the press all agreed that there was something rotten in the state of Denmark.*

something nasty in the woodshed A shocking secret, a hidden scandal, etc. The phrase comes from the comic novel *COLD COMFORT FARM* (1932) by the British novelist Stella Gibbons, in which the aged Ada Doom claims to be haunted by a terrible trauma (never detailed) that she experienced long ago, when as a young child she "saw something nasty in the woodshed." *You'd better not put yourself up for election if you have anything nasty in the woodshed.*

Somme, the (som) A battle that leads to huge losses on both sides without a decisive result being reached, or more generally a very muddy piece of ground. The Battle of the Somme on the western front in 1916 was one of the bloodiest episodes of

World War I, fought in a devastated landscape of mud and corpse-strewn trenches. The first day of the battle resulted in the British losing 60,000 men, the greatest loss on a single day ever suffered by the British army. *The atrocious weather had turned the field into something resembling the Somme. See also* FLANDERS; PASSCHENDAELE; YPRES.

Somnus (somnăs) Personification of sleep. Somnus was the god of sleep in Roman mythology, equivalent to the Greek Hypnos. He was said to be a son of Night and a brother of Death. *The call of Somnus was almost irresistible, but he knew he must stay awake until the relief arrived at dawn.*

sons of Adam *See* ADAM.

sons of Bacchus *See* BACCHUS.

sons of Belial *See* BELIAL.

sons of thunder *See* BOANERGES.

Sophie's Choice (sōfeez) An agonizingly difficult decision. The allusion is to the 1979 novel by U.S. writer William Styron (b. 1925) about a Polish woman called Sophie Zawistowska who struggles to come to terms with having to choose which of her two children should go to the gas chambers of a German concentration camp and which should survive. The book was turned into a highly successful movie, starring Meryl Streep, in 1982. *She was forced into a Sophie's Choice between her two children.*

sophistry (sofistree) The use of subtle reasoning to deceive. The word alludes to the Sophists, wandering teachers and philosophers throughout ancient Greece in the fifth and fourth centuries B.C. The word means "wise man," although the widely variant skills and motives of these teachers meant that in time it came to refer to those who cynically used their cunning to mislead or dupe others. "He looked at her imploringly, as if he would willingly have taken a lie from her lips, knowing it to be one, and have made of it, by some sort of sophistry, a valid denial" (Thomas Hardy, *Tess of the D'Urbervilles,* 1891).

Sophoclean (sofăkleeăn) Direct, simple, clear, and reasonable. The Greek playwright Sophocles (c. 496–406 B.C.) is considered perhaps the finest classical writer of tragic drama, seven examples of which survive out of a total of some 130. He is admired for his economy and simplicity of style and for his relatively straightforward approach to character and plot in such plays as *Oedipus Rex, Antigone,* and *Electra. No one present could have failed to be impressed by the Sophoclean explanation he gave of the company's actions.*

sop to Cerberus (serbărăs) A bribe or gift designed to neutralize a potential threat. In Greek mythology, Cerberus was the terrifying three-headed dog that guarded the entrance to the underworld. When a person died it was customary in classical times to place with the body a cake or some other choice offering with which to pacify Cerberus and thus gain entry to Hades unmolested. When Aeneas ventured into the underworld he went past Cerberus by feeding him a cake of honey and poppy that put him to sleep. *This offer of financial compensation is nothing more than a sop to Cerberus, a bribe to prevent the complainants from going to court.*

sound and fury Meaningless commotion and uproar. The phrase comes from William Shakespeare's tragedy *Macbeth* (1606), in which it appears in a famous speech delivered by Macbeth himself: "Life's but a walking shadow, a poor player, / That struts and frets his hour upon the stage, / And then is heard no more; it is a tale / Told by an idiot, full of sound and fury, / Signifying nothing." "Fatima had an emotional outburst and stormed out first with Giselle and the Renaissance Man in tow, taking all her sound and fury and phobias elsewhere, and everyone was profoundly relieved" (Jean Bows, *Jane's Journey*, 1991).

sounding brass or a tinkling cymbal A meaningless noise. The phrase comes from 1 Corinthians 13:1: "Though I speak with the tongues of men and of angels, and have not charity, I am become as sounding brass, or a tinkling cymbal." "I hearkened and hearkened the ministers, and read an' read at my prayer-book; but it was all like sounding brass and a tinkling cymbal: the sermons I couldn't understand, an' th' prayer-book only served to show me how wicked I was, that I could read such good words an' never be no better" (Anne Brontë, *Agnes Grey,* 1847).

sound of many waters *See* VOICE OF MANY WATERS.

sour grapes Resentment or bitter feelings, usually against something that one cannot enjoy oneself. The allusion is to Aesop's fable about a fox that on finding itself unable to reach a delicious bunch of grapes consoled itself with deciding that they were sour anyway. *He said that the book I wrote is not worth reading, but that is sour grapes because he would like to write one himself.*

South Sea Bubble A financial collapse based on a sudden failure of confidence in a doubtful project. The South Sea Bubble was the name given originally to a sudden rise and equally sudden fall in confidence in a speculative venture launched by the British lawyer Sir John Blunt in 1710. Blunt's ambitious plans involved controlling trade in the South Seas and South America; for a time the scheme prospered, but investors ultimately became nervous and in 1720 the whole project collapsed, ruining many of those connected with it. *This venture could turn into another South Sea Bubble unless more capital is found soon.*

sow dragon's teeth To plant the seeds of future conflict. The allusion is to Greek mythology, specifically to the story of Cadmus, who killed a dragon and was instructed to give half the dragon's teeth to the goddess Athena and to plant the other half in the ground. The latter sprouted into warriors who fought one another until only five were left. These survivors then accompanied Cadmus on his mission to found the city of Thebes. Athena gave her part of the teeth to the king of Colchis, who passed them on to Jason, leader of the Argonauts. Among other challenges Jason had to plant the teeth and kill the warriors who sprang up from them before he could secure the Golden Fleece (in which task he was eventually successful). *Few people realized at the time that those who agreed the compromises necessary to facilitate the state's foundation were actually sowing dragon's teeth that would lead to the loss of thousands of lives in the decades to come. See also* PYRRHIC VICTORY.

sow the wind and reap the whirlwind Those who behave irresponsibly or carelessly will find that they have to face disastrous consequences of their misdeeds later on. The expression is of biblical origin, appearing at Hosea 8:7: "For they have sown the wind, and they shall reap the whirlwind: it hath no stalk: the bud shall yield no meal: if so be it yield, the strangers shall swallow it up." In its original biblical context, it referred specifically to the idolatry of the Israelites, which proved a precursor to the Assyrian invasion. *People who behave so irresponsibly in the future will find that they sow the wind and reap the whirlwind. See also* REAP WHAT YOU SOW.

Spade, Sam *See* SAM SPADE.

Spanish Armada (ahrmahdă) A large fleet of ships or boats. The allusion is to the Spanish invasion fleet of 130 ships that sailed to England in 1588, only to be defeated in the English Channel by the English fleet under the command of Sir Francis Drake and then dashed to final destruction by storms on its way back to Spain. *There were so many canoes and kayaks on the lake that it looked like the Spanish Armada.*

Spanish Inquisition *See* INQUISITION.

spare the rod and spoil the child Children who are overindulged and never disciplined will grow up to be unruly, maladjusted individuals. This advice, often quoted in defense of corporal punishment and other forms of firm discipline, comes from Proverbs 13:24: "He that spareth his rod hateth his son: but he that loveth him chasteneth him betimes." Further support for such chastisement may be found in Proverbs 23:13–14: "Withhold not correction from the child: for if thou beatest him with the rod, he shall not die. Thou shalt beat him with the rod, and shalt deliver his soul from hell." "'I ain't doing my duty by that boy, and that's the Lord's truth, goodness knows. Spare the rod and spile the child, as the Good Book says. I'm a laying up sin and suffering for us both, I know'" (Mark Twain, *The Adventures of Tom Sawyer,* 1876).

sparrow's fall *See* FALL OF A SPARROW.

Spartacus (spahrtăkăs) Archetype of a slave who rises up in revolt against his masters. Spartacus was a Thracian slave who was forcibly recruited to the gladiator school at Capua in Italy. He managed to escape and raised an army of slaves, who achieved a series of memorable victories in battle against the legions of ancient Rome. Ultimately he was killed when his army was defeated by Crassus in 71 B.C. The story of Spartacus has inspired a novel by J. Leslie Mitchell (1951), a ballet by Aram Khachaturian (1954), and a film (1960), starring Kirk Douglas in the title role. *This lowly cleric long championed the rights of the dispossessed but like some latter-day Spartacus was doomed to defeat in the end.*

Spartan (spahrtăn) Austere; frugal; very strict, especially in relation to a person's lifestyle or upbringing. The people of Sparta, the capital city of Laconia, were renowned for their rejection of comfort and sophistication (which they were much given to early in their history) in favor of a much more rigorous, self-denying existence—adopted, it was said, at the prompting of the poet Tyrtaeus (fl. c. 650 B.C.). Great emphasis was put on physical endurance and self-discipline. Newborn babies were commonly left exposed on bare mountainsides so that the weak would die and only the strong would live to maturity. Children began military training at the age of seven, and the only respectable career was that of a soldier; mourning of those who fell in battle was discouraged. As a result the Spartans were widely respected in the ancient world as fighters, although the primitive state of their cultural life was decried by their more sophisticated neighbors, and their reluctance to accept new thinking led ultimately to defeat on the battlefield at the hands of the more sophisticated Macedonians. "But although she wondered, she could not help loving him the better for his odd combination of Spartan self-control and what appeared to her romantic and childish folly" (Virginia Woolf, *Night and Day,* 1919). *See also* LACONIC.

spear-carrier Someone who plays a minor supporting role in a play, movie, or some other context; a subordinate. The allusion is to the plays of the Shakespearean era, many of which require large numbers of nonspeaking actors playing soldiers, often literally carrying spears. *The party has already got its spear-carriers out to spread the message that their candidate is the man of the hour.*

spears into pruninghooks *See* BEAT SWORDS INTO PLOWSHARES.

Speedy Gonzales (gonzahlez) A person who gets things done quickly. The allusion is to a popular cartoon character, a nimble Mexican mouse, invented by Friz Freleng for Warner Brothers in 1953. *He's normally very slow, but put a paintbrush in his hand and suddenly he's Speedy Gonzalez.*

spheres, music of the *See* MUSIC OF THE SPHERES.

sphinx (sfinks) An inscrutable or enigmatic person. The allusion is to the Sphinx of Greek mythology, a monster with the body of a lion and the breasts and face of a woman that attacked Thebes and challenged its victims, on pain of death, to solve the seemingly insoluble RIDDLE OF THE SPHINX. Today the sphinx is best known through the surviving statue at Giza in Egypt, although the Egyptian version is male and lacks the wings that the Greek Sphinx was supposed to have. The word itself means "the strangler." "The distinction of Phipps is his impassivity. He has been termed by enthusiasts the ideal Butler. The Sphinx is not so incommunicable. He is a mask with a manner" (Oscar Wilde, *An Ideal Husband,* 1895).

Spider-Man A person who has an apparently superhuman power as a climber. The allusion is to the superhero of U.S. comic strips created by Stan Lee and Steve Ditko and popular since the 1950s. Otherwise known as Peter Parker, he acquires various spiderlike powers (such as the ability to spin webs and cling to walls) after being bitten by a mutant spider and uses them imaginatively to overcome his enemies. *He went up that skyscraper like Spider-Man.*

Spillane, Mickey *See* MICKEY SPILLANE.

spirit giveth life *See* LETTER OF THE LAW, THE.

spirit is willing, but the flesh is weak, the It is not always possible for a person to achieve or live up to the standards he or she espouses. In modern usage the line is usually quoted in circumstances where the speaker is apologizing for some moral lapse. The saying comes from Matthew 26:41, in which Christ warned his disciples to remain alert: "Watch and pray, that ye enter not into temptation: the spirit indeed is willing, but the flesh is weak." "Since then I have written many books; and though ceasing my methodical study of the old masters (for though the spirit is willing, the flesh is weak), I have continued with increasing assiduity to try to write better" (W. Somerset Maugham, *The Summing Up,* 1938). *See also* FLESH IS WEAK, THE.

Spock, Doctor *See* DOCTOR SPOCK.

Spock, Mr. *See* STAR TREK.

spoil the Egyptians To plunder an enemy, especially through deception or subterfuge. According to Exodus 12:36 the Israelite women were told to take whatever they could from their Egyptian captors before the flight from Egypt: "And the LORD gave the people favour in the sight of the Egyptians, so that they lent unto them such things as they required. And they spoiled the Egyptians." *When the workers realized their dismissal was inevitable they elected to spoil the Egyptians by stealing every tool they could lay their hands on.*

spread one's net To prepare to capture or ensnare someone or something. The expression is of biblical origin, appearing at Proverbs 29:5: "A man that flattereth his neighbour spreadeth a net for his feet." *The government will have to spread its net very wide if it is to make any significant impact on tax evasion.*

spread the gospel To spread news of some kind; to support a particular belief, outlook, etc. The allusion is to the spreading of the Christian message, as undertaken originally by Christ's disciples (Mark 16:15). "Fifa is taking a risk in spreading the World Cup gospel" (*Guardian,* January 2, 2002).

Squeers, Wackford *See* DOTHEBOYS HALL.

SS A ruthless and much feared military organization synonymous with brutal oppression. The SS, or Schutzstaffel (German for "protective echelon"), was one of the most dreaded parts of the Nazi establishment. Recruiting dedicated Nazis devoted to Adolf HITLER and its own commander Heinrich Himmler, the SS were responsible for carrying out many of the worst atrocities of the Nazi era. Its members dominated both the military and civil structures of the Third Reich. *People in the crowd complained that the soldiers had behaved like the SS, beating up protesters indiscriminately. See also* NIGHT OF THE LONG KNIVES.

stadium (staydeeăm) A sports arena with tiered seating for spectators. The word comes from the Greek *stadion,* which denoted a length of around 606 feet. This was the distance run by competitors on the sports track at Olympia, and in time the word came to be applied to the arena itself. Legend has it that Hercules himself set the length of the track at Olympia. *The competitors entered the stadium to a deafening roar.*

staff of Aesculapius (eskălaypeeăs) Emblem of the medical profession, including the American Medical Association and the Royal Medical Corps, consisting of a staff with a serpent entwined around. Aesculapius was the god of medicine or healing in Roman mythology, equivalent to the Greek Asclepius, who was reputed to have learned his skills from the centaur Chiron and become the first physician prior to being slain by Zeus for compromising the god's power over living things. *Doctors with the organization wear badges bearing the staff of Aesculapius to denote their role as healers. See also* CADUCEUS.

Stalin (stahlin) An authoritarian, tyrannical leader. Josef Stalin (Josif Vissarionovich Dzhugashvili; 1879–1953) succeeded Lenin as the leader of Communist Russia in 1922 and under his rule countless thousands of Russians were imprisoned in the GULAGS of Siberia or condemned to death, especially during the purges he instituted during the 1930s. Millions more died of starvation as a result of the disastrous collectivization of agriculture that took place under his direction. The name Stalin, incidentally, means "man of steel." *The council has come under the influence of a local Stalin, who is ready to sacrifice anyone to his will.*

Stallone, Sylvester *See* RAMBO.

Stanley, Henry Morton *See* DARKEST AFRICA; DOCTOR LIVINGSTONE, I PRESUME?

star chamber A tribunal that is noted for its severity and which operates free from the usual checks and measures. The original Star Chamber was a room in Westminster Palace in London in which a special court sat to try powerful nobles who had offended the Crown; its name referred to the gilt stars that were painted on the ceiling. The tyrannical power of the Star Chamber, which employed torture to obtain confessions, ended with its abolition by Parliament in 1641. "Finally, ministers who could not agree were sent before a 'Star Chamber' of nonspending ministers or ministers who have 'settled'" (H. Glennerster, *Paying for Welfare: The 1990s*, 1992).

star of David A symbol consisting of two superimposed equilateral triangles arranged in the form of a star. The origins of the symbol are uncertain but appear to go back to biblical times, although it is not mentioned specifically in the Bible or the Talmud. It was adopted by the first Zionist Conference in 1897 and in due course became the symbol on the flag of independent Israel. During the Nazi era, authorities implemented, beginning in 1939, the obligatory wearing of the star of David by Jews on their clothing as a "badge" displaying their racial origins. *The Jewish nation has united under the star of David and will stand together until the crisis is past. See also* SOLOMON'S SEAL.

starship Enterprise *See STAR TREK.*

stars in their courses Fate; destiny. The phrase is a quotation from Judges 5:20, which describes how "the stars in their courses fought against Sisera." ***Sisera*** was a Canaanite general who was doomed to defeat by Deborah and Barak and to his own murder at the hands of Jael, the wife of Heber (Judges 4:17–22). He has since become an archetype of a person who struggles futilely against his fate. "Thus the stars in their courses, fought for Darwin" (George Bernard Shaw, *Back to Methuselah,* 1921).

Starsky and Hutch A pair of heroic, dashing police detectives. The 1970s U.S. television series *Starsky and Hutch* introduced two stylish and likable undercover Los Angeles detectives, Dave Starsky (played by Paul Michael Glaser) and Ken Hutchinson (played by David Soul), and became one of the most popular police procedurals of its era. *They arrived in town like Starsky and Hutch, driving a big red car and wearing thick knitted sweaters.*

Star Trek Archetypal science-fiction series. First screened in 1966, the series introduced many stock features of future science-fiction programs and made stars of such characters as ***Captain Kirk***, the Vulcan ***Mr. Spock***, chief engineer Scotty (*see* BEAM ME UP, SCOTTY) and medical officer Dr. McCoy. The series following the journeys through space of the ***starship Enterprise*** continued with movies for the cinema and further television series featuring new characters. It also introduced one of the best-known examples of a split infinitive in its opening statement of the starship's mission "to boldly go where no man has gone before." *The hotel had been fitted out with so much chrome and automatic doors it looked like something out of Star Trek.*

Star Wars High technology, especially space technology. The allusion is to the six *Star Wars* movies of George Lucas (b. 1944), which began with *Star Wars* (1977) and was completed with *Revenge of the Sith* in 2005. These epic space movies traced the evolution of such memorable characters as ***Luke Skywalker*** (the young hero of the first three movies), DARTH VADER, OBI-WAN KENOBI, and YODA. The series became synonymous with the military use of space and in the early 1980s, when President Ronald Reagan announced plans to develop a system of space lasers (the Strategic Defense Initiative) to knock out nuclear missiles before they could reach their targets, the press were quick to dub the project "Star Wars." *Modern hospitals are making extensive use of Star Wars laser technology.*

stations of the cross A series of landmark events. The original Stations of the Cross recorded 14 incidents that occurred during Christ's journey from the judgment hall in Jerusalem to his death by crucifixion at Calvary: 1) Christ is condemned to death, 2) Christ receives the cross, 3) Christ's first fall en route to Calvary, 4) Christ meets his mother, 5) Simon of Cyrene is made to carry the cross, 6) Christ's face is wiped by Veronica (a woman of Jerusalem), 7) Christ's second fall, 8) Christ comforts the women of Jerusalem, 9) Christ's third fall, 10) Christ is stripped of his garments, 11) Christ is nailed to the cross, 12) Christ dies on the cross, 13) Christ's body is taken down from the cross, and 14) Christ's body is laid in the tomb. Representations of these incidents are often arranged around the interior of a church and visited in sequence for prayer and meditation, especially during Lent. *Her divorce marked the last and most important of the personal stations of the cross she would have to endure on the road to artistic self-knowledge. See also* VIA DOLOROSA.

Statue of Liberty An internationally recognized emblem of freedom. The Statue of Liberty, formally entitled "Liberty Enlightening the World," is a colossal statue of a woman in classical drapery holding aloft a burning torch and carrying a tablet bearing the date July 4, 1776. It stands on Liberty Island at the entrance to New York harbor (close to but not actually on ***Ellis Island***, which was until 1954 the main point of entry for foreign immigrants). The statue, unveiled in 1886, was the work of French sculptor Frédéric-Auguste Bartholdi (1834–1904) and was a gift from France to the United States. *He was as American as the Statue of Liberty.*

steal someone's thunder To preempt someone, and thus to deprive him or her of credit or recognition that he or she is due. The story goes that the now largely forgotten English playwright and critic John Dennis (1657–1734) conceived a simple device to produce the sound of thunder for his own play *Appius and Virginia* (1709), possibly consisting of a series of hollowed logs. The play was not a success, but his thunder device was, and Dennis was incensed when he heard it being used in a performance of William Shakespeare's *Macbeth* (1606), exclaiming: "Damn them! They will not let my play run, but they steal my thunder!" *He rushed round to tell everyone the news, only to find that someone else had got there first and stolen his thunder.*

stentorian (sten<u>tor</u>eeăn) Very loud, especially as regards speaking, or forcefully expressed. The word alludes to a Greek herald called Stentor, whose voice (according to Homer) was so loud it was equivalent to those of 50 other men. He died after losing a shouting contest with Hermes, the herald of the gods. The word itself means "voice of bronze." "The stentorian tones of the auctioneer, calling out to clear the way, now announced that the sale was about to commence" (Harriet Beecher Stowe, *Uncle Tom's Cabin,* 1852).

Stepford wives (stepfărd) Women who submerge their own personality in order to be perfect wives for their husbands. The 1974 movie *Stepford Wives*, based on a 1972 Ira Levin novel, depicted a suburban community in which all the carefully groomed wives (actually robotic copies of the original women) are dedicated solely to domestic chores and serving the needs of their husbands. All is exposed when a newlywed couple move into the community and the bride refuses to accept such unthinking chauvinist servility. A second movie version of the novel was released in 2004. *We were really surprised to find that virtually overnight her sister had abandoned her old radicalism and become a Stepford wife.*

Stephen *See* SAINT STEPHEN'S LOAVES.

stigmata (stigmahtă) The brands or other prominent marks or scars on a person's body, especially those associated with suffering or disgrace of some kind. The reference is ultimately to the Greek and Roman practice of branding slaves and criminals with a mark known as the *stigma,* but the word has particular relevance for Christians, who associate it with the wounds Christ sustained to his hands, feet, and side at the Crucifixion (John 19:16–36). Many saints and other holy people over the centuries have reportedly (and apparently miraculously) displayed similar bleeding wounds resembling those inflicted on Christ. "We know too well the child of syphilitic parents; the type is classical; the doctors can pick it out anywhere. Those little old creatures who have the appearance of having already lived, and who have kept the stigmata of all out infirmities, of all our decay" (Upton Sinclair, *Damaged Goods,* 1913).

still small voice An inner sense of right and wrong; the voice of one's conscience. In 1 Kings 19:11–13, God speaks to Elijah on Mount Horeb: "And he said, Go forth, and stand upon the mount before the LORD. And behold, the LORD passed by, and a great and strong wind rent the mountains, and brake in pieces the rocks before the LORD; but the LORD was not in the wind: and after the wind an earthquake; but the LORD was not in the earthquake: And after the earthquake a fire; but the LORD was not in the fire; and after the fire a still small voice . . . and said, What doest thou here, Elijah?" ". . . no louder, no softer; not thrusting itself on people's notice a bit the more for having been outdone by louder sounds—tink, tink, tink, tink. tink. It was a perfect embodiment of the still small voice, free from all cold, hoarseness, huskiness, or unhealthiness of any kind" (Charles Dickens, *Barnaby Rudge,* 1841).

Stockholm syndrome (stokhōm) The tendency for kidnap victims or hostages to sympathize or form a bond with their captors. The reference is to a hostage situation that developed in Stockholm, Sweden, on August 23, 1973, when four bank employees were confined in a bank vault with two bank robbers. Over the following days the kidnapped staff came to identify more closely with their kidnappers than they did with the authorities outside the bank. *It was like a mass outbreak of Stockholm syndrome when the crowd started cheering on the other team.*

stoic (stōik) Accepting one's fate without showing emotion. The word alludes to the Stoics, members of a philosophical school founded in ancient Greece in the fourth century B.C. influenced by the teachings of Zeno of Citium, they recommended the repression of emotion and advocated the supremacy of a cool-headed, rational approach. They came to be called the Stoics because they held meetings at the Painted Portico, or *Stoa Poikile,* in Athens. "At the pronounced words and the spontaneous echo that voluminously rebounded them, Captain Vere, either thro' stoic self-control or a sort of momentary paralysis induced by emotional shock, stood erectly rigid as a musket in the ship-armourer's rack" (Herman Melville, *Billy Budd,* 1924).

stolen thunder *See* STEAL SOMEONE'S THUNDER.

stolen waters are sweet pleasures acquired illegally or through otherwise dubious means are all the more enjoyable. The sentiment comes from Proverbs 9:17: "Stolen waters are sweet, and bread eaten in secret is pleasant." ". . . his eyes dancing with all the glee of a forbidden revel; and his features, which have at all times a mischievous archness of expression, confessing the full sweetness of stolen waters, and bread eaten in secret" (Sir Walter Scott, *Redgauntlet,* 1824). *See also* FORBIDDEN FRUIT.

stonewall To offer stubborn resistance to something. The term is often linked to the Confederate general Thomas J. Jackson (1824–63), who became known as "Stonewall" Jackson for the heroic action of his troops at the First Battle of Bull Run during the U.S. Civil War, after General Robert E. Lee observed "There stands Jackson like a stone wall." Jackson died after being accidentally shot by his own troops during the Battle of Chancellorsville in May 1863. In reality, the term was probably already in use before this and may have started life as a cricketing term, describing a batsman who stubbornly refuses to hit out at the ball and thus risk losing his wicket. *The witness was happy to put a name to the suspect but stonewalled when it came to giving an address.*

straight and narrow The honest or moral path. The phrase is biblical in origin, from Matthew 7:13–14, which warns that it is much easier to follow the path to eternal condemnation than it is to take the path that leads to salvation: "Enter ye in at the strait gate: for wide is the gate, and broad is the way, that leadeth to destruction, and many there be which go in thereat: Because strait is the gate, and narrow is the way, which leadeth unto life, and few there be that find it." (*Strait* in this context means "narrow.") "You can walk the straight and narrow, but with a little bit of luck you'll run amuck" (Alan Jay Lerner, "With a Little Bit of Luck," 1956).

strain at a gnat and swallow a camel To make much fuss over a relatively insignificant detail yet ignore what is important. The expression comes from Matthew 23:24, in which Christ compares the superficial attitude of the Pharisees to those who worry about the tiny insect that has fallen into their drink, while drinking down one of the largest of animals that has also fallen in: "Ye blind guides, which strain at a gnat, and swallow a camel." "Go where you may, you will attract attention; you will make an enemy of every ugly woman who looks at you. Strain at a gnat, Catherine, and swallow a camel. It's only a question of time" (Wilkie Collins, *The Evil Genius,* 1886).

strait and narrow *See* STRAIGHT AND NARROW.

Strangelove, Doctor *See* DOCTOR STRANGELOVE.

stranger and ye took me in *See* I WAS A STRANGER, AND YE TOOK ME IN.

stranger in a strange land A person who is unfamiliar with his or her surroundings and the people near him or her. The origin of this phrase is Exodus 2:22: "And she, bare him a son, and he called his name Gershom: for he said, I have been a stranger in a strange land." The name Gershom sounds like the Hebrew for "an alien there." "After thirteen years of romantic mystery, the brethren who had wronged Joseph, came, strangers in a strange land, hungry and humble, to buy 'a little food'; and being summoned to a palace, charged with crime, they beheld in its owner their wronged brother" (Mark Twain, *The Innocents Abroad,* 1869).

streets of gold A place where there are plentiful opportunities to make an easy fortune. The expression comes from Revelation 21:21, in which John describes his vision of NEW JERUSALEM (the celestial city of heaven) in terms of streets paved with gold: "And the twelve gates were twelve pearls; every several gate was of one pearl: and the street of the city was pure gold, as it were transparent glass." "Oh, London is a fine town, A very famous city, Where all the streets are paved with gold" (George Colman the Younger, *The Heir-at-Law,* 1797).

strong, out of the *See* OUT OF THE STRONG CAME FORTH SWEETNESS.

strong meat Something that arouses repulsion, fear, or anger among people of a sensitive disposition. The phrase comes from Hebrews 5:12: "For when for the time ye ought to be teachers, ye have need that one teach you again which be the first principles of the oracles of God; and are become such as have need of milk, and not of strong meat." In this original biblical context the "strong meat" refers to more advanced teachings of God that the faithful are deemed not yet capable of absorbing. *The fascinating but scandalous subject of the professor's lecture was rather strong meat for some of the more impressionable members of his audience, who begged to be excused and left in some haste.*

stumbling block An obstacle that hinders progress. The phrase occurs several times in the Bible, as in Romans 14:13: "Let us not therefore judge one another any more: but judge this rather; that no man put a stumblingblock or an occasion to fall in his brother's way." "We've studied hard and Miss Stacy has drilled us thoroughly, but we mayn't get through for all that. We've each got a stumbling block. Mine is geometry of course, and Jane's is Latin, and Ruby and Charlie's is algebra, and Josie's is arithmetic" (Lucy Maud Montgomery, *Anne of Green Gables,* 1908).

Sturm und Drang (shtuurm unt drang) A crisis involving torment, rebellion, and stress. The literal meaning of the phrase in German is "storm and stress." Named after a play of the same title (1776) by the German writer Friedrich von Klinger, the German Sturm und Drang literary movement of the late 18th century found expression in the works of Johann von Goethe (1749–1832), Johann von Schiller (1759–1805), and other writers. It involved a rejection of classicism and an impassioned adoption of the ideals of the Romantic movement, with all its accompanying rebelliousness and extravagant emotional turbulence. "Why does he have to go through all this Sturm und Drang?" (Michael Munn, *Hollywood Rogues*, 1991).

Stygian (stijăn) Dreadful; very gloomy; impenetrably dark. The word comes from the name of the ***Styx,*** the river that according to Greek mythology encircled Hades. The dead were carried across its waters by Charon the boatman. "A beam from the setting sun pierced the Stygian gloom" (H. Rider Haggard, *She,* 1887).

Stymphalian birds *See* LABORS OF HERCULES.

Styx *See* STYGIAN.

sub rosa (săb rōză) Secretly; confidentially. The rose was a great favorite of the ancient Romans and among other qualities was understood to represent secrecy, an association it acquired either through its earlier identification with the Egyptian god Horus, who listed secrecy among his virtues, or through the legend that Eros bribed Harpocrates with a rose so that he would not tell Venus of their intimacies. Consequently a rose was sometimes suspended over council tables as a reminder that any conversations that took place happened "under the rose," that is, in confidence. Similarly a bouquet of roses over a doorway was supposed to be a sign that anything said inside would be kept confidential and thus all present could speak freely. The phrase had acquired a legal connotation by the 19th century, referring to the confidentiality that exists between lawyer and client. *By mutual agreement these meetings always took place sub rosa, and no records were made of what was said.*

such a time as this *See* FOR SUCH A TIME AS THIS.

suffer fools gladly To tolerate foolish people with patience. The expression comes from 2 Corinthians 11:19: "For ye suffer fools gladly, seeing ye yourselves are wise." In the original biblical reference Paul commends the Corinthians for their forbearance, underlining that it is a proof of wisdom to tolerate those who lack it. "A clever woman and thoroughly coached, thought I. Well, zikali was never one to suffer fools, and doubtless she is another of the pawns whom he uses on his board of policy" (H. Rider Haggard, *Finished,* 1917).

suffer the little children To show greater forbearance to children and other innocents. The phrase comes from Matthew 19:14, in which Christ tells his disciples that he welcomes children to come to him for his blessing: "Suffer little children to come unto me, and forbid them not: for of such is the kingdom of heaven." *Suffer* here means "let" or "allow." (See also Luke 18:15.) *The priest frowned as the boys raced about the vestry and reflected that it was not always easy to "suffer the little children," as he so often instructed his parishioners.*

sufficient unto the day is the evil thereof It is enough to worry about one's present troubles without concerning oneself with possible future problems as well. The expression comes from the account of Christ's Sermon on the Mount at Matthew 6:33–34: "Seek ye first the kingdom of God, and his righteousness; and all these things shall be added unto you. Take therefore no thought for the morrow: for the morrow shall take thought for the things of itself. Sufficient unto the day is the evil thereof." *There's no point in getting anxious about tomorrow—sufficient into the day is the evil thereof. See also* TOMORROW WILL TAKE CARE OF ITSELF.

sulk in one's tent To retreat into moody seclusion while nursing a private grievance. The reference is to the behavior of Achilles after he lost his prize of the beautiful slave girl Briseis to his rival Agamemnon, king of Mycenae, during the Trojan War. According to Homer's *Iliad* (c. 700 B.C.), Achilles retreated to his tent and only consented to come out again after the death of his close friend Patroclus. In his absence the Greeks sustained several serious reverses on the battlefield. Variants of the phrase include to ***sulk like Achilles*** and to ***sulk like Achilles in his tent.*** *After this initial reverse the party's candidate refused to take part in any more television showdowns and instead retired to sulk in his tent.*

Sundance Kid *See* BUTCH CASSIDY AND THE SUNDANCE KID.

sun go down on one's anger, don't let the Never end the day unreconciled with those with whom one has quarreled. This proverbial advice comes from Ephesians 4:26: "Be ye angry, and sin not: let not the sun go down upon your wrath." Variants include ***don't go to bed angry.*** *Her husband recalled the saying about not letting the sun go down on one's anger and resolved to go around to their neighbors' house to apologize before dinnertime.*

Sunnybrook Farm (suneebruuk) A place where everything is unrealistically perfect. The allusion is to the children's book *Rebecca of Sunnybrook Farm* (1903) by Kate Douglas Wiggins. Rebecca herself is indomitably cheerful, loyal, and hardworking, and Sunnybrook Farm is equally divorced from the harsh realities of life. *There's no way you would confuse the South Bronx with Sunnybrook Farm.*

Superman A person with apparently superhuman powers. Superman made his first appearance in the 1930s as a comic-strip hero invented by Jerry Siegel and Joe Schuster and later became the central character in numerous movies and television series. A native of the planet Krypton, and otherwise known on earth as mild-mannered journalist ***Clark Kent***, he has fantastic strength and a range of other powers, but is susceptible to the debilitating effects of KRYPTONITE. He has a girlfriend, ***Lois Lane***, who for several decades remained innocent of his dual personality, and an archenemy in the shape of the evil ***Lex Luthor***. *Superman himself couldn't clear that amount of snow in an hour.*

Superwoman A woman who achieves more than would appear humanly possible. The allusion is to the comic-strip heroine, a female equivalent of SUPERMAN, complete with cloak and the power of flight. In modern usage, the name is often given to women who successfully combine a challenging career with a fulfilling domestic life, especially since the publication of Shirley Conran's book *Superwoman* (1975). "It's easy to think you are Superwoman and try to give everyone 100 per cent of your attention" (Linda Stoker, *Having It All*, 1991). *See also* WONDER WOMAN.

survival of the fittest The natural law that the strongest species are the species that survive in the long term. Otherwise known as the ***law of the jungle***, the phrase is closely associated with the evolutionary theories of British naturalist Charles Darwin (*see* DARWINIAN), though it appears to have been coined originally by Herbert Spencer in *Principles of Biology* (1864–67). *Things may be different where you come from, but out here it's the survival of the fittest.*

Susanna and the Elders *See* DANIEL COME TO JUDGMENT, A.

Svengali (svengahlee) A person who exercises a malign hypnotic influence over others. Svengali is a villainous impresario in the 1894 novel *Trilby* by the British novelist George du Maurier (1834–96). He exercises a pernicious influence over the young heroine of the book, singer Trilby O'Ferrall, inspiring her to sing beyond her natural ability; after Svengali dies she loses her musical powers and also dies. "Lydon's counsel alleged that Malcolm McLaren 'regards himself as a Svengali of these people to do whatever he cares without asking anybody else'" (M. Brown, *Richard Branson: The Inside Story*, 1989).

sweat of thy face *See* ADAM'S CURSE.

Sweeney Todd (sweenee tod) A murderer who cuts the throats of his victims. The allusion is to Sweeney Todd (1756–1802), the so-called ***Demon Barber of Fleet Street***, who murdered customers at his Fleet Street barber shop in London by slitting their throats with his razor and then disposed of their bodies by cutting them up and putting them in meat pies or sausages to be sold from a neighboring bakery. "The magazine was launched ceremoniously and seven weeks later was scuppered in as blatant an act of back-stabbing as Fleet Street has seen since Sweeney Todd set up shop there" (Maureen Lipman, *Thank You for Having Me*, 1990).

sweetness and light Amiable relations; harmony. The phrase first appeared in *The Battle of the Books* (1697) by the Irish satirist Jonathan Swift (1667–1745), although it later became better known as a quotation from *Culture and Anarchy* (1869) by the English poet and critic Matthew Arnold (1822–88). According to Arnold the qualities essential to "sweetness and light" are moral virtue and intellectual truth. In modern usage the phrase tends to be employed facetiously. *He thought that once he had apologized all would be sweetness and light, but he counted without the very human need for revenge.*

sword of Damocles (damăkleez) A looming threat; an impending danger. According to Greek legend Damocles was a nobleman who sought to ingratiate himself with Dionysus the Elder (405–367 B.C.) by remarking enviously upon the great happiness that Dionysus must enjoy as ruler of Syracuse. In response Dionysus invited Damocles to dine with him. Only after Dionysus had sat down to eat did Damocles realize that there was a sword suspended over his head by a single hair. Thus threatened, Damocles did not enjoy his meal and came to appreciate how Dionysus himself had to live with the perpetual fear of assassination or deposition by jealous enemies. "True, in old age we live under the shadow of Death, which, like a sword of Damocles, may descend at any moment" (Samuel Butler, *The Way of All Flesh,* 1903).

swords into plowshares *See* BEAT SWORDS INTO PLOWSHARES.

sybaritic (sibăritik) Pleasure-loving; luxurious; self-indulgent. The inhabitants of the town of Sybaris in ancient Lucania (southern Italy) were notorious for their pleasure-loving ways and their indulgence in all manner of comforts and luxuries. By the same token, any person who shows a fondness for the good things in life may be dubbed a ***sybarite.*** *The sybaritic ways of the urban young were never likely to win much approval among their elders.*

sycophant (sikōfănt, sīkōfant) A person who flatters to win favor; a parasite; a toady. The word comes from the Greek *sykon* (meaning "fig") and *phainein* (meaning "to show"). It is supposed to allude to informants who told the ancient Greek authorities about neighbors who were illegally exporting figs or helping themselves to the fruit of sacred fig trees. Another derivation suggests a link with a class of Athenian lawyers called *sycophants,* who were known to blackmail their clients with the threat of revealing their guilt, thereby "shaking the fig tree" to obtain money or other favors. *Once in power the young king disposed of the aged counselors who had advised his mother and surrounded himself with sycophants.*

Sydney Carton *See* IT IS A FAR, FAR BETTER THING THAT I DO.

Sylvester Stallone *See* RAMBO.

Symplegades (simplegădeez) Rocks or other obstacles that may prove treacherous to passing vessels. The Symplegades (meaning "clashing ones") were two moving rocks located at the entrance to the Black Sea. According to legend, these rocks would press together when a ship came between them, crushing it to pieces. The Argonauts successfully negotiated this obstacle by the ruse of sending a bird through the gap and then slipping through as the rocks opened again, sustaining only minor damage to the stern of the ship as they went through. Ever since then the Symplegades, sometimes called the ***Cyanean rocks,*** have been fused as one. "I saw fastened to a shed near the light-house a long new sign with the words 'Anglo Saxon' on it in large gilt letters, as if it were a useless part which the ship could afford to lose, or which the sailors had discharged at the same time with the pilot. But it interested somewhat as if it had been a part of the Argo, clipped off in passing through the Symplegades" (Henry David Thoreau, *Cape God,* 1865).

syrinx *See* PANPIPES.

T

tabernacle (tabernakăl) A shrine or other place of worship or by extension any building, cupboard, etc., in which something precious is preserved. The allusion is to the Tabernacle of the Old Testament, a portable sanctuary in which God was worshiped from the time of Moses to Solomon. It is described in Exodus 25–31 as a large tent (the Latin word *tabernaculum* meaning "tent") divided by a veil creating the HOLY OF HOLIES (an inner chamber), and an outer area called the Holy Place; the whole structure was surrounded by an enclosure. "Not a soul attended; one of the most anxious afternoons that he had ever known was spent by Richard in a vain discussion with Mrs. Hollister, who strongly contended that the Methodist (her own) church was the best entitled to and most deserving of, the possession of the new tabernacle" (James Fenimore Cooper, *The Pioneers,* 1823).

Tabitha *See* DORCAS SOCIETY.

table of Pythagoras (păthagorăs) The multiplication table as represented by a square divided into 100 squares. The multiplication table is traditionally credited to the Greek mathematician and philosopher Pythagoras (c. 580–c. 500 B.C.). *The table of Pythagoras is still in common use in classrooms around the world.*

Taenarum (taynahrăm) A gloomy, ominous place. Greek legend identified a cave at Taenarum, the southernmost tip of the Peloponnesus, as one of the entrances to the underworld. *He shuddered at the thought of being consigned to this melancholy hole in the ground, gaping like Taenarum, the portal to Hades.*

tail wags the dog, the *See* WAG THE DOG SYNDROME.

take a little wine Drink a small amount of wine to settle the digestion. This proverbial piece of advice comes from 1 Timothy 5:23, in which Paul advised Timothy, "Drink no longer water, but use a little wine for thy stomach's sake and thine often infirmities." *"Take a little wine," said the general, offering to fill her glass. "It will do you a world of good."*

take a rain check *See* RAIN CHECK.

take for a ride To cheat or swindle someone. The phrase originally meant "to murder someone" and has its origins in underworld slang of the 1920s, when gangsters operating in Chicago and other crime-ridden areas might remove rivals by luring them into a car and then having them murdered by an accomplice hidden in the back seat. The body was then driven away and hidden where it was unlikely to be found. *It was only when I examined my purchase more closely that I realized I had been taken for a ride—the "porcelain" ornament was made of cheap plastic.*

take in vain *See* TAKE THE NAME OF GOD IN VAIN.

take one's cross *See* BEAR/CARRY/TAKE ONE'S CROSS.

take the fifth To rely on the constitutional right not to offer evidence that might incriminate oneself. Under the Fifth Amendment to the U.S. Constitution (1789), no person can be forced to give evidence that might be damaging to their own cause in court. The phrase "take the fifth" or ***plead the fifth*** became notorious for its frequent use by witnesses called before the House Un-American Activities Committee seeking to rout out communist sympathizers in the 1950s. *When her parents interrogated her about her private life she wisely opted to take the fifth.*

take the name of God in vain To show disrespect toward God; to blaspheme. The phrase comes from the third of the Ten Commandments, as given in Exodus 20:7: "Thou shalt not take the name of the LORD thy God in vain; for the LORD will not hold him guiltless that taketh his name in vain." In modern usage the phrase is used more widely, and any act of disrespect toward another person may be described in terms of taking that person's name in vain. *His mother dropped the vase in horror. She had never heard her son take the name of God in vain before.*

take the sword, perish with the sword *See* LIVE BY THE SWORD SHALL DIE BY THE SWORD, THOSE WHO.

take the wings of the morning *See* WINGS OF THE MORNING.

take time by the forelock *See* CARPE DIEM.

take up thy bed and walk *See* RISE, TAKE UP THY BED, AND WALK.

talents *See* PARABLE OF THE TALENTS.

tale that is told Life as a transient phenomenon with no more substance or importance than a story. The phrase comes from Psalm 90:8–9, which depicts God as a refuge for the human race: "Thou hast set our iniquities before thee, our secret sins in the light of thy countenance. For all thy days are passed away in thy wrath: we spend our years as a tale that is told." In 1606 William Shakespeare wrote in *Macbeth,* "Life's but a walking shadow, a poor player, / That struts and frets his hour upon the stage, / And then is heard no more; it is a tale / Told by an idiot, full of sound and fury, / Signifying nothing." "Thus man passes away; his name perishes from record and recollection; his history is as a tale that is told, and his very monument becomes a ruin" (Washington Irving, "Westminster Abbey," 1820).

tall poppy A prominent member of society; a leader. The phrase alludes to the reply of Tarquinius Superbus, the seventh and last legendary king of Rome, when his son Sextus asked him how to subdue the inhabitants of the city of Gabii. Instead of answering in words, Tarquinius simply strode about his garden striking the heads off the tallest poppies with his stick. By this Sextus understood that if he executed all the most prominent people in the city the rest of the populace would fall in line. *Several tall poppies are* *expected to be scythed down as a result of official investigations into the industry.*

talmudic (talmoodik) Of or relating to the Talmud, a body of Jewish ethical sources. The name derives from a Hebrew root word for "study." The Talmud is a record of wide-ranging discussions of ethical matters in the early centuries of the common era (A.D.) held both in the land of Israel and in Babylonia. All such discussions followed a formula: They began with a practical question or problem to which rabbis offered a response or solution, supported by reasoned argument, biblical references, and established principles and practices of an ethical or legal nature. Consensus was sought but not always achieved, and minority opinions were recorded and credited. By the year 200 the assembled material was edited for duplication and was structured logically for ease of reference. Six major orders (topics) were delineated, and each order was further subdivided. This editing process resulted in a work known as the Mishnah (from a word meaning "repeat" or "teach"), which in turn became the focus of discussion and was further extended and embellished. The resulting work was the Gemara (from a root meaning "complete"). The Mishnah and the Gemara, as well as subsequent contributions, were dovetailed into it. By 500 there were two versions of the Talmud: the Talmud Yerushalmi (Jerusalemite) and the more substantial Talmud Bavli (Babylonian), which is thought more authoritative and is referred to more frequently. Traditional observant Jews believe the Talmud to be the "oral Torah," mirroring the written Torah. The Talmud contains some legend and folklore, but most of this material is found in the Midrash. An archaic usage of *talmudic* denoted "cryptic" or "esoteric"—a usage that was offensive to Jews. *The precepts were traced to their talmudic source.*

Tammany Hall (tamănee) A political organization or other place in which corruption is believed to be rife. Tammany Hall in New York was the headquarters of the Tammany Society, which under the leadership of ***William Marcy "Boss" Tweed*** (1823–78) sought to promote the interests of the Democratic Party. Founded in 1789, the society became notorious for bribery and corruption. It was named after a Native American chief of the Delaware tribe in the 17th century, whose name was later adopted by various groups opposed to British colonial rule. *Their methods smacked uncomfortably of Tammany Hall.*

tantalize To tease or torment someone with something desirable while at the same time preventing him or her from obtaining or enjoying it. The word alludes to the legend of Tantalus, mythical king of Phrygia and a son of Zeus. Tantalus was consigned to Hades after stealing his father's favorite dog, stealing ambrosia nectar and giving it to men, and killing his own son and serving him up as food for the gods. He was punished by being made to stand in water that retreated whenever he tried to drink it and under a bough bearing delicious fruit that remained just beyond his grasp. "To surround his interior with a sort of invidious sanctity, to tantalize society with a sense of exclusion, to make people believe his house was different from every other, to impart to the face that he presented to the world a cold originality—this was the ingenious effort of the personage to whom Isabel had attributed a superior morality" (Henry James, *Portrait of a Lady,* 1881).

Tara *See* TOMORROW IS ANOTHER DAY.

tar baby A sticky situation from which it is virtually impossible to extricate oneself. The allusion is to one of the *Uncle Remus* children's stories of Joel Chandler Harris (1845–1908), in which Brer Fox attempts to capture Brer Rabbit by tricking him into fighting with a doll covered in tar: Brer Rabbit gets stuck to the tar baby and only narrowly manages to escape. *This issue is a political tar baby that wise old campaigners know better than to tangle with.*

Tardis (tahrdis) A machine offering the possibility of traveling through time and space, or anything that looks larger on the inside than it does on the outside. The Tardis is the time machine used by the eponymous Doctor in the BBC's long-running science-fiction television series *Doctor Who*, first broadcast in 1963. From the outside it appears to be an old-fashioned blue police telephone box, but it is much larger on the inside and capable of carrying its occupants across the universe and from one era to another. Tardis is actually an acronym, short for "Time and Relative Dimensions in Space." *If I had a Tardis I would love to visit ancient Rome.*

Tarpeian rock (tahrpeeăn) A height from which a condemned person may be hurled to destruction. The reference is to Tarpeian Rock on the Capitoline from which criminals guilty of treason were thrown to their death in ancient Rome. Legend had it that it was named after Tarpeia, the daughter of the general who held the fortress on the hill against the Sabines. When the Sabines attempted to storm it, Tarpeia treacherously opened a gate to the invaders in the expectation of being rewarded with the gold bracelets they wore on their left arms but was instead crushed to death by the soldiers' shields, which they also carried on the left arms. *When the market crashed the towering stock exchange building became a Tarpeian rock from which stricken executives hurled themselves to oblivion.*

tartar (tahrter) A fearsome or formidable person, especially one with a shrewish character or very bad temper. The origins of the word lie in the Tartar (or ***Tatar***) warriors who swept through postmedieval Asia and eastern Europe, led by GENGHIS KHAN and spreading terror wherever they went. They were so called in reference to ***Tartarus,*** the Latin name for the lowest region of hell, because they seemed like demons from the underworld. According to Greek legend the region of Tartarus was reserved for the Titans and those criminals deserving of the most severe punishments. "At last Mr. Guppy came back, looking something the worse for the conference. 'My eye, miss,' he said in a low voice, 'he's a Tartar!' " (Charles Dickens, *Bleak House,* 1852–53).

Tartuffe (tahrtoof) A hypocrite. The allusion is to the central character in the French writer Molière's play *Le Tartuffe; ou, L'Imposteur* (1664), who conceals his greedy and lecherous nature beneath a show of religious piety but is finally exposed as the conman he really is. *It was only when the great man's diary was published that everyone recognized him for the Tartuffe he was beneath his public persona.*

Tarzan (tahrzan) An agile, muscular hero figure. The fictional character Tarzan was created by the British novelist Edgar Rice Burroughs (1875–1950) in *Tarzan of the Apes* (1914) and developed in numerous later stories. The loincloth-clad Tarzan was identified as the son of a British aristocrat, reared by apes after being lost in the jungle and able to summon the assistance of various animals in his many adventures, which were also filmed for cinema and television. In some versions of his adventures, he is comforted by an American companion called ***Jane***; their first meeting gave rise to the oft-quoted introduction ***me Tarzan, you Jane***. "Ken looked like a waterborne Tarzan, swinging through the air from wave to wave" (Andy Martin, *Walking on Water*, 1991).

Teapot Dome A major political scandal. The Teapot Dome scandal erupted in the United States in the 1920s, when secret payments made by the Mammoth Oil Company to drill on a government oil field at Teapot Dome in Wyoming came to light, leading ultimately to the trial and imprisonment of Secretary of the Interior Albert B. Fall (1861–1944), who had received the bribes. *Watergate developed into the biggest political scandal since the Teapot Dome.*

tears, vale of *See* VALE OF TEARS.

tears of Eos (eeos) The morning dew. The allusion is to the tears that were supposedly wept every morning by the Greek goddess Eos in mourning for her son Memnon, who was slain by Achilles during the Trojan War. *The lawns sparkled with the "tears of Eos" as the old romantic liked to say.*

teeth set on edge *See* SOUR GRAPES.

Teflon-coated Impervious to criticism or blame. The allusion is to a tough nonstick coating (tradenamed Teflon) for cooking pans and other utensils developed in the 1940s from polytetrafluoroethylene. In modern usage the term "Teflon-coated" (or simply "Teflon") is often applied to politicians, criminals, etc., who appear to be immune from any blame for their actions or associations: accusations or criticism directed at them do not "stick." *Ronald Reagan's ability to avoid personal blame for any policy failure led to him being called the Teflon President.*

Teiresias *See* TIRESIAS.

telamon (telămăn) An architectural column in the shape of a male figure. The allusion is to Telamon, a mythological king of Salamis who participated in the CALYDONIAN BOAR HUNT and was one of the Argonauts. He is also identified as the father of Ajax and Teucer. *The temple portico was supported by a dozen telamons in the Greek style. See also* CARYATID.

Telemachus *See* ODYSSEUS.

Tell, William *See* WILLIAM TELL.

tell it not in Gath (gath) Do not allow your enemies to make capital out of your misfortunes; be careful to whom you reveal your weaknesses. Gath is identified in 2 Samuel 1:17–20 as the city of the Philistines: "And David lamented with this lamentation over Saul and over Jonathan his son . . . the beauty of Israel is slain upon thy high places: how are the mighty fallen! Tell it not in Gath, publish it not in the streets of Askelon; lest the daughters of the Philistines rejoice, lest the daughters of the uncircumcised triumph." "Tell this not in Gath, lest the Scots rejoice that they have at length found a parallel instance among their neighbours, to that barbarous deed which demolished Arthur's Oven" (Sir Walter Scott, *Ivanhoe,* 1819).

Tellus (telăs) Personification of the Earth. Tellus was identified in Roman mythology as the goddess of the Earth, equivalent to the Greek GAEA. "On the following morning it was known that Lord De Terrier was with the Queen at Buckingham Palace, and at about twelve a list of the new ministry was published, which must have been in the highest degree satisfactory to the whole brood of giants.

Every son of Tellus was included in it, as were also very many of the daughters" (Anthony Trollope, *Framley Parsonage,* 1861).

Tempe, vale of (tempee) A beautiful valley. The picturesque wooded valley of Tempe in Thessaly, situated between Mount Olympus and Mount Ossa, was considered sacred to Apollo and it was here that he pursued Daphne until she forever escaped his clutches by being transformed into a laurel tree. "Indeed, it is a question if the exclusive reign of this orthodox beauty is not approaching its last quarter. The new Vale of Tempe may be a gaunt waste in Thule; human souls may find themselves in closer and closer harmony with external things wearing a sombreness distasteful to our race when it was young" (Thomas Hardy, *The Return of the Native,* 1878).

Temple, Shirley *See* SHIRLEY TEMPLE.

ten commandments A set of rules that must not, under any circumstances, be broken. The original Ten Commandments were the laws revealed by God to Moses on the top of Mount Sinai for the guidance of the Israelites (as related in Exodus 20:3–17 and Deuteronomy 5:6–21). The first four describe the responsibilities of the Israelites to God; the last six describe their responsibilities to one another. Moses carried the Ten Commandments, inscribed by the finger of God on two stone tablets, down the mountain but later smashed them to pieces in disgust when he found that in his absence his people had begun to worship an idol called the Golden Calf. Subsequently Moses returned to Mount Sinai and was presented with two new stone tablets, which were placed in the Ark of the Covenant. "The business world needs the 10 commandments of email" (*Guardian,* November 5, 2001). *See also* THOU SHALT HAVE NO OTHER GODS BEFORE ME; THOU SHALT NOT STEAL.

Tenth Muse Poetical inspiration, sometimes used in reference to a female poet or a literary woman; an inspiring or influential nontraditional art form. The allusion is to Sappho (c. 650–c. 580 B.C.), the poetess of Lesbos who was sometimes referred to as the Tenth Muse. "'You were right in telling me she would do me no good. But you were wrong in thinking I should wish to be like her.' 'Wouldn't you really like to be a tenth Muse, then, Maggie?' said Philip, looking up in her face as we look at a first parting in the clouds, that promises us a bright heaven once more" (George Eliot, *The Mill on the Floss,* 1860). *See also* MUSES.

Teresa, Mother *See* MOTHER TERESA.

Terminator, the A person who is hired to kill others or otherwise brings things to a premature end. The allusion is to the 1984 thriller of the same title starring ARNOLD SCHWARZENEGGER as a cyborg robot sent back in time to kill a future leader of mankind. The character (revived in popular sequels to the original movie) has produced memorable quotations that have entered the popular lexicon, notably ***hasta la vista, baby*** and ***I'll be back***. *He had the reputation of a troubleshooter and terminator sent into struggling companies to cut out anyone not pulling their weight.*

terpsichorean (terpsikăreeăn, terpsăkoreeăn) Of or relating to dancing. The allusion is to Terpsichore, identified in Greek mythology as the muse of choral dance and song (see MUSES) and conventionally depicted holding a lyre. "The old-fashioned fronts of these houses, which had older than old-fashioned backs, rose sheer from the pavement, into which the bow windows protruded like bastions, necessitating a pleasing chassez-dechassez movement to the time-pressed pedestrian at every few yards. He was bound also to evolve other Terpsichorean figures in respect of door-steps, scrapers, cellar-hatches, church buttresses, and the overhanging angles of walls which, originally unobtrusive, had become bow-legged and knock-kneed" (Thomas Hardy, *The Mayor of Casterbridge,* 1886).

terrible beauty Something that is at once appalling and yet awe-inspiring. The phrase was a coinage of the Irish poet and playwright W. B. Yeats (1865–1939), making its first appearance in his poem "Easter 1916," about the Easter Rising in Dublin that year, a violent rebellion that marked a significant point in the struggle for Irish independence: "Now and in time to be, / Wherever green is worn / Are changed, changed utterly: / A terrible beauty is born." The phrase has remained strongly associated with the birth of the Irish state, although it has also been applied in other contexts in succeeding years. *The image of the Twin Towers crashing to the ground remains a terrible beauty.*

tertium quid (tersheeăm kwid, terteeăm kwid) An unknown, unclassifiable, or nameless thing that has the features of two other things. The phrase is credited to the Greek philosopher and mathematician Pythagoras (c. 580–c. 500 B.C.), who once offered the following definition of a biped: "A man is a biped, so is a bird, and a third thing." According to Iamblichus (c. A.D. 250–c. 330), another Greek philosopher, the "third thing" Pythagoras had in mind was himself. "And there is another mode of dress open to him, which I can assure my readers is not an unknown costume, a tertium quid, by which semi-decorum and comfort are combined. The hunting breeches are put on first, and the black trowsers are drawn over them" (Anthony Trollope, *Hunting Sketches,* 1865).

Tethys (teethis) The sea; the third satellite of the planet Saturn. Tethys was one of the Titans of Greek mythology, a sea goddess who was the daughter of Uranus and the wife of Oceanus and by him became the mother of the sea nymphs called the oceanids. *He slipped soundlessly over the side of the boat and into the welcoming arms of Tethys, goddess of the sea.*

Teucer (tyooser) Archetype of a skilled archer. According to Greek legend Teucer was the son of Telamon and Hesione and became famous for his skills in archery with the Greek army during the Trojan War. On his return from Troy he was sent into exile by his father for having failed to avenge the death of his brother, AJAX, at the hands of Odysseus. "'But,' thought he, 'I may, like a second Teucer, discharge my shafts from behind the shield of my ally; and, admit that he should not prove to be a first-rate poet, I am in no shape answerable for his deficiencies, and the good notes may very probably help off an indifferent text'" (Sir Walter Scott, *The Antiquary,* 1816).

Thais (thayăs) A woman who uses her beauty to influence her lover. The original Thais was an Athenian courtesan of the fourth century B.C. who became the mistress of Alexander the Great. She exercised her influence over him to persuade him to order the burning of the palace of Persepolis. "'"The lovely Thais sits beside you. Take the goods the gods provide you." I often say that to my wife, till the children have got calling her Thais. The children have it pretty much their own way with us, Mr. Crawley'" (Anthony Trollope, *The Last Chronicle of Barset,* 1867).

Thalatta! (thălata) A cry of joy or triumph. Greek soldiers retreating from their Persian enemies were reputed to have exclaimed, "Thalatta! Thalatta!" (meaning "the sea! the sea!") on catching sight of the waters of the Black Sea. In modern usage the soldiers' cry is sometimes rendered as "Thalassa! Thalassa!" *Like the Greeks at the sight of their deliverance, he felt like shouting out "Thalatta! Thalatta!" at this first glimpse of his rescuers.*

Thalia (thălīă) A source of poetical or comic inspiration. Thalia was one of the MUSES of Greek mythology, identified as the muse of comedy and pastoral poetry. The word comes from the Greek *thaleia* (meaning "blooming"). *Thalia herself would appear to have sat at his elbow, guiding his pen as a young man, but in his latter years she seems to have deserted him for other rivals. See also* THREE GRACES.

Thanatos (thanătos) The personification of death. According to Greek mythology Thanatos was the son of Nyx, the goddess of night, and was identified as the god of death. In the first half of the 20th century Sigmund Freud selected *Thanatos* as a name for the universal death instinct. *This urge for self-destruction, the magnetic pull of Thanatos, is hard for some people to resist at such moments.*

that's all, folks! This is the end, there is no more. This was the famous slogan scrawled across the screen at the end of the Warner Brothers *Merry Melodies* cartoons, from 1930. Mel Blanc (1908–89), who provided the voices of many of the most popular characters in the cartoons, memorably chose "That's all, folks!" for his epitaph. *That's all, folks! The bar's closed.*

that's the way it is, and *See* AND THAT'S THE WAY IT IS.

theater of the absurd A form of drama or other entertainment that seeks to emphasize the futility and meaningless of existence, often using bizarre or unorthodox methods. The reference is to an avant-garde movement in world drama that gathered pace after World War II, championed by such playwrights as Samuel Beckett, Jean Genet, and Edward Albee. *The campaigning efforts of the extreme right had slipped into the realms of the theater of the absurd. See also* WAITING FOR GODOT.

their finest hour A moment of glory. The phrase was famously delivered by British prime minister Winston Churchill (1874–1965) in a speech broadcast on June 18, 1940, in which he sought to bolster resistance to the threat of a possible Nazi invasion of the United Kingdom: "Let us therefore brace ourselves to our duties, and so bear ourselves that if the British Empire and its Commonwealth last for a thousand years, men will still say, 'This was their finest hour.' " *Surveying the wreckage of their home after the party, the boys were forced to admit this had not been their finest hour.*

theirs not to reason why *See* OURS NOT TO REASON WHY.

Thelma and Louise Archetypes of two women who seek to assert their equality in a repressively male world. The 1991 movie *Thelma and Louise* starred Geena Davis and Susan Sarandon as two friends who behave in an increasingly lawless fashion after shooting a male attacker and being forced to go on the run from the police. The characters became icons of feminist solidarity and remain symbols of escape from a male-dominated culture. *The couple burst into the party like Thelma* *and Louise, driving all self-respecting males into the shadows.*

Themis (theemis) Personification of justice. Themis was identified in Greek mythology as the daughter of Uranus and Gaea and respected as the goddess of law and order, alongside her husband Jupiter. She is perhaps best known today through her visual representation, conventionally holding a cornucopia and a pair of scales. "By next day's post, the solicitor sent the case to London, a chef-d'oeuvre of its kind; and in which, my informant assured me, it was not necessary on revisal to correct five words. I am not, therefore, conscious of having overstepped accuracy in describing the manner in which Scottish lawyers of the old time occasionally united the worship of Bacchus with that of Themis" (Sir Walter Scott, *Guy Mannering,* 1815).

Theon's tooth (theeonz) A sharp or penetrating criticism. The allusion is to the ancient Roman poet Theon, who was noted for his biting satires. *It was clear that both actors were suffering acutely from the poisonous imprint of Theon's tooth in that morning's reviews of the performance.*

Theramenes, sandals of *See* WEAR THE SANDALS OF THERAMENES.

there is a time and a place for everything *See* TIME AND PLACE FOR EVERYTHING.

there is no joy in Mudville *See* CASEY AT THE BAT.

there is no peace for the wicked *See* NO PEACE FOR THE WICKED.

there is nothing new under the sun *See* NOTHING NEW UNDER THE SUN.

there's gold in them thar hills There are opportunities to be taken advantage of. The allusion is to the gold rushes that took place at various locations in the late 19th century, when there was literally gold to be found in the hills, although the phrase itself probably dates only from Western movies of the 1930s and 1940s. *Thousands of businesses have opened sites on the Internet, sensing there's gold in them thar hills.*

there's the rub That is where the problem lies. This is a quotation from HAMLET's famous TO BE OR NOT TO BE soliloquy in William Shakespeare's tragedy *Hamlet* (c. 1600): "To sleep, perchance to dream. Ay, there's the rub; / For in that sleep of death what dreams may come, / When we have shuffled off this mortal coil, / Must give us pause." The word "rub" in this sense refers to an obstacle or obstruction, specifically an unevenness of the ground. *There's the rub—if no one tidies up the house, we will end up living in a pigsty.*

there was no more spirit in her *See* QUEEN OF SHEBA.

there were brave men before Agamemnon *See* BRAVE MEN BEFORE AGAMEMNON, THERE WERE.

Thermopylae (thermopălee) A decisive battle or moment, especially when facing overwhelming odds. It was at the narrow pass of Thermopylae in Thessaly (the only route connecting north and south Greece) that Leonidas and 300 Spartans heroically held off a much larger invading Persian army in 480 B.C., fighting to the death after being betrayed by a Greek traitor. Their courage became a symbol of Spartan indomitability. The word itself means "hot gates." "He would much prefer not to die. He would abandon a hero's or a martyr's end gladly. He did not want to make a Thermopylae, not be Horatius at any bridge, nor be the Dutch boy with his finger in that dyke" (Ernest Hemingway, *For Whom the Bell Tolls,* 1941).

Thersites (thersīteez) Archetype of an impudent, foul-tongued critic, especially one who criticizes everyone and everything. Thersites was a trouble-making deformed Greek warrior who was killed by a blow from Achilles during the Trojan War after daring to mock him for Achilles' grief over the death of his friend Penthesilea. "And first, it may be said, there is a pelting kind of thersitical satire, as black as the very ink 'tis wrote with . . ." (Laurence Sterne, *Tristram Shandy,* 1759).

Theseus (theeseeăs) Archetype of a mythological hero and adventurer. Theseus was the son of Aegeus, the king of Athens, and the central figure in a series of legendary encounters. These episodes included the slaying of the Minotaur, the conquest of the Amazons, taking part in the Calydonian hunt, and seeking the Golden Fleece. '"I will tell you what, Mistress Mary—it will be rather harder work to learn surveying and drawing plans than it would have been to write sermons,' he had said, wishing her to appreciate what he went through for her sake; 'and as to Hercules and Theseus, they were nothing to me. They had sport, and never learned to write a bookkeeping hand'" (George Eliot, *Middlemarch,* 1871–72).

thespian (thespeeăn) An actor. The word was originally coined in tribute to the Greek poet Thespis, who is traditionally credited with having been the founder of Greek tragic drama in the late sixth century B.C. With great success Thespis introduced the actor in the guise of a figure from history or legend as an alternative to the convention of the chorus narrating the action. As an adjective *thespian* is applied to anything of or relating to the theater as a whole. "Vergil Gunch thundered, 'When we manage to grab this celebrated Thespian off his lovely aggregation of beautiful actresses—and I got to admit I butted right into his dressing-room and told him how the Boosters appreciated the high-class artistic performance he's giving us.'" (Sinclair Lewis, *Babbitt,* 1922).

Thestylis (thestilis) A rustic maiden. The allusion is to the young female slave called Thestylis who appears in the *Idylls* of the Greek pastoral poet Theocritus (c. 310–250 B.C.). *He was immediately captivated by this Thestylis and her beautiful voice and within a month had written a dozen magnificent poems in her honor.*

Thetis's hair stone (theetis) Rock crystal containing hairlike filaments. It is also called ***Venus's hair stone.*** The allusion is to Thetis, the leader of the sea nymphs known as the nereids in Greek mythology and remembered as the mother of Achilles. *Instead of leaving, the little girl reached into her bag and handed him a crystal lump of the type some people call Thetis's hair stone.*

they also serve The contribution of people behind the scenes is also valuable, though not always acknowledged. The allusion is to a quotation from the poem "On His Blindness" by the English poet John Milton (1608–74): "They also serve who only stand and wait." It is variously encountered both in its full form and in the abbreviated "they also serve." *It may not be the most glamorous of occupations, but they also serve who only stand and wait.*

they know not what they do *See* FATHER, FORGIVE THEM.

they shall not pass A declaration of resistance to an enemy. The origins of this slogan are thought to date back to World War I, being variously ascribed to Marshal Pétain or General Robert Nivelle, but it is also strongly associated with the Spanish Civil War of the 1930s, having been memorably delivered in a famous radio broadcast on July 19, 1936 to Republican supporters by Dolores Ibarruri (La Pasionaria). *The team's strategy was based on the determination that "They shall not pass!"*

they that sow the wind shall reap the whirlwind *See* SOW THE WIND AND REAP THE WHIRLWIND.

they toil not, neither do they spin *See* LILIES OF THE FIELD.

thief in the night, like a Suddenly; unexpectedly; surreptitiously. The phrase is biblical in origin, appearing in 1 Thessalonians 5:1–3, where it describes how Jesus Christ will return: "But of the times and the seasons, brethren, ye have no need that I write unto you. For yourselves know perfectly that the day of the Lord so cometh as a thief in the night. For when they shall say, Peace and safety; then sudden destruction cometh upon them, as travail upon a woman with child; and they shall not escape." "For the Son of Man cometh as a thief in the night, and there is not one of us can tell but what this day his soul may be required of him" (Samuel Butler, *The Way of All Flesh,* 1903).

thieves break through and steal *See* LAY NOT UP TREASURES UPON EARTH.

things ain't what they used to be *See* FINGS AIN'T WOT THEY USED T'BE.

things fall apart, the center cannot hold We are on the verge of chaos. This is a quotation from the poem "The Second Coming" by the Irish poet W. B. Yeats (1865–1939): "Things fall apart; the centre cannot hold; / Mere anarchy is loosed upon the world." *The question is how long the government will hold on, for when things fall apart, the center cannot hold.*

things in common, all *See* ALL THINGS IN COMMON.

things to all men, all *See* ALL THINGS TO ALL MEN.

thin red line An apparently brittle but defiant line of defense. This was originally a tag applied to the British army, specifically the 93rd Highlanders, who stood successfully against an attack by a much larger Russian force during the Battle of Balaclava in the Crimean War of 1853–56. The regiment consequently became known as the "thin red line," after the color of their uniforms, and in due course the description came to be applied to the British infantry as a whole. The variant "thin blue line" is sometimes used of the police, for similar reasons. *The troops formed a thin red line against the rioting mob.*

thirty pieces of silver The price of an act of betrayal. The allusion is to the 30 shekels of silver that was paid by chief priests to JUDAS in exchange for information about Christ's whereabouts (Matthew 26:14–16), thus setting in motion the trail of events that led to the Crucifixion. According to Matthew 27:3–5 Judas soon repented of his deed and "cast down the pieces of silver in the temple, and departed, and went and hanged himself." Thirty shekels of silver was also the compensation laid down under the law of Moses for the loss of an ox. *Rumor has it that any executive who is prepared to give evidence against the company will be offered thirty pieces of silver in the form of an official pardon. See also* ACELDAMA; POTTER'S FIELD.

Thisbe *See* PYRAMUS AND THISBE.

this is another fine mess you've got me into *See* LAUREL AND HARDY.

Thomas, doubting *See* DOUBTING THOMAS.

Thomas Gradgrind (gradgrīnd) A soulless person who believes only in hard facts and sticks unbendingly to his or her principles. The allusion is to Thomas Gradgrind, a hard-hearted retired merchant turned schoolmaster in the Charles Dickens novel *Hard Times* (1854). The novel ends tragically with Gradgrind realizing too late the damage he has caused to his own children. *Our headmaster was a real Gradgrind who had absolutely no interest in the arts.*

Thor (thor) A man of enormous strength. Thor is identified in Norse mythology as the son of Odin and Frigga and the god of thunder and war. He was renowned for his great strength, which was redoubled by the belt he wore, and was conventionally depicted wearing iron gloves and carrying a great hammer (the Mjollnir). "Thaw with his gentle persuasion is more powerful than Thor with his hammer. The one melts, the other but breaks in pieces" (Henry David Thoreau, *Walden, or Life in the Woods,* 1854).

thorn in the flesh A persistent irritation or annoyance, especially one that cannot be easily escaped. The phrase comes from 2 Corinthians 12:7, in which Paul complains about his own troubles: "And lest I should be exalted above measure through the abundance of the revelations, there was given to me a thorn in the flesh, the messenger of Satan to buffet me, lest I should be exalted above measure." The precise nature of Paul's "thorn in the flesh" has been much debated and various chronic illnesses ranging from blindness to malaria have been proposed as the cause of his discomfort. There was, perhaps significantly, a sect of Pharisees whose practice was to insert thorns into their clothing to prick their legs as they walked and make them bleed. The phrase is also encountered as ***thorn in the/one's side.*** "Sadly, it was a road accident . . . which finally took the wind from his quixotic career as bye-lection candidate, champion of lost causes, and thorn in the flesh of authority" (*Guardian,* April 7, 1986).

thorns, crown of *See* CROWN OF THORNS.

thou art the man You are the guilty person, or the person for the job in question. The quotation is biblical in origin, appearing in 2 Samuel 12:7 in the account of the adultery of DAVID AND BATHSHEBA. After Nathan told David the parable of the rich man who stole the ewe lamb belonging to his poor neighbor, David exclaimed that the rich man deserved to die, upon which Nathan replied, "Thou art the man." Nathan here was referring to David's "theft" of Bathsheba from her husband. The child who resulted from their union died a week after birth. *The girls would not listen to his denials of any involvement in the matter: It was clearly a case of "thou art the man."*

though he slay me, yet will I trust in him An expression of loyalty and faithfulness to someone, even though such loyalty may not be reciprocated. The expression comes from Job 13:15, in which Job resisted suggestions that, after all his troubles, he owed no duty of loyalty to God: "Though he slay me, yet will I trust in him: but I will maintain mine own ways before him." *The corporal gestured ruefully after the departing emperor and refused to voice any complaint at the harsh treatment he had received on the latter's orders. "Though he slay me, yet will I trust in him" was his only comment.*

thought police An oppressive secret police force, especially one that makes it its business to suppress subversive ideas. The thought police were an invention of British novelist George Orwell (1903–50) in his book *Nineteen Eighty-Four* (1949), in which they maintain constant surveillance of those suspected of wavering from prescribed thinking. Those found guilty of such transgressions are tortured at the Ministry of Love and then brainwashed or vaporized. "George Barker had taken his place in 1940 but had escaped to the United States before Pearl Harbor, for he had been followed everywhere by the 'thought police,' the sinister kempeitai, who suspected him of being a communist spy" (James Kirkup, *A Poet could not but be Gay*, 1991). *See also* BIG BROTHER; DOUBLETHINK; ROOM 101.

thousand cuts *See* DEATH BY A THOUSAND CUTS.

thousand days *See* HUNDRED DAYS.

thou shalt have no other gods before me Demand for unswerving loyalty (sometimes used ironically). This is the first of the TEN COMMANDMENTS, listed in Exodus 20 and Deuteronomy 5. *The men quickly realized that with the unyielding, yet generally just commander it was a case of "thou shalt have no other gods before me."*

thou shalt not steal Do not steal from others. This appears as the eighth of the TEN COMMANDMENTS (Exodus 20:15 and Deuteronomy 5:19). *"Thou shalt not steal," said the old woman severely as she retrieved the necklace from the little girl.*

thou shouldst be living at this hour You should be living now to witness this. This is a quotation from the poem "To Milton" by the English poet William Wordsworth (1770–1850), in which Wordsworth expressed the sentiment that the long-dead English poet John Milton (1608–74), a fellow opponent of tyrannical monarchy, would have much appreciated the triumph of the French Revolution of 1789. *"John F. Kennedy, thou shouldst be living at this hour," intoned the presenter as Neil Armstrong stepped onto the Moon.*

thrasonical (thraysahnikăl, thrăsahnikăl) Boastful; arrogant; vain. The word alludes to Thraso, a soldier in the comedy *Eunuchus* by Terence (c. 185–c. 159 B.C.), who brags of his own achievements. "Novi hominem tanquam te: his humour is lofty, his discourse peremptory, his tongue filed, his eye ambitious, his gait majestical, and his general behavior vain, ridiculous, and thrasonical" (William Shakespeare, *Love's Labour's Lost,* 1594–95).

thread of destiny *See* FATES.

three bears *See* GOLDILOCKS.

Three Graces Personifications of beauty and charm. The Three Graces were beautiful goddesses identified in Greek mythology as the sisters Aglaia, Thalia, and Euphrosyne. "As for the graces of expression, a great thought is never found in a mean dress; but though it proceed from the lips of the Woloffs, the nine Muses and the three Graces will have conspired to clothe it in fit phrase" (Henry David Thoreau, *Week on the Concord and Merrimack Rivers,* 1849).

Three Mile Island A nuclear accident threatening a widespread catastrophe. Three Mile Island was the name of a nuclear power station at Middletown, Pennsylvania, which, on March 28, 1979, was the scene of an accident resulting in the release of radioactive material threatening the lives of 36,000 people living in the area. Ever since then the term Three Mile Island has been quoted as a warning of the ever-present risk of environmental disaster associated with reliance upon nuclear power. *According to the press, we came perilously close to suffering another Three Mile Island. See also* CHERNOBYL; CHINA SYNDROME; MELTDOWN.

Three Musketeers A trio of swashbuckling heroes or loyal friends. The novel *The Three Musketeers* (1844) by the French writer Alexandre Dumas *père* (1802–70) was set in 17th-century France and related the adventures of three of the king's dashing sword-wielding musketeers, ***Athos***, ***Porthos***, and ***Aramis***, together with new recruit ***D'Artagnan***, as they sought to defend the interests of the king against the scheming Cardinal Richelieu. "She was barely seventeen, the youngest of the Three Musketeers, as they had styled themselves long ago; yet in everything except appearance she might have been at least ten years older" (Mary Gervaise, *The Distance Enchanted*, 1983). *See also* ALL FOR ONE AND ONE FOR ALL.

three-pipe problem A particularly difficult problem. The allusion is to the SHERLOCK HOLMES detective stories of the British writer Sir Arthur Conan Doyle (1859–1930), in the course of which the detective likes to consider unfathomable cases over one, two, or (rarely) three pipefuls of tobacco. *Reducing pollution in China while not hindering economic progress is a three-pipe problem for environmentalists.*

threescore years and ten The age of 70. Once considered the average length of time that a person might expect to live, the phrase comes from Psalm 90:10: "The days of our years are threescore years and ten; and if by reason of strength they be fourscore years, yet is their strength labour and sorrow; for it is soon cut off, and we fly away." "By and by we are called in to see an old baby, threescore years and ten or more old" (Oliver Wendell Holmes, *Elsie Venner,* 1861).

Three Stooges, the (stoojăz) An incompetent or comical trio. The Three Stooges were a popular cinema slapstick comedy act who starred in some 200 movies from the 1930s to the 1960s. The original Stooges were Larry Fine (Louis Feinberg; 1902–75), Moe Howard (Moses Horwitz; 1897–1975), and Curly Howard (Jerome Lester Horwitz; 1903–52), although Curly was replaced by another Howard brother, Shemp Howard (Samuel Horwitz; 1895–1955), in 1947. *Watching the three men trying to sort out the mess they had made was like watching the Three Stooges.*

three wise men *See* MAGI.

throne of grace The throne of God and, by extension, heaven. The phrase appears in the letter to the Hebrews 4:16: "Let us therefore come boldly unto the throne of grace, that we may obtain mercy, and find grace to help in time of need." The term is sometimes associated with depictions of the Trinity, with God holding the body of Christ on his knees while the Holy Spirit, in the form of a dove, hovers overhead. Other names for the throne of grace include the ***mercy seat.*** "Ah, Mr. Cassilis, my sin has found me out, you see! I am very low, very low; but I hope equally penitent. We must all come to the throne of grace at last, Mr. Cassilis" (Robert Louis Stevenson, *New Arabian Nights,* 1882).

through a glass darkly *See* SEE THROUGH A GLASS DARKLY.

through the looking-glass In weird, incomprehensible territory; in a situation where the normal rules do not apply. The allusion is to the classic children's tale *Through the Looking-Glass and What Alice Found There* (1872) by the British writer Lewis Carroll (Charles Lutwidge Dodgson; 1832–98), a book that was characterized by its topsy-turvy view of the world and comic reversal of familiar logic. *When I heard what had been decided it really felt like we had gone through the looking-glass. See also* ALICE IN WONDERLAND.

throw a curveball To unsettle an opponent by delivering a blow (real or metaphorical) that is difficult to return or respond to. The allusion is to baseball, in which a ball pitched with a spin on it is especially difficult to deal with. *The press threw the governor a curveball when they came up with some telling observations about his private life.*

throw down the gauntlet To issue a challenge. In this phrase the word "gauntlet" is used in its more familiar sense, meaning "protective glove." In medieval times, one knight might challenge another by throwing down his gauntlet; if the other knight picked the gauntlet up this meant he accepted the challenge. "Since, in 1850, the one bastion of that order which had escaped major trouble in 1848 was the Russian Empire, it was likely that at some point France would throw down the gauntlet to the tsar" (David Saunders, *Russia in the Age of Reaction and Reform 1801–1881*, 1994).

throw in the towel To give in; to concede defeat. The allusion is to boxing, in which the trainer of a losing fighter might toss a towel into the ring to signal that their side are unwilling to go on with the bout (usually because of injury to the fighter concerned). *When they were threatened with court action they decided to throw in the towel.*

throw the apple of discord *See* APPLE OF DISCORD.

throw the first stone *See* LET HIM WHO IS WITHOUT SIN CAST THE FIRST STONE.

throw to the lions To expose someone to an unpleasant fate. The phrase harks back to ancient Rome, where army deserters, common criminals, and Christians were often put to death by being sent into the arena to face wild animals. The practice reached a peak during the reign of the emperor Nero in the wake of the destruction of Rome in the fire of A.D. 64, for which the city's Christians had been blamed. *It seems the leadership has decided to cut its losses and throw the spokesman to the lions.*

Thule *See* ULTIMA THULE.

thumbs-up An indication of approval or encouragement, in which the thumb is pointed up and the other fingers are closed in a fist. This gesture is popularly supposed to have its origins in the gladiatorial arenas of ancient Rome. When a gladiator was defeated, the crowd was invited to decide his fate by showing a collective thumbs-up, in which case the gladiator was allowed to live, or a ***thumbs-down,*** in which case he was put to death. In reality no one is sure exactly what sign the crowd made with their thumbs to indicate their decision, as suggested by John Dryden's description of such a moment in his translation of the *Third Satire of Juvenal* (1693): "Influenced by the rabble's bloody will, / With thumbs bent back they popularly kill." The use of thumbs-up or thumbs-down as understood today may date back only as far as early Hollywood film reenactments of such gladiatorial contests. *The chairman has just given his thumbs-up to the new project, providing certain conditions are met in advance.*

Thursday The fifth day of the week. The day was named after THOR, the Norse god of thunder. *In Britain elections generally take place on a Thursday. In the United States Thanksgiving is always the last Thursday in November.*

Thyestean feast (thīesteeăn) A feast at which human flesh is served. The reference is to Thyestes, a Greek who committed adultery with the wife of his brother Atreus. In revenge Atreus murdered the children of Thyestes and fed them to him at a banquet. Thyestes realized what he was being offered and fled the feast, laying a curse on his brother's household. *No one ever found the body, but few dared voice the suspicion that many shared, that the unlucky parents had unwittingly taken part in a Thyestean feast.*

thy will be done An expression of acquiescence to another's wishes. The phrase comes from the Lord's Prayer, as rendered in Matthew 6:9–10: "Our Father which art in heaven, Hallowed be thy name. Thy kingdom come. Thy will be done in earth, as it is in heaven." (See also Luke 22:42.) *"Thy will be done," replied the managing director's secretary with heavy irony as she gathered together the documents he had left on the desk for her.*

Tiananmen Square (teeanănmen) An act of violent repression directed against supporters of democracy. Tiananmen Square in Beijing, China, was the scene of a huge popular demonstration in favor of democratic political reform in 1989; it ended on June 4 when the Chinese army moved in and massacred many of the unarmed students maintaining their peaceful protest in the square. *God forbid we ever see a Tiananmen Square in this country.*

tidings of great joy *See* GOOD TIDINGS OF GREAT JOY.

tilt at windmills To oppose imaginary threats or enemies. The reference is to *Don Quixote* (1605, 1615) by Miguel de Cervantes Saavedra (1547–1616), in which the deluded hero DON QUIXOTE mistakes a group of distant windmills for giants and rides off to fight them, only to impale his lance in the sails and be lifted high off the ground. In modern usage, the phrase is also sometimes employed when people commit themselves to a struggle they appear very unlikely to win. "To criticize language for being 'misleading' as to the state of affairs in the real world is to tilt at windmills, because language is not so much a limpid pool through which we are to glimpse the truth as a muddy pond full of the debris of history and ideology" (Deborah Cameron, *Feminism and Linguistic Theory*, 1992).

Timbuktu (timbuktoo) A far distant place. Timbuktu is a real place, a city in Mali in western Africa, founded in 1087. Its fabled reputation as a center of the gold trade made it a goal of 19th-century explorers, though it was not until 1828 that a French explorer managed to visit the city (by then largely in ruins) and return in one piece to describe what he had seen. *When they moved from next door to the next street it might as well have been to Timbuktu, as we haven't seen them since.*

Time, Father *See* FATHER TIME.

time and place for everything There is an appropriate time for all things and, therefore, times when certain things should not be said or done. The proverb has its origins in Ecclesiastes 3:1–8: "To everything there is a season, and a time to every purpose under the heaven: a time to be born, and a time to die; a time to plant, and a time to pluck up that which is planted; a time to kill, and a time to heal; a time to break down, and a time to build up; a time to weep, and a time to laugh; a time to mourn, and a time to dance . . . a time to get, and a time to lose; a time to keep, and a time to cast away; a time to rend, and a time to sew; a time to keep silence, and a time to speak; a time to love, and a time to hate; a time of war, and a time of peace." The saying is also encountered in the forms ***time for all things, season for all things,*** and ***to every thing there is a season.*** " 'There is a time for everything, a time to embrace, and a time to refrain from embracing; the first is now going to be mine' " (Thomas Hardy, *Tess of the D'Urbervilles,* 1891). *See also* WORD IN SEASON.

time as this, for such a *See* FOR SUCH A TIME AS THIS.

time for all things *See* TIME AND PLACE FOR EVERYTHING.

timeo Danaos et dona ferentes *See* BEWARE OF GREEKS BEARING GIFTS.

Times Square A very busy place. Times Square in New York City is famous for its bustling crowds and animated neon advertisements, which add to the atmosphere of frenetic urban activity. It is located at a crossroads, where 42nd Street and BROADWAY meet. It owes its name to the presence nearby of the former headquarters of the *New York Times* newspaper. *Traffic diversions turned the normally quiet intersection into Times Square, with horns blaring and pedestrians running for their lives.*

time to be born, and a time to die *See* TIME AND PLACE FOR EVERYTHING.

Timon (tīmăn) Archetypal misanthrope. Timon was a rich Athenian citizen who spent his entire fortune on lavish entertainments for his friends. When his money was all gone, Timon found himself deserted by his erstwhile companions and became a recluse, living in a remote cave and bitterly avoiding all human contact, with the single exception of the exile Alcibiades. He was represented on stage in William Shakespeare's play *Timon of Athens* (1605). In modern usage his name appears most frequently in the phrase to ***out-Timon Timon,*** meaning to be even more misanthropic than Timon. *A sour and embittered Timon, he lurked on the fringes of society for years, savaging anybody who ventured near him.*

Tinkers to Evers to Chance A successful display of coordinated teamwork. The allusion is to the Chicago Cubs baseball team of the early 1900s, and its stars Joe Tinker, Johnny Evers, and Frank Chance, who entered baseball history for their perfection of the double play. *The plan was to keep the ball rolling by switching the money from one partner to another and then to a third in lightning Tinkers to Evers to Chance style.*

tinkling cymbal *See* SOUNDING BRASS OR A TINKLING CYMBAL.

Tin Man *See* FRIEND OF DOROTHY.

Tin-Pan Alley The music industry. Tin Pan Alley is both the name of a district around BROADWAY and 14th Street in New York City and a nickname for Denmark Street off Charing Cross Road in London, both of which were once centers of the music industry, crowded with music promoters, publishers, and aspiring songwriters. Though all have long since moved elsewhere, the name Tin-Pan Alley is still widely used to refer to the music industry as a whole, especially to the songwriting part of it. The name itself was probably derived from the slang use of "tin-pan" to refer to a cheap, tinny-sounding piano. *He decided he needed some new songs from Tin-Pan Alley.*

Tinseltown Nickname for HOLLYWOOD. Reflecting the hollow superficial glamor of the popular film industry, the nickname was coined in the 1940s by actor and composer Oscar Levant. *It's Oscar time again and all Tinseltown will be there to join the stars on the famous red carpet.*

Tiny Tim *See* BOB CRATCHIT.

Tiphys (tifis) A pilot. According to Greek mythology Tiphys was the pilot for the Argonauts during their epic voyage of adventure. *Descended from many generations of pilots, he himself served as Tiphys to many major passenger liners plying the treacherous waters in that part of the world.*

Tiresias (tīreeseeas) Archetype of a wise old prophet. Tiresias, or ***Teiresias,*** was famed in Thebes for his prophetic gifts but was blinded by the gods for having seen Athena bathing in the fountain Hippocrene. Another version of the legend relates how Tiresias became involved in an argument between Zeus and Hera, who when Tiresias spent seven years transformed into a woman consulted him over the question of whether men or women experience more pleasure from sex. Tiresias declared that women found sex nine times more enjoyable than men and thus incurred the wrath of Hera, who blinded him in her rage. Zeus then granted Tiresias prophetic powers in compensation for the loss of his sight. It was Tiresias who revealed to Oedipus the awful truth that the latter had unwittingly murdered his father and married his mother. He was also reputed to understand the language of the birds and continued to dispense wisdom until a very advanced age. *The old man, like some venerable Tiresias, dispensed wisdom from his throne on the stoop for all the world.*

Tisiphone *See* FURIES.

titanic (tītanik) Immensely huge or powerful. The word makes reference to the Titans of Greek myth, the 12 primeval gods and goddesses identified as the sons and daughters of Uranus (the sky) and Gaea (the Earth). Legend had it that they ruled the earth in a golden age until the youngest of them, Cronus, overthrew Uranus and was subsequently himself overthrown by his son Zeus. He and the other Titans were consigned to Tartarus. By the same token a person or thing that is immensely huge or powerful may be called a ***titan.*** "On the Promenade des Anglais, where Ned Silverton hung on him for the half hour before dinner, he received a deeper impression of the general insecurity. Silverton was in a mood of Titanic pessimism" (Edith Wharton, *The House of Mirth,* 1905).

Titanic (tītanik) A doomed ship or other vessel, project, etc. The White Star liner RMS *Titanic* was considered the most luxurious liner of its day and was claimed by its designers to be unsinkable. During the night of April 14–15, 1912, however, having set sail on its maiden voyage from Southampton for the United States with 3,000 people on board, it struck an iceberg off Newfoundland and sank in under three hours, leading to the deaths of 1,513 people. The disaster subsequently acquired semimythical status and has been reenacted on the cinema screen several times. The phrase ***rearrange the deck chairs on the Titanic***, signifying a futile gesture, has also entered the annals of the political cliché. *When the funding dried up, the whole business went down like the Titanic.*

tithe of mint, anise, and cumin A relatively trivial obligation, duty, or other matter, usually in comparison with a much more significant matter that has been neglected. The phrase comes from Matthew 23:23, in which Christ criticized the Pharisees for busying themselves with trivialities while neglecting more important matters: "For ye pay tithe of mint and anise and cummin, and have omitted the weightier matters of the law, judgment, mercy and faith: these ought ye to have done, and not to leave the other undone." *This pitiful offering reminded her of the tithe of mint, anise, and cumin paid by the Pharisees, a very inadequate replacement for the total amount owed.*

Tithonus (tithōnăs) Archetype of a very old, decrepit person. According to Greek mythology Tithonus was the brother of King Priam of Troy and much admired by Eos, the goddess of the dawn, for his great beauty. When he prayed for the gift of immortality, Eos persuaded Zeus to grant him his wish, but as she had forgotten also to ask for the gift of eternal youth on his behalf, Tithonus became wizened and feeble as he aged. Unable to die, he was eventually transformed by Eos into a grasshopper. "And did you ever imagine that you and Nick, of all people, were going to escape the common doom, and survive like Mr. and Mrs. Tithonus, while all about you the eternal passions were crumbling to pieces, and your native Divorce-states piling up their revenues?" (Edith Wharton, *Glimpses of the Moon,* 1922).

tittle *See* JOT OR TITTLE.

Tityrus (titīrăs) Poetical name for a shepherd. Shepherds appear with this name in the works of early Greek poets and of the Roman poet Virgil (70–19 B.C.). It was subsequently adopted for similar characters by such English poets as Geoffrey Chaucer (c. 1342–1400) and Edmund Spenser (1552–99). "Heroes and their feats / Fatigue me, never weary of the pipe / Of Tityrus, assembling as he sang / The rustic throng beneath his favourite beech" (William Cowper, *The Task,* 1785).

Tityus (tityăs) Archetypal sufferer of great torment. According to Greek mythology Tityus was a giant who tried to rape Leto, the mother of Apollo and Artemis. As punishment he was consigned to the underworld, where a vulture perpetually tore out his liver. When he lay down on the ground his body covered nine acres. *Suddenly he envisioned the dreadful fate that could be in store for* *him, doomed to suffer eternal agony like some modern-day Tityus.*

Tiw *See* TYR.

Tobacco Road Squalid and degenerate surroundings. The allusion is to a novel (1932) of the same title written by Erskine Caldwell (1903–87), in which he vividly described the harsh realities of life among the impoverished sharecroppers of the Deep South, specifically the rural community of Tobacco Road in Georgia. *Even as a rich man living in a big house on Long Island, he never forgot his humble Tobacco Road beginnings.*

to be or not to be Should one do or not do something? This most famous of all quotations from the plays of William Shakespeare comes from his tragedy *HAMLET* (c. 1600), opening a soliloquy in which the central character debates the arguments for and against suicide. In modern usage, the phrase is commonly applied in a much wider range of contexts, often with a different verb in place of "be." *To vote or not to vote, that was the question being faced by the bulk of a politically indifferent electorate.*

to boldly go where no man has gone before *See* STAR TREK.

Todd, Sweeney *See* SWEENEY TODD.

to everything there is a season *See* TIME AND PLACE FOR EVERYTHING.

to him that hath *See* WHOSOEVER HATH, TO HIM SHALL BE GIVEN.

toil in the groves of Academe *See* ACADEMIA; GROVES OF ACADEME.

toil not, neither do they spin *See* LILIES OF THE FIELD.

Tokyo Rose (tōkeeō) A woman who betrays her country. The allusion is to Iva Ikuko Togori D'Aquino (b. 1916), a woman of Japanese descent who was born in Los Angeles and later made propaganda broadcasts for the Japanese during World War II. Though her broadcasts had little real effect upon U.S. troops serving in the Pacific, her efforts were enough to have her arrested and tried for treason; she served six years in prison. *The papers dubbed her the Soviet Union's Tokyo Rose but no one took her seriously. See also* LORD HAW-HAW.

Tolkienesque (tolkeenesk) Reminiscent of the style or subject matter of the writings of the British novelist J. R. R. Tolkien (1892–1973). Author of *The Lord of the Rings* (1954–55) and other epic tales, Tolkien has become indelibly linked in the popular imagination to a fantasy world of wizards, hobbits, and other folkloric creatures. Many details of his inventive stories were prompted by his studies as a professor of Anglo-Saxon and of English Language and Literature at Oxford. *He first attracted attention with a clever Tolkienesque short story published in a magazine when he was just twelve years old. See also* GANDALF; GOLUM; HOBBIT; ORC.

Tom and Jerry A pair of individuals who behave in a boisterous, slapstick manner. The allusion is to the classic *Tom and Jerry* cartoons made by the animators William Hanna and Joseph Barbera, featuring the comical antics of a cat called Tom and a mouse called Jerry as they seek to outwit one another (sometimes employing extreme violence). They first appeared in a 1940 cartoon called *Puss Gets the Boot*. It has been suggested that the characters' names may have been prompted by the fact that much earlier they had been applied to a pair of lively young men who featured in Pierce Egan's *Life in London; or, The Day and Night Scenes of Jerry Hawthorn, Esq, and His Elegant Friend Corinthian Tom* (1821). "It was like a Tom and Jerry cartoon to see him bang his head on the door, bounce back, look a little dazed, and then remember the terrifying 'nightmare' he was escaping from, and shoot for cover behind the sofa" (Jon Hadwick, *Owl Light*, 1991).

Tommy A soldier in the British army. Associated particularly with soldiers fighting in World War I, the nickname was actually familiar to British soldiers through most of the 19th century as a shortened form of Tommy Atkins, the name given on the specimen forms handed out to new recruits as a guide to filling out their own enlistment documents. "O it's Tommy this, an' Tommy that, an' 'Tommy, go away'; / But it's 'Thank you, Mister Atkins', when the band begins to play" (Rudyard Kipling, "Tommy," *Barrack Room Ballads*, 1892).

tomorrow is another day Fortunes can change radically from day to day. Common to the extent of being a cliché, this is the closing line of the classic 1939 movie GONE WITH THE WIND, in which it is delivered by Vivien Leigh in the guise of Scarlett O'Hara as she resolves to make up for some of her earlier mistakes by devoting her energies to restoring her neglected ***Tara*** estate: "After all, tomorrow is another day." This was also to have been the title of a sequel Margaret Mitchell planned to write to her original novel, upon which the film was based. *It is undeniable that today's events have been disappointing, but tomorrow is another day.*

tomorrow will take care of itself Do not worry about the future until it comes. The proverb comes from Christ's Sermon on the Mount: "Take therefore no thought for the morrow: for the morrow shall take thought for the things of itself" (Matthew 6:34). *His grandmother was notorious for her procrastination in such matters. She was a great believer in the philosophy tomorrow will take care of itself. See also* SUFFICIENT UNTO THE DAY IS THE EVIL THEREOF.

Tom, Uncle *See* UNCLE TOM.

Tom Paine A political radical, especially one committed to the cause of liberty. Tom Paine (1737–1809) was born in England but became identified with the cause of liberty and revolution in other countries, fighting for the Americans in the American Revolution and subsequently becoming a member of the French revolutionary parliament. His most influential publications were *The Rights of Man* (1791–92) and *The Age of Reason* (1794). *As a political thinker he was sometimes described as a modern Tom Paine.*

Tom Sawyer (soyer, soier) Archetype of a mischievous, resourceful young boy. The central character of the novel *The Adventures of Tom Sawyer* (1876) by Mark Twain (Samuel Langhorne Clemens; 1835–1910), he famously exercises his creativity to get out of school and to escape the risk of doing any hard work. *The kids on the corner seemed to have more in common with Darth Vader than they did with Tom Sawyer. See also* HUCKLEBERRY FINN.

Tom Thumb A very small person. Tom Thumb, just the size of his father's thumb, was originally a nursery tale character, whose adventures were in wide circulation by the 16th century. In the 19th century the diminutive Charles Sherwood Stratton (1838–83), just 40 inches in height, was marketed by the showmen Barnum and Bailey (*see* P. T. BARNUM) as "General Tom Thumb" and traveled to Europe, where he was presented to both Queen Victoria of England and Louis Philippe of France. *The space for the driver is so restricted you would need to be Tom Thumb to feel comfortable.*

tongues, gift of *See* GIFT OF TONGUES.

Tonto *See* LONE RANGER.

tooth for a tooth *See* EYE FOR AN EYE.

Tophet *See* GEHENNA.

Topsy Something that develops steadily under its own volition and despite the fact that no one has taken responsibility for it. The reference is to a slave girl called Topsy in the antislavery novel *Uncle Tom's Cabin* (1851) by Harriet Beecher Stowe (1811–96). When asked to account for her origins, lacking any knowledge of her parents she replies simply: "I 'spect I grow'd. Don't think nobody never made me." *Once the initial idea for the project had been formed, it continued to grow over the years, like Topsy.*

tortoise *See* HARE AND THE TORTOISE.

to the pure all things are pure *See* UNTO THE PURE ALL THINGS ARE PURE.

touch me not *See* NOLI ME TANGERE.

touch pitch and be defiled It is inevitable that if a person has dealings with wickedness he or she will be tainted with it. The proverb is from the apocryphal book of Ecclesiasticus (Sirach) 13:1: "He that toucheth pitch, shall be defiled therewith, and he that hath fellowship with a proud man, shall be like unto him." A concise variant may be found in the form ***pitch defiles.*** "Not in electioneering, Mr. Romer, any more than in any other pursuits, can a man touch pitch and not be defiled; as thou, innocent as thou art, wilt soon learn to thy terrible cost" (Anthony Trollope, *Doctor Thorne,* 1858).

touch the hem of his garment *See* HEM OF HIS GARMENT, TOUCH THE.

Tower of Babel (baybăl, babăl) A scene of general confusion and noise. The allusion is to the biblical Tower of Babel, which according to Genesis 11:4–9 was built with the intention of reaching heaven. The Tower of Babel may have been a type of Babylonian temple called a ziggurat. Ziggurats were pyramid shaped, and some may have reached more than 325 feet (100 meters) high. God thwarted the efforts of the builders by making them speak in different languages so that no one could make himself or herself understood to another. The word *Babel* itself means "gate of God." *At the international airport, he stood still for a moment and listened to the many languages being spoken all around him. It was a veritable Tower of Babel.*

Tower of London A state prison. The Tower of London, which was built on the site of a fort erected by the Romans under Julius Caesar, was constructed by the Normans under William the Conqueror in the 11th century and substantially enlarged by later monarchs. It acquired a dreaded reputation as a prison in which the state's most important prisoners were confined and sometimes executed, including several members of the royal family and the senior aristocracy. *Carry on like that and you'll end up in the Tower of London.*

Tracy, Dick *See* DICK TRACY.

trail of tears A route, real or metaphorical, that is lined with evidence of suffering. The allusion is to the Trail of Tears that the Cherokee followed when forced to abandon their ancestral lands in Georgia and to migrate to Oklahoma in 1829–43, despite their having previously won a Supreme Court decision in their favor. Around 4,000 of their number died on the journey of cold, exhaustion, and disease. *Survivors of the battle were forced to follow a thousand-mile trail of tears to safety.*

Travis Bickle (travis bikăl) Archetype of an unhinged killer. Travis Bickle is the name of the deranged Vietnam War veteran who turns killer in the 1976 movie *Taxi Driver*. Played by Robert De Niro, Bickle turns to violence in a misguided one-man crusade to clean up the streets. *He was a quiet man whom no one would have suspected of being a Travis Bickle.*

treasure in heaven *See* LAY NOT UP TREASURES UPON EARTH.

treasures upon earth, lay not up *See* LAY NOT UP TREASURES UPON EARTH.

tree is known by its fruit, the People should be judged not by their appearances but by how they act and by what they produce (for example, with reference to their offspring). The proverb is biblical in origin, coming from Matthew 12:33: "Either make the tree good, and his fruit good; or else make the tree corrupt, and his fruit corrupt: for the tree is known by his fruit." "If then the tree may be known by the fruit, as the fruit by the tree, then, peremptorily I speak it, there is virtue in that Falstaff" (William Shakespeare, *Henry IV, Part 1,* 1597–98).

tree of knowledge A source of knowledge or wisdom. The phrase appears in biblical descriptions of the GARDEN OF EDEN, in which it is identified as the Tree of Knowledge of Good and Evil (Genesis 2:9). It is the disobedience of ADAM AND EVE in disregarding God's command not to eat of the fruit of this tree that leads to their expulsion from Paradise. Today the tree is sometimes interpreted as a symbol of the truth that the gaining of knowledge necessarily requires the loss of innocence, hence the expression ***eat from the tree of knowledge*** meaning to learn such knowledge. "And so the poor child, with her soul's hunger and her illusions of self-flattery, began to nibble at this thick-rinded fruit of the tree of knowledge, filling her vacant hours with Latin, geometry, and the forms of the syllogism" (George Eliot, *The Mill on the Floss,* 1860). *See also* FORBIDDEN FRUIT.

tree of life Life or the fount of life. The tree is described in Genesis 2:9 (and elsewhere) as a central feature of the GARDEN OF EDEN: "And out of the ground made the LORD God to grow every tree that is pleasant to the sight, and good for food; the tree of life also in the midst of the garden." The tree of life is generally interpreted as a symbol of God's gift of life. (See also Proverbs 3:18 and 11:30 and Revelation 2:7 and 22:1–19.) "But we have not to do with the wars of the Mulberry Hills and the Dry Docks. We must to Rooney's, where, on the most blighted dead branch of the tree of life, a little pale orchid shall bloom" (O. Henry, *Strictly Business,* 1910).

trial by ordeal A challenge involving considerable mental or physical endurance. The allusion is to the early medieval custom of testing a person's guilt by putting them through a form of torture in the belief that if they were innocent God would prevent them from suffering injury. Accused persons might face ordeal by water (having their hand plunged into boiling water or being tossed into a pond with hands and feet tied), by fire (being forced to hold a red-hot bar or walk across heated plowshares), or by eating consecrated bread to see if they choked on it. "During this trial by ordeal the restaurant was almost empty although people kept arriving and being turned away because: 'There are no tables'" (Walter Perrie, *Roads that Move*, 1991).

tribes of Israel *See* LOST TRIBES OF ISRAEL.

tribune of the people A democratic leader, specifically one who acts as a champion of public rights. In ancient Rome the senior rank of tribune denoted a chief magistrate, who wielded great influence in the city. During the revolt of 494 B.C. two tribunes were elected by the plebeians to prevent the patricians from taking revenge on the rebels (the number was subsequently increased to 10). Tribunes were immune from prosecution and had various powers of veto at their command. "The man on the little stool behind the President, is the Capo Lazzarone, a kind of tribune of the people, appointed on their behalf to see that all is fairly conducted: attended by a few personal friends" (Charles Dickens, *Pictures of Italy,* 1845).

tried and found wanting *See* WRITING ON THE WALL.

Trigger *See* ROY ROGERS.

triple whammy *See* DOUBLE WHAMMY.

Tristan and Isolde (izoldă) Archetype of a pair of tragic lovers. According to a medieval English romance, Tristan (or Tristram) was the nephew of King Mark of Cornwall, while Isolde (or Iseult) was the daughter of an Irish king. Isolde was promised in marriage to King Mark, but when Tristan went to Ireland to bring her to Cornwall, the pair fell in love after unwittingly drinking a love potion made for the bridal couple by Isolde's mother. The story ends tragically, although there are several different versions of the events surrounding the pair's demise: in one, King Mark finds the lovers asleep in the forest, with a sword between them to keep them apart. "But always my dreadful secret lay between us, like the sword between Tristan and Isolde" (John Fowles, *The Magus*, 1988).

Triton (trītăn) A mythological sea creature; the larger of Neptune's two satellites. The Greek sea god Triton was the son of Poseidon and Amphitrite and was said to have the upper half of a human fixed to a fish's tail. He is often depicted in art and literature blowing a horn formed from a conch shell in order to calm the sea at Poseidon's approach. His name is sometimes encountered in the form ***a Triton among the minnows,*** signifying a great person among inferiors. ". . . on the right of the stage is the public fountain, with a triton in green bronze blowing from a conch; around the fountain is a stone seat; the bell of the Cathedral is ringing, and the citizens, men, women and children, are passing into the Cathedral" (Oscar Wilde, *The Duchess of Padua,* 1891).

triumvirate (trīămvirăt) Three people acting as one body. The original triumvirates were the groups of three magistrates who were appointed to fulfill various official functions in ancient Rome. The most famous triumvirate of all was the political alliance of Julius Caesar, Marcus Licinius Crassus, and Pompey the Great that wielded power from

60 B.C. "He showed her a letter which he was about to dispatch to Robespierre himself, vindicating his suspected patriotism, and indignantly demanding to be allowed to prove it by filling some office, no matter how small, under the redoubtable triumvirate which then governed, or more properly terrified, France" (Wilkie Collins, *After Dark,* 1856).

Troilus and Cressida (troylăs, kresidă) Archetypal tragic lovers. According to Homer's *Iliad* (c. 700 B.C.), Troilus was the youngest son of King Priam and Queen Hecuba of Troy and died in the course of the Trojan War. His romance with Cressida was a later invention of around the fourth or fifth century A.D. subsequently elaborated by medieval writers. "'Troilus loved and he was fooled,' said the more manly chaplain. 'A man may love and yet not be a Troilus. All women are not Cressids'" (Anthony Trollope, *Barchester Towers,* 1857).

Trojan (trōjăn) A hard-working, determined, or otherwise reliable person. The Trojans were much respected for their courage in battle, as evidenced in the course of the lengthy Trojan War against the Greeks, as related in Homer's *Iliad* (c. 700 B.C.) and Virgil's *Aeneid* (30–19 B.C.). The word, occasionally has other connotations: In William Shakespeare's day it could be used as a synonym for a robber or dissolute rogue. *He worked like a Trojan until dawn broke and the danger had passed.*

Trojan horse (trōjăn) A deception designed to undermine an enemy from within. The allusion is to the ***wooden horse*** with which the Greeks achieved the final overthrow of Troy at the conclusion of the Trojan War. According to Homer (in the *Iliad,* c. 700 B.C.) and Virgil (in the *Aeneid,* 30–19 B.C.), the Greeks built a large, hollow wooden horse and filled it with warriors before making a pretense of leaving their camps around Troy and sailing away. The Trojans, fooled into thinking the horse was an offering to the goddess Athena, dragged it within their walls. After dark the Greek warriors poured out of the horse and sacked the city. In modern usage a Trojan horse usually refers to an apparently harmless gift through which an enemy may be defeated or disrupted. The term has particular relevance in computer circles, where it can refer to an apparently innocent program or system that subsequently releases a damaging computer virus. "A 'Trojan horse' cancer treatment that slips inside tumour cells and destroys them with radiation has been successfully tested in the U.S." (*Times,* November 16, 2001). *See also* BEWARE OF GREEKS BEARING GIFTS.

Trophonius *See* CAVE OF TROPHONIUS.

Trump, Last *See* LAST TRUMP.

truth?, What is *See* WHAT IS TRUTH?

truth shall make you free, the Knowledge of the truth is the key to salvation. The sentiment is biblical in origin, appearing in John 8:31–32, in which Christ promised the Jews that if they obeyed his word, they would be his true disciples. Such knowledge—God's revelation of his truth—would set them free from sin: "If ye continue in my word, then are ye my disciples indeed; And ye shall know the truth, and the truth shall make you free." "'Well, if you won't accept Tennyson as an authority, perhaps you will believe the words of a Greater than he,' said Gilbert seriously. "'Ye shall know the truth and the truth shall make you free." I believe that, Anne, with all my heart. It's the greatest and grandest verse in the Bible—or in any literature'" (Lucy Maud Montgomery, *Anne's House of Dreams,* 1917).

Tuck, Friar *See* FRIAR TUCK.

Tuesday The third day of the week. It is named after Tiw (TYR), the Anglo-Saxon god of war and the sky. *Shrove Tuesday is the day before Lent begins, on Ash Wednesday.*

turn the other cheek To accept a personal insult or injury passively and without retaliating. The expression is biblical in origin, being quoted by Christ in the course of his Sermon on the Mount, as related in Matthew 5:38–39: "Ye have heard that it hath been said, An eye for an eye, and a tooth for a tooth: But I say unto you, That ye resist not evil: but whosoever shall smite thee on thy right cheek, turn to him the other also." "It is well, I think, that violent offences, when committed, should be met by instant rebuke. To turn the other cheek instantly to the smiter can hardly be suitable in these days, when the hands of so many are raised to strike" (Anthony Trollope, *The Last Chronicle of Barset,* 1867). *See also* EYE FOR AN EYE.

Tuscan Belonging to a relatively plain and unornamented order of classical architecture derived from the DORIC style. *The architects chose a grand but somewhat restrained Tuscan style for the portico of the bank's new headquarters in the center of the city. See also* CORINTHIAN; IONIC.

Tweed, "Boss" *See* TAMMANY HALL.

Tweedledum and Tweedledee A pair of individuals or things that are so similar they are virtually indistinguishable. The allusion is to two characters who appear in the children's fantasy *THROUGH THE LOOKING-GLASS* (1865) by Lewis Carroll. They are depicted as two very fat twin brothers with identical mannerisms and appearance and the habit of each repeating everything the other says. The names were in existence before Carroll, however, and were applied as early as 1715 to the rival composers Giovanni Bononcini and George Frideric Handel, as immortalized in a poem by the contemporary writer John Byrom: "Some say, that Signor Bononcini / Compar'd to Handel's a mere ninny; / Others aver, to him, that Handel / Is scarcely fit to hold a candle. / Strange! That such high dispute should be / 'Twixt Tweedledum and Tweedledee." "The umpires conferred, then, like Tweedledum and Tweedledee in their striped shirts, cantered over to the third man in the stands, who'd been gazing at Mrs. Sherwood at the time and missed the incident altogether, and who now waved his down-turned palms back and forth to indicate no foul" (Jilly Cooper, *Polo,* 1991).

twilight of the gods *See* GÖTTERDÄMMERUNG.

twilight zone A mysterious area between reality and fantasy, in which all manner of weird things might occur. The allusion is to the cult U.S. science-fiction television series *The Twilight Zone* (1959–63), which featured such bizarre phenomena as time warps and machines capable of independent thought and began with the words: "There is a fifth dimension beyond that which is known to men. It is a dimension as vast as space and as timeless as infinity. It is the middle ground between light and shadow, between science and superstition, and it lies between the pit of man's fears and the summit of his knowledge. This is the dimension of imagination. It is an area we call The Twilight Zone." *Things were turning out so unexpectedly it was a bit like being in the twilight zone.*

twinkling of an eye, in the Instantaneously; very quickly; in the briefest time. The phrase comes from 1 Corinthians 15:51–52, in which Paul writes about the resurrection of the dead on the return of Christ: "Behold, I shew you a mystery; We shall not all sleep, but we shall all be changed, In a moment, in the twinkling of an eye, at the last trump: for the trumpet shall sound, and the dead shall be raised incorruptible, and we shall be changed." "I don't understand these matters very well, but from Fyne's narrative it seemed as if the creditors or the depositors, or the competent authorities, had got hold in the twinkling of an eye of everything de Barral possessed in the world" (Joseph Conrad, *Chance,* 1913).

Twist, Oliver *See* OLIVER TWIST.

twist slowly in the wind To be left alone to endure prolonged public humiliation, regret, etc. The reference is to the turning of the body of a hanged man on a gibbet. The phrase is particularly associated with the public downfall of leading political figures and featured prominently during the WATERGATE scandal, when it was voiced by Richard Nixon's Assistant for Domestic Affairs John D. Ehrlichman: "I think we ought to let him hang there. Let him twist slowly, slowly in the wind." *She could have rescued him from public humiliation in front of the other parents, but she decided to let him twist slowly in the wind.*

two-edged sword Referring to something that is open to two different interpretations, such as an argument or policy that has an effect against both parties involved. The phrase comes from the Bible. Hebrews 4:12 reads: "For the word of God is quick, and powerful, and sharper than any two-edged sword, piercing even to the dividing asunder of soul and spirit, and of the joints and marrow, and is a discerner of the thoughts and intents of the heart." According to Revelation 1:16: "And he had in his right hand seven stars: and out of his mouth went a sharp two-edged sword: and his countenance was as the sun shineth in his strength.' (See also Revelation 2:12 and the apocryphal book of Ecclesiasticus [Sirach] 21:3.) "The honest soldier was confused. The lawyer's eloquence overpowered him. He felt guilty. Josephine saw his simplicity, and made a cut with a woman's two-edged sword. 'Sir,' said she coolly, 'do you not see it is an affair of money?'" (Charles Reade, *White Lies,* 1857).

two or three gathered together *See* WHERE TWO OR THREE ARE GATHERED TOGETHER.

Tyburn (tībern) A place of execution by hanging. Tyburn was the name of a location in London where public executions took place regularly from 1388 to 1783, using a triangular gallows that made it possible to hang several people at the same time. It was originally the name of a tributary of the River Thames, after which the settlement of Tyburn was named. The name was similarly applied to other places of execution around the country, such as Tyburn in York. *His career of larceny and murder finally ended at Tyburn.*

Typhoid Mary A carrier of disease. The reference is to Mary Mallon (c. 1870–1938), a household cook who was a carrier of typhoid fever, leading to the outbreak of epidemics in various locations throughout the New York area where she had worked. Immune to the disease herself, between 1904 and 1914 she passed it on to at least 51 other people, of whom three died. "Such people are infectious however, and if they are involved in food preparation and are careless about washing their hands, they may be the modern equivalent of 'Typhoid Mary,' passing Giardia on to others" (Linda Gamlin and Jonathan Brostoff, *The Complete Guide to Food Allergy and Intolerance*, 1989).

Tyr (tir) Personification of war. Tyr, or ***Tyrr*** or ***Tiw,*** was identified in Norse mythology as the son of Odin and was revered as the god of war. *Valhalla must be bursting at the seams with young warriors recently slain at the call of Tyr.*

Tyre *See* NINEVEH AND TYRE.

U

über alles (oober alez) Dominant; above all. An expression of German origin, meaning "over all," it comes from the German national anthem "Deutschland über alles," which became notorious as the anthem (1922–45) of the Nazi regime of Adolf HITLER. The phrase is commonly employed in circumstances where a person or organization is suspected of acting in a dictatorial manner. *With her sister it's a case of fun über alles, even if that means sacrificing her family and career.*

Ubi sunt? (oobee sănt) Where are they now? This lament in Latin on the transitory nature of earthly greatness has biblical origins, the words arising from a medieval reworking of David's lament for Saul and Jonathan: "The beauty of Israel is slain upon thy high places: how are the mighty fallen!" (2 Samuel 1:19). The *ubi sunt* motif became a popular theme of medieval poetry, designating "a mood or theme in literature of lament for the mutability of things" *(Oxford English Dictionary). They were among the most celebrated players of their generation, but as is so often the case in the world of sport, once they retired, their names rarely cropped up outside the usual Ubi sunt? inquiries.*

Ugly American An American who acts in an overbearing manner while abroad. The origin of the expression was the best-selling book of stories entitled *The Ugly American* (1958) by William J. Lederer and Eugene Burdick, which dealt with the United States' disastrous involvement in Southeast Asia in the postwar period. *Resentment in the region at the presence of a large number of "ugly Americans" did little to help soothe ruffled local sensibilities over what was seen as unwarranted interference from the West.*

ugly duckling An unprepossessing person or thing who against all expectations proves a great success. The reference is to the children's story "The Ugly Duckling" (first translated into English in 1846) by Danish writer HANS CHRISTIAN ANDERSEN (1805–75). Andersen's tale, often interpreted over the years on the large and small screens and in song, concerns a duckling who seems to lack the natural abilities and good looks of his young siblings, until he grows up and turns out not to be a duck at all, but a magnificent swan. The phrase is often applied to children of ordinary appearance who confound expectations by becoming great beauties as adults, but it may also be applied to a wider range of human or animal misfits, projects, commercial enterprises, etc., that exceed all predictions for them. "Even when made up with the finest cosmetics money could buy it would never be beautiful, but still . . . not bad for an ugly duckling, Sally thought, smiling wryly" (Janet Tanner, *Folly's Child*, 1991).

Ugly Sisters Two (or more) people or other entities that behave in a jealous, even cruel way toward others. The allusion is to the two Ugly Sisters in the folktale and pantomime story *Cinderella*, the ugly but vain daughters of an impoverished baron who cruelly mistreat their stepsister CINDERELLA, only to be thwarted when she wins the hand of PRINCE CHARMING. *These two female critics developed into a pair of Ugly Sisters who held every show on Broadway in their thrall.*

ultima Thule (ăltimă thoolee, ăltimă thyoolee) A far-distant place; a remote destination; the ends of the earth or the very limit of what is attainable. Latin for "farthest Thule," ultima Thule in Roman times was the northernmost limit of the known world. Thule was identified by the Greek explorer Pytheas (fl. 300 B.C.) as being located six days' sailing beyond the north of Britain (possibly Norway, Iceland, or the Shetland Islands). Pliny the Elder described Thule in *Historia Naturalis* (A.D. 77) as "an island in the Northern Ocean discovered by Pytheas, after sailing six days from the Orcades." The phrase appears in the first book of Virgil's *Georgics* (c. 36 B.C.): "Tibi serviat Ultima Thule." "My cognizance of the pit had become known to the inquisitorial agents—the pit whose horrors had been destined for so bold a recusant as myself—the pit, typical of hell, and regarded by rumor as the Ultima Thule of all their punishments" (Edgar Allan Poe, "The Pit and the Pendulum," 1843).

Ulysses *See* ODYSSEUS.

Ulysses' bow (yooliseez) Something extremely difficult to handle or that only one person is able to use effectively. Legend has it that the great bow belonging to the Greek adventurer Ulysses (ODYSSEUS) could only be drawn by the celebrated hero himself. It was through his ability to draw his bow and his skill as an archer, specifically in shooting an arrow through 12 rings, that Ulysses was recognized by his wife, Penelope, when he returned home after 20 years away. The bow, which was also reputed to have prophetic powers, was at one time the property of Eurytus of Oechalia. *So many adventurers had come to grief trying to pull off this modern Ulysses' bow that it was soon believed that no one would ever succeed in the feat.*

Uncas *See* LAST OF THE MOHICANS.

Uncle Fester *See* ADDAMS FAMILY.

Uncle Sam The United States. The United States has been personified as "Uncle Sam," depicted visually as a gaunt-looking white-bearded old showman dressed in top hat and a stars-and-stripes dress suit, since the early 19th century. It has been suggested that the name was first bandied about in the neighborhood of Troy in New York around 1812, presumably inspired by the letters "U.S." stamped on government supplies, although another theory links the name to a real Uncle Sam who handled army supplies in the neighborhood. His image was ubiquitous during World War I, when potential army recruits were encouraged by a stern-looking Uncle Sam with pointed finger over the slogan "Uncle Sam Wants You!" In modern usage the tag is employed with similar frequency both fondly and critically. "Suddenly, the Kremlin is falling over itself to get close to Uncle Sam" (Peter Cave, *Foxbat*, 1979).

Uncle Tom A black person who acts in an obsequious manner toward white people. The allusion is to the central character in the hugely popular novel *Uncle Tom's Cabin* (1852) by U.S. author and antislavery campaigner Harriet Beecher Stowe (1811–96). Uncle Tom is an aged, loyal, gentle black slave whose sufferings and ultimate martyrdom at the hands of the vicious slave owner ***Simon Legree*** vividly evoke the realities of life as a slave in the period leading up to the Civil War. He was allegedly based upon Josiah Henson (1789–1883), a black slave and Methodist preacher brought to London in 1876 to be presented to Queen Victoria. *He had been a firebrand as a youth but he had been outpaced by a new generation of black radicals who saw their elders as a generation of Uncle Toms.*

understanding heart *See* JUDGMENT OF SOLOMON.

under the aegis of *See* AEGIS.

under the sun *See* NOTHING NEW UNDER THE SUN.

unequally yoked Improperly or unsuitably linked in a very close partnership (usually by marriage). The phrase is biblical in origin, being a quotation from 2 Corinthians 6:14 in which Paul warns the Corinthians, "Be ye not unequally yoked together with unbelievers." The phrase has been variously applied to marriages between Christians and non-Christians and more generally to any pair of partners deemed ill matched. *The two nations entered a coalition against their common enemy, but it quickly became apparent that they were unequally yoked.*

unerring as the dart of Procris (prokris) Undeviating; deadly accurate. According to Greek legend the jealous Procris deserted her husband, Cephalus, and was presented by the sympathetic Diana with a dog that always caught its prey and a dart that always hit its target and then returned to its owner's hand. Unfortunately when Procris hid in some bushes to spy on her husband and any lover he might be with, she made too much noise, and thinking he was being stalked by a wild beast, Cephalus hurled his javelin into the bushes, killing her. Upon discovering his mistake Cephalus killed himself out of grief. *This last shaft was as unerring as the dart of Procris and left its victim stunned.*

unforgivable sin *See* UNPARDONABLE SIN.

unicorn A fabulous animal resembling a white horse with a single horn in the middle of its forehead, most familiar today as an emblem in heraldic devices. Its name derives from the Latin *unus cornus* ("one horn"). The unicorn made its first appearance in literature in the writings of Ctesias around 400 B.C. and was subsequently mentioned in many medieval bestiaries. Originally described as having a lion's tail, a stag's legs, and a horse's head and body, the unicorn was believed to be very fierce but also fatally attracted by chastity, allowing it to be tricked into laying its head in the lap of a young virgin and thus captured. Allusions to the unicorn in modern iconography usually invoke the creature's identification with chastity, although Christian tradition sometimes also depicts Christ as a unicorn. *He came to think of her as some elusive unicorn, uncatchable and remote from the ordinary world of men.*

unkindest cut of all, the The most hurtful of injuries or insults, especially one delivered by a person previously thought to be a friend. The allusion is to William Shakespeare's play *Julius Caesar* (1599), in which Mark Antony shows the crowd the "most unkindest cut of all" made in the assassinated Caesar's mantle by the dagger wielded by Marcus Brutus, Caesar's supposed friend. "He followed this with the unkindest cut of all: 'Or is it that he is afraid I will ask him for money?'" (Philip Callow, *Van Gogh: A Life*, 1990).

unknown God An unidentified god or other object of veneration. The phrase alludes to the biblical story of Paul, who was on the way to speak to a group of skeptical Greek philosophers in Athens when he noted an altar inscribed with "TO THE UNKNOWN GOD" (Acts 17:23). On meeting his audience he asserted that all he aimed to do was to identify the god whom they already worshiped. It is thought that such altars were originally erected by Greeks as votive offerings when they were unsure which god they should thank. The phrase has been used in many contexts, including the title of John Steinbeck's novel *To a God Unknown* (1933). *This benefaction of an unknown God prompted many of the workers to offer silent prayers of thanks.*

unpardonable sin An offense (sometimes relatively trivial) that is considered certain to attract the condemnation of others. Although the phrase, sometimes rendered in the form ***unforgivable sin,*** does not actually appear in the Bible, it is the conventional way of describing the sin of blasphemy against the Holy Spirit (see Matthew 12:31–32 and Luke 12:10). The *NIV Thematic Reference Bible* defines the unforgivable sin as "The willful, outwardly expressed and impenitent slander against the Holy Spirit, when Jesus Christ's mighty works, clearly performed by the power of the Holy Spirit, are attributed to Satan, thus subjecting Christ to public disgrace" (p. 2,074). In general modern usage the phrase is sometimes employed in a parodic sense in reference to some minor social transgression or overstepping of accepted boundaries. "After all, for a seaman, to scrape the bottom of the thing that's supposed to float all the time under his care is the unpardonable sin" (Joseph Conrad, "Heart of Darkness," 1902).

unto dust shalt thou return You will not live forever. The phrase is biblical in origin, appearing in various forms at Genesis 2:7 and 3:19, Job 10:9 and 33:6, and Isaiah 64:8. It appears in Genesis 3:19 in the fuller form "dust thou art, and unto dust shalt thou return." In biblical usage dust and clay are symbols of mortality. Job subsequently echoes the phrase in protest at God's actions toward him: "Remember, I beseech thee, that thou hast made me as the clay; and wilt thou bring me into dust again?" (Job 10:9). Henry Wadsworth Longfellow, in "A Psalm of Life," wrote: "Dust thou art, to dust returnest." Today the term is most familiar in the form ***ashes to ashes, dust to dust,*** a phrase frequently spoken in the course of burial services. "Life is real! Life is earnest! / And the grave is not its goal; / Dust thou art, to dust returnest, / Was not spoken of the soul" (Henry Wadsworth Longfellow, "A Psalm of Life," 1839).

unto the pure all things are pure How a person sees something and the influence that he or she exerts on it depend largely on the nature of his or her own moral character. The saying comes from the letter of Paul to Titus: "Unto the pure all things are pure: but unto them that are defiled and unbelieving is nothing pure; but even their mind and conscience is defiled" (Titus 1:15). The line is sometimes quoted in defense of an individual's right to read whatever he or she chooses to read or in other defenses of freedom of choice. *The priest refused to believe that what he was being told could be true, but then unto the pure all things are pure.*

untouchable A law enforcer or other government agent who is immune to being bribed. The allusion is to a famously incorruptible group of detectives called the Untouchables that was led by ***Eliot Ness*** (1903–57) of the U.S. Department of Justice against the notorious AL CAPONE gang in Chicago during the 1920s. Their adventures, detailed by Ness himself in a book entitled *The Untouchables* (1947), later inspired a popular television series and a movie (1987), both with the same title. *A team of untouchables has been put together to find out how far the corruption in the department has really gone.*

upstairs, downstairs The contrast between the upper and lower classes. The phrase alludes to the fact that in the great houses of former times the kitchens and other rooms that were the province of the servants were usually located on the lower floors, while the owners of the buildings conducted their lives in the floors above. The phrase became doubly familiar as the title of a popular BBC television series, broadcast around the world in the 1970s, about life in a large London home in the early decades of the 20th century. *He specializes in stories about upstairs, downstairs in modern Manhattan. See also* HUDSON.

Urania *See* MUSES.

Uranus (yoorănăs, yooraynas) A planet in the solar system, seventh in distance from the Sun. In Greek mythology Uranus was a personification of the sky, a god who ruled the universe and who by his own mother, Gaea (the Earth), fathered the Titans and Cyclopes. He was subsequently overthrown by his son Cronus, who thus separated heaven from earth. *The old lady warned him that his life would never be easy because of the baleful influence of Uranus in his birth chart.*

Uriah *See* LETTER OF URIAH.

Uriah Heep (yooriă) An obsequious, untrustworthy hypocrite. The allusion is to the clerk of the name in Charles Dickens's novel *David Copperfield* (1849–1850) who deceitfully pretends to be the "'umble servant" of the lawyer Mr. Wickfield while stealing money from his business. The loathsome Heep's deceit is finally revealed and his plot to force Wickfield into letting him marry his daughter comes to nothing. *He was horrified to find that his assistant was a Uriah Heep who had brought the family business to the brink of ruin.*

U.S. cavalry A force that arrives in the nick of time to save the situation. The allusion is to the many Western movies made over the decades in which a troop of the U.S. 7th Cavalry arrives just in time to save beleaguered heroes from attack by hostile Native Americans. The arrival of help just in time is likely to be hailed with a thankful "***here come the cavalry***" delivered in more or less reverent tones according to the severity of the situation. "One must resist seeing Bakhtin as the U.S. Cavalry, riding in to rescue a threatened humanism from howling poststructuralists" (Bernard Bergonzi, *Exploding English*, 1990).

use a little wine *See* TAKE A LITTLE WINE.

Usher, House of *See* HOUSE OF USHER.

usual suspects *See* ROUND UP THE USUAL SUSPECTS.

utopia (yootōpeeă) An ideal society or a perfect place or paradise. The word comes ultimately from the Greek for "no place," but owes its modern familiarity largely to the fact that the English statesman and philosopher Sir Thomas More (1478–1535) used it as the title of a book (1516) in which he described an imaginary ideal society, situated on an island, in which reason held sway. The adjective ***utopian*** is usually employed in the sense of "idealistic," with the implication that whatever is being discussed is also unrealistic. "Assumptions vary: some people take the more recent past as their benchmark, others look to a more distant Utopia" (J. Finch, *Family Obligations and Social Change*, 1989).

V

Vader, Darth *See* DARTH VADER.

Valentine's Day massacre *See* SAINT VALENTINE'S DAY MASSACRE.

Valentino (valănteenō) A handsome, sexually attractive male, especially one who has such qualities to excess. The allusion is to movie star Rudolph Valentino (Rodolfo di Valentina d'Antonguolla; 1895–1926), who became a heart-throb for silent-movie audiences through such films as *The Sheikh* (1921) and *Blood and Sand* (1922) before his early death from peritonitis. "I don't care if he looks like Rudolph Valentino and goes in every bistro in the country every night of the year" (Alice T. Ellis, *Pillars of Gold*, 1993).

vale of tears Life as a series of misfortunes and sadnesses. The image of life as a vale of tears is believed to have biblical origins, being derived originally from the Valley of Baca (the Hebrew *bakah* meaning "weeping") mentioned in Psalm 84:5–6. Baca trees are balsams that exude gum in tearlike drops. "I excused myself and dropped to the rear of the procession, sad at heart, willing to go hence from this troubled life, this vale of tears, this brief day of broken rest, of cloud and storm, of weary struggle and monotonous defeat" (Mark Twain, *A Connecticut Yankee in King Arthur's Court,* 1889).

vale of Tempe *See* TEMPE, VALE OF.

Valhalla (valhală) The afterworld, where the souls of the brave go after death. According to Norse mythology, Valhalla is situated in Asgard and is connected to Earth by a rainbow bridge. It consists of a vast banqueting hall with walls of gold and a roof made of warriors' shields. Here the souls of heroes slain in battle spend eternity engaging in mock battles, feasting with Odin and recounting their exploits. The wounds they sustain in combat are magically healed each day. In modern usage Valhalla may denote any place (real or otherwise) to which only the bravest or most distinguished of persons may be admitted in recognition of their achievements. "At first it looked like a vast blue fort or Valhalla; but when they began to tuck the coarse meadow hay into the crevices, and this became covered with rime and icicles, it looked like a venerable moss-grown and hoary ruin" (Henry David Thoreau, *Walden, or Life in the Woods,* 1854).

Valkyrie (valkiree, valkăree) A formidable woman, especially one of statuesque proportions and Nordic appearance. In Norse mythology the Valkyries were the 12 beautiful blond handmaidens of Odin who roamed battlefields on flying horses picking out the bravest of the slain and carrying them to VALHALLA where they might spend eternity in the company of other great heroes. The word *Valkyrie* literally means "chooser of the slain." In modern usage the Valkyries are most familiar from Wagnerian opera, in which they are conventionally depicted in horned Viking helmets and armor. "The lawn-mower was sincerely intended to pass longitudinally over the body of Mr. Collins from heel to head; and it was the time for a death-song. Black Valkyrie hovered in the shrieking air" (Booth Tarkington, *Penrod,* 1914).

valley of dry bones A situation in which life seems impossible; the abode of death. The phrase is a reference to Ezekiel 37, in which God puts Ezekiel "down in the midst of the valley which was full of bones . . . and, lo, they were very dry. And he said unto me, Son of man, can these bones live?" (Ezekiel 37:1–3). On God's command through the prophet, the bones rise up and live again. (The episode is usually considered an allegory of the restoration of Israel.) The valley of dry bones symbolizes a situation in which hope is completely gone because of the irreversibility of death. "As the dry bones shook and came together in that dreadful valley of Ezekiel's, so now a philosophical theorem, cerebrally entertained, began to stir and heave and throw off its gravecloths, and stood upright and became a living presence" (C. S. Lewis, *Surprised by Joy,* 1955).

valley of Jehoshaphat (jăhōshăfat) A location for the final judgment of the nations; any place where a final reckoning shall be held. The valley of Jehoshaphat is referred to in Joel 3:2, but since the name Jehoshaphat is a play on words for "Jehovah is judge," and the prophets were more concerned with the certainty and reality of future judgment than in its exact location, the language is probably metaphorical and its precise location is not known. ". . . nothing was to be found but dry, sapless, mouldering, and disjointed bones, such as those which filled the valley of Jehoshaphat" (Sir Walter Scott, *Ivanhoe,* 1820). *See also* JUDGMENT DAY.

valley of the shadow of death A situation in which death is close by or imminent. The phrase comes from Psalm 23:4: "Yea, though I walk through the valley of the shadow of death, I will fear no evil: for thou art with me; thy rod and thy staff they comfort me." John Bunyan, in *PILGRIM'S PROGRESS* (1678), gives a fuller description of the valley: "The Valley it self . . . is as dark as pitch: we also saw there Hobgoblins, Satyrs, and Dragons of the Pit: We heard also in that Valley a continual howling and yelling, as of a People under unutterable misery; who there sat bound in affliction and Irons: and over that Valley hangs the discouraging cloud of confusion, death also doth always spread his wings over it: in a word, it is every wit dreadful, being utterly without Order." Other writers have generally accepted the gloomy nature of the valley. "One would have thought Inverary had been the Valley of the Shadow of Death, the inferior Chiefs showed such reluctance to approach it" (Sir Walter Scott, *A Legend of Montrose,* 1819).

vandal A person who deliberately defaces or otherwise spoils property. The original Vandals were a nomadic Teutonic people from central Europe (originally of Scandinavian origin) whose warlike behavior contributed to the final destruction of the Roman Empire in the fourth and fifth centuries A.D. They overran Gaul, Spain, and North Africa and sacked Rome in 455, causing widespread destruction to great works of art and buildings. The Vandals were especially notorious for looting and laying waste the lands that fell into their hands. "Though she did think that Uncle Tom had been worse than any vandal in that matter of selling her lover's magnificent works, still she was ready to tell of his generosity" (Anthony Trollope, *Ayala's Angel,* 1881).

Vanderbilt (vanderbilt) A very wealthy person, a tycoon. Cornelius Vanderbilt (1794–1877) established his family's fortune in the railroad and shipping businesses. He went on to use much of his vast wealth for charitable purposes. *You'd think he was a Vanderbilt the way he has been throwing his money around.*

van Gogh (van gō) A talented artist, especially one who is mentally anguished. Dutch artist Vincent van Gogh (1853–90) suffered from depression that was intensified by lack of recognition as an artist during his own lifetime, which ended with his suicide at the age of 37. He has since been hailed as a leader of the Postimpressionists and as one of the world's greatest artists of all time. *His paintings sell pretty well but let's face it, he's no van Gogh.*

Vanity Fair A town or other place that is notable for corruption and vice, or the world of men, with all its follies and lusts, generally. The phrase comes from *PILGRIM'S PROGRESS* (1678, 1684) by John Bunyan (1628–88), in which Vanity Fair is the name given to a fair held in the town of Vanity, the attractions of which include all manner of vice and sin. The phrase is best known today as the title of a novel by William Makepeace Thackeray (1811–63), published 1847–48, in which he similarly satirizes the follies of contemporary society. *He feared that if his daughters were set loose in the world they would soon fall prey to the temptations of Vanity Fair.*

vanity of vanities An act or belief that is considered entirely futile. The word *vanity* today generally signifies personal pride or conceit, but in its original biblical context the word suggested rather the notions of meaninglessness, emptiness, futility, or idolatry. The word appears many times in the Bible, notably in Ecclesiastes 1:2: "Vanity of vanities, saith the Preacher, vanity of vanities; all is vanity." The phrase is sometimes rendered in Latin as ***vanitas vanitatum*** or in another quotation from the same verse as ***all is vanity.*** "Oh how vain it is, the vanity of vanities, to live in men's thoughts instead of God's!" (Lytton Strachey, *Eminent Victorians,* 1918).

Van Winkle, Rip *See* RIP VAN WINKLE.

veil of Isis *See* LIFT THE VEIL OF ISIS.

veil of the temple rent A revelation or a moment of revelation. The image of a torn veil as a symbol of revelation is biblical in origin, referring to the moment of Christ's death on the cross, when "behold, the veil of the temple was rent in twain from the top to the bottom" (Matthew 27:51). (See also Mark 15:38, Luke 23:45, and Hebrews 6:19–20, 9:6–9, and 10:19–20.) The veil in question was the curtain in the Temple at Jerusalem that separated the Holy Place from the HOLY OF HOLIES (the innermost room of the tabernacle) (see Exodus 26:31). "The fact that the curtain prevented ordinary worshipers from entering the 'Most Holy Place' came to be seen as pointing to the much deeper separation between God and sinful humanity. The curtain thus came to be a symbol of the barrier placed between God and humanity by human sinfulness. At the time of the crucifixion of Jesus Christ, the curtain of the temple was torn. This dramatic event, noted in the Gospels, is seen as a symbol of one of the chief benefits brought about by the death of Jesus Christ: the barrier between God and humanity caused by sin has been torn down, so that there is now free access for believers to God on account of Christ's death" (*NIV Thematic Reference Bible,* p. 1,099). Legend has it that the veil was spun by the VIRGIN MARY herself. The image of the torn veil was variously taken up, for example, at the time of the Reformation (when it represented the abolition of the official priesthood), by Romantic poets (who used it as an image of the search for personal truth or liberty), and by many other writers as a simple image of spiritual, sexual, or other revelation. *This last thunderous communication brought him understanding. At last the veil of the temple was rent, and he comprehended for the first time how he had been betrayed.*

venereal *See* VENUS.

vengeance is mine My revenge over my enemy is complete. Generally quoted today by those who are gloating over some victory against their rivals, the phrase comes from the Bible, although it was originally meant to convey the desirability of leaving matters of retribution to divine providence. It appears in its original context in the form of a quotation of Paul writing to the Romans: "Dearly beloved, avenge not yourselves, but rather give place unto wrath: for it is written, Vengeance is mine; I will repay, saith the Lord" (Romans 12:19, quoting Deuteronomy 32:35). "'Thank God, that kept thine hand from blood-guiltiness, rash young man!' answered the curate. 'Vengeance is mine, saith the Lord, and I will repay it'" (Sir Walter Scott, *Kenilworth,* 1821).

veni, vidi, vici *See* I CAME, I SAW, I CONQUERED.

Venus (veenăs) The archetype of a feminine beauty. Venus was the Roman goddess of fertility and love and the equivalent of the Greek Aphrodite. According to mythology she emerged from the sea, variously from the foam of the waves or out of a seashell. She was herself the mother of Eros. In modern usage any woman described as a Venus is considered exceptionally beautiful. Other derivatives of the name of Venus include the adjective ***venereal,*** which variously refers to the genitalia and related sexual matters, especially to sexually transmitted diseases. "The sleeping Faun that lay in the alcove by the doorway had its twin brother that slumbered, and the silver Venus that stood in the sunlight held out her arms to a Venus as lovely as herself" (Oscar Wilde, *A House of Pomegranates,* 1891).

Venus's hair stone *See* THETIS'S HAIR STONE.

vesta (vestă) A type of short match, found commonly in the home since its introduction early in the 20th century. The name is an allusion to Vesta, the Roman goddess of the hearth and the equivalent of the Greek Hestia, who was widely worshiped throughout the Roman Empire. Her sacred fire at the Temple of Vesta in the Forum at Rome was kept burning by specially chosen maidens known as the ***vestal virgins.*** These attendants were trained from the age of 10 and were expected to keep themselves pure; if they were found to have been unfaithful they faced death or severe punishment. In modern usage any woman who is deemed to place undue (or hypocritical) importance on her own chastity is likely to be accused of acting ***like a vestal virgin.*** *The young man struck a vesta against the rough wall and by its feeble light strained to see further into the room.*

via Dolorosa (veeă dolărōsă, veeă dōlărōsa) A painful or sorrowful experience; a period of suffering; any unfortunate series of events leading to a melancholy conclusion. Literally translated from Latin as "sad road," the original via Dolorosa was the route taken by Christ through Jerusalem on his way to the Crucifixion after his condemnation by Pontius Pilate (Matthew 27:31–33, Mark 15:20–22, Luke 23:26–33, and John 19:16–17). Although the site of Pilate's judgment hall is not known and the modern city plan bears little relation to that of 2,000 years ago, tradition identifies a particular route as that taken by Christ on his way to Golgotha, complete with 14 STATIONS OF THE CROSS marking the locations of certain events that took place in the course of the procession. "She was well aware that directly Mrs. Neale received her money she went round the corner to drink ardent spirits in a mean and musty public-house—the unavoidable station on the Via Dolorosa of her life" (Joseph Conrad, *The Secret Agent,* 1907).

vials of wrath Vengeance, especially on the wicked. The allusion is biblical, referring, in the vision of John in Revelation 15:7, to the vials (bowls) "full of the wrath of God" that the seven angels will pour on the earth. With the emptying of the vials will come seven terrible plagues or other terrible afflictions (part of the Last Judgment). The image usually appears nowadays in the phrase ***empty the vials of one's wrath*** (signifying to discharge one's anger), although the phrase has made many appearances in literature, including in Joseph Conrad's *Typhoon* (1902), in which an approaching storm is described as "something formidable and swift, like the sudden smashing of a vial of wrath."

Vicar of Bray A person who changes his or her principles to suit the times. The allusion is to a song of the early 18th century that celebrated the memory of a 16th-century vicar of Bray in Berkshire who was notorious for changing his religious stance, switching from Catholic to Protestant and vice versa as the times demanded in order to keep his living through the various religious upheavals that took place under the Tudors: "And this is the law, I will maintain, / Unto my dying day, Sir, / That whatsoever King shall reign, / I will be the Vicar of Bray, sir!" "When Margaret finally foundered, some hoped that he had gone down with the ship, but here he was as buoyant as the Vicar of Bray" (Julian Critchley, *The Floating Voter*, 1993).

Victorian (viktoreeăn) Stern, prudish, strait-laced, old-fashioned. The Victorian period lasted from the coronation of Queen Victoria in London in 1837 to her death in 1901. The period saw Britain emerge as the world's leading industrial and military power, with an empire that extended across the globe. It also witnessed a significant rebellion against the relatively lax moral standards of the preceding period and a greater value being placed upon self-reliance, restraint, and piety. Later generations came to view the Victorians, for all their other achievements, as smug, narrow-minded, and censorious. *We all thought it was very Victorian of the vicar when he refused to allow us to hold a fund-raising disco in the church hall.*

Vietnam (veeetnahm, vyetnahm) The Vietnam War, or a situation that looks set to become a disaster on a similar scale. The trauma of the Vietnam War (1965–73), which cost over 55,000 U.S. lives, is reflected in the fact that it is customarily referred to as "Vietnam," without any further need for clarification. This remains true more than 30 years after the war ended. In some respects this constitutes a more accurate way of referring to the conflict, as a state of war was never actually formally declared. *The last thing the White House wants in Iraq is another Vietnam.*

Village, the *See* GREENWICH VILLAGE.

Vincent van Gogh *See* VAN GOGH.

Virgin Mary Archetype of a virtuous, innocent woman. As the virginal mother of Christ (see Matthew 1:16–25 and Luke 1–2), Mary has special significance for Christians, especially within the Roman Catholic tradition. *She stared back at them unblinking, the Virgin Mary herself, and it was almost impossible to believe she could be guilty of the charges being laid at her feet. See also* QUEEN OF HEAVEN; ROSE WITHOUT A THORN.

visit the cave of Trophonius *See* CAVE OF TROPHONIUS.

Vladimir *See* WAITING FOR GODOT.

Vlad the Impaler *See* DRACULA.

voice crying in the wilderness A lone voice of protest raised against prevailing opinion, typically one expressing views that meet with an indifferent or openly hostile reception. The original voice in the wilderness was that of JOHN THE BAPTIST, who preached about the coming of Christ: "In those days came John the Baptist, preaching in the wilderness of Judaea, and saying, Repent ye: for the kingdom of heaven is at hand. For this is he that was spoken of by the prophet Esaias [Isaiah], saying, The voice of one crying in the wilderness, Prepare ye the way of the Lord, make his paths straight" (Matthew 3:1–3). (See also Mark 1:3, Luke 3:4, and John 1:23.) The phrase is typically applied to prophets whose words of warnings or advice are generally ignored. *She did her best to stop the committee from voting against the proposal, but hers was a voice crying in the wilderness, and the suggestion was thrown out.*

voice from the whirlwind Through the workings of nature God communicates to human beings. In Job 38:1 it is Job himself who hears the voice of God in a whirlwind, rebuking him for his complaints about the sufferings he has experienced and subsequently offering him comfort. In modern usage the phrase may refer to any message or moral that emerges out of a desperate situation. *Like a voice from the whirlwind, just when it seemed all hope was lost came the realization that if the submerged car was full of water it should become much easier to open the door and escape.*

voice in the wilderness *See* VOICE CRYING IN THE WILDERNESS.

voice of many waters A tremendous noise, specifically one considered equal to the crashing sound of the sea. The phrase comes from Psalm 93:4, which reads: "The LORD on high is mightier than the noise of many waters, yea, than the mighty waves of the sea." It is also encountered as the ***noise of many waters*** and as the ***sound of many waters.*** "I saw the mighty walls rushing asunder—there was a long tumultuous shouting sound like the voice of a thousand waters—and the deep and dank tarn at my feet closed suddenly and silently over the fragments of the House of Usher" (Edgar Allan Poe, "The Fall of the House of Usher," 1839).

voice of the turtle is heard in the land, the A call to love; the coming of spring. The phrase comes from the biblical Song of Solomon 2:11–12, in which it refers to the call of the turtledove heralding the coming of spring: "For, lo, the winter is past, the rain is over and gone; The flowers appear on the earth; the time of the singing of birds is come, and the voice of the turtle is heard in our land." "But he did; he told us at prayers in the Pilgrims' tent, last night, and he seemed as if he was reading it out of the Bible, too, about this country flowing with milk and honey, and about the voice of the turtle being heard in the land" (Mark Twain, *The Innocents Abroad,* 1869).

volcano A mountain or other opening in the Earth's crust from which fire and molten matter issue periodically; any potentially explosive situation. The word has its roots in the name of Vulcan, the Roman god of fire and metalworking and the equivalent of the Greek Hephaestus. Although made lame by an injury resulting from his being thrown from heaven by his father, Jupiter, for taking his mother Juno's side in a quarrel, and described as very ugly in appearance, Vulcan became the husband of the beautiful but faithless Venus. Working at his forge, Vulcan created the thunderbolts hurled by Zeus and the suit of armor worn by Achilles. He also modeled the first mortal woman, Pandora, from clay. Other words that come from the name include ***vulcanist,*** a person who studies volcanoes, and ***vulcanize,*** to improve the natural properties of rubber by treating it with chemicals. "'Pray be serious,' remonstrated Neelie. 'We are both sitting on a volcano'" (Wilkie Collins, *Armadale,* 1866).

Voltaire (vol<u>tair</u>) A preeminent man of letters. The allusion is to the French philosopher, writer, and poet Voltaire, the pseudonym under which François-Marie Arouet (1694–1778) published his many admired plays, essays, and other writings. A leading figure of the ENLIGHTENMENT, who freely criticized the faults of contemporary society, he set a high intellectual standard to which many later writers and thinkers have aspired. Voltaire is said to have arrived at his pseudonym through an anagram of his real name, in the form *Arouet l(e) j(eune)* ("Arouet the younger"), with *v* for *u* and *i* for *j*, although another theory suggests it was derived from *Veauterre* ("valley land"), the name of an estate he bought near Asnières-sur-Oise. *It may not be too much of an exaggeration to call him America's Voltaire.*

Vronsky, Count *See* ANNA KARENINA.

W

Wackford Squeers *See* DOTHEBOYS HALL.

Wacky Races A chaotic car race or other disorganized scramble of some kind. The allusion is to a popular long-running children's cartoon series of the same title first broadcast in 1969–70. Featuring such outlandish characters as DICK DASTARDLY, Penelope Pitstop and the Slag Brothers, it was loosely based on a 1965 movie starring Jack Lemmon and Tony Curtis, *The Great Race*. "Roger, however, had a few tricks of his own to counter with and a long hot summer season in Yarmouth was turned into 'The Wacky Races'" (Marti Caine, *A Coward's Chronicles*, 1990).

wages of sin Suffering of some kind as a punishment for the sins that a person may have committed. The phrase comes from Romans 6:23, in which Paul writes, "The wages of sin is death; but the gift of God is eternal life through Jesus Christ our Lord." In modern usage the suffering or punishment under consideration may be no more than a slight sense of guilt. " 'The wages of sin, Watson—the wages of sin!' said he. 'Sooner or later it will always come. God knows, there was sin enough,' he added, taking up a brown volume from the table" (Sir Arthur Conan Doyle, *A Study in Scarlet*, 1887).

Wagnerian (vargnereeăn) In a manner reminiscent of the musical works of the German composer Richard Wagner (1813–83). Wagner's operas are well known for their grandiose and melodramatic nature as well as for their epic length, hence the application of the term Wagnerian to anything that seems overlong or larger-than-life. *The project was Wagnerian both in its scope and its duration.*

wag the dog syndrome The strategy of doing something to distract attention from something else. The allusion is to the 1997 movie *Wag the Dog*, in which a U.S. president sanctions war with Albania in order to divert the attention of the press from a sex scandal. The ultimate source for the name of the syndrome is presumably the expression "the tail wags the dog," which refers to a situation that is dominated by a relatively unimportant element. *Call me an old cynic, but this looks to me like a prime example of wag the dog syndrome.*

wailing wall A place where people gather to lament their woes. The allusion is to the Wailing Wall (also called the *Western Wall*) in Jerusalem, supposedly the only part of Herod's Temple left intact after the building was destroyed by the Romans in A.D. 70 and thus the focus for lamentations over the fall of Israel. This holy site is revered by Jews, who flock to pray there and to slip pieces of paper bearing prayers and requests between the stones. *The paper has an agony column that acts as a sort of wailing wall for those people working in the industry who feel they have been short-changed by their employers.*

waiting for Godot (godō) Waiting at length for something to happen, especially something that is unlikely ever to take place. The allusion is to Samuel Beckett's celebrated play *Waiting for Godot* (1952), in which two tramps, named ***Vladimir*** and ***Estragon***, wait for someone called Godot, who never comes. An eloquent comment upon the futility of existence, the play confounded and fascinated contemporary critics and audiences and has since exercised a profound influence upon world drama. Beckett himself denied that Godot was God. "It was an appealing image, and an appealing movement for radicals hunting their red snark, and tired of waiting for Godot" (Nigel Fountain, *Underground: The London Alternative Press*, 1988).

Walden (woldăn) An idyllic rural retreat. The allusion is to the book *Walden; or, Life in the Woods* (1854) by U.S. writer Henry David Thoreau (1817–62), in which the author describes two years he spent living in seclusion in a cabin in the woods on Walden Pond in Concord, Massachusetts, seeking to escape the complications of the modern urban world and to regain contact with nature. *After ten years in the big city, he longed for a Walden to escape to and bought a lonely cottage a couple of hours out of town.*

walk on water To achieve the apparently impossible and emerge unscathed. The allusion is to the biblical episode (related in Mark 6:45–56 and Matthew 14:22–33) describing how Christ rescued his disciples during a storm by walking to their boat over the water of the Sea of Galilee. *Over the years his performances on the soccer field won him countless fans, many of whom believed he could walk on water if he chose to.*

walk with God *See* ENOCH.

walls have ears Say nothing, as it is all too easy to be overheard. Though probably much older, the expression is most familiar as a slogan of World War II warning people to be guarded in their conversation lest they let slip information that could be useful to enemy agents. *I would tell you everything here and now, but walls have ears.*

walls of Jericho (jerikō) A seemingly invincible obstacle that is miraculously overcome without a blow being struck. The reference is to the biblical episode of the fall of the city of Jericho before the Israelites. Joshua 6:1–20 describes how Joshua and his forces, bearing the Ark of the Covenant, surrounded Jericho for six days. On the seventh day they awaited a signal from their leader "when the people heard the sound of the trumpet, and the people shouted with a great shout, that the wall fell down flat, so that the people went up into the city, every man straight before him, and they took the city." *Like the walls of Jericho, the board's objections against the proposal collapsed as soon as promises of substantial compensation were received.*

Wall Street The financial center of the United States. The allusion is to the street in lower Manhattan in New York where the Stock Exchange and other banking and insurance concerns have their headquarters. The term is now commonly used fairly loosely to refer to the U.S. stock market and big business in general. The wall in the street's name was a wooden structure built by Dutch settlers in the 17th century to defend New York from attack by the English. The term often occurs in connection with the infamous Wall Street Crash of 1929, when a collapse in share prices triggered the GREAT DEPRESSION. *Several Wall Street analysts believe a global recession may be just around the corner.*

Walt Disney *See* DISNEYFICATION; DISNEYLAND.

Walter Mitty (mitee) A daydreamer who escapes reality by whiling away the time imagining himself or herself in different roles. The allusion is to a short story called "The Secret Life of Walter Mitty" (1939) by U.S. humorist James Thurber (1894–1961), which describes how a henpecked husband called Walter Mitty finds relief in his fantasies. The story was filmed in 1947 with Danny Kaye in the central role. "Many men basically have a Walter Mitty attitude to housework" (V. Donald, C. Orton, C. Dudley, and S. Ward, *What Every Woman Should Know About Retirement*, 1987). *See also* BILLY LIAR.

Waltons, the (woltănz) Stereotype of a large, loving family living in the impoverished American Midwest during the depression. The Waltons, with their clean-living all-American values, first appeared in a semiautobiographical novel and film (1963) written by Earl Hamner Jr. but are perhaps best remembered today as the stars of an immensely popular, if saccharine-sweet, television series (1972–81). *With all those mutual congratulations and teary-eyed expressions of affection going on it was like a particularly mushy episode of The Waltons.*

Wandering Jew A person who changes address frequently and never seems to settle long in one place. The reference is to a medieval legend which identifies the Wandering Jew as a Jew who taunted Christ on his way to be crucified, or refused to let him rest at his door; for this sin he was cursed to wander the world restlessly until the Day of Judgment. In some versions of the legend he is described as a cobbler and given the name ***Ahasuerus***. Various reports of sightings of the Wandering Jew have been made over the centuries, most recently in Salt Lake City in 1868. "And Carl, pointing the bow of his fiddle at me, 'Here comes our wandering Jew, my other little brother, Izzy-Jack' " (Jack Caplan, *Memories of the Gorbals*, 1991).

wander in the wilderness To languish as an outcast while out of office, in exile, or otherwise out of favor. The phrase, typically used in the context of party politics, is biblical in origin. It appears several times but is best known in reference to the period the Israelites spent wandering in the wilderness after their flight from Egypt under the leadership of Moses. Moses is quoted in Numbers 14:33 warning his people that it will be many years before their exile comes to an end: "Your children shall wander in the wilderness forty years." *After his expulsion from the party he spent nearly a decade wandering in the wilderness, quite unable to reclaim his position in the political limelight.*

war in heaven Conflict or disagreement at the highest level of an organization, company, or other institution or group. The allusion is to Revelation 12:7–9, which describes John's vision of a battle fought between the angels and Satan: "And there was war in heaven: Michael and his angels fought against the dragon; and the dragon fought and his angels, And prevailed not; neither was their place found any more in heaven." *Shortly after, rumors* *began to spread that those controlling the project had had a falling-out and war had broken out in heaven.*

War of Jenkins's Ear *See* JENKINS'S EAR, WAR OF.

war to end all wars, the World War I. This expression was first adopted while the war was still continuing, presumably in a halfhearted attempt to make the slaughter seem more justified. It may have been suggested originally by an H. G. Wells book entitled *The War That Will End War* (1914), but was soon shown to be a hollow sentiment with the outbreak of World War II, among other conflicts. "Tolkien himself fought in 'the war to end all wars,' but saw his sons fighting in the one after that" (T. A. Shippey, *The Road to Middle-Earth*, 1982).

washed in the blood of the lamb Redeemed by faith or otherwise purified. The phrase comes from Revelation 7:14, which describes a host of people in white robes before the throne of God: ". . . they which came out of great tribulation, and have washed their robes, and made them white in the blood of the Lamb." "Make them clean, oh God; wash away their offences in the blood of the Lamb; and when their spirits pass, oh receive Thou them into the heaven of the just" (H. Rider Haggard, *Allan Quatermain,* 1887).

wash one's hands of To refuse to accept guilt for some misdeed or to involve oneself further in a dubious or apparently ill-fated enterprise. The expression alludes to the episode in Matthew in which PONTIUS PILATE washes his hands to emphasize his refusal to accept any responsibility for crucifying Christ after the mob has rejected his offer of a pardon in favor of Barabbas: "When Pilate saw that he could prevail nothing, but that rather a tumult was made, he took water, and washed his hands before the multitude, saying, I am innocent of the blood of this just person: see ye to it" (Matthew 27: 24). *Following his dismissal as manager of the team he washed his hands of them and refused to accept any responsibility for any further disappointments in the competition.*

watch and pray Be alert and put your trust in God. The expression is biblical in origin, occurring in Matthew 26:41 and Mark 14:38 (where Christ is speaking to his disciples at Gethsemane). "I shall expect your clear decision when I return this day fortnight. Meantime, watch and pray that you enter not into temptation: the spirit, I trust, is willing, but the flesh, I see, is weak. I shall pray for you hourly" (Charlotte Brontë, *Jane Eyre,* 1847).

Watergate (wahtergayt) The political scandal that shook the United States in the 1970s and resulted in the resignation of President Richard Nixon and the besmirching of the U.S. political establishment as a whole. Watergate was actually the name of an apartment complex in Washington, D.C., which was the scene of a break-in that led to the uncovering of official attempts to conceal a high-level conspiracy in which Nixon himself was implicated. Ever since then the term Watergate has been synonymous with political corruption. "Many teachers know of their own cover-up operations, and fear lest a personal Watergate scandal be revealed" (Guy Claxton, *Being a Teacher*, 1989). *See also* ALL THE PRESIDENT'S MEN; DEEP THROAT; -GATE; SMOKING GUN.

water into wine The miraculous transformation of something ordinary into something much more valuable. The allusion is to the biblical episode describing the ***marriage in Cana,*** during which Christ turned water into wine for the guests at a marriage feast (John 2:1–11). *The play went down well enough, but the critics were generally agreed that you can't turn water into wine.*

Waterloo (wahter<u>loo</u>) A final, climactic defeat, especially one from which there is no hope of recovery. The allusion is to the Battle of Waterloo fought between the French armies of NAPOLEON and those of Britain and her allies under the command of the duke of Wellington on June 18, 1815 near the village of Waterloo in Belgium. Napoleon's comprehensive defeat ended his reign once and for all and resulted in his permanent exile to the remote island of SAINT HELENA. Ever since then those who are seen to suffer a serious defeat may be said to ***meet their Waterloo***. *As far as his future in competitive athletics was concerned, this was his Waterloo.*

waters of Babylon *See* BY THE RIVERS OF BABYLON.

water, water everywhere and not a drop to drink Though something may appear to be in plentiful supply, it is not actually in a form that is of any use. The allusion is to the poem "The Rime of the Ancient Mariner" (1798) by the English poet Samuel Taylor Coleridge (1772–1834), which includes the lines: "Water, water everywhere, / And all the boards did shrink; / Water, water everywhere / Nor any drop to drink." *The flooding contaminated the water supply, prompting residents to lament that there was water, water everywhere and not a drop to drink.*

Watson, Doctor *See* DOCTOR WATSON.

waving the bloody shirt Rousing popular feeling; fomenting unrest or rebellion. The allusion is to the post-Civil War era when Republicans metaphorically waved the bloody shirt to remind voters that in their opinion the Democratic Party was to blame for causing the war and the bloodshed that had ensued. *When he changed the subject to argue that the current administration had the blood of U.S. casualties in Iraq on its hands he was accused of waving the bloody shirt.*

way it is, and that's the *See* AND THAT'S THE WAY IT IS.

Wayne, Bruce *See* BATMAN AND ROBIN.

Wayne, John *See* JOHN WAYNE.

way of all flesh *See* GO THE WAY OF ALL FLESH.

way of a man with a maid, the The mysterious nature of relationships between the sexes. This reference to the mystery of sexual attraction is of biblical origin, appearing at Proverbs 30:18–19: "There be three things which are too wonderful for me, yea, four which I know not: The way of an eagle in the air; the way of a serpent upon a rock; the way of a ship in the midst of the sea; and the way of a man with a maid." *What on earth she saw in him I shall never know, but I suppose that's the mystery of the way of a man with a maid.*

way of transgressors, the The troubled, difficult lives of those who refuse to live by the law. The expression comes from Proverbs 13:15: "Good understanding giveth favour: but the way of transgressors is hard." "It is not enough to tell me that you worked hard to get your gold. So does the Devil work hard. The way of transgressors may be hard in many respects" (Henry David Thoreau, *Life Without Principle,* 1863).

weaker vessel Womankind; "a person less able to withstand physical or mental strain, temptation or exploitation, than others" (*Oxford Dictionary of Current Idiomatic English,* vol. 2, p. 579). The phrase comes from 1 Peter 3:7: "Likewise, ye husbands, dwell with them according to knowledge, giving honour unto the wife, as unto the weaker vessel, and as being heirs together of the grace of life; that your prayers be not hindered." The phrase is sometimes applied to people of either sex who are considered less capable than others but is generally avoided in contemporary usage as misogynistic and offensive to women. "'I'll give up smoking to please you, if you will give up something to please me,' said Prince, seeing a good chance to lord it over the weaker vessel at small cost to himself" (Louisa May Alcott, *Eight Cousins,* 1875).

wealth makes many friends The rich are never short of friends attracted by their wealth. The proverb is of biblical origin, appearing at Proverbs 19:4 in the form "Wealth maketh many friends; but the poor is separated from his neighbour." *She was a great believer in the old saw that wealth makes many friends and had no doubt that as soon as her son had snared a rich wife, they would be surrounded permanently by admirers.*

weariness of flesh *See* OF MAKING MANY BOOKS.

wear the sandals of Theramenes (theramăneez) To change one's views according to the prevailing fashion. Theramenes (died c. 404 B.C.) was a Greek aristocrat who was notorious for his vacillating opinions and loyalties. *The vice president was accused of wearing the sandals of Theramenes, altering his standpoint for electoral gain.*

weaver's shuttle Something that goes very quickly, especially life. The phrase comes from Job's consideration of his own death: "My flesh is clothed with worms and clods of dust; my skin is broken, and become loathsome. My days are swifter than a weaver's shuttle, and are spent without hope" (Job 7:5–6). "She slid the length of the room; her tender shoulders swayed; her feet were deft as a weaver's shuttle; she laughed, and enticed Babbitt to dance with her" (Sinclair Lewis, *Babbitt,* 1922).

web of Penelope *See* PENELOPE.

wedding in Cana *See* WATER INTO WINE.

Wednesday The fourth day of the week. It was originally called Woden's Day, Woden being the Old English rendering of ODIN, the ruler of the gods and the god of wisdom, war, and culture in Norse mythology. *Ash Wednesday marks the beginning of Lent.*

week is a long time in politics, a Situations can change very quickly in the world of politics. This observation is usually credited to British prime minister Harold Wilson (1916–95) speaking to lobby correspondents after the 1964 general election. It is generally assumed to mean that political circumstances change very rapidly, although Wilson himself insisted that what he had in mind was that politics should be judged on a longer timescale. *No one expected the home secretary to ride the storm, but a week is a long time in politics.*

weeping and gnashing of teeth The expression of extreme frustration, grief, or regret. The phrase comes from the biblical episode in which Christ foresees the Day of Judgment and describes the severe punishment of those who reject him:

". . . but the children of the kingdom shall be cast out into outer darkness: there shall be weeping and gnashing of teeth." (Matthew 8:12). (See also Matthew 22:13, 24:51, and 25:30 and Luke 13:28.) "There was weeping and wailing and gnashing of teeth in the camp of the outsiders now" (Mark Twain, *Life on the Mississippi,* 1883).

we few, we happy few A band of confederates. The phrase comes from William Shakespeare's play *Henry V* (1598), specifically from a famous speech in which the young King Henry exhorts his exhausted army to defeat the much larger French army at the imminent Battle of Agincourt: "We few, we happy few, we band of brothers . . . And gentlemen in England now a-bed / Shall think themselves accurs'd they were not here, / And hold their manhoods cheap whiles any speaks / That fought with us upon Saint Crispin's day." *We few, we happy few who have been assigned to the night shift.*

weighed in the balances and found wanting *See* WRITING ON THE WALL.

well done, good and faithful servant A compliment to someone on a job well done (sometimes intended ironically). The phrase is a quotation from Matthew 25:14–30, in which Christ relates the PARABLE OF THE TALENTS. *The general made an attempt to wipe the soup off his sleeve, then gazed wearily at the waiter as if to say "well done, good and faithful servant."*

Weller, Sam *See* SAM WELLER.

we're not in Kansas anymore We are entering unfamiliar, menacing territory. This is a quotation from the 1939 movie *The Wizard Of Oz*, in which the line is spoken by Dorothy shortly after she finds herself transported by a twister from her native Kansas to the fantastical land of Oz: "Toto, I have a feeling we're not in Kansas anymore." *Looking at all the weird people round here, we're clearly not in Kansas anymore. See also* FRIEND OF DOROTHY; WIZARD OF OZ.

we shall fight them on the beaches We shall do whatever is necessary to achieve victory. This expression of stalwart resistance to enemy invasion is a quotation from one of the most celebrated speeches delivered by British prime minister Winston Churchill (1874–1965) during the course of World War II, forming part of a speech delivered to the House of Commons on June 4, 1940, following the evacuation of British soldiers from Dunkirk: "We shall fight in France, we shall fight on the sea and oceans, we shall fight with growing confidence and growing strength in the air, we shall defend our island, whatever the cost may be, we shall fight on the beaches, we shall fight on the landing grounds, we shall fight in the fields and in the streets, we shall fight in the hills; we shall never surrender." *"We shall fight them on the beaches," his father murmured as he saw the massed ranks of his in-laws bearing down on them. See also* CHURCHILLIAN.

West, Mae *See* MAE WEST.

we wuz robbed We were cheated of victory. This familiar expression of indignation at defeat is actually a quotation dating back to June 21, 1932, when it was famously shouted into the microphone by U.S. boxing manager Joe Jacobs after his boxer, German heavyweight champion Max Schmeling, had been defeated on points by Jack Sharkey. *Say what you like about the game, but I reckon we wuz robbed.*

whammy *See* DOUBLE WHAMMY.

What hath God wrought! What great things God has done! The sentiment comes from Numbers 23:23 and is remembered today chiefly through its being chosen as the first message to be transmitted by telegraphy on May 28, 1844. *A suggestion that trips to the Grand Canyon should be publicized under the slogan "What hath God wrought!" was not taken seriously by most present at the meeting.*

What is a man profited, if he shall gain the whole world? Material wealth and power is ultimately of no consequence. The sentiment was voiced by Christ in Matthew 16:26 and Mark 8:36, in which he compares transient earthly riches with a person's immortal soul: "For what is a man profited, if he shall gain the whole world, and lose his own soul? or what shall a man give in exchange for his soul?" "Only last Sunday dear Mr. Scoles had been so witty in his sermon, so sarcastic: 'For what,' he had said, 'shall it profit a man if he gain his own soul, but lose all his property?' " (John Galsworthy, *The Forsyte Saga,* 1922).

What is man? A reminder that human beings are but one element in the order of things. According to Psalm 8:4–5 human beings rank below God and a little lower than the angels but above the beasts: "What is man, that thou art mindful of him? and the son of man, that thou visitest him? For thou hast made him a little lower than the angels, and hast crowned him with glory and honour." "What is man but a mass of thawing clay? The ball of the human finger is but a drop congealed" (Henry David Thoreau, *Walden,* 1854).

What is truth? What value does the truth have? This cynical observation is recorded in John 18:37–38 as Pontius Pilate's reply to the following assertion by Christ: "To this end was I born, and for this cause came I into the world, that I should bear witness unto the truth. Every one that is of the truth heareth my voice. Pilate saith unto him, What is truth?" " 'The whole truth?' Miss Bart laughed. 'What is truth? Where a woman is concerned, it's the story that's easiest to believe' " (Edith Wharton, *The House of Mirth,* 1905).

whatsoever a man soweth, that shall he also reap *See* REAP WHAT YOU SOW.

whatsoever thy hand findeth to do One should dedicate oneself fully to the task in hand or to one's work in general. The expression comes from Ecclesiastes 9:10: "Whatsoever thy hand findeth to do, do it with thy might, for there is no work, nor device, nor knowledge, nor wisdom, in the grave, whither thou goest." *The old cleric rolled up his sleeves and beamed at them both. "Whatsoever thy hand findeth to do," he said, with a shrug.*

wheat and tares *See* PARABLE OF THE WHEAT AND TARES.

wheel of fortune Fortune; fate. FORTUNA was the Roman goddess of fortune, who was variously prayed to, thanked, or blamed for the fickle workings of fate. She was conventionally depicted with a wheel in her hand, a symbol of inconstancy. Humans were often represented bound to the wheel and rising or falling as Fortune turned it. "Fortune good night; / Smile once more; turn thy wheel" (William Shakespeare, *King Lear,* 1607).

wheels within wheels A complicated and interconnected arrangement of forces or circumstances that typically exerts an obscure or surreptitious influence upon events. The allusion is to Ezekiel 1:16, in which Ezekiel describes his vision: "The appearance of the wheels and their work was like unto the colour of a beryl: and they four had one likeness: and their appearance and their work was as it were a wheel in the middle of a wheel." "Gertrude, truth is a very complex thing, and politics is a very complex business. There are wheels within wheels. One may be under certain obligations to people that one must pay" (Oscar Wilde, *An Ideal Husband,* 1895).

when in Rome, do as the Romans do One should conform to the manners, customs, and way of life practiced in one's surroundings. This piece of proverbial advice is generally credited to Saint Ambrose and appears in the text of his *Advice to Saint Augustine,* written in A.D. 387. The legend goes that this was the reply Ambrose gave when approached by Augustine (in correspondence from Milan) on the question of whether he should fast on Saturday, as they did in Rome, or ignore this custom, as they did in Milan. This sage saying is often clipped to ***when in Rome.*** Equivalents in other cultures include the advice "Never wear a brown hat in Friesland." *I don't like kissing total strangers, but in this country it's considered impolite not to, and when in Rome we must do as the Romans do.*

when the going gets tough, the tough get going Some people only produce their best efforts when circumstances are at their most testing. This became well known as a favorite slogan of Joseph P. Kennedy (1888–1969), father of U.S. president John F. Kennedy, although it has also been credited to American football coach Knute Rockne (1888–1931). It enjoyed a new lease of life as a publicity line for the 1985 movie *The Jewel of the Nile.* "Although he never grew much above 5 ft 5 ins, Bremner was always in the thick of disputes and played according to the old motto, when the going gets tough, the tough get going" (Stuart Cosgrove, *Hampden Babylon*, 1991).

where neither moth nor rust doth corrupt *See* LAY NOT UP TREASURES UPON EARTH.

where's the beef? Where is the substance in what is being claimed? This expression was widely heard in the 1980s when it was used by Democratic presidential nominee Walter Mondale to question policies put forward by his rival Gary Hart. Mondale in turn had borrowed it from an advertising campaign launched in 1984 by the Wendy International hamburger chain, which featured an elderly lady thus criticizing the inadequate amount of meat in a rival company's products. *That all sounds very well, but where's the beef?*

where the carcass is, there will the eagles be gathered People tend to gather where they see an opportunity to obtain some benefit for themselves. The proverb comes from Matthew 24:28: "For wheresoever the carcase is, there will the eagles be gathered together." Sometimes the phrase is encountered with ***vultures*** instead of *eagles. The press had already learned the news and descended upon the house, confirming that "where the carcass is, there will the eagles be gathered."*

where there's no vision, the people perish People cannot exist without having hopes and dreams to aim for. This is a quotation from Proverbs 29:18: "Where there is no vision, the people perish: but he that keepeth the law, happy is he." *Now that their last hope of rescue had disappeared, many gave up the struggle to go on, for where there's no vision, the people perish.*

where two or three are gathered together Wherever people meet in small groups. The phrase is biblical in origin, coming from Matthew 18:20, in which Christ reassures his followers that wherever they meet, he himself will be with them: "For where two or three are gathered together in my name, there am I in the midst of them." The expression is particularly associated with religious gatherings but is sometimes used in a more general sense for small gatherings of any kind. "Very singular to look into it: how a kind of order rises up in all conditions of human existence; and wherever two or three are gathered together, there are formed modes of existing together, habitudes, observances, nay gracefulnesses, joys!" (Thomas Carlyle, *History of the French Revolution,* 1837).

whiff of grapeshot A taste of battle or a show of force. The expression is particularly associated with the outbreak of the French Revolution in 1795 and Thomas Carlyle's description of how the young NAPOLEON successfully suppressed a mob of his opponents on the streets of Paris. Napoleon was an artillery officer by training and packed his cannon with grapeshot, which comprised masses of cast-iron balls that spray outward when fired. *It's funny how a whiff of grapeshot can make a man change his mind about things.*

whip the offending Adam To punish someone for his or her sins in order to improve the future character. The reference is to Adam as the first man to disobey God and to fall into sin (Genesis 3). The use of Adam's name as a synonym for sin is also encountered in the expression ***the old Adam,*** describing sin in general terms. "Consideration, like an angel, came / And whipped the offending Adam out of him" (William Shakespeare, *Henry V,* 1599).

Whistler's Mother A severe-looking woman. The allusion is to the painting *Arrangement in Grey and Black, No. 1: The Artist's Mother* (1871–72) by the U.S. artist James McNeill Whistler (1834–1903). The model for the painting was Whistler's own mother, though his main preoccupation was the use of color and the arrangement of shapes within the painting rather than the subject itself. The story goes that his mother offered to help after the artist's regular sitter did not turn up; also, that Whistler originally intended to have his model standing, but allowed his mother to be seated as she found standing for long periods uncomfortable. *She had absolutely no sense of humor and sat through the whole show poker-faced, like Whistler's Mother.*

white as snow *See* SINS BE AS SCARLET.

whited sepulchre (sepălker) Someone or something that appears dignified and perfect from the outside but is actually corrupt within. The image is biblical in origin, coming from Matthew 23:27, in which Christ likens the Pharisees to the whitewashed tombs (made of stone or otherwise set in caves) of the dead: "Woe unto you, scribes and Pharisees, hypocrites! for ye are like unto whited sepulchres, which indeed appear beautiful outward, but are within full of dead men's bones, and of all uncleanness." In the time of Christ, Jewish tombs were usually painted white in order to discourage the living from accidentally touching and thus defiling them. "Surely it is high time that the whited sepulchre of the BBC is acquainted with the reality that licence fees can be withheld" (*Daily Telegraph,* September 17, 2001).

Whitehall The British government. Whitehall is the name of a busy London road close to the

Houses of Parliament and the location of many government and civil service offices. It takes its name from a royal palace (originally a mansion called York Place, belonging to Cardinal Wolsey), which was called White Hall by Henry VIII. It was largely destroyed in 1698 in a fire that left only the Banqueting Hall standing. *No one is sure what Whitehall will make of this latest development.*

white man's burden The supposed duty of the white races to govern and educate other, more "backward," races of the world. A notion that harks back to the days of the British Empire, when many less-developed countries came under British colonial rule, the concept was perhaps best expressed by Rudyard Kipling in his poem "The White Man's Burden" (1899): "Take up the White Man's Burden—/ Send forth the best ye breed—/ Go bind your sons to exile / To serve your captives' need." It is now viewed as a redundant relic of the imperial past. *No one talks about the white man's burden anymore, though many third world countries continue to operate under the shadow of the rich West.*

white smoke A sign that an important decision has finally been reached. The allusion is to the voting practices at the Vatican when the ballots are collected to elect a new pope. At the end of each round of voting among the cardinals the ballots themselves are burned together with an added chemical (originally wet straw), producing black smoke and thus advising the crowds outside the Vatican that no decision has yet been made. When agreement is finally reached white smoke is released from the chimney by burning the ballots alone. *There is no sign yet of white smoke from Camp David to tell the world that the rift between the parties has been healed.*

whither thou goest, I will go Expression of complete devotion by a committed follower. The saying is of biblical origin, spoken by RUTH when promising to accompany her mother-in-law, Naomi, to Bethlehem: "Intreat me not to leave thee, or to return from following after thee: for whither thou goest, I will go; and where thou lodgest, I will lodge: thy people shall be my people, and thy God my God. Where thou diest, will I die, and there will I be buried" (Ruth 1:16–17). "'I fear, my lord,' the girl answered timidly. 'Then give me the basket.' 'Nay, my lord, whither thou goest there I go also'" (H. Rider Haggard, *King Solomon's Mines,* 1886).

who dares wins Those who are prepared to take risks are the most likely to succeed. Famous as the motto of Britain's SAS (Special Air Service), an elite commando unit, since 1942, it was originally the motto of Brigadier Robert Yerburgh, Lord Alvingham (1889–1955). *It was a dangerous mission, with no certainty of success, but who dares wins.*

whole duty of man Religious faith or something else considered as a person's essential duty in life. The phrase comes from Ecclesiastes 12:13: "Let us hear the conclusion of the whole matter: Fear God, and keep his commandments: for this is the whole duty of man." ". . . to buy it for as little as he could possibly give, and sell it for as much as he could possibly get; it having been clearly ascertained by philosophers that in this is comprised the whole duty of man—not a part of man's duty, but the whole" (Charles Dickens, *Hard Times,* 1854).

whom God hath joined together let no man put asunder No one should come between husband and wife. This now-formulaic phrase from the marriage service ("The Form of Solemnization of Matrimony" of the *Book of Common Prayer*) warns third parties not to separate a married couple. The phrase is a quotation from Matthew 19:6 and Mark 10:9, appearing as Christ's response to questions put to him about divorce. It is sometimes quoted (often facetiously) in other contexts when separation threatens two people or things that should not be parted. "'The Church don't recognize divorce in her dogma, strictly speaking,' he says: 'and bear in mind the words of the service in your goings out and your comings in: What God hath joined together let no man put asunder'" (Thomas Hardy, *Jude the Obscure,* 1895).

Whore of Babylon (babilon) A personification of corruption and sexual depravity. The allusion is to Revelation 17:1–7, which describes a whore mounted upon a scarlet beast with seven heads and 10 horns and with the words "Mystery, Babylon the Great, the Mother of Harlots and Abominations of the Earth" written on her forehead: "The woman was arrayed in purple and scarlet colour, and decked with gold and precious stones and pearls, having a golden cup in her hand full of abominations and filthiness of her fornication." In its biblical context the Whore of Babylon was a metaphor for Rome, pictured as the embodiment of corrupt earthly power. The Puritans later adopted the name as an insulting epithet for the Roman Catholic Church, and eventually it came to be used more generally. It also appears as the ***Scarlet Whore of Babylon.*** "I'd marry the W—of Babylon rather than do anything dishonourable!" (Thomas Hardy, *Jude the Obscure,* 1895).

whoring after other gods Abandoning one's previous loyalties in favor of a new master. The expression comes from Judges 2:17, which refers to the lapse of the Israelites when they abandon God to worship pagan Canaanite gods (whose worship includes ritual prostitution). *For some years the senator's loyalty had been suspect, but this was the first time he had been openly accused of whoring after other gods.*

whosoever hath, to him shall be given Those who already have something are sometimes rewarded with more before those who have nothing. This saying of Christ is recorded in Matthew 13:11–12 when explaining why he used parables: "Because it is given unto you to know the mysteries of the kingdom of heaven, but to them it is not given. For whosoever hath, to him shall be given, and he shall have more abundance: but whosoever hath not, from him shall be taken away even that he hath" (Matthew 13:11–12). (See also Matthew 25:29, Mark 4:25, and Luke 8:18 and 19:26.) *The tax cuts for the wealthy is a straightforward case of "whosoever hath, to him shall be given."*

whosoever will save his life shall lose it Those who are preoccupied only with their own interests will in the long run be disappointed. The expression appears in Matthew 16:24–25, as well as in Mark 8:35 and Luke 9:24 and 17:33, where Christ tells his disciples: "If any man will come after me, let him deny himself, and take up his cross and follow me. For whosoever will save his life shall lose it: and whosoever will lose his life for my sake shall find it." *Their action could be judged foolhardy in the extreme, but then again, whosoever will save his life shall lose it.*

Wicked Witch of the West A woman who is deemed to behave in a wicked manner. The Wicked Witch of the West is the evil witch who seeks to rob Dorothy of her precious ***ruby slippers*** in L. Frank Baum's book *The Wizard of Oz* (1900), filmed in 1939. She dissolves, however, when Dorothy throws a bucket of water over her. *He had never got on with his mother-in-law, whom he referred to as the Wicked Witch of the West. See also* FRIEND OF DOROTHY; WIZARD OF OZ.

widow's cruse (krooz) A small but apparently never-ending supply of something. The allusion is to a biblical episode describing how Elijah sought help from a widow of Zarephath during a time of drought and famine. Elijah had been relying on the water of the brook Cherith and on food brought to him night and morning by ravens as sources of sustenance. But when the brook dried up God instructed him to seek out the widow, even though she had only "an handful of meal in a barrel and a little oil in a cruse" to offer him. In reward for this generosity, Elijah promised her that "The barrel of meal shall not waste, neither shall the cruse of oil fail, until the day that the Lord sendeth rain upon the earth" (1 Kings 17:12–14). *Like the widow's cruse of biblical fame, it seemed that the young hoodlum's supply of feeble jokes knew no end.*

widow's mite A small offering from someone who can ill-afford it. The allusion is to an episode described in Mark 12 and Luke 21, in which Christ favorably compares the tiny amount of money paid into the treasury by a poor widow with the larger amounts given by those who are better off: ". . . this poor widow hath cast more in, than all they which have cast into the treasury: for all they did cast in of their abundance; but she of her want did cast in all that she had, even all her living" (Mark 12:43–44). A *mite* was the lowest denomination in ancient Jewish coinage. "'Twas the boy's 'mite,' and, / like the 'widow's,' may / Perhaps be weigh'd / hereafter, if not now" (Byron, *Don Juan,* 1819–24).

wife, Lot's *See* LOT'S WIFE.

wife, Potiphar's *See* POTIPHAR'S WIFE.

Wild Bill Hickok *See* DEAD MAN'S HAND.

Wild Bunch An unruly group of people. The original Wild Bunch was a gang of outlaws who spread terror throughout the Old West under the leadership of Butch Cassidy (*see* BUTCH CASSIDY AND THE SUNDANCE KID) in the 1890s. They robbed banks and trains until around 1902, by which time most of the various gang members had been killed or imprisoned. Their escapades were brought to the big screen in the classic Western movie *The Wild Bunch* (1969). "The wild bunch were giggling helplessly as I was escorted, proud and unprotesting, to the exit" (Ian Breakwell, *Seeing in the Dark*, 1990).

wilderness, voice crying in the *See* VOICE CRYING IN THE WILDERNESS; WANDER IN THE WILDERNESS.

wild geese Mercenary soldiers. The term was originally applied to the Irish Jacobites who fought in mainland Europe after the deposition of the Catholic James II in 1689, getting involved in various conflicts—though it is by no means clear that the term was thus employed at the time. The earliest application of it to such soldiering appears to date only from 1845 and Michael Barry's poem "Spirit of the Nation": "The wild geese, the wild geese, 'tis long since they flew, / O'er the billowy ocean's bright bosom of blue." The term is today particularly associated with the mercenaries from various countries who offered their services to the Congolese government when the Congo was threatened with rebellion in 1964, events brought to the big screen in the 1978 film *The Wild Geese*, starring Roger Moore, Richard Harris, and Richard Burton. *Several African states are rumored to have* *recruited wild geese with wide experience in different theaters of war to bolster their military forces.*

Wilkins Micawber (wilkinz măkahber) An incurable optimist. Wilkins Micawber is a character in the novel *David Copperfield* (1849–50) by the British novelist Charles Dickens (1812–70). Always confident, even in the face of imminent disaster, that "something will turn up," he was based upon the author's own father, who spent much of his life struggling to cope with a burden of crushing debt. "The labour movement bewitched by the enemy, bothered and bewildered by the passivity of the people, waits like Micawber for something to turn up" (Beatrix Campbell, *Wigan Pier Revisited*, 1985).

William Tell A legendary medieval hero. The 15th-century Swiss hero William Tell was renowned for his skill with the crossbow. Legend relates how he was challenged by the Austrian governor Hermann Gessler to shoot an apple off his own son's head: he succeeded and later killed Gessler himself, thus paving the way for Swiss independence. The story has, however, no basis in historical fact. *It was the greatest father and son act since William Tell shot the apple off his son's head.*

will it play in Peoria? *See* PLAY IN PEORIA.

Willy Loman (lōman) Archetype of a disillusioned, failed businessman. Willy Loman, driven to suicide by the collapse of his family and professional life, is the central character in the play *Death of a Salesman* (1949) by U.S. playwright Arthur Miller (1915–2005). His sad fate is often interpreted as a searing indictment of the failure of the American Dream. *Her father was a Willy Loman who rarely cracked a smile after getting back from work.*

wind bloweth where it listeth, the The spirit, or the mind, moves wherever it chooses. The expression comes from John 3:6–8, in which Christ explains to Nicodemus the Pharisee what it means to be BORN-AGAIN: "That which is born of the flesh is flesh; and that which is born of the Spirit is spirit. Marvel not that I said unto thee, Ye must be born again. The wind bloweth where it listeth, and thou hearest the sound thereof, but canst not tell whence it cometh, and whither it goeth: so is every one that is born of the Spirit." "You are a happy man, Frank—you go and come, as the wind bloweth where it listeth" (Sir Walter Scott, *Rob Roy*, 1817).

windmills, tilt at *See* TILT AT WINDMILLS.

wind of doctrine A changeable belief, especially one subject to a sudden whim or enthusiasm. The expression comes from Ephesians 4:14, in which Paul advises the Ephesians that there were many false teachings that would all too readily turn immature believers away from the right path: "Henceforth be no more children, tossed to and fro, and carried with every wind of doctrine." *She drifted from one school of thought to another, seemingly incapable of resisting being blown along by every wind of doctrine that wafted in her direction.*

wings of a dove The power of flight, especially from oppression of some kind. In Psalm 55:6 the narrator yearns for the wings of a dove in order to escape the hostilities of his enemies: "And I said, Oh that I had wings like a dove! for then would I fly away, and be at rest." This biblical exclamation is usually quoted as ***Oh, for the wings of a dove!*** "Pray don't suppose I write in anger; I am only sorry and disheartened. My state of mind resembles David's. If I had the wings of a dove, I would flee away and be at rest" (Wilkie Collins, *Armadale,* 1866).

wings of the morning A swift passage. The phrase comes from Psalm 139:9–10: "If I take the wings of the morning, and dwell in the uttermost parts of the sea; Even there shall thy hand lead me, and thy right hand shall hold me." Thus to ***take the wings of the morning*** means to make swift progress from somewhere. "'Fast enough,' said the Antiquary; 'the gentleman wished to take the wings of the morning, and bolt in the what d'ye call it,—the coach and four there'" (Sir Walter Scott, *The Antiquary,* 1816).

win one for the Gipper (giper) To make a special effort in the face of difficult odds for the sake of someone. The allusion is to George Gipp (1895–1920), a legendary player for the Notre Dame football team until his premature death from pneumonia at the age of 25. As he lay dying Gipp told the team's coach Knute Rockne: "Some time, Rock, when the team is up against it, when things are wrong and the breaks are beating the boys—tell them to go in there with all they've got and win just one for the Gipper." On November 10, 1928, when Notre Dame were struggling against Army, Rockne passed on Gipp's request, telling the team to win one for the Gipper: The exhortation worked and Notre Dame won the game. Some have questioned the veracity of this legend, pointing out that Gipp never referred to himself as the Gipper, but it has become a cherished piece of U.S. sports history nonetheless. The U.S. actor (and later president) Ronald Reagan played the role of George Gipp in a 1940 film of Rockne's life, and the nickname "the Gipper" stayed with him throughout his subsequent political career. *If ever there was a time to win one for the Gipper, this is it.*

winter of our discontent *See* NOW IS THE WINTER OF OUR DISCONTENT.

wisdom crieth in the streets Sensible advice is made known widely, but sometimes also meaning that such wisdom is ignored. The expression comes from Proverbs 1:20: "Wisdom crieth without; she uttereth her voice in the streets." *In times like these all reason flies out of the window, and wisdom crieth in the streets.*

wisdom is better than rubies It is preferable to be wise than rich. This is a quotation from Proverbs 8:11: "For wisdom is better than rubies; and all the things that may be desired are not to be compared to it." The sentiment is also encountered in the form ***wisdom is better than wealth.*** *She was very beautiful and very rich, it is true, but she was not very bright, and wisdom, they say, is better than rubies.*

wisdom of Solomon *See* JUDGMENT OF SOLOMON.

wise as serpents and harmless as doves Shrewd but innocent. The expression comes from Matthew 10:16, in which Christ instructs his 12 apostles: "Behold, I send you forth as sheep in the midst of wolves: be ye therefore wise as serpents, and harmless as doves." ". . . with little or no sharpness of faculty or any trace of wisdom of the serpent, nor yet quite a dove, he possessed that kind and degree of intelligence which goes along with the unconventional rectitude of a sound human creature" (Herman Melville, *Billy Budd,* 1924).

wise as Solomon *See* JUDGMENT OF SOLOMON.

Wise Men *See* MAGI.

Wise Men of Gotham *See* GOTHAM.

wise virgins *See* PARABLE OF THE WISE AND FOOLISH VIRGINS.

witch-hunt A systematic campaign to root out subversive elements of one kind or another. The allusion is to the notorious hunts for people suspected of practicing witchcraft that were prosecuted throughout much of Europe and, later, in parts of the Colonial America from the late medieval period until the late 17th century. The stereotypical targets of such campaigns were impoverished old peasant women who had fallen out with their neighbors, although in some regions such as Germany the emphasis was upon accusing wealthier members of society in the expectation of confiscating their property for the state. Nowadays, the term is applied freely to any concerted effort to unearth enemies of the state, political or social misfits, etc. "In the coming witch-hunt thousands of people were to be deprived of their livelihood and reputation but, as we now know, the most serious spies went undetected" (Peter Lewis, *The Fifties: Portrait of a Period*, 1989).

Witch of Endor (endor) Archetypal witch or medium with supernatural powers. The reference is to the sorceress of Endor, who (according to 1 Samuel 28:3–25) on the command of King Saul summoned up the spirit of the prophet Samuel; the spirit warned the king of his imminent defeat and death in battle against the Philistines. "I merely lit that fire because I was dull, and thought I would get a little excitement by calling you up and triumphing over you as the Witch of Endor called up Samuel. I determined you should come; and you have come! I have shown my power" (Thomas Hardy, *The Return of the Native,* 1880).

Wizard of Oz A person who is believed, however mistakenly, to hold the solution to some problem or other. The allusion is to L. Frank Baum's celebrated children's book (1900) of the same title, which was turned into a classic of the musical cinema when filmed in 1939. Most people are unaware that Baum wrote numerous sequels to this first book. At the end of the book it is revealed that the wizard is no wizard at all, but an old man who has been blown to Oz in a balloon from his home in Omaha. *People have great faith in the managing director, but he's not the Wizard of Oz. See also* END OF THE RAINBOW; FRIEND OF DOROTHY; MUNCHKIN; WE'RE NOT IN KANSAS ANYMORE; WICKED WITCH OF THE WEST; YELLOW-BRICK ROAD.

Woden; Wodin *See* ODIN.

woe is me Expression of self-pity at one's own plight. The expression appears several times in the Bible, for example, in Isaiah 6:5, when the prophet sees the Lord in his holiness and is then utterly dismayed at his own sin: "Then said I, Woe is me! for I am undone; because I am a man of unclean lips, and I dwell in the midst of a people of unclean lips: for mine eyes have seen the King, the LORD of hosts." The phrase is particularly associated with Jeremiah in the following lament: "Woe is me, my mother, that thou hast borne me a man of strife and a man of contention to the whole earth!" (Jeremiah 15:10). "Woe is me when all men praise me!" (George Bernard Shaw, *Saint Joan,* 1924).

woe to them that are at ease in Zion *See* AT EASE IN ZION.

wolf in sheep's clothing A person or thing that appears to be harmless but is masking its real, harmful nature. The allusion is to Matthew 7:15, in the Sermon on the Mount, in which Christ condemns FALSE PROPHETS who claim to be genuine; in reality they maliciously destroy the faithful: "Beware of false prophets, which come to you in sheep's clothing, but inwardly they are ravening wolves." The expression also evokes Aesop's fable about the wolf that disguises itself in a sheep's skin in order to evade detection by its intended prey. *The stranger gave the impression of being the friendliest and most trustworthy of men, but as things turned out he was a wolf in sheep's clothing.*

wolf shall dwell with the lamb *See* LION SHALL LIE DOWN WITH THE LAMB.

woman taken in adultery *See* GO AND SIN NO MORE; LET HIM WHO IS WITHOUT SIN CAST THE FIRST STONE.

Wonderland *See* ALICE IN WONDERLAND.

wonders of the world *See* EIGHTH WONDER OF THE WORLD.

Wonder Woman A woman who proves herself capable of seemingly superhuman achievements. The allusion is to a comic-book heroine modeled on SUPERMAN, who made her first appearance in 1942, the creation of Charles Moulton Marston and Harry Peter. Armed with a magic lasso, she later became an icon of the feminist movement. In modern usage the tag is commonly applied, like SUPERWOMAN, to any woman who successfully combines, or attempts to combine, an active home life with a full-time career. *She must be Wonder Woman to manage the things she does.*

wooden horse *See* TROJAN HORSE.

Woodstock Icon of the HIPPIE movement of the 1960s. Farmland near the town of Woodstock in New York State became the venue, in August 1969, for an almost legendary rock concert featuring such artists as Joan Baez, Arlo Guthrie, and Jimi Hendrix. It marked the zenith of hippie culture and is fondly remembered for its celebration of antiestablishment values and individual freedom. *To the end of his days, he never got Woodstock out of his system.*

Wooster, Bertie *See* JEEVES.

Word, the The word of God; Jesus Christ, the second person of the Trinity, representing the communication of God to people. A translation of the Greek *logos,* the term appears in John 1:1: "In the beginning was the Word, and the Word was with God, and the Word was God." "The use of *logos* bonds not only the being of the God-man Jesus into one fused personality, but also bonds the natural and supernatural aspects of the written *logos.* Jesus the living Word, like the written Word, becomes the place of meeting, where God's hidden glory is unveiled and the Father becomes known" (Lawrence O. Richards, *Expository Dictionary of Bible Words,* 1985).

word and deed, in As one says and does. The expression is found in Romans 15:18, "to make the Gentiles obedient, by word and deed," and is alluded to in 2 Corinthians 10:11, "Let such an one think this, that, such as we are in word by letter when we are absent, such will we be also in deed when we are present," and in 1 John 3:18, "My little children, let us not love in word, neither in tongue; but in deed and in truth." ". . . she believed them still so very much attached to each other, that they could not be too sedulously divided in word and deed on every occasion" (Jane Austen, *Sense and Sensibility,* 1797–98).

word in season A timely warning or piece of advice. The phrase is biblical in origin, appearing in Isaiah 50:4 in the course of one of the Servant Songs: "The Lord GOD hath given me the tongue of the learned, that I should know how to speak a word in season to him that is weary: he wakeneth morning by morning, he wakeneth mine ear to hear as the learned." (See also 2 Timothy 4:2.) "'Or if there should be any little hitch between 'em,' thought the Captain, meaning between Walter and Mr. Dombey, 'it only wants a word in season from a friend of both parties, to set it right and smooth, and make all taut again'" (Charles Dickens, *Dombey and Son,* 1848). *See also* TIME AND PLACE FOR EVERYTHING.

Word made flesh The embodiment of an idea or truth. The phrase comes from the Bible, appearing in John 1:14, which refers to the Word of God as Jesus Christ, hence God as a human being: "And the Word was made flesh, and dwelt among us, (and we beheld his glory, the glory as of the only begotten of the Father,) full of grace and truth." *Their leader was a magnificent figure, tall, handsome and courageous—heroism made flesh.*

Word of God *See* WORD, THE.

work the oracle *See* ORACLE.

worm that dieth not The conscience or something else that continues to exert a troubling influence. The phrase comes from Mark 9:43–44, which quotes Christ as saying, ". . . it is better for thee to enter into life maimed, than having two hands to go into hell, into the fire that never shall be quenched: Where their worm dieth not, and the fire is not quenched." ". . . his lord felt, amid all the pomp and magnificence we have described, the gnawing of the worm that dieth not" (Sir Walter Scott, *Kenilworth,* 1821).

wormwood and gall *See* GALL AND WORMWOOD.

worship the golden calf *See* GOLDEN CALF.

worth one's salt *See* SALARY.

would you buy a used car from this man? This man is probably not trustworthy. This expression is strongly associated with U.S. president Richard Nixon, having been used by the Democratic Party as a campaign slogan in 1968, though it is said to have made its first appearance in connection with Nixon as early as 1952. Nixon became president, but the slogan acquired a new resonance when he was forced to resign during his second term as a result of the WATERGATE scandal. *He is enjoying greater popularity in the polls than ever before, but you have to ask yourself would you buy a used car from this man?*

wrath of Agamemnon (agămemnon) Extreme anger. According to Greek mythology when Agamemnon, king of Mycenae, was told that in order to appease the god Apollo he must return his prize, a Trojan girl named Chryseis, to her father, his anger knew no bounds. Unable to defy Apollo, he returned the girl but then demanded Achilles' prize, a girl named Briseis, provoking a violent quarrel between them. "The frogs and the mice would be nothing to them, nor the angers of Agamemnon and Achilles" (Anthony Trollope, *Barchester Towers,* 1857). *See also* BRAVE MEN BEFORE AGAMEMNON, THERE WERE.

wrath to come A future punishment or revenge. The phrase is biblical in origin, appearing in Matthew 3:7, Luke 3:7, and 1 Thessalonians 1:10, referring each time to the wrath of God for sinners at JUDGMENT DAY. "Must I beg to him then? Must I kneel to him? Must I ask him to save me from the wrath to come?" (Anthony Trollope, *Lady Anna,* 1874).

Wreck of the Hesperus (hespărăs) An appalling disaster or other dreadful event or sight. The allusion is to a shipwreck that occurred off the coast of Massachusetts in 1839, when the schooner *Hesperus* struck an offshore reef and was lost. The event was commemorated in a famous poem, "The Wreck of the Hesperus" (1840), which became a favorite choice for public recital during the Victorian period: "It was the schooner Hesperus, / That sailed the wintry sea; / And the skipper had taken his little daughter, / To bear him company." *She staggered out of the swamp looking like the wreck of the Hesperus.*

writing on the wall A warning of imminent catastrophe or failure. The allusion is to the biblical story of BELSHAZZAR'S FEAST, which relates how King Belshazzar entertained a thousand nobles at a magnificent banquet at the royal palace, the food served on golden vessels looted from the Temple at Jerusalem (Daniel 5:1–28). The occasion ended in consternation when a spectral hand appeared and wrote the enigmatic words ***"mene, mene, tekel, upharsin"*** on the palace wall. Belshazzar was seized with fear (see BELSHAZZAR'S PALSY) and offered a share of his kingdom to any astrologer who could interpret the message. He was subsequently informed by Daniel that the words meant "MENE; God hath numbered thy kingdom, and finished it. TEKEL; Thou art weighed in the balances, and art found wanting. PERES; Thy kingdom is divided, and given to the Medes and Persians" (Daniel 5:26–28). That very night the Median and Persian armies swept into Babylon, conquering it and slaying Belshazzar. The phrase is also encountered as ***handwriting on the wall.*** "As the government announces plans to regulate its special advisers, is the writing on the wall for these little Machiavellis?" (*Guardian,* June 25, 2001).

Wuthering Heights (wăTHering) A desolate, weather-beaten, comfortless place. The allusion is to the novel (1847) of the same title by Emily Brontë, which takes its name from the moorland farmstead that is home to the turbulent HEATHCLIFF. "Wuthering" means "wild weather" in Yorkshire dialect. *He had promised his aunt a comfortable luxury hotel so she was not best pleased when she found herself in Wuthering Heights.*

Xanadu (zanadoo) A magnificent, exotic residence or other place, especially one with mystical qualities. The allusion is to Samuel Taylor Coleridge's unfinished poem "Kubla Khan" (1816), which begins with a reference to the great summer residence of the Mongol emperor Kublai Khan (1215–94) at Shang-du, north of Beijing: "In Xanadu did Kubla Khan / A stately pleasure-dome decree." Coleridge was drawing upon a description of the palace at Shang-du written by Samuel Purchas in *Purchas his Pilgrimage* (1613), in which it was said to encompass 16 miles of land, with fertile meadows, pleasant springs, and a sumptuous house. Centuries later Xanadu was the name was given to the vast mansion built by the fictional Charles Foster Kane in the movie *CITIZEN KANE* (1941). "Oxford was my Xanadu" (Irene Young, *Enigma Variations*, 1990).

Xanthippe (zanthipee, zantipee) An ill-tempered, peevish, shrewish woman; a nag. The original fifth-century B.C. Xanthippe, or ***Xantippe,*** was the wife of the Greek philosopher Socrates, who acquired a notorious reputation for her scolding of her husband, variously attributed to her impatience at her husband's neglect of her in favor of philosophical discussion and to his lack of interest in practical matters, specifically the business of making a living. Another school of thought has it that Socrates deliberately held his celebrated discussions in the open air primarily to escape his wife's censorious attentions. William Shakespeare subsequently referred to Xanthippe in her role as the archetypal nag in *The Taming of the Shrew* (c. 1593): "Be she as foul as was Florentius' love, / As old as Sibyl, and as curst and shrewd / As Socrates' Xanthippe, or a worse, / She moves me not." She reappears in a similar role in many other works, including the novel *Tom Jones* (1748) by Henry Fielding: " 'By this Xanthippe' (so was the wife of Socrates called, said Partridge)—'by this Xanthippe he had two sons, of which I was the younger.' "

xanthous (zanthăs) Yellowish or reddish-yellow; having yellowish hair and a light complexion. The word is descended from the name of the Xanthus River (meaning yellow river), the ancient Greek name for the river Scamander and hence the name also of the city that sprang up on its banks. Legend has it that the river was named by the poet Homer, who noted how the fleeces of local sheep were stained golden red by its silt-laden waters. Another derivation, though, suggests a link with a Greek hero of the same name who reputedly routed a force of Trojans on the banks of the river. *They watched as a xanthous stain spread through the sluggish water.*

xenocratic (zenōkratik) Chaste; continent; unimpressed by wealth. Xenocrates (396–314 B.C.) was a Greek philosopher who combined the ideas of Pythagoras with those of his own teacher, Plato. Xenocrates' sense of personal virtue was so strong that he was immune even to the temptations proffered by the renowned courtesan Laïs, as alluded to by the Italian poet Ludovico Ariosto: "Warmed by such youthful beauty, the severe / Xenocrates would not have more been chaste" (*Orlando Furioso*, 1532). *She behaved with xenocractic indifference to all the fine things that were paraded before her by her wealthy admirers.*

Xerxes (zerkseez) A powerful leader. The original Xerxes I (c. 519–465 B.C.), king of Persia, attacked Greece at the head of a vast army of more than 2.5 million men, defeating his enemies at Thermopylae (480) but subsequently having to retreat after his fleet was scattered at the Battle of Salamis the same year and his army overcome at Plataea in 479. He was eventually murdered by Artabanus, the commander of his own bodyguards. The name *Xerxes* is usually associated with military and political leaders but may occasionally be applied more widely, as in Herman Melville's *Moby-Dick* (1851), in which it was applied to a stallion: "He was the elected Xerxes of vast herds of wild horses, whose pastures in those days were only fenced by the Rocky Mountains and the Alleghanies." *See also* ESTHER.

X-Files The world of the paranormal. The allusion is to the popular U.S. television series *The X-Files* (1993–2002), which starred David Duchovny and Gillian Anderson as FBI agents ***Fox Mulder*** and ***Dana Scully***, investigators into incidents of an apparently paranormal nature. *All this talk of lights in the sky and little green men is very X-Files, don't you think? See also* MEN IN BLACK.

Y

yahoo (yahhoo) A rude, uncivilized person, a brute. The allusion is to the satire *Gulliver's Travels* (1726) by the Irish writer Jonathan Swift (1667–1745), in which the disgusting, savage Yahoos are one of the outlandish races visited by Lemuel GULLIVER. The uncouth and philistine behavior of these creatures, who resemble human beings, marks them out from the gentle and civilized Houyhnhnms, a race of horses who are the Yahoos' masters. *The bar was packed with yahoos roaring, brawling, and throwing up. See also* BROBDINGNAGIAN; LAPUTA; LILLIPUTIAN.

Yahweh *See* JEHOVAH.

Yankee Doodle (yankee doodăl) An American or, more specifically, a New Englander. The reference is to the popular song "Yankee Doodle," which was originally sung by English soldiers during the French and Indian War (1755–63) at the expense of American colonists, who were shabbily dressed by comparison and exhibited little sense of fashion in their appearance: "Yankee Doodle came to town / Riding on a pony; / Stuck a feather in his cap / And called it Macaroni." *The Yankee Doodle, with his sunhat, loud check shirt, and cameras, became a familiar sight in picturesque English market towns and tourist sites from the 1950s.*

Year Zero A point at which the old way of doing things is replaced by new thinking. The term has dark connotations, the most famous Year Zero being 1975, when the notorious Khmer Rouge regime in Cambodia began a bloody systematic purge of everyone who had been connected with the previous government. "The year 1936 was Year Zero for macroeconomics" (J. A. Trevithick, *Involuntary Unemployment*, 1992). *See also* KILLING FIELD.

yellow-brick road The apparent way to happiness, or the route to solving a problem or realizing one's desires. The Yellow-Brick Road features prominently in Frank L. Baum's children's book *The Wizard of Oz* (1900), filmed in 1939, as the route paved with yellow bricks down which Dorothy and her companions make their way to see the WIZARD OF OZ himself in the City of Emeralds in the hope that he will grant their various desires. In the big-screen adaptation the road was the subject of one of the film's most memorable songs, "Follow the Yellow-Brick Road." In modern usage, the term is often applied to quests that do not necessarily meet with expectations when completed. "The road that led to the sea was her own 'yellow brick road' leading to excitement and adventure" (E. Nash, *Strawberries and Wine*, 1993). *See also* FRIEND OF DOROTHY.

yellow press The sensationalist newspapers. The expression alludes to a first attempt to introduce color printing in the course of a circulation battle between Joseph Pulitzer's *New York World* and William Randolph Hearst's *New York Journal* in 1895. An issue of the *New York World* included a comic strip by Richard Outcault in which a child—"The Yellow Kid"—appeared in a long yellow shirt. Soon many papers were publishing comic strips in color to attract new readers. Subsequently all attempts by newspapers to attract a wider readership through such gimmicks, or through the use of sensationalist attention-grabbing headlines and so forth, were dubbed "yellow" journalism. "When she read about his new marriage she said, The yellow press have caught him, poor boy" (S. Bedford, *A Compass Error*, 1993).

Yoda (yōdă) A wise person, especially one of diminutive and comical appearance. Yoda is a character in the immensely successful *STAR WARS* films of George Lucas, the first of which was released in 1977. Apart from his great wisdom and his odd appearance (his small furry figure being crowned with long pointed ears), his most endearing (or irritating) feature is his habit of juggling the usual order of words in sentences. *The professor is our very own Yoda, telling us exactly what to do when the rest of us are stumped.*

Yossarian *See* CATCH-22.

young Lochinvar *See* LOCHINVAR.

young Turk An ambitious and capable young man, especially one who supports radical reform (typically in the field of politics or business). The allusion is to a political party called the Young Turks, which attracted widespread support among students following its foundation in Geneva in 1891 and led ultimately to the overthrowing of Sultan Abdul Hamid in 1908 and the transformation of Turkey into a modern European state under Mohammed V. The Young Turks remained highly influential within Turkey until the end of World War I, when the party was dissolved. "The young Turk of theoretical physics could not have guessed that this very point in classical optics, probed by Wien, was to be of importance in one of the most fundamental papers he was subsequently to write" (J. C. Polkinghorne, *The Quantum World*, 1984).

your country needs you It is your patriotic duty to serve your country. This slogan dates from World War I, specifically to a British recruiting poster that had the words "Your country needs you!" under a portrait of the impressively mustachioed ***Lord Kitchener*** (1850–1916), the hero of Khartoum, pointing belligerently at the viewer. *It's time to step up to the plate—your country needs you!*

Ypres (eepră) A bitter battle resulting in huge numbers of casualties but little tactical gain. The First Battle of Ypres took place in and around the town of Ypres in Belgium from October 20 to November 18, 1914, not long after the outbreak of World War I. The massive number of losses on both the Allied and German sides for virtually no territorial advantage established a pattern that was to be repeated time and again over the next four years. The Second Battle of Ypres took place between April 22 and May 25, 1915, and witnessed the first military use, by the Germans, of chlorine gas. *Ypres gave a new meaning to stalemate. See also* FLANDERS; PASSCHENDAELE; SOMME, THE.

Z

Zeboiim *See* ADMAH AND ZEBOIIM.

zephyr (zefer) A gentle breeze; a soft wind. The allusion is to Zephyrus, the god of the west wind in Greek mythology, identified as the son of Astraeus and Aurora and the father of Xanthus and Balius (the two immortal horses of Achilles) by the Harpy Podarge. The west wind itself was sometimes referred to by the name Zephyrus, which might itself have come ultimately from the Greek *zophos* (meaning "darkness" or "west"). "He felt a zephyr curling about his cheek, and turned. It was Bathsheba's breath—she had followed him, and was looking into the same chink" (Thomas Hardy, *Far from the Madding Crowd,* 1874).

Zeus (zoos) The king of the gods in Greek mythology and thus, by association, any person who makes decisions or dispenses advice from a position of apparently unquestionable authority. The son of Cronus and Rhea, he was reputed to rule heaven and earth from his seat on Mount Olympus in Thessaly and to be the father of many gods, demigods, and mortals. He is conventionally depicted with the lightning bolts that he could aim at will at those who displeased him. The name is thought to have come originally from the Greek for "bright." His equivalent in Roman mythology was the supreme god JUPITER. *For a short time the president was credited with having the insight and all-encompassing authority of a Zeus. See also* EIGHTH WONDER OF THE WORLD.

Zeuxis (zooksis) An artist noted for the realism of his or her work. The original Zeuxis, a fifth-century B.C. Greek painter famed for the verisimilitude of his painting, was a native of Heraclea in southern Italy. He is remembered chiefly for the contest in which and he and his younger rival, Parrhasius, attempted to outdo each other with the realism of their still lifes. Zeuxis painted a bunch of grapes so realistic that birds tried to eat the fruit, but he subsequently admitted defeat when Parrhasius invited him to pull aside the curtain concealing his painting, only to find when he tried to grip the cloth that the curtain itself was painted. *Alone among the new generation of artists she has donned the mantle of Zeuxis through the lifelike character of her work.*

Zion (zīon) The name of the hill on which the city of Jerusalem was first built and sometimes called David's City. In biblical times, the city of Jerusalem grew significantly, and Mount Zion is now in the southeast of the old city of Jerusalem. In poetic and prophetic writing of biblical times, *Zion* referred to Jerusalem as a whole (for example, Isaiah 2:3 and 33:14) and even for the land

and people of Judah as a whole (for example, Isaiah 10:24; 51:11, 16; and 59:20). The phrase ***Daughter(s) of Zion*** meant Jerusalem and its inhabitants, both male and female (see Isaiah 1:8 and Song of Solomon 1:5). Sometimes, confusingly, other parts of Jerusalem were also referred to as Zion, as is the case in Joel 3:17 and 21, which is actually indicating the Temple Mount. Zion has significance for Christians and Jews. For Christians, it signifies the church of God or the kingdom of heaven (as in Isaiah 4:2–6, Hebrews 12:22, and Revelation 14:1). For Jews, as early as the destruction of the first Temple and the exile of the Jews to Babylonia (586 B.C.), it expressed the yearning of the Jewish people for their homeland. Most famously this use of Zion appears in Psalm 137: ". . . we wept when we remembered Zion." This longing to return also found expression in Jewish prayer, which sometimes reflects the belief that God's presence has also been exiled from Zion. For example, one of the prayers said three (or more) times a day has, "Let our eyes behold Your return in mercy to Zion." The term *Zionism* first appeared in the 19th century. It encapsulated the idea of building up the land and the people and mostly referred to the movement to enable Jews in the diaspora to return to the land of Israel. Here, again, *Zion* represented Israel. The Zionist movement has taken many forms, and the term *Zionist* is shared by organizations with varying emphases in their political philosophies. Labor Zionists, for example, focus on Jewish self-determination and self-development. Religious Zionists focus on the land of Israel as a gift from God and the responsibility of Jews to fulfill God's commandments in the land of Israel, including the commandment to inhabit the land. Since the creation of the state of Israel, Zionism has concentrated on the defense and development of Israel and continues as a movement for the upbuilding of the land and people. "Glorious things of thee are spoken, / Zion, city of our God! . . . / Blest inhabitants of Zion, / Washed in the Redeemer's blood— . . . / Saviour, if of Zion's city / I through grace a member am, . . . / Solid joys and lasting treasure / None but Zion's children know" (John Newton, "Glorious things of thee are spoken," Olney Hymns, 1779).

Zoilus (zoylăs) A spiteful critic. The allusion is to a Greek rhetorician of the name who lived in the fourth century B.C. and became notorious for his witty, biting remarks about the works of Isocrates, Plato, and Homer, among others, earning him the nickname "the Thracian Dog." It was specifically for his attacks on Homer's epics that he earned yet another moniker: "Homeromastix" (Homer's scourge). His most outrageous remarks concerning the writings of Homer included his dismissive description of the companions of Ulysses on the island of Circe as "weeping porkers." "The duty of the critic is to act as judge, not as enemy, of the writer whom he reviews; a distinction of which the Zoilus of the Messenger seems not to be aware" (Edgar Allan Poe, *Criticism,* 1850).

zombie A dull-witted person. The allusion is to the undead zombies supposedly raised by voodoo magic. Zombie was originally the name of a python god worshipped by various West African tribes. "You wouldn't want to lay the family heirloom on a horse ridden by a zombie, would you?" (John Francome, *Stone Cold*, 1990).

Zorro (zorō) An expert swordsman. The allusion is to the black-masked, black-caped hero of stories written by Johnson McCulley, the first of which appeared in 1919. They have since been filmed many times, with the role of Zorro being taken by the likes of Douglas Fairbanks, Tyrone Power, and Antonio Banderas. The name Zorro itself comes from the Spanish for "fox" or "cunning." *He waved his umbrella around his head like a short, indignant Zorro.*

Zuleika (zoolīkă) Archetype of a femme fatale. Zuleika Dobson, in the 1911 novel of the same name by Max Beerbohm (1872–1956), is a beautiful young woman who brings heartbreak and destruction to the many Oxford undergraduates who fall irrevocably for her charms. Beerbohm is said to have based this, his most famous character, upon the actress Constance Collier (1878–1955), to whom he was once engaged. *Who is this Zuleika who has turned a dozen grown men into whimpering children?*

Index

This index does not include allusions that are entries in the book; those allusions are listed alphabetically. The index lists concepts related to the entries, in order to help readers find allusions that are relevant to a particular topic or theme.

S

T

Y

Z